W9-CUT-304

OH$12.95

Quasi-Experimentation

Design & Analysis Issues for Field Settings

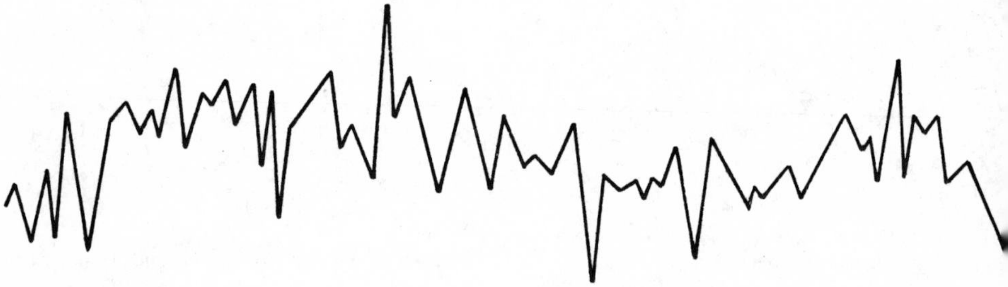

Quasi-Experimentation

Design & Analysis Issues for Field Settings

Thomas D. Cook   NORTHWESTERN UNIVERSITY

Donald T. Campbell   SYRACUSE UNIVERSITY

Rand McNally College Publishing Company • Chicago

To Fay, whose spirit
will never be pulled from its essence,
despite Mephisto's misguided efforts.

Sponsoring editor: Louise Waller
Project editor: Gayle Fankhauser
Designer: Willis Proudfoot
Cover illustrator: Arles Day

79 80 81 10 9 8 7 6 5 4 3 2
Copyright © 1979 by Rand McNally College Publishing Company
All rights reserved
Printed in U.S.A.
Library of Congress Catalog Card Number 76-17157

Contents

Preface ix

1 Causal Inference and the Language of Experimentation 1

Introduction 1
The Language of Experimentation 2
The Concept of Cause 9
  Causation and the Positivist Tradition 10
  Essentialist Theories of Causation 14
  John Stuart Mill and Causation 18
  Popper and Falsificationism 20
  The Activity Theory of Causation 25
  An Evolutionary Critical-Realist Perspective 28
Implications of the Analysis of Causation 30

2 Validity 37

Statistical Conclusion Validity 39
  Introduction 39
  Some Major Threats to Statistical Conclusion Validity 41
  The Problem of "Accepting" the Null Hypothesis 44
Internal Validity 50
  Introduction 50
  Threats to Internal Validity 51
  Estimating Internal Validity in Randomized Experiments and
    Quasi-Experiments 55
  Threats to Internal Validity That Randomization Does Not Rule Out 56
  Assessing the Plausibility of Internal Validity Threats If a Randomized Experiment
    Has Been Implemented 58
Construct Validity of Putative Causes and Effects 59
  Introduction 59
  List of Threats to the Construct Validity of Putative Causes and Effects 64
  Construct Validity, Preexperimental Tailoring, and Postexperimental
    Specification 68
External Validity 70
  Introduction 70
  List of Threats to External Validity 73
  Models to Be Followed in Increasing External Validity 74

Relationships Among the Four Kinds of Validity 80
   Internal Validity and Statistical Conclusion Validity *80*
   Construct Validity and External Validity *81*
   Issues of Priority Among Validity Types *82*
Some Objections to Our Validity Distinctions 85
Some Objections to Our Tentative Philosophy of the Social Sciences 91

3 Quasi-Experiments: Nonequivalent Control Group Designs 95
Notational System 95
Three Designs That Often Do Not Permit Reasonable Causal Inferences 95
   The One-Group Posttest-Only Design *96*
   The Posttest-Only Design with Nonequivalent Groups *98*
   The One-Group Pretest-Posttest Design *99*
Some Generally Interpretable Nonequivalent Control Group Designs 103
   The Untreated Control Group Design with Pretest and Posttest *103*
   The Nonequivalent Dependent Variables Design *118*
   The Removed-Treatment Design with Pretest and Posttest *120*
   The Repeated-Treatment Design *123*
   The Reversed-Treatment Nonequivalent Control Group Design with Pretest and
     Posttest *124*
   Cohort Designs in Formal and Informal Institutions with Cyclical Turnover *126*
   A Posttest-Only Design with Predicted Higher-Order Interactions *134*
   The Regression-Discontinuity Design *137*

4 The Statistical Analysis of Data from Nonequivalent Group Designs
***Charles S. Reichardt* 147**
Introduction 147
Nonequivalent Group Designs Without Controlled Selection 148
   Elementary Analysis of Variance (ANOVA) *150*
   Analysis of Covariance (ANCOVA) with a Single Covariate *153*
   Analysis of Covariance with Multiple Covariates *170*
   Analysis of Variance with Blocking or Matching *175*
   Analysis of Variance with Gain Scores *182*
   Rationales for the Analysis *185*
   General Guidelines for Analyzing Data from Nonequivalent Groups Without
     Controlled Selection *196*
Analysis of the Regression-Discontinuity Design 202

5 Quasi-Experiments: Interrupted Time-Series Designs 207
Introduction 207
   Types of Effects *208*
Simple Interrupted Time Series 209
Interrupted Time Series with a Nonequivalent No-Treatment Control Group Time
   Series 214
Interrupted Time Series with Nonequivalent Dependent Variables 218
Interrupted Time Series with Removed Treatment 221
Interrupted Time Series with Multiple Replications 222
Interrupted Time Series with Switching Replications 223
Some Frequent Problems with Interrupted Time-Series Designs 225
   Gradual Rather Than Abrupt Interventions *226*
   Delayed Causation *227*
   "Short" Time Series *228*
   Limitations of Much Archival Data *230*

6   The Statistical Analysis of the Simple Interrupted Time-Series Quasi-Experiment
Leslie J. McCain and *Richard McCleary*   **233**

Introduction   233
The Problem with Ordinary Least Squares Regression   234
Autoregressive Integrated Moving Average (ARIMA) Models   235
  The Deterministic and Stochastic Components of a Time Series   235
  Defining ARIMA (p, d, q)   236
  Noise Model Identification   240
  Estimation of φ and θ Values   251
  Diagnosis   251
ARIMA Seasonal Models   253
  Multiplicative ARIMA Seasonal Models   253
  Identifying the Seasonal Model   255
The Intervention Components   261
  Abrupt, Constant Change   262
  Gradual, Constant Change   263
  Abrupt, Temporary Change   264
  Which Transfer Function Should Be Used?   265
Summary of the Modeling Strategy   268
  Identification   268
  Estimation   268
  Diagnosis   268
  Intervention Hypothesis Test   269
Three Examples   270
  The Effects of Charging for Calls to Directory Assistance   270
  The Effects of a Flood on a Local Economy   278
  The Effects of a Gun Control Law on the Incidence of Armed Robbery   282
Conclusion   292

7   Inferring Cause from Passive Observation   **295**

Treatment as a "Dummy Variable" in a Regression Analysis   298
Causal Modeling by Path Analysis   301
Cross-Lagged Panel Correlations   309
The Causal Analysis of Concomitancies in Time Series   *Melvin M. Mark*   321
  Ordinary Least Squares (OLS) Regression When Trend or Seasonality Is Present   321
  OLS Regression When Trend and Seasonality Are Absent or Removed   324
  Generalized Least Squares (GLS) Regression   326
  Distributed Lag Models   327
  The Simple Cross-Correlation Function   327
  Prewhitening by the Presumed Cause   330
  The Independent Prewhitening of Both Series   331
  Spectral Analysis Methods   333
  Some Generic Problems   335
  Issues Not Addressed   338
Concluding Comments on Moving from Passive Observation to Deliberate Manipulation   339

8   The Conduct of Randomized Experiments   **341**

Introduction   341
  The Functions of Random Assignment   341
  What Random Assignment Does Not Do   342
  When Random Assignment Is Not Feasible or Desirable   344
  This Chapter   346

Major Obstacles to Conducting Randomized Experiments in Field Settings   347
  Withholding the Treatment from No-Treatment Control Groups   347
  Faulty Randomization Procedures   350
  Sampling Variability and the Number and Choice of Units for
    Randomization   354
  Treatment-Related Refusals to Participate in the Planned Experiment   356
  Treatment-Related Attrition from the Experiment   359
  Heterogeneity in the Extent of Treatment Implementation   366
  The Treatment in the No-Treatment Control Group   367
  Unobtrusive Treatment Implementation   369
Situations Conducive to Randomized Experiments   371
  When Lotteries Are Expected   372
  When Demand Outstrips Supply   374
  When an Innovation Cannot Be Delivered in All Units at Once   375
  When Experimental Units Can Be Temporarily Isolated: The Equivalent Time
    Samples Design   377
  When Experimental Units Are Spatially Separated or Interunit Communication Is
    Low   378
  When Change Is Mandated and Solutions Are Acknowledged to Be Unknown   380
  When a Tie Can Be Broken   381
  When Some Persons Express No Preference Among Alternatives   381
  When You Can Create Your Own Organization   382
  When You Have Control over Experimental Units   383
Conclusion   384

References   387

Name Index   397

Subject Index   401

Preface

This book presents some quasi-experimental designs and design features that can be used in many social research settings. The designs serve to probe causal hypotheses about a wide variety of substantive issues in both basic and applied research. Each design is assessed in terms of four types of validity, with special stress on internal validity. Although general conclusions are drawn about the strengths and limitations of each design, emphasis is also placed on the fact that the relevant threats to valid inference are specific to each research setting. Consequently, a threat that is usually associated with a particular design need not invariably be associated with that design.

The first chapter of the book briefly surveys some of the philosophy of science literature on causation. It particularly deals with philosophy of science perspectives that emphasize the relationship between deliberately manipulating objects and perceiving their consequences. These perspectives are then related to the practice and logic of experimentation. We adopt a critical-realist perspective, positing that causal connections are "real" but imperfectly perceived, and we particularly stress epistemological theories that restrict the analysis of causation to the analysis of manipulable causes—factors that can be varied "at will."

The second chapter lists some of the many plausible alternatives that hinder the interpretation of the findings from field research. These alternatives are listed under four headings. Threats to statistical conclusion validity are factors that can lead to invalid conclusions about whether a presumed cause and effect covary. Threats to internal validity are factors that can lead to invalid conclusions about whether a relationship between manipulated or measured variables reflects a causal influence from one of them to the other. Threats to the construct validity of putative causes and effects can lead to invalid conclusions about the construct labels that should be attached to manipulations and measures. Threats to external validity are factors that lead to invalid conclusions about the extent to which results can be generalized across populations, settings and times. Some critiques of this conceptualization of validity are then enumerated and briefly discussed.

Chapters 3 through 6 form the core of the book. They are concerned with quasi-experimental designs and modes of analyzing the data that result from them. The chapter on the analysis of data from research with nonequivalent groups is by Charles S. Reichardt, Psychology Department, University of Denver. The analysis of data for interrupted time-series experiments is by Leslie J. McCain, Department of Sociology, State University of New York at Buffalo, and Richard McCleary, Department of Criminal Justice, Arizona State University.

Chapter 7 deals with causal inference from designs that lack most of the characteristic features of experimental research. The equivocality of final causal inferences is stressed throughout the discussion. The chapter considers regression adjustments to equate nonequivalent groups measured only after a treatment, path analysis, cross-lagged panel correlation, and statistical techniques designed to assess the causal relationship between two time series. We are grateful to Melvin M. Mark of the Psychology Department, Pennsylvania State University, for writing this last section.

The final chapter is concerned with randomized experiments. Such experiments are sometimes possible in field research, and we outline some obstacles to their implementation, some ways of overcoming these obstacles, and some ways of recognizing the situations where random assignment is most feasible. The chapter presents a cautious advocacy of randomized experiments. It is an advocacy because of the high quality of causal inferences that can be made and because the many successfully implemented randomized experiments indicate that such experiments can be successfully carried out. But it is a cautious advocacy for two reasons. First, random assignment is only relevant to internal validity and even then does not rule out all internal validity threats. Second, we stress the need to design randomized experiments so as to have interpretable quasi-experimental fall-back options in case the planned random assignment cannot be implemented or breaks down after implementation.

Evanston, Illinois   T. D. C.
March 1979   D. T. C.

ACKNOWLEDGMENTS

As with all books, debts are owed by the authors. First, we thank the many generations of graduate students at Northwestern University who have helped us to clarify our ideas by their worried looks, their perceptive comments, and their need to relate what we were saying to their own backgrounds of study. The students came from all the social science disciplines, both basic and applied. We hope that what they helped us achieve will help other students and research practitioners whose intellectual backgrounds and substantive interests are equally diverse.

We are also grateful to the many colleagues who read portions of the manuscript as it evolved and shared with us and our contributors their reactions and suggestions. Among these people are Robert F. Boruch, William G. Cochran, Lee J. Cronbach, Leonard W. Dintzer, David A. Kenny, J. Jack McArdle, Barbara A. Minton, David R. Rogosa, and Jerry Ross. Richard A. Hay, Jr., further aided the project by assisting with generating many of the figures in chapter 6 and by responsively maintaining the program SCRTIME.

Several organizations must also be acknowledged for their support of the research and preparation of this volume. Thomas Cook's contribution was partially funded by a grant from the Russell Sage Foundation and by grants and contracts from the National Science Foundation (EPP-76-02376, DAR-76-20889, and DAR-78-09368). Donald Campbell's work was partially funded by a National Science Foundation Grant (BNS-782-6810 and its predecessors). Charles Reichardt's contribution was partially funded by a National Science Foundation Graduate Fellowship, a National Science Foundation Grant (GSOC-7103704), a National Science Foundation Contract (NSF-C-1066), a National Institute of Education Contract (NIE-C-74-0115), and a faculty research grant from the University of Denver. The work of Leslie McCain was partially supported by a National Science Foundation Grant (BNS-782-6810) and a research fellowship from the Center for Urban Affairs at Northwestern University. Richard McCleary's work was partially supported by the Center for Urban Affairs at Northwestern University and a National Science Foundation Grant (AEN-18810). The work is the responsibility of the authors and not that of the agencies that kindly supported them.

Two other special debts are owed. One is to JoEllen Bendall and Karen Mills, who for several years worked with cheerfulness and perseverance on the typing and management of this book under chaotic conditions in which only swineherds would feel comfortable. The other debt is to Louise Waller, Gayle Fankhauser, and Sue Baugh of Rand McNally, who first supported us, then cajoled us, and finally badgered us into producing a book that was only four years behind schedule.

CREDITS

Quotation in chapter 1, pp. 3–4: E. G. Boring, The nature and history of experimental control. *American Journal of Psychology*, 1954, 67, 577–78. Published by the University of Illinois Press. Copyright 1954 by the Board of Trustees of the University of Illinois. Reprinted by permission.

Figure 1.3: D. T. Campbell, Prospective: Artifact and control. In R. Rosenthal and R. L. Rosnow (Eds.), *Artifact in behavioral research*. New York: Academic Press, 1969. Reprinted by permission.

Figures 5.2 and 5.3: E. E. Lawler, III, and J. R. Hackman, The impact of employee participation in the development of pay incentive plans: A field experiment. *Journal of Applied Psychology,* 1969, *53,* 467–71. Copyright 1969 by the American Psychological Association. Reprinted by permission.

Table 7.4: G. Vigderhaus, Forecasting sociological phenomena: Application of Box-Jenkins methodology to suicide rates. In K. F. Schuessler (Ed.), *Sociological methodology 1978*. San Francisco: Jossey-Bass, 1977. Reprinted by permission.

Figure 7.17: R. Jessor and S. L. Jessor, *Problem behavior and psychosocial development: A longitudinal study of youth,* p. 242. New York: Academic Press, 1977. Reprinted by permission.

Figure 7.18: L. B. Lave and E. P. Seskin, *Air pollution and human health,* p. 136. Baltimore: The Johns Hopkins University Press. Copyright 1977 by The Johns Hopkins University Press. Reprinted by permission.

Figure 7.19: R. Atkin, R. Bray, M. Davison, S. Herzberger, L. Humphreys, and U. Selzer, Cross-lagged panel analysis of sixteen cognitive measures at four grade levels. *Child Development,* 1977, *48,* 944–52. Copyright 1977 by The Society for Research in Child Development, Inc. Reprinted by permission.

Table 8.1: Rand Corporation, *A million random digits*. Santa Monica, Calif.: Rand Corporation, 1955. Reprinted by permission.

Quotation in chapter 8, pp. 357–58: H. W. Riecken, R. F. Boruch, D. T. Campbell, W. Coplan, T. K. Glennan, J. Pratt, A. Rees, and W. Williams, *Social experimentation: A method for planning and evaluating social innovations,* pp. 58–59. New York: Academic Press, 1974. Reprinted by permission.

Quasi-Experimentation

Design & Analysis Issues for Field Settings

Causal Inference and the Language of Experimentation

INTRODUCTION

The major purpose of this book is to outline the experimental approach to causal research in field settings. We hope that our work will prove useful to persons interested in both theoretical and applied social research. The book is addressed to two contrasting audiences. One group consists of persons trained in laboratory research who want to conduct their current work in the real world where conditions are more difficult to control, and who want to make this transition with a minimal loss in the quality of causal inference and with a greater awareness of the particular ambiguities they will usually have to accept in interpreting the results of their field research projects. The second audience is of social scientists who are acquainted primarily with descriptive research where the investigator does not manipulate or intrude upon the processes being observed, who are aware of the dangers of inferring causation from passive observational data, and who are nonetheless interested in inferences about effects, benefits, influences and the like. Our hope is that such social scientists will learn from this book how to collect the kinds of data and perform the kinds of statistical analyses that will render causal inferences as sound as possible.

Since the book is largely about drawing causal inferences in field research, we obviously need to define cause. Part of this chapter is devoted to this topic. We shall deliberately adopt an outmoded position derived from Mill's inductivist canons, a modified version of Popper's falsificationism, and a functionalist analysis of why cause is important in human affairs. We will contrast our "critical-realist" position with some of the many other philosophical beliefs about causation.

In chapter 2 we shall introduce a set of terms for understanding some of the modifications to classical experimental designs that work in field settings necessitates. We have adopted many of the terms developed by Campbell (1957) and Campbell and Stanley (1963) in their systematic attempt to explicate the threats to valid inference that arise when the major features of laboratory research with humans are not present (e.g., random assignment, physical isolation of respon-

dents, short duration of the experimental treatment). Their efforts have been substantially extended in our present work.

In chapters 3 through 7 we describe a variety of forms that designs with non-comparable (i.e., nonrandomized) groups can assume, and present an outline of how the data collected within such design frameworks might be statistically analyzed. These chapters stress the assumptions that have to be accepted before responsible inferences about the causal impact of treatments can be drawn from particular designs and data analyses.

Even though most of the controls associated with the laboratory cannot—and should not—be created in field settings, classical designs based on random assignment can nevertheless sometimes be implemented in such settings. In chapter 8, we discuss a variety of factors which prevent the use of random assignment in field settings or which cause the randomization to break down before the study is completed. Strategies that may overcome these obstacles are stressed. Chapter 8 is concerned, therefore, with the implementation of randomized experimental designs in the field rather than with the form of such designs.

The present book is not intended to be a definitive treatise on field research. Many topics central to such a purpose will only be lightly touched upon, including: how to check on the importance of one's guiding research questions; how to physically sample respondents; how to construct and validate measures; how to collect qualitative data; how to present research findings. Nor is the book a comprehensive treatise on evaluation research. Although it may be of some relevance, we do not discuss such crucial evaluation issues as: how to incorporate into the evaluation the concerns of various constituencies with an interest in the eventual findings; how to discover whether the program is being implemented in anything like the promised form; how to use qualitative or quantitative knowledge about a program to assess whether much of the research resources should be devoted to answering questions about causal impact; how to measure and use in the analysis details about the heterogeneity of a program or project.

Instead, the book is intended to help persons who conduct both basic and applied research, who have already decided that they want a causal question answered, and who are prepared to look elsewhere for details about how to carry out field operations that, while significant for a study, may be less important in answering the causal questions posed in that study. In applied fields, such as evaluation, causal questions usually have an explicit context that at least specifies the population of persons who might be affected by a putative cause. For example, the sponsors and practitioners of research often ask causal questions about a specific kind of person who lives or works in a particular type of setting. Although we discuss sampling and measurement issues implicated by the context surrounding causal questions, we are more concerned with the experimental designs and statistical analyses that facilitate causal inference.

THE LANGUAGE OF EXPERIMENTATION

The word *experiment* denotes a test, as when one experiments with getting up two hours earlier to see if this makes one's working day more productive. The test is usually of a causal proposition: for example, does garlic or curry add a better

flavor to certain rice dishes? There are some uses of the concept of experiment where the link with cause is not immediately obvious, yet still paramount. For instance, an airplane is "experimental" only if one wants to test whether it flies faster, more efficiently, or more safely than some alternative.

The notion of a "trial" or deliberate manipulation is also linked to experimenting. Actually getting up earlier on some mornings is the most direct way of evaluating how one's productivity changes; using curry on some occasions and garlic at others will enable one to evaluate which seasoning improves the rice dish; and without flying the experimental airplane, it will be difficult to test. There are, of course, both deliberate and unplanned trials based on simulating real manipulations and experiences, as when one tries to imagine the different tastes that garlic or curry might cause, or when one "pilots" the airplane in a simulator. But these are proto-trials, as it were, and more credibility is attributed to tests based on actual eating or flying than to simulated tests.

Deliberate trials have long been used to test causal propositions. Our ancestors probably did not start out with a plan to strike flints together until sparks were produced. At some point they probably observed an accidental fire caused by lightning or sparks, and they also noted that rubbing stone against stone caused sparks. From this, they could have developed and tested the hypothesis that such sparks combined with flammable material can produce a flame. A much later example of a deliberate trial is illustrated in the following story from Boring (1954), an example from seventeenth-century field research that is redolent with features of modern science.

> In 1648 the Torricellian vacuum was known to physics in general and to Pascal in particular. This is the vacuum formed at the upper closed end of a tube which has first been filled with mercury and then inverted with its lower open end in a dish of mercury. The column of mercury falls in the tube until it is about 30 inches high and remains there, leaving a vacuum above it. Pascal was of the opinion that the column is supported by the weight of the air that presses upon the mercury in the dish (he was right; the Torricellian tube is a barometer) and that the column should be shorter at higher altitudes where the weight of the atmosphere would be less. So he asked his brother-in-law, Perier, who was at Clermont, to perform for him the obvious experiment at the Puy-de-Dôme, a mountain in the neighborhood about 3,000 feet ("500 fathoms") high as measured from the Convent at the bottom to the mountain's top. On Saturday, September 19, 1648, Perier, with three friends of the Clermont clergy and three laymen, two Torricellian tubes, two dishes and plenty of mercury, set out for the Puy-de-Dôme. At the foot they stopped at the Convent, set up both tubes, found the height of the column in each to be 26 old French inches plus 3 1/2 Paris lines (28.04 modern inches), left one tube set up at the Convent with Father Chastin to watch it so as to see whether it changed during the day, disassembled the other tube and carried it to the top of the mountain, 3,000 feet above the Convent and 4,800 feet above sea-level. There they set it up again and found to their excited pleasure that the height of the mercury column was only 23 French inches and 2 Paris lines (24.71 inches), much less than it was down below, just as Pascal had hoped it would be. To make sure, they took measurements in five places at the top, on one side and the other of the mountain top, inside a shelter and outside, but the column heights were all the same. Then they came down, stopping on the way

to take a measurement at an intermediate altitude, where the mercury column proved to be of intermediate height (26.65 inches). Back at the Convent, Father Chastin said that the other tube had not varied during the day, and then, setting up their second tube, the climbers found that it too again measured 26 inches 3 1/2 lines. These are reasonable determinations for these altitudes, showing about the usual one inch of change in the mercury column for every 1,000 feet of change in altitude.

In this experiment there was no elaborate design, and it took place 195 years too soon for the experimenters to have read John Stuart Mill's *Logic*. Yet experimental control and Mill's Method of Difference were used. How important it was for them to have left a barometer at the base of the Puy-de-Dôme to make sure that changes in the tube that they carried up the mountain were due to elevation and not to general atmospheric changes or to other unknown circumstances! How wise of the party at the top to have made the measurement under as many different conditions as they could think of with altitude constant! How intelligent of them to take a reading on the way down and thus to turn Mill's Method of Difference into his Method of Concomitant Variation!

Despite the creative use of experimental design features from the seventeenth century onward, it was not until the past century or so that experimental design notions became systematized. This systematization at first emphasized physical control of conditions—isolation, insulation, sterilization, strong steel chamber walls, soundproofing, lead shielding against Hertzian waves, and so forth. Much more recently, as biological research moved from the laboratory to the open field, the modern theory of experimental control through randomized assignment to treatment emerged. In agricultural work the emphasis is usually on whether a new practice or technique will increase the yield per acre. Note that, unlike Pascal's work in physics, this problem implies a particular single cause, the effects of which the researcher would like to evaluate. To do this, he or she creates different agricultural plots and deliberately assigns to each a different type of seed, fertilizer, method of raking, or whatever is under investigation. We shall refer to these possible causes as *treatments,* though the term *independent variables* could also have been used. We shall refer to possible effects of the treatment as *outcomes,* though the term *dependent variables* could also have been used and will occasionally be mentioned. Outcomes can, of course, be measured at many time intervals before, during, and after an experiment. As we shall see later, the scheduling of outcome measurement is one of the more important tools an experimenter has for detecting effects and for attributing them to the treatment.

To infer treatment effects, one needs a comparison. If the researcher applied fertilizer and then measured the yield, a number—produce per acre—would result. But we would not know if a larger or smaller number would have been obtained without the fertilizer. Many sources for comparison exist in experimentation— most have different purposes and not all are equally efficacious for any one purpose. The researcher, for example, could compare this year's yield in the experimental plot with last year's yield from the same plot; or he or she could compare this year's yield with that of some neighboring plot. The first of the comparisons would not be very useful, since crop yields depend on many factors (rainfall, sun, and so forth) which change from year to year. The second compari-

son is more useful; however, a neighboring plot may have a slightly different soil composition or be slightly more shaded. Either of these might account for observed differences in crop yield.

Although it would help to apply the old and new fertilizer to several plots, the number of plots in each treatment group may not by itself help causal inference. More important is the manner in which treatments are assigned. If all the plots treated with the new fertilizer are located on the southern side of an agricultural station (perhaps because these plots are nearer to where the new fertilizer is delivered), and if all the plots with the old fertilizer are on the northern side, then clearly one set of plots will get more sun than the other. Thus, any differences in crop yield between plots with one fertilizer rather than the other may be attributed to differences in sunlight and not to differences in the fertilizer used.

One of the great breakthroughs in experimental design was the realization that random assignment provided a means of comparing the yields of different treatments in a manner that ruled out most alternative interpretations. Random assignment requires experimental units, which can be plots of land in agriculture, individual persons in social psychology experiments, intact classrooms in education studies, and even neighborhoods in some criminal justice research. Treatments are then assigned to these units by some equivalent of a coin toss, a process of random selection which determines the treatment that each receives. Given a sufficient number of units relative to the variability between units, the random selection procedure will make the average unit in any one treatment group comparable to the average unit in any other treatment group before the treatments are applied.

In our hypothetical agricultural example, the plots of land to which the new fertilizer is to be applied would be dotted haphazardly around the part of the agricultural station set aside for this experiment and would be interspersed with the haphazardly arranged plots to which the old fertilizer is to be applied. When there is random assignment, any differences in yield observed at the close of the experimental period cannot be due to differences in the number of sunlight hours from plot to plot since the plots receiving one treatment are, *on the average,* identical to those receiving the other treatment. In addition, differences in yield cannot be due to differences in the composition of soil from plot to plot since the soil is comparable, *on the average,* in the new and old fertilizer plots. Of course, each individual plot remains different from any other, just as each human is different from every other in a social experiment. However, the average plot in each agricultural treatment group is initially comparable, just as in social experiments the average human in each treatment group is initially comparable. Random assignment is the great *ceteris paribus*—that is, other things being equal—of causal inference. Its dependence on having many units per group has the beneficial side effect of permitting multiple tests or replications since the basic experiment is, in a sense, recreated in all treatment plots. Indeed, the error terms that are used for testing treatment effects indirectly assess whether the findings can be replicated.

All experiments involve at least a treatment, an outcome measure, units of assignment, and some comparison from which change can be inferred and hopefully attributed to the treatment. *Randomized experiments* are characterized by the

use of initial random assignment for inferring treatment-caused change. It is more difficult to assign individuals or larger social groups to treatments at random than it is to assign agricultural plots. It is also more difficult to assign individuals to treatments at random in field settings than in laboratory settings. The field researcher is often a guest at the sites where he or she works while the laboratory researcher has almost total control over the setting and acts as the respondent's host. Such considerations imply that random assignment will be less frequent with humans than with objects and less frequent with humans in the field than in the laboratory.

Although the term was not coined until later, Stouffer (1950) and Campbell (1957) placed a special emphasis on *quasi-experiments*—experiments that have treatments, outcome measures, and experimental units, but do not use random assignment to create the comparisons from which treatment-caused change is inferred. Instead, the comparisons depend on nonequivalent groups that differ from each other in many ways other than the presence of a treatment whose effects are being tested. The task confronting persons who try to interpret the results from quasi-experiments is basically one of separating the effects of a treatment from those due to the initial noncomparability between the average units in each treatment group; only the effects of the treatment are of research interest. To achieve this separation of effects, the researcher has to explicate the specific threats to valid causal inference that random assignment rules out and then in some way deal with these threats. In a sense, quasi-experiments require making explicit the irrelevant causal forces hidden within the *ceteris paribus* of random assignment.

Several distinctions are traditionally made among types of quasi-experiments. *Nonequivalent group designs* are typically those in which responses of a treatment group and a comparison group are measured before and after a treatment. This would be the case where two school classes are compared to each other and measures, perhaps of achievement, are collected at the beginning and end of the school year. *Interrupted time-series designs* are those in which the effects of a treatment are inferred from comparing measures of performance taken at many time intervals before a treatment with measures taken at many intervals afterwards. For example, attendance at school might be observed every day for a year and then every day for the next year following a new school policy about attendance. As we shall see in chapter 5, many interrupted time-series designs are improved (i.e., frequently occurring alternative interpretations are ruled out) by combining the longitudinal component of time series with the cross-sectional comparability of nonequivalent group designs.

The term *correlational-design* occurs in older methodological literature, most often to refer to efforts at causal inference based on measures taken all at one time, with differential levels of both effects and exposures to presumed causes, being measured as they occur naturally, without any experimental intervention. We find the term *correlational* misleading since the mode of statistical analysis is not the crucial issue. We discuss such methods in chapter 7 using the term, "Passive Observational Methods" to replace Correlational Methods.

The reduced possibilities for control available in field settings led to the development of the theory of quasi-experiments and to a refined specification of the controls needed if random assignment has not been achieved. Lack of control has

other consequences, however, and these help determine the difference in form between most laboratory and field experiments. In the laboratory, one is more likely to be able to implement parametric studies in which many levels of a treatment are manipulated across a wide range. For example, some disadvantaged students might receive no extra tutoring, some 1 hour per week, others 2 hours, others 4, others 8, and others 16. Parametric studies are useful because they permit one to detect inflection points in curves (i.e., between which two levels of tutoring does achievement begin to rise most dramatically). Also, with their wide range researchers often can detect effects they might miss if only two levels of a treatment are varied and the most extreme one is still not powerful enough to cause an impact.

Controlled settings also make it easier to implement factorial experiments where all the levels of one treatment are crossed with all the levels of another. For instance, one might want to compare one hour of tutoring with four hours of tutoring per week and whether the tutoring is done by a peer or an adult. If the treatments were factorially combined, four groups would be created: one hour of tutoring from a peer, one hour from an adult, four hours from a peer, and four hours from an adult. Factorial experiments are useful because they allow us to test whether the two treatments interact (i.e., combine together) in nonadditive fashion so that the effect of four hours of tutoring from a peer would exceed the sum of the advantage conferred by four hours of tutoring with an adult and one hour of tutoring with a peer. We do not want to suggest that experimental control is necessary for all parametric and factorial analyses. We only want to suggest that it facilitates inferences about the form of causal relationships.

The advantages of experimental control for inferring causation have to be weighed against the disadvantages that arise because we do not always want to learn about causation in controlled settings. Instead, for many purposes, we would like to be able to generalize to causal relationships in complex field settings, and we cannot easily assume that findings from the laboratory will hold in the field. Even in agriculture, the transition from the controlled experiment at the research station to the average practice on a farm is always problematic. Even if fertilizer *A* is superior to *B* in controlled experiments, it may not be superior in the special type of soil found in, say, southeast Georgia; or a particular farmer may not want, or be able, to use the fertilizer according to the guidelines developed from agricultural experiments and printed on the bag. However, the difference between the conditions of initial testing and those desired for implementation would probably be less marked in agriculture than with any social phenomena in which the initial testing either took place in a laboratory study that lasted 50 minutes per respondent or took place in a few minutes in some street location. Most of the social phenomena of theoretical and practical social interest from which we want to generalize occur in markedly less controlled settings than either the laboratory or the staged short-term experiment along one block of a street.

The term *control* is used in several different senses in research design, and we need to be precise regarding our usage. One sense refers to the ability to control the situation in which an experiment is being conducted so as to keep out extraneous forces. The lead shields, soundproof rooms, and sterile test tubes of the natural scientist are all means of controlling irrelevant forces that could affect

the outcome of an experiment and lead to spurious causal inferences. In social research, the laboratory is sometimes used to control extraneous sources of variance. However, some research topics demand field settings. Relatively more control can be obtained in some such settings (the school room or prison) than in others (the home or the neighborhood), and it is important to note that the amount of control is at issue and not whether there is control or not. No environment offers total control.

A second sense of control concerns the ability to determine which units receive a particular treatment at a particular time. Such control over the independent variable is necessary if random assignment to treatments is to take place, for random assignment rarely occurs unless someone (and it need not be the researcher) determines that scarce resources (i.e., treatments) should be distributed by some form of lottery. Control over the independent variable clearly helps separate the effects attributable to a treatment from the effects attributable to irrelevancies that are correlated with a treatment. Since control is not an all-or-nothing proposition, a researcher often can help determine who gets which treatment, even though he or she has no power to compel a random allocation to treatments. We shall see later that even this degree of control can improve inferences about cause.

The term control is also used in a third sense as in statements such as: "We attempted to control for respondents' knowledge of the experimental hypothesis by deliberately giving all respondents a false hypothesis"; or, "We attempted to control for the possibility that the persons exposed to the treatment were more experienced than those who were not by measuring the amount of experience each respondent had had and then controlling for it in the statistical analysis." Here the sense relates to a particular identified threat to valid inference that one has attempted to eliminate by the way the procedures of the study were designed and implemented (the first example above) or by measuring the potential threat and then in some manner using the measure in the data analysis to rule out the threat (the second example).

The three senses of control all involve ruling out threats to valid inference. In the first sense, the experimenter's control over the research environment serves as an omnibus means of ruling out threats, so much so that in some natural sciences the particular threats being ruled out need never be explicated and considered individually. It is as though they are handled automatically. In the second sense, control over the independent variable helps to separate effects of the treatment and of correlates of the treatment. With random assignment this unconfounding may once again be so automatic that the threats being ruled out need never be explicated individually. In the third sense, awareness of single threats is paramount, and research design becomes a matter of identifying the relevant threats and ruling them out through research design or through the constructs that are validly measured. Whatever its manifestation, the major function of control is the same: to rule out threats to valid inference. (A second function is to add precision, the ability to detect true effects of smaller magnitude.) However, since experimentation in field settings cannot readily use control in our first sense, but must use it in the last two senses, we can readily anticipate that causal inference will be much more problematic in field than in laboratory settings.

CAUSAL INFERENCE AND THE LANGUAGE OF EXPERIMENTATION

It might be thought that control in either of the first two senses can be discarded and that the researcher can instead explicate and measure all the relevant threats to valid inference. However, the importance of using experimental methods in less controlled field settings became clear after many attempts were made to infer causation from descriptive studies that were not experimental in form and that followed the logic of conceptualizing, measuring, and attempting to control statistically for threats. Cross-sectional surveys were the most widely used vehicle for providing the multivariate data needed for such causal analysis. At first, cross-tabulations were used to control for alternative explanations to the preferred one; later, researchers used multiple regression techniques under a variety of different guises. For all these techniques, it was assumed that statistical controls were adequate substitutes for experimental controls and that the functions served by random assignment, isolation, and the rest could be served just as effectively by passive measurement and statistical manipulation. The belief became widespread that random assignment was not necessary because one could validly conceptualize and measure all of the ways in which the people experiencing different treatments differed before their treatment was implemented, and that one could rule out any effects of such initial group differences by statistical adjustment alone. (Some researchers believed that *all* extraneous sources of variation in the dependent variable [that isolation and reliable measurement largely deal with] could be conceptualized, validly measured, and then partialled out of the dependent variable.) The difficulties inherent in fully modelling initial group differences, validly measuring each of the concepts in the model, and then removing the variance attributable to these concepts seem to us more conspicuous today than ten years ago. This is true even among the sociologists, political scientists, and economists who are most widely associated with using correlational data for purposes of inferring cause (Duncan, 1975; Heise, 1975; Rivlin, 1971).

Thus, there were two major reasons for using experimental designs in theoretical and practical research in field settings. The first was an increasing unwillingness to conduct experimental tests in controlled—and usually laboratory—settings that were irrelevant for both theory and practice. The second arose out of a dissatisfaction with nonexperimental alternatives for inferring causation. (The nature of this dissatisfaction will become clearer after reading chapter 7.) To this we add a third reason—that the deliberately intrusive and manipulative nature of experimentation is closely related to some philosophy of science conceptions of a particular type of cause, to most persons' everyday understanding of the notion of cause, and to the way that most changes would have to be made to improve our environment by introducing successful new practices and weeding out harmful ones. In the following sections we discuss in detail such philosophical and pragmatic concepts of cause.

THE CONCEPT OF CAUSE

Often when we discuss effects of events or programs we fall into a casual, sometimes careless, use of the words *cause* and *effect*. This is particularly the case when we are challenging interpretations of data and pointing to the need to rule

out alternative explanations. In well-controlled laboratory experiments causal inference may be so certain that cause and effect are rarely used. But in field research, the explicit use of causal concepts cannot be avoided. As a result, we encounter the full range of problems associated with causation, problems philosophers have encountered for centuries.

The epistemology of causation, and of the scientific method more generally, is at present in a productive state of near chaos. In our treatment of causality we shall touch upon only a small part of the current ferment. (See the bibliography in Brand [1976] for a fuller discussion.) We are far from satisfied with our treatment here and find in it no completely satisfying resolution to the major problems of causality. But we do not have the kind of experience it might take to bring even a personally perceived order out of the current literature. Our problem is magnified when one considers that many more concepts of cause can be found in historical reviews of philosophical thinking about causality (Bunge, 1959; Wallace, 1972 and 1974) than we shall touch upon here. However, a brief discussion is in order.

Causation and the Positivist Tradition

Perhaps the most famous positivist analysis of cause is that of David Hume. His analysis stressed three conditions for inferring cause: (a) contiguity between the presumed cause and effect; (b) temporal precedence, in that the cause had to precede the effect in time; and (c) constant conjunction, in that the cause had to be present whenever the effect was obtained. Of these conditions, the last is the most important and most positivistic.

The requirement of constant conjunction equates causal inference with the observation of regularities, of dependency between the presumed cause and effect. Hume stresses that all we observe even in the most mechanistic push-pull examples of apparent causation are billiard balls striking each other and stationary balls moving after they have been struck. No cause is directly observed in such examples, only coincidence in space and time. And if one "sees" cause as the billiard balls move, Hume believed this was a problem for psychology and not logic. Hume's denial of all conceptual status to unobserved phenomena led him and others to base conclusions about cause solely on the observation of past correlations between variables—a basis that is logically inadequate.

It is not difficult to see how Hume's analysis justified the equating of causation with powerful prediction and successful forecasting, even though to postpositivists it would be unthinkable to assume that a high correlation between the hair length of students and their opposition to the war in Vietnam implies any causal relationship at all. One would first want to know what other factors might cause both long hair and opposition to the war. We reject Hume, therefore, and many others following him (Russell, 1913; Pearson, 1892; and Norman Campbell, 1920) who have claimed that high correlations demonstrate, or are synonymous with, causation. However, we do agree with Hume that once one conceives of causation in terms other than correlation, it becomes an unobservable factor about which necessarily fallible inferences are made because they are only indirectly linked to observables. While we agree with the positivists that cause cannot be directly demonstrated, we disagree regarding the conclusions to be drawn from this posi-

tion. If they invoke cause at all, it is only when high correlations are involved; but we want to base causal inferences on procedures that reduce the uncertainty about causal connections even though this uncertainty can never be reduced to zero.

Bertrand Russell (1913) has made one of the most cited attacks on the notion of causation from a positivist perspective. He looked to the physics and astronomy of his day as the most mature sciences, and he noted their lack of concern with unobservables and the explicitness and parsimony of the functional relationships that physicists sought to test. He asked why the concept of cause is needed since it is not implied by functional relationships of mathematical form ($\epsilon = mc^2$ would be a current example). In Einstein's famous formula, any of the three variables can be expressed on the left side (traditionally reserved for an effect where one is appropriate), and none of them implies cause. Russell's point of view is positivist, rejecting unobservables (like cause), and seeking to establish explicit functional laws between continuously measured observables in a closed system where the correlations between variables is well-nigh perfect. Russell's viewpoint on this issue is close to that of Norman Campbell (1920).

Suppes (1970) has pointed out Russell's error, at least with respect to recent physics, for his review of major physics journals revealed a significant number of articles with "cause" in the title. Moreover, while not all functional relationships imply cause, many do. For instance, in the gas laws, careful experimentation determined what happens to volume and pressure when temperature is deliberately varied. Russell did not examine the role that testing causal relationships plays in establishing the fundamental, observed data from which functional relationships are induced.

Although Russell was incorrect in asserting that physicists do not use cause, it seems to us that he would have been correct if he had stated that cause plays a lesser overt role in the natural sciences than in other areas of life, including the social sciences. Self-conscious concern about the limitations of causal inference that one often sees when social scientists discuss individual studies seems to be less frequent among natural scientists. This is because natural scientists routinely employ research procedures unavailable in field research with human beings, and these procedures lead them to take cause for granted. Four of these procedures are: (1) An isolation of the phenomenon under investigation from external sources of influence. This is achieved by conducting laboratory research in enclosed settings that exclude extraneous sounds, chemicals in the air, and the like. (2) Dependent variables that are often inert and would not be expected to change over time for reasons other than the cause under investigation. (3) Explicit and precise theories specifying the exact size of an expected effect, whether it be the expansion of a metal or the change in a moon's orbit. (4) Measurement instruments whose calibration and usage is so fine relative to the size of the predicted effect that repeated tests can be made of how closely the observed data fit the expected pattern.

The availability of such features differs from one natural science to another, with the laboratory controls of the physicist not being available to, say, the astronomer. However, some combination of these features is available to most natural scientists, while rarely available to most social and many biological scientists. Thus, less overt preoccupation with causal relationships among natural scientists does not imply they attach less importance to causation. Because of their theories

and procedures they may be more able to take the testing and inferring of cause for granted. Were these theories and procedures to change, our guess is that the natural scientist's concern with cause would be just as self-conscious as the social scientist's.

Though we reject the positivist's claim that causation is unnecessary because it is unobservable, we agree with Russell and Norman Campbell who have attacked the use of the terms *necessary* and *sufficient* causal conditions when referring to the results of analyses of two-category, present-absent data. Consider Figure 1.1 which presents a continuous causal function. Alternate dichotomization points are presented which generate the three 2 × 2 matrices in Figure 1.2. In the first of these matrices, where the two dichotomization points A and A' happen to intersect on the function line, we find a relationship such that the cause is both necessary and sufficient for the effect, in the classical sense of these words. That is, each time the cause is absent, so is the effect, and each time the cause is present, the

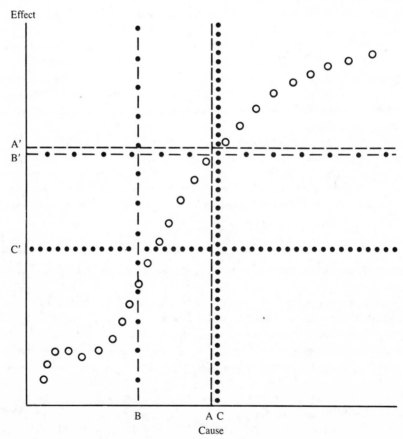

Figure 1.1. Continuous causal function with alternate dichotomization points generating the all-or-none instances A, B, or C of Figure 1.2.

	Cause absent	Cause present	Cause absent	Cause present	Cause absent	Cause present
Effect present	0	9	0	9	5	9
Effect absent	16	0	9	7	11	0
	A		B		C	
	The cause is both necessary and sufficient		The cause is necessary but not sufficient		The cause is sufficient but not necessary	

Figure 1.2. Three classic types of cause derived by arbitrary differences in the points of dichotomization for the same continuous function shown in Figure 1.1.

effect also appears. If we dichotomized at points B and B′ on the continuous cause and effect axes, we would obtain the second matrix which illustrates a necessary but not sufficient cause. That is, when the cause is absent, the effect is absent; but when the cause is present, the effect appears sporadically. When the dichotomization is at points C and C′, the third matrix results in which the cause is sufficient but not necessary. Here, when the cause is absent, the effect is sometimes present and sometimes absent; but when the cause is present, the effect is always present. The point to be emphasized is that the same continuous causal function resulted in substantially different conclusions about the nature of the causal relationship, with the conclusion depending on such a trivial concern as where the dichotomization takes place along the continuous cause and effect variables.

The positivist's denial of causation is conceptually linked to other research-related beliefs. In critical common sense there is a tendency to distinguish between the evidence of the senses and the real world which one seeks to know through perception. The working scientist usually makes a parallel distinction between his often fallible meter readings and the physical processes he is seeking to diagnose or confirm through his laboratory instruments. Positivism clear back to Comte and Hume has argued against this dualism of evidence and reality. Try as you will, argued Hume, you can find no relation between one billiard ball's motion and the motion of another ball it strikes other than coincidence in space and time. Do not therefore needlessly presume, he argued, an additional underlying causal necessity or a separate reality from the evidence of your senses. One aspect of this empiricist monism has been a resistance to positing unobserved entities, leading Mach to deny the existence of atoms in the heyday of success for the atomic theory in chemistry. It is represented in the preference for "intervening variables" over "hypothetical constructs" in that more recent classic paper by MacCorquodale and Meehl (1948). Most pervasively it is represented in the dogma of operational definitions for *theoretical* terms (Bridgman, 1960; Bergmann, 1958) by the notion that number of hours since feeding or percentage of normal body weight or score on an anxiety scale *defined* the theoretical variable *drive*, and that specific performance measures *defined* response strength. Empirical monism led to advocating repeated use of one particular measuring instrument which was given a privileged theory-defining role, or the impractical and theory-confusing dogma that each

alternative measuring process and each improvement in instrumentation defined a separate theoretical concept.

It was in the form of operational definitions that the unacceptability of positivist empiricist monism first became apparent. Although Boring in 1923 defined intelligence as what the intelligence tests measured, fortunately Louis Terman paid no attention and set to work revising the best such test, the 1916 Stanford Binet, to remove biases inferred from departures of his data from theoretical expectations. A physicist knows on both theoretical and practical grounds that galvanometer readings are influenced by friction, inertia, and other laws however much these may be minimized by jeweled bearings, lightweight needles, and theory-based compensatory corrections. A large proportion of any experimental physicist's meter readings are discarded because the instruments are judged to be malfunctioning since the readings do not match expectations of what they should be. One-variable, "pure" measuring instruments are an impossibility. *All* measures involve many known theoretical variables, many as yet unknown ones, and many unproven presumptions, as Duhem (1962) so plausibly illustrated long ago. None can be "definitional" of a single theoretical variable. This is unavoidably so in physics, although often only marginally important. It is much more so in the social sciences where a very small part of any treatment variable or outcome measure is specified by corroborated theory. Psychology's revolt against definitional operationalism first appeared in discussions of test validity introducing the concept of construct validity (Cronbach and Meehl, 1955; Campbell and Fiske, 1959) and was sharply rejected on logical positivist grounds (Bechtold, 1959, answered by Campbell, 1960. See also Webb, et al., 1966). The corrective recommended, which we discuss in chapter 2, was not to abandon "operations," but to use multiple operations each recognized as fallible (Campbell and Fiske, 1959).

On definitional operationalism and empiricist monism more generally the predecessors of this book were clearly post-logical-positivist, although perhaps at first not completely so. In Campbell (1957) and Campbell and Stanley (1963, 1966) both treatments (causes) and observations (measures of effects) are discussed as equivocal exemplifications of intended theoretical variables, as complex products of many determinants, as containing not only random error but also systematic bias due to irrelevant components. However, the presentations are distinctly atheoretical and show some traces of the positivist reluctance to refer to variables which are only indirectly and imperfectly observed, as in speaking of "generalizing to other X's and O's" rather than of the construct validity of treatment implementations and measures, as in Cook and Campbell (1976) and this volume.

Essentialist Theories of Causation

We can use the term *essentialist* to describe philosophers who argue that the term cause should only be used to refer to variables that explain a phenomenon in the sense that these variables, when taken together, are both necessary and sufficient for the effect to occur. This position equates cause with a constellation of variables that necessarily, inevitably, and infallibly results in the effect. Philosophers who restrict cause to observable necessary and sufficient conditions (or sufficient conditions that operate when all the necessary conditions are met) reject as

causes those factors which are known to bring about effects sometimes, but not always. There is a distinct mechanistic tone to discussions of causes as necessary and sufficient antecedent conditions. We doubt very much whether the search for such causes is likely to be fruitful. Few social science theories of today have the background of most natural science theories, nor are they based on empirical relationships that have been tested through considerable research in relatively controlled settings which approximate closed systems (e.g., as has been the case with the gas laws). As Bhaskar (1975) has noted, the point about closed systems is crucial, since causal relationships among a small set of variables can best be studied in closed systems from which all known extraneous forces are excluded.

In field research, we have to expect that outside variables will always impinge on a dependent variable, making the results sensitive to forces other than those in the explicit theoretical system. Like Suppes (1970), we are convinced that observed causal relationships in the social sciences will be fallible rather than inevitable and that the connections between antecedents and consequences will be probabilistic. This is not to deny that social scientists can better approximate inevitable causal connections by studying the contingency conditions that codetermine when a particular putative cause affects an outcome. We merely deny that they will ever be totally successful in this attempt. Probabilistic relationships are, of course, anathema to most essentialists who seek explicit functional laws that express inevitable relationships among a set of observables and in this sense provide a complete causal understanding of a particular event.

The essentialist position on cause is associated with reductionism, with shifts in the level at which causal mediating constructs are postulated. For instance, to understand the conditions that are necessary and sufficient for an electric switch to cause a bulb to burn, one has to understand the principles and constructs of electricity. Once this understanding has been achieved, one can then set about developing a rather long list of factors that have to be present if the light bulb is to be illuminated. Unfortunately, understanding can take place at many different levels of reduction, and in the case of the light being turned on it would be possible to seek explanatory concepts at an even lower level of micromediation, perhaps in terms of particle or even subparticle behavior. An important strategic question facing essentialists is in the choice of the level of mediation where they believe it will be possible to discover variables that inevitably and necessarily produce a given effect. Since we eschew such ultimate understanding of the multiple causes of particular effects, this strategic question need not worry us here. Our concern is less with understanding the causal determinants of a phenomenon than in assessing how reasonable it is to assume that particular manipulable causes usually produce a given result.

In their search for ultimate causes, usually at a micromediational level, essentialists do not require that a cause has to precede its effect. Indeed, they require that the two variables be simultaneously related. If they are not, processes might *sometimes* occur during the delay interval that are necessary for the effect. Unless these processes are completely specified, essentialist causation cannot be inferred; and if they are specified, then causation will better approximate simultaneity since the causal powers that immediately affect the dependent variable can be included in the causal constellation and more proxy variables can be discarded. Gasking

(1955, p. 479), who is by no means an essentialist, gives the following example to illustrate the point:

> Iron begins to glow when its temperature reaches a certain point. I do not know what that temperature is: for the sake of the illustration I will suppose it to be 1000°C., and will assume that iron never glows except at or above this temperature. Now, if someone saw a bar of iron glowing and, being quite ignorant of the physical facts, asked: "What makes that iron glow? What causes it to glow?" we should answer: "It is glowing because it is at a temperature of 1000°C. or more." The glowing, B, is caused by the high temperature, A. And here the B that is caused is not an event subsequent to the cause A. Iron reaches 1000°C. and begins glowing at the same instant. Another example: current from a battery is flowing through a variable resistance, and we have a voltmeter connected to the two poles of the battery to measure the potential difference. Its reading is steady. We now turn the knob of our variable resistance and immediately the voltmeter shows that the potential difference has increased. If someone now asks: "What caused this increase?" we reply: "The increase of the resistance in the circuit." But here again the effect was not something subsequent to the cause, but simultaneous.

In the first of his examples, Gasking makes the point that the state of being at 1000°C. causes (by which he means at a somewhat micromediational level) the iron to glow and that glowing will result as soon as the temperature reaches 1000°C. We have no difficulty here in accepting a causal explanation which does not require a temporal delay between the cause and effect. However, it would not be possible to test Gasking's proposition unless there was sufficient variation in temperature to show that no glowing occurs if the temperature is below 1000°C. and glowing always occurs at higher temperatures. If we consider, for the moment, the experimental manipulation of temperature, a short lapse in time would presumably be required after applying heat to the metal before its temperature is raised to 1000°C. Tests of a simultaneous-appearing causal proposition about states call for procedures that permit variations in the presumed cause to be related to later variations in the presumed effect. Such tests involve the producing of A in order to produce B, and the producing of A precedes the state of B being achieved.

Gasking's second example is more explicitly manipulative, for he writes of turning "the knob of our variable resistance." Even if the potential difference changed exactly when the variable resistance reached the crucial level, it is worth noting that this change occurred after the variable resistance was made to vary. Though causal explanations at a micromediational level need not require that the cause precede the effect, the *testing* of causal relationships does require a temporal precedence of changes in the cause over changes in the effect prior to reaching a particular state.

Bertrand Russell has brought up an important temporal issue that, as a positivist, he uses to discredit the idea of causation, but that also has implications for essentialist thinking about cause. If one acknowledges the possibility of direct causation from A to B, then the question arises: How does one specify the length of the delay between when A changes and B responds? If the response is instantaneous but fleeting, then a delayed measure of B will fail to detect it. If the

response is delayed, too premature a measure of B will not detect it. The problem is not just operational, concerned with the choice of time intervals in a particular research project. It is fundamental, because the time problem implies that questions about A causing B are meaningless unless they include some time interval within which the effect will occur. The paucity of most social science theories means that we can rarely specify such an interval.

The problem is also fundamental since delayed causes would appear to exert their influence in conjunction with mediating variables. Some philosophers and practitioners of science therefore have preferred to forgo the analysis of delayed causation and instead have advocated that research efforts should be diverted towards discovering the ahistorical and often more micro-level field forces which directly mediate delayed effects. Thus, in psychotherapeutic work a researcher with this orientation would not be concerned with historical forces in a client's past that affect behavior in the present but would instead be concerned with the client's current behavior and motives as they relate to the present environmental pressures. Mapping the current causal forces in a respondent's field, while neglecting the historical forces that impinge on the present, lies at the root of such movements as Lewin's (1951) espousal of field theory in social psychology and the rationale offered for behavior modification in clinical research. According to Suppes (1970), this approach also accounts for the dominance of field theories in physics once electromagnetic concepts came to be accepted. Suppes (pp. 31–32) cites a remarkably explicit statement by the physicist Maxwell (1892) favoring the neglect of delayed causation and the study, instead, of any variables in the present through which delayed causes may have exerted their influence. The essentialist concern, once again, is to make explicit any causal chains that might operate through time and to study only the last link of the chain as it directly impinges on the persons or objects being studied.

The essentialist's insistence on infallible and necessary causal relationships leads one to confound high correlation with cause and to question why necessary and sufficient conditions should precede effects (as in the previous iron example). It can also cause one to question why cause should operate in only one direction— from A to B. Functional relationships imply reversible causation, as when an increase in pressure can cause an increase in temperature, and an increase in temperature can cause an increase in pressure. Moreover, some reversible relationships are what we shall call mutually reciprocating within limits, as would be the case if an increase in temperature caused an increase in pressure which, without any further external stimulation, caused an increase in temperature.

We readily acknowledge the usefulness and reasonableness of positing the reversible and mutually reciprocating causes implied by the descriptive functional relationships to which positivists and essentialists aspire. In practice, however, bi-directional causes lead to problems, at least in the short run. In so-called correlational studies the problem of distinguishing which is the cause and which the effect is well known; and in a single experimental study it is not possible to vary an independent variable that is also the dependent variable. Nonetheless, in a program of research it is usually possible to manipulate a causal construct in one study and then to manipulate the effect from such a study so that it becomes the cause in a second one. Further, the cause in the first study would become the

dependent variable in the second. Programmatically, then, reversible causes can be distinguished. In many cases, mutually reciprocating causes can be partially detected at a more micro-level, provided that it is possible to observe valid and sensitive indicators of the cause and effect constructs within a time flow.

In their different ways, both positivists and essentialists aspire to a level of explicitness that we find unrealistic at the present time. The positivists sought to replace unexplicit links in the process of knowing with completely explicit observations (be they atomic sense data, protocol sentences, or observational statements) and with completely explicit deductions from these observations. Essentialists seek to understand completely the multiple causal determinants of a particular effect so that they can be explicit about the factors that necessarily and inevitably produce the effect. Against such explicitness and induction we would like to counterpose our own position which echoes that of Campbell and Stanley (1963) who, emphasizing the inevitable ambiguity and equivocality of experimental results which depend on many deep-seated unproven presumptions, claimed that experiments *probe but do not prove* causal hypotheses. In support of this departure from both positivism and what we have called essentialism, Campbell and Stanley (1963) cited Hanson (1958) and Popper (1959) with approval.

John Stuart Mill and Causation

While it would be wrong to classify John Stuart Mill as a nonpositivist—his debt to Hume is considerable, and he attacked Comte as being not enough of a positivist—it is worth stressing some nonpositivist and nonessentialist aspects in his thinking about cause. Mill held that casual inference depends on three factors: first, the cause has to precede the effect in time; second, the cause and effect have to be related; and third, other explanations of the cause-effect relationship have to be eliminated. The third criterion is the difficult one; and Mill's most significant contribution—for causal analysis purposes—consists of his work on the methods of agreement, differences, and concomitant variation related to this third criterion. The Method of Agreement states that an effect will be present when the cause is present; the Method of Difference states that the effect will be absent when the cause is absent; and the Method of Concomitant Variation implies that when both of the above relationships are observed, causal inference will be all the stronger since certain other interpretations of the covariation between the cause and effect can be ruled out.

To illustrate, we can imagine a billiard cue (A) striking a billiard ball which moves (B). This illustrates the Method of Agreement, since when A is present B occurs. Imagine now observing a cue lying in its rack (i.e., not-A) with the ball on the table. The ball will not move (i.e., not-B) without the cue (or some substitute mediator) striking it. This illustrates the Method of Difference. The two methods together make it possible to infer that a billiard ball can roll if it is struck by a billiard cue and that a cue in the room is not sufficient to make the ball roll. At its core, the Method of Concomitant Variation involves examining a somewhat complex pattern of data in order to induce whether a treatment is associated with an effect and whether some rival causal explanations can be ruled out on the basis of when the treatment and effect are and are not related. In this case, the major alternative explanation eliminated is that the ball would have rolled even if the cue

had not struck. The concept of a control group is implicit here and is clearly central in Mill's thinking about cause.

There are research contexts where random assignment, the physical isolation of units, and the like fulfill the same ends as Mill's canons. Where such design features are not available, as is usually the case in field research, the researcher has to make explicit the inferential threats which remain implicit in controlled settings where the procedural niceties of isolation and random assignment are possible. Mill's great contribution was to realize that the comparison of situations where a particular threat to valid inference was or was not operating provided the key for assessing whether the threat might account for any observed relationship between the cause under study and its possible effect. Though he was not as explicit as modern methodologists about the nature of these threats and the difficulties of making comparisons, and though he was clearly more prone to infer causation from observed regularities than we would be, his contribution to our thinking about cause has been seminal. A careful reading of chapters 3 through 7 will reveal how often a modified form of Mill's canons is used to rule out identified threats to valid inference.

Mill was explicit about the fact that some ways of inferring covariation and temporal precedence have greater value for inferring cause than others. Boring (1954) nicely expresses Mill's preference: "[He] remarked that mere agreement would indicate that night is the cause of day, and day is the cause of night, since the sequence is universal, and he noted that we can be more certain that agreement indicates cause when the antecedent term in the conjunction of events can be established at will without dependence on other events . . ." (p. 212). Mill himself wrote: "It thus appears that in the study of various kinds of phenomena which we can, by a voluntary agency, modify or control, we can in general satisfy the requirements of the Method of Difference but that by the spontaneous operations of nature these requisitions are seldom fulfilled" (cited in Boring, p. 212).

Mill's dissatisfaction with naturally occurring sequences of covariation even when temporal precedence is clear stems from his realization that in nature two forces can vary because a third impinges on the two and makes them covary even though they are not themselves causally related. For instance, day and night covary but do not imply cause; height and weight are correlated but neither causes the other since genetics and nutrition probably cause both. Productivity and worker satisfaction may increase in a factory, with satisfaction preceding productivity. But this sequence need not imply cause, for an increase in wages might cause each dependent variable to change, with the change in satisfaction occurring sooner than the change in productivity. Think how much simpler causal inference would be if the independent variable—satisfaction—were varied as Mill preferred, that is, "at will" by the researchers. In such a case, some workers might experience a planned event that increased their satisfaction without directly influencing productivity, other than through satisfaction, while other workers might experience a planned event that has no effect on satisfaction or productivity shifts other than those that would have normally occurred during the course of the study. Mill's Method of Concomitant Variation and his stress on the researcher's active control, where possible, over the independent variable directly reflects his concern with the third and most difficult necessary condition for confidently inferring

cause—that there should be no alternative interpretations of why when *A* varied, *B* varied afterwards.

Popper and Falsificationism

Among more contemporary philosophers of science, Popper (1959) has been the most explicit and systematic in recognizing the necessity of basing knowledge on ruling out alternative explanations of phenomena so as to remain, the researcher hopes, with only a single conceivable explanation. Such a theory has general implications for all knowledge processes, and our discussion will reflect this. However, we urge the reader to interpret the following discussion particularly in terms of ruling out alternative interpretations of *causal hypotheses*.

Popper's thinking is based on an acceptance of Hume's critique of induction (e.g., to say that night has always followed day does not logically justify the inductive conclusion that night will always follow day). Accepting this critique entails denying the possibility of confirmatory knowledge based on generalizing from particular observations to general scientific propositions. However, Popper claims that deductive knowledge is logically possible and that deductions from a scientific proposition can be tested by comparing the deduced pattern of relationships with the obtained pattern. If the data fit the pattern, this supports the theory to the provisional extent that no other known theory can account for the pattern. But such corroboration can never prove the theory to be true, although failures to confirm the prediction can falsify the theory under test.

The debate between the "confirmationist" position of the logical positivists and Popper's "falsificationist" alternative needs discussion even in a brief review such as this, particularly since both points of view have been rejected by recent post-positivists. Both points of view assume that experimental and observational "facts" can often be generated that are relevant to the validity of a theory and yet independent enough of the theory to be used in evaluating its validity. This shared assumption has come under vigorous attack, as we will discuss below.

Both the confirmationist and falsificationist assume that scientific theories can be used to generate quantitative predictions as to the outcome of scientific experiments and that these predictions, many of which are about causal relations, can be compared with the data. Let us grant this assumption while noting that such predictions also require many background assumptions. There are technical quibbles at this point also, particularly since the observed data never exactly match a quantitative prediction and thus they "fail to confirm" or "falsify" every theory and every numerically specified causal hypothesis. However, let us tentatively agree that on important issues the relevant scientific community can divide outcomes into three categories that are clear in the extremes even if blurred at the borders: (1) confirmed (or corroborated) predictions, (2) ambiguous outcomes, and (3) disconfirmed or falsified predictions. (The degree of precision required for a confirmation varies widely at various stages of a science and even within the same stage for various data types.)

While the scientific community may reach such decisions, they are far from compelling or immune to criticism. What is currently referred to as the "Quine-

Duhem thesis" (Quine, 1953; Duhem, 1962) points out that because of all of the background assumptions that might be wrong—flaws in the equipment, the effects of unknown or wrongly disregarded physical processes, and the like—any outcome can be rationally distrusted and explained away by ad hoc hypotheses that alter the background assumptions. This is obviously true of the disconfirmed predictions, but the same criticism can be leveled against confirmations, which may be pseudo-confirmations made on the basis of a coincidence of such flaws. Such coincidences, however, seem much less likely than spurious falsifications, since many possibilities exist for erroneous assumptions or flaws each of which individually could explain a nonconfirmation. Falsification can thus be regarded as particularly equivocal. Nonetheless, the scientific community does arrive at usable consensus on falsifications (or anomalies) as well as on confirmations of theoretical predictions.

It is in relating these outcomes to the choice among theories that a central distinction between the confirmationist and falsificationist positions emerges. Let us first consider confirmations. The empiricist monism of the positivist leads to the interpretation that the theory which produced the prediction remains a useful, economical summary and predictor of experience. The ambiguity that comes from recognizing that this theory is only one of many different theories that might do equally well with present and past data is not regarded as relevant, for theory is not regarded as a description of real unobserved underlying processes, but rather as but a convenient summarizer and predictor. The "confirmation" achieved is confirmation of usefulness, rather than of the truth of the theory in any realist sense.

Popper's falsificationism, on the other hand, stresses the ambiguity of confirmation. For him, corroboration gives only the comfort that the theory has been tested and has survived the test, that even after the most impressive corroborations of predictions, it has only achieved the status of "not yet disconfirmed." This status of "not yet disconfirmed" is rare and precious in any advanced science, but it is far from the status of "being true."

The error of referring to data as proving the truth of a theory can be stated in terms of an old class of logical fallacies such as "affirming the consequent," "modus tollens," or "the error of the undistributed middle term." While often dismissed as a logical triviality, as a misuse of deductive logic for an inductive situation, or as a ponderous restatement of the truism that scientific truths are never proven with logical certainty, the logical predicament referred to in the situation can usefully be interpreted in relevant ways, and indeed provides a framework in which our emphasis is on plausible rival hypotheses. In choosing, however tentatively, a "true" theory, the scientist as critical-realist operates in a practical way knowingly using an invalid deductive schema of the following sort:

> If Newton's theory A is true, then it should be observed that the tides have period B, the path of Mars shape C, the trajectory of a cannonball form D.
> Observation confirms B, C, and D.
> Therefore Newton's theory A is true.

We can see the fallacy of this argument by viewing it as an Euler diagram, Figure 1.3. The invalidity comes from the existence of the cross-hatched area, i.e., other possible explanations for B, C, and D being observed. But the syllogism is not useless. If observations inconsistent with B, C, and D are found, these validly falsify the truth of Newton's theory A. The argument is thus highly relevant to a winnowing process, in which predictions and observations serve to weed out the most inadequate theories, including the most inadequate causal hypotheses that might seem at first to "explain" a given phenomenon. However, if the predictions are confirmed, the theory remains one of the possible true explanations. This asymmetry between logically valid rejection and logically inconclusive confirmation is the main thrust of Popper's emphasis on falsifiability.

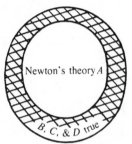

Figure 1.3. Relation of theory to facts (Campbell, 1969a).

It is our inescapable predicament that we cannot prove a theory or other causal proposition. We must work within the limitations diagrammed. *We as scientists try in some practical way to "empty" the cross-hatched area, to make it as small as possible.* We do this by expanding as much as we can the number, range, and precision of confirmed predictions. The larger and more precise the set, the fewer will be the alternative explanations, even though this number still remains in some sense infinite. But as practicing scientists, we in fact pay little or no attention to the mere logical possibility of alternative theories, to the merely logical existence of a cross-hatched area. Toulmin (1961, pp. 113–15) has stated the point well:

> Again, philosophers sometimes assert that a finite set of empirical observations can always be explained in terms of an infinite number of hypotheses. The basis for this remark is the simple observation that through any finite set of points an infinite number of mathematical curves can be constructed. If there were no more to "explanation" than curve-fitting, this doctrine would have some bearing on scientific practice. In fact, the scientist's problem is very different: In an intellectual situation which presents a variety of demands, his or her task is—typically—to accommodate some new discovery to the scientist's own inherited ideas, without needlessly jeopardizing predecessors' intellectual gains. This kind of problem has an order of complexity quite different from that of simple curve-fitting: Far from a scientist having an infinite number of possibilities to choose between, it may be a stroke of genius to imagine even a single one.

It is only when there exist actually developed alternative explanations, that is, when there are known contents to the cross-hatched area, that validity questions arise for theories and other causal hypotheses whose predictions have been confirmed. It was because there were no actually developed rivals that Newton's theory was regarded as certainly true for 200 years, even by such critical epistemologists as Kant. The cross-hatched area was empty in any practical sense. But the logical correctness of Hume's analysis of scientific truth is brought home as a relevant problem for scientific induction by the subsequent overthrow of Newton's theory for that of Einstein.

The situation is in fact even sloppier than this. When a theory such as Newton's has no near rivals and predicts exquisitely well an enormous range of phenomena, we tend to forgive it a few wrong predictions. Thus, as Kuhn (1962) emphasizes, there were known in Newton's day systematic errors of prediction, as of the precession of the perihelion of Mercury, which would have invalidated the theory at that time had Einstein's theory been available. The truer picture is one of a competition between developed and preponderantly corroborated theories for an overall superiority in pattern matching (Campbell, 1966), that is, in matching a pattern of predictions to a pattern of data.

Thus the only process available for establishing a scientific theory is one of eliminating plausible rival hypotheses. Since these are never enumerable in advance, or at all, and since these are usually quite particular and require quite unique modes of elimination, this is inevitably a rather unsatisfactory and inconclusive procedure. But the logical analysis of our predicament as scientific knowers, from Hume to Popper, convinces us that this is the best we can do.

Let us grant that due to the considerations raised in the Quine-Duhem thesis and in the section on the theory-ladenness of facts that follows, singular discordant facts, or discordant facts alone, rarely falsify theories unless they are accompanied by alternative theories that are more in accord with the facts. While it would be wrong to state simply that theories are falsified by alternative theories alone, the usual essential is a combination of alternative theory *and* discordant facts. This leads to an emphasis upon a rivalry of theories in an environment of experimental and observational facts. For this rivalry, Popper has used a natural selection analogy in his 1935 presentation (1959; see also Ackermann, 1970; Toulmin, 1972; Campbell, 1974), and he stresses the use of criticial evidence of all kinds. The rigid thesis that *any* discordant observation falsifies a theory is an oversimplified stereotype of Popper's views created almost entirely by his critics. Popper himself emphasizes tests with multiple validation criteria that permit one theory to be preferred over another. He does not stress a single test being used to reject the theory in the absence of a competitor.

Popper's perspective on falsification depends on the assumption that theories can be compared with each other. This assumption is currently under attack by postpositivists (Hanson, 1958; Kuhn, 1962; Feyerabend, 1975). In challenging positivist beliefs in the possibility of uninterpreted observation statements which provide a theoretically neutral basis for testing theories, the postpositivists have claimed that all observations ("facts") are presumptive and are impregnated with the theory or paradigm under which they were collected. The relevant slogan is one of the "theory-ladenness of facts." Our concern is with the corollary that,

because facts are laden with a particular theory, the relative merits of theories cannot be estimated by comparing each theory's predictions with "objective (i.e., theory-free) facts."

We share the postpositivists' belief that observations are theory-laden and that the construction of sophisticated scientific apparatus and procedures for data presentation usually involve the explicit or implicit acceptance of well-developed scientific theories, over and above the theory being tested. However, we reject the position that observations are laden with only a single theory or paradigm.

We can see the error contained in this *single*-theory-ladenness by going back to Duhem who in 1908 (1962) provided detailed concrete illustrations of the multiple-theory-ladenness of the measures produced by the physics experiments of his day. His work remains the richest demonstration of the truism. While he used the multiple-theory-ladenness of facts as an important part of his general argument for the logical and often practical inconclusiveness of experimental tests of theories, his emphasis on the multiplicity of theories and ordinary beliefs supports the cumulative continuity of physics. In the great scientific revolutions, most of the facts and apparatus, as theory laden as they are, still remain available for comparative tests which help assess the relative merits of extant and new rival theories.

Recently Kuhn (1976) has explicitly limited his use of the term *incommensurability of theories* to mean not mathematically equivalent rather than not comparable. He has also given at least partial acceptance to Stegmüller's (1976) reformulation of Kuhn's position. One aspect of this position is a distinction between T-theoretical terms, which are theoretical relative to a specific theory T, and T-nontheoretical terms which are theory-laden with theories other than T and which function more or less as "observation terms" were to function when theory T is being tested. The implication is that some of the previous arguments that appeared to undercut Popper's belief that observations can falsify theories may not be as powerful as once thought.

Our objection to current connotations of the postpositivist critique goes further. We find much to value in the laboratory scientist's belief in "stubborn facts" that "speak for themselves" and which have a firm dependability greater than the fluctuating theories with which one tries to explain them. Modern theorists of science—Popper, Hanson, Polanyi, Kuhn, and Feyerabend included—have exaggerated the role of comprehensive theory in scientific advance and have made experimental evidence seem almost irrelevant. Instead, exploratory experimentation unguided by formal theory, and unexpected experimental discoveries tangential to whatever theory motivated the research, have repeatedly been the source of great scientific advances, providing the stubborn, dependable, replicable puzzles that have justified theoretical efforts at solution. The experimental physicists feel that their incontrovertible laboratory data serve to keep the speculative theorists honest—an indispensable role in the process of science. Of course, when analytically examined, these stubborn, incontrovertible facts turn out to involve both commonsense presumptions and trust in the truth of many well-established theories that are no longer challenged and that make up the shared core of belief of the science in question. In addition, some of these stubborn facts prove to be

undependable, become reinterpreted as experimental artifacts, or prove to be laden with the dominant focal theory under attack and disappear once it has been replaced. But the great bulk of factual base is not so, and remains dependable. In some areas of psychology, the difficulties of replicating experimental results are so great that this emphasis will seem inappropriate. Perhaps such areas should put more emphasis on achieving such stubborn facts and less emphasis on elaborate theorization until there are indeed dependable factual puzzles worthy of the theoretical effort.

Popper's work relates to epistemology in general rather than the epistemology of causal inferences in particular. However, his work is totally germane to the logic of drawing causal inferences. Indeed, it implies (1) a logical stress on falsifying causal propositions and on giving the status of "not yet disproven" to data patterns that corroborate a particular causal hypothesis but do not rule out all plausible alternative causal hypotheses; (2) a need to collect data which will confront the causal propositions under test, recognizing that convincing data-based refutations require multiple disconfirmations from a variety of strong tests and that the data from any one refutation test are not "objective" in the sense of being free of all theoretical assumptions; and (3) a need to collect data which confronts causal propositions by putting them in competition with other plausible causal propositions, so that a winnowing of the weaker causal hypotheses can take place and a smaller number of hypotheses remains. But whereas Popper is concerned with differentiating between alternative grand theories, the perspective we shall adopt in differentiating among causal hypotheses is less grandiose in implication. Most of the alternatives to the proposition that, say, school desegregation causes an increase in white flight to the suburbs revolve around the possibility that an observed increase in white flight would have occurred without school desegregation, or is an artifact of how white flight is measured, and so on. Such alternatives are threats to the validity of causal inferences but are hardly alternative theories as that term is generally used. Rather, they are more in the nature of theoretical "nuisance factors." Yet these are the alternatives most often confronting practicing researchers who attempt to probe causal relationships by trying to rule out alternative explanations for an observed change, particularly when this change conforms to an expected data pattern suggesting that it could be due to the presumed causal aspect whose influence is being tested.

The Activity Theory of Causation

Many philosophers of science (e.g., Collingwood, 1940; Gasking, 1955; Suppes, 1970; von Wright, 1971; Harré and Madden, 1975; and Whitbeck, 1977) have pointed out that in everyday language the concept of cause implies manipulation. Causes are what we can manipulate to make something happen—the switch is thrown and the light goes on, the edges of the curtains are pulled and the curtains move across the windows, the motorist stopped by a police officer says he is on the way to the hospital and the officer decides not to give him a ticket, the teacher gives an F on the first quiz and the student drops the course, the Federal Reserve Board increases the money supply and inflation increases, the Supreme Court passes the Bakke verdict and some professional schools change their admis-

sion policies. None of the manipulations in these examples invariably produce the intended effects, and the probability of obtaining the effect decreases the more "social" the examples become and the more delayed the response.

This everyday sense of cause has been the starting point for philosophical analyses of what is now often called the activity theory of cause. Perhaps the earliest clear exposition of the theory is given by Collingwood (1940). He distinguishes between three senses in which the term cause is used. The first is as follows: "That which is 'caused' is the free and deliberate act of a conscious and responsible agent, and 'causing' him to do it means affording him a motive for doing it" (p. 285). To illustrate this sense, Collingwood uses examples from history and refers to questions of the form: What caused the Boston Tea Party? What caused Napoleon to invade Russia? These illustrations highlight that both the presumed cause and effect are human activities, with motives and intention heavily involved.

Collingwood's second sense, expressed in rather severe English, is this: "That which is 'caused' is an event in nature, and its 'cause' is an event or state of things by producing or preventing which we can produce or prevent that whose cause it is said to be" (p. 285). Collingwood exemplifies this sense of cause by referring to the manipulation of a switch which causes an electric bulb to give out light. He might also have referred to a vaccine which, when administered, prevents the incidence of some disease. Collingwood is explicit that this sense of the word cause is bound up with the idea of a practical science which informs us about the consequences of performing particular acts. Engineering and medicine are disciplines that, in his day, Collingwood considered to be implicitly adopting this sense of cause.

Collingwood presumably makes a distinction between these two senses of cause to avoid confusing human intentions with physical manipulations. As previously stated, we are less inclined to make a distinction between causes that reflect intention and causes that do not. In each case, an act or series of acts are involved that, when carried out, are aimed at producing or preventing some effect or event. We find the similarity between Collingwood's first and second senses more useful than the distinction between them.

His third sense of cause is close to the essentialist's. He writes that cause is involved when "that which is 'caused' is an event or state of things, and its 'cause' is another event or state of things standing to it in a one-to-one relation of causal priority: i.e., a relation of such a kind that (a) if the cause happens or exists the effect also must happen or exist, even if no further conditions are fulfilled, (b) the effect cannot happen or exist unless the cause happens or exists, (c) in some sense which remains to be defined, the cause is prior to the effect; for without such priority there is no telling which is which" (pp. 285–86). Collingwood's third sense of cause is the one which in the late 1930s he saw being used in basic research where the aim was to explain a phenomenon so fully that we arrive at *the* inevitable cause of some unique event.

Collingwood carefully points out that the ability to control B through manipulating A does not presume a full explanation of why this causal relationship exists. Few children, for instance, can explain why a light goes on when they flick a

switch, but they know that flicking a switch turns on the light. Sometimes, of course, the switch will fail to make the light go on. At such moments we are particularly aware of how inadequate our causal knowledge is of the mediational process whereby a switch turns on a light. We also come to realize that the light does not *inevitably* follow once the switch is manipulated. A full specification of *the* cause for an electrician would require reference to other concepts such as wires joining one part of the electrical system to another, electricity being available, light bulbs being made of the proper materials, and so forth. However, a full specification of *the* cause for physicists might be quite different, being highly reductionist and micromediational, probably invoking concepts about the level of subparticles. *The* cause of the light going on is some complex arrangement of multiple factors, which philosophers call conditions, but they might be different factors at different levels of reduction for persons with different backgrounds! No wonder Scriven (1971; 1975) doubts the usefulness of explanatory causes because of the "irreducible" nature of the concept and the different explanatory causal systems that can be applied to the same phenomena by different groups of people.

At any one level of reduction, how can one specify all of the conditions that make up the causal antecedent of, say, a light going on? Collingwood notes that in some sciences some conditions are more valued than others. He cites the following hypothetical case: "Suppose someone claimed to have discovered the cause of cancer (in Collingwood's third sense, that is), but added that his discovery would be of no practical use because the cause he had discovered was not a thing that could be produced or prevented at will. Such a person would be ridiculed by his colleagues in the medical profession. His 'discovery' would be denounced as a sham" (p. 300). Collingwood's point is that causal explanations are often valued for the leads they give about factors that can be manipulated. If the essential cause of some effect does not imply controlling the effect (e.g., cancer) through manipulating some factor, then knowledge of that cause is not considered useful by many persons. Collingwood again makes his point about the special importance of the manipulable parts of the essential cause by imagining a car that cannot climb a steep hill. A basic scientist might be able to explain why the car cannot climb the hill in terms of the laws of physics. However, such forces will only indirectly suggest what he should do to get the car up the hill. On the other hand, a mechanic, without understanding physics, might be able to explain that the car is only functioning on three cylinders and that four cylinders are needed to give the car enough power to get up the hill, given the slope of the hill, the weight of the car, and so on.

Gasking (1955) takes causation in Collingwood's second sense and likens the partial information it gives to recipes in cooking. In order to achieve a particular type of Schwarzwälder Kirschtorte, we would take a recipe designed to bring about that particular desired outcome and would follow it, ending up with or "causing" a finished cake. We would not need to have an understanding of why particular ingredients are used, why only so much of each ingredient is required, why the mixing proceeds in a certain order, why the oven has to be preheated, and so on. Nor, in a more reductionistic and micromediational sense, would we need to know the chemical composition of the ingredients or the chemical reactions that take place once mixing and cooking occur. All

we would need to know to bring about the effect is that a causal recipe exists that can be followed. Simple causal relationships are more at issue with recipes than essentialist causal explanations.

Knowledge of what is likely to happen if something is deliberately varied has great practical value for social policy. Without causal knowledge one cannot easily bring about desired changes or eliminate undesirable states. If we think back to Collingwood's hypothetical example of discovering the essential cause of cancer, the point is that a cause which does not imply actions to prevent or cure cancer are less useful than a cause with action implications. To control cancer requires knowing how to act with respect to diets, the air we breathe, or the tissue that is to be cut out. In a similar vein, to control inflation does not imply knowing all the causes of inflation but simply those that we can do something about. Knowledge of causal manipulanda, even the tentative, partial, and probabilistic knowledge of which we are capable, can help improve social life. What policy makers and individual citizens seem to want from science are recipes that can be followed and that usually lead to desired positive effects, even if understanding of the micromediational processes is only partial and the positive effects are not *invariably* brought about.

The image of a recipe brings to mind the current limitations of learning about manipulable causal forces in the social world. Recipes usually specify multiple ingredients and precise quantities from which only a small deviation is allowed. In addition, the ingredients often are mixed and prepared in a set order, with a precise oven temperature for cooking. When reliable knowledge of causal relationships in the social world also depends on multivariate causal interconnections, on the exact specification of levels for each causal force, and on specific orders of combining variables, acquiring reliable causal knowledge will be difficult and causal connections will simply not repeat from one instance to the next. Since the causal manipulanda of social policy interest can rarely be finely adjusted, we may have to content ourselves at present in more complex settings with manipulanda that only sometimes bring about intended effects. With more research and other experiences, the contingency variables on which causal impact codepends will probably be specified, and knowledge of causal relationships will then improve in reliability.

An Evolutionary Critical-Realist Perspective

Overlapping with the activity theory of causation is a biological evolutionary perspective with intellectual origins quite different from the ordinary language philosophy of the followers of Wittgenstein and Austin, from which much of activity theory has emerged. From the evolutionary perspective (e.g., as reviewed by Campbell, 1974) humanity's strong and stubborn psychological predispositions to infer causal relations (Heider, 1944; Michotte, 1963) can be seen as the product of a biological evolution of brain-mind processes, which has resulted in a psychic unity concerning causation. This unity is, in general, adaptive because it will often validly reflect causal processes that can and do occur in the real world; but it will not fit the world perfectly and some of the ''causes'' that humans perceive will reflect passive relationships of concomitancy that have no accurate implications for changing one's behavior to adapt more effectively to external circumstances.

Such an evolutionary perspective, when couched in a critical-realist mode, enables us to recognize causal perceptions as "subjective" or "constructed by the mind"; but at the same time it stresses that many causal perceptions constitute assertions about the nature of the world which go beyond the immediate experience of perceivers and so have objective contents which can be right or wrong (albeit not always testable). The perspective is realist because it assumes that causal relationships exist outside of the human mind, and it is critical-realist because it assumes that these valid causal relationships cannot be perceived with total accuracy by our imperfect sensory and intellective capacities. And the perspective is evolutionary because it assumes a special survival value to knowing about causes and, in particular, about manipulable causes.

The theory of natural selection implies that the object content of subjective causal perceptions about middle-sized objects and events has been accurate enough in the evolutionary past to be useful. As a result we have highly developed organs for seeing such objects and events and for analyzing their interrelationships. With macroscopic or galactic objects, or events that occur in nanoseconds or millenia, our organs are not at all highly developed. Knowledge of such objects and events may not have been very useful in our distant past. Evolutionary theory would also lead us to believe that the highly presumptive *causal inferences* which humans have drawn about the relationships between middle-sized objects and events (e.g., Does raising a stick cause the apple which I cannot reach to fall out of the tree?) have survival value. More importantly, they may have a survival value greater than a less presumptive perception of environmental concomitancies that are devoid of causal imputation (e.g., The sun rising a little later each morning is associated with apple trees losing their leaves).

This evolutionary perspective brings us to an important distinction between mere correlation and truly causal relationships, between forecasting and diagnosing manipulable causes which will enable us to change the world. Most animals and many plants have adaptations enabling them to exploit the predictively useful correlations among the sensed variables of their environments. Indeed, it is the existence of such relationships that makes sense organs adaptive. For many of these species, this adaptation is passive, involving differential response to environmental change but no action to change the environment. Thus an anchored shellfish may monitor the sun and tides with adaptive openings and closings of the valves that permit it to feed. But it cannot take any action to modify its environment. However, other species go beyond a passive diagnosis of concomitancies among the sensed A's and B's and focus special attention on that subset of concomitancies for which the organism's manipulation of A will produce a change in B. Such species try, therefore, to assess whether fires, huts made of different fabrics, and increased physical exertion will help one keep warm when the weather cools; and they will strive to use sticks and ladders to get down fruit from trees. In our evolutionary scenario, it is these species that would develop brain-mind systems giving causal perceptions and causal inferences, diagnostic of *manipulable* relationships. We human beings are preeminently such a species, and our intuitive concept of causality is a product of an evolutionary adaptation like the one sketched above.

Unfortunately, the phenomenal, experiential unity of the concept of causality leads us humans to expect a logical certainty and singular essence when we experience "cause." But meticulous logical analyses by philosophers show that there is a hodgepodge of nearly contradictory essences in the cause-effect relationship: antecedence-subsequence and simultaneity, nonidentity yet immediate proximity. From the evolutionary point of view, causality may well be such a logical hodgepodge of nonentailing but useful clues in the diagnosis of dependably manipulable correlations on the basis of fragmentary and momentary perceptual evidence.

From such an evolutionary perspective, the "subjective," "constructed-in-the-mind," "going-beyond-the-data-given" status of causal inferences is not incompatible with the general descriptive validity of the causal imputations resulting. Such a view is not entirely alien to Kant's and is a part of a frequently noted evolutionary interpretation of the Kantian categories (reviewed in Campbell, 1974, pp. 441–47). For Kant, causality was a synthetic a priori category, synthetic meaning descriptive of the nature of the world rather than logically true. For us human beings the concept of cause may be a priori in the sense that we are born with it rather than learning it in our own lifetime, and this may be why we have such strong predispositions to perceive and infer cause even when none is there.

In this evolutionary view, as with the activity theory, the concept of causality is closely linked to intentions and purposes. Most causal inferences are about attributes of the world that are particularly relevant to an active, intrusive, willful organism. While trying out manipulations is the best practical (although imperfect) mode of discovering and confirming causal inferences, our evolutionary history has made us also predisposed to generate causal inferences from passively observed concomitancies involving changes we ourselves have not manipulated. Thus early humans no doubt observed and causally interpreted the correlation between burning wood and warmth long before they learned how to control fire. Causal inferences derived from observing such concomitancies are more likely to generate false information about causal connections. Some of these false positives are easily winnowed out when the putative cause is manipulated and the expected results do not occur. But other "causal" inferences derived from correlational evidence cannot be so easily falsified, as is indicated by the failure to discover sooner that witch doctors cannot cause rain. Since from the evolutionary perspective causal inferences are much better validated when confirmed by manipulation, this view also suggests that experimentation is a natural outgrowth of a focus on causal laws.

IMPLICATIONS OF THE ANALYSIS OF CAUSATION

The several notions of causality we have briefly described all share much with each other and with ordinary usage. With the positivists we share the recognition that causation and concomitance are closely related, even while we disagree about the nature of that relationship. We are willing to assert that causes have a real nature, albeit one that can only be imperfectly grasped. With the later positivists who wanted to substitute continuous mathematical functions for causal laws, we agree in rejecting the older notions of necessary and/or sufficient causes where the causes and effects occur in but one of two states: present or absent.

With the essentialists we share a willingness to consider underlying causes not given in the observational data and a longing for utterly dependable causal relations, even though we recognize that we will not discover such with the macro-causal levels and unclosed systems found in biology, psychology, and the social sciences.

From J. S. Mill we take three important criteria for inferring cause: (1) covariation between the presumed cause and effect; (2) the temporal precedence of the cause; and (3) the need to use the "control" concept implicit in his Method of Concomitant Variation to rule out alternative interpretations for a possible cause and effect connection. We also note Mill's preference for tests of causal propositions which involve the active manipulation of causal agents, since theoretical and spurious causal forces are usually confounded in nature and most can be clearly unconfounded when putative causes are varied "at will."

From Popper's work, we recognize the necessity to proceed less by seeking to confirm theoretical predictions about causal connections than by seeking to falsify them. For Popper, the process of falsification requires putting our theories into competition with each other. We believe that such competition can be achieved, even though the observations made in tests are not theory-free and there can be no guarantee that the researcher has conceptualized all the relevant alternative theories. At most, he or she can conceptualize the "plausible" alternatives. Our emphasis differs from Popper's in that we stress attempts to gain knowledge by pitting causal hypotheses not against other explanatory or descriptive theories but against mundane nuisance factors which suggest that an observed relationship may not be causal or may involve different constructs than those in which the investigator is interested. Like Popper, we stress the need for *many* tests to determine whether a causal proposition has or has not withstood falsification; such determinations cannot be made on one or two failures to achieve predicted results.

From the activity theorists of causation, we take the idea that the causal laws of greatest practical significance and closest correspondence to common sense definitions of cause are those laws involving manipulable causes. These are causes we can do something about, and they can be likened to recipes for action. But, like recipes, such action may have to be based on a host of causal variables and specific interrelationships among these variables. When the relevant variables cannot be specified, causal knowledge will be problematic and probabilistic. However, some of the causal connections can be dependable even when we do not understand the processes that mediate an effect.

From evolutionary epistemology we take the idea that humanity may have evolved with a special need to detect aspects of the environment that can be changed to bring about desired states. We might presume that knowledge about such changes is most dependably achieved by manipulating the environment, observing the immediate results, and inferring causal connections between the two. If so, much of the causal knowledge so achieved will be both valid and useful. Some valid causal knowledge is undoubtedly inferred from concomitancies that are not associated with direct manipulation, but much invalid knowledge is presumably also generated from such evidence. At least, this is what the psychological research suggests that deals with the prevalence and immediacy of the causal attributions that are generated from observing events that happen to be

related in time and space. Given the need to attribute cause, we might also presume that some of the causal knowledge derived from manipulation will be invalid, especially where a long time interval is thought to elapse between the manipulation and the outcome or where irrelevant manipulations are correlated with valid causal events, as when a witch doctor chooses to do a rain dance at, say, the sight of dark clouds.

If we now juxtapose the points made above with the logic of experimentation, we note a close correspondence. Most experiments require the manipulation of putative causes and thus are restricted to the subset of all causes that are manipulable. Moreover, experiments are epitomized by control over the independent variable. This permits us to falsify many of the mundane nuisance alternative interpretations that challenge causal inference, nowhere more so than when random assignment occurs. Experiments often involve control groups, and these in their turn contribute to ruling out other alternative interpretations by a process similar to Mill's Method of Concomitant Variation. The experiment is modest, seeking only to elucidate whether a particular cause or a restricted set of causes has an effect. It is not aimed at a comprehensive explanation of all the causal forces that determine a particular outcome; nor is it usually aimed at establishing sufficient causes and their necessary counterparts. Rather, it is aimed in the short term at probing probabilistic causes. In a sense, our analysis of causation leads us to a conception of cause that avoids an essentialist explanation and settles for probing probabilistic causal connections. However, our analysis of causation also leads us to prefer experimentation—one of the less modest methodological tools for field research—because a major requirement for experimentation (manipulability) closely mirrors the type of cause in which we are most interested.

Our position on causation is perhaps best summarized by the eight statements below. In these, the term *molar* refers to causal laws stated in terms of large and often complex objects. *Micromediation* refers to the specification of causal connections at a level of smaller particles than make up the molar objects and on a finer time scale.

1. *Causal assertions are meaningful at the molar level even when the ultimate micromediation is not known.* They are meaningful in the sense that they can be right or wrong and that, given proper conditions, they can be tested. Let us expand on Collingwood's (1940) illustration of the wall switch turning on an electric light bulb. It seems meaningful to assert that, when activated, a particular light switch A causes a lightbulb B to burn. As individuals, we have often verified such an assertion, as when we have tried to find which of several switches controlled a particular bulb. We also accept as meaningful and open to criticism the causal assertions that the electric current flowing into the bulb caused the light and that the heat of the filament in the lightbulb caused the light (with the implication that any other way of heating the filament to the same temperature would also have produced the light). Further, it is meaningful to us to assert that, where the wall switch is heat-sensitive, as in some elevators, the warmth of our finger caused the light to go on. Indeed, many of us have experimented with this proposition by holding hot or cold fingers in front of the heat-sensitive switch. We also find meaningful the assertion that an instructor's need to grade papers at night

caused her to switch on the light, even though this assertion is about a motivational cause and reflects intention. The admonition from one person to another not to read in such poor light, the advertising campaign to save energy, and a change in the cost of electricity are all meaningful and testable causes for a light being switched on or off. Thus, we find it advantageous to conceive of molar causes that imply human intention as well as molar causes of the traditional push-pull variety associated with physics and mechanics (e.g., flicking the switch causes the light to go on). Such causal assertions are helpful primarily because they imply knowledge about how to control the environment; and they are meaningful because they can be tested and are subject to verification as being largely right or wrong. Given these points, we do not find it useful to assert that causes are "unreal" and are only inferences drawn by humans from observations that do not themselves directly demonstrate causation.

2. *Molar causal laws, because they are contingent on many other conditions and causal laws, are fallible and hence probabilistic*. If the light bulb has burned out, if a wire has broken, if the electrical power station has failed, if the contacts in the switch have corroded or become too loose, if the insulation has worn thin permitting an alternative route for electrical flow other than through the bulb, if the intention to turn on the light is swamped by incompatible intentions that dominate a person's attention and action, then the occurrence of the cause may not produce the effect. To those of us who use causal concepts as a part of ordinary common sense, we realize that causes do not invariably produce their usual effects. Yet the fallible nature of molar causal relationships perplexes philosophers seeking a logical foundation for the concept of cause. Such philosophers focus on ultimate micromediation, on causal essences. They hope to treat as causes only those factors that *inevitably* produce a given outcome, that are both necessary and sufficient for the result. There are many important philosophical issues about micromediation and the criterion that causes should inevitably produce a particular effect. However, we can avoid taking a stand on these since we are reconciled to the fact that in the social sciences the causal explanations we will be dealing with will be molar and contingently causal rather than ultimately micromediational and inevitable. We are also reconciled to the belief that, where any one of the contingent conditions is not as assumed, manipulating the cause may not produce the effect. Given the difficulties in conceptualizing and testing all the relevant contingent conditions, many genuine effects will appear to occur sporadically. Only later will the conditions become clear under which the cause more frequently leads to the effect. As a result, the evidence supporting molar causal laws will usually be probabilistic; it is probably the case that the more molar the causal assertion and the longer and more unspecified the assumed micromediational causal chain, the more fallible the causal law and the more probabilistic its supporting evidence.

3. *The effects in molar causal laws can be the result of multiple causes*. We can turn on the light by other means than flicking the switch. For instance, if the light switch is left in the "on" position, we can turn the light off and on by any other break in the circuit or by scraping the insulation off two wires and touching them together (light off) and then respacing them (light on). It is clear from this exam-

ple that, as we go down the causal chain, any link can be potentially activated by those before it and that many of the contingencies assumed in a molar law can become a manipulated cause. We can also conceive of multiple causation at the same molar level. For instance, an instructor may decide to switch on the light in order to do her grading, because she has nothing else to do, because she does not feel sleepy yet, or because she is curious about how a particular student did.

Multiple causation gives rise to the problem of spurious causation, for we are not sure whether a particular treatment or some other cause produced an observed effect. In discussing spurious causal inferences, we have in the past, and may again in this book, inadvertently imply single causation, with assertions about *the* cause. When we use such an expression we are not discussing the *only* possible cause of some unique effect; we are referring to the manipulated cause of an effect *in a particular research project*. From a wider perspective such a cause is only one of many that could have produced a given effect. Indeed in conducting factorial experiments, the researcher recognizes that effects may have multiple causes that do not always act in a simple additive fashion.

4. *While it is easiest for molar causal laws to be detected in closed systems with controlled conditions, field research involves mostly open systems.* The concept of a closed system appears in the technical philosophical discussion of causal laws, particularly regarding questions of necessity and the inevitability of a particular cause or causes producing a unique event. We would like to extend the concept to include physical and social isolation, for these can produce nearly closed systems. Thus, the soundproofing, lead shielding, thick steel walls, and so forth of the laboratory strongly resemble closed systems, forcibly excluding all the undesired contingency states and alternative causes that have been recognized and allowing for any special conditions that are necessary for a molar causal law to operate. This is quite unlike the situation in field settings where the disturbing contingencies and alternative causes are greater in number, are less likely to be known, and will usually be more difficult to control. Insulation of the wires connecting the light switch, lightbulb, and power source provides a closed system to a minor degree in Collingwood's example, and one can imagine how many more contingencies would operate if wires were not so well insulated. In laboratory experiments, the manipulation of the cause comes from outside the closed system; it is what the economists would call an exogenous variable. Similarly, the light switch is an access point for forces or messages from outside the largely closed system of insulated wires. The best way to test causal relationships is to make controlled intrusions into a closed system.

When the system is more open—as with field research in the social sciences— multiple causation and the operation of contingent causes are more of a problem. In providing people with income supplements of different levels in order to study their effects on, perhaps, the number of days worked, it is not possible, nor desirable for most purposes, to shield respondents from all the other factors that affect working conditions (inflation rates, the availability of credit to finance new businesses, the supply of local housing, convenient roads, attractive work environment, and so on). Nor is it possible to control all of the factors on which an effect of income supplements might be based (alternative job opportunities, landlords raising rents when

they realize respondents have more money, and the like). The more open the system, the more fallible will be causal inferences. Until contingency conditions are more fully specified, which is a process that can take many, many years, molar causal relationships in society may not be reproduced easily.

5. *Dependable intermediate mediational units are involved in most strong molar laws*. This is perhaps a restatement of the previous point. However, it calls attention to the fact that, in biological systems, some complex molar units have acquired such dependability that they may operate as unproblematic units in still more molar causal chains. The individual nerve cell is one such unit. Until one is sick, it is an unproblematic unit that dependably and causally contributes to human functioning at more molar levels. Larger, more complex servosystem units may similarly function. For instance, a traditional goal for military training is to turn the individual soldier into an unproblematic unit who dependably responds to orders. Dependable intermediate mediation is involved in all *strong* causal laws. Undependable mediation—as when nerve cells malfunction or soldiers refuse to respond to orders—results in weaker and less dependable molar laws.

In biological and social units, where purposes, goals, cybernetic systems or servomechanisms are involved, molar dependability may be achieved by substituting alternative micromediational links. Thus, if an extra homework assignment causes the room to be lighted at midnight, this effect can be mediated by candles if the electrical power source is out. If the rat's hunger causes the animal to press a lever, this can be mediated by pulling the lever with its jaw when its paws are tied. The substitution of mediating mechanisms, and the intention implicit in this, poses no problem for our concept of cause, nor for cause as it is understood in ordinary language. Nor does it make experimentation any less relevant as a means of testing causal hypotheses (though it does suggest the need to probe how effects come about). However, deliberate substitution of mechanisms is a dramatic departure from the physical push-pull billiard ball examples of causation, calling into question philosophical analyses based on describing causation exclusively in terms of the physical domain. At the molar level we are discussing, it is as meaningful to make the causal assertion that raising the thermostat setting caused the temperature in the room to rise as it is to assert the more direct, mechanical causal relation that increasing the fire in the furnace caused an increase in temperature. In each case, a contingent assertion can be corroborated or falsified at a probabilistic level.

6. *Effects follow causes in time, even though they may be instantaneous at the level of ultimate micromediation*. For philosophers concerned with restricting cause to factors that are both necessary and sufficient for a unique effect which is inevitably produced, it is important that the cause and effect occur simultaneously. If they are separated in time, even briefly, other variables in the micromediational causal chain may have produced the effect, so that the putative cause is not primary.

This philosophical requirement violates everyday language where a cause has to precede an effect. It also violates the working assumption of most scientists interested in biological, psychological and social relations. Their training and experience lead them to expect that a cause, whether of the purposive or passive push-pull variety, should precede its effect. This working assumption is probably

well founded, for at the more molar level at which biologists and social scientists work ultimate micromediation and causal necessity are not at issue. Instead, the aim is to discover points in the causal chain where changes in one variable lead to changes in another. Delayed causal connections imply real storage processes (Rozelle and Campbell, 1960), as with bank accounts or energy storage in fatty tissues. Such storage processes, plus the present-day realism where one does not look for ultimate causes in the social sciences, lead us to accept the idea of delayed causation while not ruling out that within some logical framework, ultimate causes should have instantaneous effects.

7. *Some causal laws can be reversed, with cause and effect interchangeable.* In the gas laws which relate volume, pressure, and temperature to each other, the semiclosed laboratory equipment makes possible the external intrusion of a change in any one of the three while holding the others constant. Consequently, we know that experimentally decreasing volume increases temperature and pressure; that experimentally varying temperature changes pressure if volume is held constant, and the like. But such reversible conditions cannot be assumed for all correlations, even those obtained under laboratory control. For instance, we might well show that the expertise of a communicator changes someone's attitude about a particular topic; but it is less clear that a change in attitude will cause a change in how the person views the expertise of the communicator, though it might. However, in a clearer case, if providing food stamps to a family improved the nutritional status of children, it would be almost impossible to show the reverse—that improving the nutritional status of the children causes the family to get food stamps.

8. *The paradigmatic assertion in causal relationships is that the manipulation of a cause will result in the manipulation of an effect.* This concept of cause has been implicit in all the foregoing examples, and philosophers claim that it reflects the way causation is understood in everyday language. Causation implies that by varying one factor I can usually make another vary. For many valid causal laws we may not in practice be able to manipulate the putative cause at will, if at all. This has grave consequences for our ability to test the law, but it does not negate its truthfulness. However, it does decrease the immediate practical importance of the law, for it suggests that the causal powers implicit in the law cannot be easily used to make desirable changes in persons or environments. Putative causal factors that cannot be varied may be involved in correlational relationships with their presumed effects. But since it is the case that not all dependable laws of concomitance are causal laws (e.g., it is dependable that night follows day, but not at all clear that night causes day), it is dangerous to infer causation from observed regularities or dependencies between variables. If we define the meaningfulness of causes in terms of their ability to create testable, dependable, and planned changes, then the most meaningful causes are those which can be deliberately manipulated. Such a concept of cause mirrors the unique feature of experimentation—the manipulation of putative causes.

2

Validity

We shall use the concepts *validity* and *invalidity* to refer to the best available approximation to the truth or falsity of propositions, including propositions about cause. In keeping with the discussion in chapter 1, we should always use the modifier "approximately" when referring to validity, since one can never know what is true. At best, one can know what has not yet been ruled out as false. Hence, when we use the terms valid and invalid in the rest of this book, they should always be understood to be prefaced by the modifiers "approximately" or "tentatively."

One could invoke many types of validity when trying to develop a framework in which to understand experiments in complex field settings. Campbell and Stanley (1963) invoked two, which they called "internal" and "external" validity. Internal validity refers to the approximate validity with which we infer that a relationship between two variables is causal or that the absence of a relationship implies the absence of cause. External validity refers to the approximate validity with which we can infer that the presumed causal relationship can be generalized to and across alternate measures of the cause and effect and across different types of persons, settings, and times.

For convenience, we shall further subdivide the two validity types of Campbell and Stanley. Covariation is a necessary condition for inferring cause, and practicing scientists begin by asking of their data: "Are the presumed independent and dependent variables related?" Therefore, it is useful to consider the particular reasons why we can draw false conclusions about covariation. We shall call these reasons (which are threats to valid inference-making) threats to *statistical conclusion validity,* for conclusions about covariation are made on the basis of statistical evidence. (This type of validity was listed by Campbell [1969] as a threat to internal validity. It was called "instability" and was concerned with drawing false conclusions about population covariation from unstable sample data. We shall later consider "instability" as one of the major threats to statistical conclusion validity.)

If a decision is made on the basis of sample data that two variables are related, then the practicing researcher's next question is likely to be: "Is there a *causal* relationship from variable A to variable B, where A and B are manipulated or measured variables (operations) rather than the theoretical or otherwise generalized constructs they are meant to represent?" To answer this question, the researcher has to rule out a variety of other reasons for the relationship, including the threat that B causes A and the threat that C causes both A and B. The first of these threats is usually handled easily in experiments, as we shall see later. The latter is not so easily dealt with, especially in quasi-experiments. Much of the researcher's task involves self-consciously thinking through and testing the plausibility of noncausal reasons why the two variables might be related and why "change" might have been observed in the dependent variable even in the absence of any explicit treatment of theoretical or practical significance. We shall use the term *internal validity* to refer to the validity with which statements can be made about whether there is a causal relationship from one variable to another in the form in which the variables were manipulated or measured.

Internal validity has nothing to do with the abstract labeling of a presumed cause or effect; rather, it deals with the *relationship* between the research operations *irrespective of what they theoretically represent*. However, researchers would like to be able to give their presumed cause and effect operations names which refer to theoretical constructs. The need for this is most explicit in theory-testing research where the operations are explicitly derived to represent theoretical notions. But applied researchers also like to give generalized abstract names to their variables, for it is hardly useful to assume that the relationship between the two variables is causal if one cannot summarize these variables other than by describing them in exhaustive operational detail. Whether one wants to test theory about the effects of "dissonance" on "attitude change," or is interested in policy issues relating to "school desegregation" and "academic achievement," one wants to be able to make generalizations about higher-order terms that have a referent in explicit theory or everyday abstract language. Following the lead of Cronbach and Meehl (1955) in the area of measurement, we shall use the term *construct validity of causes or effects* to refer to the approximate validity with which we can make generalizations about higher-order constructs from research operations. Extending their usage, we shall use the term to refer to manipulated independent variables as well as measured traits. We shall base inferences about constructs more on the fit between operations and conceptual definitions than on the fit between obtained data patterns and theoretical predictions about such data patterns—more on what Campbell (1960) called trait validity than what Cronbach and Meehl (1955) termed nomological validity. We shall not ignore nomological validity, however.

The construct validity of causes and effects was listed by Campbell and Stanley (1963) under the heading of "external validity," and it is what experimentalists mean when they refer to inadvertent "confounding."[1] (That is, was the effect

---

[1]Confounding is sometimes done deliberately in more complex experimental designs, e.g., Latin squares or incomplete lattice designs. Such deliberate confounding is meant to achieve efficiency at the cost of reduced interpretability for some carefully chosen interactions that are considered implausible or that are of little theoretical or practical significance.

due to the planned variable X, or was X confounded with "experimenter expectancies" or a "Hawthorne effect," or was X a "negative incentive" rather than "dissonance arousal"?) As such, construct validity had to do with generalization, with the question: "Can I generalize from this one operation or set of operations to a referent construct?" Given this grounding in the need to generalize, it is not difficult to see why Campbell and Stanley linked generalizing to abstract constructs with generalizing to (and across) populations of persons, settings, and historical moments. Just as one gains more information by knowing that a causal relationship is probably not limited to particular operational representations of a cause and effect, so one gains by knowing that the relationship (1) is not limited to a particular idiosyncratic sample of persons or settings of a given type, and (2) is not limited to a particular population of Xs but also holds with populations of Ys and Zs. We shall use the term *external validity* to refer to the approximate validity with which conclusions are drawn about the generalizability of a causal relationship to and across populations of persons, settings, and times.

Our justification for restricting the discussion of validity to these four types is practical only, based on their apparent correspondence to four major decision questions that the practicing researcher faces. These are: (1) Is there a relationship between the two variables? (2) Given that there is a relationship, is it plausibly causal from one operational variable to the other or would the same relationship have been obtained in the absence of any treatment of any kind? (3) Given that the relationship is plausibly causal and is reasonably known to be from one variable to another, what are the particular cause and effect constructs involved in the relationship? and (4) Given that there is probably a causal relationship from construct A to construct B, how generalizable is this relationship across persons, settings, and times? As stated previously, each of these decision questions was implicit in Campbell and Stanley's explication of validity, with the present statistical conclusion and internal validities being part of internal validity and with the present construct and external validities being part of external validity. All we have done here is to subdivide each validity type and try to make the differences among types explicit. We want to stress that our approach is entirely practical, being derived from our belief that practicing researchers need to answer each of the above questions in their work. There are no totally compelling logical reasons for the distinctions.

STATISTICAL CONCLUSION VALIDITY

Introduction

In evaluating any experiment, three decisions about covariation have to be made with the sample data on hand: (1) Is the study sensitive enough to permit reasonable statements about covariation? (2) If it is sensitive enough, is there any reasonable evidence from which to infer that the presumed cause and effect covary? and (3) if there is such evidence, how strongly do the two variables covary?

The first of these issues concerns statistical power. It is vital in reporting and planning experiments to analyze how much power one has to detect an

effect of a given magnitude with the variances and sample sizes on hand. In planning studies, the power analysis usually consists of discovering the sample size required for detecting an effect of desired magnitude, given the expected variances. The major practical difficulties besetting such an analysis are, first, obtaining agreement as to the magnitude of desired impact, and second, finding acceptable variance estimates (other data sets are often used for the second purpose). Once these difficulties are overcome, the required sample sizes can be computed according to formulae given in most statistical texts.

When an experiment has been completed, power analyses usually have a different function. The known variances and sample sizes are used to compute the magnitude of effect that could have been "reasonably" detected in the study at hand. ("Reasonably" is often taken to mean "with 95% confidence.") If the magnitude of the detectable effect seems low to most persons, one would tentatively conclude that the experiment was powerful and that the null hypothesis might be provisionally accepted. However, if the magnitude estimate seems high, then it is not clear whether the absence of covariation is due to the true absence of a relationship or to the experiment being so weak that reasonably sized true effects could not be detected. Power analyses are desirable in any report of a study where the major research conclusion is that one variable does not cause another.

In research probing causal hypothesis, statistical analyses are primarily used for deciding whether a presumed cause and effect covary. In many studies, a decision about covariation is made by comparing the degree of covariation and random error observed in the sample data to an a priori specified risk of being wrong in concluding that there is covariation. This risk is specified as a probability level (usually 5%), and we speak of setting α at .05. The 5% level is arbitrary, and if we want more protection against being wrong in claiming there is covariation, then one simply lowers the probability level. Observed relationships below the specified probability level are treated as though they are "true," while those above it are treated as though they are "false." However, as statistics texts make clear in their discussions of Type I and Type II error, we can be wrong in concluding that the population means of various treatment groups truly differ even when the obtained probability level is below the specified one. We can also be wrong in concluding that they do not differ relative to the variances when the probability level is above the specified level.

Many traditions have developed in the data analysis field for assessing, not whether covariation can be inferred, but the amount of covariation. When the scale on which the outcome variable is measured has some commonsense referent, effects can be expressed in terms of the treatment causing, say, an average increase in income of $1,000 per annum per person, or a reduction in prison recidivism of 20% over two years. With other scales, magnitude estimates are more difficult to interpret, and one wonders what an average treatment effect of five points on some academic achievement test "means" when it cannot be validly translated into an estimate of, say, grade level or mental age. This is why some researchers do not like to express the magnitude of impact directly in terms of the original scale but prefer to estimate it indirectly as the additional variance that the treatment permits one to predict in the dependent variable.

Magnitude estimates have a considerable advantage over estimates of whether covariation can reasonably be inferred since they are less dependent on sample size. (Note that very small effects will be statistically significant given a large enough N of units.) This dependence on sample size leads many statisticians to prefer estimates of the magnitude of covariation over inferences about whether it is reasonable to presume any covariation at all. Nonetheless, as we shall use the term, *statistical conclusion validity* refers to inferences about whether it is reasonable to presume covariation given a specified α level and the obtained variances. As such, statistical conclusion validity seems more closely related to tests of statistical significance than to magnitude estimates. Our stress on statistical significance is because decisions about whether a presumed cause and effect covary logically precede decisions about how strongly they covary. Moreover, in most reports where magnitude estimates are given without corresponding statistical significance tests it is usually presumed that the estimates of, say, the difference between two means are statistically significant.

Fortunately, decisions about covariation and its magnitude are not independent, for statistical significance depends on the relationship between a magnitude estimate and a standard error. Consequently, information about whether covariation can be presumed and about how much can be presumed is almost always available somewhere in a research report, though each type of information is not always equally stressed.

We would prefer to see research reported in terms of both statistical significance and magnitude estimates that are bounded by confidence intervals. In this sense, research conclusions might take the following form: "The treatment caused a statistically significant increase in the income of families of four. In tests similar to the one conducted, the effect in 95% of the cases would be an increase of between $400 and $1,600 per year." Bounded magnitude estimates realistically reflect the sources of error in social research which limit our confidence in conclusions. If widely used, they would decrease the current dependence on speciously precise point estimates, e.g., "The average increase in income was $1,000 per year." When sample sizes are small, it is particularly dangerous to rely on statistical significance as the sole editing mechanism that allows us to differentiate between magnitude estimates that are and are not worth treating as different from zero. With small samples, power analyses should be reported to illustrate the magnitude of the effect that could have been detected given the sample sizes, the variances obtained in the study, and the chosen α level.

Some Major Threats to Statistical Conclusion Validity

Below is a list of some threats to drawing valid inferences about whether two variables covary. Later we shall present lists of threats to the other kinds of validity. In listing threats, we have been guided by our own research experience and by our substantive reading about factors that can lead to spurious inferences. No list of threats is the perfect one; and ours outlines forces that we believe plausibly occur in basic or applied research in field settings. But though we consider each threat plausible, we do not believe that each operates

with equal frequency or that each affects outcome variables to the same degree. Indeed, empirical research has been conducted on identified threats to try to establish the conditions under which they are likely to affect responses so that data-based estimates of plausibility can be made. For instance, on the basis of a program of research into how pretest measurement affects behavior in laboratory experiments, Lana (1969) was led to conclude that pretest sensitization is probably less of a threat than was previously feared. In the last analysis, systematic research and carefully considered experience should influence the practicing scientist's concern about the likelihood of each of the threats we have identified and have provisionally labeled as plausible. Moreover, we anticipate that persons with an interest in basic research will see some of the listed threats as more plausible than persons who are interested in more applied work, and vice versa. We also anticipate that the threats we will discuss for statistical conclusion validity and for the three other types of validity will be modified as experience accumulates.

Low Statistical Power

The likelihood of making an incorrect no-difference conclusion (Type II error) increases when sample sizes are small, and α is set low. Moreover, statistical tests differ considerably in power, with some being notably low—for example, tests of the difference between independent correlations (Cronbach and Snow, 1976). Cohen's (1970) book on statistical power gives a preliminary introduction to the topic for social scientists.

Violated Assumptions of Statistical Tests

Most tests of the null hypothesis require that certain assumptions be met if the results of the data analysis are to be meaningfully interpreted. Thus, the particular assumptions of a chosen statistical test have to be known and—where possible—tested in the data on hand. For example, with the analysis of covariance, the regression of the posttest on the first-order covariates should be homogeneous and the groups being compared should be equivalent. Each of these assumptions can be checked to some degree, the former by examining scatterplots and the latter by comparing pretest means. Not all assumptions are equally important. For instance, like other multiple regression techniques, the analysis of variance is robust to violations of normality but is less robust to violations of the assumption of uncorrelated errors (Lindquist, 1953). Since the importance of particular assumptions depends on the test being conducted, it is desirable to consult standard statistical references to check one's understanding about the test's assumptions and to learn how to circumvent any problems with assumptions that might arise with a particular data set.

Fishing and the Error Rate Problem

The likelihood of falsely concluding that covariation exists when it does not (Type I error) increases when multiple comparisons of mean differences are possible and there is no recognition that a certain proportion of the comparisons will be significantly different by chance. Ryan (1959) has distinguished between the error rate per comparison ("the probability that any one of the

comparisons will be incorrectly considered to be significant"), the error rate per experiment ("the expected number of errors per experiment") and the error rate for experiments in general ("the probability that one or more erroneous conclusions will be drawn in a particular experiment").

The last two are the most important, and Ryan has illustrated one method of adjusting for the error rate per experiment. This involves computing a new t value which has to be reached before significance at a given α level can be claimed. The new t is obtained by taking the desired α (e.g., .05) and dividing it by the number of possible comparisons so as to give an adjusted proportion (p) that will be lower than .05. Then, the t value corresponding to this adjusted p is looked up in the appropriate tables. It will, of course, be higher than the t values normally associated with $\alpha = .05$. This higher value reflects the stringency required for obtaining a more accurate level of statistical significance when multiple tests are made. A second method for dealing with the error rate problem involves using the conservative multiple comparison tests of Tukey or Scheffé which are discussed in most moderately advanced statistics texts. When there are multiple dependent variables in a factorial experiment, a multivariate analysis of variance strategy can be used for determining whether any of the significant univariate F tests within a particular main or interaction effect are due to chance rather than the manipulations.

The Reliability of Measures

Measures of low reliability (conceptualized either as "stability" or "test-retest") cannot be depended upon to register true changes. This is because unreliability inflates standard errors of estimates and these standard errors play a crucial role in inferring differences between statistics, such as the means of different treatment groups. Some ways of controlling for unreliability include (1) using longer tests for which items or measures have been carefully selected for their high intercorrelations, or (2) using more aggregated units, e.g., groups instead of individuals, since a group mean will be more stable than individual scores. However, the increase in reliability due to aggregation is counterbalanced by a decrease in the number of degrees of freedom that results. (3) Occasionally the standard corrections for unreliability presented in textbooks can be used, but with great caution—particularly if the reliability estimate is low.

The Reliability of Treatment Implementation

The way a treatment is implemented may differ from one person to another if different persons are responsible for implementing the treatment. There may also be differences from occasion to occasion when the same person implements the treatment. This lack of standardization, both within and between persons, will inflate error variance and decrease the chance of obtaining true differences. The threat—which is pervasive in most kinds of field experiments (see Boruch and Gomez, 1977, for a statistical analysis) — can most obviously be controlled by using all the available opportunities to make the treatment and its implementation as standard as possible across occasions of implementation. In some instances, despite best efforts to standardize, treatments will have con-

siderable unplanned variability in how they are implemented. It is always wise to try and understand and measure this heterogeneity and to use the measures in the data analysis. The advantages and disadvantages of doing this are outlined in chapters 3 and 4.

Random Irrelevancies in the Experimental Setting

Some features of an experimental setting other than the treatment will undoubtedly affect scores on the dependent variable and will inflate error variance. This threat can be most obviously controlled by choosing settings free of extraneous sources of variation or by choosing experimental procedures which force respondents' attention on the treatment and lower the salience of environmental variables. In many complex field settings these suggestions will be very difficult to implement. In such cases the need will be to measure the anticipated sources of extraneous variance which are common to all the treatment groups in *as valid a fashion as possible* in order to introduce the measures into the statistical analysis. Monitoring the experiment in its initial stages will suggest other setting variables which will probably add to the error variance and which, if reliably measured, could be introduced into the analysis to reduce error.

Random Heterogeneity of Respondents

The respondents in any of the treatment groups of an experiment can differ on factors that are correlated with the major dependent variables. Occasionally certain kinds of respondents will be more affected by a treatment than others, and this—as we shall soon see—is a matter of external validity. At other times respondent variables do not interact with the treatment but are related to outcomes. When this happens, the error variance will be inflated. This threat can obviously be controlled by selecting homogeneous respondent populations, but this is often at some cost to external validity. Alternatively, the relevant respondent characteristics can be reliably measured and, under the appropriate circumstances (see Elashoff, 1969), used for blocking or as covariates. It is also worth noting that the threat is reduced when within-subject error terms are appropriate—that is, when they depend not on differences between persons but on differences between occasions of responding within the same persons. The advantages of within-subject designs can be most simply illustrated in pretest-posttest designs where the reduction in error depends on the correlation between each respondent's pre- and post-scores: the higher the correlation, the greater the reduction in the error term.

The Problem of "Accepting" the Null Hypothesis

It is frequently stated in the literature on experimental design that the null hypothesis cannot logically be proven. There are two reasons for this. First, there is always the possibility, however remote, that statistics have failed to detect a true difference. Second, we cannot know what would have resulted if the treatment had been more powerful, or a statistical test of greater power had been used, or if the statistical analysis had extraneous sources of respondent or setting variance which correlate with the dependent variable. (For a discussion

of the logic of accepting the null hypothesis see Cook, Gruder, Hennigan and Flay, 1979.)

These arguments are logically compelling. But while we cannot prove the null hypothesis, in many practical contexts we have to make decisions and act *as though* the null hypothesis were true. This is especially the case in applied research, where decisions have to be based on imperfect knowledge which only suggests that a treatment has had no detectable effect. The issue then becomes: By what standards should one estimate the confidence that can be placed in "accepting" the null hypothesis, particularly if a decision has to be based on the results of a single experiment?

Situation 1

When an explicit directional hypothesis guides the research, it is sometimes possible to conclude with considerable confidence that the derived effect was not obtained under the conditions in which the testing occurred. This conclusion is easiest to draw when the results are statistically significant and in the opposite direction to that specified in the hypothesis or when the results, though not statistically reliable, are contrary to the derived prediction and are found in a vast majority of reasonably powerful subgroup analyses, e.g., at different sites. But note here that the issue is not acceptance of the hypothesis of no-difference, but acceptance of the hypothesis that a particular predicted effect was not obtained.

Yet even when the results are opposite to what was expected, it is still useful to check whether influential suppressor variables might be obscuring a smaller true effect in the predicted direction. For example, Campbell and Boruch (1975) have maintained that true effects of compensatory education programs have been obscured in much past research because the experimental groups receiving compensatory treatments came from economically poorer homes than did the more affluent control group children whose parents' incomes made them ineligible for the compensatory program. Since the children in experimental groups usually come from homes that are associated with lower achievement levels and slower growth rates over time, Campbell and Boruch argue that two countervailing forces are set up in compensatory education experiments. First there are differences in growth rates, which cause experimentals to gain *less* than controls over time. Second, there are true treatment effects which cause experimentals to gain *more* than would randomized controls. The net effect of these two forces can be the misleading appearance of either no treatment effect or even a harmful effect.

Situation 2

A situation where no-difference findings are generally interpretable is when point estimates of the size of a desired effect are available (e.g., we want an increase of more than 2% on one variable or an increase of at least ten points on some other). This specification, when combined with variance estimates, allows us to compute—before any data are collected—the sample size required for inferring at a given confidence level that a difference of the desired size would have been observed if it had truly occurred. Thus, if the number of observations in a completed study is at least equal to the number specified in the prestudy analysis, and if the variances used for computing the desired sample size are similar to

those that were actually obtained in the study, then one can compute with a known level of confidence whether a specified point standard has been exceeded with the data on hand. This is clearly a desirable situation for any data analyst.

Let us illustrate the above points by describing a section from a report on the effects of manpower training programs on subsequent earnings. Aschenfelter (1974) knew that training costs were about $1,800 for each trainee. He estimated that a return of at least 10% on this investment (i.e., $200) would be adequate for declaring the manpower training program a "success." Then, assuming equal numbers of persons in the experimental training group and the no-training control group, and knowing from previous data that the standard deviation in income was about $2,000 for white males, Aschenfelter calculated that about 1,600 persons would be needed in the experiment if a true effect of at least $200 was to be detected with 95% certainty. However, Aschenfelter further calculated that if he were to break down the data by two race and two sex groups, he would need a total of 6,400 respondents—1,600 in each subgroup. Knowing this, he was then in a position to assess whether he had the necessary resources to design an experiment of this size or whether he would be better served by using some other technique for trying to evaluate the training program.

Unfortunately, it is rare to have valid variance estimates and a prior point estimate of the size of an expected effect. The problem of specifying expected effect sizes is sometimes political, largely because a publicized point estimate can become a reference against which a social innovation is evaluated. As a result, even if an innovation has had *some* ameliorative effect, it may not be given much credit if it failed to have the *promised* effect. It is no small wonder, therefore, that the managers of programs prefer less specific statements such as "We want to increase achievement," or "We want to reduce inflation" to statements such as "We want to increase achievement by two years for every year of teaching" or "We want to reduce inflation to 5% a year." The problem of specifying magnitudes is also sometimes one of "consciousness," for the issue may simply not be considered in designing the research. Alternatively, it may be silently considered by some persons but never brought to the level of discussion for fear that different parties to the research may disagree on the level of effect required to conclude that a treatment has made a significant, practical difference.

Situation 3

Even when no magnitude-of-effect estimate is available, it is still possible to use information about sample sizes and variances in order to calculate *retrospectively* the size of any effect that could have been detected in a particular experiment with, say, 95% confidence. This magnitude can then be inspected and interpreted. At times it will seem so unreasonably large that the only responsible conclusion is that the experiment was not powerful enough to have detected a true effect. For instance, in the Aschenfelter case a sample size of 400, split equally between experimentals and controls, would have required the experimentals to earn considerably more than $200 on the average if a true effect were to be detected at the 5% level. How reasonable is it to expect an average increase in earnings over $200 in the first working year after graduating from a job-training program? The answer to this cannot be definitive since no criteria exist for assess-

ing reasonableness. Nonetheless, the figure seems to us to be very high. We would strongly advise anyone whose research results in a no-difference conclusion to conduct the retrospective analysis indicated above.

Situation 4

When data are first analyzed, it is often the case that the estimate of the treatment effect (say, a difference between sample means) is statistically nonsignificant but in the expected direction. Typically, efforts are then made to "reduce the error term" used for testing the treatment effect—a topic that we shall now discuss.

Obviously, it is desirable to design the research initially so as to minimize this error. For instance, "Student" (1931) reexamined an experiment which compared how four months of free pasteurized milk affected the height and weight of Scottish school children when compared to four months of raw milk. About 5,000 students received each type of milk. "Student" maintained that the same statistical power (and much lower financial costs) would have resulted had only 50 sets of identical twins been used. This is because weight and height are highly correlated for monozygotic twins, leading to lower error terms than those associated with differences between nonrelated children. In light of modern knowledge, we might not want to design the study in the way "Student" suggested because of nonstatistical considerations. For example, would parents seek to supplement one of their twin's diets if they knew that the other was receiving a school-provided supplement, and how generalizable would findings from 50 sets of twins be? Nonetheless, "Student's" point is important, and it suggests designing research *wherever possible* so as to have small error terms, provided that the means of reducing the error do not trivialize the research.

Perhaps the best way of reducing the error due to differences between persons is to match *before* random assignment to treatments. (This, we shall soon see, is quite different from matching as a substitute for randomization. While matching prior to randomization can increase statistical conclusion validity and permit tests to discover in which particular subgroups a treatment effect is obtained, matching as an alternative to randomization often leads to statistical regression artifacts that can masquerade as treatment effects.) The best matching variables are those that are most highly correlated with posttest scores. Normally the pretest is the best single matching variable since it is a proxy for all the social and biological forces that make some individuals or aggregates of individuals different from others. The actual process of matching is simple. One takes all the scores on the matching variable, ranks them, and places them into blocks whose size corresponds to the number of experimental groups (say, three). Then, the three persons in the first block are randomly assigned to one of the experimental groups, the next three in the next block are randomly assigned, and so on until all the cases are assigned. The data that result from such a design can then be analyzed as coming from a Levels $\times$ Treatment design. The same logic basically holds when matching takes place on multiple variables, but the problem of finding matches is harder. (Matching will be discussed in greater detail in several of the chapters to come.)

Given random assignment to treatment conditions, it is nonetheless possible to match retrospectively after all the data have been collected. With large sample

sizes, retrospective matching will result in treatment groups that have comparable proportions of units with the characteristic on which matching takes place. However, the major disadvantage of this technique compared to prospective matching is that subgroups with few members (e.g., blacks in many settings) can be disproportionately represented in each treatment group, with very few persons in one of the groups. This makes it difficult to estimate treatment effects for the subgroups in question. But this problem aside, ex post facto blocking can be extremely useful both because effects of the blocking variable can be removed from the error term and because the interaction of the blocking variable with the treatment can be assessed.

When there is no interest in testing how the dependent variables are related to the matching or blocking variable, an alternative method of reducing the error term can be used that loses fewer degrees of freedom. It requires using multiple regression strategies involving variables which are correlated with the dependent variable *within treatment groups* and whose effects are to be partialled out of the dependent variable. Covariance analysis is one such strategy. The extent to which covariance analysis reduces error depends on the correlation between the covariates (the lower the better) and the correlation of each of them with the dependent variable (the higher the better). But two words of caution are required about such multiple regression adjustments. First, important statistical assumptions have to be demonstrably met for the results of the analysis to be meaningful, especially the assumption of homogeneous regression within treatment groups. Second, in experiments with non-comparable groups, the analysis will reduce error but will rarely adjust away all the initial differences between groups. Thus, the function of reducing error—which makes covariance so useful with both randomized experiments and quasi-experiments—should not be confused with the purported function of making groups equivalent. Equivalence is not needed with randomized experiments and is rarely achieved by regression adjustments with quasi-experiments. (For an extended discussion of these last points see chapters 3 and 4.)

Both matching and multiple regression adjustments assume that measures have been made of the variables for which adjustments are to be made. Failure to measure them means that error terms cannot be reduced to reflect the way that person or setting variables are related to the major outcome measures of an experiment. Increasing one's confidence in accepting the null hypothesis demands *valid* measurement of the variables that are most likely to affect posttest scores.

There is little point in reducing the error variance due to differences among persons and settings if the outcome measures are so unreliable that they cannot register true change. Thus, the experimenter has to be certain to begin with reliable measures. Alternatively, the experimenter has to try and develop even more reliable measures after an experiment is under way by adding items to tests, by rescaling, or by aggregating data. But whether or not attempts are undertaken to increase reliability, it is important that internal consistency estimates and test-retest correlations be displayed in a research report. The reader can at least judge for himself the extent to which measures may have been capable of registering true changes.

Statistical procedures exist for correcting for unreliable measurement. This means that analysis of "true" scores should be possible. (Details of this procedure

are available in many standard texts, including McNemar, 1975.) These correctional procedures can often be misleading in practice. First, there are many ways of conceptualizing reliability, each of which implies a different reliability measure and different numerical estimates of the amount of reliability. Second, for any one kind of reliability, its own reliability will not be directly known. And third, reliability-adjusted values do not logically correspond with the values that would have been obtained had there been perfectly reliable measurement. This is perhaps most dramatically illustrated by reliability-adjusted correlations in excess of 1.00, or by the fact that a nonsignificant r of, say, $-.10$ must inevitably result in a higher adjusted value *of the same sign*, whereas the population correlation may have been $+.04$. Great caution must be exercised, therefore, in the use of reliability adjustments. It would be naive to present the results only for adjusted data or, when adjusted results are presented, to use only one estimate of reliability. A range would be better.

Each of the foregoing strategies can reduce error terms. Consequently, it is advisable for purposes of statistical conclusion validity to use as many as possible of the following design features. (1) Each person might be his own control (i.e., serve in more than one experimental group); (2) samples might be selected that are as homogeneous as possible (monozygotic twins are merely the extreme of this); (3) pretest measures should be collected on the same scales that are used for measuring effect; (4) matching might take place, before or after randomization, on variables that are correlated with the posttest; (5) the effects of other variables that are correlated with the posttest might be covaried out; (6) the reliability of dependent variable measures might be increased; or, (7) occasionally the raw scores might be adjusted for unreliability. In addition, (8) estimates of the desired magnitude of effect should be elicited, where possible, before the research begins. Even when no such estimate can be determined, (9) the absolute magnitude of a treatment effect should be presented so that readers can infer for themselves whether a statistically reliable effect is so small as to be practically insignificant or whether a nonreliable effect is so large as to merit further research with more powerful statistical analyses. It should not be forgotten that all of these strategies have negative consequences if uncritically used and that all of them require trade-offs that will become more obvious later. Moreover, most of them are more problematic when analyzing data from quasi-experiments than data from randomized experiments.

Situation 5

Having tried to make the error term as small as possible, the researcher will encounter a problem if the data analysis still fails to result in statistically significant effects. All one can then conclude is that this particular example of this particular treatment contrast had no observable effects. One cannot easily draw conclusions about what would have happened if each treatment had been more homogeneously implemented (i.e., each person or unit in a group had received exactly the same amounts of the treatment) or if the experimental contrast had been larger (i.e., the mean difference between groups had been greater on some measure designed to assess the strength of the treatment implementation).

As we shall see later, quasi-experimental analyses can sometimes be conducted to assess these two possibilities by capitalizing upon the fact that measures

of treatment implementation can be made which estimate presumed differences in the strength of the treatment. Such differences can then be associated with estimates of the magnitude of changes between a pretest and posttest in order to determine if the two are related. While such analyses should definitely be conducted, chapters 3 and 4 will illustrate that great care must be exercised in interpreting the results. This is because individuals will normally have voluntarily chosen to expose themselves to treatments in different amounts, and so the kind of person at one treatment level is likely to be different from a person at another level. Nonetheless, if sophisticated quasi-experimental analyses of the kind in chapters 3 and 4 still fail to result in covariation between the treatment and outcome measures, then the analyst can be all the more confident in accepting the null hypothesis.

INTERNAL VALIDITY

Introduction

Once it has been established that two variables covary, the problem is to decide whether there is any causal relationship between the two and, if there is, to decide whether the direction of causality is from the measured or manipulated A to the measured B, or vice versa.

The task of ascertaining the direction of causality usually depends on knowledge of a time sequence. Such knowledge is usually available for experiments, as opposed to most passive observational studies. In a randomized experiment, the researcher knows that the measurement of possible outcomes takes place after the treatment has been manipulated. In quasi-experiments, most of which require both pretest and posttest measurement, the researcher can relate some measure of pretest-posttest change to differences in treatments.

It is more difficult to assess the possibility that A and B may be related only through some third variable (C). If they were, the causal relationship would have to be described as: $A \rightarrow C \rightarrow B$. This is quite different from the model $A \rightarrow B$ which most clearly implies that A causes B. To conclude that A causes B when in fact the model $A \rightarrow C \rightarrow B$ is true would be to draw a false positive conclusion about cause. Accounting for third-variable alternative interpretations of presumed A-B relationships is the essence of internal validity and is the major focus of this book.

Although in the examples that follow we shall deal primarily with the possibility of false positive findings, it should not be forgotten that third variables can also threaten internal validity by leading to false negatives. The latter occur whenever relationship signs are as below. In the case to the left, an increase in A causes an increase in both B and C, but the increase in C causes a decrease in B. Thus,

the net effect of A and C on B would be to tend to obscure a true $A \to B$ relationship. In the case depicted in the center, an increase in A would cause an increase in B and a decrease in C, while a decrease in C would cause a decrease in B. Once again, the effects of A and C would tend to cancel each other out. In the final case, an increase in A would cause a decrease in both B and C, and the decrease in C would cause a countervailing increase in B.

Let us give an example of the second of these three relationships. Imagine that A is tutoring and B is academic achievement. Imagine, further, that tutoring is given to the weaker students academically and is withheld from the stronger, this process of selection into the treatment being C. Since tutoring is negatively related to initial achievement, we have $A \twoheadrightarrow C$. Being weaker, the students with tutoring would be expected to gain less over time than their fellow students for a number of reasons that have nothing to do with tutoring (e.g., slower rates of learning from other sources). Hence, $C \twoheadrightarrow B$. Thus, if tutoring did raise achievement ($A \xrightarrow{+} B$) but the children who received tutoring were expected to gain less from schooling anyway (that is, $C \twoheadrightarrow B$), then the effects of tutoring and of lower expected growth rates would countervail. In the special case where the two forces were of equal magnitude, they would totally cancel each other out. In cases where one force was stronger than the other, the stronger cause would prevail but its effect would be weakened by the countervailing cause. We hope that our later examples, which emphasize internal validity threats and false positive findings, will not blind readers to the effects that such threats can have in leading to false negative findings because of the operation of suppressor variables.

It is possible for more than one internal validity threat to operate in a given situation. The net bias that the threats cause depends on whether they are similar or different in the direction of bias and on the magnitude of any bias they cause independently. Clearly, false causal inferences are more likely the more numerous and powerful the validity threats and the more homogeneous the direction of their effects. Though our discussion will be largely in terms of threats *taken singly,* this should not blind readers to the possibility that multiple internal validity threats can operate in cumulative or countervailing fashion in a single study.

Threats to Internal Validity

Bearing this brief introduction in mind, we want to define some specific threats to internal validity.

History

"History" is a threat when an observed effect might be due to an event which takes place between the pretest and the posttest, when this event is not the treatment of research interest. In much laboratory research the threat is controlled by *insulating* respondents from outside influences (e.g., in a quiet laboratory) or by *choosing dependent variables* that could not plausibly have been affected by outside forces (e.g., the learning of nonsense syllables). Unfortunately, these techniques are rarely available to the field researcher.

Maturation

This is a threat when an observed effect might be due to the respondent's growing older, wiser, stronger, more experienced, and the like between pretest and posttest and when this maturation is not the treatment of research interest.

Testing

This is a threat when an effect might be due to the number of times particular responses are measured. In particular, familiarity with a test can sometimes enhance performance because items and error responses are more likely to be remembered at later testing sessions.

Instrumentation

This is a threat when an effect might be due to a change in the measuring instrument between pretest and posttest and not to the treatment's differential impact at each time interval. Thus, instrumentation is involved when human observers become more experienced between a pretest and posttest or when a test shifts in metric at different points. The latter can happen, for instance, if intervals are narrower at the ends of a scale than at the midpoint, resulting in so-called ceiling or basement effects. (Basement effects are also called "floor" effects.)

Statistical Regression

This is a threat when an effect might be due to respondents' being classified into experimental groups at, say, the pretest on the basis of pretest scores or correlates of pretest scores. When this happens and measures are unreliable, high pretest scorers will score relatively lower at the posttest and low pretest scorers will score higher. It would be wrong to attribute such differential "change" to a treatment because it might be due to statistical regression.

Statistical regression is not an easy concept to grasp intuitively. It might help you understand it if you think of your own academic test taking. You may sometimes have surprised yourself by doing worse than you expected, perhaps because you didn't sleep well the night before, you read the questions too quickly and misunderstood them, there may have been someone with an infuriating cough in front of you, or because the test just happened to have had a disproportionately high number of items from a part of the curriculum that you had not studied in detail. Any or all of these factors could have depressed your scores, and they can be conceptualized as error factors that do not reflect true ability. Consequently, the next time you took a test on the same or similar subject matter your scores would probably be higher and would more accurately reflect your ability. This is because, all things being equal, you will be less likely to have been deprived of sleep, less likely to have read the questions too quickly, less likely to have had someone with a cough sit in front of you, and less likely to have received questions from parts of the curriculum that you had studied the least.

Viewed more generally, statistical regression (1) operates to increase obtained pretest-posttest gain scores among low pretest scores, since this group's pretest scores are more likely to have been depressed by error; (2) operates to decrease obtained change scores among persons with high pretest scores since their pretest scores are likely to have been inflated by error; and (3) does not affect obtained

change scores among scorers at the center of the pretest distribution since the group is likely to contain as many units whose pretest scores are inflated by error as units whose pretest scores are deflated by it. Regression is always to the population mean of a group. Its magnitude depends both on the test-retest reliability of a measure and on the difference between the mean of a deliberately selected subgroup and the mean of the population from which the subgroup was chosen. The higher the reliability and the smaller the difference, the less will be the regression.

Selection

This is a threat when an effect may be due to the difference between the kinds of people in one experimental group as opposed to another. Selection is therefore pervasive in quasi-experimental research, which is defined in terms of different groups receiving different treatments as opposed to probabilitistically equivalent groups receiving treatments as in the randomized experiment.

Mortality

This is a threat when an effect may be due to the different kinds of persons who dropped out of a particular treatment group during the course of an experiment. This results in a selection artifact, since the experimental groups are then composed of different kinds of persons at the posttest.

Interactions with Selection

Many of the foregoing threats to internal validity can interact with selection to produce forces that might spuriously appear as treatment effects. Among these are selection-maturation, selection-history, and selection-instrumentation. Selection-maturation results when experimental groups are maturing at different speeds. Such group differences in growth rates typically occur, for example, when middle-class and lower-class children are compared at two different time intervals on some test of cognitive knowledge. In this situation, the children from more affluent backgrounds tend to gain at a faster rate than the others. Selection-history (or local history) results from the various treatment groups coming from different settings so that each group could experience a unique local history that might affect outcome variables. (The interaction can also occur with randomized experiments if a treatment is only implemented at one or two sessions—usually with large groups of respondents. In such cases, the treatment will be associated with any unique events that happened during the few sessions which provided all the data about a particular treatment's effects.) Selection-instrumentation occurs when different groups score at different mean positions on a test whose intervals are not equal. The best known examples of this occur when there are differential "ceiling" and "floor" effects, the former being when an instrument cannot register any more true gain in one of the groups, and the latter when more scores from one group than another are clustered at the lower end of a scale.

Ambiguity About the Direction of Causal Influence

It is possible to imagine a situation in which all plausible third-variable explanations of an *A-B* relationship have been ruled out and where it is not clear

whether *A* causes *B* or *B* causes *A*. This is an especially salient threat to internal validity in simple correlational studies where it will often not be clear whether, for example, less foreman supervision causes higher productivity or whether higher productivity causes less supervision. This particular threat is not salient in most experiments since the order of the temporal precedence is clear. Nor is it a problem in those correlational studies where one direction of causal influence is relatively implausible (e.g., it is more plausible to infer that a decrease in the environmental temperature causes an increase in fuel consumption than it is to infer that an increase in fuel consumption causes a decrease in outside temperature). Nor is it necessarily a problem in correlational studies when the data are collected at more than one time interval, for then one knows something about temporal antecedence. However, ambiguity about the direction of causal influence is a problem in many correlational studies that are cross-sectional.

Diffusion or Imitation of Treatments

When treatments involve informational programs and when the various experimental (and control) groups can communicate with each other, respondents in one treatment group may learn the information intended for others. The experiment may, therefore, become invalid because there are no planned differences between experimental and control groups. This problem may be particularly acute in quasi-experiments where the desired similarity of experimental units may be accompanied by a physical closeness that permits the groups to communicate. For example, if one of the New England states were used as a control group to study the effects of changes in the New York abortion law, any true effects of the law would be obscured if New Englanders went freely to New York for abortions.

Compensatory Equalization of Treatments

When the experimental treatment provides goods or services generally believed to be desirable, there may emerge administrative and constituency reluctance to tolerate the focused inequality that results. Thus, in nationwide educational experiments such as Follow Through, the control schools, particularly if equally needy, tended to be given Title I funds earmarked for disadvantaged children. Since these funds were given to the supposed "no-treatment controls" in amounts approximately equivalent to those coming to the experimental schools, the planned contrast obviously broke down. Several other experimental evaluations of compensatory education have encountered the same problem. It exemplifies a problem of administrative equity that must certainly occur elsewhere, including among units of industrial organizations. Such focused inequities may explain some administrators' reluctance to employ random assignment to treatments which their constituencies consider valuable.

Compensatory Rivalry by Respondents Receiving Less Desirable Treatments

Where the assignment of persons or organizational units to experimental and control conditions is made public (as it frequently must be), conditions of social competition may be generated. The control group, as the natural underdog, may be motivated to reduce or reverse the expected difference. This result is particularly likely where intact units (such as departments, plants, work crews, and the

like) are assigned to treatments, or if members of the control group will be at a disadvantage if a treatment is successful. As an example, Saretsky (1972) has pointed out that the success of performance contracting—paying commercial contractors according to the size of learning gains made by students—would threaten the job security of school teachers. Many would think that they could be replaced by contractors or that their professional role might be redefined because of the contractors. Given this threat, Saretsky has suggested that the academic performance of children taught by teachers in the control groups of the OEO Performance Contracting Experiment could have been better during the experiment than it had been in past years. The net effect of atypically high learning gains by controls, if it occurred, would be to diminish the difference in learning between control students taught by their regular teachers and experimental children taught by outside contractors. Saretsky (1972) describes other examples of the phenomenon of special effort by the controls. He calls this effort a "John Henry effect" in honor of the steel driver who, when he knew his output was to be compared to that of a steam drill, worked so hard that he outperformed the drill and died of overexertion. (Compensatory rivalry is very like compensatory equalization in that each is a response to the focused inequity that inevitably results when treatments differ in desirability, as they do if valuable resources are being distributed. However, compensatory equalization is a response of administrators and compensatory rivalry is a response of those in the less desirable treatment groups.)

Resentful Demoralization of Respondents Receiving Less Desirable Treatments

When an experiment is obtrusive, the reaction of a no-treatment control group or groups receiving less desirable treatments can be associated with resentment and demoralization, as well as with compensatory rivalry. This is because persons in the less desirable treatment groups are often relatively deprived when compared to others. In an industrial setting the persons experiencing the less desirable treatments might retaliate by lowering productivity and company profits, while in an educational setting, teachers or students could "lose heart" or become angry and "act up." Any of these forces could lead to a posttest difference between treatment and no-treatment groups, and it would be quite wrong to attribute the difference to the planned treatment. Cause would not be from the planned cause, A, given to a treatment group. Rather, it would be from the inadvertent resentful demoralization experienced by the no-treatment controls.

Estimating Internal Validity in Randomized Experiments and Quasi-Experiments

Estimating the internal validity of a relationship is a deductive process in which the investigator has to systematically think through how each of the internal validity threats may have influenced the data. Then, the investigator has to examine the data to test which relevant threats can be ruled out. In all of this process, the researcher has to be his or her own best critic, trenchantly examining all of the threats he or she can imagine. When all of the threats can plausibly be eliminated, it is possible to make confident conclusions about whether a relationship is probably causal. When all of them cannot, perhaps because the appropriate data are not available or because the data indicate that a particular threat may indeed have

operated, then the investigator has to conclude that a demonstrated relationship between two variables may or may not be causal. Sometimes the alternative interpretations may seem implausible enough to be ignored and the investigator will be inclined to dismiss them. They can be dismissed with a special degree of confidence when the alternative interpretations seem unlikely on the basis of findings from a research tradition with a large number of relevant and replicated findings.

Invoking plausibility has its pitfalls, since it may often be difficult to obtain high inter-judge agreement about the plausibility of a particular alternative interpretation. Moreover, theory testers place great emphasis on testing theoretical predictions that seem so implausible that neither common sense nor other theories would make the same prediction. There is in this an implied confession that the "implausible" is sometimes true. Thus, "implausible" alternative interpretations should reduce, but not eliminate, our doubt about whether relationships are causal.

When respondents are randomly assigned to treatment groups, each group is similarly constituted on the average (no selection, maturation, or selection-maturation problems). Each experiences the same testing conditions and research instruments (no testing or instrumentation problems). No deliberate selection is made of high and low scorers on any tests except under conditions where respondents are first matched according to, say, pretest scores and are then randomly assigned to treatment conditions (no statistical regression problem). Each group experiences the same global pattern of history (no history problem). And if there are treatment-related differences in who drops out of the experiment, this is interpretable as a consequence of the treatment. Thus, randomization takes care of many threats to internal validity.

With quasi-experimental groups, the situation is quite different. Instead of relying on randomization to rule out most internal validity threats, the investigator has to make all the threats explicit and then rule them out one by one. His task is, therefore, more laborious. It is also less enviable since his final causal inference will not be as strong as if he had conducted a randomized experiment. The principle reason for choosing to conduct randomized experiments over other types of research design is that they make causal inference easier.

Threats to Internal Validity That Randomization Does Not Rule Out

Though randomization conveniently rules out many threats to internal validity, it does not rule out all of them. In particular, imitation of treatments, compensatory equalization, compensatory rivalry, and demoralization in groups receiving less desirable treatments can each threaten internal validity even when randomization has been successfully implemented and maintained over time. Some of these threats will usually cause spurious differences (e.g., demoralization in the controls). However, other threats will tend to obscure true differences, especially by making no-treatment control groups perform atypically. This last happens with the imitation of treatments, compensatory equalization, and compensatory rivalry. We want to make clear that, while randomized experiments are superior to quasi-experiments with respect to internal validity, they are not perfect.

Most of the threats that randomization does not rule out result from the focused inequities that inevitably accompany experimentation because some peo-

ple receive one treatment and others receive different treatments or no treatment at all. Since much social experimentation is ameliorative, treatments have to differ in desirability by virtue of the very research problem (e.g., the different payment levels in a compensatory education or an income supplement program, or the different amounts of time that can be spent away from cell-block confinement in a prison experiment on "rehabilitation"). Obviously, individual respondents want to receive the more desirable treatments. In the same vein, officials want to avoid salient inequities which can lead to charges that they favored some respondents over others in distributing treatments.

It is rare in our society to have valuable resources distributed on a random basis. *Instead, we expect them to be distributed according to need, merit, seniority or on a "first come, first served" basis.* The point is that distributing resources by lottery violates the meritocratic and/or social responsibility norms which regulate and justify most differences in rewards and opportunities in the United States. This is not to say that lotteries are never used in resource distribution. They seem to be convenient, for instance, in distributing sudden "windfalls" or universally undesired resources (e.g., a lottery was used for inducting young men into the U.S. armed services after 1969). Nonetheless, distribution by merit or need is more common than distribution by chance, and the latter often violates expectations about what is "just." It is this which leads to randomization exacerbating some internal validity threats.

The extent of an administrator's apprehension about randomization probably depends on four subjective estimates: (1) the differences in desirability between treatments; (2) the probability that individuals will learn of treatment differences; (3) the probability that organized constituencies will learn of these differences; and (4) how much the various constituencies will feel that their interests are affected by the most likely research outcomes. Some research questions make it difficult to rule out all of an administrator's apprehensions since, first, they absolutely require treatments that differ in desirability (e.g., what is the effect of extra payments to schools?). Second, scarce research resources require geographical contiguity (e.g., we can only do the study in one school district). Third, it seems to be part of an administrator's job to consider how various constituencies might react to focused inequities and to fear the worst (e.g., what will the teachers' union or the PTA think if resources are distributed by chance instead of by need or merit?). And fourth, administrators know that constituency representatives want to get the best possible advantages for their charges and want to avoid any potential harm to them (e.g., a teachers' union official might think: If performance contracting works in schools, then the role of the classroom teacher could be reduced in scope and importance—do we want that?). Such considerations highlight both the difficulties of gaining permission to randomize and of ruling out the threat of compensatory equalization when randomization has taken place.

The only other internal validity threat that can operate in a randomized experiment is differential mortality from the treatment groups. While such differences can be interpreted as a consequence of the treatment—and as a result will often be very important—they have the undesirable side effect of obscuring the interpretation of other results. This is because the units remaining in one treatment group may not be comparable on the average to those in another group. Thus, if there

were differential attrition from, say, an experiment on the effect of income supplements on the motivation to find work, we would not be sure if a relationship between the dollar value of a supplement and the number of days worked was due to the supplement reducing the number of days worked or to selection differences associated with the kinds of persons who remained in each treatment condition for the entire experiment. Treatment-correlated attrition leads to the possibility of a selection confound. We might readily surmise that such attrition is all the more likely the more the treatments differ in desirability.

With the exception of differential mortality and the selection problems that follow from it, the threats to internal validity which random assignment does not rule out are caused by atypical behavior on the part of persons in no-treatment control groups or groups that receive less desirable treatments. Such behavior represents an unplanned but nonetheless causal consequence of the planned experimental contrast. Even when there is a valid causal relationship at the operational level, one may wonder how differences in B can be interpreted as the result of threats to internal validity. Internal validity is, after all, concerned with threats that cast doubt on whether there is a valid *causal* connection, and the threats we are discussing do not deny the validity of a causal connection. The answer is in one sense simple. Internal validity refers to doubt about whether there is a causal connection from A-as-manipulated (or measured) to B-as-measured; on the other hand, the threats to internal validity which we are discussing (e.g., resentful demoralization of the controls) cast doubt on whether the causal connection is from A to B or is from A's comparison group to B. (In another sense, this issue is academic, for causal inference always depends on the *contrast* between A and A's comparison, irrespective of whether A or the comparison causes the observed changes in the dependent variable. Given our emphasis on the desirability of identifying *active* causal agents, it is important to identify whether A or its comparison accounts for change, since knowing the active causal agent allows one to know what to manipulate. This is why we specify internal validity in terms of the pattern of influence from A to B rather than in terms of the pattern of influence from the contrast between A and its comparison to B).

Assessing the Plausibility of Internal Validity Threats If a Randomized Experiment Has Been Implemented

The possibility of a selection artifact resulting from differential attrition can best be empirically assessed in two ways. First, an analysis is called for of the proportion of respondents, originally assigned to each experimental condition, who actually provide posttest data. Differences in this proportion across treatments indicate a differential dropout. Second, an analysis is called for of the pretest scores in each treatment group computed on the basis of all those who provided posttest data. This gives a preliminary indication of whether the dropouts differed across groups on the background characteristics that are most likely to affect posttest scores (i.e., those that are highly correlated with pretest scores on the same test). We will deal with these points in greater detail in chapter 8.

An assessment of imitation, compensatory equalization, or compensatory rivalry can often be made by direct measures in the experimental and control groups of the process that the independent variable was meant to affect. Thus, if a

treatment were meant to provide money to some schools but not others, the finances of both kinds of schools would need examining. If a treatment was expected to make experimental children view an education television program, it would be necessary to measure how often they watch the show and how often the controls watch it. A small or nonexistent experimental contrast would suggest that imitation, compensatory equalization, or compensatory rivalry may have occurred. Thus, measures of the exact nature of the treatment in *all* treatment and control groups are absolutely vital in any experiment. The sooner such measurements are taken, the easier it will be to detect unexpected patterns of behavior in the experiment and control groups and the easier it will be to take corrective action.

It will normally be easy to use background information to find out if controls had contact with experimentals and copied them or to find out if administrators provided additional resources to some units from nonexperimental sources. It will normally not be as easy to assess whether compensatory rivalry took place, though direct measures of verbal expressions of such rivalry by the controls can give a lead, as can indications of whether control group performance is greater than would be expected. Saretsky (1972), it will be remembered, tried to determine this in the performance level in past years in the same classes, but he probably ran into a regression problem. Nonetheless, if used with care, the use of secondary data from past classes can be useful for attempting to assess the magnitude of any compensatory rivalry. Such data could also be useful for assessing resentful demoralization, because this threat leads to the testable prediction that performance should be atypically low in the control group during the experiment.

CONSTRUCT VALIDITY OF PUTATIVE CAUSES AND EFFECTS

Introduction

Construct validity is what experimental psychologists are concerned with when they worry about "confounding." This refers to the possibility that the operations which are meant to represent a particular cause or effect construct can be construed in terms of more than one construct, each of which is stated at the same level of reduction. Confounding means that what one investigator interprets as a causal relationship between theoretical constructs labeled *A* and *B*, another investigator might interpret as a causal relationship between constructs *A* and *Y* or between *X* and *B* or even between *X* and *Y*.

In the discussion that follows we shall restrict ourselves to the construct validity of presumed causes and effects, since these play an especially crucial role in experiments whose raison d'être is to test causal propositions. But it should be clearly noted that construct validity concerns are not limited to cause and effect constructs. All aspects of the research require naming samples in generalizable terms, including samples of people and settings as well as samples of measures or manipulations. Even with internal validity and statistical conclusion validity, inferences have to be made about abstract constructs: viz "cause" and "reliable change" or "reliable differences."

The reference to the level of reduction in the definition of "confounding" is important, because it is always possible to "translate" sociological terms

into psychological ones, or psychological terms into biological ones. For example, participative decision making could become conformity to membership group norms on one level, or some correlate of, say, the ascending reticular activating system on another. Each of these levels of reduction is useful in different ways and none is more legitimate than any other. But such "translations" from one level to another do not involve the confounding of rival explanations that is at issue here.

Before we continue our abstract characterization of construct validity, some concrete examples of well-known construct validity concerns may help. In earlier medical experiments on drugs, the psychotherapeutic effect of the doctor's helpful concern was confounded with the chemical action of the pill. So, too, were the doctor's and the patient's belief that the pill should have helped. To circumvent these problems and to increase confidence that any observed effects could be attributed to the chemical action of the pill *alone*, the placebo control group and the double-blind experimental design were introduced. (The first of these involves giving a chemically inert substance to respondents, and the second requires that neither the person prescribing the pill nor the person evaluating its effects knows the experimental condition to which the patient has been assigned.)

In industrial relations research, the Hawthorne effect is another confound which causes uncertainty about how operations should be labeled. If we assume for the moment that productivity was increased in the original Hawthorne studies by the planned experimental intervention, the issue for construct validity purposes is: Was the increase due to shifts in illumination (the planned treatment) or to the demonstrated administrative concern over improved working conditions (the "Hawthorne effect") or to telling the women how well they were doing their work (an inadvertent correlate of increasing the illumination)?

Construct validity concerns begin to surface at the planning and pilot-testing stages of an experiment when attempts are made to fit the anticipated cause and effect operations to their referent constructs, whether these are derived from formal social science theory or from policy considerations. Such "fitting" to the construct of interest is best achieved (1) by the careful preexperimental explication of constructs so that definitions are *clear* and in conformity with public understanding of the words being used, and (2) by data analyses directed at some of the four following points, preferably all of them.

First, a test should be made of the extent to which the independent variables alter what they are meant to alter. This is done by assessing whether the treatment manipulation is related to direct measures of the process designed to be affected by the treatment. (This is called "assessing the 'take' of the independent variable.") Second, a test should be conducted to assess whether an independent variable does not vary with measures of related but different constructs. For instance, a manipulation of "communicator expertise" should be correlated with reports from respondents about the communicator's level of knowledge, but it should not be correlated with attributions about cognate constructs, such as trustworthiness, congeniality, or power. If there are such correlations, it is difficult to differentiate effects due to expertise from those due to the other variables. Third, the proposed dependent variables should tap into the

factors they are meant to measure. Normally, some form of inter-item correlation can suggest this. And fourth, the dependent variables should not be dominated by irrelevant factors that make them measures of more or less than was intended. Thus, the outcome construct, like the treatment construct, has to be differentiated from its particular cognates.

As we have detailed the procedure, assessing construct validity depends on two pro esses: first, testing for a *convergence* across *different* measures or manipulations of the same "thing" and, second, testing for a *divergence* between measures and manipulations of related but conceptually distinct "things." Our position should not be interpreted to imply that construct validity absolutely depends on having information about both convergences and divergences, for it is clearly desirable to have information about convergences even when nothing is known directly about divergences. Indeed, other discussions of construct validity have restricted themselves to convergences, even while noting that a close correspondence between different types of measures of the same thing is less meaningful if there are similar measurement irrelevancies associated with each measure, as when only paper-and-pencil or observational measures of the same construct are made—see Campbell and Tyler, 1957; Cronbach and Meehl, 1955; Cronbach, Glesser, Nanda, and Rajaratnam, 1972. However, as Campbell and Fiske (1959) suggest, a construct should be differentiated from related theoretical constructs as well as from methodological irrelevancies. (For an example of differentiation from other theoretical constructs in basic research, see Cook, Crosby and Hennigan, 1977; and for an example in applied research, see the differentiation of viewing "Sesame Street" from "being encouraged to view 'Sesame Street' by paid professionals," Cook et al., 1975.)

We can illustrate these points by considering a possible experiment on the effects of supervisory distance. Suppose we operationalized "supervision" as a foreman standing within comfortable speaking distance of workers (e.g., ten feet). This particular operationalization would exclude distances that were beyond speaking but not beyond seeing, and the treatment might be more exactly characterized as "supervision from speaking distances." It would be dangerous to generalize from such a specific treatment to the general "supervision" construct, especially if supervision has different consequences when it comes from shorter and longer distances. To lessen this possibility, it would be useful if supervisory distance were systematically varied by means of planned manipulations. That is not always possible. However, it would still be useful if supervision *inadvertently* varied across a wide range of distances because foremen differed in their behavior from day to day. Careful analysis of the effects of spontaneous variation in distance would then allow us to test whether we can generalize from one supervisory distance to another. If we can, we can generalize with greater confidence to the general construct of "supervision," whereas if we cannot, we would like to restrict our generalization to "supervision from ten feet or less."

The foremen might also differ from each other, or might themselves differ from day to day, in whether they supervise with a smile or in an officious manner. Neither the smile nor the officiousness would seem to be necessary components of most definitions of "supervision." Hence, the researcher might

hope that such irrelevant behaviors would occur with different frequency across instances where supervisory distance was manipulated, and that data analyses could be conducted to differentiate the effects of supervision and, say, smiling. If the effects of supervision depended on whether the supervisor did his work with a smile or officiously, important contingencies would be specified that determine the particular type of supervision that causes a particular effect. Such contingency-specifying restrictions to generality are very important. They more accurately delimit the causal construct, which might be "supervision with a smile" rather than the more general but less accurate "supervision."

The kind of specification we have just been discussing concerns variables that are inadvertently manipulated at the same time as the intended treatment or that are inadvertently measured as part of an effect construct. It is more difficult to spell out the implications for construct validity of "developmental sequences," which are the processes that causally follow from the treatment and mediate its consequences. For example, close supervision by a foreman might mean that workers can ask for, and receive, task-relevant feedback that increases the quality or quantity of their performance. Alternatively, workers might feel resentment that their freedom is being curtailed by the supervision and might work less. The feedback and resentment process are consequences that presumably depend on who the foreman or worker is, how past relations have been in the particular work environment, and so forth. The researcher, therefore, faces the following dilemma: Should the treatment be specified as, say, "closeness of supervision," or "closeness of supervision which leads to task-relevant feedback"? The latter is probably the construct that led to the observed effects even though it was not the planned causal construct. We are presently inclined not to include developmental sequences under the heading of construct validity since they do not have to do with the correspondence between an operational treatment or measure and its referent construct. However, developmental sequences are very important in their own right. They help specify why a particular treatment is effective and so contribute to developing theory about the conditions under which the treatment will or will not be expected to have the observed effect. It will not have the effect, for instance, in any setting where manipulating the treatment fails to elicit a change in the developmental process that mediates the effect.

Our discussion of construct validity thus far has implied that a common definition exists of all the constructs about which we would like to test propositions. This is manifestly untrue. It is difficult enough to get an accepted formal definition of, say, being black in the U.S. today (How much African blood makes someone black? Is blackness sociological rather than biological?), let alone a widely accepted formal definition of a less grounded construct such as aggression. (Does aggression of necessity entail "intent to harm"? Does it include verbal as well as physical acts?)

Practically speaking, it would be much simpler if there were accepted definitions; but from a certain philosophical perspective, it is fortunate that we cannot in reality achieve widely accepted definitions of most constructs. This is because propositions about constructs are more reliable if they have been successfully tested, not only across many overlapping operational representations

of a single definition of a construct, but also across representations of many overlapping definitions of the *same* construct. Think how much utility there is in knowing that for many propositions about aggression it is irrelevant whether or not one defines aggression to include "intent to harm," for the same relationships hold with or without the inclusion of intent. And think how accurate and specific our propositions would be if we had information allowing us to differentiate between propositions that are valid for intentional but not unintentional aggression. Our advocacy of multiple operationalism overlaps, therefore, with an advocacy of multiple formal definitionalism, provided that all the definitions seem reasonable to most members of a given language group even though not necessarily accepted by all the members of that group.

Though the construct validity of causes and effects has to do with theoretical concepts, it would be a mistake to think that construct validity should only be a concern of the theoretician. First, many treatments in applied research are complex packages of variables rather than indicators of apparently unidimensional constructs. Consequently, it will often be difficult to describe and reproduce the total package, making replication more difficult than if the causal components of the package had been well specified and their independent contributions had been explored. Second, if one knows which components of a treatment are most responsible for an effect, it would be more efficient to reproduce just these features than it would be to reimplement the more expensive total package. For instance, "Sesame Street" was evaluated using a treatment where children and their parents were encouraged to watch the show on a weekly or monthly basis by paid professionals who left toys, books, and games about the show in the home. This total effort increased viewing but cost between $100 and $200 per child per viewing season over and above the costs of producing and distributing the show. Since viewing the show without such encouragement costs $1 to $2 per child per viewing season, would it not be useful to know whether the educational impact observed because of encouragement might be due to viewing the show ($1 to $2) as opposed to factors associated with being encouraged that have nothing to do with viewing—factors that cost between $100 and $200 per child? Third, since construct validity involves the fit between operations and referent constructs, it requires a rigorous definition of the referent construct. In policy research, this means being highly explicit about the nature of the problem under investigation and thereby reducing the chances of conducting "irrelevant" research. For instance, what is the hoped-for causal construct to which we want to make generalizations—viewing "Sesame Street" under the conditions most children spontaneously view it, or viewing "Sesame Street" in a context of visits from paid professionals when "Sesame Street"–related artifacts, not paid for by the parents, are in the home?

It is our distinct impression that most applied experimental research is much more oriented toward high construct validity of effects than of causes. This is entirely understandable, for what one wants to see is evidence that the social problem being addressed is at least partially ameliorated—not any problem, but *the* major problem as generally conceived. Thus, great care goes into measuring outcomes, for unless a rigorous measure of "recidivism" or "employ-

ment'' or ''academic achievement'' is used which most competent persons believe to be reasonable, the research is likely to be seen as ''irrelevant.'' While a focus on impact is entirely reasonable in applied research, this focus is often accompanied by a restricted interest in understanding the contingencies on which impact depends. More frequent measurement of the dimensions of the multivariate treatment and more frequent internal data analyses aimed at assessing the contribution of each component to any observed effect would greatly improve applied social research that uses experiments.

It is also our impression that applied researchers are more concerned than basic researchers with the range of cause and, especially, effect constructs over which a relationship can be generalized. In studies of school desegregation, for example, the implications of finding in an urban school district that the achievement of minority school children increased to a small degree would possibly be different if researchers had asked questions about ''white flight'' from the city than if such questions had not been raised. The whole concern with the unanticipated side-effects of innovations reflects a realistic understanding of the utility of having a net of dependent variable measures that tap into many constructs, some of which have been developed after explicit attempts to think through what may be unexpected effects. In our treatment here, construct validity will deal largely with attempts to generalize from operations to constructs but generalizing across constructs will be very briefly considered.

List of Threats to the Construct Validity of Putative Causes and Effects

Here is our list of some threats to construct validity. They all have to do either with the operations failing to incorporate all the dimensions of the construct, which we might call ''construct underrepresentation,'' or with the operations containing dimensions that are irrelevant to the target constructs, which we might call ''surplus construct irrelevancies.'' The list concentrates mostly on the fit between constructs and the way that the research problem is conceptualized, and devotes less attention to generalizing across constructs. Getting the initial question ''right'' is not as important a construct validity issue as getting one's operations to reflect one's research constructs. The list that follows is about the latter.

Inadequate Preoperational Explication of Constructs

The choice of operations should depend on the result of a conceptual analysis of the essential features of a construct. For instance, by consulting dictionaries (social science or otherwise) and the past literature on a topic, one would find that ''attitude'' is usually defined as a stable predisposition to respond. This stability is understood either (a) as a consistency across modes of responding to an attitude object (affective, cognitive, and behavioral), or (b) as a consistency in individual responses across time (i.e., as a positive correlation between responses to the same measure given at different time intervals). Such an analysis suggests the inadequacy of the usual procedure of measuring preferences or beliefs at a single time and then calling these responses ''attitude.'' (For an extended discussion of this subject, see Cook and Flay, 1978.)

To give another example, many definitions of aggression include both the intent to harm others and the fact that harm results from actions. This is to distinguish between (a) the black eye one boy gives another as they collide coming round a blind bend, (b) the black eye that one boy gives another to get his candy (instrumental aggression) or to harm him (noninstrumental), and (c) the verbal threat by one child to another that he will give him a black eye unless the other boy gives him some candy.

Since intent and physical harm are stressed in the definition above—which is not the only one possible—only (b) above is adequate as an example of the construct "aggression," though it will not be adequate for the minority of persons who prefer some other definition of the term. A precise explication of constructs is vital for high construct validity since it permits tailoring the manipulations and measures to whichever definitions emerge from the explication. Sometimes, several formal definitions are reasonable. Resources and the extent to which one formal definition is preferred over others in the local language community will then play important roles in determining the formal definitions used in the research.

Mono-Operation Bias

Many experiments are designed to have only one exemplar of a particular possible cause, and some have just one measure to represent each of the possible effect constructs. Since single operations both underrepresent constructs and contain irrelevancies, construct validity will be lower in single exemplar research than in research where each construct is multiply operationalized in order to triangulate on the referent. There is rarely an adequate excuse for single operations of effect constructs, since it is not costly to gather additional data from alternative measures of the targets. There is more excuse for having only one manipulation of a possible causal construct. This is because increasing the total number of treatments in a factorial design can lead either to very large sample research or to small sizes within each cell of the design should it not be possible to increase the total sample size. Moreover, if one lets irrelevancies in the treatment presentation vary spontaneously from occasion to occasion, this threatens statistical conclusion validity, even though any treatment effects that emerge despite the inflated error are presumably not due to those irrelevancies. Nonetheless, there is really no substitute for deliberately varying two or three exemplars of a treatment, *where possible*. Hence, if one were interested in the expertise of a communicator, one might use, say, three fictitious sources: a distinguished male professor from a well-known university, a distinguished female research scientist from a prestigious research center, and a famous science journalist from West Germany. Then, the variance due to the difference between these sources can be examined to test whether the different combinations of irrelevancies (sex, affiliation, nationality, or academic standing) differently affected responses and whether each expert singly—and the three combined—caused the expected outcome. If sample size did not permit analyzing separately by source, the data could be combined from all three. The investigator could then test whether expertise was effective despite the irrelevant sources of heterogeneity.

Mono-Method Bias

To have more than one operational representation of a construct does not necessarily imply that all irrelevancies have been made heterogeneous. Indeed, when all the manipulations are presented the same way, or all the measures use the same means of recording responses, then the method is itself an irrelevancy whose influence cannot be dissociated from the influence of the target construct. Thus, if all the experts in the previous hypothetical example had been presented to respondents in writing, it would not logically be possible to generalize to experts who are seen or heard. Thus it would be more accurate to label the treatment as "experts presented in writing." To cite another example, attitude scales are often presented to respondents without apparent thought to (a) using methods of recording other than paper-and-pencil, (b) varying whether the attitude statements are positively or negatively worded, or (c) varying whether the positive or negative end of the response scale appears on the right or left of the page. On these three points depends whether one can test if "personal private attitude" has been measured as opposed to "paper-and-pencil nonaccountable responses," or "acquiescence," or "response bias."

Hypothesis-Guessing Within Experimental Conditions

The internal validity threats called "resentful demoralization" and "compensation rivalry" were assumed to result because persons who received less desirable treatments compared themselves to persons who received more desirable treatments, making it unclear whether treatment effects of any kind occurred in the treatment group. Reactive research may not only obscure true treatment effects, but also result in effects of diminished interpretability. This is especially true if it is suspected that persons in one treatment group compared themselves to persons in other groups and guessed how the experimenters expected them to behave. Indeed, in many situations it is not difficult to guess what the experimenters hope for, especially in education or industrial organizations. Hypothesis-guessing can occur without social comparison processes, as when respondents know only about their own treatment but persist in trying to discover what the experimenters want to learn from the research.

The problem of hypothesis-guessing can best be avoided by making hypotheses (if present) hard to guess, by decreasing the general level of reactivity in the experiment, or by deliberately giving different hypotheses to different respondents. But these solutions are at best partial, since respondents are not passive and can always generate their own treatment-related hypotheses which may or may not be the same as the experimenters'. Learning an hypothesis does not necessarily imply either the motivation or the ability to alter one's behavior because of the hypothesis. Despite the widespread discussion of treatment confounds that are presumed to result from wanting to give data that will please the researcher—which we suspect is a result of discussions of the Hawthorne effect—there is neither widespread evidence of the Hawthorne effect in field experiments (see reviews by D. Cook, 1967; Diamond, 1974), nor is there evidence of a similar orientation in laboratory contexts (Weber and Cook, 1972). However, we still lack a sophisticated and empirically corroborated theory of the conditions under which hypothesis-guessing (a) occurs, (b) is

treatment specific, and (c) is translated into behavior that (d) could lead to erroneous conclusions about the nature of a treatment construct when (e) the research takes place in a field setting.

Evaluation Apprehension

Rosenberg (1969) has reviewed considerable evidence from laboratory experiments which indicates that respondents are apprehensive about being evaluated by persons who are experts in personality adjustment or the assessment of human skills. In such cases respondents attempt to present themselves to such persons as both competent and psychologically healthy. It is not clear how widespread such an orientation is in social science experiments in field settings, especially when treatments last a long time and populations do not especially value the way that social scientists or their sponsors evaluate them. Nonetheless, it is possible that some past treatment effects were due to respondents being willing to present themselves to experimenters in ways that would lead to a favorable personal evaluation. Being evaluated favorably by experimenters is rarely the target construct around which experiments are designed. It is a confound.

Experimenter Expectancies

There is some literature (Rosenthal, 1972) which indicates that an experimenter's expectancies can bias the data obtained. When this happens, it will not be clear whether the causal treatment is the treatment-as-labeled or the expectations of the persons who deliver the treatments to respondents. This threat can be decreased by employing experimenters who have no expectations or have false expectations, or by analyzing the data separately for persons who deliver the treatments and have different kinds or levels of expectancy. Experimenter expectancies are thus a special case of treatment-correlated irrelevancy, and they may well operate in some (but certainly not all) field settings.

Confounding Constructs and Levels of Constructs

Experiments can involve the manipulation of several discrete levels of an independent variable that is continuous. Thus, one might conclude from an experiment that A does not affect B when in fact A-at-level-one does not affect B, whereas A-at-level-four might well have affected B if A had been manipulated as far as level four. This threat is a problem when A and B are not linearly related along the whole continuum of A; and it is especially prevalent, we assume, when treatments have only a weak impact. If they do, because low levels of A are manipulated, and if conclusions are drawn about A without any qualifications concerning the strength of the manipulation, then misleading negative conclusions can be drawn. The best control for this threat is to conduct parametric research in which many levels of A are varied and many levels of B are measured.

Interaction of Different Treatments

This threat occurs if respondents experience more than one treatment which is common in laboratory research but quite rare in field settings. We do not

know in such an instance whether we could generalize any findings to the situation where respondents received only a single treatment. More importantly, we would not be able to unconfound the effects of the treatment from the effects of the context of several treatments. The solution to this problem is either to give only one treatment to respondents or, wherever possible, to conduct separate analyses of the first and succeeding treatments which respondents received.

Interaction of Testing and Treatment

To which kinds of testing situations can a cause-effect relationship be generalized? In particular, can it be generalized beyond the testing conditions that were originally used to probe the hypothesized cause-effect relationship? The latter is an especially important question when the pretesting of respondents is involved and might condition the reception of the experimental stimulus, although the previously cited work of Lana (1969) suggests that pretest sensitization is far from omnipresent. We would want to know whether the same result would have been obtained without a pretest, and a posttest-only control group is necessary for this. Similarly, if repeated posttest measurements are made, we would want to know whether the same results would be obtained if respondents were posttested once rather than at each delay interval. We would want to know whether the effect does or does not have to be specified as including the frequency of posttest measurement. The recommended solution to this problem is to have independent experimental groups at each delayed-test session.

Restricted Generalizability Across Constructs

When social science results are presented to audiences, it is very common to hear comments such as: "Yes, I accept that the youth job-training program increases the likelihood of being employed immediately after graduation. But what does it do to adaptive job skills—punctuality, the ability to follow orders, and so on?" When such questions can be answered, we have a fuller picture of a treatment's total impact and are more likely to gain a comprehensive assessment of the program. Sometimes treatments will affect dependent variables quite differently, implying a positive effect on some construct and an unintended negative effect on another. While it is impossible to measure all the constructs that a particular treatment could affect, it is useful to explore with other persons how a treatment might influence constructs other than those that first come to mind in the original formulation of the research question. Particularly in the program evaluation area, we could cite many studies where the guiding research questions were not well explored and where it would have been feasible to collect more outcome measures, making the research more useful.

Construct Validity, Preexperimental Tailoring, and Postexperimental Specification

Our presentation of the construct validity of putative causes and effects has thus far emphasized the researcher critically (a) thinking through how a construct should be defined, (b) isolating the cognate constructs from which any particular construct has to be differentiated, and (c) deciding which measures or manipula-

tions he can use to index the particular hypothetical construct of interest. Then, we emphasized both (d) the need to have multiple measures or manipulations wherever possible. This need does not deny that some measures are better than others but merely indicates that no single measure is perfect and also indicates (e) the need to present the manipulations or measures in multiple delivery modes. All of these points are geared toward helping the researcher answer the major conceptual questions guiding the research, whether the questions are theoretical or applied.

Data analyses do not always produce the desired results that suggest high construct validity. Consider, first, direct measures which are collected to test whether the treatment varied what it should have varied and did not vary what it was not supposed to have varied. If a reliable measure of, say, communicator credibility suggests that a communicator was not perceived to be more credible in one experimental group than another, then it is not easy to say that credibility caused any effects that may have been inferred from the outcome data. The investigator is then forced to become a detective whose goal is to use whatever means are available to specify what might have caused the observed effects if credibility did not.

Next, consider what might happen if the data indicate that a manipulation affected two reliably measured exemplars of a particular construct but not three others that were equally well measured. How is the effect to be labeled in this case, since the planned label does not fit all the results and so seems inappropriate? Feldman's (1968) experiment in Boston, Athens, and Paris offers a concrete example of this. He used five measures of "cooperation" in an effort to test whether compatriots receive greater cooperation than foreigners. The measures were giving street directions; doing a favor by mailing a lost letter; giving back money that one could easily, but falsely, claim as one's own; giving correct change when one did not have to; and charging the correct amount to passengers in taxis. The data suggested that giving street directions and mailing the lost letter were differently related to the experimental manipulations than were foregoing chances to cheat in ways that would be to one's advantage. Thus, the data forced Feldman to specify two kinds of "cooperation" (involving low-cost favors versus foregoing one's own financial advantage) where initially he had tailored his measures to reflect what he had hoped was the unitary construct of cooperation. Moreover, since his respecification of the constructs came after the data were received we can place less confidence in them than might otherwise have been warranted This is not to downplay Feldman's research, which was exemplary given his research question. If he had not had the five measures, a much less differentiated—and hence less accurate—picture would have emerged of the differences in help given to compatriots and foreigners.

The important point is that construct validity consists of more than merely assessing the fit between planned constructs and the operations that were tailored to these constructs. One can use the obtained pattern of data to edit one's thinking about both the cause and effect constructs, and one can suggest, *after the fact,* other constructs that might fit the data better than those with which the experiment began. Often, the data force one to be more specific in one's labeling than originally planned, as in the Feldman example or with the research of Parker (1963), who set out to test whether the introduction of television caused a decrease in per capita library circulation. He finally concluded that it did for the circulation of

fiction books but not for the circulation of factual ones. The process of hypothesizing constructs and testing how well treatment and outcome operations fit these constructs is similar whether it occurs before the research begins or after the data are received. The major difference is that in the later stage one specifies constructs that fit the data, whereas in the earlier stage one derives operations from constructs.

In their pathfinding discussion of construct validity, Cronbach and Meehl (1955) stressed the utility of drawing inferences about constructs from the fit between patterns of data that would be predicted if a particular theoretical construct was operating and the multivariate pattern of data was actually obtained in the research. They used the term "nomological net" to refer to the predicted pattern of relationships that would permit naming a construct. For instance, a current version of dissonance theory predicts that being underpaid for a counterattitudinal advocacy will result in greater belief change than being overpaid, provided that the individual who makes the advocacy thinks he has a free choice to refuse to perform the advocacy. The construct "dissonance" would therefore be partially validated if experimental data showed that underpayment caused more belief change than overpayment but only under free choice conditions. However, the fit between the complex prediction and the complex data only facilitates belief in "dissonance" to the extent that other theoretical constructs could not explain this same data pattern. Bem (1972) obviously believes that reinforcement constructs do as good a job of complex prediction in this case as "dissonance."

We have implicitly used the "nomological net" idea in our presentation of construct validity. First, we discussed the usefulness—for labeling the treatment—of examining whether the planned treatment is related to direct measures of the treatment process and is not related to cognate processes. Second, we discussed the advantages of determining in what ways the outcome variables are related to treatments and the type of treatment that could have resulted in such a differentiated impact. For instance, if the introduction of television decreases the circulation of fiction but not fact books, one can hypothesize that the causal impact is mediated by television taking time away from activities that are functionally similar—such as fantasy amusement—but not from functionally dissimilar activities—such as learning specific facts. However, our emphasis has differed slightly from that of Cronbach and Meehl (1955) inasmuch as we are more interested in fitting cause and effect operations to a generalizable construct (see Campbell, 1960—the discussion of "trait validity") than we are in using complex predictions and data patterns to validate entirely hypothetical scientific constructs like "anxiety," "intelligence" or "dissonance." However, we readily acknowledge that the way the data turn out in experiments helps us edit the constructs we deal with, as when we find that a foreman's "supervision" has different consequences from less than ten feet as opposed to more than ten feet.

EXTERNAL VALIDITY

Introduction

Under external validity, Campbell and Stanley originally listed the threat of not being able to generalize across exemplars of a particular presumed cause or effect construct. We have obviously chosen to incorporate this feature under con-

struct validity as "mono-operation bias." The reason for listing this threat differently from Campbell and Stanley is not fundamental. Rather it is meant to emphasize that most researchers want to draw conclusions about constructs, but the Campbell and Stanley discussion had a flavor of definitional operationalism, although a *multiple* definitional operationalism. We have tried to avoid this flavor by invoking construct validity to replace generalizing across cause and effect exemplars. The other features of Campbell and Stanley's conceptualization of external validity are preserved here and elaborated upon. They have to do with (1) generalizing to particular target persons, settings, and times, and (2) generalizing across types of persons, settings, and times.

Bracht and Glass (1968) have succinctly explicated external validity, pointing out that a two-stage process is involved: a target population of persons, settings, or times has first to be defined and then samples are drawn to represent these populations. Very occasionally, the samples are drawn from the populations with known probabilities, thereby maximizing the final representativeness discussed in textbooks on sampling theory (e.g., Kish, 1965). But usually the samples cannot be drawn so systematically and are drawn instead because they are convenient and give an intuitive impression of representativeness, even if it is only the representativeness entailed by class membership (e.g., I want to generalize to Englishmen and the people I found on streetcorners in Birkenhead, England, belong to the class called Englishmen). Accidental sampling, as it is technically labeled, gives us no guarantee that the achieved population (a subset of Englishmen who hang around streetcorners in Birkenhead) is representative of the target population of which they are members. Consequently, we find it useful to distinguish among (1) target populations, (2) formally representative samples that correspond to known populations, (3) samples actually achieved in field research, and (4) achieved populations.

One of many examples that could be cited to illustrate these last points concerns the design of the first negative income tax experiment. Practical administrative considerations led to the study being conducted in a few localities within New Jersey and in one city in neighboring Pennsylvania. Since the basic question guiding the research did not require such a restricted geographical location, the New Jersey-Pennsylvania setting must be considered a limitation which reduces one's ability to generalize to the implicit target population of the whole United States. (To criticize the study because the achieved sample of settings was not formally representative of the target population may appear unduly harsh in light of the fact that financial and logistical resources for the experiment were limited, and so sampling was conducted for convenience rather than formal representativeness. We shall return to this point later. *For the present, however, it is worth noting that accidental samples of convenience do not make it easy to infer the target population,* nor is it clear what population is actually achieved.)

Generalizing *to* well-explicated target populations should be clearly distinguished from generalizing *across* populations. Each is germane to external validity: the former is crucial for ascertaining whether any research goals that specified populations have been met, and the latter is crucial for ascertaining which different populations (or subpopulations) have been affected by a treatment, i.e., for assessing how far one can generalize. Let us give an example.

Suppose a new television show were introduced that was aimed at teaching basic arithmetic to seven-year-olds in the United States. Suppose, further, that one could somehow draw a random sample of all seven-year-olds to give a representative national sample within known limits of sampling error. Suppose, further, that one could then randomly assign each of the children to watching or not watching the television show. This would result in two randomly formed, and thus equivalent, experimental groups which were representative of all seven-year-olds in the United States. Imagine, now, that the data analysis indicated that the average child in the viewing group gained more than the average child in the nonviewing group. One could generalize such a finding *to* the average seven-year-old in the nation, the target population of interest.

This is equivalent to saying that the results were obtained *despite possible variations in how much different kinds of children in the experimental viewing group may have gained from the show*. A more differentiated data analysis might show that the boys gained more than the girls (or even that only the boys gained), or the analysis might show that children with certain kinds of home background gained while children from different backgrounds did not. Such differentiated findings indicate that the effects of the televised arithmetic show could not be generalized *across* all subpopulations of seven-year-old viewers, even though they could be generalized *to* the population of seven-year-old viewers in the United States.

To generalize across subpopulations like boys and girls logically presupposes being able to generalize to boys and girls. Thus, the logical distinction between generalizing to and across should not be overstressed. The distinction is most useful for its practical implications insofar as many researchers who are concerned about generalizing *across* populations are usually not as concerned with careful samplings as are persons who want to generalize *to* target populations. Many researchers with the former focus would be happy to conclude that a treatment had a specific effect with the particular achieved sample of boys or girls in the study, irrespective of how well the achieved population of boys or girls can be specified.

The distinction between generalizing to target populations and across multiple populations or subpopulations is also useful because commentators on external validity have often implicitly stressed one over the other. For instance, some persons discuss external validity as though it were only about estimating limits of generalizability, as is evidenced by comments such as: "Sure, the treatment affected seven-year-olds in Tucson, Arizona, and that was your target group. But what about children of different ages in other areas of the United States?" Other commentators discuss external validity exclusively in terms of the fit between samples and target populations, as is evidenced by comments such as: "I'm not sure whether the treatment is really effective with children who have learning disabilities, for if you look at the pretest achievement means for the groups in your experiment, you'll see that they are as high as the test publisher quotes for the national average. How could children with learning disabilities have scored so high? I doubt that the research really involved the kind of child you said it did."

Finally, we make the distinction between generalizing to and across in order to emphasize the greater stress that we shall place in this presentation on generalizing

across. The rationale for this is that formal random sampling for representativeness is rare in field research, so that strict generalizing to targets of external validity is rare. Instead, the practice is more one of generalizing across haphazard instances where similar-appearing treatments are implemented. Any inferences about the targets to which one can generalize from these instances are necessarily fallible and their validity is only haphazardly checked by examining the instances in question and any new instances that might later be experimented upon. It is also worth noting that the formal generalization to target populations of persons is often associated with large-scale experiments. These are often difficult to administer both in terms of treatment implementation and securing high-quality measurement. Moreover, attrition is almost inevitable, and so the sample with which one finishes the research may not represent the same population with which one began the research. A case can be made, therefore, that external validity is enhanced more by a number of smaller studies with haphazard samples than by a single study with initially representative samples if the latter could be implemented. Of course, it should not be forgotten that all the haphazard instances of persons and settings that are examined can belong to the class of persons or settings to which one would like to be able to generalize research findings. Indeed, they should belong to such a class.

List of Threats to External Validity

Tests of the extent to which one can generalize across various kinds of persons, settings, and times are, in essence, tests of statistical interactions. If there is an interaction between, say, an educational treatment and the social class of children, then we cannot say that the same result holds across social classes. We know that it does not. Where effects of different magnitude exist, we must then specify where the effect does and does not hold and, hopefully, begin to explore why these differences exist. Since the method we prefer of conceptualizing external validity involves generalizing across achieved populations, however unclearly defined, we have chosen to list all of the threats to external validity in terms of statistical interaction effects.

Interaction of Selection and Treatment

In which categories of persons can a cause-effect relationship be generalized? Can it be generalized beyond the groups used to establish the initial relationship—to various racial, social, geographical, age, sex, or personality groups? Even when respondents belong to a target class of interest, systematic recruitment factors lead to findings that are only applicable to volunteers, exhibitionists, hypochondriacs, scientific do-gooders, those who have nothing else to do, and so forth. One feasible way of reducing this bias is to make cooperation in the experiment as convenient as possible. For example, volunteers in a television-radio audience experiment who have to come downtown to participate are much more likely to be atypical than are volunteers in an experiment carried door-to-door. An experiment involving executives is more likely to be ungeneralizable if it takes a day's time than if it takes only ten minutes, for only the latter experiment is likely to include those people who have little free time.

Interaction of Setting and Treatment

Can a causal relationship obtained in a factory be obtained in a bureaucracy, in a military camp, or on a university campus? The solution here is to vary settings and to analyze for a causal relationship within each. This threat is of particular relevance to organizational psychology since its settings are on such disparate levels as the organization, the small group, and the individual. When can we generalize from any one of these units to the others? The threat is also relevant because of the volunteer bias as to which organizations cooperate. The refusal rate in getting the cooperation of industrial organizations, school systems, and the like must be nearer 75% than 25%, especially if we include those that were never contacted because it was considered certain they would refuse. The volunteering organizations will often be the most progressive, proud, and institutionally exhibitionist. For example, Campbell (1956), although working with Office of Naval Research funds, could not get access to destroyer crews and had to settle for high-morale submarine crews. Can we extrapolate from such situations to those where morale, exhibitionism, pride, or self-improvement needs are lower?

Interaction of History and Treatment

To which periods in the past and future can a particular causal relationship be generalized? Sometimes an experiment takes place on a very special day (e.g., when a president dies), and the researcher is left wondering whether he would have obtained the same cause-effect relationship under more mundane circumstances. Even when circumstances are relatively more mundane, we still cannot logically extrapolate findings from the present to the future. Yet, while logic can never be satisfied, "commonsense" solutions for short-term historical effects lie either in replicating the experiment at different times (for other advantages of consecutive replication, see Cook, 1974a) or in conducting a literature review to see if prior evidence exists which does not refute the causal relationship.

Models to Be Followed in Increasing External Validity

In many instances researchers know that they want to generalize to specific target populations of persons, settings, or times. This is particularly the case in much applied research, although it is also found among basic researchers interested in contingency theories (e.g., a theory of schizophrenia, or of behavior in street settings which require the ability to make references about schizophrenics and street settings, however these are defined). Clearly, when target populations are specified, it is necessary that the research samples be "representative" in some way.

In other instances, the researchers may not have specific populations in mind. This is most likely to be the case with someone developing a general theory, but it is also sometimes appropriate in developing more limited theories or conducting applied research. For instance, the applied researcher in education may have fourth-grade inner-city children as the primary intended target population. But he or she may not have a specific target group of persons in mind for giving the achievement tests. Yet if all the posttest measurement is conducted by middle-class testers hired for the particular project, the researcher cannot extrapolate

beyond such testers. In a sense, he or she has drawn an unintended secondary sample with an unclear population referent that has no intrinsic interest, and without further evidence no generalization beyond such testers is warranted. How much better it would be if the irrelevant factor of tester social status were not fixed but varied. Then, one could analyze the data to test whether similar effects were obtained despite background differences among testers—that is, one could test whether it is possible to generalize *across* factors like tester status that are irrelevant to major research goals.

When a target population has been specified, it is appropriate—where possible—to draw up a sampling frame and select instances so that the sample is representative of the population within known limits of sampling error. Many textbooks on sampling theory exist and are informative about the advantages and disadvantages of drawing samples in different ways. Formally speaking, the most representative samples will be those that are randomly chosen from the population, and it is possible for these randomly selected units to be randomly assigned to various experimental groups. We might label the first stage in such a two-stage randomization process as following the *random sampling for representativeness model*.

It is probably only feasible to follow this model when sampling intended primary targets of persons, the more so if generalization to a limited setting is required (e.g., to residents of Detroit, rather than the whole United States). However, random sampling for representativeness is theoretically possible on a larger scale, particularly if multistage area sampling of, say, the whole nation is undertaken. But studies on this scale require considerable resources. Moreover, while it is clear that the model can be followed for some issues where it is important to generalize to particular target populations of persons, it is less clear whether it is often feasible to generalize to target settings, except where these are highly restricted. For instance, by selecting a representative national sample of persons, one should be able to generalize to various geographical settings (i.e., cities, towns, and the like). But regions do not exhaustively define settings, and the nationwide representative experiments of which we are aware—all of which embed treatments within polling studies—take place in the respondents' homes rather than in the street or in factories. While a restriction to living rooms is desirable for anyone interested in generalizing to settings where opinion polls typically take place, it is less desirable for the majority of researchers who have no such particular target setting in mind. The point to be noted is that the model of random sampling for representativeness requires considerable resources which are probably more readily available for sampling target populations of persons than of settings or historical times and which are probably more available for restricted populations of persons (e.g., inhabitants of Detroit) than for the United States at large.

A second model for increasing external validity is the *model of deliberate sampling for heterogeneity*. Here the concern is to define target classes of persons, settings, and times and to ensure that a wide range of instances from within each class is represented in the design. Thus, a general educational experiment might be designed to include boys and girls from cities, towns, and rural settings who differ widely in aptitude and in the value placed on achievement in their home settings. The task would then be to test whether an educational innovation has

comparable effects in each of the subgroups of children and settings. If the achieved sample sizes do not permit this, then the task would be to test whether the innovation has observable effects *despite* differences between kinds of children and kinds of settings. The first task involves an obvious attempt at multiple replication, either by testing for interactions of the treatment and student characteristics or by statistical tests of whether treatment has any observed effects within each group. The second task involves testing whether a treatment effect is obtained even though differences between persons and settings are not taken into account in the data analysis and are inflating the error terms that are used for testing treatment effects.

Deliberate sampling for heterogeneity does not require random sampling at any stage in the sampling design. Hence one cannot—technically speaking—generalize from the achieved samples to any formally meaningful populations. All one has are purposive quotas of persons with specified attributes. These quotas permit one to conclude that an effect has or has not been obtained across the particular variety of samples of persons, settings, and times that were under study, which is like saying: "We tried to have children of Types I and II in the experiment in order to see if the effect would hold with each of them. It did. We're not sure how well one can generalize from our particular achieved samples of children to children of Type I and Type II in general, but at least we learned that the effect holds with at least one sample of Type I children and at least one sample of Type II children. What we cannot do with any confidence is specify the populations of children involved." To have a sample of persons in an experiment with Type I characteristics is not at all sufficient for formally concluding that we can generalize any findings to the average Type I persons.

When one samples nonrandomly, it is usually advantageous to obtain opportunistic samples that differ as widely as possible from each other. Thus, if it were possible, one might choose to implement a treatment both in a "Magnet School," that is, a school established to exemplify teaching conditions at their presumed best, and also in one of the city's worst problem schools. If each instance produced comparable effects, then one might begin to suspect that the effect would hold in many other kinds of schools. However, there is a real danger in having only extreme instances at each end of some implicit, impressionistic continuum. This can best be highlighted by asking: "What would you conclude about external validity if an effect were obtained at one school but not the other?" In this case, one would be hard pressed to conclude anything about the effects of the innovation in the majority of schools between the extremes. For this reason, it is especially advantageous if deliberate sampling for heterogeneity results in at least one instance of the impressionistic mode of the class under investigation as well as instances at each extreme. In other words, at least one instance should be representative of the "typical school" of a particular city (or nation), and at least one instance representing the best and worst schools.

The model of deliberate sampling for heterogeneity is especially useful in avoiding the pitfall of restricted inference that results from the failure to consider sampling questions about secondary targets of inference (e.g., the social class of educational testers as opposed to the social class of school children). Unless one has good reasons for matching the class of testers and children, the model based

on seeking heterogeneity indicates that it would be unwise to sample from a homogeneous group of testers with a common background. Comparable background does not mean identical testers, of course, for testers of any one class differ from each other in a multitude of ways. Nonetheless, social class is relatively homogeneous, should plausibly affect test scores, and is an irrelevant source of homogeneity that can often be made heterogeneous at little or no extra cost.

Deliberate purposive sampling for heterogeneity is usually more feasible than random sampling for representativeness. Imagine conducting an experiment in a school district to which you want to generalize. You could draw up a list of schools and randomly select a number of them in order to generalize with confidence. But resources and politics often prevent working with so many schools. Instead, the researcher is often lucky if he can afford (or be granted) access to more than one or two schools—an achieved sample of convenience. This being so, the researcher should seek convenient samples which differ considerably on attributes that he or she especially wants to generalize across and should take care not to be inadvertently restricted to populations, particularly those of secondary interest.

A third model for extending external validity is the *impressionistic modal instance model*. Here, the concern is to explicate the kinds of persons, settings, or times to which one most wants to generalize and then to select at least one instance of each class that is impressionistically similar to the class mode. We alluded to this strategy earlier in detailing the desirability of having at least one school similar to the average school in a district. To achieve this aim is simple. Where comprehensive records exist, one can detail the average size of schools, average achievement levels, average per capita expenditure, and so forth, and choose one or more schools that most closely approximate the modal school characteristics that have been "drawn up." Should there be no obvious single mode, one can then define the multiple modes and try to obtain at least one sample of each. Thus, in many urban school districts, one might find three modes corresponding to all-black, all-white, and heavily desegregated schools. Then a choice of one group from each class would be called for. Where no suitable archive measures exist, it should nonetheless be possible for the researcher to sample the opinions of experts and interested parties to obtain their impression of what the average school or student is like. A composite impression is then derived for all the single impressions, and this composite forms the framework for deciding the order in which potential respondents (or which access-granting authorities) should be approached for permission to do the study in their locale.

The definition and selection of modal instances is probably most easy in consultant work or project evaluation where very limited generalization is required. For instance, an industrial manager knows that he or she wants to generalize to the present work force in its current setting carrying out its present tasks the effectiveness of which is measured by means of locally established indicators of productivity, profitability, absenteeism, lateness, and the like. The consultant or evaluator then knows that he or she has to select respondents and settings to reflect these circumscribed targets. A feasible method is to concentrate on sampling impressionistically modal instances if sampling has to be carried out at all. (The evaluator might also do well to select out exemplary instances in order to gain a

preliminary understanding of what a business or project is capable of. But that is another matter.)

The determination of modal instances is more difficult the closer one comes to theoretical research. This is because target populations are less likely to be specified. For instance, in testing propositions about "helping" behavior, it is not desirable to generalize only to workers who are presently employed in a particular factory, working at a particular task, and producing a particular product. The persons, the settings, the task, and the product would be irrelevant to any helping theory. Yet—logically speaking—the factors incorporated into a particular test of a proposition about helping determine the external validity of the findings, and the researcher presumably does not welcome this restriction. Instead, he or she would like to generalize to all persons (in the United States? beyond our shores?), all settings (the street, the home, the factory?), and all tasks (helping someone who has fainted, helping the permanently disabled?). The feasibility of confident generalizations of such breadth is low, and the most that the basic researcher can do is to attempt to replicate his or her original findings across settings with different restrictions or to wait until others have conducted the replications. Sampling for heterogeneity is at issue here rather than sampling to obtain impressionistically modal instances that the researcher cannot convincingly define.

It should be clear by now that, where targets are specified, the model of random sampling for representativeness is the most powerful model for generalizing and that the model of impressionistic modal instances is the least powerful. The model of heterogeneous instances lies between the two. However, the last model has advantages over the other two in that it can be used when no targets are specified and the major concern is not to be limited in one's generalizations. Moreover, it can be used with small numbers of samples of convenience. In many cases the random selection of instances results in generalizing to targets that are of minimal significance for persons whose interests differ from those of the original researcher's. For instance, to be able to generalize to all whites living in the Detroit area, while of interest for some purposes, is generally of little interest to most people. However, it is worth noting that whites in Detroit differ in age, SES, intelligence, and the like so that it is possible to test whether a particular treatment can have similar effects *despite* such differences. In addition, subgroup analyses can be conducted to examine generality across subpopulations. In other words, formal randomization from populations of low interest can be used to test causal relationships across heterogeneous subpopulations. In other words, an important function of random samples is to permit examining the data for differential effects on a variety of subpopulations. Given the negative relationships between "inferential" power and feasibility, the model of heterogeneous instances would seem most useful, particularly if great care is made to include impressionistically modal instances among the heterogeneous ones.

In the last analysis, external validity—like construct validity—is a matter of replication. It is worth noting that one can have multiple replication both *within* a single study—subgroup analyses exemplify this—and also *across* studies—as when one investigator is intrigued by a pattern of findings and tries to replicate them using his or her own procedures or procedures that have been closely modeled on the original investigators'.

Three dimensions of replication are worth noting. First, is the simultaneous or consecutive replication dimension, with the latter being preferable since it offers some test, however restricted, of whether a causal relationship can be corroborated at two different times. (Generalizing across times is necessarily more difficult than generalizing across persons or settings.) Second is the independent or nonindependent investigator dimension, with the former being more important, especially if the independent investigators have different expectations about how an experiment will turn out. Third is the dimension of demonstrated or assumed replication. The former is assessed by explicit comparisons among different types of persons and settings where some persons did or did not receive a particular treatment. The latter is inferred from treatment effects that are obtained with heterogeneous samples, but no explicit statistical cognizance is taken of the differences among persons, settings, and times. Demonstrated replication is clearly more informative than assumed, for to obtain an effect with a mixed sample of, say, boys and girls, does not logically entail that the effect could be obtained separately for both boys and girls. It only entails that the effect was obtained despite any differences between boys and girls in how they reacted to the treatment.

The difficulties associated with external validity should not blind experimenters to practical steps that can be taken to increase generalizability. For instance, one can often deliberately choose to perform an experiment at three or more sites where different kinds of persons live or work. Or, if one can randomly sample, it is useful to do so even if the population involved is not meaningful, for random sampling ensures heterogeneity. Thus, in their experiment on the relationship between beliefs and behavior about open housing, Brannon et al. (1973) chose a random sample of all white households in the metropolitan Detroit area. While few of us are interested in generalizing to such a population, the sample was nonetheless considerably more heterogeneous than that used in most research, despite the homogeneity on the attributes of race and geographical residence.

In addition, our three models for increasing external validity can be used in combination, as has been achieved in some survey research experiments on improving survey research procedures (Schuman and Duncan, 1974). Usually, random samples of respondents are chosen in such experiments, but the interviewers are not randomly chosen; they are merely impressionistically modal of all experienced interviewers. Moreover, the physical setting of the research is limited to one target setting that is of little interest to anyone who is not a survey researcher—the respondent's living room—and the range of outcome variables is usually limited to those that survey researchers typically study—that is, those that can be assessed using paper and pencil. However, great care is normally taken that these questions cover a wide range of possible effects, thereby ensuring considerable heterogeneity in the effect constructs studied.

Our pessimism about external validity should not be overgeneralized. An awareness of targets of generalization, of the kinds of settings in which a target class of behaviors most frequently occurs, and of the kinds of persons who most often experience particular kinds of natural treatments will, at the very least, prevent the designing of experiments that many persons shrug off willy-nilly as "irrelevant." Also, it is frequently possible to conduct multiple replications of an experiment at different times, in different settings, and with different kinds of

experimenters and respondents. Indeed, a strong case can be made that external validity is enhanced more by many heterogeneous small experiments than by one or two large experiments, for with the latter one runs the risks of having heterogeneous treatment, measures that are not as reliable as they could be, and measures that do not reflect the unique nature of the treatment at different sites. Many small-scale experiments with local control and choice of measures is in many ways preferable to giant national experiments with a promised standardization that is neither feasible nor even desirable from the standpoint of making irrelevancies heterogeneous.

RELATIONSHIPS AMONG THE FOUR KINDS OF VALIDITY

Internal Validity and Statistical Conclusion Validity

Drawing false positive or false negative conclusions about causal hypotheses is the essence of internal validity. This was a major justification for Campbell (1969) adding "instability" to his list of threats to internal validity. "Instability" was defined as "unreliability of measures, fluctuations in sampling persons or components, autonomous instability of repeated or equivalent measures," all of which are threats to drawing correct conclusions about covariation and hence about a treatment's effect. (What precipitated the need for this additional threat was the viewpoint of some sociologists who had argued against using tests of significance unless the comparison followed random assignment to treatments. See Winch and Campbell, 1969, for further details.)

The status of statistical conclusion validity as a special case of internal validity can be further illustrated by considering the distinction between bias and error. Bias refers to factors which systematically affect the value of means; error refers to factors which increase variability and decrease the chance of obtaining statistically significant effects. If we erroneously conclude from a quasi-experiment that A causes B, this might either be because threats to internal validity bias the relevant means or because, for a specifiable percentage of possible comparisons, sample differences as large as those found in a study would be obtained by chance. If we erroneously conclude that A does not affect B (or cannot be demonstrated to affect B), this can either be because threats to internal validity bias means and obscure true differences or because the uncontrolled variability obscures true differences. Statistical conclusion validity is concerned not with sources of systematic bias but with sources of random error and with the appropriate use of statistics and statistical tests.

An important caveat has to be added to the preceding statement that random errors reduce the risk of statistically corroborating true differences. This does not imply that random errors invariably inflate standard errors or that they never lead to false positive conclusions about covariation. Let us try to illustrate these points. Imagine multiple replications of an unbiased experiment where the treatment had no effect. The distribution of sample mean differences should be normal with a mean of zero. However, many individual sample mean differences will not be zero. Some will inevitably be larger or smaller than zero, even to a statistically significant degree.

Imagine, now, the same assumptions except that bias is operating. Because of the bias, the distribution of sample mean differences will no longer have a mean of zero, and the difference from zero indicates the magnitude of the bias. However, the point to be emphasized is that some sample mean differences will be as large when there is bias as when there is not, although the proportion of differences reaching the specified magnitude will vary between the bias and nonbias cases depending on the direction and magnitude of bias. Since sampling error, which is one kind of random error, affects both sample means and variances, it can lead to both false positive and false negative differences. In this respect, sampling error is like internal validity. But it is unlike internal validity in that it cannot affect population means. Only sources of bias—threats to internal validity—can do the latter.

Construct Validity and External Validity

Making generalizations is the essence of both construct and external validity. It is instructive, we think, to analyze the similarities and differences between the two types of validity. The major similarity can perhaps best be summarized in terms of the notion of statistical interaction—that is, the sign or direction of a treatment effect differs across populations. It is easy to see how person, setting, and time variables can moderate the effectiveness of a treatment. It is probably also easy to see how an estimate of the effect may depend on such threats to construct validity as the number of treatments a respondent receives or the frequency with which outcomes are measured. It may be less easy to see how a treatment effect can interact with (i.e., depend on) the particular method used for collecting data (mono-method bias), or the expectancies of the persons implementing a treatment (experimenter expectancies), or the guesses that respondents make about how they are supposed to behave (hypothesis-guessing). But in all these instances an internally valid effect can be obtained under one condition (say, when paper-and-pencil measures of attitude are used) and a different, but still valid, effect may result when attitude is measured some other way.

Specifying the factors that codetermine the direction and size of a particular cause-effect relationship is useful for inferring cause and effect constructs. This is because some of the causes or effects that might explain a particular relationship observed under one condition may not be able to explain why there are different causal relationships under other conditions. It should especially be noted that specifying the populations of persons, settings, and times over which a relationship holds can also clarify construct validity issues. For instance, suppose a negative income tax causes more married women than men to withdraw their labor from the labor market (see the summary statements of the four negative income tax experiments in Cook, Del Rosario, Hennigan, Mark, and Trochim, 1978). Such an action might suggest that the causal treatment can be understood, not just in monetary terms but also in terms of a possible shift in economic risks (i.e., where the family breadwinner is guaranteed an income, the withdrawal of his or her labor could have extremely serious consequences if the income guarantee were withdrawn or if the guaranteed sum failed to rise with inflation. But where a source of more marginal income is involved—as

with some married women—the withdrawal of their labor is less critical since the family is not so heavily dependent on that one source of income.) Other interpretations of why men and women are affected differently are also possible. Their existence highlights the difficulty of inferring causal constructs where the clarifying inference is indirect, being based on differences in responding across populations rather than on attempts to refine the causal operations directly so that they better fit a planned construct. The major point to be noted, however, is that both external and construct validity are concerned with specifying the contingencies on which a causal relationship depends and all such specifications have important implications for the generalizability and nature of causal relationships. Indeed, external validity and construct validity are so highly related that it was difficult for us to clarify some of the threats as belonging to one validity type or another. In fact, two of them are differently placed in this book than in Cook and Campbell (1976). These are "the interaction of treatments" and "the interaction of testing and treatment." They were formerly included as threats to external validity on grounds that the number of treatments and testings were part of the research setting. On reflection, however, we think they are more useful for specifying cause and effect constructs than for delimiting the settings under which a causal relationship holds, though they obviously can serve both purposes.

The major difference between external and construct validity has to do with the extent to which real target populations are available. In the case of external validity the researcher often wants to generalize to specific populations of persons, settings, and times that have a grounded existence, even if he or she can only accomplish this by impressionistically examining data patterns across accidental samples. However, with cause and effect constructs it is more difficult to specify a particular construct—what, for instance, *is* aggression? Any definitions would be disputed and would not have the independent existence of, say, the population of American citizens over 18 years of age. Even though the latter is a theoretical construct, it is obviously more grounded in reality than such constructs as "attitude towards authority" or "a negative income tax."

Issues of Priority Among Validity Types

Some ways of increasing one kind of validity will probably decrease another kind. For instance, internal validity is best served by carrying out randomized experiments, but the organizations willing to tolerate these are probably less representative than organizations willing to tolerate passive measurement. Second, statistical conclusion validity is increased if the experimenter can rigidly control the stimuli impinging on respondents, but this procedure can decrease both external and construct validity. And third, increasing the construct validity of effects by multiply operationalizing each of them is likely to increase the tedium of measurement and to cause either attrition from the experiment or lower reliability for individual measures.

These countervailing relationships—and there are many others—suggest how crucial it is to be explicit about the priority ordering among validity types in planning any experiment. Means have to be developed for avoiding all unnecessary trade-offs between one kind of validity and another, and to minimize the

loss entailed by the necessary trade-offs. However, since some trade-offs are inevitable, we think it unrealistic to expect that a single piece of research will effectively answer all of the validity questions surrounding even the simplest causal relationship.

The priority among validity types varies with the kind of research being conducted. For persons interested in theory testing it is almost as important to show that the variables involved in the research are constructs A and B (construct validity) as it is to show that the relationship is causal and goes from one variable to the other (internal validity). Few theories specify crucial target settings, populations, or times to or across which generalization is desired. Consequently, external validity is of relatively little importance. In practice, it is often sacrificed for the greater statistical power that comes through having isolated settings, standardized procedures, and homogeneous respondent populations. For investigators with theoretical interests our estimate is that the types of validity, in order of importance, are probably internal, construct, statistical conclusion, and external validity.

We also estimate that the construct validity of causes may be more important for such researchers than the construct validity of effects, particularly in psychology. Think, for example, of how simplistically "attitude" is operationalized in many persuasion experiments, or "cooperation" in bargaining studies, or "aggression" in studies of interpersonal violence. Think, on the other hand, about how much care goes into demonstrating that a particular manipulation varied "cognitive dissonance" and not reactance, communicator expertise and not experimenter expectancies or evaluation apprehension. Might not the construct validity of effects rank lower than statistical conclusion validity for most theory-testing researchers? If it does, this would be ironic since multiple operationalism makes it easier to achieve higher construct validity of effects than of causes.

Much applied research has a different set of priorities. It is concerned with testing whether a particular problem has been alleviated by a treatment—recidivism in criminal justice settings, achievement in education, or productivity in industry (high internal validity and high construct validity of the effect). It is also crucial that any demonstration of change in the indicator be made in a context which permits either wide generalization or generalization to the specific target settings or persons in whom the researcher or his clients are particularly interested (high interest in external validity). The researcher is relatively less concerned with determining the causally efficacious components of a complex treatment package, for the major issue is whether the treatment as implemented caused the desired change (low interest in construct validity of the cause). The priority ordering for many applied researchers is something like internal validity, external validity, construct validity of the effect, statistical conclusion validity, and construct validity of the cause.

For the kinds of causal problems we have been discussing, the primacy of internal validity should be noted for both basic and applied researchers. The reasons for this will be given below, and they relate to the often considerable costs of being wrong about the magnitude and direction of causal relations, and the often minimal gains in external validity that are achieved in moving from

initial accidental samples of convenience that belong in the class to which generalization is desired to other types of samples. Consequently, jeopardizing internal validity for the sake of increasing external validity usually entails a minimal gain for a considerable loss.

There is also a circular justification for the primacy of internal validity that pertains in any book dealing with experiments. The unique purpose of experiments is to provide stronger tests of *causal* hypotheses than is permitted by other forms of research, most of which were developed for other purposes. For instance, surveys were developed to describe population attitudes and reported behaviors while participant observation methods were developed to describe and generate new hypotheses about ongoing behaviors *in situ*. Given that the unique original purpose of experiments is cause-related, internal validity has to assume a special importance in experimentation since it is concerned with how confident one can be that an observed relationship between variables is *causal* or that the absence of a relationship implies *no cause*. The relative desirability of randomized experiments over quasi-experiments becomes even clearer in this context, for the former allows stronger tests of causal hypotheses than the latter. This is not to say that the randomized experiment guarantees a perfect test of internal validity. Far from it. However, it usually allows a stronger test than most quasi-experiments; and most of the quasi-experiments we discuss in chapters 3 and 5 of this volume permit stronger tests than the nonexperiments we shall discuss in chapter 7.

Though experiments are designed to test causal hypotheses, and internal validity is the sine qua non of causal inference, there are contexts where it would not be advisable to subordinate too much to internal validity. Someone commissioning research to improve the efficiency of his own organization might not take kindly to the idea of testing a proposed improvement in a laboratory setting with sophomore respondents. A necessary condition for meeting such a client's needs is that he can generalize any findings to his own organization and to the indicators of efficiency that he regularly uses for monitoring performance. Indeed, his need in this respect may be so great that he is prepared to sacrifice some gains in internal validity for a necessary minimum of external validity. We would tend to agree with him if increasing internal validity meant going outside his organization or organizations like his own into some completely different type of setting, e.g., the psychological laboratory. In most cases, the desirable minimum of external validity would be that the achieved samples of persons, settings, and measures belong to the specified target "populations," however accidental the samples finally achieved happened to be. However, we would be less inclined to agree with him if class membership were not enough and he insisted on, say, the formal random sampling of respondents when this type of selection precluded random assignment to treatments, which it might if it were feared that many of the potential respondents would refuse to be in the study if random assignment to treatments took place. In this last case, the gain in external validity in moving from accidental samples to samples that were *initially* formally random would not usually seem worth the loss in internal validity that is associated with going from random to systematic assignment to treatments.

Many basic researchers specify target populations when they formulate their guiding research questions, and they want to test causal theories about specific classes of persons (e.g., alcoholics) or settings (e.g., urban ghettoes), for their research would be trivialized by any procedures that increased internal validity through conducting research with groups other than alcoholics or in settings other than ghettoes. Thus, when targets of generalization are specified in guiding research questions, cognizance has to be taken of this in designing an experiment, and instances should be chosen that at least belong in the class to which generalization is desired. Unfortunately, being a member of a class does not necessarily imply being representative of that class.

SOME OBJECTIONS TO OUR VALIDITY DISTINCTIONS

A number of criticisms of the original Campbell and Stanley distinction between internal and external validity have recently appeared, and we wish to discuss them here (Gadenne, 1976; Kruglanski and Kroy, 1975; Hultsch and Hickey, 1978; Cronbach, in preparation). These critics make partially overlapping but also independent criticisms which we shall address one by one.

The first objection is to the claim that random assignment rules out all threats to internal validity. The argument is made that it is *in principle* impossible to rule out all validity threats because the true cause of an observed effect may be either the planned treatment, or procedural correlates of the treatment, or the interaction of the treatment and the procedures in which the treatment is embedded. The critics cite Rosenthal's work on experimenter expectancies to support this point, arguing that such expectancies are just one of many conceivable, and some as yet inconceivable, forces that operate in an experiment and can be treatment related.

On one level this is an important point, highlighting theorists' concerns with generalizing from operationalized independent variables to theoretical causal constructs. But the objection does not take into account the fact that Campbell and Stanley conceived of procedural variables, like experimenter expectancies, as threats to external and not internal validity. This is because such threats cast doubt on whether a causal relationship can be generalized beyond particular settings (e.g., where the experimenter had an hypothesis about the outcome of the study). They do not cast doubt on whether there was a causal relationship from the independent-variable-as-manipulated to the dependent-variable-as-measured. Indeed, the critics seem quite prepared to acknowledge that causal inference is involved in studies where the experimenters' expectancies may play a role, and their concern is with how the treatment should be labeled. Is it an effect of a particular theory-relevant construct or of the theoretical irrelevancy of "experimenter expectancies"? Such an issue of "confounding" has been discussed in this chapter as an issue of construct validity, while in Campbell and Stanley it was an issue of external validity and was never an issue of internal validity.

Nonetheless, the critics do perform an essential service, for it is indeed false to claim that randomization controls for all threats to internal validity. For instance, one can set up a randomized experiment but still have systematic

selection because of differential attrition. Moreover, the process of distributing valued resources on a random basis (instead of by need or merit, say) can lead to the operation of threats like compensatory rivalry or compensatory equalization. These, in their turn, can lead to false inferences about the effects of a treatment. While randomization is the best single means of increasing our confidence in causal inferences, it is not a panacea. Indeed, a book devoted to quasi-experiments implies that randomized experiments are not achievable at will. In the chapter devoted to randomized experiments we will stress the need to design interpretable quasi-experiments along with randomized experiments so the researcher has strong alternative designs should the initial random assignment to treatments break down. Though this book advocates random assignment, it does so in a more explicitly qualified manner than its predecessors.

The second objection made by the critics is that Campbell and Stanley, while explicitly rejecting inductive inference, nonetheless base their concept of external validity on inductive inference—going from samples to populations. At first glance this seems to be a telling criticism, for the language of external validity is the language of generalizing from samples of persons and settings to populations of persons and settings. However, it should be noted that in previous discussions, Campbell (1969b) has stressed that, because of the problem of induction, all generalization in the social sciences is particularly presumptive and that external validity is inherently more problematic than even internal validity whose bases are more obviously deductive.

It should also be noted that the relationship of samples to populations can be specified in deductive terms that permit falsification. For instance, if one conducts an experiment with a random sample drawn from a well-designated universe (say, the city of Detroit), one can rule out the threat that the universe is biased towards white or male or upper-income inhabitants of the city either by understanding what random selection is and then examining how it was implemented in the experiment in question, or by comparing background characteristics of the sample with (hopefully, recent) census data on the population. Stated more formally, the threat to be ruled out is: There is a race bias in the study. One deduces from this that the percentages of persons from different races who are in the sample should not differ from the percentages in the population to a greater degree than is warranted by sampling error. This deduction is testable by collecting data on the race of persons in the sample. If the percentages differ from what is expected on the basis of the (hopefully, recent) census, it would not be false to say that there is probably a race bias. However, if the percentages are as expected from the census, then it would be false to say there is a race bias though there may be other sources of bias.

External validity can also be deductively tested when sampling is carried out to achieve heterogeneity rather than formal representativeness. The postulate is, say: The treatment does not affect black inhabitants of Detroit. The deduction is: The effect will not be observed among blacks. The falsifying test of this is to examine empirically whether there is a causal relationship among blacks. If there is, one cannot say that the causal relationship generalizes to all blacks, but one can at least say that the relationship is not false when tested with a particular biased sample of blacks. If there is no causal relationship

among blacks, one can confidently conclude that the effect does not hold with all black inhabitants of Detroit. It is simply not the case, therefore, that external validity rests on a base of inductive inference that flies in the face of the acknowledged limitations of inductive inference.

Campbell and Stanley included under external validity threats having to do with generalizing from manipulations and measures to target constructs. Their discussion of these issues was explicitly nonpositivist, espousing multiple operationalism. Nonetheless, there was a flavor of positivism in that the inductive framework may have encouraged readers to think that the operations "somehow" were the constructs, that an observed response really was "aggression" or "love." The present book, in distinguishing between external and construct validity, has been written to avoid such a positivist flavor and to stress that constructs are hypothetical entities not "corporeally" represented by samples of operations.

A third objection the critics make is to note that all guiding research propositions must be couched in general/universal terms whereas internal validity is couched in the language of causal connections involving research operations. The critics wonder how one can have any validity internal to an experiment when the propositions whose validity is being tested are phrased in general terms external to the experiment (e.g., *A* is "causally" related to *B*). The concern with the universal nature of research propositions goes beyond internal validity, of course, as can be seen in the fact that the guiding research propositions are likely to be phrased as: "What is the *causal* effect of *school desegregation* on the *academic achievement* of *children in the public schools* of *Evanston* in *1969?*" Or, "What was the *causal* effect of a *guaranteed income* on the *labor force participation* of *working poor persons* in *New Jersey and Scranton, Pennsylvania, between 1969 and 1972?*" Given the universal terms in these propositions, critics point out that validity depends on the fit between research operations and referent constructs (construct validity) or populations (i.e., external validity). Most critics invoke Brunswik at one point or another and call for a "representative" social science in which (1) the target populations and constructs are clearly stated and sampling takes place so as to represent these populations in the research operations; and (2) the targets are not conceived solely in terms of respondents—the representativeness of settings and procedures is also crucial for Brunswik and his followers.

We have a great deal of sympathy with the position that all aspects of research design test propositions of a general and universal nature and that sampling is the means by which one approximates representing general constructs about causes, effects, types of people, or the like. However, it is easier to conceive of the representativeness of constructs and populations than of relationships among variables. How does one, for instance, sample to represent "causality"? We find it difficult to imagine representative samples of causal instances. Instead, we think that testing the nature of an observed relationship between an independent and dependent variable has to revolve around the particularities of a single study—around details concerning covariation, temporal precedence, and the ruling out of alternative interpretations about the nature of the relationship in the experiment on hand. Of course, we do not deny that the

notion of "cause" is an abstract one and that the single study only approximates causal knowledge. But we believe it is confusing to insist that internal validity is a contradiction in terms because all validity is external, referring to abstract concepts beyond a study and not to concrete research operations within a study. It is confusing because the choice of populations and the fit between samples and populations determines representativeness, whereas neither populations nor samples are necessary for inferring cause.

Nonetheless, the critics make a very useful point, for if the goals of a research project are formulated well enough to permit specifying target constructs and populations, then the research operations have to represent these targets if the research is to be relevant either to theory or to policy. Moreover, a focus on representativeness has historically entailed a heightened sensitivity to unplanned and irrelevant targets that unnecessarily limit generalizability, as when all the persons who collect posttest achievement data in an early childhood experiment with economically disadvantaged children are of the same social class. Clearly, relevant research demands representativeness where target constructs or populations are specified. It also demands heterogeneity where irrelevant populations could limit the applicability of the research. Though we advocate putting considerable resources into the preexperimental explication of relevant theory or policy questions—and hence targets—this should not be interpreted in any way as an exclusive focus. As we tried to demonstrate in the discussion of both construct and external validity, it is sometimes the case that the data, once collected and analyzed, force us to restrict (or extend) generalizability beyond the scope of the original formulation of target constructs and populations. The data edit the kinds of general statements we can make.

For instance, in his experiment on the help given to compatriots and foreigners, Feldman (1968) wanted to generalize to "cooperation." He deduced that if his independent variable affected cooperation, he would find five dependent variable measures related to his treatment. But only two were related, and the data outcomes forced him to conclude tentatively that his treatment was differently related to two kinds of cooperation. Similarly, the designers of the New Jersey Negative Income Tax Experiment wanted to generalize to working poor persons, but the data forced them tentatively to conclude that working poor blacks responded one way to the treatments, working poor persons who were Spanish speaking reacted another way, and working poor whites probably did not respond to the treatments at all. The point is this: While it is laudable to sample for representativeness when targets of generalization are specified in advance—and we heartily endorse such sampling—in the last analysis it is the patterning of data outcomes which determines the range of constructs and populations over which one can claim a treatment effect was obtained. One has always to be alert to the data demanding a respecification of the affected populations and constructs and to the possibility that the affected populations and constructs will not be the same as those originally specified.

A fourth objection has been directed towards Campbell and Stanley's stress on the primacy of internal over external validity. The critics argue that no kind of validity can logically have precedence over another. Of what use, critics say, is a theory-testing experiment if the true causal variable is not what the

researchers say it is; or of what use is a policy experiment about the effects of school desegregation if it involves a school in rural Mississippi when most desegregation is in large, northern cities where white children have fewer alternatives to public schools than in the deep South? This point of view has been best expressed by Snow (1974). He uses the term "referent validity" to designate the extent to which research operations correspond to their referent terms in research propositions of the form: "Counseling for pregnant teenagers improves their mental health" or "The introduction of national health insurance causes an increase in the use of outpatient services." Without using our terminology, Snow notes that such propositions usually contain implicit or explicit references to populations, settings, and times (external validity), to the nature of the presumed cause and effect (construct validity), to whether the operations representing the cause and effect covary (statistical conclusion validity), and to whether this covariation is plausibly the result of causal forces (internal validity).

For a study to be useful, the argument goes, each part of the proposition should be given approximately equal weight. There is no need to stress the causality term over any other. Other critics (Hultsch and Hickey, 1978; Cronbach, in preparation) take the argument one step further and stress the primacy of external over internal validity. Hultsch claims that if we have a target population of special interest—for example, the educable mentally retarded—then it is better to test causal propositions about this group on representative samples. He maintains this should be done even if less rigorous means have to be used for testing causal propositions than would be the case if a study was restricted to easily available but nonrepresentative subgroups of the educable mentally retarded or to children who were not educable and retarded. Cronbach (in preparation) echoes this argument and adds, first, that in much applied social research the results are needed quickly and, second, that a high degree of confidence about causal attribution is less important in the decisions of policy-makers (broadly conceived) than is confidence in knowing that one is working with formally or impressionistically representative samples. Consequently, Cronbach contends that the time demands of experiments with experimenter-controlled manipulanda and the reality of how research is (and is not) used in decision making suggest a higher priority for speedy research using available data sets, simple one-wave measurement studies or qualitative studies as opposed to studies which, like quasi-experiments, take more time and explicitly stress internal validity.

It is in some ways ironic that the charge of neglecting external validity should be leveled against one of the persons who invented the construct and elevated its importance in the eyes of those who restricted experimentation to laboratory settings and who wrote about experimentation without formally mentioning the special problems that arise in field settings. But this aside, we have no quarrel *in the abstract* with the point of view that, where causal propositions include references to populations of persons and settings and to constructs about cause and effect, each should be equally weighted in empirical tests of these propositions. The real difficulty comes *in particular instances* of research design and implementation where very often the investigator is forced to make undesirable choices between internal and external validity. Gaining a representative sample of educable, mentally retarded students across the whole nation demands considerable resources.

Even gaining such a sample in a few cities located more closely together is difficult, requiring resources for implementing a treatment, ensuring its consistent delivery, collecting the required pretest and posttest data, and doing the necessary public relations work. Without such resources, one runs the risk of a large, poorly implemented study with a representative sample or of a smaller, better implemented study where the small sample size limits our confidence in generalizing.

Since random sampling is so rare for purposes of achieving representativeness, it is useful to consider the trade-off between internal and external validity when heterogeneous but unrepresentative sampling is used or when impressionistically modal but unrepresentative instances are selected that at least belong in the general class to which generalization is desired. Samples selected this way will have unknown initial biases, since not all schools will volunteer to permit measurement, even fewer schools will agree to deliberate manipulation of any kind, and the sample of schools that *will* agree to randomized manipulation will probably be even more circumscribed than the sample of schools that agrees to measurement with or without quasi-experimentation. The crucial issue is this: Would one do better to work with the initially more representative sample of schools in a particular geographical area that volunteered to permit measurement, even though no deliberate manipulation took place? Or would one rather work with a less representative sample of schools where both measurement and deliberate manipulation took place?

Solving this problem boils down, we think, to asking whether the internal validity costs of eschewing deliberate manipulation and more confident causal inferences are worth the gains for external validity of having an initially more representative sample from which bias-inducing attrition will nonetheless take place. Any resolution must also consider two other factors. First, the study which stresses internal validity has at least to take place in a setting and with persons who belong in the class to which generalization is desired, however formally unrepresentative of the class they might be. Second, the study which stresses external validity and has apparently more representative samples of settings and persons will result in less confident causal conclusions because more powerful techniques of field experimentation were not used or were not used as well as they might have been under other circumstances.

The art of designing causal studies is to minimize the need for trade-offs and to try to estimate in any particular instance the size of the gains and losses in internal and external validity that are involved in different trade-off options. Scholars differ considerably in their estimate of gains and losses. Cronbach maintains that timely, representative, but less rigorous studies can still lead to reasonable approximations to causal inference, even if the studies are nonexperimental and of the kind we shall discuss—somewhat pessimistically—in chapter 7. Campbell and Boruch (1975), on the other hand, maintain that causal inference is problematic with nonexperimental and single-wave quasi-experiments because of the many threats to internal validity that remain unexamined or have to be ruled out by fiat rather than through direct design or measurement. The issue involves estimating how to balance timeliness and the quality of causal inference, whether the costs of being wrong in one's causal inference are not greater than the costs of being late with the results.

Consider two cases of timely research aimed at answering causal questions which used manifestly inadequate experimental procedures. Head Start was evaluated by Ohio-Westinghouse (Cicirelli, 1969) in a design with only one wave of measurement of academic achievement. The conclusion—Head Start was harmful. Analysis of the same data using different statistical models appeared to corroborate this conclusion (Barnow, 1973); to reverse it completely, making Head Start appear helpful (Magidson, 1977); or to result in no-difference findings (Bentler and Woodward, 1978). Since we do not know the effects of Head Start, any timely decisions based on the data would have been premature and perhaps harmful. The second example worth citing is the Coleman Report (Coleman et al., 1966). In this large-scale, one-wave study it was concluded that black children gained more in achievement the higher the percentage of white children in their classes. This finding was used to justify school desegregation. However, better designed subsequent research has shown that if blacks gain at all because of desegregation (which is not clear), they gain much less than was originally claimed. It is important, we feel, not to underestimate the costs of producing timely results about cause, particularly its direction, which turn out to be wrong. Clearly, the chances of being wrong about cause are higher the more one deviates from an experimental model and conducts nonexperimental research using primitive one-wave quasi-experiments.

Since timeliness is important in policy research—though less so for basic researchers for whom this book is also intended—we shall devote some of the next chapter to quasi-experimental designs that do not require pretests and to ways in which archives can be used for rigorous and timely causal analysis. In the end, however, each investigator has to try to design research which maximizes all kinds of validity and, if he or she decides to place a primacy on internal validity, this cannot be allowed to trivialize the research.

We have not tried to place internal validity above other forms of validity. Rather, we wanted to outline the issues. In a sense, by writing a book about experimentation in field settings, we are assuming that readers already believe that internal validity is of great importance, for the raison d'etre of experiments is to facilitate causal inference. Other forms of knowledge about the social world one more accurately or more efficiently gained through other means—e.g., surveys or participant observation. Our aim differs, therefore, from that of the last critics we discussed. They argue that experimentation is not necessary for causal inference or that it is harmful to the pursuit of knowledge which will be useful in policy formulation. We assume that readers believe causal inference is important and that experimentation is one of the most useful, if not *the* most useful, way of gaining knowledge about cause.

SOME OBJECTIONS TO OUR TENTATIVE PHILOSOPHY OF THE SOCIAL SCIENCES

Protests against "scientism" have been prominent in recent commentaries on the theory of conducting social science. Such protests focus on inappropriate and blind efforts to apply "the scientific method" to the social sciences. Critics argue that quantification, random assignment, control groups and the deliberate intrusion

of treatments—all techniques borrowed from the physical sciences—distort the context in which social research takes place. Their protest against scientism is often linked with the now-pervasive rejection of the logical positivist philosophy of science and is frequently accompanied by a greater emphasis on humanistic and qualitative research methods such as ethnography, participation observation, and ethno-methodology. Critics also point to the irreducibly judgmental and subjective components in all social science research and to the pretensions to scientific precision found in many current studies.

We agree with much of this criticism and have addressed the issue in our previous work (Campbell, 1966, 1974, 1975; Cook, 1974a; Cook and Cook, 1977; Cook and Gruder, 1978; Cook and Reichardt, in press). However, some of the critics of scientism (Guttentag, 1971, 1973; Weiss and Rein, 1970; Hultsch and Hickey, 1978; Mitroff and Bonoma, 1978; Mitroff and Kilman, 1978; Cronbach, in preparation) have cited Campbell and Stanley (1966) and Cook and Campbell (1976) as prime examples of the scientistic norm to which they object. While the identification of our previous work with scientism oversimplifies and blurs the issues, we acknowledge that in this volume, as in the past, we advocate using the methods of experiments and quantitative science that are shared *in part* with the physical sciences. We cannot here comment extensively on these criticisms of our background assumptions, which go beyond criticisms of causation issues alone. But we can indicate in broad terms the approach we would take in responding to these objections.

First, we of course agree with the critics of logical positivism. The philosophy was wrong in describing how physical science achieved its degree of validity, which was not through descriptive best-fit theories and definitional operationalism. Although the error did not have much impact on the practice of physics, its effect on social science methods was disastrous. We join in the criticism of positivist social science when *positivist* is used in this technical sense rather than as a synonym for "science." We do not join critics when they advocate giving up the search for objective, intersubjectively verifiable knowledge. Instead we advocate substituting a critical-realist philosophy of science, which will help us understand the success of the physical sciences and guide our efforts to achieve a more valid social science. Critical realists (Mandelbaum, 1964) or "metaphysical realists" (Popper, 1972), "structural realists" (Maxwell, 1972), or "logical realists" (Northrop, 1959; Northrop and Livingston, 1964) are among the most vigorous modern critics of logical positivism. Critical realists particularly concerned with the social sciences identify their position with Marx's materialist criticism of idealism and positivism, e.g., Bhaskar, 1975, 1978; Keat and Urry, 1975.

Second, it is generally agreed that the social disciplines, pure or applied, are not truly successful as sciences. In fact, they may never have the predictive and explanatory power of the physical sciences—a pessimistic conclusion that merits serious debate (Herskovits, 1972; Campbell, 1972). This book, with its many categories of threats to validity and its general tone of modesty and caution in making causal inferences, supports such pessimism and underscores the equivocal nature of our conclusions. However, it is sometimes forgotten that these threats are not limited to quantitative or deliberately experimental studies. They also arise in *less formal, more commonsense, humanistic, global, contextual integrative and*

qualitative approaches to knowledge. Even the "regression artifacts," identified with measurement error, are an observational-inferential illusion that occurs in ordinary cognition (see Tversky and Kahnman, 1974, and Fischoff, 1975).

We feel that those who advocate qualitative methods for social science research are at their best when they expose the blindness and gullibility of specious quantitative studies. Field experimentation should always include qualitative research to describe and illuminate the context and conditions under which research is conducted. These efforts often may uncover important site-specific threats to validity and contribute to valid explanations of experimental results in general and of perplexing or unexpected outcomes in particular. We also believe, along with many critics, that quantitative researchers in the past have used poorly framed questions to generate quantitative scores and that these scores have then been applied uncritically to a variety of situations. (Chapters 4 and 7, in particular, highlight some of the abuses associated with traditions of quantitative data analysis which have probably led to many specious findings.) In uncritical quantitative research, measurement has been viewed as an essential first step in the research process, whereas in physics the routine measures are the products of past crucial experiments and elegant theories, not the essential first steps. Also, the definitional operationalism of logical positivists has supported the uncritical reification of measures and has encouraged research practitioners to overlook the measures' inevitable shortcomings and the consequences of these shortcomings. A fundamental oversight of uncritical quantifiers has been to misinterpret quantifications as replacing rather than depending upon ordinary perception and judgment, even though quantification at its best goes beyond these factors (Campbell, 1966, 1974, 1975). Experimental and quantitative social scientists have often used tests of significance as though they were the sole and final proof of their conclusions. From our perspective, tests of significance render implausible only *one* of the many plausible threats to validity that are continually arising. Naive social quantifiers continue to overlook the presumptive, qualitatively judgmental nature of *all* science. In contrast, the tradition we represent, with its heavy use of the word "plausible," stresses that the scientist must continually judge whether a given rival hypothesis will explain the data. Qualitative contextual information (as well as quantitative evidence on tangential variables) has long been recognized as relevant to such judgments.

Valid as these criticisms are, it is not enough merely to point out the limitations of our methods. Critics should be able to offer viable alternatives. To be superior to the techniques described in the next six chapters, however, the proposed qualitative methods would have to eliminate more of the threats to validity listed in this chapter than do the quantitative methods. In this regard, it is refreshing to note that our humanistic colleague, Howard Becker (1978), has tried to rule out some of the validity threats in research which uses photographs either as evidence or as the means of presenting final research results, no quantification having intervened. Others conducting qualitative research under nonlaboratory conditions also recognize the equivocal nature of any causal inferences drawn from their observations. Many sociologists, anthropologists and historians have attempted to avoid causal explanations, aiming instead for uninterpreted description. Yet careful linguistic analysis of their reports shows that they are rarely successful. Their

understandings, insights, meanings, analysis of intentions and the like are strongly colored by causal conclusions even when the terms "effects," "gains," "benefits" and "results" are carefully avoided.

Most of the critics also write as if they were advocating an alternative social science approach that, when implemented, would remove the equivocality of inference plaguing our research efforts. Examples of such new approaches are rare and, when offered, are not impressive. The best of qualitative social science joins with us and much of the significant literature in recognizing and emphasizing the ambiguity of social science situations. Such an emphasis should help us relinquish the hope for a simple social science rather than try to provide a "superior route" to such a dubious goal.

The methodology presented in this book is a product of a critical dialectic that has continued over the past several decades. In this dialectic, social scientists have criticized each other's attempts to draw causal inferences; in answer to these criticisms, practitioners have collected additional data or conducted secondary analyses. We believe that the threats to validity and methodological arrangements we present in this book would arise from such a critical exchange even without the physical science paradigm. If the starting point for investigating an issue was qualitative humanistic scholarship, the results of the scholarship would, we believe, be criticized in terms of specific rival alternative interpretations like those we have defined. Answering these criticisms would lead, we also believe, to reinventing quantification, control groups, the arbitrary intrusions of experimental manipulations, and randomization, since recognizing threats would lead to a need for mechanisms that rule out such threats. Yet in most real world settings, even these ingenious devices will not be enough; and confident estimates of effects, gains, and the like must be tentative at best and subject to correction. We hope that our long list of threats will encourage such modesty and caution in drawing conclusions regardless of whether the approach is humanistic or scientific.

However, the list of threats to validity should not leave the readers with the belief that reasonably dependable causal knowledge cannot be achieved in the social sciences. Indeed, we hope that this book will help guide the search for and recognition of such dependable connections. The techniques presented in the following chapters should be of some assistance in ruling out as many threats to validity as possible and reducing the number of plausible alternative interpretations of the data. But we wish to stress that causal inferences will never be proved with certainty since the inferences we make depend upon many assumptions that cannot be directly verified. This predicament should not discourage us since it is not unique to social science and is shared in varying degrees by the successful physical sciences (Kuhn, 1961; Toulmin, 1972).

3

Quasi-Experiments: Nonequivalent Control Group Designs

NOTATIONAL SYSTEM

This chapter discusses some quasi-experimental designs which attempt to partition respondents into nonequivalent groups that receive different treatments or no explicit treatment at all. None of the designs presented here includes time-series data. In outlining the designs we shall use a notational system in which X stands for a treatment, O stands for an observation, subscripts 1 through n refer to the sequential order of implementing treatments $(X_1 \ldots X_n)$ or of recording observations $(O_1 \ldots O_n)$. A dashed line between experimental groups indicates that they were not randomly formed. A wavy line between nonequivalent groups indicates that they can be considered cohorts, a term that will be defined later.

This notational system gives all the information that is required for describing experimental designs. It does not, of course, give all the information required for designing research. Indeed, a monograph on research design would have to deal with how research questions are formulated, how sampling is carried out to achieve representativeness, when causal inferences can reasonably be drawn, how data should be analyzed, and how results should be communicated to various interested parties. In this book we shall concern ourselves in detail with how the scheduling of treatments and observations helps in making causal inferences, and how the experimental data might be analyzed statistically in order to support causal inferences. All other questions of research design are treated only in the detail necessary for making our points about causal inference.

THREE DESIGNS THAT OFTEN DO NOT PERMIT REASONABLE CAUSAL INFERENCES

The three designs below are frequently used in social science research. While they are often useful for suggesting new ideas, they are *normally* not sufficient for permitting strong tests of causal hypotheses because they fail to rule out a number of plausible alternative interpretations.

It should not be forgotten that experimental design is only one way to rule out alternative interpretations and that sometimes threats can be ruled out in nondesign ways. This is especially the case when particular threats seem implausible in light of accepted theory or common sense or when the threats are validly measured and it is shown in the statistical analysis that they are not operating. With the designs under consideration, we should therefore expect some instances where few, if any, threats to internal validity are plausible even though the scheduling of treatments and measures does not by itself rule out most of the relevant threats. Though we believe that the three designs we shall examine below are *generally* uninterpretable, we urge the reader not to conclude that studies using them are *invariably* uninterpretable. Indeed, we shall later cite one example where causal inference seems reasonable.

The One-Group Posttest-Only Design

This design is diagrammed below. As can be seen, it involves making observations only on persons who have undergone a treatment, and then only after they have received it. If this were all of the information we had about the variable and about the population, the design would be totally uninformative.

$$X \quad O$$

One basic deficiency is the lack of pretest observations from persons receiving the treatment. As a result, one cannot easily infer that the treatment is related to any kind of change. A second deficiency is the lack of a control group of persons who did not receive the treatment. Without this control it is difficult to conceptualize the relevant threats and to measure them individually. In most contexts one needs time-relevant data from no-treatment control groups to check on maturational trends. One also needs information from such groups to check on any other causally irrelevant factors that could affect posttest scores and prevent one from inferring what the posttest mean would have been in the treatment group had there been no treatment.

Our predecessors have probably been mistaken in identifying the design we are discussing as "The One-Shot Case Study." Single-setting, one-time-period case studies as used in the social and clinical sciences occur in settings where many variables are measured at the posttest; contextual knowledge is already rich, even if impressionistic; and intelligent presumptions can be made about what this group would have been like without X. These three factors can often serve the same roles that pretest measures and control groups do more formally in more elaborate experimental designs. It may even be that in hypothesis-testing case studies, the multiple implications of the thesis for the multiple observations available generate "degrees of freedom" analogous to those coming from numbers of persons and replications in an experiment (Campbell, 1975). However that may be, and while recognizing that the epistemology of humanistic scholarly approaches needs much further elaboration, certainly the case study as normally practiced should not be demeaned by identification with the one-group posttest-only design. However, one would often recommend with the case study that scholarly effort should be redistributed so as to provide explicit evidence about conditions prior to the presumed

cause and about contemporary conditions in social settings without the treatment that are similar to the setting in which the case study is taking place. All inference is comparative, and it is usually optimal to have comparable sorts of evidence, comparable degrees of detail and precision, about conditions prior to the implementation of a treatment and about factors that occur simultaneously with the treatment.

A consideration of some of the conditions under which posttest observations on a single treatment group may result in reasonable causal inference may be of help at this point. Scriven's (1976) concept of the "modus operandi" approach provides one valuable perspective, based upon considering police detective approaches. When a thief commits a crime he leaves behind a series of clues which perhaps indicate when he entered a building, by which means he entered, which types of goods he stole or left behind, and so on. The experienced detective examines these clues and relates them to what is known about the preferred operating style of identified burglars, ruling out some potential suspects because their usual mode of breaking and entering differs from what is observed. Having reduced the universe of likely suspects (i.e., causes), the detective then searches for further clues in the hope of narrowing down the number of suspects to one or two. The researcher can sometimes function as a detective, noting the level of different variables and using this information to rule out some threats to both internal and construct validities. For example, in education a case study might reveal that a new mathematics curriculum stresses algebra over geometry and arithmetic and that, after completing the curriculum, a particular group of children scores well above national norms in algebra but not in geometry and arithmetic. To the extent the researcher can rule out alternative possibilities (e.g., the difference is due to chance, or existed before the new curriculum began), it is provisionally warranted to infer causation.

Three points need stressing about the modus operandi example we have just cited. First, the experimental design is no longer that of a simple case study with a single dependent variable measured at one time. The design has become more complex and has many dependent variables that are expected to have different levels. (Making the design even more complex by adding respondents' posttest recollections of how they were at the pretest can also help. If one is prepared to assume that such retrospective pretests are valid, one can then examine the data for differences in the amount of change between different constructs.)

Second, some causes, like some burglars, leave their unique "signature" on the effect. For example, if a specific poison is found in the victim's blood, compelling causal inferences can be established if the prevalence of that chemical is rare, if its sources are few or unique, and if spatial and temporal contiguity can be established that links the victim to sources of that particular chemical. On further examination, such cases turn out to be those in which the causal hypotheses involved are already established, and the "base rates" for their distribution known. To establish that a single factory using vinyl chloride is the culprit for neighborhood and employee cancers requires a much less elaborate experimental design than one set up to determine which air and water pollutants may be cancer producing. The notion of "signed causes" may be usefully extended even back into laboratory research. Consider the one-group posttest-only design in a study of

the effects of rehearsing a nonsense syllable list when compared to a study of the effects of a movie on some social attitude. The nonsense syllable list is a "signed cause," and the base rate for people at large being able to recite these 12 nonsense syllables in the specific order in which they were presented in an experiment can be assumed to be extremely low. But for the social attitude example, innumerable communications in ordinary daily life are potential causes. To give an attitude survey only to those who have just seen the movie would normally tell us nothing about the movie's impact on the attitude. (However, the illustrations that respondents use in open-ended responding and the justifications for the attitudes that respondents advance might turn up plausible "signed causes" testifying to the movie's impact as opposed to the impact of other attitude-influencing forces.)

Third, one point can be made about both simple case studies with a single novel dependent variable (e.g., a nonsense syllable list or death due to vinyl chloride poisoning) and more complex case studies with different predictions for different dependent variables. Their interpretability depends on being able to make confident inferences about change and on being able to rule out more threats to internal validity than is normally the case with a simple case study that has a single outcome variable which can be multiply influenced. The functional requirements are to assess change and to rule out alternative interpretations. Though the case study and other one-group posttest-only designs are generally poor at achieving these ends, they are not always so. At times multiple dependent variables are available and realistic assumptions about change and alternative interpretations of change can be made. Moreover, the case study is useful for purposes unrelated to inferring causation, such as assessing whether there was a treatment and how well it was delivered, or generating new hypotheses about the phenomenon under investigation.

The Posttest-Only Design with Nonequivalent Groups

Often a treatment is implemented before the researcher can prepare for it, and so the research design is worked out after the treatment has begun. Such research is often said to be ex post facto. However, research of this kind does not necessarily imply the absence of pretest observations, for archival records can often be used to establish what the pretest scores of the various experimental units were. We shall understand ex post facto here in a more restricted sense than is often used—as research where there are no pretest observations on the same or equivalent scales for which posttest observations are available.

If we add to the case study a single nonequivalent control group that does not receive the treatment, we arrive at the design diagrammed below.

$$\begin{array}{cc} \overline{X \quad O} \\ \text{- - - - -} \\ \overline{ \quad O} \end{array}$$

Its most obvious flaw is the absence of pretests, which leads to the possibility that any posttest differences between the groups can be attributed either to a treatment effect or to *selection* differences between the different groups. The plausibility of

selection differences in research with nonequivalent groups usually renders the design uninterpretable.

The posttest-only design with nonequivalent groups can be more complicated than appears above, especially if multiple groups are involved that receive the treatment with different dosages. This would be the case, for instance, if one nonequivalent group of parolees had one year's counseling, another group had nine months, another group six months, another three months, and another none. Such a design would take the form below, with the subscript indicating the treatment period in months.

$$
\begin{array}{cc}
\hline
X_{12} & O \\
\hline
X_9 & O \\
\hline
X_6 & O \\
\hline
X_3 & O \\
\hline
X_0 & O \\
\hline
\end{array}
$$

If the length of the treatment were related to posttest scores, this would be consistent with the possibility that the treatment had causally influenced the outcome measure, say, recidivism. But it would not be strong evidence, for one would have to rule out the possibility that the persons least likely to go back to prison were selected for the longer parole period. This could happen because the persons making the selection wanted the parole counseling to appear beneficial or because the ex-offenders who were likely to stay in the counseling treatment longer were those least likely to drop out of the experiment as a result of committing crimes.

A tradition has developed in economics and sociology of trying to overcome the lack of pretest measures by seeking out pretest measures which correlate with the posttest within experimental groups *but are not measured on the same scale as the posttest*. This means that more easily retrieved measures such as age, sex, social class, race, place of birth, or residence are substituted for the absent pretest. We shall leave discussion of this particular modification of the posttest-only design until we deal with designs that have both pretests and nonequivalent groups.

The One-Group Pretest-Posttest Design

This design is one of the more frequently used designs in the social sciences and is diagrammed below.

$$
\begin{array}{ccc}
\hline
O_1 & X & O_2 \\
\hline
\end{array}
$$

It can be seen that pretest observations (O_1) are recorded on a single group of persons, who later receive a treatment (X), after which posttest observations are made (O_2). Since the use of this design is so widespread, we would like to illustrate its weaknesses using a hypothetical example.

Imagine the case where the supervisory style of foremen is altered in a work setting and where the change is expected to increase productivity. Imagine, further, that the posttest level of productivity is reliably higher than the pretest level. One might want to attribute such an increase to the change in supervisory style. However, the change might alternatively be due to *history* in the sense that other events could have happened between the pretest and posttest that affected productivity. Some of these could have occurred within the work setting (e.g., a new salary scale might have been implemented, union policies might have changed, or a new training program might have been introduced). Other events could have taken place outside of the work setting (e.g., a new export drive might have been started nationally, or the weather might have become warmer, allowing workers to feel better or become better acquainted). Any of these events, or others, *could* have affected productivity. In order to rule them out, the researcher has to make the case either that they are implausible in the particular context of a given study or that they are plausible but did not actually operate. Data are usually required for making the second case, and either common sense, or theory, or experience are required for buttressing the argument of implausibility. If he or she cannot rule out a particular history threat, then the researcher has to admit that he or she cannot draw confident causal conclusions because a frequently plausible threat cannot be ruled out.

Consider, next, *statistical regression*. Why should supervisory styles be changed? One reason might be that productivity is low and needs to be increased. Now, productivity in any one year can be low because of a genuinely stable decline in productivity or because productivity has been consistently low for some time. But it might also be *low in any one year* because of random factors like an atypical strike or delays in the delivery of raw materials or other "errors" in the method of measuring productivity. Such random factors mean that the impetus for change will be negatively correlated with productivity, and this is tantamount to deliberately choosing a year of extremely low productivity for conducting one's experiment. What will happen in such a case is that productivity will probably increase in the next year as it regresses towards the grand mean of the productivity trend. In other words, by choosing to change one's work practices when productivity is low one can capitalize upon random fluctuations in productivity.

A more common form of regression artifact for this design arises when a special program is given only to those with extreme scores on the pretest, as would happen with a compensatory education program that is given only to low-achieving children. Selecting out low scorers will produce a spurious improvement if the pretest-posttest correlation is less than 1.00. The magnitude of the spurious regression effect will depend on (a) how far the correlation is below unity (McNemar, 1940) and (b) how far the low scorers are below their population mean. In a similar vein, if an advanced training program were given to the best salespeople of one year and was in fact totally ineffective, it would nonetheless probably appear to reduce the sales volume of its graduates when their pretest-posttest performance is compared to that of other salespeople. What is important to note is that the amount of regression is negatively related to how highly each salesperson's sales volume is correlated from year to year, and is positively related to how far the pretest year deviates from the average sales volume of the average salesperson.

Even when the pretest-posttest correlation is high, a posttest increase in productivity could be accounted for in terms of *maturation*. Typically, productivity levels do not stay constant from year to year, being subject to systematic fluctuations as well as to the random fluctuations that lead to statistical regression. Whenever productivity is systematically rising over the years or is subject to systematic cyclical fluctuations within any one year, a posttest increase over pretest levels can appear in the design under discussion. This increase would not be unambiguously attributable to the supervisory change. It could alternatively be attributed to workers becoming more experienced, or to machinery becoming more and more sophisticated, or to the average height and weight of United States males being on the increase, or whatever. This threat is particularly relevant because many of the factories that allow outside investigators to conduct research may be proud of the fact that they are getting better and better. Of course, productivity sometimes systematically decreases, and cyclical trends decrease as well as increase. Hence, with the design under discussion, maturation can sometimes lead to spurious decreases as well as spurious increases.

In some contexts there are nondesign ways of directly estimating whether maturation could plausibly account for pretest-posttest differences. Consider the productivity example again; imagine that the pretest and posttest are separated by a year and that the mean level of experience (years worked in an organization) increases by a year between pretest and posttest. If the pool of *pretest scores were sufficiently large,* one could regress productivity onto years worked. If the resulting regression line were flat and the correlation of experience and productivity was therefore zero, then the maturation hypothesis would be rendered implausible because it presupposes that the experience gained during a year's work affects productivity. However, if there were a simple linear relationship, one could then use the regression equation derived from the pretest scores in order to predict the productivity change expected in a year. This could then be used to assess if the one-year change predicted from the pretest scores alone was different from the actual change obtained during the year.

Though it is useful, care must be taken with such an estimation procedure. First, with obtrusive measures a problem arises because the expected posttest performance is derived from a pool of pretest scores where measurement has taken place only once. Consequently, if the expected and obtained scores differed, this might be either because the posttest was affected by the treatment or because knowledge gained at the first testing altered performance on the subsequent testing. Second, problems can arise if the expected maturation is assessed from a pool of persons who contribute pretest scores and if some of these persons then drop out of the study so that the pretest and posttest groups are less than totally comparable. Differences between expected and obtained scores might then be due to selection. Finally, it is worth noting that the mean posttest experience must inevitably be different from the mean pretest experience if maturation is occurring and the analyses are restricted to persons who provide both pretest and posttest data. As a result, the pretest data cannot be used to assess the relationship between experience and productivity for that part of the experience distribution which is represented in the posttest but not in the pretest. All one can do is assume that the relationship in this part of the distribution can be inferred by extrapolating from

the way in which productivity and experience are related *for the particular range of pretest experience scores.*

Though we have focused on history, maturation, and regression as frequent competing explanations in the one-group pretest-posttest design, it would be incorrect to think that they are the only relevant ones. *Testing* is an obvious addition to the list. This is because exposure to an outcome measure at one time can lead to shifts in performance at another. For instance, in education a pretest can be the impetus to learning the correct answers to items and thus increase the posttest level of performance. *Instrumentation* can also be a threat if, for reasons that are relevant or irrelevant to the experiment, the definition of an outcome measure is changed. This might happen, for example, if the definition of what constitutes a "serious" traffic accident is modified in some record-keeping system.

Occasionally there will be specific settings where the threats of history, maturation, regression, instrumentation, and testing are implausible or can be convincingly ruled out via direct measurement. In those settings, the one-group pretest-posttest design will be interpretable. Unfortunately, these settings are likely to be rare. To rule out effects of history, the respondents would have to be *physically isolated* from historical forces that affect productivity. To rule out statistical regression, we would require a *series of pretest observations* from which it could be inferred that the introduction of the treatment was not associated with extreme values of the pretest. However, since the one-group pretest-posttest design is defined as having only one pretest observation, nothing can be known of the pretest trend except in very rare circumstances where the phenomenon under investigation is known to be nonchanging. Alternatively, regression would be implausible if the pretest-posttest correlation were close to 1.00, since the magnitude of regression depends upon the unreliability of the measures and unreliable measures have lower test-retest correlations. Though high test-retest correlations are not unknown, they are often closer to .40 than to 1.00 with social measures and time intervals of about a year. As for maturation, *a long series of pretest observations* would obviously permit testing the threat sensitively, but it is by definition not available. A less sensitive test would be to use a regression procedure like the one described for the purpose of estimating maturation numerically, though this requires accepting certain assumptions. If neither of these empirical strategies were feasible, one would then have to deal with a maturation threat by using common sense, theory, or experience to assess the plausibility of assuming whether maturation was or was not occurring in the specific context of a specific research project.

Consider how much more fortunate the physicist is when compared to the behavioral scientist who works in field settings. The physicist can use a laboratory to create physical isolation, and he or she often works with objects that do not change over the time period of an experiment. This being so, history, maturation, and regression are not problematic, and the data from single-group pretest-posttest changes are often causally interpretable. Consider, next, the cultural anthropologist who wants to investigate how a new tool (e.g., the axe) has affected a remote tribe that has been "untouched by the modern world." This researcher, too, can use physical isolation (e.g., a dense jungle setting) and the presumption of stable pretest trends with respect to outcomes in order to help causally interpret certain

kinds of pretest-posttest shifts. The social scientist, on the other hand, has fewer of the advantages of the physicist or the cultural anthropologist working in ''remote'' areas, for the social scientist is trying to answer causal questions in more complex social settings where the entities being studied are clearly amenable to change for reasons that have nothing to do with the experiment.

The practical question is, therefore: When can physical isolation be achieved or assumed by the social scientist? When can he or she assume stable pretest trends given that no pretest data are available for empirically assessing the trend? In our opinion, social scientists working in field settings will rarely be able to give confident answers to these questions *unless they are working with novel outcome variables and short pretest-posttest time intervals*. This means that we should usually not expect hard-headed causal inferences from the simple before-after design when it is used by itself, though inferences may be possible under the special conditions noted above. However, we will often achieve some knowledge using the design, even when pretest-posttest intervals are long and the outcome variables are subject to multiple influence other than the treatment. This is because the design permits ruling out some competing threats to validity and it often suggests hypotheses worth further exploration. Our hope is that persons considering the use of this design will hesitate before resorting to it and will decide to incorporate into it some of the design adjuncts we shall mention later.

SOME GENERALLY INTERPRETABLE NONEQUIVALENT CONTROL GROUP DESIGNS

In this section, we shall distinguish eight kinds of generally interpretable nonequivalent control group designs. These can be labeled (a) no-treatment control group designs, (b) nonequivalent dependent variables designs, (c) removed-treatment control group designs, (d) repeated-treatment designs, (e) reversed-treatment nonequivalent control group designs, (f) cohort designs, (g) posttest-only designs with predicted higher-order interactions, and (h) regression-discontinuity designs. These designs are not in any way qualitatively different from the ones we labeled ''generally interpretable.'' They merely make it possible to rule out more threats to internal validity. Readers would do themselves a disservice if they treated the designs to follow as qualitatively distinct from those already presented.

Our separate discussion of the designs that follow should not blind the reader to the importance of incorporating more than one of them into the work that he or she does. The designs have different strengths and weaknesses, and their creative mixture within a single study can significantly increase our confidence in making causal attributions. We hope, therefore, that the reader will pay particular attention to some of the studies we shall deal with in detail (e.g., Broadbent and Little, 1960; Lawler and Hackman, 1969; and Lieberman, 1956). These studies were improved by creatively mixing the design features that we shall treat separately for pedagogic convenience alone.

The Untreated Control Group Design with Pretest and Posttest

The design is diagrammed below. It is perhaps the most frequently used design in social science research and is fortunately often interpretable. It can, therefore,

be recommended in situations where nothing better is available. Because of its frequent usage, we shall deal with it in considerable detail.

$$
\begin{array}{ccc}
O_1 & X & O_2 \\
\hline
O_1 & & O_2
\end{array}
$$

Our discussion will be in two parts. In this chapter, we shall detail how much the interpretation of outcomes from this design depends on the particular pattern of findings. To do this, we shall discuss five different outcomes, using the first one to illustrate the most likely threats. For heuristic reasons, the discussion will be phrased in terms of group differences in pretest-posttest gains. In the next chapter, four ways of statistically analyzing the data from the basic design will be outlined, and it will be concluded that a simple analysis of pretest-posttest gain is normally inappropriate. Thus, our heuristic focus on gains in this chapter should not be interpreted to imply that the data from the pretest-posttest design with nonequivalent groups should be analyzed as simple gain scores.

Outcome 1. The basic design under discussion usually controls for all but four threats to internal validity. One uncontrolled threat is that of *selection-maturation.* This arises when the respondents in one group are growing more experienced, more tired, or more bored than the respondents in another group. To help understand this, imagine the situation where a new practice is introduced into one of two settings where identical tasks are being performed and where the treatment group outperforms the controls at the pretest. If the treatment increased productivity, we would expect a posttest difference between groups that was larger than the pretest difference, as Figure 3.1 illustrates. But we would also expect this pattern of data if the treatment and control groups differed because the former were, say, brighter on the average and were using their aptitude to gain new knowledge at a faster rate than the controls.

Figure 3.1 has been drawn to illustrate the special situation where there is no growth at all among the controls who have reached a stable level of performing by the pretest. When the data are of this form, the major issue that the investigator has to face is: How plausible is it to postulate causally irrelevant growth patterns that only affect the experimental group? In many instances, it will be much easier to think of reasons why the experimentals and controls should be maturing at different rates *in the same direction* than it will be to think of reasons why one group should be changing in one direction while the other group is not changing at all. For instance, different growth rates in the same direction are common in education contexts or in contexts where people are expected to gain through experience. In other instances, it will be easier to think of reasons why neither group should be growing than to think of reasons why one should be growing and the other not. If plausibility or, preferably, the direct analysis of pretest data to assess growth rates within conditions indicates that no growth would be expected in either group during the experiment, then when the experimental outcomes are as depicted in Figure 3.1, one need not worry too much about selection-maturation.

However, if the threat cannot be ruled out, despite the absence of all measured pretest-posttest growth in the controls, then it must be taken seriously.

A second problem arises with *instrumentation*. It is not clear with many scales that the intervals are equal, and change is often easier to detect at some points on a scale than others. Scaling problems are presumably more acute the greater the nonequivalence of the experimental groups and the farther apart they are on the scale, especially if any of the group means approaches one end of the scale where ceiling or floor effects are likely. An inspection of the pretest and posttest frequency distributions within each treatment group will suggest whether instrumentation problems are plausible. If they are, the distributions will be skewed and/or the group means and variances will be correlated. Sometimes, the raw data can be rescaled so as to reduce the problem, while at other times a careful choice must be made of intact and unmatched groups that score at about the middle of a scale and close to each other.

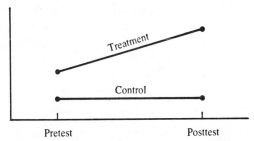

Figure 3.1. First outcome of the no-treatment control group design with pretest and posttest.

A third problem has to do with *differential statistical regression*. Consider the consequences of having a predetermined experimental group of low scorers (say, children eligible for Head Start) and then selecting no-treatment controls from the children nearby so that their scores will be as close as possible to the experimental mean, yet still above it on the average since they are not eligible for Head Start. Knowing this, the researcher might put in a special (but misguided) effort to select as controls children with particularly low scores, arguing that the best approximation for creating equivalent groups is to form groups with minimal differences. But the deliberate selection of low scorers is a form of matching which will result in the control group mean regressing to its population baseline, as in Figure 3.1. The experimentals, on the other hand, would not be expected to change since they were not selected for their low scores. Such differential regression could obviously result in the Figure 3.1 pattern of outcomes.

A fourth problem relates to the interaction of selection and history. We shall call this *local history*, events other than the treatment which affect the experimental group but not the control group, or vice versa. Imagine introducing some par-

ticipative decision-making procedure to a group of day workers while leaving decision making as it was among night workers. Imagine, further, that the investigator was interested in seeing whether participative decision making induced higher work morale. Now, if the experiment started in the early spring and ended by midsummer we might expect the increasingly warm weather to have a greater effect on the work morale of day workers than of night workers. This is only one of many possible examples, of course, and the plausibility of a local history explanation has to be examined within the particular context of specific research settings when the nonequivalent control group design is used.

Outcome 2. There is a pattern of selection-maturation interaction which is both more common and more lawful than the one that would be represented by Figure 3.1. This pattern occurs when nonequivalent groups are growing at different average rates in a common direction, as in Figure 3.2. Such differences in growth rate will usually be reflected in pretest differences. When the differential growth continues for the total course of an experiment (in the absence of other forces which affect observed growth, such as ceiling effects), it will result in larger posttest than pretest differences between groups. This pattern will have nothing to do with the effects of a treatment, but it may seem to the unwary as if it does.

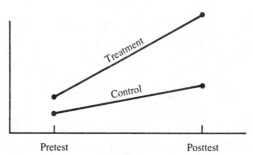

Figure 3.2. Second outcome of the no-treatment control group design with pretest and posttest.

It is common in quasi-experimental research in many substantive areas to find differences in growth rates, particularly when respondents self-select themselves into receiving a treatment. For when self-selection occurs, treatments are more likely to become available to the specially meritorious or to persons with keen desires to "improve themselves." Since the "meritorious" or the "keen" will usually be intrinsically more able or more exposed to opportunities for change, the "meritorious" or "keen" will change faster over time. Thus a selection-maturation difference can masquerade as a treatment effect.

Several clues are available for assessing whether nonequivalent groups may be maturing at different rates over time. First, if the group mean differences are a

result of biased social aggregation or selection only, then the differential growth between groups should also be occurring within groups. To help understand this, imagine two groups of children, one of which receives an educational treatment and is composed of children with more ability, on the average, than the controls. The experimentals might very well gain more than the controls over time for reasons associated with the children's innate abilities. But more importantly for our present purposes, on many measures of educational achievement we would expect the more able among the experimentals to gain more than the less able *among the experimentals*. The point is that many patterns of selection-maturation should lead to increased *within-group* variances at the posttest when compared to the pretest. In estimating the plausibility of a selection-maturation threat, it is always important to inspect the variances, particularly when the obtained outcomes are like those depicted in Figure 3.2. Second, the plausibility of selection-maturation can be estimated by plotting *pretest* outcome scores against the maturational variable (e.g., age or years of experience) for the experimental and control groups separately. If the regression lines differ in linear slope, this is presumptive evidence of differential average growth rates.

The growth pattern we have been describing up to this point is one associated with phrases like "the rich get richer" or "the able become more able." This pattern is characterized by a constant increase over time in the mean difference between nonequivalent groups and by within-group variances that increase with their respective group means. But there are many, many ways in which two or more groups can differ from each other over time in the absence of a treatment effect, and there is no *logical* need for the difference between groups to be increasing at a constant rate. Instead, much more complex patterns of growth differences can be imagined (e.g., simple linear growth in one condition and quadratic growth in another, or quadratic growth in one condition and cubic in another). However, in our experience (largely influenced by educational experiments), it is more common to have linearly increasing group differences over the time span of an experiment than it is to have more complex forms of group differences. But what is most common in our experience is not synonymous with what is possible in the context of a particular research problem.

Since it is important to be able to identify the particular pattern of maturation that would be expected in each group in the basic research design, attempts should be made to estimate at least the gross pattern of maturational differences. As we have seen, the pretest data are sometimes appropriate for this. So, too, is background theory, for descriptive longitudinal data sometimes exist from populations similar to those in an experiment. Consider the case in education. Here, many data sets describe how those who initially had a higher level of achievement came to grow further ahead of their lower-scoring contemporaries on most achievement measures, resulting in a constant increase in group differences. But for certain skills (e.g., the notion of conservation) we suspect that learning gains may come about abruptly as children reach the "stage" where the skill can be learned. For skills like conservation, constant increases would not be expected. Instead, sharp discontinuities in the growth pattern would be expected in each group and at different times across groups.

Unfortunately, the necessary longitudinal descriptive information is not available in other substantive areas, and estimates of group differences in maturational patterns will have to be made on the basis of experience or guesswork. Neither of these is, alas, suitable for numerically estimating particular group growth rates in a specific study (e.g., estimates of the form: the change in income for each month of age is X dollars). Nor are they suitable for even estimating gross differences in pattern (e.g., the average expected change in income is greater in group A than in group B).

Thus far, we have treated selection-maturation as though it were the only threat to internal validity that could operate if the outcome pattern in Figure 3.2 resulted. This is clearly not the case. All the other threats listed for the outcome in Figure 3.1 apply to Figure 3.2. Take local history as an example. One group can obviously experience different local events between the pretest and posttest, and these can masquerade as treatment effects. Take instrumentation as another example. Since nonequivalent groups usually differ at the pretest, there is the distinct possibility of floor or ceiling effects that affect one group differently from another. In some educational experiments the higher-scoring group's true achievement shift from pretest to posttest may be underestimated because of a floor effect. Actually, these threats do more than make the interpretation of the data pattern in Figure 3.2 hazardous. They also make it difficult to use the pretest data for estimating the gross expected maturation pattern within each treatment group.

Basically, Figures 3.1 and 3.2 differ in their implications for how plausible is the threat of differential growth. Figure 3.1 suggests that no change would be expected between the pretest and the posttest, and this increases the likelihood that the observed change in the experimental group is due to the treatment. However, to accept this assumption about the control group the researcher has to ask: (1) "Might there have been change in the control group to which the measures were not sensitive?" If the answer to this is negative, the researcher also must ask (2) "Though no change occurred among the controls, how sure can I be that there would also have been no change in the nonequivalent treatment group in the absence of a treatment?" Figure 3.2 suggests that the no-treatment controls might well be changing over time and that the research is not tapping into a no-change situation. It does more than that, however. It also suggests that the group with greater pretest advantages may be changing at a faster rate than the group with fewer pretest advantages. This being so, the researcher has to ask: "How can I test whether there is differential growth?" and "How can I estimate the pattern of the differential growth?" We shall see in the next chapter that differential change patterns of the form "the rich get richer" (i.e., a constant increase in group mean differences over time) are more amenable to statistical analysis than other forms of differential change. Whatever the thoughts one has about selection-maturation, one cannot afford to ignore local history, differential instrumentation shifts, differential testing, and differential statistical regression as other possible interpretations of the outcome patterns depicted in both Figure 3.1 and Figure 3.2.

Outcome 3. Our discussion of the nonequivalent no-treatment control group design has thus far focused on the outcome where the treatment group is superior

to the controls at the pretest and appears to be even more superior at the posttest. Let us now look at Figure 3.3 which shows the related outcome where the pretest superiority is diminished or eliminated by the posttest.

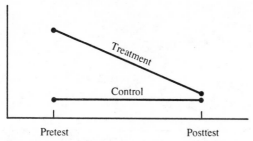

Figure 3.3. Third outcome of the no-treatment control group design with pretest and posttest.

This particular outcome was obtained from a sample of black third, fourth, and fifth graders in a study of the effects of school integration on academic self-concept (Weber, Cook and Campbell, 1971). At the pretest, black children who attended all-black schools had a higher academic self-concept mean than black children who attended integrated schools in the same school district. But after formal school integration had taken place, the initially segregated and initially integrated black children did not differ. While the basic logic of experimental design with control groups involves starting with equality between groups and finishing with differences between them, we should be alert to "catch up" designs in which the "control group" already has the treatment which the experimental group receives between pretest and posttest. Of course, all of the problems described for Figures 3.1 and 3.2 are still relevant, especially the possibility of a selection-maturation interaction.

Outcome 4. A fourth possible outcome of the no-treatment control group design with pretest and posttest is depicted below. Its salient characteristics are that the controls initially outperform the experimentals and that the difference between experimentals and controls is greater at the pretest than the posttest. This is a particularly interesting outcome since it is the one desired when organizations introduce compensatory inputs to increase the performance of groups who have started out at a disadvantage (as in some educational contexts) or where performance did not seem up to par for other reasons (as happens in industry when changes are made to improve poor performances).

This outcome is subject to the typical scaling (i.e., instrumentation) and local history (i.e., selection × history) threats that were discussed earlier. But two special aspects stand out. First, regression is more of a threat than it is when the outcome is as depicted in Figure 3.1. When no attempt has been made to match

groups and one is instead dealing with stable group differences, regression is normally not a threat if the research outcome is similar to the one depicted in Figure 3.1. This is because we would have no reason to expect respondents in the treatment condition to regress upwards from their higher pretest scores.

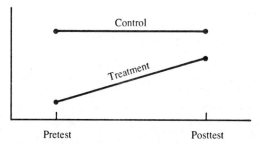

Figure 3.4. Fourth outcome of the no-treatment control group design with pretest and posttest.

But the situation can be very different, as in the case illustrated in Figure 3.4, if the treatment is deliberately given to experimental group members *because their scores are unexpectedly low*. This will lead to regression upwards by the posttest and to the data pattern shown in Figure 3.4. We would expect such regression because there is likely to be an especially large error component determining an unexpectedly low pretest mean (as opposed to a low pretest mean which reflects a stable pattern of poor performance and measures having a large true score and a small error variance component). To assess the likelihood of statistical regression, it is important to explore *why* low-scoring groups are assigned a particular treatment.

Second, the outcome in Figure 3.4 is particularly useful since it rules out the previously mentioned cumulative pattern of selection-maturation where persons scoring lower at the pretest could be expected to be even further behind at the posttest. When this common maturational pattern is presumed to operate, the outcome in Figure 3.4 would imply that the treatment had had an effect *despite* the lower expected pretest-posttest change among respondents in the treatment group. In other words, the treatment was so powerful that it overcame a countervailing force which tended to obscure a true treatment effect. Of course, it should not be assumed that all maturational trends follow the pattern of the higher-scoring group spontaneously changing faster than the lower-scoring group. This assumption has to be checked against the growth patterns reflected in the pretest scores or against any general laws that might be applicable to a given research area. Nonetheless, outcome four rules out all possibilities of differential linear growth that are based upon members of the higher-scoring pretest group growing at a faster average rate than members of the lower-scoring pretest group. Less common patterns of selec-

tion-maturation would have to be invoked as alternative explanations of the findings in Figure 3.4.

Outcome 5. Bracht and Glass (1968) have noted the desirability of basing causal inferences on interaction patterns like that in Figure 3.5. Here the trend lines cross over and the means are significantly different from each other in one direction at the pretest and in the opposite direction at the posttest. The important point is not the crossover per se, since any interaction tells us that trend lines differ. The important point concerns the pattern of switching mean differences, for this tells us that the low-scoring pretest group (the "experimentals") has overtaken the high-scoring control group. None of the other interaction patterns that we have presented thus far does this, nor is it done if the trend lines cross but the two posttest means do not differ.

There are several other reasons why Figure 3.5 is usually more interpretable than other outcomes of the nonequivalent control group design. First, the plausibility of an alternative scaling interpretation is reduced, for no logarithmic or other transform will remove the interaction. Moreover, any reference to a "ceiling" effect mediating the crossover is inappropriate. While this effect might explain why a lower-scoring pretest group comes to score as high as a higher-scoring

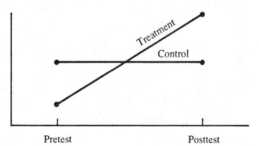

Figure 3.5. Fifth outcome of the no-treatment control group design with pretest and posttest.

group, it would not explain how the lower-scoring group then drew ahead. A more convincing scaling artifact would have to be based on the notion that there is some true change in the lower-scoring group but that it is inflated because the scale intervals make change easier for both low- and high-scoring units than for units scoring closer to the grand mean. Note, though, that this entails postulating the exacerbation of a true effect and not the mediation of an artifactual effect.

Second, the Figure 3.5 outcome renders a regression alternative explanation less likely. When groups are selected on the basis of pretest scores or variables related to pretest scores, there is reason to suspect that a low treatment mean might be regressing to a higher grand mean. However, it is rarely reasonable to expect that this grand mean will be higher than that of the higher-scoring control

group. It would have to be, however, if statistical regression were to explain why the experimental group overtakes the control group and significantly differs from it at the posttest.

Third, Cook et al. (1975) have commented on the interpretability of Figure 3.5 when a selection-maturation threat is feared. They reanalyzed some of the Educational Testing Service (ETS) data on the effectiveness of "Sesame Street" and found that children in Winston-Salem who had been encouraged to view the show knew reliably less at the pretest than children who had not been so encouraged. By the posttest, however, the treatment group knew reliably more than the control group, thereby resulting in a data pattern that resembled Figure 3.5. The selection-maturation problem is reduced in this case because so few documented maturation patterns can be described in terms of trends that meet and cross over as opposed to trends that never meet and grow continuously further apart. Of course, complicated forms of selection-maturation cannot be ruled out if the data are as in Figure 3.5. For instance, Cook et al. had to probe the possibility that the encouraged children were both younger and brighter than those in the control group—that they scored lower at the pretest because they were younger and changed more over time because they were brighter. Fortunately, data analysis indicated that the encouraged and nonencouraged groups did not differ in age or pretest measures of cognitive aptitudes that are often considered stable.

Though the outcome in Figure 3.5 is usually interpretable, any attempt to set up a design to achieve it involves considerable risk and should not be undertaken lightly. This is especially true in growth situations where a true treatment effect would have to countervail against a lower expected growth rate in an experimental group. Where this possibility exists, a no-difference finding would not make it clear whether a treatment effect had or had not been obtained for two countervailing forces could have cancelled each other out. Even if there were a difference, this would much more readily take the form of Figure 3.4 than Figure 3.5. Figure 3.4 is much less interpretable than Figure 3.5 on a variety of grounds. It is one thing to comment on the interpretative advantages provided by a crossover interaction with reliable and switching pretest and posttest differences, and it is quite another to obtain the data pattern.

We have discussed these five outcomes of the no-treatment control group design because the basic design is widely used and its interpretability depends, in part, on the particular outcomes obtained in a research project. The investigator who plans to employ this design would do well to ponder, before data collection, which outcomes are interpretable and which forces may countervail against obtaining such outcomes. In particular, the researcher has to consider the risk of equivocal findings resulting from studies where the no-treatment controls outperform the experimentals at the pretest. To be sure, outcomes of low equivocality *can* result if pretest differences favor the controls (see Figure 3.5), but they are less likely than the more ambiguous Figure 3.4 outcomes.

The Untreated Control Group Design with Proxy Pretest Measures

Sometimes it is not possible to collect pretest measures from respondents either on the same instrument as is used at the posttest or on a parallel form of the instrument. Instead, the researcher has to seek out pretest measures which he or she

hopes will correlate with posttest scores within each group, despite being different in form from the posttest scores. The need for different measures is most striking when novel responses are involved—say, in an experiment where the consequences of a preliminary algebra curriculum are to be evaluated, for it would not make sense to give a preexperimental algebra test to children who have never had algebra. Instead, one might give them a general test of mathematical aptitude. Different pretest measures are also needed when evaluating the consequence of an ongoing practice, since in this case it may not be possible to collect any measures other than those found in the archives or those where changes are not likely to be affected by the treatment (e.g., stable characteristics like age, sex, or socioeconomic status).

Such variables function in the design and analysis as proxies for the pretest. The hope is that proxy pretests will be correlated with the posttest within each treatment group, thereby serving two purposes. First, statistical power will be increased if scores on the proxy pretest are related to posttest scores. Second, a preliminary indication will be evident of the way in which selection operates, for the proxy variables may suggest some of the specific initial differences between groups. The basic difficulty with proxy pretests is that they usually correlate less well with posttest scores than do pretests that are collected on the same instrument as the posttest. Consequently, proxies are less adequate than similar pretests for increasing statistical power and for understanding the particular ways in which the posttest scores may be related to initial group differences. (The reader should not infer from this that pretests collected on the same instrument are perfect—far from it.) Pretest-posttest correlations are inevitably imperfect even when the same treatment is used and the measures are corrected for attenuation. For instance, the factorial composition of a measure can change, from one time to another—as when an algebra test gives weight to both algebraic ability and reading skill when used with younger children at a pretest but taps only into algebraic skill when used at the posttest when the children are older. Though the algebra test may have the same apparent form at each testing session, it is not quite the same test each time. The advantage of similar-appearing pretests over proxy pretests are only relative, as we shall see in the next chapter.

The proxy pretest design is diagrammed below. The new subscripts, A and B, refer to different measures. It can be seen from the figure that the design is identical in all ways to the simple pretest-posttest design with nonequivalent groups except for the A and B subscripts.

$$
\begin{array}{ccc}
\hline
O_{A1} & X & O_{B2} \\
\hline
O_{A1} & & O_{B2} \\
\hline
\end{array}
$$

Let us consider a concrete example of the design. Imagine a large firm that offers a year-long business leadership evening course to all of its first-year executives. Some 30 of the new junior executives take it, another 50 cannot fit it in, are not interested, or have other reasons. At the end of the year, all of the executives are given a test of Business Leadership Skills (O_{B2}), which hopefully has been

developed independently of the curriculum materials. Let us imagine further that statistically significant differences are found on the O_{B2} measure at the posttest and they favor the alumni of the course. Now, skeptics might allege that the alumni would have had better leadership skills even without the course. So, an effort might be made to control for this probability by using personnel selection test scores in each man's file. Imagine, further, that within each group, tests of General Ability, Social Intelligence, and Interpersonal Dominance are found to correlate substantially with the scores on Business Leadership Skills, and so an equally weighted composite of standard scores is formed which correlates .70 within each group. This composite is O_{A1}.

If the course alumni and their controls turn out not to have differed on O_{A1} (or any of its components), this provides reasonable assurance that the groups did not differ on the shared components producing the correlation between O_{A1} and O_{B2}. In such a case, the use of the proxy pretest would increase the interpretability of the quasi-experiment, although the possibility of pretreatment differences on unmeasured components of O_{B2} remains. If, however, a group difference is found on O_{A1}, the usual procedures of matching, covariance, partial r, or multiple regression will almost always *under-adjust*, and the practitioner of these procedures will misleadingly package this under-adjustment as a treatment effect. Indeed, when the correlation between O_{A1} and O_{B2} is .00, no adjustment will take place, and all of the pretest differences will remain in the posttest. When the correlation is substantial and less than 1.00, some of the pretest differences will be removed but not all. Hence, we would erroneously conclude from posttest group differences in leadership skills that the course was effective when, in fact, the posttest difference might be due to selection. It is only when the correlation of O_{A1} and O_{B2} is 1.00 (when corrected for unreliability in O_{B2}) that the adjustment will be adequate and all the group pretest differences will be removed from the posttest. Such a high correlation is unlikely between a posttest and a proxy pretest, and it is this fact that makes the proxy pretest design so difficult to interpret. (An extended discussion of this issue can be found in chapter 7.)

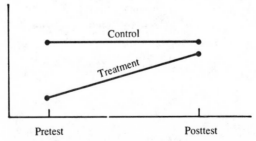

Figure 3.6. Hypothetical pretest and posttest means of a treatment and nonequivalent control group.

The hypothetical example we have just discussed refers to the situation where there is a reliable posttest difference between nonequivalent groups. Sometimes, when there is no such difference, the ex post facto design under discussion has been used to infer that there is no treatment effect. Here, too, one can be in error. Figure 3.6 gives the hypothetical pretest and posttest means for two nonequivalent groups measured on the same scale at each time interval. The group scoring the lowest at the pretest should be considered the treatment group. If we only had posttest information we would conclude from Figure 3.6 that the posttest means did not differ. Now, if we had pretest scores that correlated highly with posttest scores, a statistical adjustment like covariance analysis would reveal a difference between the adjusted posttest scores, with the treatment mean being higher. But if the pretest scores did not correlate highly with the posttest, which is more likely with proxy variables, there will be little adjustment of the posttest means and no reliable differences would be obtained. However, such differences might have been found with the same posttest data if we had better pretest measures. What this implies is that any no-difference conclusion based on the use of proxy pretest variables might be false, reflecting the inadequacies of the design rather than the ineffectiveness of the treatment. (Campbell and Erlebacher, 1970, have discussed this special case of the ex post facto design in greater detail, and the interested reader should consult that reference.)

The Untreated Control Group Design with
Separate Pretest and Posttest Samples

The basic pretest-posttest design with nonequivalent groups is sometimes used with a further modification. Instead of the same units being measured at each time interval in the nonequivalent treatment groups, separate samples are used in each group at each time interval. The design is most often needed when the researcher strongly suspects that pretest measurement will affect posttest responses in a way that could easily lead to incorrect inferences about cause. The actual design is diagrammed below, with the vertical line indicating noncomparability across time.

$$
\begin{array}{c|ccc}
O & X & O \\
\hline
O & & O \\
\end{array}
$$

The strongest context where this design can be used is when the pretest and posttest groups in each treatment condition are selected at random so that they are representative of the same population. In other words, the design is strongest where there is no vertical dotted line! The caveat, even when pretest and posttest are each random samples from the same population, is that the pretest and posttest groups are only comparable (1) within the limits of sampling error, so that with smaller and heterogeneous samples of respondents, comparability is problematic; (2) the pretest and posttest groups have to be comparable *after* the process of selecting, so that comparability is not achieved if the selection process is *implemented* in biased fashion or if the persons refusing to be measured are, on the average, different at each time interval; and (3) even if the pretest and posttest

groups are comparable, the treatment and control groups are not. Hence most of the threats to internal validity that are relevant to the nonequivalent control group design where the same units are measured at the pretest and posttest still apply when different units are measured at each time.

The difficulties of implementing the design under question can be illustrated by considering an experiment on how lawn mower use is affected by public advertisement campaigns and face-to-face contacts, each of which is designed to inform people about how to use their power lawn mowers more safely (Kerpelman et al., 1978). Part of the total design involved the use of independent pretest and posttest samples in each of two towns, one of which received the ads plus face-to-face contact and the other served as no-treatment controls. Within each town, the selection of respondents was made randomly at both the pretest and posttest, and implementation of the sampling design was left to different research subcontractors at each site. Analysis of the demographic background characteristics of respondents revealed a highly similar pretest-posttest profile at one site, being presumptive evidence that the major assumption of the design was met. However, the pretest and posttest samples had a different profile at another site. The cause of this site difference was not clear, but its implications were. It meant that the greater changes in knowledge of lawn mower safety found at the treatment site when compared to the control site were causally ambiguous: were they due to the treatment or to differences in the composition of the pretest and posttest samples at the one site?

Anyone considering the use of a nonequivalent group design with unique pretest and posttest samples should first assess, in very critical fashion, whether the need for separate pretest and posttest groups is compelling. If *and only if* it is, the researcher should then pay special attention to (1) how the samples are drawn, (2) how the sampling design is implemented and (3) which variables are measured as indirect checks on the comparability of samples. Variables should be chosen because one would not expect them to be affected by the treatment and because such variables would be expected to influence posttest performance. Needless to say, such variables should be reliably measured. However, even if the measures meet these conditions, their use as tests of comparability is still indirect, since it is logically impossible in the posttest-only group to measure the most crucial aspect of comparability—pretest performance. Anyone using this design should check on the background comparability of the pretest and posttest samples as soon as the posttest data are in, for it may well be that the sampling design has been incorrectly implemented and can be reimplemented before the data collection staff has been disbanded. Alternatively, if the data collection phase has come to a complete halt, the only thing that can be done when the pretest and posttest samples appear noncomparable at any one site is to examine the data to find out whether the noncomparability is general or is limited to a specific subsample. In the study of Kerpelman et al. an impressive correspondence was obtained within each treatment group between the pretest and posttest profiles of all the respondents who had not gone to college, but no such correspondence was found with respondents who had attended college. In such a case, it may be reasonable to assume that the sampling requirement of the design has been carried out as planned with *some* of the total set of respondents (i.e., those who had not gone to college).

The design with separate pretest and posttest samples is weak, and should not be attempted unless a clear indication exists that resources permit no stronger design. Even then, the design has to be implemented in such a way that great care is devoted to the sampling and data collection phases, for without independent evidence of the comparability of pretest and posttest samples the design is nearly worthless for purposes of inferring cause. This is because the simplest form of selection will usually provide a plausible alternative interpretation. Moreover, the design will often be low in statistical power given the absence of information about the relationship of the pretest to the posttest within each treatment group.

The Untreated Control Group Design with Pretest Measures at More Than One Time Interval

This design is a variant on the most commonly used untreated control group design, and is diagrammed below.

$$\begin{array}{cccc} O_1 & O_2 & X & O_3 \\ \hline O_1 & O_2 & & O_3 \end{array}$$

It can be seen that the only addition to the basic design is an antecedent pretest of the same form used at the posttest.

The advantages of pretests at two (or more) time points are considerable. We saw earlier how a significant threat to internal validity with the untreated control group design is selection-maturation. Adding a pretest permits one to see whether the nonequivalent groups are in fact growing apart at different rates between O_1 and O_2, at a time when the treatment could not have affected the scores. Of course, one has to be careful in using the two pretests to estimate possible differences in growth rates for three reasons. First, the growth rates will be fallibly estimated, given measurement error. Second, scaling artifacts might make the measured growth between O_1 and O_2 unrepresentative of what we would expect between O_2 and O_3. And third—even in the absence of fallible measurement and imperfect scales—we would still have to assume that the rate of growth between O_1 and O_2 in each group would have continued between O_2 and O_3. This is testable for the untreated control group but not for the crucial treatment group. These difficulties notwithstanding, the second pretest can help considerably in assessing the plausibility of selection-maturation.

This is not the only benefit of this design. If the O_2 observations were atypical in either of the groups and we have no O_1 measures, a spurious treatment effect could emerge because of statistical regression. But with a prior pretest one can quickly see whether the O_2 level is inexplicably high or low when compared to O_1. A third benefit of the design cannot perhaps be fully appreciated at this point, for it has more to do with inferential statistical analysis than design. In some instances, it is desirable to be able to estimate the correlation between observations taken from a single group across a known time interval. To compute the correlation between O_2 and O_3 in the treated group gives an unclear estimate of what the correlation would have been had no treatment been given, which is the crucial information needed for the statistical analysis. Consequently, the O_2–O_3

correlation from the untreated group is often used as the best estimate of the corresponding correlation in the treated group. However, a good case can be made that the O_1–O_2 correlation in the treated group will usually be a better estimate than the O_2–O_3 correlation in the untreated group. Since correlations are sensitive to the length of the test-retest interval, it is desirable to have the same interval between O_1 and O_2 as between O_2 and O_3. This is why the design with multiple pretests has been drawn with equal intervals.

Adding a pretest clearly helps the interpretation of possible causal relationships. Why, then, is the design not used more often? One reason may be relative ignorance, but another is surely that the design is often unfeasible. In many situations, one is fortunate to be able to delay the treatment implementation in order to obtain a single pretest let alone two. Sometimes, archives will make the second pretest possible, though with archives the researcher can often extend the pretest "time series" for many more than two intervals. Unfortunately, time is not the only feasibility constraint. Some persons responsible for authorizing research expenditures are loath to see money spent for any features of experimental design other than the posttest measurement of persons who have received particular treatments. It is difficult to get such persons to spend money on untreated control group respondents; and we suspect that it will also be even more difficult to get them to spend money on more than one pretest. Nonetheless, where the time frame or the archival record system permits, it is useful to try to persuade authorities to allow two pretests on the same measure taken at different times.

The Nonequivalent Dependent Variables Design

By itself, this is one of the weakest interpretable quasi-experiments. We discuss it for two reasons. First, it can be implemented when resources allow measurement of only a single treatment group. Second, nonequivalent dependent variables can strengthen causal interpretation when *added* to other quasi-experimental designs. The design is diagrammed below in a form which highlights its similarity to the untreated control group design:

O_{1A}	X	O_{2A}	A and B represent different
O_{1B}		O_{2B}	measures from a single group.

However, the essence of the design is that *a single group* of persons is involved. These are pretested on two scales, one of which is expected to change because of the treatment (O_A) and the other is not (O_B). Hence, use of the design is restricted to theoretical contexts where differential change is predicted. If the research is conducted without hypotheses, the design reduces to being a simple one-group pretest-posttest design with multiple dependent variables. Any pattern of differential change might be due to chance, ceiling/basement effects, or to differences in reliability between the measures. These last points are important, for when change and no-change are predicted, it is imperative to demonstrate that the predicted no-change variable has been reliably measured and would probably have registered true effects had they occurred.

Findings using the nonequivalent dependent variables design are only interpretable when the two outcome variables are conceptually similar and each would be affected by most of the plausible alternative interpretations of the obtained effect, other than the treatment. To take an exaggerated example, it would be trivial to demonstrate that a new industrial machine was related to a pretest-posttest difference in productivity (O_A) but not to differences in hair styles (O_B). Rather, one would want to show that the machine caused a difference in, say, the quantity of production during its hours of operation (O_A) but not during the hours when it was down and different machines were used (O_B). The importance of the two related but different dependent variables comes from the fact that alternative interpretations, such as history, would be expected to affect productivity whether the experimental machine was operating or not.

Let us illustrate by an actual example how the credibility of this design depends on initial expectations that both variables A and B should be affected by any plausible alternative interpretations of an apparent treatment effect. Broadbent and Little (1960) surveyed the literature from laboratory experiments on the effects of noise on industrial productivity. They concluded that "the effect of noise is to increase the frequency of momentary lapses in efficiency rather than to produce decline in rate of work, gross failures of coordination, or similar inefficiency." They set out to test this in an industrial setting where personnel have the job of perforating the edge of film. This was a particularly fortunate work setting since, for payment reasons, measures of the rate of work and the number of broken films were routinely collected and archived. The number of broken films was one of the operational definitions of "momentary lapse," a variable that should be affected by noise. The amount of work performed while machines were working was one measure of "rate of work," a variable that should not be affected by noise. Moreover, it was possible to obtain the relevant archival data both before and after a workroom was experimentally treated and the noise level was reduced. A comparison of before-after changes showed that there were fewer "momentary lapses" after the noise was reduced—and that neither rate of work nor absenteeism was affected when noise was reduced. Without the literature review and the hypotheses it generated, it would probably not have been possible to predict that noise should affect the number of momentary lapses but not the rate of work.

The use of the nonequivalent dependent variables design is not restricted to industrial contexts, of course. It can be used in education where one is attempting to assess, for example, the effectiveness of a new curriculum on geometry. One would expect geometry scores to increase if the curriculum were successful, but one would not expect scores to change on tests measuring the ability to manipulate fractions. If such differential change was obtained, simple maturation or testing effects would be ruled out, since these would presumably increase scores on each test, not just on one of them. In marketing contexts, one would expect a drive to increase sales of a particular washing machine detergent not to affect the sales of cosmetic soaps. However, an increase in the general level of affluence, or a general increase in the concern for cleanliness, would be expected to affect sales of both washing machine detergents and cosmetic soaps.

In our previous discussion of the Broadbent and Little (1960) quasi-experiment, we distorted their design somewhat in order to make the general point.

Consideration of what they actually did and found is useful because it reveals the fundamental weakness of the simple nonequivalent dependent variables design. The investigators found that the rate of work increased in the room where the noise had been experimentally reduced, and they attributed this to historical factors. They were able to do this because their design wisely included a nonequivalent control group work area where the noise had not been experimentally reduced. Thus, the investigators were able to demonstrate that the noisy and less noisy rooms did not differ in the rate of work but did differ in the number of momentary lapses. Without this control for the effects of history, Broadbent and Little would have had some difficulty in explaining why the rate of work increased and lapses decreased in the less noisy work areas. This was, after all, the very outcome that they did not want because it would not have supported the propositions about the *differential* effects of noise that were derived from laboratory experiments. The nonequivalent dependent variables design is entirely dependent on contrasting patterns of change and no-change, and it cannot handle the pattern of general change that Broadbent and Little obtained in their reduced-noise condition alone. Thus, nonequivalent dependent variables are probably better used as part of a larger design rather than a complete design in itself.

As we have presented the design thus far, it has only two variables and two waves of measurement. We would like now to set the nonequivalent dependent variables design into a broader "pattern-matching" context. The design is obviously strongest where differentiated patterns of change are predicted that allow many alternative interpretations to be ruled out. The probability of ruling out threats depends in part on the specificity of the predicted data pattern so that interpretability increases (1) with the number of dependent variables for which predictions are made—the two-variable/two-wave case is merely the simplest case of the more general design—and (2) with the specificity of numerical or sign predictions made.

The most important point to be noted is that the *prospective* consideration of plausible alternative interpretations will sometimes incline the researcher to predict a data pattern involving multiple variables against which the obtained data can be matched to assess how well the data corroborate the expected pattern and how well alternative interpretations are ruled out. (Since some effects would be expected by chance in the multivariable-multiwave case, it is advisable, where possible, to have two measures of each relationship.) In any event, nonequivalent dependent variables designs based on multiple variables and multiple measurement waves will often permit ruling out all plausible threats to internal validity. But if these threats are not made explicit before data collection begins, it is unlikely that all the variables will be measured that are required for matching obtained data with a pattern of relationships that logically rules out threats to valid causal inference.

The Removed-Treatment Design with Pretest and Posttest

It is sometimes not feasible to obtain even a nonequivalent control group. In such a situation one is forced to create conditions that closely approximate meet-

ing the conceptual requirements of a no-treatment control group. The design that we outline below does this in many instances.

$$O_1 \quad X \quad O_2 \qquad O_3 \quad \bar{X} \quad O_4$$

In essence, the design calls for a simple one-group pretest-posttest design (see from O_1 to O_2). But a third wave of data collection is added (see O_3), after which the treatment is removed from the treatment group ($\bar{X}$ symbolizes this), and a final measure is taken after the treatment has been removed (O_4). Thus, from O_1 to O_2 is the experimental sequence, as it were, while the sequence from O_3 to O_4 serves as a no-treatment control for the sequence from O_1 to O_2. Note that the same group of units is involved throughout the whole design.

In this design, we would expect an effective treatment to cause a difference between O_1 and O_2 that is opposite in direction to the difference between O_3 and O_4. However, since it is possible that the initial effects of the treatment might increase or even dissipate between O_2 and O_3, it is important to add that there has to be a noticeable discontinuity after $\bar{X}$ (as in Figure 3.7). If there is not, and if there is a smooth trend from O_2 to O_4, then any difference between O_3 and O_4 that was different from the experimental $O_1 - O_2$ difference might be due to the treatment having no long-term effect rather than to the treatment effect dissipating because it was removed.

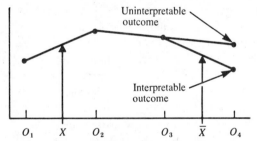

Figure 3.7. Generally interpretable outcome of the removed-treatment design.

Only four problems seem to arise with the interpretable outcome in Figure 3.7. First, it might be difficult to obtain the pattern of statistical effects necessary for statistical conclusion validity, since this would require both that $(O_1 - O_2) \neq (O_3 - O_4)$ and that $(O_2 - O_3) \neq (O_3 - O_4)$.

A second problem concerns construct validity of the cause. Since many treatments are ameliorative in nature, removing them might not only be hard to defend ethically but may also arouse frustration in respondents that should be correlated with indexes of aggression, satisfaction, and perhaps performance. Such considerations indicate that sometimes it will not be possible to implement the design,

especially if a deliberate choice has to be made by research personnel to remove an ameliorative treatment.

Third, there are many instances where respondents voluntarily decide to discontinue their exposure to a treatment for reasons that have no obvious relationship to the fact that social research is taking place. The design is most likely to be used, therefore, when subjects self-select themselves out of the treatment group. But very special care has to be taken when this happens. To illustrate the need for care, imagine someone who becomes a foreman (X), develops promanagerial attitudes between O_1 and O_2, dislikes his new contact with managers, and becomes less promanagerial by O_3. This person would be a likely candidate for resigning from his position or for being relieved of it ($\overline{X}$). Any continuation of his less promanagerial attitudes after changing from a foreman back to a factory worker would result in an $O_3 - O_4$ difference that differed from the $O_1 - O_2$ difference. Thus, the researcher has to decide whether the $O_3 - O_4$ difference reflects spontaneous maturation or the change of jobs. The maturation explanation would be more likely if the $O_3 - O_4$ difference were similar to the $O_2 - O_3$ difference (see the outcome marked "uninterpretable" in Figure 3.7) but would be less likely if the $O_3 - O_4$ difference were greater than the $O_2 - O_3$ difference (see the "interpretable" outcome in Figure 3.7). A rise in promanagerial attitudes between O_1 and O_2 and a decline in promanagerial attitudes between O_3 and O_4 that was greater than the $O_2 - O_3$ decline would strongly suggest that entering a new role causes one to adopt the attitudes appropriate to that role.

Fourth, it is advantageous with this design that the observations be made at equal time intervals. This permits a control for any spontaneous linear changes that take place over a given time period. A simple comparison of the differences between $O_2 - O_3$ and $O_3 - O_4$ would be meaningless if the $O_3 - O_4$ time interval were longer than the $O_2 - O_3$ interval. This is because a constant rate of decay would reveal larger $O_3 - O_4$ differences than $O_2 - O_3$ differences. As we shall later see with time-series designs, it is often possible to estimate rates of change per time interval so that the equal spacing of observations loses many of its advantages. But a sensitive estimate of the spontaneous rate of change is not possible with the design under consideration since two of the time differences might be affected either by the treatment or its removal. This increases the reliance on equal intervals, though they control only for simple linear patterns of spontaneous change.

Lieberman (1956) used a simpler version of the removed-treatment design in his examination of the attitude change that follows role change. He obtained samples of foremen who lost their new positions and reverted to being workers again. Lieberman had three waves of measurement: before becoming a foreman, after becoming a foreman, and after reverting back to worker status. The part of his design under discussion differed, therefore, from the one we have outlined since only one measurement was made between the treatment and the removal of the treatment. Hence, we are unable to attribute any differences between his $O_1 - O_2$ and his $O_2 - O_3$ measures as due to a shift in the attitude of former foremen who became workers again or to the fact that foremen whose attitudes were becoming less managerial were selected for demotion. In addition, the statistical analysis of the three-wave design could involve contrasting the $O_1 - O_2$ difference with the

$O_2 - O_3$ difference, a procedure that uses the O_2 observations twice. If, through sampling error, the O_2 mean were raised, this would necessarily be reflected in an $O_1 - O_2$ difference of a different algebraic sign (and hence implied causal direction) from the $O_2 - O_3$ difference. Such a difference would occur even if nothing had happened as a result of the treatment! Having two observations between the treatment and removal of the treatment rules out these possibilities in the design we have advocated.

The Repeated-Treatment Design

When the investigator has access to only a single research population it will sometimes be possible to introduce the treatment, fade it out, and then reintroduce it at a later date. Obviously, this design is most viable in contexts where the initial effects of the treatment are transient or do not prevent the treatment from having an even stronger effect when it is reintroduced. The design is diagrammed below.

$$O_1 \quad X \quad O_2 \quad \bar{X} \quad O_3 \quad X \quad O_4$$

The most interpretable outcome of this design is when O_1 differs from O_2, O_3 differs from O_4, and the $O_3 - O_4$ difference is in the same direction as the $O_1 - O_2$ difference. The design is of the general type associated with Skinnerians, and the basic logic behind it was used in the original Hawthorne studies (Roethlisberger and Dickson, 1939). It may be remembered that in some of those studies women factory workers were separated from their larger work groups and were given different kinds of rest periods at different times so that the experimenters could investigate the effects of rest on productivity. In some cases, the same rest period was introduced at two different times; if we were to regard only these repeated rest periods, we would have the basic design under discussion here.

One threat to internal validity comes from the possibility of cyclical maturation—that is, productivity is being affected by regularly occurring systematic factors. For example, if O_2 and O_4 were recorded on Tuesday morning and O_1 and O_4 on Friday afternoon, any differences in productivity might be related to differences in daily performance rather than to a treatment. It would be preferable, therefore, if such cyclical factors could be ruled out. A second threat to internal validity can arise if there is resentment when the treatment is removed between O_2 and O_3. If this were to happen, O_3 would be decreased and an $O_3 - O_4$ difference might be erroneously attributed to a replication of the treatment's effect when it was in fact due to removing a source of frustration by reinstating the treatment.

When the basic design is used as it was in the Hawthorne studies, it is particularly vulnerable on grounds of external and statistical conclusion validity. For example, many of the performance graphs in Roethlisberger and Dickson (1939) are of individual women workers, and in the Relay Assembly Row Experiment there was a grand total of only six women! Moreover, there appears to be considerable variability in how the women reacted to treatments (particularly the Mica Splitting Room Experiment). We cannot be sure to what extent results would be statistically significant if the analyses were based on summing across all the women. (We cannot help but note in passing how closely the Hawthorne studies

parallel the design of Skinnerian experiments. There is the same preference for few subjects and repeated reintroduction of the treatment, and there is the same disdain for statistical tests.) Of course, the repeated treatment design does not *require* that there be a small population or an absence of statistical tests. These are merely correlates of the use of this design in the past. We would strongly urge the use of larger samples and statistical tests.

Construct validity is a major threat because respondents may well notice the introduction, removal, and reintroduction of the treatment with the consequence that they can guess and respond to a hypothesis about the purpose of the study. It is worth noting that this can occur even when there is none of the obtrusive observation or special group status that was involved in the original Hawthorne experiments. When respondents are reacting to their special status in an experiment or to a hypothesis they might have guessed, we cannot be sure how the treatment should be labeled. This design is better, therefore, when there are unobtrusive treatments and a long delay between the treatment and its reintroduction. It is also desirable that there be no confounding of cycles and reintroductions of the treatment. Hence, the design is best of all when the reintroductions are frequent and randomly distributed across time blocks. (This last point will be discussed later when we deal with randomized experiments, particularly the Equivalent Time Samples Design.)

The Reversed-Treatment Nonequivalent Control Group Design with Pretest and Posttest

This design can be diagrammed

$$
\begin{array}{ccc}
O_1 & X+ & O_2 \\
\hline
O_1 & X- & O_2
\end{array}
$$

where $X+$ represents a treatment that is expected to influence an effect in one direction and $X-$ represents the conceptually opposite treatment that would be expected to reverse the pattern of findings in the $X+$ group.

Morse and Reimer (1956) probably used this design to investigate how decision-making procedures that were either "democratic" (i.e., participative) or "hierarchically controlled" affected productivity and job satisfaction. The hypothesis was that the "democratic" procedure would increase productivity and satisfaction but the hierarchically controlled procedure would decrease them. To test this, Morse and Reimer developed a design that involved the use of four divisions in an organization, two of which were assigned to each experimental condition. While it is not clear from the report whether the assignment of treatments to the four divisions was done on a random basis, the small number of experimental units makes it difficult to believe that the treatment and control groups would have been comparable at the pretest even if random assignment had taken place. Indeed, at one point in their report Morse and Reimer commented that the two experimental groups tended to differ in pretest satisfaction, and tables in the report indicate a possible group pretest difference in respondents' perception of the locus of decision making. Thus, for our present illustrative purposes, we shall consider

the Morse and Reimer study as a quasi-experiment, the results of which indicated that satisfaction increased between pretest and posttest in the "democratic" decision-making group and decreased in the "hierarchically controlled" group. It is precisely such a pattern of change in opposite directions that is indicative of a treatment effect. But, as always, alternative interpretations have to be considered.

Respondents in the Morse and Reimer study probably did not select themselves into work divisions, and the work divisions probably did not select themselves into being in one experimental group or the other. If these suppositions are correct, selection-maturation would probably not be a major threat to the internal validity of the interpretation of findings. We would have no reason to suspect that the two groups were spontaneously maturing in different directions. What makes a selection-maturation interaction less likely in this design than in many others is that the only interaction pattern that can alternatively explain the findings is the rare one where maturation operates *in different directions* in each group rather than the more typical maturational pattern where change occurs *at different rates in the same direction* in each group. The reversed-treatment control group design is often stronger with respect to internal validity than its simpler alternatives because selection-maturation cannot usually explain changes in opposite directions.

The reversed-treatment design with nonequivalent groups is stronger than the no-treatment control group design with respect to construct validity. This is because the theoretical causal variable has to be rigorously specified if a test is made that depends on one version of the cause affecting one group one way and another group the other way. Moreover, many of the irrelevancies associated with one treatment will be different from those associated with the reversed treatment. To understand these points better, what would have happened if Morse and Reimer's design had involved only a "democratic" decision-making group and a no-treatment control group. A steeper pretest-posttest satisfaction slope in the "democratic" group could have been attributed to the new locus of decision making or to a Hawthorne effect. But the plausibility of a Hawthorne effect is lessened when we note the pretest-posttest decrease in satisfaction in the "hierarchically controlled" group. This is because awareness of being in a research study is typically considered to elicit socially desirable responses (higher productivity or greater satisfaction, rather than less desirable responses such as decreased satisfaction). It is the high construct validity of the cause which makes the reversed-treatment design potentially more appropriate for theory-testing research than the no-treatment control group design.

The last statement should not be taken to mean that the reversed-treatment design is flawless with regard to specifying the causal construct. Morse and Reimer found that productivity was greater at the posttest than the pretest in both the "democratic" and "hierarchical" decision-making groups. If we accept for the moment that these data indicate an increase in productivity (which is not clear in the absence of a no-treatment control group), the possibility arises that a Hawthorne effect may have caused the productivity change. This is because the productivity measure, unlike satisfaction, did not show the expected changes in opposite directions. The moral of this is that the potentially high construct validity

of the reversed-treatment design depends on the research revealing changes in opposite directions. When change is in the same direction in both groups, we are left in the same position as with the relatively uninterpretable one-group pretest-posttest design, i.e., there is change, but we do not know whether the same type of change would have occurred even in the absence of a planned treatment. To be maximally interpretable, the reversed-treatment design needs (1) a placebo control group which receives a treatment that is not expected to influence productivity or satisfaction except through a Hawthorne effect and (2) a no-treatment control group which would provide a no-cause baseline.

We should also not forget that, in many organizational contexts, ethical and practical drawbacks prevent the implementation of some kinds of reversed treatments. It is not, after all, useful or humane to introduce treatments that will harm people or productivity. Indeed, the understandable preference for ameliorative and prosocial treatments makes reversing such treatments problematic. Given this, it will often not be possible to reverse treatments deliberately, and we should instead expect to use the design in question mostly when reversals are unplanned. Since reversed treatments will often be unpopular, it may be difficult to unconfound effects attributable to the planned aspects of the reversal from effects attributable to any unplanned affective consequences that follow from receiving an unpopular treatment.

A problem of statistical conclusion validity is associated with the reversed-treatment design. Imagine that a simple analysis of variance resulted in a statistically significant interaction of experimental groups and time of testing, with the posttest differences being greater than the pretest ones. We would not know from this whether the effect was the result of (a) sampling error, (b) only one of the treatments causing its expected effect or (c) both treatments causing effects in opposite directions. Significant pretest-posttest differences *within each group* would decrease the chances of (a) above but would not discriminate between (b) and (c) in many cases. This is because at times it would be reasonable to assume that at least one of the pretest-posttest differences was due to group-specific maturation and not to the treatment or its reversal. Interpreting the direction of change would be even more problematic if only one of the two differences were significant. While it would seem at first glance that the significant difference represents directional change, this need not be so, for the single difference might be due to maturation. To remove ambiguity about whether there is treatment-correlated change in one but not the other treatment group we need a no-treatment control group. Indeed, researchers who are particularly interested in the direction of change should think twice before using a reversed-treatment design in the absence of a no-treatment control group. However, with a mixed design of a treatment/reversed-treatment, and no-treatment group, researchers would be in a very strong position. It would be even stronger if they could add a fourth group of placebo controls.

Cohort Designs in Formal and Informal Institutions with Cyclical Turnover

Many formal institutions are characterized by regular turnover as one group of persons graduates to another level of the institution. Schools provide an obvious

example of this as children move from grade to grade. So, too, do many businesses as one group of trainees follows another. Such systematic turnover patterns are not confined to institutional settings in the normal use of that expression. For instance, children follow each other within families, sharing much the same home environment and differing genetically from each other only in random fashion. We shall use the term "cohort" to denote groups of respondents who follow each other through formal institutions or informal institutions like the family. Such cohorts are useful for experimental purposes because (1) some cohorts receive a particular treatment while preceding or following cohorts that do not, (2) it is often reasonable to assume that a cohort differs in only minor ways from its contiguous cohorts, and (3) it is often possible to use archival records for comparing cohorts who have received a treatment with cohorts who were in the same institutions before the treatment began or after it was discontinued.

The crucial feature that makes cohort designs particularly useful for drawing causal inferences is that a "quasi-comparability" can often be assumed between the cohorts that do and do not receive a treatment—between, say, the fourth grade class one year and the fourth grade class the next year. How reasonable it is to assume quasi-comparability in a particular research setting depends on how similar the cohort groups are on the average in background characteristics, including organizational history. The degree of achieved comparability will never be as high with cohorts as with random assignment. Indeed, the virtue of cohort designs is only relative, based on the fact that cohort groups are likely to be more similar to each other than are treatment groups which do not share the same home or work environment. Since cohort designs do not automatically rule out selection, they gain additional strength if the data analysis shows that cohort groups with and without the treatment do not systematically differ on reliably measured third variables that are believed to be possible mediators of a treatment effect. While the strong measurement of such variables obviously cannot rule out selection threats associated with unmeasured variables, it can at least rule out some particular types of selection.

Our discussion of cohort designs will be divided into two sections. The first deals with designs that recognize differences in the degree to which various respondents experience a treatment. The second deals with designs that can be used if the treatment is more homogeneous and respondents have little opportunity to regulate how much of the treatment they receive. The latter would be the case, for example, when evaluating the effects of a curriculum in schools or training centers. We shall not deal with the growing use of cohort designs to try to unconfound the effects of age (i.e., growing older), birth cohort (i.e., being born within a given time span), and period of history (i.e., the events occurring between any two time intervals). Using the data from sample surveys of cohorts to unconfound these effects is a task that demographers and developmentalists in particular have set themselves, and the inferential pitfalls that make their task difficult are outlined in Glenn (1977).

The Cohort Design in Which Treatment Partitioning Is Possible

Minton (1975) wanted to examine how the first season of "Sesame Street" would affect the Metropolitan Readiness Test scores of a socially heterogeneous

sample of kindergarten children. She located a kindergarten where the test was used at the end of the child's first year. However, she had no data from a control group of children who did not watch the show during the season. Fortunately, though, she had access to the Metropolitan scores of the children's older siblings from earlier years when they had been the same age as the "Sesame Street" viewers but the show had not been on the air. She was able, therefore, to compare the postkindergarten knowledge level of children who were "Sesame Street" viewers with the knowledge level of their siblings when they terminated kindergarten in the years before "Sesame Street." The essential design can be diagrammed below, with the wavy line indicating a restricted degree of selection nonequivalence. The purpose of the design is to test whether the two observed groups differ.

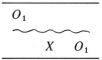

The design as it stands is not strong. First of all, there might be a selection problem since the older siblings are more likely to be first-borns and any differences between O_1 and O_2 might be due to comparing groups with different percentages of first-borns. It would be desirable, therefore, if effects of ordinal birth condition could be either assessed, reduced, or eliminated. One way of reducing the threat would be by analyzing the data separately for second-born older children and their third-born siblings, for third-born children and their fourth-born siblings, and so forth on the assumption that ordinal position makes more of a difference with first- and second-borns or penultimate and last-borns than with children in the middle (Zajonc and Markus, 1975).

The design is also weak with respect to history, for the older and younger siblings in the design could have experienced events other than "Sesame Street" which affected knowledge levels in one cohort more than the other. An indirect way of partially examining this threat would be to break down the cohorts into those whose kindergarten experience was separated by one, two, three, or more years to see if the greater learning of the younger group held over these particular sets of unique historical events. This procedure would be less than optimal, of course, because there would be no control for the historical events other than "Sesame Street" that took place in the same year the show was introduced.

Another control for history would have been to split the children into viewers and nonviewers or, if this were not possible, into heavy and light viewers. If "Sesame Street" were effective, we would then expect a statistical interaction— with larger knowledge differences between the heavy and light viewers than between their respective siblings. The reason for this is that, in the absence of a treatment effect, there would be no reason to assume that the difference in knowledge between heavy and light viewers of "Sesame Street" should vary in any way from the difference between their siblings who would presumably have become heavy and light viewers respectively if "Sesame Street" had been available to them. In particular, we would expect the heavy and light viewers to experience the same general history. Partitioning respondents into treatment groups based on the

extent of their experience with the treatment greatly strengthens the internal validity of this particular cohorts design. It is difficult to come up with plausible alternative interpretations when the data look like Figure 3.8.

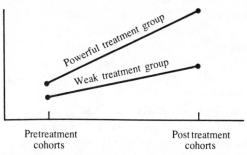

Pretreatment
cohorts

Post treatment
cohorts

Figure 3.8. Interpretable outcome of a posttest-only cohort design with two treatment levels.

Partitioning has a further advantage for internal validity. If the conditions of testing differ between the earlier and later cohorts, then testing alone might cause higher scores in the later experimental group than the earlier control one. Partitioning respondents by the length of exposure to the treatment rules out a simple testing threat, for there is no reason why testing should have a greater effect in the longer exposure treatment group when compared to the shorter exposure group. For a number of reasons, then, we advocate partitioning respondents and implementing the modified design below, where X_1 and X_2 indicate quantitative differences in the extent of treatment implementation.

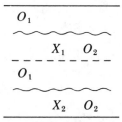

Though Minton had none of the controls for history and testing listed above—since she did not partition by length of viewing—her design was slightly more complicated than we have portrayed it, and the complications increase interpretability. She collected data on all six subtests of the Metropolitan Readiness Test, and found that the mean of the "Sesame Street" cohorts differed from their siblings' mean on only a single subtest, knowledge of letters. Since content analyses of the first year's programming of "Sesame Street" (Ball and Bogatz, 1970) have shown that more time was spent teaching letters than anything else, it might be assumed that a test of letter skills would be more sensitive to program effects than other tests. In a sense, then, the design that Minton used involved *both* cohort

groups *and* nonequivalent dependent variables. In her case, however, the different status of each dependent variable was ascertained after the show's first season was over and not before. It is clearly more problematic to infer the different conceptual status of dependent variables after the fact than before it!

Instead of using siblings as cohorts, Ball and Bogatz (1970) in their evaluation of "Sesame Street" used older children from the local neighborhood. Their experimental design involved taking a sample of children and testing them before "Sesame Street" went on the air and six months later. Some of the children's ages ranged between 47 and 52 months at the pretest and between 53 and 58 months at the posttest. These were called the posttest cohort. Other children's ages ranged from 53-58 months at the pretest and 59-65 months at the posttest. These were called the pretest cohort. By considering just the posttest scores of the posttest cohort (then aged 53-58 months) and just the pretest scores of the pretest cohort (then also aged 53-58 months) Ball and Bogatz created a design where it was hoped that an effect of "Sesame Street" would be inferred if the posttest cohort of 53-58 months was more knowledgeable than the pretest cohort of 53-58 months.

When this design is used, maturation cannot easily explain any differences between the means of the pretest and the posttest cohorts. This is because they are of equivalent age and so are presumably at comparable maturational stages. A selection effect is also not likely, provided that the analysis included data from *all* the available children in each age cohort. As a check on the comparability of pretest and posttest cohorts, background characteristics can be measured. Indeed, Ball and Bogatz measured a variety of demographic background characteristics and showed that the cohorts did not differ from each other on any of the variables. As we have outlined it thus far, the design differs from Minton's only in using neighborhood children of different birthdates as cohorts instead of siblings of different birthdates. Consequently, we might anticipate that the design is vulnerable to a history interpretation. It might be, for example, that something which affects learning occurred at about the same time that "Sesame Street" was introduced or older pretest cohorts may have experienced unique events before the younger cohorts were born that affected the older cohorts' knowledge. Or the older children may have been at particularly sensitive maturational stages when they learned information also available to the younger cohorts but less meaningful for them. Also, the design as portrayed here and as implemented by Ball and Bogatz has a unique testing problem, since the scores of the pretest cohort came from a first pretest measurement wave while the scores of the posttest cohort were from a second wave of measurement (i.e., from the posttest after having been pretested six months earlier). Thus, it would not be clear whether any obtained differences between cohorts were due to the treatment or to differences in the frequency of measurement.

The problems of history and testing can be eliminated by following Ball and Bogatz's extension to their basic design. They used measures of the frequency of viewing "Sesame Street" to partition each cohort into four separate groups that differed in the level of reported viewing. The results are displayed in Figure 3.9, and an analysis of variance showed that the differences in knowledge between the

various viewing groups were greater among the posttest cohort than the pretest one. Since the cohorts were of the same mean age, of comparable social background within the different viewing groups, and experienced the same history and testing sequences (all posttest cohorts were pretested), an interaction outcome like the one that Ball and Bogatz obtained can account for all the threats to internal validity that we have discussed thus far.

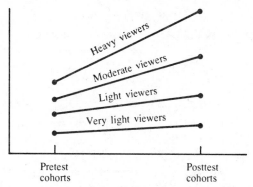

Figure 3.9. Interpretable outcome of a selection cohorts design with pretest and posttest cohorts.

The selection cohorts designs we have outlined are very useful (1) when age or experience can alternatively account for results in a pretest-posttest design or (2) when no pretest measures of experimentals are available. The data from such designs are especially interpretable in causal terms if there are different levels of a treatment and the data analysis reveals that these statistically interact with the cohort groups.

The Cohort Design in Which No Treatment Partitioning Is Possible

We have seen previously how history, selection, and some forms of testing are especially likely to be threats to internal validity in the simplest cohort designs. In much research these threats can be dealt with by separating out individuals and giving some a treatment while withholding it from others. But such separation is rarely possible in research with intact organizations. Here, a treatment has to be made available to all, and hard-headed causal inferences have to depend on making use of the fact that all the members of some organization received a treatment one year while none of their cohorts received it in previous years. The problem then becomes: How does one explicate and control for all the threats that operate when comparing cohorts?

We have previously noted Saretsky's (1972) claim that the no-treatment control group children in the Performance Contracting Experiment performed better than would have been expected on the basis of previous years. What Saretsky was

trying to demonstrate was that something associated with the child or teacher knowing that he or she was in a control group enhanced learning. It is not clear how Saretsky tested this causal hypothesis. Let us assume for pedagogic purposes that he compared the average grade equivalent gain in control group classes with the average gain from classes of the same grade taught in previous years when there was no awareness of being in a study. Thus, the design would be of the form below where O_1 and O_2 represent scores for the earlier cohort and O_3 and O_4 represent scores for the other cohort at a later date. Obviously, this design—which we might call "the institutional cycles design"—can be extended back over time to include multiple "control" cohorts rather than the single one pictured here. Indeed, it seems that Saretsky reported data for two preexperimental years.

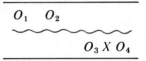

$$O_1 \quad O_2$$
$$O_3 \ X \ O_4$$

How would one control for *selection* deflating the mean difference for the earlier control cohort or inflating the difference for the later experimental cohort? One way of approximating a test would be to examine the background characteristics of students in each cohort to see if they are comparable on the available measures. If they are, and if the measures are plausibly related to the outcome variables, then a selection threat is all the less likely. Another way would be to draw all of the siblings out of the total sample and restrict the data analyses to them. Another would be to test whether the teachers were the same in each cohort, restricting the analyses to teachers who were equally represented in each cohort.

How could one attempt to rule out *testing*? The particular testing threat involved with the design under discussion is that at least one of the four tests was atypically administered or scored. Sometimes, there are data available about this, but often the assumption is made that school testing is a routine affair with which students and teachers are familiar so that testing should not differ by years. This argument is, of course, based on plausibility alone; and it would be useful if additional data on the issue could be made available.

History is the most salient and troublesome threat in the institutional cycle design when evaluating the effects of an innovation, for history might either have decreased the performance of the earlier control cohorts or increased the performance of the later treatment cohorts. Here, it can help to have a *series* of control cohort years, for if the pretreatment years are comparable to each other and only the posttreatment year differs from any other, then it is not plausible to claim that performance in the pretreatment cohorts was atypically low. The search for an alternative interpretation based on history can thus be limited to events that occurred in the treatment year and not earlier. Sometimes, no particular history threats will come to mind. But, in general, we would be in a stronger position to deal with history during the treatment year if a nonequivalent, no-treatment control group could be found and measured during the critical year. Or, failing this, the design could be greatly strengthened if nonequivalent dependent variables were specified, some of which should be affected by history while others should not be.

The plausibility of a history threat can be examined if the research question is slightly different and if, instead of wanting to know the effects of a new practice (e.g., participating in a performance contracting experiment as control respondents), one wants to know the effects of a long-established practice (e.g., what is the effect of asking second graders to do one-half hour of homework each school night). If one had access to past school records, or if one had a two-year period in which to do the research, then a design like the one sketched below might be possible. The first cohort group consists of children measured at the end of the second grade; the second consists of children from the next year's cohort when they reached the second grade and were measured at the beginning and end of that school year; and the third group consists of children who enter second grade the year after the second cohort group. The spacing of the observations is meant to represent the fact that O_1 and O_2 are not simultaneously observed, nor are O_3 and O_4. Interpretation is easier, of course, if measurement is simultaneous. This particular design is discussed in greater detail by Campbell and Stanley (1963), who call it the "Recurrent Institutional Cycle Design."

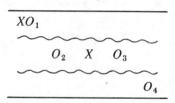

An approximate control for history is provided if, in addition to O_3 being greater than O_2, O_1 surpasses O_2, and O_3 surpasses O_4. These last comparisons suggest that a treatment has been effective at two different times so that any historical force would have had to operate twice if it is to explain both $O_1 > O_2$ and $O_3 > O_4$. Selection is also ruled out in this version of a cohort design since, quite apart from the similarity (but nonequivalence) of cohorts, the same persons are involved in the $O_2 - O_3$ comparisons. The remaining problem that affects cohort designs—testing—is not ruled out since all the comparisons involve contrasting a first testing (O_2 or O_4) with a second testing (O_1 and O_3). This is why Campbell and Stanley recommended extending the design further by splitting the middle group that is both pretested and posttested into random halves, one of which receives a pretest, treatment, and posttest sequence while the other receives a treatment and posttest but no pretest. Any differences between these two groups at the posttest would presumably be due to repeated measurement; the failure to obtain differences or even strong but unreliable trends suggesting differences would indicate that repeated measurement is not a problem.

Though the three-group design that we have outlined is practical for use in institutional settings where everyone has to receive a treatment, it has one major drawback over and above testing (which in some concrete situations will seem an implausible threat). The drawback is that interpretability depends on a complex pattern of outcomes in which three contrasts are all statistically reliable in similar ways. Since two of these contrasts involve O_2, a chance elevation of O_2 would have disastrous implications. This implies that the design should only be used with reliable measures and large samples.

A Posttest-Only Design with Predicted Higher-Order Interactions

In some circumstances no pretest information is available and it is desirable to test a causal relationship. Unfortunately, there are few quasi-experimental designs which permit this, and pretests are an absolute necessity for most designs unless some form of cohort or interaction strategy is used. (It is a different matter with randomized experiments. Pretests can be dispensed with since randomization ensures the probabilistic equivalence of the different treatment groups at the pretest. However, it is advisable to collect pretest data nonetheless, for without it difficulties may arise in designing a "fallback" quasi-experiment that is interpretable. The need for such a fallback is acute when the comparability of treatment groups is not maintained over the course of an experiment, as would be the case if there were higher attrition from the experiment in some treatments than in others.)

Let us illustrate how, in the absence of pretest information, interaction predictions can be used with intact groups for providing relatively strong inferences about cause. Nisbett and Kanouse (1969) were interested in testing the idea that overweight persons lack the ability to discriminate the internal body cues that indicate hunger. Hence, the authors hypothesized that among overweight persons there would be no relationship between the time of last eating and the amount of grocery purchases, but that there would be such a relationship among persons of normal weight who do pay attention to internal cues which indicate how hungry they are. To test this, Nisbett and Kanouse asked customers who entered a supermarket when they had last eaten, and they also observed the customers' weights and the size of their grocery bills. The data analysis revealed that body weight (coded as overweight or normal) and the reported number of hours since last eating (a variable with six levels) statistically interacted to determine the size of the grocery bill. As predicted, there was positive correlation between purchases and time since last eating among normals but, unlike the prediction, there was a *negative* correlation of these variables among the overweight.

A major difficulty with this design is selection. Assume for the moment that persons of normal weight who wait the longest time between meals are more likely to have jobs. (After all, it is more difficult for social and practical reasons to eat at work than at home.) If this were the case, normal persons who had gone longer without eating might well be more affluent and have more money to spend on food. This would explain the pattern of discrimination that Nisbett and Kanouse predicted for normals. But it would not explain the pattern among the overweight. However, if we further assume that the overweight persons who go longer without eating may do so because they are less affluent, then they should have less to spend on groceries than their overweight counterparts who have recently eaten. This would explain the negative relationship among the overweight. Alternatively, the overweight persons who have not eaten for a comparatively long time might be abstaining in order to diet, and this might also be related to lower grocery purchases. The point is that various selection mechanisms *could* explain the interaction of body weight and time since last eating, though a different selection mechanism has to be invoked for each weight group.

A second potential problem with this design relates to the specificity of the predicted outcomes and the difficulty of obtaining such specific patterns of data.

Nisbett and Kanouse predicted that there would be no relationship between purchases and time since last eating among the overweight who are relatively insensitive to internal hunger cues. But they unexpectedly obtained a negative relationship among the overweight. The authors needed, therefore, to explain this unexpected pattern. Since they had creatively collected estimates of intended purchases from shoppers as they entered the supermarket, they were able to show that the overweight persons who had gone longer since last eating both intended to buy less and actually did buy less. This was interpreted as demonstrating that the purchasing behavior of overweight persons was probably determined by their expectations about purchasing rather than by their internal hunger cues. The corollary of this is that normal persons' behavior should be determined more by their internal hunger cues than by their expected purchasing. However, the evidence for this was ambiguous. While the difference between what normals expected to buy and what they actually bought increased over five levels of time-since-last-food, it deviated markedly from this pattern among normals who had not eaten for more than five and one-fourth hours. Persons in this last group actually bought *less* than they intended, even though the theory predicted that they should have been more sensitive to their internal hunger cues than others and that they should have been the most prone of all to buy on impulse, thereby buying more than they intended.

The moral is clear and is illustrated in our earlier discussion of case studies with multiple "outcome" variables and predictions about which areas should be affected in which ways if a certain variable were the "cause." The moral is that causal interpretation tends to be facilitated as the predicted interaction between nonequivalent groups grows more complex. But the chance of obtaining so many data points in the predicted order decreases with the number of data points predicted. There are many reasons for this, including chance, selection differences in intact groups which influence data patterns but are irrelevant to theory, and theories that are partially or totally incorrect. Replication is crucial when making higher-order interaction predictions. This helps control for chance fluctuations.

The importance of the relative complexity of the interaction predictions can be further illustrated from an archival quasi-experiment by Seaver (1973) who was interested in examining the effects of a teacher's performance expectancies on students' academic achievement. To do this, Seaver located from school records a group of children whose older siblings had obtained high or low achievement scores and grades in school. He then divided the two groups of younger children into those who had had the same teacher as their sibling and those who had had a different teacher. This resulted in a 2 × 2 design (same or different teacher crossed with high- or low-performing sibling). Seaver predicted that children with high-performing siblings would out-perform children with low-performing siblings by a greater amount if they had had the same teachers as their siblings than if they had had a different teacher.

Seaver obtained the predicted interaction on several subsets of the Stanford Achievement Test, and the means indicated support for the teacher expectancy hypothesis. Moreover, it is not easy to invoke a selection alternative interpretation. The one that springs most readily to mind is that children who had low-performing siblings might be assigned to teachers with a reputation for "handling difficult chil-

dren" who also happen to teach very little. Alternatively, children with high-performing siblings might be assigned to teachers with a reputation for stimulating potential "stars." But this simple selection explanation cannot be correct since children who had had different teachers were also labeled as low or high performers and so should have also been sent to a particular kind of teacher. The only selection interpretation which can be invoked is rather complicated and will not strike some readers as very plausible. It is that the children who had had different teachers were those who would have gone to teachers with reputations for dealing with high or low performers if this had been possible, but that they did not go because it was not possible. The best ways to examine this last threat in detail would be to have definite information that the assignment of teachers to children was haphazard or to have teachers equally represented in all cells of the design.

Two questions about the construct validity of the treatment in the Seaver study can be raised. First, it is assumed that it was the teacher's expectancy about the child's performance that influenced that performance. It is also possible, though probably less plausible, that it was the child's expectancy about the teacher's skill or friendliness toward the child and his or her family that influenced the child's learning. It would not be easy to dissociate these two interpretations unless one had either an experimenter-controlled manipulation of the child's and the teacher's expectancy or one had questionnaire or interview data which showed that children who manifested an expectancy effect did not expect teachers to teach them differently because they had taught their siblings. Second, there is no evidence from the study indicating why expectancy influenced performance. Was the apparent effect due to teachers calling less on children with poor-performing siblings, or to teachers reinforcing them differently, or to teachers publicly attributing less ability or motivation to them, or some other reason? Of course, the Seaver study was designed to answer questions about whether an expectancy effect could be demonstrated at all in a nonreactive archival quasi-experiment, and an examination of process variables was not intended. This was probably just as well, for archival experiments tend to be weak on process since they are typically set up to record performance outcomes and not the processes mediating performance.

The investigator who has only posttest data is indeed fortunate if he or she can translate the research hypothesis into an interaction in which one group of respondents is superior to some other group in one experimental condition and is inferior in another. Nisbett and Kanouse succeeded in doing this, as did Seaver. The major threat to the single-interaction design is that of selection, and the basic design's interpretability depends in large measure on how well selection artifacts can be explicitly ruled out or rendered less plausible. One technique for reducing the plausibility of selection is to make the interaction hypothesis involve a second- or third-order interaction. However, it is ironic that, on the one hand, interpretability increases with the *specificity* of predictions about particular statistics or particular interaction patterns; on the other hand, the *probability of obtaining* specific and expected data outcomes decreases with the very specificity of the predictions! Nonetheless the interaction prediction designs we have just outlined are very useful if carefully interpreted.

The Regression-Discontinuity Design

When people or groups are given awards or those in special need are given extra help, one would like to discover the consequences of such provisions. A regression-discontinuity design is often appropriate for these situations. The logic behind the design is simple. Imagine that respondents can be classified according to scores on a quantified continuum with a specified cutting point. Persons who score above the point gain, say, an award, while those who score below it do not. If the award had any influence on a particular outcome variable, a discontinuity should appear at the cutting point when separate regression lines are computed for the two groups. This is because the persons above the cutting point should have had their outcome scores increased by the award while those below the point should not have.

To illustrate this, imagine the situation in which one has a continuous interval scale measure of pretest organizational performance, perhaps output level or grades. One then gives a bonus to those persons who score above a particular output or school grade level—to be followed by an evaluation of the award's effects on subsequent performance. One could draw a graph with pretest output level along the horizontal and posttest output level along the vertical. A scat-

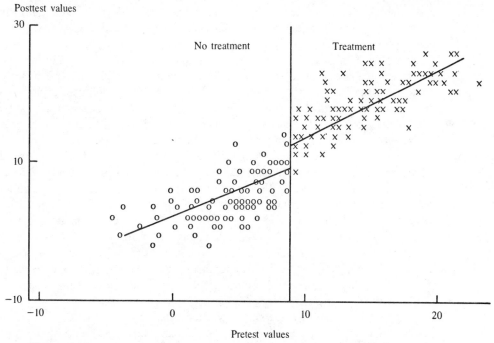

Figure 3.10. Hypothetical outcome of a pretest-posttest regression-discontinuity quasi-experiment.

terplot could then be computed which relates each person's posttest score to his or her pretest score. If the award were effective, there should be a discontinuity when fitting separate regression lines to the individuals above and below the pretest performance cutting point. Such a hypothetical case is portrayed in Figure 3.10.

Portraying the data from the regression-discontinuity design in this fashion highlights the similarity to the way some treatment effects would appear in a randomized experiment when posttest scores are plotted as a function of pretest scores. In the case of the randomized experiment, a main effect of the treatment would make the regression line of the treated group higher than that of the control group. If there were no interaction of treatment and pretest, this would hold for all values of the pretest. In the regression-discontinuity case where awards are dispensed, the treatment is successful, and only a main effect is obtained, a treatment effect would look the same except that all the control cases above the cutting point, and all the experimental cases below it, would be missing.

The similarity in regression plots indicating a simple main effect of the treatment is not the principal resemblance between the regression-discontinuity design and the randomized experiment. In the nonequivalent group designs discussed in this chapter the selection and selection-maturation processes were at best imperfectly known. Sometimes, descriptive data from populations similar to but not identical to those being examined can help ascertain gross selection differences and, where such data are longitudinal, can help ascertain selection-maturation. But such descriptive data rarely allow exact estimates of the selection confound for particular samples. In other cases, pretest data are available from units that differ in age or experience and who themselves will provide the posttest data of interest. Estimates of selection-maturation can then be generated for different groups on the assumption that within-group changes for a specific time period before the treatment would be identical to changes during the (equivalent length) pretest-posttest time period. In many other cases, only imperfect proxies are available for describing selection differences such as sex, race, place of birth, and the like.

In all the above cases, knowledge of the selection and related selection-maturation processes is at best imperfect and dependent on accepting unverified assumptions. With regression-discontinuity, as with random assignment, the selection process is known perfectly in theory. In the regression-discontinuity case, selection is based on the fallible scores used for assigning persons to the treatment or control groups. In the randomized experiment, assignment is based on a lottery and the average person in one treatment group is similar to the average person in another. As with the randomized experiment, it is knowledge of the selection process that makes the regression-discontinuity design so potentially amenable to causal interpretation.

It may occur to some readers that effects can be obtained other than a discontinuity in the level of the regressions at the cutting point—which corresponds to a simple main effect of the treatment. For example, the slope of the regression lines might differ on each side of the cutting point. At first glance, this difference in slope would imply an interaction of the pretest and treatment such that the persons on the treatment side of the point do better or worse depending on where their scores fall above the cutting point. For instance, suppose the National Science Foundation awarded individual fellowships to graduate students solely on the basis

of Graduate Record Examination scores—which is not the case. An evaluation of the awards' effectiveness using a regression-discontinuity design might seem to imply, when regression slopes differ and the steeper one is on the awards side of the cutting point, that fellowships have more of an impact on students whose GRE scores are among the highest than on students whose scores just qualified them for fellowships. However, the interpretation of differences in slope is extremely diffi-cult, if not impossible, in the absence of intercept differences.

The following discussion of the regression-discontinuity design is divided into two sections. The first deals with the use of pretest scores to classify units and assign them to treatments, and the second with the use of quantitative scores other than the pretest. This distinction has no theoretical importance, and is made only to remind readers that the regression-discontinuity design can be used when no pretest measures are available.

Regression-Discontinuity with Similar-Appearing Pretest Measures

Seaver and Quarton (1976) used the regression-discontinuity design to exam-ine how college students' grades in one quarter were affected by making the Dean's list on the basis of their grades from the previous quarter. The investiga-tors obtained grades for 1,002 students for the quarters before and after the list was published; their sample included persons who did and did not qualify for the

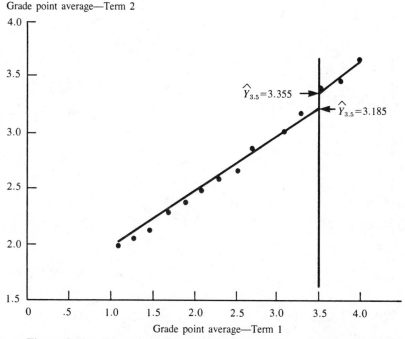

Figure 3.11. Regression of grade point average Term 2 on grade point average Term 1 for the non-Dean's list and Dean's list groups.

distinction. We would expect students who made the list to do better than those who did not for a variety of reasons. The issue with regression-discontinuity analysis is whether the rewarded students perform better than others by a higher factor than would have been the case without the reward.

Seaver kindly provided Joyce Sween and the authors of this book with his data, which Sween has replotted. When plotted as individual scores instead of the array means in Figure 3.11, it looks as though grades are curvilinearly related to each other across quarters. Since the plot of 1,002 scores is complex, we have replotted the data in Figure 3.12 using finer array means than Seaver and Quarton, and we have fitted both curvilinear and linear regressions to the data. Obviously, a strong case can be made for curvilinearity in the data.

What are the consequences of the underlying relationship being curvilinear? As Figure 3.12 shows, fitting a curvilinear trend produces no evidence of a dis-

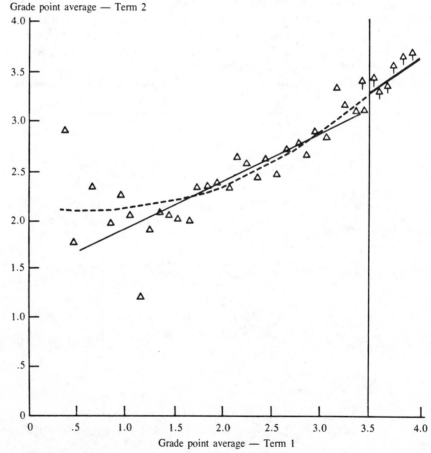

Figure 3.12.   Plot of column means for Seaver-Quarton data.

QUASI-EXPERIMENTS: NONEQUIVALENT CONTROL GROUP DESIGNS

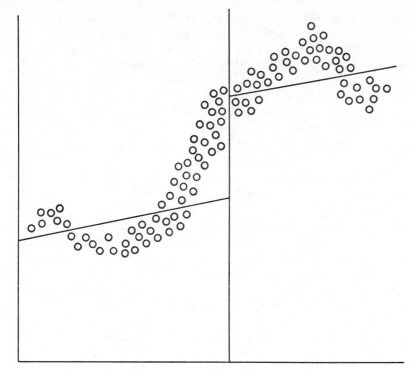

Figure 3.13. The consequences of fitting inappropriate linear regressions when the underlying regression is not linear.

continuity at the cutting point and so no evidence that making the Dean's list had any effect. In other words, when linear regressions are fitted to the data on each side of a cutting point, *but one or more of the regressions are not in fact linear,* spurious intercept differences can emerge. So, too, can spurious slope differences.

The point we are making can perhaps best be understood by considering the hypothetical example in Figure 3.13 where the scatterplot portrays an underlying nonlinear relationship. Fitting linear relationships gives a discontinuity at the cutting point; fitting a nonlinear regression does not. Imagine, now, that the underlying distribution was of a J-form and that the tail at the high end of the pretest distribution in Figure 3.13 did not exist. Then, it would not be appropriate to fit a linear regression to the data at the lower end of the pretest continuum, but it would be appropriate at the higher end. However, if linear regressions were fitted on both sides of the cutting point, a discontinuity in both level and slope would be obtained. The major threat to internal validity with the regression-discontinuity design is of selection-maturation—the possibility that change between the pretest and posttest does not follow a simple linear pattern across the whole of the pretest distribution.

Seaver and Quarton were actually sensitive to this threat. But instead of examining the form of their data more closely for the broader range of cases who did not make the Dean's list, they chose another strategy. They reasoned that, if there were spurious selection-maturation, then it should appear in the data when the pretest in Figure 3.11 was used as the posttest and the previous quarter's grades were used as the pretest. When this analysis was conducted, it produced no discontinuities. However, the test is not as accurate as critically examining scatterplots to examine whether nonlinear forms of regression fit the data better than linear forms. If they do, regressions of a higher order than the linear have to be fit; otherwise spurious causal conclusions will result.

Another set of problems with the regression-discontinuity design arises from the fact that in most social settings the treatment is made available only to a small percentage of the persons who score at one of the extremes of the quantitative continuum. This is not, of course, a necessary feature of the regression-discontinuity design, though it is certainly to be expected in many cases where the design is appropriate. Being restricted to the most needy and the most meritorious, the regression-discontinuity design is therefore weak when researchers wish to generalize to other kinds of persons. For instance, in an example to be presented later, it is shown that Medicaid significantly increased the number of visits that poor persons reportedly made to doctors. This effect, while small in average magnitude (though visually dramatic), represents many millions of dollars per year. Some health planners would like to be able to estimate how the demand for medical services will increase once we have some form of a national health insurance program where individuals of all kinds do not pay for medical services directly. How confident would one feel generalizing to the United States at large from the Medicaid experience with the most-poor and least-healthy? (In practice, of course, one would not rely solely on Medicaid for an estimate of the demand for health services—some labor unions have won completely free medical services for their members, and some cities have private medical schemes allowing unlimited free medical services).

The dependence on small numbers of extremely high or low scores raises a more technical problem: It is often difficult to estimate with any reasonable certainty the shape of the distribution of scores on the short side of the cutting point. Yet, as we shall see in chapter 4 where the statistical analysis of data from the regression-discontinuity design is discussed, it is important to be able to estimate this distribution in order to determine if it can be considered simply an extension of the distribution found on the long side of the cutting point.

A difficulty that can often be anticipated with the regression-discontinuity design is that the cutting point will not be as clearcut as our discussion may suggest. In particular, we can anticipate that some persons will be allowed access to the treatment, not because of need or merit, but because they are friends of friends, or are particularly skillful at manipulating the persons responsible for permitting access, or are owed some type of social debt. A lack of clarity about the cutting point is especially likely when the cutting point is widely known, for this may give rise to special pressures to help some persons achieve the cutting point score. For instance, the Irish government publishes the passing score on various national examinations in education. A frequency distribution of the

number of children obtaining all possible scores on the physics exam shows a less than expected number of students scoring just below the cutting point and a higher than expected frequency just above it (Greaney, Kellaghan, Takata and Campbell, in preparation). It seems likely, therefore, that examiners gave students scoring just below the cutting point "an extra helping hand." In many social service settings, clients disguise part of their income if they suspect that full disclosure will take them above a cutting point for eligibility for services. Indeed, some professionals may deliberately condone such practices because the cutting points for eligibility seem so arbitrary to them.

A major problem when cutting points are fuzzy is that the systematic deviations around the cutting point can masquerade as treatment effects. Imagine a social service setting where the clients know the income cutoff point for obtaining supplementary social services. Some will report their income to be lower than it actually is. In order to examine whether obtaining supplementary services increased the social mobility aspirations of children, we might plot the income of a wide range of parents against the mobility aspirations of their children. Let us suppose that the overall relationship is linear and positive, indicating that higher incomes are associated with higher aspirations. However, one group of parents whose reported incomes fall below the cutting point will have actual incomes above it. The aspiration scores of their children will be higher than those of parents who have comparable reported income but lower actual income. Combining the scores of all persons with comparable reported incomes will artifactually increase the obtained scores of those children who score just below the cutting point. As a result, we will have a reduced intercept difference at the cutting point and spurious differences in slope.

Since achieving the cutting point permits access to scarce and desired resources, we should always anticipate that cutting points will be unclear and that some individuals will gain what, strictly speaking, they should not receive. Where such individuals can be identified, the solution is to drop them from the analysis and proceed as though they were not part of the study. (It is always desirable, of course, to try and understand the pressures that lead to such "biased" [but probably sociologically lawful] assignments.) If it is not possible to identify all the individuals who received treatments for which they were not strictly eligible, then an estimate should be made of the range around the cutting point in which biased assignments are likely to have occurred. This range is then treated as the cutting point, and the analysis proceeds with a hatched area demarcating the cutting range rather than with a straight line at a particular cutting score. The logic of the analysis is the same whether a range or cutting point is used, although statistical sensitivity will be greater with a point.

Quantified Multiple Control Groups, Posttest-Only Design

Using the pretest to classify units on a merit or need basis is merely a special case of a more general principle. The principle states that regression-discontinuity designs are possible wherever units can be ordered along some quantifiable dimension which is systematically related to assignment of treatment. We can illustrate this by referring to a study by Lohr (1972; Wilder, 1972), who was interested in exploring the effects of Medicaid. The program was designed to make medical

care available to the very poor (income under $3,000 per family per year) by means of federal government payments. One important question was whether the poor would actually take advantage of the new medical policy.

Lohr's data can be displayed to plot the mean visits to the doctor per family per year as a function of annual family income (each measure was based on interviews done in connection with the Current Population Reports). The relationship of the two variables is portrayed in Figure 3.14, where it can be seen that the number of visits per year systematically decreases as income decreases. The one discontinuity from this trend is for families with an income under $3,000, where the number of medical visits sharply increases and even tends to exceed the number of visits made by the more affluent families. Since these data indicate that Medicaid might have increased medical visits by the poor, we have to ask ourselves the perennial question: Are there any plausible alternative interpretations of the relationship?

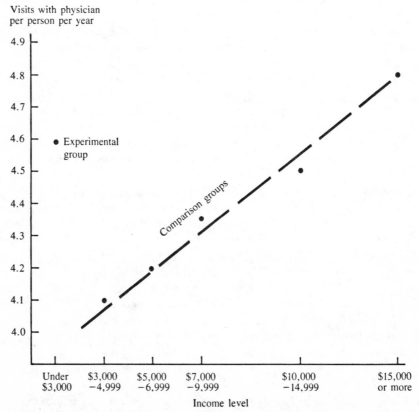

Figure 3.14. Quantified multiple control group posttest-only analysis of the effects of Medicaid. (After Lohr, 1972; Wilder, 1972.)

The chronically sick aside, visits to the doctor are presumably highest among the aged. Income is also lower among the aged. Thus, if the aged fell disproportionately into the lowest-income category, the relationship in Figure 3.14 might reflect a special selection phenomenon. Against this fact, we have to consider that there is no reason why the aged should be so heavily represented in the lowest-income group rather than spread more systematically across each lower-income group. Fortunately, the relationship of age to income is ultimately an empirical issue and national demographic data exist for checking it. It is perhaps more important to note that persons over 65 are eligible for Medicare as well as Medicaid and that there are indications that many older persons use both programs. Hence, an evaluation of Medicaid by itself should be restricted to persons under 65 years of age, though an evaluation of the program in its social context should also include separate analyses of persons over 65. Thus, there is good reason for wanting to see the Figure 3.14 data presented separately for families where no one is eligible for Medicare and for families where someone is eligible.

A different age explanation is based on the possibility that medical visits are most needed by pregnant women and young children. Hence, we have to consider whether the lowest-income group was disproportionately composed of persons prone to pregnancy and large families. If so, they might have had more frequent visits to doctors even before Medicaid, though such visits were presumably to state hospitals on a nonpayment basis. There is every need, therefore, to disaggregate the data even further to examine the relationship of income to medical visits among persons of different family sizes as well as at different age levels.

A different kind of possible selection bias cannot be ruled out merely by disaggregating on the basis of demographic factors that are routinely measured in surveys and that can be easily used in archival studies. Some families in the lowest-income group were eligible for assistance from many programs, some of which mandated (and paid for) medical visits by recipients and their children as a precondition for receiving aid or for continuing to receive it. The issue, therefore, arises: Were the disproportionately frequent visits to doctors by the poor the result of Medicaid meeting a need or a response to the pre-Medicaid requirement of other programs that a doctor be consulted? If the latter, no effect of Medicaid would need to be invoked. This problem would be easy to solve if we knew something about the programs in which family members were enrolled, especially those requiring work-related and welfare-related physical checkups. Only if data on mandated checkups were collected at the time of the survey could disaggregation on this variable take place. Without foresight, however, the required information would probably not be collected. In that case, the best one could do would be to consult the most reliable data available on the number of persons eligible for mandated medical visits and determine (1) if such eligibility related to income in the discontinuous manner suggested by Figure 3.14 and (2) was of a magnitude that could plausibly account for the pattern in that figure.

Another possible alternative interpretation is based on selection-maturation. This interpretation suggests that the demand for medical care was greatest among the poor, that the supply of doctors was increasing year by year, and that the new supply could only find outlets among those sections of the population whose prior

demands had not been met and whose physical state required urgent care. Against this, however, is the fact reported to us by Lohr that, though the number of doctors per capita increased between 1960 and 1970, the number *in medical practice* did not. Presumably, some doctors went into medical research or into non-medical careers.

A final threat to internal validity arises because the direction of causality is not clear from Figure 3.14. Did Medicaid cause an increase in medical visits, or did the desire for medical visits by the sick and hypochondriac lead these persons to underreport their true income both to doctors and to interviewers in order to continue the pretense that they were eligible for such programs? An indirect check of this might be possible by using nonmedical surveys to estimate the proportion of persons in each of the income categories in Figure 3.14. The "opposite direction of causality" explanation would be ruled out if equal proportions fell into each income category in each type of survey. (However, this test is only approximate, for sick persons might generalize their underreporting of true income to all surveys, whether oriented to medical services or not.)

What perhaps should be emphasized regarding most of the threats to internal validity we have listed is that their plausibility can be assessed without undue effort by consulting available archives in order to disaggregate the data from Figure 3.14 or to collect additional data that rule out specific alternative explanations. Thus, our list of threats should not discourage researchers; like other lists for other projects, it should spur into action those persons whose interest lies in strengthening a particular causal inference.

It should be noted that the Lohr-Wilder data actually cover three waves, one coming before Medicaid. As displayed in Riecken et al. (1974, Fig. 4.18), the data for the year prior to Medicaid indicated that doctors devoted the lowest level of attention to the least financially advantaged group, which—as Figure 3.14 shows—was not the case after Medicaid. Such a change invalidates many of the alternative interpretations listed above that were presented here for pedagogical reasons.

Some important problems of construct validity should also be mentioned with respect to Lohr's quasi-experiment. Given the stimulation of demand by Medicaid and the apparent inelasticity of supply, does an increase in the quantity of care for the poor entail a decrease in the quality of care for them and for others? Furthermore, is the dependent variable appropriately labeled as "an increase in physician visits" or as "a *temporary* increase in physician visits"? The frequency of chronic and ill-monitored disease is presumably higher among the poor and might well be decreased by Medicaid, thereby leading to a later decrease in visits as more and more chronic problems are cured or detected before they become worse.

4

The Statistical Analysis of Data from Nonequivalent Group Designs

by CHARLES S. REICHARDT

INTRODUCTION

In this chapter we will explore the logic behind the analysis of data from non-equivalent group designs and offer suggestions on the best way to apply this logic in practice. The discussion is not highly mathematical, as a reasonable understanding of the topic, as complex as it may be, does not require elaborate formulae. Instead, the discussion is directed to researchers who have only an elementary working knowledge of statistics. Algebraic results which would be helpful to more sophisticated readers are included as footnotes and serve to supplement the text but are *not* required for understanding.

Following the discussion in the previous chapter, we will distinguish between two classes of nonequivalent group designs: regression-discontinuity designs where the selection procedure is explicitly determined by a measured, quantitative dimension and designs where selection is not so constrained. We label the first class "designs with controlled selection" and the second class "designs without controlled selection." Since the selection process is controlled to some extent in all designs, these labels should not be interpreted literally. Rather, they indicate differences in the degree and type of control that is exercised in the assignment procedure.

The present discussion is primarily concerned with the analysis of nonequivalent group designs without controlled selection. We stress these designs for the following reasons. First, nonequivalent group designs without controlled selection are far more common in practice than nonequivalent group designs with controlled selection. Second, the analysis of these types of designs is generally more difficult and less salutary than the analysis of designs with controlled selection. Third, the rudiments of the analysis of designs with controlled selection, regression-discontinuity designs, are well presented in the preceding chapter. And fourth, the discussion of the analysis of designs without controlled selection lays the necessary foundation for the treatment of the analysis of the regression-discontinuity design, which will be found at the end of this chapter.

NONEQUIVALENT GROUP DESIGNS
WITHOUT CONTROLLED SELECTION

For the sake of simplicity, we shall restrict the discussion to the simple non-equivalent group design with a single experimental group and a single no-treatment control group. This restriction imposes virtually no loss in generality since, with only minor changes, the discussion can be readily adapted to more complex designs. In addition, we assume that the respondents in each treatment group have been observed at the same time both prior to the treatment (a pretest measure) and after the treatment (a posttest measure). While we assume that only one posttest measure is of interest, the discussion could be generalized to incorporate multiple posttests (cf. Bock, 1975). It is prudent, however, to allow for the possibility of having a number of different pretest measures.

We shall refer to the respondents as individuals, although larger groups (e.g., classes, schools, businesses, cities, states, and so forth) may be the real unit in the design and analysis. Of course, we also assume that individuals have *not* been randomly assigned to the treatment and control groups but rather that they have been assigned by some overt or covert, uncontrolled nonrandom process (e.g., self-selection or selection based on need or merit). Most likely, the nonrandom selection procedure produces groups that are nonequivalent.

It is important to examine carefully what we mean by equivalent and non-equivalent. In a true experiment with random assignment, the treatment groups are considered initially equivalent (though this equivalence can later be vitiated if there is differential attrition from the two groups). The label "equivalent" does *not* imply that the two groups would have *identical* mean scores on any variables measured at the pretest. Rather, it indicates that *if* the random assignment procedure were repeated over and over again so that the sample sizes in the two groups became infinitely large, the two groups would then have *identical* means (or medians, variances, or the like) on all variables measured at the pretest. Thus our use of the term *equivalent* denotes an equivalence of expected (population) values and not an equivalence of obtained (sample) values. We use the term *nonequivalent* in a similar manner; assuming that if the same nonrandom selection process were repeated over and over again, the two treatment groups would *differ* in a number of ways. For example, if the assignment to treatment conditions were based partly on the individual's level of income (e.g., high-income individuals mostly assigned to one group and low-income individuals to the other), then the two groups would have different expected mean levels on income and would undoubtedly have different expected mean levels on a wide range of other characteristics related to income level. Thus in using the term nonequivalent, we mean that the *expected* values of at least one characteristic of the groups are not equal even in the absence of a treatment effect.

Of course, a selection procedure which is not formally random (i.e., assignment of individuals based on a table of random numbers) may still be sufficiently haphazard so that it is "random in effect" (Lord, 1963). We believe, however, that most nonrandom assignment procedures, in practice, produce groups that conform to our definition of nonequivalence—i.e., the groups have different expected values on at least one and probably a number of characteristics.

To understand the nature of the group nonequivalence, then, one must understand the selection process and how it differs from being random. As obvious as this may sound, this reasoning is not always understood. For example, even in the face of an obviously nonrandom selection process, a researcher might argue that the groups are essentially equivalent because the mean pretest difference between the groups is "small." Although such evidence is suggestive, it is *not* sufficient to establish that the groups are equivalent, and indeed it may be quite misleading. In particular this argument fails to recognize that, even if the expected group pretest difference is zero, the groups *still* might have large expected differences on *other* variables which may affect the posttest scores and, thereby, be critically important in interpreting the data. Thus, one can only understand the nature of group differences by examining the selection process along with the pretest scores.

Such an understanding is an important step in the data analysis, though, of course, much more is required. In analyzing data from the nonequivalent group design, the purpose is not merely to *describe* the performance in groups of individuals, though that is useful. Rather, the purpose of the analysis is to determine the *effect* of an experimental treatment in contrast to a control condition. Usually this entails a comparison of the posttest scores in the two groups. Yet selection differences resulting from the nonrandom assignment may produce posttest differences between the groups even in the absence of a treatment effect. Therefore, to get a "reasonable" estimate of the treatment effect, the analysis must properly recognize or, as is sometimes said, *control* for the effects of these initial differences.

In addition, the analysis must also adjust for any differences caused by local history effects, compensatory rivalry, resentful demoralization, and the like. The present discussion, however, will largely ignore these problems. This is not because these threats to validity are unimportant. Quite the contrary, these problems can bias the analysis of the nonequivalent group design just as badly as they can bias the analysis of the randomized experiment. Indeed, some of these threats are likely to be more of a problem in the former than in the latter. In particular, local history effects are probably more likely to be associated with nonequivalent groups than with equivalent groups. Rather, the reason for ignoring these problems here is that the steps taken toward their resolution are the same in both situations, and the purpose of the present discussion is to focus on those issues most endemic to the nonequivalent group design. It is the presence of selection differences which most distinguishes the nonequivalent group design from the randomized experiment and which will therefore demand our attention. But even though the discussion ignores these other problems, they should not be ignored in the analysis.

A number of statistical methods are available with which to attack the problem of separating the effect of the treatment from the effect of selection differences. Four very simple and common ones are elementary analysis of variance (ANOVA), analysis of covariance (ANCOVA) either with a single covariate or multiple covariates, analysis of variance with blocking or matching (matching), and analysis of variance with gain scores (gain score analysis). Because these techniques are so common and form the logical basis for more elaborate procedures, we will discuss each technique at length. This discussion will focus on

two sets of issues. First, what is the underlying model for each procedure, what are its general characteristics, and what is the treatment effect estimate that it provides? Second, how and why might the treatment effect estimate be biased?

Though we are mainly concerned with how the four statistical techniques (ANOVA, ANCOVA, matching, and gain score analysis) behave in quasi-experiments, we shall also consider to some extent how they function in the randomized experiment. The four techniques were originally developed for the randomized experiment and occasional reference to that context should be helpful. In particular, it is useful to compare the treatment effect estimate generated by each of the four statistical models when assignment has been random. With a few simplifying, but reasonable assumptions, it can be shown that the expected value of this estimate is the same in each model. Thus, the models agree, or are compatible, where randomized experiments are concerned. But, of course, we should not overlook the fact that even in the randomized experiment, estimates from the models will generally differ in precision (i.e., some models provide an estimate of the treatment effect which has less variance than other estimates). In addition, some models offer more insight into the structure of the data than others, especially with respect to detecting interactions of the treatment with individual characteristics of the experimental units.

On the other hand, in nonequivalent group designs, each model generally has a *different* expected value for the estimate of the treatment effect which makes the models incompatible. This means that, in this context, the characteristics and likely biases of each method should be considered separately.

The purpose of this discussion is not to prove that one method is preferable to any other in analyzing data from nonequivalent group designs. Rather the appropriate conclusions can be summed up in two parts. First, each of these statistical procedures, and indeed any procedure, for the analysis of the nonequivalent group design can be biased under different circumstances. That is, no analysis technique exists that can be blindly applied to all sets of data with foolproof results. Rather, the analysis must be carefully tailored to fit each research situation. Second, this tailoring cannot be done in an automated and thoughtless fashion. While there are several logical frameworks (or rationales) to guide the researcher in tailoring the analysis to fit the specific research setting, a great deal of knowledge and thought on the part of the researcher is still required.

The rest of the discussion of the nonequivalent group design without controlled selection identifies four rationales for the analysis (unrelated to the above four statistical procedures) and describes the knowledge that the researcher must have in order to implement them. General recommendations for the analysis are also provided.

Elementary Analysis of Variance (ANOVA)

The Model

For our simple pretest-posttest design with two nonequivalent groups, the elementary ANOVA is perhaps the simplest model of the structure of the data. It specifies three components which determine the level of posttest responding.

The first is the *grand mean* of the posttest scores across all individuals, a value that serves to locate the average response on the measurement scale in question. The second is the *treatment effect*, which is the average value that the treatment adds to, or subtracts from, the posttest scores in the treatment group. The third is the (so-called) *error* or residual, which represents the effects of all other factors that contribute to differences between the scores. Thus, the error represents the influences of unreliable measurement and reliable individual differences between the respondents. In addition, the ANOVA model makes certain assumptions about the errors, namely that they are random variables which are normally and independently distributed with a mean of zero and constant variance. It should be noted, however, that the pretest scores do not enter into the model.[1]

That the errors in the two groups have the same (zero) mean is necessary both for the treatment effect estimate to be unbiased and for traditional significance tests to be correct. The other specifications concerning the errors are also required for standard significance tests, but violating them does not bias the estimate of the treatment effect. Since the emphasis in this chapter is on potential biases, we shall not be concerned with these latter assumptions about the distribution of the errors. This is not to imply that these assumptions are unimportant. While even substantial violations of some assumptions (e.g., constant variance and normal distribution of the errors) have only slight effects on the integrity of significance tests, moderate violations of other assumptions (e.g., independence of the errors) can have considerable effects (see Glass, Peckham, and Sanders, 1972; Lindquist, 1953; and Scheffé, 1959).

A weakness of the elementary ANOVA model is that the treatment effect is indexed as an average increase or decrease in responding so that the model does not allow for the possibility that the magnitude of the treatment effect might differ across characteristics of the individuals. Thus the model precludes learning about treatment interaction effects that might help specify the nature and generality of the treatment's particular impact. This limitation cannot be

---

[1]Algebraically, the model is

$$\text{(a) } Y_{ij} = \mu + \alpha_i + \epsilon_{ij}$$

(1)

$$\text{(b) } \epsilon_{ij} \sim NID \ (0, \sigma_\epsilon^2)$$

where Y_{ij} is the posttest score for the jth individual (j goes from 1 to n) in the ith treatment group (given our simple two-group example, $i = 1$ or 2, or $i = E$ or C for experimental and control), μ is the overall mean, α_i (technically $\alpha_E - \alpha_C$) is the treatment effect, and ϵ_{ij} is the error. The second line of the above model is just a shorthand way of writing that the errors are normally and independently distributed with mean zero and constant variance, σ_ϵ^2. The estimate of the treatment effect is

$$\hat{\alpha}_E - \hat{\alpha}_C = \bar{Y}_{E\cdot} - \bar{Y}_{C\cdot}.$$

where the symbol ˆ denotes the standard least squares estimate and the bar ‾ denotes a mean where summation is taken over the subscript that has been replaced by a dot.

rectified without adding to the model measured factors (such as the pretest) which take into account individual characteristics.

Another (and related) weakness of the elementary ANOVA is that, under many circumstances, it has less power to detect true differences than the ANCOVA, matching, or gain score analysis. This relative lack of power occurs because the model "explains" only that portion of the variation of the posttest scores that results from the treatment effect. All other variation, including the variation that could be "explained" by the pretest, is relegated to the error term against which the treatment effect is compared. This means that small treatment effects are more likely to go undetected in the elementary ANOVA than in other methods which can use pretest information to remove some of the variation from the error terms and thereby increase the power of the significance test.

Bias

In the elementary ANOVA model, the treatment is assumed to be the *sole* cause of any expected difference in posttest performance between the experimental and control groups. We have argued, however, that when groups are not randomly assigned to treatment conditions, another source of expected difference is possible—namely, selection differences associated with group non-equivalence. The ANOVA model does *not* take these differences into account. Therefore, when selection differences are present so that the groups are expected to differ in posttest performance even in the absence of a treatment effect, the ANOVA procedure is biased. Because selection differences are very likely to arise in quasi-experimental research in the social sciences, the ANOVA model is seldom used in this fashion with such data.

However, the ANOVA could also be used in a two-step procedure which employs both the pretest and posttest scores. First, the *pretest* scores would be analyzed with the elementary ANOVA model. If the result is not statistically significant, the groups are assumed to be equivalent. A result of "no difference" is then used to justify the second step where the ANOVA model is applied to the posttest scores. Though such a two-step procedure is possibly better than a procedure which ignores the pretest scores altogether, it is still likely to be biased. As we have argued, this is because the equivalence of the groups cannot be adequately determined on the basis of pretest scores alone. Yet the two-stage procedure rests on this faulty assumption. An example may illustrate the difficulty. Assume that group differences are expected to increase (relative to within-group variability) over time not because of a treatment effect but because of selection-maturation. In this case the mean difference between the groups on the pretest might be small, and the first step of the procedure would not reject the null hypothesis. But this failure to reject the null hypothesis does not justify assuming that the groups are equivalent because, with selection-maturation, the group difference can increase over time in a manner completely unrelated to the treatment. Thus the ANOVA on the posttest scores may very well lead to a statistically significant but spurious result.

Analysis of Covariance (ANCOVA) with a Single Covariate

The Model

The ANCOVA with a single covariate extends the elementary ANOVA by including the pretest measure in the model in the form of a linear regression.[2] Using the pretest ("covariate" in ANCOVA terminology) in this way provides an adjustment for initial differences between the groups. In the randomized experiment, the adjustment generally serves to increase the precision of the treatment effect estimate but (under certain general conditions) does not change the expected value of the estimate as compared to the estimate in the elementary ANOVA. In the nonequivalent group design, the adjustment can still increase precision, but it usually alters the expected value of the treatment effect estimate as compared to the ANOVA. Our discussion will focus largely on how well this adjustment accounts for initial differences between nonequivalent groups.

The ANCOVA model is perhaps best described pictorially. Consider Figure 4.1 where the pretest scores vary along the horizontal axis and the posttest scores along the vertical. Each individual in the experiment contributes one point to the graph. This point is jointly determined by his or her pretest and posttest scores (X and Y, respectively). The conglomerate of these points for all individuals forms two scatterplots—one for each treatment group. These are detailed as ellipses in the figure, with the ellipse that is shifted to the right representing the scores in the experimental group and the one shifted to the left representing the control group scores.

If you look along the horizontal axis in the figure, you will see that the pretest mean in the experimental group is higher than in the control group. If you look along the vertical axis, you will see marginal distributions that depict how posttest scores are dispersed. In our example, the lower distribution is from the control group and the upper distribution is from the experimental group. Drawn through each scatterplot is a regression line of the posttest scores

---

[2]Algebraically, the model is

$$\text{(a) } Y_{ij} = \mu + \alpha_i + \beta(X_{ij} - \bar{X}..) + \epsilon_{ij}$$

(2) $\text{(b) } \epsilon_{ij} \sim NID\ (O, \sigma_\epsilon^2)$

(c) X is fixed (i.e., nonstochastic). If X is considered to be a random variable, it must be independent of the errors, ϵ.

where β is the coefficient of the within-group linear regression of the posttest Y on the pretest X, and $\bar{X}..$ is the overall mean on the pretest. (Often $\bar{X}..$ is omitted from the model. This makes no difference in the above standard form of the ANCOVA but does matter when the standard model is extended as discussed in footnote 3.) Otherwise, the subscripts, variables, and parameters are similar to those in the preceding ANOVA model, though their values may be different. The consequences of violating the distributional assumption (2b) are somewhat different than in the ANOVA, though we shall not consider them here. The interested reader is referred to Atiqullah (1964), Elashoff (1969), and Glass, Peckham, and Sanders (1972) for a discussion of some of these issues. The estimate of the treatment effect is:

$$\hat{\alpha}_E - \hat{\alpha}_C = (\bar{Y}_{E\cdot} - \bar{Y}_{C\cdot}) - \hat{\beta}\ (\bar{X}_{E\cdot} - \bar{X}_{C\cdot})$$

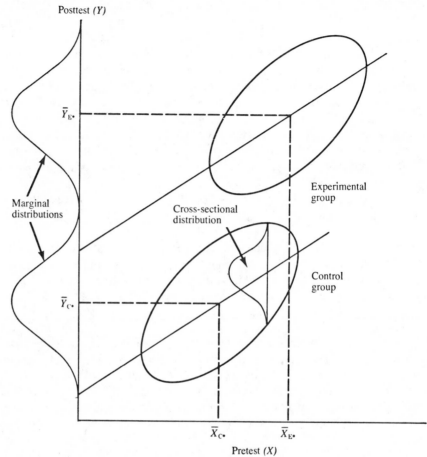

Figure 4.1. Plot of pretest versus posttest scores—estimate of treatment effect in ANCOVA model and reduction in error variance compared to ANOVA.

on the pretest scores. If the data actually conform to the ANCOVA model, the expected regression lines would be linear and parallel, as in the figure, and the observed regressions could be used to predict (within each group) the "best" estimate of posttest ability for any individual given his or her pretest score. The treatment effect is represented in the ANCOVA model as the displacement of one regression line above or below the other, or in other words, as the difference between the intercepts where the regression lines intersect the vertical axis. Assuming the ANCOVA model is correct, there appears to be a positive treatment effect in Figure 4.1 because the regression line in the experimental group is displaced above the regression in the control group or, alternatively,

because the intercept in the experimental group is higher than in the control group.[3]

Consider, next, Figure 4.2. The ellipses once again indicate that the groups have different distributions of pre- and posttest scores and parallel, linear regression lines. But this time, the regression lines overlap and intersect the vertical axis at the same intercept. Thus, the ANCOVA would find this to be a null case of no treatment effect.

The intuition behind this geometrical interpretation of the treatment effect estimate is straightforward. The relevant question is whether the experimental group outperformed the control group on the posttest by more than should be expected on the basis of initial selection differences. In essence, the ANCOVA attempts to answer this question by using a matching procedure whereby for any given *pretest* value it takes the predicted posttest values for the treatment and control groups and examines the difference between them. To see this, first note that the regression line in each group provides an estimate of the average posttest score for each given pretest score. In other words, if we know an individual's pretest score we can use the estimated regression line to get a reasonable prediction of the individual's posttest score. Now select an arbitrary pretest score and compare the predicted posttest scores in the two groups. One finds that this difference is equal to the vertical displacement between the two regression lines. Thus the estimate of the treatment effect in the ANCOVA is the difference between the predicted posttest scores of individuals in the two groups who have been "matched" on pretest scores. A statistically significant difference then "suggests" that one group would have significantly outperformed the other on the posttest *if the groups had started with the same pretest scores*. The similarity between the ANCOVA and an explicit matching procedure is further explored in the section on matching.

---

[3]Whether or not the true (population) regression lines are actually linear and parallel, the standard ANCOVA model that we have presented (footnote 2) makes this assumption and therefore fits the observed regressions so that they are constrained to be linear and parallel. However, the standard model can be elaborated so as to encompass both nonlinear and nonparallel regressions. Nonlinear regressions can be specified by including higher-order terms in X [e.g., $\gamma(X_{ij} - \bar{X}..)^2$, $\delta(X_{ij} - \bar{X}..)^3$] in the model. Nonparallel regression surfaces are specified by allowing the regression coefficients (β, γ, δ, etc.) to vary across groups (e.g., specifying β_i, γ_i, δ_i). In particular this latter adjustment allows for the possibility of a treatment interaction where the effect of the treatment varies according to the individual's pretest level. Allowing for interactions does, however, raise another difficulty. Since the displacement between nonparallel regression lines is not a constant, the researcher must decide at what point the displacement should be measured so as to obtain an appropriate estimate of the "main" effect of the treatment. By including the pretest in the model as a deviation from the overall mean ($X_{ij} - \bar{X}..$), the researcher is choosing to measure the displacement at the overall mean on the pretest. So, in a simple model, the treatment main effect estimate becomes:

$$\hat{\alpha}_E - \hat{\alpha}_C = (\bar{Y}_E. - \bar{Y}_C.) - \hat{\beta}_E (\bar{X}_E. - \bar{X}..) + \hat{\beta}_C (\bar{X}_C. - \bar{X}..)$$

But if the deviation form is not used, the treatment main effect estimate is calculated as the difference between the intercepts (i.e., where $X = 0$) so that in a simple model

$$\hat{\alpha}_E - \hat{\alpha}_C = (\bar{Y}_E. - \bar{Y}_C.) - \hat{\beta}_E (\bar{X}_E.) + \hat{\beta}_C (\bar{X}_C.)$$

This would seldom seem appropriate. Cochran (1969) provides a rationale for choosing between several different comparisons, though we feel that the first one presented above is generally the most appropriate.

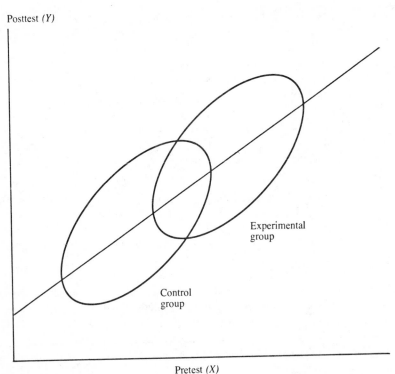

Posttest *(Y)*

Experimental
group

Control
group

Pretest *(X)*

Figure 4.2. Plot of pretest versus posttest scores revealing null case for ANCOVA model.

As previously noted, under certain general conditions the expected value of the treatment effect estimate in the ANCOVA is the same as in the ANOVA when analyzing data from randomized experiments. This is because the expected pretest difference between the groups is zero, so the expected scatterplots of the data from the treatment and control groups are not displaced in the horizontal direction—as with the quasi-experimental data in Figures 4.1 and 4.2—but either fall on top of one another (no treatment effect) or are displaced in the vertical direction only (a treatment effect). When there is no expected horizontal displacement, the expected difference between the intercepts of the regression lines (the ANCOVA estimate) is equal to the expected difference between the mean posttest scores (the ANOVA estimate).

However, in both the true and quasi-experiment, the ANOVA and ANCOVA estimates generally differ in precision. This is because the ANCOVA reduces the size of the error variance by including the pretest scores directly in the model. This reduction can be demonstrated pictorially. Consider, once again, Figure 4.1 where the marginal distribution of the posttest scores for each treatment group is graphically represented on the vertical (*Y*) axis. It is the variance of these distributions that is attributed to error in the ANOVA. By incorporating the pretest, the

ANCOVA spreads these marginal distributions into the two-dimensional scatter-plots represented by the ellipses. From the shape of these ellipses, one sees that part of the variance in the posttest scores is "predictable" by the pretest scores. That is, if the pretest scores of two individuals from the same group differ, one expects the posttest scores to differ in the direction specified by the regression line. Thus by knowing the pretest scores, one is better able to predict the posttest scores. The ANCOVA operates in exactly this manner, removing part of the variance of the posttest by using the pretest as a predictor and assigning to error only the variance of the cross-sectional distribution of the scatterplots. Since the variance of the cross-sectional distribution is smaller then that of the marginal distribution, the ANCOVA has a smaller error variance than the ANOVA.

The size of the difference in error variance between the ANOVA and ANCOVA depends on how highly the pretest and posttest are correlated within treatment groups. The higher the absolute value of the correlation, the greater is the reduction in error variance, though little reduction occurs until the correlation is above .3 or .4.[4] In addition, the precision of the ANCOVA estimate will be lower when the groups are nonequivalent than when they are randomly formed.[5]

With data from the nonequivalent group design, the estimates of the treatment effect in the ANCOVA and ANOVA generally differ not only in precision, but also in expected value. This can be understood by considering Figure 4.3. We might suppose that the ellipses represent the distributions of the entire joint *populations* of pretest and posttest scores in the two treatment groups, so that we are dealing with expected values and not differences due to sampling variation. In Figure 4.3(a) a large mean posttest difference $(\bar{Y}_C. - \bar{Y}_E.)$ exists between the groups. The ANOVA model would label this a negative treatment effect since the control group outperformed the experimental group. But as no intercept difference exists between the regression lines (i.e., $\alpha_C = \alpha_E$), the ANCOVA model would

---

[4]The reduction in error variance is demonstrated by the relation

$$\sigma_\epsilon^2 = \sigma_Y^2 (1 - \rho_{XY}^2)$$

where σ_ϵ^2 and σ_Y^2 are, respectively, the error variances in the ANCOVA and ANOVA models, and ρ_{XY} is the pooled within-group pretest-posttest correlation.

A more accurate comparison of the precision between the ANCOVA and ANOVA, however, must take account of the variability in the ANCOVA estimate due to the variance of the estimate of the slope, β. Adding this variability, the error variance σ_ϵ^2 becomes "effectively about"

$$\sigma_Y^2(1 - \rho_{XY}^2)[1+ \frac{1}{2(n-2)} + \frac{nD^2}{4(n-2)\sigma_X^2}]$$

where D is the expected pretest difference between the groups [i.e., $D = E(\bar{X}_E. - \bar{X}_C.)$], n is the within-group sample size, and σ_X^2 is the variance of the pretest scores within groups (Cochran, 1953, 1957). In the true experiment, $D = 0$ so the last term drops out of the above equation. In the non-equivalent group design, however, D is generally not equal to zero, and this obviously reduces the precision of the ANCOVA estimate.

[5]The effect that the expected pretest difference between the groups has on the precision of the ANCOVA has already been noted in footnote 4. The intuition behind this finding comes from examining the estimate of the treatment effect as presented in footnote 2. The estimate involves the term $\hat{\beta}$ $(\bar{X}_E. - \bar{X}_C.)$. So a larger pretest difference $(\bar{X}_E. - \bar{X}_C.)$ amplifies any "mistake" made in estimating β and correspondingly leads to a less precise estimate. This decrease in precision can also be explained as an increase in the degree of multicollinearity (cf. Johnston, 1972; or Theil, 1971).

find *no* treatment effect. In Figure 4.3(b), the intercept difference is smaller than the mean posttest difference, but both differences favor the same group. Hence, the ANOVA and ANCOVA would agree that the control condition was superior to

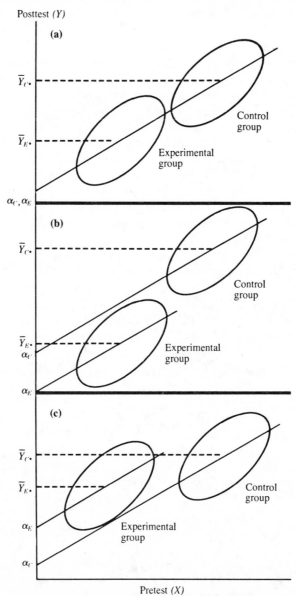

Figure 4.3. Comparison of treatment effect estimates in ANOVA and ANCOVA for three possible outcomes of nonequivalent group design.

the experimental condition but would disagree about the size of the effect. In Figure 4.3(c), the ANOVA and ANCOVA models would completely disagree as to which treatment condition is superior, since the estimate of the treatment effect in the one is the reverse of the other. That is, the posttest mean of the control group is higher than the mean of the experimental group, suggesting that the treatment effect was negative (if one trusts the ANOVA). However, the intercept in the experimental group is higher than the intercept in the control group, suggesting that the treatment effect was positive (if one believes the results of the ANCOVA).

Bias

Since the ANCOVA introduces an adjustment for group pretest differences which can substantially alter the expected value of the treatment effect estimate when compared to the ANOVA, the critical question is whether this adjustment removes all the bias due to selection differences. In other words, does the ANCOVA model provide an unbiased estimate of the treatment effect in quasi-experimental research? In discussing this question, we first consider the case where the pretest and the posttest are *operationally identical* measures. By this we mean that the measures or observations are physically or structurally the same, as with two measures of height using the same scale or two measures of vocabulary skills using the same or strictly parallel tests. The case where the pretest and posttest are *operationally unique* is considered in a later section below. This distinction is somewhat arbitrary, but it does serve a useful pedagogic purpose.

When we consider identical or parallel tests, it is easy to construct an artificial example where the ANCOVA model would properly correct for the effects of selection differences. First, assume that both the pretest and posttest are perfectly reliable measures, which means that they contain no measurement error. And second, assume that the individuals being studied and the environments with which they interact do *not* change between the pretest and posttest observations and that there is no treatment effect. Under these strict conditions, an individual's pretest score would equal his or her posttest score. The plot of the posttest versus pretest scores for the treatment and control groups would produce a straight line with a slope equal to one and an intercept equal to zero (as in Figure 4.4(a), for example). Then, regardless of the manner in which individuals were selected into treatment conditions, the ANCOVA model would correctly suggest that there was no treatment effect. That is, the scores for the two groups would fall along the same line and have the *same* intercept. A "well-behaved" data pattern of this kind would also provide a perfect baseline from which to judge the impact of a treatment. For example, a treatment which had a constant effect would raise or lower the regression line of the experimental group by that constant amount, and the ANCOVA would give the proper interpretation once again.

Of course, research in the behavioral sciences rarely if ever has both perfectly reliable measurement and no pretest-posttest change other than that due to the treatment effect. With the present state of the art, few behavioral traits can be measured *without* error, especially when the individual person is the unit of analysis. In addition, individuals often change through processes of maturation, learning, fatigue, and the like, and they may be affected by changes in the en-

vironment, not the least of which may be the presence of a pretest observation. Lord (1958, p. 440) has described this situation for educational contexts:

> Even though the pretest and posttest consist of the same questions and are physically identical, it is quite possible to maintain that the student has changed drastically during the course of instruction and that, even though we eliminate practice effect from consideration, the test no longer measures the same thing when given after instruction as it did before instruction.

And Bryk and Weisberg (1977, p. 951) emphatically concur with this sentiment:

> [One is] typically examining systems that are fundamentally dynamic. Individuals are growing and changing in interaction with one another and the environment even in the absence of any external intervention. The pretest and posttest represent two snapshots of a continuous growth process.

Thus it is probably appropriate in many situations to conclude that, when collected at different times, even well-constructed and carefully implemented operationally identical measures are fallible indicators of a naturally evolving behavior pattern, rather than perfect measures of the same stable trait.

We now want to consider how measurement error and a variety of kinds of change can bias the estimate of the treatment effect in the ANCOVA when it is employed with nonequivalent groups. This is not to suggest that measurement error and change always produce biases in the ANCOVA treatment effect estimate—they do not. For example, if the pretest and posttest contained the same measurement error, these two sets of scores can still be equal and the ANCOVA again justified by the above logic. Similarly, the ANCOVA can properly handle some forms of change between the pretest and posttest as described below. Nonetheless, biases can arise from these two sources and the examples should make this clear. We should be quick to note that a full understanding of the bias in the ANCOVA as applied to quasi-experimental data requires knowledge not only of measurement error and change (i.e., the relationship of the pretest to the posttest) but also knowledge of the nature of selection differences. For this reason, we always include a description of the assumed selection differences in each example. A more complete explication of the nature of biases in ANCOVA is provided by Cronbach et al. (1977) and the statistically sophisticated reader is referred to that work.

Measurement error in the pretest. Most researchers admit that their observations contain a certain amount of random measurement error, though they have come to expect the amount of error to vary depending upon the type of observation. In addition, many researchers believe that random measurement error, like random sampling variation, introduces *no* bias into the ANCOVA. Unfortunately, they are only half correct. Random measurement error in the posttest is like random sampling variation in that it will reduce the precision of the estimate of the treatment effect but not introduce a bias. Random measurement error in the *pretest*, however, not only reduces precision but can also bias the estimate of the regression slope and thus bias the estimate of the treatment effect. This can be demonstrated in the following way, which borrows heavily from Lord's (1960) conceptualization.

Imagine, first, the ideal case we mentioned above of (1) an operationally identical pretest and posttest containing no measurement error and (2) no change in individuals over time. Further, assume that selection into treatment groups is

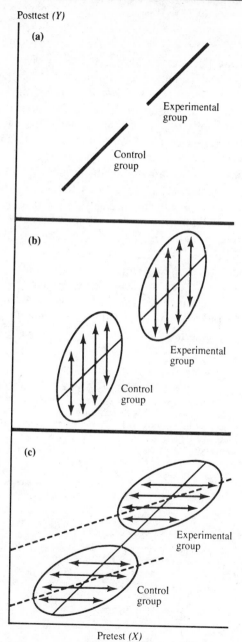

Figure 4.4. Effects of measurement error on ANCOVA.

based solely on true pretest ability. Then scatterplots of the data would look something like the plot in Figure 4.4(a). In this situation, no treatment effect would be inferred by the ANCOVA since there is no intercept difference between the regression lines. Consider, now, the effects of introducing random measurement error into the posttest scores (Y). This will equally distribute error (as indicated by arrows) above and below the true regression lines resulting in scatterplot ellipses as in Figure 4.4(b). Since the ANCOVA fits the estimated regression lines so that deviations in the Y direction are minimized, and since the errors are "symmetrically" distributed in that direction, measurement error in the posttest produces no bias in the estimate of the slopes and hence in the estimate of the treatment effect. Indeed, both the estimated regression lines and treatment effect are the same as those in the error-free case save for random sampling fluctuations.[6]

Quite a different outcome results from measurement error in the pretest (X). Error of this kind serves to increase the pretest variance and, thereby, elongates the ellipses, as indicated by the arrows in Figure 4.4(c). This elongation makes scatterplots that are "symmetrically" distributed around the true regression slope (solid lines) in the X direction but "nonsymmetrically" distributed around the true regression lines in the Y direction. The "nonsymmetry" in the Y direction can be seen by drawing arrows from the true regression lines *upwards* and *downwards* to the edge of the ellipses and noting that these arrows generally have different lengths. Given its least squares criterion for fitting lines, the ANCOVA would fit the estimated regressions so that they pass more through the length of the scatterplots (the dashed line in Figure 4.4(c)) resulting in an *underestimate* of the true regression slopes. This underestimate leads to an intercept difference between the regressions and the conclusion that there was a treatment effect when none existed.[7]

---

[6]Readers who are unfamiliar with ANCOVA, multiple regression, or ordinary least squares (OLS) algebra may not intuitively see why the regression lines in Figure 4.4(b) should be fit the way they are. In particular, the question often arises as to why the regression lines do not pass through the "length" of the ellipses (i.e., correspond to the major axes of the ellipses). The fact of the matter is that the ANCOVA fits the regression lines so that the sum of the squares of the deviations around the lines *in the Y direction* is minimized. For "nicely behaved" plots as in Figure 4.4(b) this means that at each point the "size" of the deviations above the line should equal the size of the deviations below the line. By carefully inspecting the regression lines and the arrows in Figure 4.4(b), the reader will see that this symmetry is indeed achieved but that this would no longer hold if the regression lines were fit in any other position.

[7]Our discussion assumes a very simple model of measurement error. Algebraically, let X^*_{ij} and Y^*_{ij} be the perfectly measured pretest and posttest scores with $Y^*_{ij} = \beta X^*_{ij}$ (the text specifies $\beta = 1$). Further, assume that X^*_{ij} and Y^*_{ij} are normally distributed *within the groups* with variances $\sigma^2_{x^*}$ $\sigma^2_{x^*}(= \beta^2\sigma^2_{x^*})$, respectively. To introduce measurement error, we let X_{ij} and Y_{ij} be the fallibly measured scores with

$$X_{ij} = X^*_{ij} + u_{ij}$$
$$Y_{ij} = Y^*_{ij} + v_{ij}$$

where u_{ij} and v_{ij} are the errors of measurement and are assumed (1) to be normally distributed with mean zero and variances σ_u^2 and σ_v^2, respectively, and (2) to be independent of each other and of the true scores X^*_{ij} and Y^*_{ij}. Under these conditions, pedagogically useful results are not easily obtained with the algebra of expectations but do follow from the algebra of probability limits which may be

Because of the way random measurement error attenuates the estimates of the regression slopes, the bias that it produces in the treatment effect estimate is always in one direction. To understand this, we must first distinguish between underadjustment and overadjustment biases. As the name suggests, an underadjustment bias means that too little correction is made for the effects of selection differences. The result is that the treatment given to the group scoring highest on the posttest is made to appear better than it really is. To see this, think of the treatment effect estimate as being composed of two parts: the posttest difference between the groups and a correction that is subtracted to adjust for selection differences. If too little is subtracted to adjust for selection differences (an underadjustment), the group with the higher mean posttest score will appear to do relatively better than it should. On the other hand, an overadjustment bias occurs when too much is subtracted to adjust for selection differences so the group with the higher mean posttest score appears to do relatively worse than is really the case. Since an ANOVA makes no correction for selection differences, its bias is always an underadjustment. In contrast, since an ANCOVA does make an adjustment for the effect of selection differences, its bias could, at least in theory, be an overadjustment or an underadjustment. The bias in ANCOVA caused solely by random measurement error, however, is unidirectional.

Assuming that a perfectly measured pretest would provide an unbiased treatment effect estimate (and this is a very strict assumption), random measurement error in the pretest results in an *underadjustment*. The reason is that as errors in the pretest increase in size, the treatment effect estimate in the ANCOVA converges toward the ANOVA estimate which completely ignores the pretest. This can best be seen when the pretest is completely unreliable, for then the pretest and posttest would not be related, the regression slopes would be equal to zero, and

---

thought of (with varying degrees of accuracy) as expectations in large samples. The probability limit of the estimated regression coefficient when using the fallible observations, X_{ij} and Y_{ij} is

$$plim\ (\hat{\beta}) = \rho_{XX}\beta$$

where ρ_{XX} is the within-group reliability of X [i.e., $\rho_{XX} = \sigma^2_X{}^* (\sigma^2_X{}^* + \sigma_u{}^2)$]. Since ρ_{XX} takes on values between 0 and 1, the effect of measurement error is to attenuate the slope of the observed regression (i.e., to make it closer to zero). Measurement error also alters the probability limit of the treatment effect estimate from

$$E(\bar{Y}^*_{E\cdot} - \bar{Y}^*_{C\cdot}) - \beta E(\bar{X}^*_{E\cdot} - \bar{X}^*_{C\cdot})$$

with perfectly reliable measurement to

$$E(\bar{Y}^*_{E\cdot} - \bar{Y}^*_{C\cdot}) - \rho_{XX}\beta E(\bar{X}^*_{E\cdot} - \bar{X}^*_{C\cdot})$$

in the case of fallible measurement. If the former estimate removes all of the initial "bias" that is created by selection differences, the latter does not, leaving a portion $(1 - \rho_{XX})$ which depends upon the reliability of the pretest measure. While our emphasis is on the nonequivalent group design, the algebra also applies to the true experiment but with some different conclusions. In the latter situation measurement error in the pretest results in the same "bias" (i.e., inconsistency) in the estimate of the regression slope β but leaves the treatment effect estimate "unbiased" (consistent) because $E(\bar{X}^*_{E\cdot} - \bar{X}^*_{C\cdot}) = 0$.

A model such as that presented here is probably the most commonly assumed model of measurement error in the social sciences (aside from naively assuming that measurement error does not exist). However, more elaborate and varied models of measurement error are possible and often plausible and will have correspondingly different effects upon the behavior of the ANCOVA (see Berkson, 1950; and Cochran, 1968b).

the ANCOVA would be reduced to the ANOVA. In our earlier example, the initially most able group was labeled the treatment condition. Using ANCOVA with the fallibly measured pretest would not have adjusted for all of the selection differences favoring the more able group and would have made the treatment look beneficial. Had the treatment been given to the less able group in our example, the conclusion would have been reversed; the treatment would have looked *harmful* when, in fact, it had had no effect.

Measurement error in the pretest can therefore produce spurious treatment effects when none exist. But it can also result in a finding of no intercept difference when a true treatment effect exists, or it can produce an estimate of the treatment effect which is in the opposite direction of the true effect.

So far we have restricted consideration to the case where the ANCOVA would be unbiased if the pretest were perfectly measured. What happens when we relax this assumption and consider pretest measurement error together with other sources of bias (e.g., differences in growth patterns)? In this case, random measurement error in the pretest still biases the treatment effect estimate in the ANCOVA toward underadjustment. However, as we shall demonstrate below, the bias due to growth can lead to either an overadjustment or an underadjustment. Therefore, depending upon the relative size and direction of each of these forces, the total bias may be in either direction.

Because random measurement error always tends to bias the ANCOVA with a single covariate toward underadjustment and because error is virtually always present in social science measurements, we would suspect that the ANCOVA with a single pretest is biased more often in the underadjustment than the overadjustment direction. But this does not mean that an overwhelming proportion of ANCOVA estimates are so biased, since there are ample sources of overadjustment bias. Rather, the above statement represents a reasonable guess when no other information is available.

Change between the time of the pretest and posttest which is irrelevant to the treatment. Not all forms of growth invalidate the ANCOVA. Indeed, under certain conditions the ANCOVA will properly model differential growth between the groups. For example, if in the absence of a treatment effect the rate of change in the mean difference between the groups is equal to the slope of the regression lines, then the null hypothesis of the ANCOVA is appropriate. The point is that the conditions under which the ANCOVA is appropriate are very restrictive. Explicitly, the ANCOVA properly models differential growth *between* groups only when that growth is perfectly mirrored by the growth patterns that occur *within* the groups. This is because the regression slope is used to correct for between-group differences but is itself estimated solely from the pattern of change arising within the groups. Unfortunately, within-group relationships do not always mirror between-group relationships in practice. And when these two growth patterns differ, a bias arises when using the ANCOVA in the nonequivalent group design.

In the discussion below, we provide three examples where the within-group relationships do not parallel the between-group differences. These examples are neither exhaustive of all possible types of growth that might bias the ANCOVA as

used in the nonequivalent group design, nor are they mutually exclusive. In practice, the researcher will have to examine the respondents, the research setting, and selection differences to determine the forces that might be operating to bias the ANCOVA treatment effect estimate.

1. *Identifiable subpopulations starting at the same level on the pretest and growing at different rates.* One can usually identify subpopulations of individuals whose pretest performance might be similar but who would tend to grow differentially over time. For example, at some age adolescent males and females tend to be the same height, but after that point the boys clearly outgrow the girls on the average. Or the salary of young college graduates might at first be the same as that of experienced but "less-educated" workers, yet the college graduates will often out-earn the less educated over time. If the treatment groups were divided according to these subpopulations, an ANCOVA model would be inappropriate. This is because the two groups would start at the same pretest level, but the greater natural growth of one group compared to the other would *displace* the regression line (of posttest scores on pretest scores) of the faster-growing group *above* the regression line of the other group. This spurious displacement would produce an intercept difference quite independently of any treatment effect.

Although we assumed above that the two subpopulations of individuals started at the *same* pretest level, this is not a necessary condition for bias to arise. Growth will invalidate the ANCOVA whenever within-group growth is not predictive of between-group growth, as with boys' and girls' heights at many stages of development. Here initial height is positively correlated with later height *within* a group of boys or girls, since individuals who are tall compared to their group at one point in time tend to remain taller than the average of their group. However, this within-group relationship is clearly not predictive of between-group changes, since the between-group changes take the form of a *crossover pattern*. That is, at early ages boys are generally shorter than girls but clearly surpass them at later ages.

Admittedly these examples are rather unusual in the sense that few research projects would attempt to study the effect of a treatment on the heights of growing children and choose to use such obviously nonequivalent groups as boys and girls. Yet for these biases to arise, the assignment to treatments does *not* have to be strictly divided according to sex. The assignment procedure need only *favor* the selection of one sex into one of the groups to bias the ANCOVA. Thus, assignment of different proportions of boys and girls to the two groups can produce a bias that is determined by the degree of nonequivalence; the larger the difference in the split between boys and girls in the two groups, the larger the bias.

2. *Trait instability and irrelevance.* Individuals need not undergo drastic change for the ANCOVA to be invalidated. The ANCOVA may be inappropriate even if the overall group performance remains stable over time but, relative to those in their group, individuals exhibit fluctuations in scores from time to time. Lord (1963) has written of a "dynamic equilibrium" which would be involved, for example, when the mean weight of a group remains stable over time but individuals randomly vary about the mean. Such a model might be appropriate for, say, a population of adults measured over a ten-week period. Although the weight of most adults remains relatively stable in the long run, short-term fluctuations are found that reflect changes in eating patterns or the amount of exercise. In

this case, we could imagine that a pretest measure of weight consists of the "true" average weight plus a "random" fluctuation which would be relatively independent of the fluctuation on the posttest ten weeks later. Although these random fluctuations in the pretest are reliable (for all practical purposes, weight can be measured without error), they would function just like measurement error in the pretest and attenuate the estimated regression between posttest and pretest. Then in a nonequivalent group design where selection was based solely on the individual's average true weight, a biased estimate of the treatment effect would result.

The point is that other factors in the pretest besides measurement error can lead to an attenuation in the estimated regression slope and thereby to an underadjustment bias in the treatment effect estimate. Indeed, *any* component of the pretest scores which is unrelated to both the posttest scores and selection differences will tend to produce an underadjustment bias (Cronbach et al., 1977). Measurement error in the pretest is only one such component; random fluctuation in weight is another. Similar instabilities or irrelevant fluctuations undoubtedly are also observed with more behaviorally relevant traits than weight. Indeed, many characteristics—attitudes, personal expenditures on nondurable goods, knowledge of current events, and the like—are probably more likely to fluctuate than weight.

3. *Changing structure of behavior*. Growth is often considered to be univariate. But when complex behaviors are involved, change can be multivariate. Cronbach and Furby (1970, p. 76) conveyed this message to researchers who are concerned with psychological measures:

> Even when [the pretest] and [posttest] are determined by the same operation, they often do not represent the same psychological processes (Lord, 1958). At different stages of practice or development different processes contribute to performance of a task. Nor is this merely a matter of increased complexity; some processes drop out, some remain but contribute nothing to individual differences within an age group, some are replaced by qualitatively different processes.

In other words, behavior is often best described as a combination of various separate and somewhat independent characteristics or processes which become disproportionately important at various times. For instance, voting behavior might be explained as a reaction to a number of different political issues whose relative importance or salience changes over time. Or total consumer expenditure might be explained as a reaction to independent and varying price changes on a number of different commodities.

Not surprisingly, the changing structure of behavior can bias the ANCOVA. Let us provide an example which draws heavily upon the insight in Cronbach et al. (1977).

Imagine using a nonequivalent group design to determine the benefits of a special program of mathematics instruction directed at grade school children. While the operationally identical pretest and posttest were designed to measure mathematical reasoning, factor A, they are also influenced by reading ability, factor B. Let the pretest performance be jointly determined by factors A and B in the

ratio of 1:Ω where, for the sake of this argument, the value of Ω is left unspecified. If Ω is greater than one, reading speed influences performance more than mathematical ability while, if Ω is in between zero and one, the reverse is true. Now suppose that the relative importance of mathematical and reading ability on the posttest is in the ratio of 1:0.25. That is, by the time of the posttest, mathematical reasoning plays a larger role in performance on the test than does reading ability. In this fashion, the example allows the structure of the pretest scores to differ from the structure of the posttest. That is, performance is determined by two factors (mathematical and reading skills) whose relative influence changes over time. Setting Ω equal to different values would allow for different changes. Finally, assume that assignment to treatment conditions tends to separate individuals according to overall true ability, equally weighting reading and mathematical skills. As a result, brighter students generally go into the experimental group and the less bright go into the control condition.

Under these conditions the ANCOVA treatment effect estimate depends upon how the structure of the pretest scores relates to both the structure of the posttest scores and the pattern of selection differences. In particular the bias in the estimate will vary in size depending upon the value of Ω (the relative importance of reading compared to mathematical ability in the pretest) and the amount of measurement error in the pretest.

For example, the relationship of Ω to the bias in the ANCOVA (and ANOVA) is presented in Figure 4.5 both for the case of a pretest with and without measurement error.[8] Several aspects of this plot are worthy of note. Considering a pretest which is measured without error, there are only two values of Ω for which the ANCOVA would lead to an unbiased estimate. First, if $\Omega = 0.25$, the structure of the pretest parallels the reliable portion of the posttest structure. Second, if $\Omega = 1$, the pretest mirrors the selection process (somewhat similar to the circum-

---

[8]The details of this example are as follows. Traits A and B are independent and distributed as N(0,1). The structure of the pretest, X, and posttest, Y, scores are

$$X_i = A_i + \Omega B_i + U_i$$
$$Y_i = A_i + 0.25B_i + V_i$$

where the subscript i references individuals and where the errors of measurement U_i and V_i are $NID(0, \sigma_u^2)$ and $NID(0, \sigma_v^2)$, respectively, and are independent of each other and of A and B. The treatment assignment is represented by a dummy variable

$$T = \begin{cases} 1 & \text{if } (A_i + B_i + 0.1C_i) \geq 0 \\ -1 & \text{if } (A_i + B_i + 0.1C_i) < 0 \end{cases}$$

where C is distributed as $N(0,1)$, is independent of A, B, U, and V, and represents a degree of randomness in the selection process. The estimate of the treatment effect in the ANCOVA becomes effectively

$$\frac{1}{\delta}\left[\frac{(\Omega - .25)(\Omega - 1) + \sigma_u^2(1.25)}{(\delta^{-2} - 2)(1 + \Omega^2) + (1 - \Omega)^2 + \delta^{-2}\sigma_u^2}\right]$$

where $\delta \cong \pi^{1/2}$. While the estimate for the ANOVA model is:

$$\delta(1.25)$$

So assuming that we are dealing with the null case, these formulae represent the bias in the estimates. For the pretest without measurement error, σ_u^2 has been set equal to zero, while for the pretest with measurement error, σ_u^2 has been set equal to one.

stances in the regression-discontinuity design; also see Cain, 1975; Cronbach et al., 1977; Goldberger, 1972b, 1972c; and Kenny, 1975c).

For all other values of Ω the bias is either positive or negative (i.e., under- and overadjustment, respectively), and for extreme values of Ω the ANCOVA is even more biased than the ANOVA (the dotted line). Thus the ANCOVA adjustment based on the pretest may be worse than no adjustment at all. The fact that the region of overadjustment bias in Figure 4.5 is smaller than the region of underadjustment bias should not necessarily lead one to conclude that the former is less likely to arise. This is because the pretest is probably more likely to have an Ω that falls in the region of overadjustment ($.25 < \Omega < 1.00$) than in many other areas.

Adding measurement error to the pretest attenuates the adjustment so that the ANCOVA estimate tends to converge around the ANOVA estimate. With a relatively "large" amount of measurement error (as in the figure), the ANCOVA estimate would be biased for all values of Ω. In other words, the plotted values for the bias do not cross the horizontal axis of zero bias. But with a "moderate" amount of error (not plotted) the attenuating effect of measurement error could

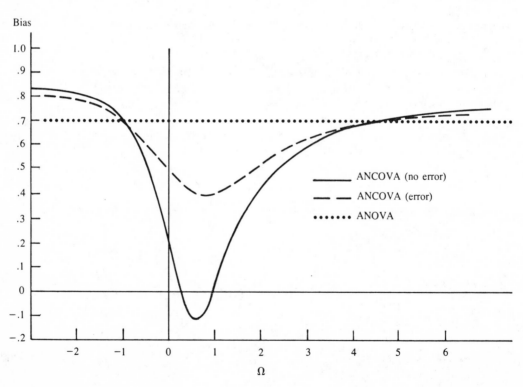

Figure 4.5. Bias in ANCOVA treatment effect estimate as a function of the structure of pretest.

perfectly counterbalance a negative bias from an Ω somewhere between the values of 0.25 and 1.00 and lead to an unbiased estimate.

Given the very elementary model presented here, the most likely specifications (a moderate amount of measurement error in the pretest and $0 < \Omega < 2$, perhaps) would generally lead to an underadjustment. Hence the ANCOVA would probably be preferred to the ANOVA but would most likely still be biased, and the direction of bias could not be taken for granted.

Other complications. Three additional aspects of the analysis warrant attention because they can influence the degree of bias in the ANCOVA. These topics are (1) operationally unique pretest and posttest measures, (2) nonlinear regression lines, and (3) nonparallel regression lines.[9]

1. *Operationally unique pretest and posttest measures.* So far our discussion has emphasized the biasing effects of measurement error in the pretest and change over time when the pretest and posttest are operationally identical measures. Although similar problems can arise when the pretest and posttest are operationally unique, additional complications are also possible. Even if there were no measurement error and no change between the time of the measures, a bias can still arise in the treatment effect estimate because of the nature of the differences between the measures. For example, we might simultaneously measure the age and height of a group of boys and a group of girls and use age as a "pretest" in an ANCOVA to adjust for selection differences in height between the groups. Most likely we would find an intercept difference between the regression lines in the two groups even in the absence of any experimenter-induced treatment. This is because even at the same age boys and girls tend to differ in height. So age by itself does not completely account for all the selection difference in height between boys and girls—not a very surprising finding. But we want to emphasize particularly that this bias arises even though the simultaneous measurement of age and height rules out any time-based change and even though age can be measured with sufficient accuracy to eliminate measurement error of any consequence.

By introducing this additional indictment of operationally unique measures, we do not mean to imply that it is always better to use operationally identical measures since this is not the case. In using a rationale to guide the analysis, one will find that it is the underlying relationship between the measures and not their nominal characteristics that is most important. The point of the discussion is merely the obvious one that an ANCOVA with an operationally unique pretest can also be biased.

2. *Nonlinear regression lines.* There is, of course, no guarantee that, as assumed by the standard ANCOVA model, the true regression lines will be linear (i.e., *straight* lines). Indeed, growth between the pretest and posttest, differences between operationally unique measures, and measurement error in the pretest (Lindley, 1947; Cochran, 1970) can each make the regression lines nonlinear

---

[9]We do not consider another complicating case where the pretest is measured after or during the treatment implementation so that it might be affected by the treatment. Cochran (1957) and Smith (1957) provide a discussion of this circumstance and show why interpretation of the results from the ANCOVA can be extremely difficult.

(i.e., curved). When the regression surface is nonlinear, use of the standard ANCOVA model can lead to different results from those obtained with a "better fitting" ANCOVA model which properly takes account of nonlinearity (Cochran and Rubin, 1973; and Rubin, 1973b). But while many nonlinearities can be adequately fit by making adjustments to the standard ANCOVA model (see footnote 3), even the best-fitting model does not necessarily lead to an unbiased estimate of the treatment effect since spurious intercept differences are still a possibility. For example, within a group of boys or girls the regression of posttest on pretest height may be curved rather than linear. But even after planning the analysis to conform to a curved regression surface, a spurious intercept difference would probably still be found since boys, even when starting out at the same height as girls, tend to grow faster.

3. *Nonparallel regression lines.* Other difficulties arise because of nonparallel regression surfaces in the two groups. The standard ANCOVA model assumes parallel regressions but can be easily adapted to handle nonparallel regressions, as demonstrated in footnote 3 (which also discusses some of the difficulties of interpretation that arise with this alteration). But as with the nonlinear case, allowing for nonparallel regressions does not eliminate the possibility of bias in the estimate of the main effect of the treatment. In addition, it is generally difficult in quasi-experimental research to reach appropriate conclusions about the cause of the non-parallel regressions.

In the random experiment, nonparallel regression surfaces can often be unambiguously attributed to a treatment interaction effect whereby the impact of the treatment varies across the levels of the pretest scores. With equivalent groups the major rival hypothesis for a treatment interaction is a floor or ceiling effect. But since these effects generally alter the shape of the distributions of the scores by making them skewed, the data can be examined to assess the plausibility of this alternate explanation. So in the absence of evidence for a floor or ceiling effect, significantly different regression slopes in the two groups can be reasonably interpreted as evidence of a treatment effect interaction.

Interpreting nonparallel regression surfaces is more problematic with nonequivalent groups. This is because the difference in slopes could be due not only to ceiling and floor effects but also to differential growth between the groups, or to differences between the groups in the reliability of the pretest measurement, as well as to the treatment having a differential impact across levels of the pretest. Indeed, we believe that "spurious" interactions are likely to be present in nonequivalent groups. Since one cannot always discriminate between these multiple causes by examining the data, separating out the treatment-related portion of an observed interaction will be difficult in practice.

Analysis of Covariance with Multiple Covariates

The Model

The ANCOVA model can easily be extended to include multiple pretest measures or covariates. In other words, a number of different pretreatment measures could have been collected on each individual and each of these mea-

sures could be included in the ANCOVA model.[10] Intuitively, the inclusion of multiple covariates produces an adjustment for initial group differences on each of the measured traits just as an adjustment was produced by the ANCOVA with a single pretest. The only difference as compared to the simple ANCOVA is that now the adjustment is done simultaneously on several measures rather than on just one. The treatment effect estimate is still based on the difference between the regression line intercepts in the two groups, but now the regression lines are calculated using all the pretest measures simultaneously.

There are two reasons why one might want to incorporate multiple covariates in the ANCOVA. First, just as the ANCOVA with a single pretest can increase the power of the analysis as compared to the ANOVA, the inclusion of multiple pretests in the ANCOVA can increase the power of the analysis as compared to the ANCOVA with a single pretest. Of course, one must be careful here since adding pretests which are completely unrelated to the posttest will actually *decrease* the precision. These pretests add nothing to the analysis, yet each one subtracts one degree of freedom from the error term. Nonetheless, if carefully chosen, additional pretests can substantially increase the power of the analysis. Second, by including additional pretests, one can make a further adjustment for initial group differences on these variables. This is one way to improve the model and hopefully arrive at less biased estimates of the treatment effect. For example, the researcher may realize that because of differential growth between the groups, an ANCOVA with a single pretest is likely to be biased. But the researcher may be able to collect a measure which predicts the differential growth. By including that measure in the ANCOVA along with the original pretest, the analysis could—theoretically—take account of both initial differences in ability and initial differences in growth rates, providing an unbiased treatment effect estimate. Of course, in practice there is still a good possibility that even the multiple pretest ANCOVA is biased.

Bias

The sources of bias in the ANCOVA with multiple covariates are essentially the same as in the ANCOVA with a single covariate so we shall touch upon them only briefly. Measurement error and other forms of irrelevant variance in any one of the pretest measures can again bias the treatment effect estimate. But unlike the case of a single covariate, adding measurement error to one covariate when there are several does *not* necessarily shift the estimate

---

[10]Algebraically, the model is

(3)
  (a) $Y_{ij} = \mu + \alpha_i + \beta_1(X_{1ij} - \bar{X}_{1..}) + \beta_2 (X_{2ij} - \bar{X}_{2..}) + \ldots + \beta_{K..}(X_{K..ij} - \bar{X}_{K..}) + \epsilon_{ij}$
  (b) $\epsilon_{ij} \sim NID\ (0, \sigma\epsilon^2)$
  (c) If the X's are stochastic, they are independent of error, ϵ

where β_k and $X_{kij}(\kappa = 1, \ldots, \kappa)$ are the regression coefficients and multiple covariates, respectively. All other symbols are defined as before. Nonlinear and nonparallel regression can be specified by adding terms for each covariate as was done in the case of a single covariate (see footnote 3). The treatment effect estimate is:

$$\hat{\alpha}_E - \hat{\alpha}_C = (\bar{Y}_E. - \bar{Y}_C.) - \hat{\beta}_1(\bar{X}_{1E}. - \bar{X}_{1C}.) - \hat{\beta}_2(\bar{X}_{2E}. - \bar{X}_{2C}.) - \ldots - \hat{\beta}_K(\bar{X}_{KE}. - \bar{X}_{KC}.)$$

toward an underadjustment. This can be intuitively appreciated by once again considering the case of ANCOVA with a single covariate. There we saw that adding random measurement error to the covariate shifts the estimate toward an underadjustment in a manner such that the estimate becomes more similar to that of the ANOVA where no covariate is used at all. Indeed, adding more and more error to the covariate brings the ANCOVA estimate closer and closer to that of the ANOVA. In other words, adding measurement error to a covariate is akin to removing the covariate from the analysis.

The same thing happens in the multiple covariate case, only there, adding measurement error to one covariate shifts the estimate toward the value that would be obtained if that covariate were removed from the model but all the other covariates remained.[11] To see how this can result in a shift toward an overadjustment bias, imagine that when all the covariates are perfectly measured and included in the ANCOVA model, the result is unbiased. Further, suppose that if one covariate is removed, the estimate is an overadjustment. This is not unreasonable since overadjustment biases are possible in the multiple covariate case just as they are in the single covariate case. Then if the omitted covariate is included in the model but with measurement error, adding more and more error will lead to more and more of an *overadjustment* bias in the treatment effect estimate.

Perhaps an artificial example will help fix the idea. Assume that the posttest scores, *Y,* are determined in equal proportion by two independent and reliable

---

[11]To prove this algebraically, assume that in matrix notation

$$Y_{N \times 1} = Z_{N \times 1}\beta_{1 \times 1} + X_{N \times K}\Gamma_{K \times 1} + \epsilon_{N \times 1}$$

where Y is the matrix of posttest scores, Z is the matrix of the scores on the one covariate singled out to receive random measurement error, X is the matrix of scores on the K covariates including the treatment assignment, β and Γ are matrices of regression coefficients, and ϵ is the matrix of residuals. Then the (OLS) estimates of the parameters are

$$\begin{bmatrix} \hat{\beta} \\ \hdots \\ \hat{\Gamma} \end{bmatrix} = \begin{bmatrix} Q & Z'X \\ \hdotsfor{2} \\ X'Z & X'X \end{bmatrix}^{-1} \begin{bmatrix} Z'Y \\ \hdots \\ X'Y \end{bmatrix}$$

where $Q = Z'Z + \sigma^2$, and σ^2 is the variance due to additional random measurement error in Z. After some tedious but straightforward algebra, the estimates can be shown to equal

$$\begin{bmatrix} \hat{\beta} \\ \hdots \\ \hat{\Gamma} \end{bmatrix} = \begin{bmatrix} \dfrac{Z'Y - Z'CY}{Q - Z'CZ} \\ \hdotsfor{1} \\ DY + \dfrac{DZZ'CY - DZZ'Y}{Q - Z'CZ} \end{bmatrix}$$

where $C = X(X'X)^{-1}X'$ and $D = (X'X)^{-1}X'$. Clearly, as σ^2 gets larger, $\hat{\beta}$ approaches zero and $\hat{\Gamma}$ approaches DY which is the OLS estimate from the model with Z excluded.

From this result, it is also possible to show that $\hat{\Gamma}$ approaches DY monotonically as σ^2 increases. By definition,

$$\begin{aligned} Q - Z'CZ &= \sigma^2 + Z'(I - C)Z \\ &= \sigma^2 + Z'(I - C)(I - C)'Z \quad \text{[because } (I - C) \text{ is idempotent]} \\ &= \sigma^2 + F'F \end{aligned}$$

where $F' = Z'(I - C)$. Substituting this result into the estimate of Γ, it can be seen that $\hat{\Gamma}$ changes monotonically with σ^2 since $F'F$ is always nonnegative.

	Y	T	$X_1{}^*$	$X_2{}^*$	X_1	X_2
Y	1.00					
T	.46	1.00				
$X_1{}^*$	.70	.77	1.00			
$X_2{}^*$	.77	.36	.65	1.00		
X_1	.59	.65	.84	.54	1.00	
X_2	.65	.30	.54	.84	.46	1.00

Table 4.1 Hypothetical correlation matrix for covariates with and without measurement error.

factors and by random measurement error, and that the treatment assignment— the dummy variable T—is determined solely by one of these factors. Further, assume that two covariates, $X_1{}^*$ and $X_2{}^*$, are available which are determined in unequal proportion by these same two factors. In particular, $X_1{}^*$ is more heavily influenced by the factor that determines the treatment assignment than by the other factor, and $X_2{}^*$ is the converse. Finally, assume that $X_1{}^*$ and $X_2{}^*$ are measured without error but that X_1 and X_2 are also available and are identical to $X_1{}^*$ and $X_2{}^*$, respectively, except that they contain random measurement error. We shall set the reliability of X_1 and X_2 equal to 0.7. Table 4.1 presents a possible correlation matrix for variables such as these. The following results are based upon this matrix assuming that it contains population values.[12]

Assume for the sake of this illustration that there is no treatment effect so that the expected value of an unbiased treatment effect estimate will equal zero. If the variances of Y and T are set equal to one, the treatment effect estimate in the ANOVA is 0.92, which is an underadjustment. An ANCOVA using $X_1{}^*$ as a single covariate gives a treatment effect estimate of -0.41,

---

[12]Table 4.1 was generated by assuming

$$Y_i = A_i + B_i + \epsilon_{Yi}$$

$$T_i = \begin{cases} 1 \text{ if } B_i \geq 0 \\ -1 \text{ if } B_i < 0 \end{cases}$$

$$X_{1i}{}^* = .25A_i + B_i$$

$$X_{2i}{}^* = 2A_i + B_i$$

$$X_{1i} = .25A_i + B_i + \epsilon_{1i}$$

$$X_{2i} = 2A_i + B_i + \epsilon_{2i}$$

where i references individuals, A and B are the reliable factors, the ϵ's are measurement errors, and all are normally distributed and independent of one another. The variances of A, B, and ϵ_Y were all set to be equal. The variances of ϵ_1 and ϵ_2 were set so that X_1 and X_2 had reliabilities equal to 0.7. The correlation between X_1 and $X_1{}^*$ and between X_2 and $X_2{}^*$ is then equal to the square root of the reliability, or 0.84.

which is obviously an overadjustment. On the other hand, an ANCOVA using X_2^* as a single covariate gives a treatment effect estimate of 0.42 which, while an underadjustment, is less so than the ANOVA estimate.

If both the perfectly measured covariates, X_1^* and X_2^*, are used in the ANCOVA, the treatment effect estimate equals zero and so is unbiased. But if either covariate is measured with error, the estimate is biased and the bias can be in either direction. That is, X_1 and X_2^* generate a treatment effect estimate in the ANCOVA of 0.27, while X_1^* and X_2 generate a treatment effect estimate in the ANCOVA of -0.18. Thus adding measurement error to one covariate shifts the estimate toward an overadjustment while adding it to the other shifts the estimate toward an underadjustment.

This same logic can be used to show that if enough measurement error is added to *all* of the covariates, the ANCOVA estimate eventually converges toward that of the ANOVA. This is simply because adding sufficient measurement error to all the covariates eventually has the same effect as if they were all removed from the model. But in the short run, measurement error in the multiple covariate case can lead to overadjustment as well as underadjustment biases.

Even if all the covariates are measured without error (which seems unlikely), the analysis can still be biased. The examples of bias caused by change between the time of the pretest and posttest in the ANCOVA with a single covariate are not directly applicable to the multiple covariate ANCOVA, but the nature of the bias is the same. Probably the best explanation is that a bias in the ANCOVA with multiple covariates can arise because the analysis does not take into account the effect of *all* selection differences between the groups. In other words, while the covariates that are included in the model control for the effects of initial differences on some characteristics, they do not control for initial differences on other critical dimensions. And depending upon the nature of the differences that are overlooked, the bias in the analyses can either be an overadjustment or an underadjustment.

For example, a researcher might want to determine how effective driver education classes are in promoting safe driving. The posttest measure of interest might be the number of traffic violations for which each individual is cited during the first year after obtaining a driver's license. An operationally identical pretest would not be of much use here since few individuals would have received any tickets, say, for speeding during the year prior to receiving a driver's license. Instead, the researcher would have to rely on a series of operationally unique pretests which, hopefully, would account for all the relevant differences between those who attended the classes and those who did not.

At this point, we can only speculate about the traits on which these two groups of individuals might differ and which would also lead to differences in the number of traffic violations. Perhaps those who take a course in driver education are more motivated to be safe drivers, or are more fearful of accidents, or are more law-abiding and so feel more compelled to learn all the proper procedures, or are more interested in lowering their insurance costs (if completing the course provides a discount), than those who do not attend such classes. On the surface, all of these presumed group differences would appear to make

the class participants safer drivers than the nonparticipants regardless of the effect of the driver education course. Thus these differences should be taken into account in comparing the two groups lest the course appear to be more beneficial than it really is.

We can well imagine, then, the researcher setting out to measure these variables and performing an ANCOVA using all of the measures as covariates. Even if the variables were measured without error, would the treatment effect be unbiased? Or is it possible that the researcher overlooked one or more critical variables? Perhaps, the groups also differ in ways that, if ignored, would tend to make the driver education course look less beneficial than it really is. For instance, perhaps those who attend the course do so because they are unskilled at such tasks and realize that they need help. Or perhaps those who attend will end up driving more frequently than those who do not attend. In both cases, those who attend would have been more likely to be involved in, say, car accidents than those who do not attend even if the driver education class had not been offered. Thus ignoring these group differences could lead to an underestimate of the effect of the treatment. This could be a case then where the researcher would have controlled for the effect of some but not all of the relevant selection differences between the groups.

A researcher might try to overcome this problem by including in the model all available variables in the hope that this accounts for most of the selection differences. Such a strategy not only ignores the problem of measurement error and irrelevance but implies, in the extreme, that every possible characteristic should be measured and included in the model. Even if such a measurement could be made, an infinite number of variables cannot be included in a statistical analysis which has only a finite number of respondents. It would seem better to follow one of the rationales presented below which provides the logic for choosing variables to measure and for designing a statistical model with which to use them.

Analysis of Variance with Blocking or Matching

The Model for a Single Pretest

We begin by considering blocking or matching with a single pretest. When using blocking or matching in a randomized experiment, individuals are first ranked and then separated into groups (blocks or pairs) according to their pretest scores. The individuals within each block or pair are then randomly assigned to treatment conditions. For example, if a total of 40 individuals are available for a study with two treatment conditions, respondents could be divided into five blocks of eight each, with four individuals within each block being randomly assigned to each of the treatment conditions. Alternatively, the individuals could be matched to make 20 pairs with one individual from each pair then being randomly assigned to each treatment. There are, of course, still other ways of dividing up the individuals prior to random assignment.

In the nonequivalent group design, individuals are blocked or matched on the basis of pretest performance *after* the groups have been formed. Thus, in blocking, individuals in the experimental and control groups are separately

ranked and placed into groups that have similar pretest scores. For example, one block might contain all those with scores from 1 to 4, while another block would contain those with scores from 5 to 8, and so forth. Individuals are discarded from the analysis if they belong to a block that has no respondents from the other treatment condition. As in the randomized case, block membership is then entered into the statistical analysis together with the treatment assignment, so that the effects of the treatment, the blocks, and their interaction can be tested.[13] Specifically, the treatment effect is estimated from the posttest difference between the treatment groups within each block.

In matching, individuals are paired so that, according to some criterion, they have comparable pretest scores. Again, individuals are discarded if reasonable matches cannot be found. The pair assignment is then used as a factor in the data analysis, but there is no test for the interaction of the treatment across levels of the pretest.[14] The treatment effect is estimated from the posttest difference between pairs.

In the randomized experiment, it is easy to see that, by separating out the effects of the blocks and interactions, the randomized block design can substantially increase the power of the analysis as compared to the elementary ANOVA

---

[13]Algebraically, the model is

(4)

$$\text{(a)} \quad Y_{ijk} = \mu + \alpha_i + \beta_j + (\alpha\beta)_{ij} + \epsilon_{ijk}$$

$$\text{(b)} \quad \epsilon_{ijk} \sim NID(0, \sigma_\epsilon^2)$$

where the block effects β_j represent mean differences in posttest performance between the blocks and the interaction terms $(\alpha\beta)_{ij}$ represent any variable effect of the treatment across blocks. The subscript j references the blocks, k refers to individuals within block-treatment cells while, as before, i indexes treatment groups. The estimate of the treatment effect depends on the nature of the blocking and the (somewhat arbitrary) restrictions placed on the parameters. When the block-treatment cells have equal sample sizes, the standard restrictions are that the block and interaction effects sum to zero [$\Sigma_j\beta_j = 0$, $\Sigma_j(\alpha\beta)_{ij} = 0$ for all i, and $\Sigma_i(\alpha\beta)_{ij} = 0$ for all j]. Under these conditions, the treatment effect estimate becomes

$$\hat{\alpha}_E - \hat{\alpha}_C = (\overline{Y}_{E..} - \overline{Y}_{C..})$$

There are other common forms of blocking, however. In stratification each treatment group contributes equal size samples to each block, but sample sizes can vary across blocks. In this case the above estimate is generally still used for the treatment main effect. On the other hand, in subclassification the sample sizes from each treatment condition are not necessarily equal even within a block. The treatment effect estimate is usually based on a weighted sum of the mean differences in each block

$$\hat{\alpha}_E - \hat{\alpha}_C = \Sigma_j W_j(\overline{Y}_{Ej.} - \overline{Y}_{Cj.})$$

where W_j is the weight ($\Sigma_j W_j = 1$) chosen to minimize the variance of the estimate (cf. Cochran, 1965).

The consequences of violating the distributional assumptions (4b) in the block design are effectively the same as in the elementary ANOVA, and the reader is referred to the references cited in that discussion (particularly Scheffé, 1959).

[14]Matching is simply blocking taken to an extreme where each pair becomes a separate block. However, with only one individual in each block per treatment condition, the model for the blocking analysis (footnote 13) must be somewhat modified since the interaction term $(\alpha\beta)_{ij}$ cannot be distinguished from the individual error term ϵ_{ijk}. The result is that no test for an interaction can be made. In the case where there are only two treatment conditions, the analysis effectively reduces to the pair difference t test, and the estimate of the treatment effect becomes

$$\hat{\alpha}_E - \hat{\alpha}_C = \overline{Y}_{E.} - \overline{Y}_{C.}$$

where the means are calculated only for those individuals who have been matched.

without blocking. Myers (1972) provides a general comparison of the difference in precision between these two methods while Feldt (1958) demonstrates how the error variance in the blocking strategy decreases as the pretest-posttest correlation increases and the heterogeneity of pretest scores within a block decreases.[15] One way to decrease the error variance is to increase the number of blocks, since this decreases the variance of the pretest scores within a block.

A reasonable appraisal of efficiency, however, must also take into account the number of degrees of freedom in the error term. As the number of blocks increases, the degrees of freedom in the error term decrease, which decreases the power of the F test. Thus an increase in the number of blocks has two countervailing effects on efficiency, and as a result, maximum efficiency is obtained with a finite number of blocks. This number depends upon the pretest-posttest correlation, the number of treatment groups, and the sample size. The reader is referred to Feldt (1958) and Myers (1972) for a thorough discussion of this matter and for the means of determining the optimum number of blocks for given research settings.

Taking the preceding comments into consideration, it is also possible to compare the efficiency of the randomized block design to that of the ANCOVA in the context of true experiments. Assuming that the regression surfaces in the two groups are linear and parallel and that the optimal number of blocks has been chosen, Feldt (1958) takes differences in degrees of freedom into account and concludes that for within-group pretest-posttest correlations of between 0 and .4 the treatment effect estimate in the block design is more precise than in the ANCOVA. This conclusion is reversed when the correlation is larger than .6 (see also Cox, 1957).

In the nonequivalent group design, it is not as easy to compare the relative precision of blocking and ANCOVA. As we noted above, the ANCOVA loses precision as the mean pretest difference between the groups increases. But it can be seen from the discussion below that, as this mean difference increases, so does the number of individuals who have to be dropped from the blocking design because there are no respondents from the other treatment group with comparable pretest scores. This decrease in sample size obviously reduces the precision of the treatment effect estimate in the block design, and it is not yet clear for the nonequivalent case when ANCOVA offers more precision than blocking and vice versa.

---

[15]Feldt (1958) assumes that the treatment and the blocking variable do not interact and that the regressions of Y on X within each group are linear. His derivation also takes into account the fact that in most practical applications of the blocked design error variances will differ across blocks, thereby violating the assumption of homoscedasticity. To allow for this, Feldt denotes the average error variance in the blocked design by $\bar{\sigma}_\epsilon^2$ and shows that it relates to the error variance in the elementary ANOVA, σ_Y^2, by the formula

$$\bar{\sigma}_\epsilon^2 = \sigma_Y^2[1 - \rho_{XY}^2(1 - \frac{\bar{\sigma}_X^2}{\sigma_X^2})]$$

where ρ_{XY} is the (within-treatment-group) pretest-posttest correlation, $\bar{\sigma}_X^2$ is the average variance of the pretest scores within the blocks, and σ_X^2 is the overall pretest variance. Thus, the larger the correlation ρ_{XY} and the smaller the average heterogeneity of pretest scores within a block, $\bar{\sigma}_X^2$, the smaller is the average error variance in the block design.

However, there are some undeniable advantages to using the block design instead of either the elementary ANOVA or the ANCOVA. Compared to the elementary ANOVA, the block design permits the additional test of whether the treatment and blocks interact. Compared to the ANCOVA, blocking does not require the researcher to specify the general shape of the regression of posttest on pretest scores, since, as specified, the block and interaction effects can adapt to any shape.

Bias

The intuitive reason for using a blocking or matching strategy in the nonequivalent group design is straightforward. Since the groups are nonequivalent, they cannot be directly compared. But if we compare only those individuals from the two groups who have similar pretest scores, then it appears as if we are controlling for initial selection differences. However, a number of biases are likely to arise, and to understand them we must examine the estimate of the treatment effect in greater detail.

Let us begin by considering the pair-matching procedure where the researcher pairs an individual from the experimental group with an individual from the control group so that, according to some criterion, they have comparable pretest scores. When dealing with nonequivalent groups, this procedure generally entails omitting some individuals from the analysis because reasonable matches cannot be found. Moreover, the omission of individuals tends to be systematic. This can be seen in Figure 4.6 where the populations of scores from the two groups are represented by ellipses. Obviously, individuals in the experimental group with pretest scores *below* X_a cannot be matched with anyone from the control group since no one in that group has a pretest score below X_a. Conversely, matches cannot be found for individuals in the control group who have pretest scores *above* X_b.

Because of this systematic dropping of individuals, the estimate of the treatment effect with matched-pair samples tends to differ systematically from that of the elementary ANOVA where individuals are not discarded. In most situations, the expected value of the treatment effect estimate in the matching strategy also differs from the expected value of the treatment effect estimate in the ANCOVA with the single pretest as covariate. But the difference is often small because pair-matching and ANCOVA are very similar. Indeed, the expected values of the treatment effect estimates in matching and ANCOVA are identical when the true regression lines in the two treatment groups are linear and parallel and when matching uses pairs whose observed pretest scores match exactly.

This equivalence is demonstrated in Figure 4.6 where parallel linear regression lines pass through the data. Taking the thin slice of all individuals who have pretest scores exactly equal to X' (as in Figure 4.6), the expected value of the posttest difference between matched pairs is simply the expected difference between the posttest scores at that value of X (labeled $\bar{Y}_{CX}'.$ and $\bar{Y}_{EX}'.$). Since the regression lines pass through these same points, the difference between the expected posttest scores at X' also represents the displacement (intercept difference) between the regressions. Indeed, given the assumption of linear and parallel regressions, the displacement between the lines and the expected matched-pair difference will be the same for *any* value of X. Thus by selecting individuals

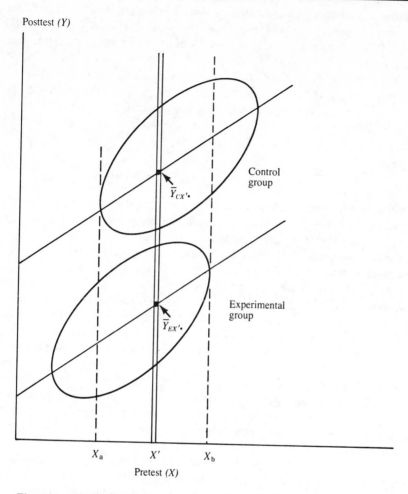

Posttest (Y)

Control
group

$\overline{Y}_{CX'\bullet}$

Experimental
group

$\overline{Y}_{EX'\bullet}$

X_a X' X_b

Pretest (X)

Figure 4.6. Demonstration of systematic discarding of individuals from matching analysis and a comparison of matching to ANCOVA.

who are perfectly matched on the basis of observed pretest ability, one is "physically equating" nonequivalent groups in the same manner as the ANCOVA "statistically equates" them.

In practice, however, the situation is less salutary because it is generally difficult to find exact matches (i.e., individuals from each group with identical scores on the pretest). Instead, the researcher has to be satisfied with using matches which are close but not perfect. As a result of imperfect matching, less of an adjustment for preexisting differences is obtained with matching than with the ANCOVA, and so more underadjustment tends to result. In fact, assuming parallel linear regressions, Cochran and Rubin (1973; Rubin, 1973a, 1973b) demonstrate that the estimate of the treatment effect from pair-matching tends to lie between the estimates from ANCOVA and ANOVA.

Cochran and Rubin (1973) have examined several different pair-matching schemes and have provided calculations which indicate the extent of the adjustment made by each method. Take, for instance, caliper-matching where individuals are chosen to form a pair if their pretest scores are as close as, or closer than, a given number of units. We shall designate this interval as C. Assuming that the standard ANCOVA would remove *all* of the bias created by selection differences, the amount of *bias reduction* provided by caliper-matching depends upon the ratio of the width of the caliper interval, C, to the standard deviation of the pretest scores within the treatment groups, σ_X. For selection differences of "moderate" size, some rough figures are:

C/σ_X	1	.8	.6	.4	.2
bias reduction	76%	84%	90%	95%	99%

(Cochran, 1972). Hence with a tight caliper-matching (e.g., where $C/\sigma_X = .2$), one would remove virtually all the bias (conditional, of course, on the very strict assumption that the ANCOVA estimate is itself unbiased!).

Other pair-matching strategies are available, but are probably best suited for application where one of the groups (most likely the control group) has a large number of individuals who can be treated as a reservoir from which to choose matches for the other group. Under the same conditions outlined for caliper-matching, these methods also tend to underadjust compared to the ANCOVA.

Let us now consider blocking. This is most widely used when the pretest is categorical (e.g., membership in political parties) though it is still applicable, of course, when the pretest is continuous and scores are grouped (e.g., scores between 1 and 4 are in one block, from 5 to 8 in another, and so forth). All scores which fall into the same block are then considered, in essence, to be matched. Consequently, it should not be surprising to note that the result of a blocking analysis is similar to that from both pair-matching and ANCOVA (assuming parallel linear regressions).

But blocking tends to provide even less of an adjustment for group nonequivalence than does pair-matching. Assuming, once again, that the ANCOVA would be unbiased, the amount of bias removed varies with the number of blocks. For "moderate" selection differences, the relationship is roughly:

number of blocks	2	3	4	5	6
bias removed	64%	79%	86%	90%	92%

(Cochran, 1968a). Thus, as the number of blocks increases, the effectiveness of the blocking strategy approaches that of the ANCOVA. Cochran and Rubin (1973; Cochran, 1965, 1968a) provide further discussion of these methods in regard to both bias and relative precision.

The obvious drawback to blocking and matching strategies is that under conditions of linear homogeneous regressions, they merely converge on the same result as the ANCOVA. The case where the regressions are not linear and parallel is somewhat more complex. Suffice it to say here that, in this case, the blocking and matching strategies converge on the same result that is obtainable from a modified ANCOVA which properly takes account of nonlinear and nonparallel regressions (see footnote 3 and the section "Other complications"). Thus, the same biases

that are present in the ANCOVA will also be present in matching and blocking methods. In particular, as in the ANCOVA, random measurement error in the pretest reduces the adjustment made by matching in direct proportion to the pretest reliability (Cochran, 1968a; Cochran and Rubin, 1973). Thorndike (1942) described this problem as a regression artifact. Individuals from nonequivalent groups who are matched on the basis of a fallible pretest would not be matched on the posttest because the posttest scores would have regressed toward their respective group means, giving the false appearance of a treatment effect.

This regression artifact can be demonstrated in the same manner used to show that measurement error leads to a bias in the ANCOVA. (Campbell and Erlebacher, 1970, and Campbell and Boruch, 1975, provide a description of this regression artifact from a different perspective using simulated examples.)

Referring back to Figure 4.4, it will be recalled that, with the outcomes illustrated in 4.4(a), the ANCOVA would find no treatment effect. As the scores are plotted in that panel, matching would be impossible because the pretest scores in the two groups do not overlap. One can well imagine, however, that if the pretest scores did overlap (i.e., if the plots for the two groups were moved toward each other along the common regression line), an effective matching strategy would lead to the same conclusion of no treatment effect. Next, consider 4.4(b) where measurement error has been added to the *posttest*. Again, the ANCOVA would conclude that there is no treatment effect, and matching would again be impossible since the pretest scores still do not overlap.

Finally, consider 4.4(c) where measurement error has been added to the pretest. Here, matching would be feasible since some individuals in the control group have the same *observed* pretest score as some individuals in the experimental group. But these individuals are obviously not matched on the basis of their true ability since, as we have seen in 4.4(a), the *true* pretest scores from the two groups do not overlap. Rather, the matching is based on the measurement error, and the direction of the measurement error in the matched pairs is different in the two groups. That is, the matched individuals from the more able experimental group have negative errors, while those from the lower-ability control group have positive errors. On the posttest, however, the scores of these "matched" individuals will regress toward their true ability, producing a difference between the pairs which favors the more able experimental group. This is because the posttest scores are uninfluenced by the measurement error in the pretest, and this measurement error was the only reason why the individuals appeared similar to begin with. Thus the posttest scores will reveal the true nature of the difference in ability between the two groups of individuals, thereby producing a spurious treatment effect estimate in the matching strategy, just as a spurious intercept difference arises in the ANCOVA.

In a similar fashion, each of the other biases in the ANCOVA can be shown to have a counterpart in the matching or blocking analysis. In addition, matching and blocking have two practical drawbacks. First, the question of how close the matches have to be (or how many blocks must be used) to have an "effective" strategy cannot always be clearly answered in practice. In other words, is removing 95% of the bias (as compared to the ANCOVA) necessary for an effective strategy or is 90% bias reduction sufficient? The application of the ANCOVA is

far less ambiguous. And second, when no overlap occurs between the groups on the pretest scores, matching and blocking cannot be done. Even when there is some overlap, there may not be *enough* for an effective analysis. On the other hand, blocking and matching can be very useful alternatives to ANCOVA when the shape of the regression surface is either unknown or difficult to model. This is because, as we noted, blocking and matching do not require that this shape be specified.

Blocking and Matching with Multiple Pretests

As with ANCOVA, blocking and matching can be used with several pretest measures. In this case, individuals are blocked or matched on all of the variables simultaneously so that individuals who are matched or put in the same block have similar scores on all of the pretest measures. Once again, it is the posttest difference between the treatment groups within the matched pairs or blocks that is the basis of the treatment effect estimate.[16]

The similarity between matching and ANCOVA for the case of a single pretest directly carries over to the case of multiple pretests. That is, an effective matching or blocking analysis using multiple pretests converges on the same result as a multiple covariate ANCOVA which properly takes account of nonlinearities and interactions. So the biases in the ANCOVA will again be shared by matching or blocking. However, an additional complication arises with matching and blocking on several variables. It becomes increasingly difficult to find close matches as the number of matching variables increases, and using inexact matches can again provide an underadjustment as compared to ANCOVA. For this reason, it is often easier to implement effectively an ANCOVA strategy than a blocking or matching analysis when using multiple pretests.

Analysis of Variance with Gain Scores

The Model for Simple Gain Score Analysis

An analysis of variance using gain scores examines the difference, or change, in performance from the pretest to the posttest. The basic assumption is that a treatment effect would lead to more (or less) change in the experimental group than in the control group. The model for the analysis is identical to the elementary ANOVA except that the gain score (posttest minus pretest) is the dependent variable rather than just the posttest alone.[17] Hence, the gain

---

[16]The algebraic model for blocking or matching with multiple pretests is a straightforward expansion of the model for a single pretest, though with numerous pretests the full model can become quite elaborate. Appropriate models and estimates of treatment effects are provided in discussions of factorial designs in most texts on analysis of variance. Rubin (1976a, 1976b) also provides a useful analytic discussion of multivariate matching.

[17]Algebraically, the gain score model is:

$$\text{(a) } Y_{ij} - X_{ij} = \mu + \alpha_i + \epsilon_{ij}$$

(5)

$$\text{(b) } \epsilon_{ij} \sim NID (0, \sigma\epsilon^2)$$

where X represents the pretest scores and the other variables, parameters, and subscripts are as labeled in the elementary ANOVA model (footnote 1). Concerns for the distributional assumptions (5b) are

score model looks for differences in mean *change* between the two groups rather than differences in mean *posttest scores*. The result is that in the nonequivalent group design, except under special conditions, the gain score analysis tests a different null hypothesis than the elementary ANOVA. Similarly, the expected value of the treatment effect estimate in the gain score analysis generally differs from that in ANCOVA and blocking or matching.[18]

In the randomized experiment, the gain score analysis is generally less precise than either the ANCOVA or the matching or blocking analysis.[19] Indeed, the gain score analysis may very well be *less* precise than the elementary ANOVA on posttest scores alone.[20] However, in the nonequivalent group design, the precision of the gain score analysis is not related to the size of the mean pretest difference between groups, as is precision in the ANCOVA and blocking or matching. Which analysis is most precise when used with nonequivalent groups, therefore, depends heavily upon the particular circumstances of the research project.

A weakness of the gain score analysis as presented here is that, like the elementary ANOVA, it does not provide a test for the presence of an interaction of the treatment with the pretest. Nonetheless, other variables could be added to the gain score model, in the same manner as they would be added to the ANCOVA model, to provide tests for interaction of the treatment with

---

similar to those for the ANOVA model, and the references cited in that discussion are also appropriate here. The estimate of the treatment effect in the gain score analysis is:

$$\hat{\alpha}_E - \hat{\alpha}_C = (\bar{Y}_{E.} - \bar{Y}_{C.}) - (\bar{X}_{E.} - \bar{X}_{C.})$$

The same test for the presence of a treatment effect could be obtained in a repeated measures ANOVA where the treatment effect is represented by the interaction of treatment groups and time of testing (cf. Porter and Chibucos, 1974). In passing, we might also note that if gain scores are used as the dependent variable in the ANCOVA, in place of the posttest scores, the same estimate of a treatment effect is obtained as in the original ANCOVA (cf. Werts and Linn, 1970).

[18]This can be seen by comparing the treatment effect estimate of the gain score analysis in footnote 17 with the estimate of the ANCOVA in footnote 2.

[19]Assuming that there is no treatment effect interaction, the error variance in the gain score analysis, σ_ϵ^2, is related to the error variance in the elementary ANOVA on posttest scores, σ_Y^2, as

$$\sigma_\epsilon^2 = \sigma_Y^2(1 - \rho_{XY}^2) + (1 - \beta)^2\sigma_X^2$$

where ρ_{XY} is the pretest-posttest correlation, σ_X^2 is the variance of the pretest scores, and β is the linear regression coefficient of Y on X, all within groups (see Porter, 1973; Porter and Chibucos, 1974). Thus *if* $\beta = 1$, the gain score analysis would have error variance

$$\sigma_\epsilon^2 = \sigma_Y^2(1 - \rho_{XY}^2)$$

which would lead to a *more precise* estimate of the treatment effect than either ANCOVA (see footnote 4) or the blocking or matching design (assuming the regression surfaces are linear, see footnote 15). However, as the first equation above also reveals, the precision of the gain score analysis is greatly reduced as β departs from the value of unity. In the true experiment, unless β is very close to 1, both the ANCOVA and the blocking or matching analysis will have greater precision than the gain score analysis (Cox, 1957; Feldt, 1958).

[20]In terms of power, the gain score analysis will only be preferred to the elementary ANOVA when $0 < 1/\beta < 2$ (Cox, 1957). So, for example, if $\beta < .5$, the gain score analysis is less precise than the elementary ANOVA which only uses the posttest scores. Elashoff and Snow (1971) provide an example where this occurred in practice, but the original investigators used the gain score analysis nonetheless.

these variables. But, of course, adding variables to the gain score model tends to alter the treatment effect estimate just as it does in the ANCOVA model.

Bias

The null hypothesis of the gain score analysis is that the mean difference between the groups is the same on the pretest as on the posttest. In other words, the mean pretest difference is used as a standard against which to judge how large the mean posttest difference should be in the absence of a treatment effect. Obviously, the mean pretest difference is an inappropriate standard when the pretest and posttest are operationally unique measures. This is because, even in the absence of *any* change, nonequivalent populations are not likely to differ by exactly the same amount on one measure (the pretest) as they do on a different measure (the posttest). However, even when the pretest and posttest are operationally identical, a number of biases are likely to arise. This fact was demonstrated in the previous chapter where the discussion was covertly phrased in terms of a gain score analysis since mean differences in the pretest and posttest were the basis for comparison. In that discussion, anything other than the treatment which produced a different mean change over time in one group than in the other group was shown to bias the analysis. The most notable threats to validity that were discussed included selection-maturation interactions, instrumentation (floor and ceiling effects), and problems of regression. Except in the rare cases where it is known that these threats are not present or where the size of the bias caused by these threats can be exactly specified numerically, the gain score analysis must be used with caution.[21]

Standardized Gain Score Analysis

Kenny (1975c) has proposed an alternative (standardized) gain score analysis which is appropriate for a particular type of selection-maturation interaction called the fan-spread pattern. This pattern of growth occurs when the initially more able or advantaged group of individuals grows at a faster rate than the less able group, so that the gap between them increases with time (e.g., the rich get richer).

The reasoning behind this spreading gap is that (1) the advantaged individuals achieved their initial superiority because they had a faster rate of growth than the less advantaged, and (2) this faster rate of growth will continue into the future, thereby further increasing the gap between the groups.

The fan-spread model also assumes that the increasing mean gap between the groups is accompanied by an increase in the variability of performance within the groups. In other words, as the groups tend to grow further apart, so do the individuals within the groups. Specifically, the model states that the average difference between the groups increases in direct proportion to the

---

[21]Gain scores have also received much deserved criticism when used for estimating the pattern of growth in individuals separately in contrast to their use in a model of the effect of a treatment (Cronbach and Furby, 1970; Lord, 1956, 1958, 1963), though this topic is beyond the concerns of the present discussion.

pooled within-group standard deviation of the scores.[22] Alternatively, this model can be described in correlational form. When the treatment assignment, T, is represented as a dummy, 0 or 1, variable, the fan-spread pattern specifies that the correlation between the pretest and treatment assignment equals the correlation between the posttest and treatment assignment:

$$\rho_{XT} = \rho_{YT}$$

This pattern of change is justified from an alternative perspective by Campbell and Boruch (1975).

If this particular pattern of fan-spread growth is expected under the null hypothesis, a test for a treatment effect can be made by comparing the above two correlations (Kenny, 1975c). Alternatively, a test could be made by using a standardized gain score analysis. In this procedure, the pretest and posttest scores are divided by their respective pooled within-group standard deviations. These standardized scores are then entered into a gain score analysis.[23]

Of course, no guarantee can be made that the fan-spread model is appropriate for any given research problem. Indeed, the fan-spread pattern is an explicit model of one very specific pattern of change which the data may or may not approximate. Obviously, when the data do not conform to this pattern, the standardized gain score analysis will be biased.

Rationales for the Analysis

So far in this chapter, we have presented a number of statistical techniques that could be used to analyze data from nonequivalent group designs that do not

---

[22]Algebraically,

$$\frac{\bar{X}_{E\cdot} - \bar{X}_{C\cdot}}{\sigma_X} = \frac{\bar{Y}_{E\cdot} - \bar{Y}_{C\cdot}}{\sigma_Y}$$

where σ_X and σ_Y are the pooled within-group standard deviation of X and Y respectively.

[23]Algebraically, the standardized scores are

$$X_{ij}^{Stand} = X_{ij}/\sigma_X$$
$$Y_{ij}^{Stand} = Y_{ij}/\sigma_Y$$

where σ_X and σ_Y are, as before, the pooled *within-group* standard deviations. These scores are then subtracted ($Y_{ij}^{Stand} - X_{ij}^{Stand}$) and entered into the gain score analysis in the same way that the raw scores would have been. The same null hypothesis is tested if, instead of using the standardized gain scores, $Y_{ij}^{Stand} - X_{ij}^{Stand}$, one uses an index of response $Y_{ij} - KX_{ij}$ with the unstandardized pretest and posttest scores and $K = \sigma_Y/\sigma_X$ (the ratio of pooled within-group standard deviations). This is also the *preferred* method because it produces results in the same scale or metric as the raw gain score analysis, ANCOVA, blocking or matching analysis, and ANOVA. If the reliability of the pretest differs from that of the posttest, Kenny (1975c) suggests an additional modification whereby the scores are standardized to have equivalent true score variances. This can be done (assuming a model of random measurement error) by using the index $K = (\sigma_Y/\sigma_X) \sqrt{\rho_{YY}/\rho_{XX}}$ where the latter term is the square root of the ratio of the within-group reliabilities. This adjustment is necessary because the fan-spread model is presumed to apply to the pattern of the true scores and not to the scores as fallibly measured. The treatment effect estimate is:

$$\hat{\alpha}_E - \hat{\alpha}_C = (\bar{Y}_{E\cdot} - \bar{Y}_{C\cdot}) - K(\bar{X}_{E\cdot} - \bar{X}_{C\cdot})$$

By comparing this estimate to that from the other previous models, one can see that the expected value of the treatment effect estimates from each model generally differ in the case of nonequivalent group designs.

have controlled selection. We have also demonstrated how each technique can be substantially biased by various sets of circumstances that may arise in social science research. Indeed, no statistical technique exists which can automatically take into account the effects of selection differences and thereby provide an unbiased treatment effect estimate under *all* circumstances. The obvious conclusion is that none of the above techniques or any others should be blindly or thoughtlessly used to analyze data from nonequivalent group designs.

The point of this critique is not to condemn particular statistical methods. Rather, it is only the *use* of these procedures in a *blind and arbitrary* fashion, without concern for the requirements of the analysis, that is criticized. The above methods can be of great use but only if they are thoughtfully and appropriately applied. It must be remembered that a statistical technique specifies a model for the data. As the structure and interrelationships of the data vary across settings, so must the structure of the model if appropriate conclusions are to be reached. Thus the statistical model must be carefully tailored to fit the unique characteristics and demands of the data at hand. No "magical" statistical techniques exist that will accomplish this tailoring automatically; the model fitting must be done by the researcher.

Of course, the purpose of tailoring is not simply to build a model that describes the data. If that were the case, the analyst could well proceed by trial and error, simply interacting with the data and refining the model until an adequate fit is obtained. Instead, the task of analysis is to disentangle the effect of the treatment from the effect of selection differences. Or, to state it in another way, the task of analysis is to rule out selection differences as an alternative explanation for the alleged treatment effect. An analysis of this nature must be guided by some logic other than mere data description. This is because description by itself does not rule out threats to validity. That requires an understanding of the processes and conditions that influenced the data and not just knowledge of what the data look like.

Several justifiable approaches to this task of ruling out selection differences as a rival explanation are available. The first step in the analysis is to decide which approach (or rationale) to employ. The second step is to use one's knowledge about how the data were generated to tailor a model in conformance with the chosen rationale.

A rationale is not a specific statistical model but rather a broad framework to use in specifying a statistical model which is appropriate for the situation and which will properly take the effect of selection differences into account. In particular, a rationale (1) provides a logical procedure for predicting how the experimental group would have performed had it not received the treatment and (2) specifies what knowledge and assumptions are needed to justify that prediction. As such, a rationale plays a guiding role, providing an explicit listing of the requirements for the analysis.

After choosing a rationale, the researcher must specify a statistical model that conforms to the requirements laid out by that rationale. That is, the rationale provides an outline for tailoring the model to the data but the researcher must fill in the specific details. This involves identifying, for the situation at hand, the underlying constructs required for implementing the rationale and determining how to operationalize them. For example, one rationale to be presented requires

identifying the causal determinants of posttest responding, while another requires identifying the variables underlying the selection process. Such specification obviously relies heavily on the knowledge and expertise of the researcher.

In the following discussion, we outline four different rationales for the analysis of nonequivalent group designs without controlled selection and offer some suggestions on how to implement them in practice. While these four rationales provide the most obvious means of generating a fair comparison between nonequivalent groups, other approaches will undoubtedly be advocated in the future so one should not feel constrained by the present list. Which rationale is the best one to follow depends on the requirements of the rationale and the situation. These will be discussed in more detail below.

Rationale I: Causal Model of the Posttest

If *all* the causal determinants of performance on the posttest are measured *perfectly* and if individuals in the two nonequivalent groups are perfectly matched on all these measures, the mean posttest difference between the two matched groups would be a reasonable indicator of a treatment effect. That is, if the samples are matched on all of the true underlying causes of posttest behavior except for differences in treatment imposition, any reliable posttest differences between the matched samples can be reasonably attributed to the treatment. For example, the present perspective justifies the use of identical twins as matched pairs to investigate the influence of environment on human intelligence. To determine the effect of environment, one might conceive of it as a treatment that has been dispensed to individuals in a nonrandom fashion. Most likely, some would argue that this treatment assignment produces selection differences on genetic factors which could also influence intelligence. Therefore these differences must be taken into account if the research results are to be convincing to all critics. In other words, the research setting parallels that of a nonequivalent group design, only the treatment is a continuous rather than dichotomous classification. According to the present rationale, matching on all the causal determinants of intelligence, besides the treatment which consists of all environmental variation, would be one solution to the problem of controlling for selection differences. Of course, the only other causes of intelligence, besides the environment, are genetic and the only way to match individuals perfectly on their genetic makeup is to compare identical twins.

Unfortunately, applying this rationale in practice is not always as easy as defining it. We have stated the rationale in terms of a matching procedure. Alternatively, one could think of the comparison in terms of the ANCOVA strategy (being careful to take proper account of the shape of the regression surfaces). As we have shown, the mechanics of these analyses are relatively straightforward. But the logic of the rationale rests on more than mechanics. It also requires the specification and accurate measurement of the causal determinants of the posttest or, as we might say, construction of a causal model for the posttest. Since the design itself cannot supply an appropriate causal model, the analyst must specify the model using substantive theory and knowledge. Obviously, there is much room for error.

We might distinguish between two parts of this model-building process: specifying the appropriate underlying causal constructs and accurately measuring them. In turn, accurate measurement can be divided into two components: reliability and validity. For our purposes, we define a reliable observation as one that does not contain random measurement error. A valid observation then is one that does not contain systematic irrelevant variation, i.e., it measures the intended trait without any systematic discrepancy. In a previous example, short-term fluctuations in weight were seen to be irrelevant components in the measurement of a person's long-term mean weight. Or, consider using chronological age as a substitute for a measure of physical maturity. While age can be measured with virtually perfect reliability and is highly correlated with physical maturity, the correlation is not perfect because individuals reach puberty at different ages.

We have already seen how measurement error and irrelevant components can bias the treatment effect estimate in ANCOVA. Since most social science measures suffer from one or both of these ailments, the researcher should either correct the ANCOVA or matching strategies or use alternative procedures so that these difficulties are taken into account in the analysis. In a later section, we consider some of these corrections and alternatives.

Unfortunately, these procedures do not address the other potential flaw in causal model building: misspecifying the underlying causal variables. As it turns out, an adequate causal model need not be complete, that is, contain *all* of the causal determinants of the posttest. Variables may be excluded from the model as long as their total contribution to the posttest is orthogonal to each of the variables (including the treatment assignment) retained in the model.[24] Generally, this means that the model needs to contain only those causal determinants on which there are initial group differences. Nonetheless, if the researcher fails to include all the variables required to satisfy this minimum causal model, the results can be severely biased just as the ANCOVA can be substantially biased by some forms of change between the pretest and posttest.

We might also note that the present rationale provides the logical foundation for the analysis of data from passive observational studies (see chapter 7). Though the potential pitfalls apply with equal force, many researchers have been willing to accept the stringent requirements of causal modeling in that context and have tried to do the best that is possible with the limited knowledge available. The researcher is well advised, however, to accept the assumptions of the causal model cautiously and to remain open to the possibility that the model is misspecified. Unfortunately, many types of misspecification are almost impossible to detect on the basis of the data alone. Thus, although there are some quality checks on the model (cf. Costner and Schoenberg, 1973; Sörbom, 1975), their use does not guarantee that the final model will be appropriate.

Rationale II: Model of the Assignment Process

Matching individuals on the variables underlying the selection process (either by physically pairing scores or by statistically equating them via

---

[24]For a more complete introduction to causal modeling and a fuller explication of these issues, the reader might consult Blalock (1964) or Duncan (1975).

ANCOVA) is the logical basis for the second rationale. For example, in a setting where individuals are self-selected into the treatment conditions, assignment may be determined by the level of the individuals' motivation and need so that all other influences are essentially random. That is, once motivation and need are taken into account, individuals in the two groups differ only in ways that are unrelated to posttest responding. Then if motivation and need can be accurately measured, these variables could be used in a matching or ANCOVA strategy to provide reasonable estimates of the treatment effect.

To see why such analyses would be appropriate, let us consider a hypothetical selection procedure that is controlled by the researcher. Imagine that individuals with the same degree of motivation and need are randomly assigned to treatment conditions but that the proportion assigned to each condition varies with the degree of motivation and need. For example, 90 percent of the individuals with high motivation and high need might be randomly assigned to the experimental group while only 10 percent of the individuals with low motivation and low need might be randomly assigned to that condition. This allows the groups to be nonequivalent since the experimental individuals would systematically have higher scores than the control individuals on variables correlated with motivation and need. Yet while the groups as a whole are nonequivalent, individuals in the two treatment conditions who are matched on motivation and need are equivalent. This is because, given the same degree of motivation and need, selection into the treatment conditions is random. Thus any reliable posttest difference between these matched pairs could reasonably be attributed to the treatment. Thus a matching strategy, or alternatively an ANCOVA which properly models the shape of the regression surfaces, would be an appropriate analysis (also see Rubin, 1977).

Of course, the same result is accomplished if, instead of controlling the selection process to be partly random, the researcher models an uncontrolled selective procedure so that all determinants of selection are taken into account except those unrelated to the posttest. In some cases of self-selection, perhaps a sufficient model would consist of the two variables of motivation and need, as we have assumed. In most cases of uncontrolled selection, however, identifying and accurately measuring the critical variables underlying an uncontrolled selection process would be difficult. Again, an ANCOVA or matching strategy can be biased if the researcher fails to include all the variables necessary to model the selection process or if these variables are not accurately measured.[25] For this reason, corrections and alternatives for ANCOVA and matching which properly take into account inaccurate measurement are recom-

---

[25]To be sure, in certain situations a variable that is fallibly measured might be the appropriate variable to include in the model and therefore would not lead to a bias. For example, a high school senior might decide to self-select into a treatment such as college, because of a high score on a standardized test. Certainly that test score would contain measurement error, but since the measurement error itself is a part of the selection decision, it is the unreliable variable and not true ability that models this individual's choice. However, in the vast majority of research settings where selection is not controlled, it is the true underlying trait and not the fallible measure of it that determines selection and so should be used in the model. For example, in most cases of self-selection it will be the individual's true level of need and motivation, and not need and motivation as the researcher fallibly measures them, that guides selection. Similarly, for most high school seniors it is true ability, among other variables, and not a score on a national exam, that is the determining factor in deciding to attend college.

mended. These procedures are the same as those recommended for the first rationale and are considered below. Unfortunately, little can be done in the analysis to avoid a misspecification of the model such as omitting a critical variable.

To preview the discussion of the regression-discontinuity design, we might note here that the analysis of that design relies on the logic of the present rationale. Following this logic, the analysis of the regression-discontinuity design is made easy, as compared to the nonequivalent group design without controlled selection, because the determinants of group assignment are known.

Analysis Techniques for Rationales I and II

It has long been recognized that the presence of measurement error or other irrelevance in the independent variables (i.e., pretests) can bias the matching or ANCOVA strategies. We will briefly examine some of the statistical palliatives that might be used to counteract the effects of these inaccuracies. Some of these procedures have been solely concerned with the problems caused by measurement error while other developments have explicitly and simultaneously addressed the problems of both measurement error and irrelevance. However, from the present perspective, we must remember that correcting the ANCOVA or matching strategies for the effects of irrelevance and measurement error will not guarantee an unbiased treatment effect estimate unless the pretests, if they have been accurately measured, provide an adequate model of either the posttest or the assignment process.

Madansky (1959) provides a review of some of the early methods that were developed to correct for the effects of measurement error in a regression analysis with a single independent variable. More recently, Cochran (1968b) has offered a comprehensive summary of the nature of measurement error and the difficulties it produces in both univariate and multiple regression, as well as in ANCOVA. Lord (1960) was one of the first to address a solution to the problem of measurement error explicitly in the context of ANCOVA. His large sample method uses a duplicate (parallel) pretest measure to correct for the presence of measurement error in a single covariate ANCOVA. Since then numerous other procedures have been developed for the single covariate ANCOVA.

The correction suggested by Porter (1967) is probably the simplest computationally and conceptually and so we consider it here. Porter's correction is based on the assumption that the measurement error in the pretest is not correlated with the true score or with the measurement error in the posttest.[26] As we have seen (footnote 7), measurement error of this type attenuates the estimate of the regression slope by a factor that depends on the within-group pretest reliability and thereby biases the treatment effect estimate. Porter has therefore suggested using a measure of the within-group pretest reliability to correct for the bias in the slope estimate and in so doing to correct for the bias in the treatment effect estimate. This can be done by regressing each pretest score toward its group mean to produce an adjusted pretest score. The adjusted score is then used in the ANCOVA

---

[26]DeGracie and Fuller (1972) propose a correction for the single covariate ANCOVA which allows the errors of measurement in the pretest and posttest to be correlated. Sörbom's (in press) model, which is discussed later, handles correlated errors in the multiple covariate ANCOVA.

model to compute the treatment effect estimate just as the original pretest would have been used if no correction had been made.[27]

This adjustment obviously requires an estimate of the reliability. Porter and Chibucos (1974, p. 450) suggest that this "should be a parallel form estimate, or if that is impossible, a short time lapse test-retest estimate." They further, and very sensibly, add that "when there is doubt as to the correct value of the reliability coefficient . . . a range of likely values should be considered." Often, a parallel form estimate or a short-term test-retest reliability estimate will not be available and there may be only an internal consistency estimate (e.g., Cronbach's coefficient alpha). The latter is likely to be an inflated estimate of the former because of linked errors due to shared irrelevance from within the single testing session (Cronbach and Furby, 1970). This makes the use of internal consistency estimates as single estimates in the correction procedure questionable. However, they might be very useful as upper end points in the recommended bracketing strategy, which examines a range of reliability values. Where available, reliability estimates provided by test publishers should be used very cautiously. This is because these estimates are likely to be internal consistency estimates and because they are probably calculated from a different population than is involved in the particular experiment at hand.

Other potential difficulties arise in the use of the reliability correction. First, since an estimate of reliability is used in the correction instead of the true value of the reliability which is unknown, the F test is technically not valid. However, Porter's (1967) Monte Carlo results indicate that the behavior of the F test is not seriously affected when standard distributional assumptions are met (although the study only considered the case where the pretest scores were distributed normally). Second, and more critically, the correction method is based on a specific model of the structure of measurement error, and while such a model is plausible for many common measurement procedures in the social sciences, not *all* measurement error will conform to it. This makes Cochran's (1968b) discussion of more complex forms of measurement error particularly worthy of attention. Finally, the correction assumes that the reliability of measurement is the same in each treatment condition. If it is not, the investigator could use a separate correction in each group (cf. Director, 1974).

Though in its original form, Porter's adjustment was concerned only with correcting for the bias due to measurement error, the procedure could be modified to handle other forms of irrelevance as well, as long as the irrelevance conforms to the necessary assumptions. Along these lines Campbell and Boruch (1975) suggested that under some circumstances the within-group reliability estimate in Porter's procedure might be replaced by an estimate of the within-group pretest-posttest correlation. When the irrelevant components in the pretest and posttest

---

[27]Algebraically, the adjusted pretest score is

$$X_{ij}^{adj} = \bar{X}_{i.} + \hat{\rho}_{XX}(X_{ij} - \bar{X}_{i.})$$

where $\hat{\rho}_{XX}$ is an estimate of the within-group pretest reliability and $\bar{X}_{i.}$ is the group mean on the pretest. Thus each group of scores is separately regressed (by a factor of $\hat{\rho}_{XX}$) toward its respective group mean.

account for equal proportions of the total variance in each measure, which is most plausible when the measures are operationally identical and when these components behave like random measurement error, Campbell and Boruch's suggestion would correct for the effects of irrelevance as well as measurement error.

Prior to these developments, Thorndike (1942) had proposed an equivalent correction for the effects of measurement error in the matching strategy. Thorndike suggested that before the pretest scores are used for matching, they should be regressed toward their group means in direct proportion to the test's reliability. Obviously, this parallels Porter's procedure and thus rests on the same assumptions. However, an additional difficulty arises in using this correction in the context of matching. In regressing the pretest scores, the size of the matched sample is reduced. The reason for the loss of sample size is that the overlap between the groups on the regressed pretest scores is less than the overlap on the unadjusted scores. Indeed, it is possible that after the adjustment there would be no overlap at all so that matching would be impossible. In addition, it becomes increasingly difficult and complex to make corrections when there are multiple pretests. For these reasons, adjustments for the effects of measurement error and irrelevance are probably better handled in the ANCOVA framework.

Even in that framework, the algebraic complexity of the adjustment is greatly increased when one corrects for the effects of measurement error and irrelevance in multiple covariates simultaneously. Because of this complexity we will limit our discussion to an overview of one class of approaches to the problem. This set of procedures is derived from the work of Jöreskog (1970a, 1970b, 1973, 1974, 1977; also see Long, 1976).

Jöreskog's models are in two parts. One part is the structural equation model which specifies the relationship between the variables as perfectly measured (i.e., the relationship between the true underlying constructs). This model can include multiple covariates. The second part is the measurement model which specifies how the measured variables are related to these unobserved constructs. Generally, at least two measured variables must be included in the measurement model for each construct. The interrelationship between the measured variables is then used to separate the presumed underlying true constructs from the irrelevant and error components in each measure. In other words, Jöreskog's procedures provide for multiple measures to triangulate upon the shared constructs. Obviously, if these procedures are to be used, the study must be designed so that an appropriate set of measures is available.

The starting point in the analysis is the researcher's specification of the structural model of either the posttest behavior or the assignment process. The researcher then specifies the measurement model for how the observed variables relate to the underlying constructs and how, if at all, the irrelevant components in the measures are interrelated. If the unknown parameters in both parts of the model are all identified (i.e., can be uniquely estimated) and if the variables have a multivariate normal distribution, maximum-likelihood estimates for the parameters, including the estimate of a treatment effect, are provided. Standard errors and tests of statistical significance which are valid in large samples can also be generated. In addition, a goodness-of-fit test and other information can be used to

modify the model when its fit to the data is inadequate (cf. Costner and Schoenberg, 1973; and Sörbom, 1975).

Keesling and Wiley (1976) provide one adaptation of these procedures that fits the unique specifications of the ANCOVA model although, explicitly, their model is only concerned with correcting for the effects of measurement error. Linn and Werts (1977), Magidson (1977), and Rindskopf (1978) have also adopted these general methods to fit the demands of the nonequivalent group design and have allowed their models to take irrelevance as well as measurement error into account (also see Bentler and Woodward, 1978; and Magidson, 1978). However, Sörbom's (in press) extension of these procedures into the realm of ANCOVA models offers the most general and efficient formulation.[28] His elaborate model provides for both irrelevance and measurement error and also allows the model specification and parameters to differ from group to group (e.g., it provides for treatment interactions).

Of course, we should be quick to note that none of these procedures are panaceas for the problems encountered in the nonequivalent group design. First, they only address the problems of measurement error and irrelevance. If the pretests, as accurately measured, do not provide an adequate model of the posttest or of the assignment process, the analysis will still be biased even if the effects of measurement error and irrelevance are properly eliminated. And second, these procedures only counteract the problems of measurement error and irrelevance if the structure and interrelationships of these components are properly specified. The researcher could misspecify the structure of the irrelevant components, for example, by incorrectly assuming that the measurement errors in the pretest and posttest are uncorrelated, or by including variables in the model that do not properly triangulate on the desired construct. Nonetheless, these procedures can be very useful tools when used carefully, with their limitations clearly in mind.

Rationale III: The Cronbach, Rogosa, Floden and Price Formulation

In a sense, the third rationale is a combination of the first two rationales. It is based on the analytic formulation of Cronbach et al. (1977), which details the potential biases in the ANCOVA when applied to data from the nonequivalent group design.

The Cronbach et al. formulation revolves around two hypothetical constructs: the ideal covariate and the complete discriminant. The former is the best possible predictor of posttest performance that can be formed on the basis of all a priori characteristics of the individuals. (Or, in our terminology, it is a complete causal model of the posttest.) The latter, complete discriminant, represents selection differences between the groups as completely as possible (or is a complete model of the assignment process). As we have seen, a covariate which corresponds to either the ideal covariate or the complete discriminant can be used in the ANCOVA to generate an unbiased treatment effect estimate. Cronbach et al. (1977) further show how the bias using an arbitrary covariate depends upon the interrelationship

---

[28]A computer program to implement this procedure (LISREL V, cf. Jöreskog and Sörbom, 1978) is currently being developed (Sörbom, personal communication).

between that covariate and these two constructs. The implication is that knowledge about the relationship of an arbitrary covariate to both of these constructs can be used to fix limits on the size of the bias.

Indeed, Cronbach (personal communication of a draft of an argument; also see Reichardt, 1979) has developed a procedure which does just that. The first step is to use the data at hand to estimate the ideal covariate and the complete discriminant. Then using both substantive knowledge and knowledge of the research setting, the analyst must fix limits in correlational terms on how close these estimates come in predicting each construct. With certain additional assumptions, these limits can be translated into brackets on the size of the bias in the treatment effect estimate. That is, the limits are used to generate a range of values which are believed to encompass the size of the true treatment effect.

When the data provide good estimates of the ideal covariate and the complete discriminant, the range of values presumed to encompass the treatment effect is relatively narrow and there is little uncertainty about its true size. Conversely, when the data provide poor estimates, the range of values is relatively wide and there is much uncertainty. Thus, the information gained in the analysis is a direct function of the quality of the data, not an inappropriate result.

Rationale IV: Models of Change or Growth

Knowledge of what the pattern of growth or change would have been in the experimental group if it had not received the treatment can be used to estimate the treatment effect. Specifically, the prediction of the amount of growth that would have occurred under null conditions is compared with the growth that was actually obtained. Any reliable discrepancy between these two values is attributed to the treatment. This is the logic of the fourth rationale.

Several ways to go about making this prediction are possible. The standardized gain score analysis, for example, was based on a prediction of this sort. We consider here two different approaches whose application requires special design features. Both procedures also require that the pretests and posttests are operationally identical measures. Otherwise change is not well defined. This does not mean, however, that change is necessarily well defined when the measures are nominally the same. As we previously noted, because change can be multidimensional, even nominally identical observations can measure quite different attributes at different stages of development. The analyst must be careful to check that the expectations about growth are consistent, not with the nominal characteristics of the measures, but with the underlying traits that they tap.

If the mean growth in the experimental group can be accurately predicted with reference only to that group's past performance, a control or comparison group is not necessary. That is, under some conditions the pretest can adequately serve for purposes of comparison. Such comparisons are particularly useful when the treatment is applied universally so that no one is untreated, when for other reasons the available control groups are not adequate for implementing other rationales, or simply when the control and experimental groups are so different that a comparison based on past behavior appears more useful then a comparison with another group. But even though a control group may not be required for the present ratio-

nale, it can often still be used to good advantage by providing a check on some of the model assumptions.

One way to predict the growth that would occur in the absence of a treatment effect is to measure performance over a number of time periods prior to the start of the treatment and then extrapolate the observed pattern of growth into the future. This is the logic behind the interrupted time-series designs that are considered in chapters 5 and 6 (and also part of the logic behind the untreated control group design with pretest measures at more than one time interval which was considered in chapter 3). Briefly, a baseline of measures is collected both before and after the treatment and the patterns of growth plotted in each. If the patterns change at the point where the treatment is introduced and if there is no other reason for an abrupt change at that point, the change can reasonably be attributed to the effect of the treatment.

Of course, a number of factors, such as shifts in instrumentation and history effects, can produce changes coincident with the treatment. These perils of the analysis are treated in the following chapters and the reader is strongly encouraged to consult that discussion before implementing such a design. We discuss the design here only to mention some technical aspects of the analysis when time-series data are obtained from a group of individuals.

In chapter 6, discussion of the analysis of the interrupted time-series design is concerned only with data from a single experimental unit—an individual, an organization, a city, and the like. In that case, the analysis requires data from a substantial number of time points, often 20 to 30 as an absolute minimum. However, when data are collected on a group of individuals, as in the present context, the analysis can be performed on far fewer time points. Perhaps as few as four observations, two before and two after the treatment, would suffice under some circumstances. Because of these differences and because of the need to incorporate data from many individuals, appropriate analysis strategies may also differ from one context to the other.

One approach to the analysis in the present context is the generalized multivariate analysis of variance (MANOVA) procedure introduced by Pothoff and Roy (1964) and subsequently elaborated by Khatri (1966), Jöreskog (1970b), and Tubbs, Lewis and Duran (1975), among others. Morrison (1976) presents a useful overview of this procedure, though not explicitly in terms of the interrupted time-series design. Alternatively, a pseudo-generalized least squares precedure (cf. Hibbs, 1974) could be developed for group time-series data which would be a direct extension of the Box and Jenkins (1976) procedures described in chapter 6. Both of these approaches would take into account the nature of the dependence between repeated observations of each individual, a step that is required if significance tests are to be appropriate (see chapter 6).

A second approach in predicting growth is embodied in the logic of the selection cohort design. As described in the previous chapter, this design relies on cohorts of similar individuals who pass through the same developmental cycle. Consider the selection cohort design used by Ball and Bogatz (1970) and previously described in chapter 3. In that analysis a pretest cohort of children who were between the ages of 47 and 52 months at the pretest (and between 53 and 58

months at the posttest) were compared to a posttest cohort of children who were between the ages of 53 and 58 months at the pretest. Instead of dividing the children up into two discrete groups in this fashion, the analysis could have used age in a more continuous fashion. Such an analysis strategy was offered by Cook et al. (1975) and Bryk and Weisberg (1976). In the simplest such strategy, the pretest scores of all the children are regressed onto the measure of age and this regression used to predict the mean posttest response (again for all the children) in the absence of a treatment effect.

To understand how this is done, we must examine that regression in detail. If the cohorts are truly similar except for differences in age (and if there are no history effects), the regression of the pretest on age will depict the aggregate pattern of maturation. Specifically, if the regression is linear, the slope of the regression line is an estimate of the mean increase in performance for a unit change in age. Then the regression slope multiplied by the length of time between the pretest and pottest equals the predicted change from the pretest to the posttest under null conditions. Adding this predicted growth to the mean score on the pretest gives the predicted mean posttest score.

While these manipulations are easily interpreted, they do not provide easily calculable significance tests (see Bryk and Weisberg, 1976; and Strenio, Bryk and Weisberg, 1977). For this reason, an alternative but logically identical procedure might be preferred. This alternative takes the form of a matching procedure. For example, a child who was 55 months old at the time of the posttest can be matched with a child who was 55 months old at the time of the pretest. If the age groups are similar, these individuals are matched in terms of predicted growth. Thus, in the absence of any other threat to validity, a reliable difference can be attributed to the treatment. However, one problem can arise in using this matching strategy or, alternatively, in using ANCOVA. The problem is that both a child's pretest and posttest scores are included in the analysis although in different matched pairs. The result is that the scores across pairs would not be independent since the two values from each individual are almost certainly correlated. This violates an assumption of the matching and ANCOVA analyses. However, the same comparison could be made in a multivariate analysis of covariance (MAN-COVA) which would properly take this additional complication into account.

Of course, the analysis of the selection cohort design rests on the assumption that the cohorts, or age groups, in our example are essentially equivalent. When this is not the case, the effect of selection differences should be taken into account in predicting the pattern of growth. The advantage of the selection cohort design, however, is that by choosing the cohorts carefully, selection differences can often be kept to a minimum. Other potential biases, such as history and testing effects, also deserve attention (see chapter 3).

General Guidelines for Analyzing Data from Nonequivalent Groups Without Controlled Selection

Random assignment of individuals to treatment conditions does not solve all the problems that are encountered in statistical analyses. Nonetheless, it is very useful—a point that can best be appreciated by understanding the difficulties that

arise when randomization and other controls on selection are absent. The benefits of randomization are based on the fact that there are no expected differences between the treatment groups at the beginning of the experiment. With adequate care and precaution, this group equivalence can often be maintained throughout the experiment, leading to a simple and unbiased comparison between the treatment and control groups on the posttest observation.

Without randomization, selection differences between the groups are almost inevitably introduced at the start of an experiment. While the groups might sometimes turn out to be similar without an objective random assignment procedure (i.e., because the assignment was haphazard, even if not formally random) such comparability is rare in the social science situations with which we are most familiar. Common forms of nonrandom assignment, such as self-selection and selection based on need or merit, typically reflect subtle biases and result in groups with reliable and often substantial preexisting differences. To reach appropriate conclusions about cause, the effects of such selection differences must be differentiated from the effects of the treatment.

We have examined four common statistical techniques and some of the reasons why they might be biased when used to analyze data from the nonequivalent group design. The difficulties we have discussed are not minor annoyances or implausible occurrences. Quite the contrary! With the present state of the art in the social sciences, any one of these statistical methods could be biased enough so that a useful treatment might look harmful and a harmful treatment might look benign or even beneficial. Rather than using one of these four standard procedures in an arbitrary fashion, we strongly recommend that the analysis be carefully planned in accordance with a logical rationale for taking the effects of selection differences into account. Only in this fashion can the analysis be properly tailored to fit the unique demands of the data at hand. Yet this tailoring is not a simple task. It requires extensive knowledge of the underlying processes that have generated the data. Generally such information is only partly available. Since the rest is guesswork, the researcher cannot have complete confidence that the analysis properly takes into account all potential biases. As Lord (1967, p. 305) has forcefully concluded:

> With the data usually available for such studies, there simply is no logical or statistical procedure that can be counted on to make proper allowances for uncontrolled preexisting differences between groups.

Cochran and Rubin (1973, p. 417) offer a similar opinion:

> If randomization is absent, it is virtually impossible in many practical circumstances to be convinced that the estimates of the effects of treatments are in fact unbiased.

Does this mean that the statistical analysis of data from the nonequivalent group design is worthless? We think not. However, the researcher must be especially diligent and careful in analyzing quasi-experimental data and in drawing causal conclusions from the analysis. Likewise, readers of reports based on quasi-experimental designs have to be skeptical and only accept conclusions about cause

if the data have been intelligently and thoroughly analyzed and if the weaknesses of the statistical methods that the authors used have been taken into consideration in formulating the conclusions.

We believe that the statistical analysis of nonequivalent group designs is facilitated (1) by a careful planning of the design so as to have available as much of the information that is required for the analysis as possible and to anticipate analysis difficulties; (2) by a rigorous and exhaustive examination of the data with multiple and open-minded analyses to try to discern the many contributing forces that are likely to be operating; and (3) by an explicit and public appraisal of the validity of the findings and the plausibility of alternative explanations. These three points are discussed in more detail below.

Planning and Design

The design of a nonequivalent group quasi-experiment should always be guided by a rationale for the analysis. That is, the design should be carefully planned and implemented so as to ensure that all the ingredients necessary for an adequate analysis are available. For some rationales, this requires procedures for measuring the determinants of posttest responding, of group assignments, or both. For this reason, the planning of the design demands not only a technical mastery of research and statistical methodology but also a mastery of the subject matter under investigation. Only with a thorough understanding of the research setting and the behavior under study can the researcher hope to collect the appropriate measures and to anticipate the potential biases. Some of these biases can then be eliminated by design. Others will have to be carefully measured and controlled for in the analysis, with the full understanding, of course, that this control will probably be less than perfect.

Which rationale is best to follow is not always easy to decide. Implementing a rationale demands a careful mix of experimental control, planned observation, and substantive knowledge—a mix that can change from one rationale to the next. For example, specifying a causal model of posttest responding is largely a substantive task while predicting growth or change might be more a matter of design, involving the observation of similar cohorts or the collection of a time series of observations.

Given the present state of the art in social science research, we believe that employing experimental control, where possible, is generally superior to relying on substantive knowledge, and this has important implications for choosing and implementing a rationale. For example, it is usually much more difficult to specify an appropriate causal model of the posttest, since this relies on substantive knowledge which may not be available, than it is to specify an appropriate analysis for the selection cohort design, assuming that this design has been carefully controlled to make the cohorts as alike as possible. In similar fashion, it is almost always easier to specify an appropriate model of the assignment process when that process has been constrained to follow a preset pattern, as in the regression-discontinuity design, than it is if the selection process is unconstrained. Another way of saying the same thing is that it is usually better to eliminate, or at least try to reduce, the impact of threats through the design of the study than to try removing their effects in the statistical analysis. Since all the threats that are specific to the nonequivalent

group design stem from the presence of selection differences between the groups, the researcher should, above all, try to control the selection process so as to work with groups that are as similar as possible. Randomization is one way of doing this, as is the use of selection cohort designs. Alternatively, the selection procedure could be controlled, as in the regression-discontinuity design, so that the model of group assignment is known. Thus, when these forms of experimental control are possible, we strongly favor the regression-discontinuity and selection cohort designs over other types of nonequivalent group designs.

Designing the study so as to incorporate the elaborated predictions of a well-specified theory is also to be preferred. That is, by envisaging as many different and variable consequences of the theory or causal hypotheses as possible and by carefully planning the study to detect them, the researcher will have more extensive opportunity to verify or falsify the presence of a treatment effect. Examples of designs which make use of this logic were scattered throughout the discussion in chapter 3 and include designs with nonequivalent dependent variables, with treatment partitioning, and with predicted higher-order interactions.

Unfortunately, such forms of experimental control and design elaboration will often not be possible. In these situations a more extensive measurement plan will be required. For example, designing the study so that multiple measures of each construct are obtained is essential if the ANCOVA is to be corrected for the biasing effects of irrelevance in the independent variables. In addition, the lack of experimental control often makes the choice between rationales more difficult. Generally, we would expect that the researcher has a better understanding of the selection process and the pattern of growth than of the causal determinants of posttest responding. When this is the case, it is probably better to plan the measurement operations so as to implement those rationales that depend upon the former knowledge than to try to implement a rationale that depends upon the latter. In other cases, however, the converse will be true. About all that can be suggested is that the researcher carefully examine his or her knowledge of the research situation, in consultation with other knowledgeable individuals, and plan to implement that rationale (or rationales) which seems best suited to the specific research problem.

The point is that in foregoing the powerful experimental control of random assignment, the researcher must be especially diligent to provide the raw materials for estimating the treatment effect by other means. This will generally require more and more reliance on substantive knowledge and theory, as the degree of experimental control decreases.

Analysis

The analysis should be guided by a clear and logical rationale for taking into account the effects of selection differences. When the study has been designed with a rationale in mind, devising a plan for the analysis will usually be straightforward although its practical implementation may not be easy. On the other hand, when the study has been carelessly designed with no regard for a rationale, a practical plan for the analysis may be extremely difficult to develop. Nonetheless, a rationale should still be used so that the difficulties of the analysis and therefore the likely equivocalities of the results are appreciated. Again, which rationale is

best to follow will depend upon the nature of the research setting and the amount of substantive knowledge. As noted, we would often expect that the researcher has a better understanding of the selection process and the nature of growth than of the causal determinants of posttest responding. Whether this knowledge can be adequately used, however, depends on whether the necessary data are available.

In performing the analysis, the researcher should explicitly try to rule out as many potential biases as possible. This is best accomplished by placing the treatment and potential biases in competition with each other as alternative explanations for the results and then directing the analysis so as to choose between them. In most situations this strategy will entail multiple analyses of the data, with each analysis aimed at estimating the effects of different patterns of potential biases.

The first step in this process is to sift through the data descriptively to see what they suggest. This information is then combined with the researcher's knowledge of (1) the subject matter, (2) the causal forces underlying the measured variables, (3) the selection process, and (4) the specific research setting, to suggest which analyses are plausible and to build appropriate models. When uncertainty about the appropriate model specification exists, a range of specifications should be used to encompass all the reasonable possibilities. In this way, a plausible *set* of models is developed which form the basis for multiple analyses of the data.

These multiple analyses are then used to bracket the size of the treatment effect within a range of plausible values. This was the logic behind using a range of different reliability estimates to bracket the proper correction for measurement error in the ANCOVA. We would further suggest incorporating within a bracket the results of analyses based on competing assumptions which take into account all of the potential biases (including those such as local history effects) and not just those due to measurement error.

This suggestion has much in common with the logic of the third rationale which was based on the work of Cronbach et al. (1977). Remember in that procedure, a range of estimates encompassing the likely treatment effect is generated, and the size of this bracket depends on the ability of the observed variables to model the posttest behavior and group assignment. Clearly, it is more appropriate to provide a plausible range of values than to report only a single estimate when uncertainty about the proper model specification exists. In the face of such uncertainty, a single point estimate is simply misleading in its apparent precision. For this reason, we strongly recommend the third rationale since it directly takes uncertainty into account.

As an example of an alternative bracketing procedure, consider how Cook et al. (1975) attempted to estimate the effect of viewing "Sesame Street" by using various different but reasonable analysis techniques which presumably had different likelihoods of revealing significant treatment effects. For instance, it was evident in the data that viewers knew more than nonviewers at the pretest, came from more affluent homes with more educated parents and, it was assumed, would mature at a faster rate over time. Because of this initial and presumably substantial difference and because the pretest contained appreciable measurement error, it was believed that a simple ANCOVA analysis would most likely underadjust for selection differences and so overestimate the effect of "Sesame Street." Similarly, it was anticipated that a correlational analysis which used each child's obtained

viewing score to create a treatment variable with several categories would overestimate treatment effects. To bracket the effects of the treatment, Cook et al. (1975) conducted an age cohorts analysis which was believed to be relatively bias free. However, it had low precision because many children had to be omitted from the analysis and because pretest scores were used in the analysis in a way that did not increase the precision of the estimate. Fortunately, each analysis reached the same conclusion, thereby adding to the interpretability of the outcomes and the credibility of the analysis (if one accepts the plausibility of the initial assumptions). Further, Cook et al. sought support for the results from an independent analysis of the same data by Kenny (1975b) and an independent study by Minton (1975). Thus, bracketing took place within the overall analysis strategy, and independent corroborations of the bracketed results were obtained both in the *same* data set analyzed differently by another researcher and in *another* data set.

Drawing Conclusions and Reporting Results

Making sense out of results from multiple analyses is difficult if they lead to different inferences about the treatment effect. Again, the role of judgment and subject-matter knowledge is paramount in solving the resulting puzzle. Regardless of the final conclusion reached by the investigator, all of the evidence and all of the assumptions underlying the analyses should be made public, as should all alternative interpretations of the data that both have and have not been ruled out. In this regard, Cochran (1965) suggests that researchers add a "validity of results" section to their reports. In such a section it would be important to defend the assumptions that were made in particular analyses, and to discuss the reasons one has for ruling out any threats as implausible. Such an appraisal of the evidence for and against rival hypotheses might be divided into two parts: one for those alternative hypotheses the analyst thinks have been ruled out by the data, and the other for those which were not ruled out either because of insufficient data or because their plausible impact appeared to be large enough to account for all of the observed effect.

In weighing all this evidence, the researcher should examine the results of related studies to see if they agree or if the disagreements can be explained in terms of a bias that was present in one study but not in the other. Similarly, consistency of results *within* the study itself is important. But consistency must be interpreted cautiously, for it is possible that the results all agree because of a common bias which has been overlooked.

When it appears that all plausible biases have been taken into account and a treatment effect emerges in spite of them all, conclusions can be made with reasonable confidence. Typically, a large degree of uncertainty will remain regardless of how much data sifting, careful reasoning, and creativity goes into the analysis. The size and direction of some biases will probably still be largely unknown, and one or more of them may provide a reasonable alternative explanation for any alleged treatment effect. In social science research where randomization is not present, it is difficult to avoid such equivocalities. The analyst must not only be prepared to accept this admittedly unsatisfactory verdict but must act accordingly. The standard practice in interpreting the results should be to label the conclusions as "tentative."

Such honesty will reflect well on the analyst, for it shows that he or she appreciates the difficulties involved in drawing causal conclusions from quasi-experimental data. When important questions are raised and left unanswered, an honest appraisal of the results also directs the attention of the scientific community toward replicating the study. For in the end, our hypotheses are confirmed only through replications which provide additional insight.

ANALYSIS OF THE REGRESSION-DISCONTINUITY DESIGN

In general, the analysis of data from the regression-discontinuity design is far more salutary than the analysis of data from nonequivalent group designs without controlled selection. Rather than having to guess about the nature of the group assignment process, the researcher has constrained the selection procedure to follow a prespecified pattern. Knowledge of this pattern can then be used to set up a justifiable experimental-control comparison. In particular, with appropriate precaution, the difference or discontinuity at the cutting point between the regression surfaces in the two groups can be taken as evidence of a treatment effect. This comparison is readily made in an ANCOVA with the pretest as a single covariate.[29]

Because we have been so disparaging of the ANCOVA procedure as used in other contexts, it may be worthwhile to describe briefly why it is appropriate here. In particular, we should emphasize that measurement error and irrelevance in the selection variable does not bias the analysis. As noted previously, if the variables that completely account for group assignment (save for essentially random differences) can be accurately measured, these measures can be used as covariates in an ANCOVA to provide an unbiased estimate of the treatment effect. When the selection is not controlled, the underlying determinants of selection are generally not measured accurately. So corrections need to be made for the effects of measurement error and irrelevance in the observed variables if the underlying causes of selection are to be properly modeled. For example, self-selection is usually determined by an individual's true level of motivation, not by motivation as measured. Because the measure of motivation is a fallible indicator of the true level of motivation and because it is this true level which underlies the selection process, we must take the inaccuracies of measurement into account in building a model for the analysis.

On the other hand, in the regression-discontinuity design it is the pretest as measured and not an underlying construct that determines selection. Even if the pretest is fallibly measured, this measurement error and irrelevance are a part of the selection criterion and need not, indeed should not, be corrected for in the

---

[29]One must be careful, however, that it is the displacement between the regression lines *at the cutting point* that is estimated. When the ANCOVA allows for nonparallel regression surfaces in the two groups, the displacement between the regression lines is measured at a point determined by how the pretest scores are entered in the model (see footnote 3). To measure the displacement at the cutting point, X', the pretest scores, X, should be rescaled as $X - X'$, and this new variable should be used in the model specification.

analysis. In other words, selection is based on the observed pretest so that this measured variable accounts for group assignment without the need for any correction.

Often the analysis of the regression-discontinuity design is restricted to estimating the discontinuity between the regression lines in the two groups only at the cutting point. Of course, in estimating the treatment effect just at the cutting point, we learn nothing about potential treatment effect interactions. Mapping out the full shape of an interaction would require extrapolating the estimated regression line for the experimental group into the region of the pretest where there is only control group data and, likewise, extrapolating the control group regression line into the region where there is only experimental group data. By the very nature of this process, there is no appropriate data in the region of the extrapolation with which to check the accuracy of the extrapolated regressions. In other words, the extrapolation rests completely on assumptions. This does not mean that the analysis should not be performed, only that its tenuous nature should be appreciated. Often the researcher should be content with just estimating the treatment effect at the cutting point since even this step will rest on many unvalidated assumptions.

In estimating the treatment effect at the cutting point, biases from two sources can arise. First, the analysis relies on the implicit assumption that in the absence of a treatment effect the regression surface would be continuous at the cutting point. Since a discontinuity in the regression can be caused by factors other than the treatment, this assumption may be incorrect. Unless the size of such spurious discontinuities is known or can be estimated, little can be done in the analysis to correct for this effect.

Second, the ANCOVA may be misspecified so that the shape of the regression surface is not properly modeled. Since the treatment effect is measured as a difference between the estimated regressions, a misspecification of the regression lines can bias the treatment effect estimate. An example of such a "pseudo-discontinuity" bias was provided in chapter 3. As we have noted previously, biases due to improperly modeling the regression surface can arise in other designs as well. For this reason, we have emphasized that nonlinearities should be taken into account whenever the ANCOVA model is used.

Correctly modeling the shape of the regression surface can be a difficult task. Though no definitive approach is available, a number of suggestions can be offered (and might also prove useful in other designs). The analyst should start by plotting the raw data to see what shapes are suggested. A useful adjunct is to group the data into intervals along the pretest and plot the mean of the posttest in each of these "columns." This serves to smooth the data so that the underlying regression surfaces stand out more clearly. It may also help to plot the column means of the posttest for varying column widths, since, depending upon the characteristics of the data, some aggregations will be more revealing than others.

Assuming that rough shapes are apparent in the plots, the analyst can proceed to model statistically the regression surface in each group. The most commonly used though not infallible procedure is step-wise polynomial fitting (cf. Bock, 1975; and Kerlinger and Pedhazur, 1973; also see footnote 3). In general, the

model specification should allow the regressions to differ across the groups (i.e., should include interaction terms) since forcing the regressions to be parallel in the presence of an interaction can again produce a pseudo-discontinuity. Unfortunately, even with these precautions, the polynomial model that results from the step-wise procedure may not be adequate.[30] For this reason, it is probably best to examine by eye how well the statistical models fit the data. Along this line, an exploratory sifting through various models would not be unreasonable. In this way one could choose a model depending upon how well it fit the data both statistically and visually. Of course, by sifting through the data in this manner one is capitalizing to some degree on chance. As a result, the probability levels of the statistical tests should be treated with considerable caution. One should also be careful not to choose a model simply because its estimate of a treatment effect is in the desired direction.

Because of the limitations of polynomial fitting, other procedures are being developed. These include methods based on work by Spiegelman (1976) and Sacks and Ylvisaker (1976) which require only very general information about the shape of the underlying surfaces. Undoubtedly, they also have their limitations (one of them being that the necessary calculations are very complicated), but these are not completely understood at this point.

An additional problem will arise for any fitting procedure when one of the treatments is given to only a relatively small group of individuals out on the tail of the distribution of the pretest. For example, such a situation arose in the study of the effects of Medicaid as presented in chapter 3. In this case only those with incomes less than $3,000 a year were eligible to receive the benefits of Medicaid. Obviously this category includes only a narrow range of individuals at the end of the income distribution. The problem is that it is difficult to estimate reliably a regression of the posttest on the pretest in a group that has very little variance in pretest scores. This in turn means that the treatment effect estimate in the regression-discontinuity design would also be estimated unreliably.

Two solutions to this problem exist for polynomial fitting. First, interactions can be ignored and the regression surfaces fit by forcing them to be parallel in the two groups. In this way the data in the larger group is used to help estimate the

---

[30]While in theory any surface can be fit by a polynomial model of sufficiently high degree, polynomial fitting has severe limitations in practice. First, the appropriate polynomial may be of infinite order and cannot be fit with a finite data set. A ceiling or floor effect might, for example, create a nonlinear regression surface that would require an infinite polynomial for a proper fit. Second, even if the polynomial is of finite degree, there is no method guaranteed to provide an unbiased estimate of the true surface.

If a low-order polynomial model fits the data, it is better to err on the side of overfitting the model (including more high-order terms than necessary) than underfitting it (omitting a low-order term that should be included). The reason is that when a low-order polynomial is correct, underfitting leads to a bias while overfitting does not. Overfitting does, however, reduce the precision of the estimate and should not be carried to an extreme. A backward selection, step-wise procedure (cf. Draper and Smith, 1966) is consistent with this preference for overfitting since it first considers higher-order models. However, it retains the higher-order terms only if they significantly contribute to the explanatory power of the model. On the other hand, if an infinite order polynomial is the proper model, it is not clear whether an inadequate higher-order model should be preferred to an inadequate lower-order model. Thus it is not clear if the backward selection procedure, which tends to favor higher-order models, is to be preferred.

regression surface in the smaller group, though with some bias if interactions are present. Second, interactions can be allowed but the treatment effect estimated by extrapolating the regressions to the point on the pretest equal to the mean in the smaller group.[31] In other words, instead of estimating the treatment effect at the cutting point, it is estimated at the pretest mean in the smaller group. This too can obviously be biased as an estimate of the treatment effect at the cutting point. However, the bias in both of these procedures is usually small when the range of pretest values in that one treatment group is small.

Finally, we should note that generating the same level of confidence in the results of a regression-discontinuity design as in the results of a randomized experiment requires a larger sample size in the former. Assuming that the pretest and posttest follow a bivariate normal distribution, Goldberger (1972b) demonstrated that the relative efficiency of the analysis of the randomized experiment as compared to the analysis of the regression-discontinuity design is approximately 2.75. In other words, if the randomized experiment had a sample of 100, the regression-discontinuity design would need a sample of 275 for the analysis to have approximately equal power. This, however, assumes that the shape of the regression surfaces are known. When the shape is unknown, an even larger sample in relative terms may be required if the regression-discontinuity design is to yield as credible results as the randomized experiment.

---

[31]This is done by subtracting the pretest mean of the group in the tail of the distribution, $\bar{X}_j$ from the pretest scores, X, to form a new variable, $X - \bar{X}_j$, which is then used in the ANCOVA model (see footnotes 3 and 29).

5

Quasi-Experiments:
Interrupted Time-Series
Designs

INTRODUCTION

A time series is involved when we have multiple observations over time. The observations can be on the same units, as when particular individuals are repeatedly observed; or they can be on different but similar units, as when annual third-grade achievement scores are displayed for a particular school over a series of years. In this latter case, different children will be in the class each year. *Interrupted* time-series analysis requires knowing the specific point in the series when a treatment occurred. The purpose of the analysis is to infer whether the treatment had any impact. If it did, then we would expect the observations after the treatment to be different from those before it. That is, the series should show signs of an "interruption" at an expected point in time.

Our presentation in this chapter will depend heavily on logic, common sense, and background theory for identifying and trying to rule out relevant threats to validity. We shall not be concerned here with the statistical analysis of interrupted time-series data or with the problems of statistical conclusion validity that the data analysis highlights. However, a discussion of the appropriate data analysis is in chapter 6, which should definitely be consulted before anyone collects and analyzes his or her own time-series data. Indeed, the interested reader may find it useful to go beyond chapter 6 and consult more comprehensive (and complicated) discussions of time-series analysis (e.g., Box and Jenkins, 1976; Glass, Willson and Gottman, 1975; Hibbs, 1974; and Box and Tiao, 1975).

Interrupted time-series designs have previously been listed and discussed by Campbell and Stanley (1963, pp. 37–43), Campbell (1969b, pp. 412–17); Riecken et al. (1974), and Glass, Willson, and Gottman (1975). The presentation that follows goes over much of the same ground, but introduces some variants on the basic design and discusses some practical problems in implementing time-series studies. We shall begin by presenting the most simple interrupted time series, and from there we shall work our way to more complicated versions. The

attentive reader will gradually come to see that the designs in this chapter combine the basic interrupted time series with many of the design variants that we outlined in chapter 3 for strengthening the interpretability of the basic nonequivalent control group design.

Types of Effects

A posttreatment time series can be affected by a treatment in several different ways. First, there may be a sharp discontinuity at the point of the interruption. We can illustrate this by considering a short series with 20 observations, 11 before the intervention and 9 after it. If the mean values for the pretreatment series were 2, 3, 4, 5, 6, 7, 8, 9, 10, 11, and 12 and the corresponding values for the posttreatment series were 10, 11, 12, 13, 14, 15, 16, 17, and 18, then we would conclude that the values decreased following the intervention, for the 12th observation is a 10 and not the expected 13. The change from a mean value of 12 to 10 is variously called a change in *level* or *intercept,* since (1) the level of the series drops, and (2) the pre- and posttreatment slopes would have different intercepts if extrapolated to a common origin.

The second type of change concerns the slope of the series following interruption. For instance, if the pretreatment mean values are 2, 3, 4, 5, 6, 7, 8, 9, 10, 11, and 12 and the posttreatment values for a similarly spaced series are 14, 16, 18, 20, 22, 24, 26, and 28, then we can see that before the treatment the series shifted one score unit per time unit, while after it there were two score units of change per time interval. Such a change is variously called a change in *drift, trend* or *slope*.

Though changes in level and slope are the most common forms of change, they are not the only ones possible. For instance, posttreatment changes will occur in the variances around each mean when a treatment makes people more homogeneous in their beliefs or actions. Also, the pattern of seasonality can be affected, as would happen if there were one kind of seasonal trend before a treatment but a different one after it. It is likely, for example, that the introduction of air conditioning caused a new relationship between time of the year and the amount of time spent indoors. Though changes in intercept and slope are the principal effects one examines, researchers should remain open-minded about other effects that can be detected in an interrupted time-series analysis.

Effects can be characterized along another dimension. A *continuous* effect is one that does not decay over time. Hence, a shift in level of X units is obtained both immediately after an intervention and for a ''considerable'' time period afterwards; or a shift in slope persists for a long time in terms of the total series length. A *discontinuous* effect is one which does not persist over time. Usually, we find that an initial effect drifts back towards the preintervention level or slope as the effect wears off. This is especially likely to be the case if the intervention is introduced and then later removed, but it also occurs where the treatment is left in place. Sometimes, a discontinuous effect can take the opposite form, with an effect becoming larger over time. However, in our experience this is rare. The time-series analyst should be sensitive to describing any effects in terms of the extent to which they are continuous or discontinuous.

Effects can also be characterized as *instantaneous* or *delayed* in their initial manifestation following the treatment. Instantaneous effects are usually simpler to interpret, for their onset can be matched exactly to the time of intervention. Delayed effects are more difficult to interpret, especially if there is no theoretical specification of how long a delay should elapse before an effect is expected. The difficulty with interpreting delayed effects arises because the extended time period between the treatment and the first visible signs of a possible impact usually allows a larger number of plausible alternative interpretations than happens with an instantaneous effect. For the most part, in this chapter we shall deal with instantaneous effects or with delayed effects where a strong theory specifies the delay interval (e.g., biology leads us to expect a nine-month delay between the start of a family-planning campaign and the first indications of effects on the birth rate). Our discussion of delayed effects will have to wait until we outline interrupted time-series designs with switching replications.

It is important to note that the effects researchers look for in an interrupted time-series study can be characterized along all three dimensions simultaneously. That is, the indicators of the effect (the level, slope, variance, and pattern of seasonality) can be combined with the permanence of the effect (continuous or discontinuous) and with the type of impact (immediate or delayed). While most of the examples in this chapter deal with immediate and continuous changes in level, delayed and discontinuous changes in level and slope are also briefly considered.

SIMPLE INTERRUPTED TIME SERIES

This, the most basic, time-series design requires one experimental group and multiple observations before and after a treatment. The design is diagrammed below.

$$O_1 \quad O_2 \quad O_3 \quad O_4 \quad O_5 \; X \; O_6 \quad O_7 \quad O_8 \quad O_9 \quad O_{10}$$

We shall begin the discussion of this design with examples from the classic studies of the British Industrial Fatigue Research Board in the early 1920s which introduced our present period of experimental quantitative management science. These were the studies which inspired, and were eclipsed by, the Hawthorne studies. While their methodology leaves much to be desired by present standards, it was a great forward leap in the direction here advocated and was probably stronger than the methodology used in the Hawthorne studies.

Figure 5.1 comes from Farmer (1924). He concluded that shortening the workday from ten to eight hours improved hourly productivity. With modern methodological concerns, we cannot be so sure. First, there is the possibility of a maturation alternative interpretation, since an upward self-improvement trend is visible before the treatment which we assume could have continued even without the change to an eight-hour day. One of the major advantages of a time series over other forms of quasi-experimental analysis is that we can assess the maturational trend prior to some intervention.

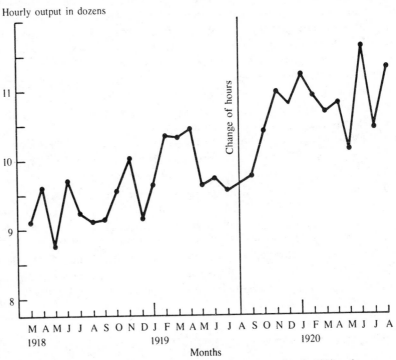

Hourly output in dozens

Change of hours

M A M J J A S O N D J F M A M J J A S O N D J F M A M J J A
1918   1919   1920
Months

Figure 5.1. Change in hourly productivity as a result of shifting from a ten-hour to an eight-hour work day. (After Farmer, 1924.)

A second threat to internal validity is apparent in Figure 5.1 since there may be a seasonal trend. (The change in the number of hours worked was introduced in August 1919. Note that in 1918 August was a low month followed by an upward trend, as it was in 1919 when the change was introduced.) The possibility of a cyclical trend masquerading as a treatment effect is reduced because there is no evidence of a summer slump in 1920. However, without a large time series it is impossible to rule out the possibility that the apparent treatment effect after August 1919 is due to most Augusts being different from following months.

Figure 5.2 gives time-series data from a quasi-experiment by Lawler and Hackman (1969) where the threats to validity are somewhat different from those in the previous example. The treatment was the introduction of a participative decision-making scheme to three groups of men doing janitorial work at night, and the dependent variable was absenteeism (the proportion of possible work hours actually worked). A noteworthy feature of Figure 5.2 is that a false picture would have been given if there had been only a single pretest and a single posttest. The total pretest data reveal that the last pretest measure is atypically low and, as a consequence, statistical regression will almost certainly be inflating the difference between the last pretest and the first posttest measure. A strength of time-series

designs is that they allow assessment of the pretest time trend, thereby permitting a check on the plausibility of a regression alternative explanation of findings.

The major threat to internal validity with most single time-series designs is a main effect of history—the possibility that forces other than the treatment under investigation came to influence the dependent variable immediately after participative decision making was introduced. For example, there might have been a police drive to clean streets of criminals at night, or some of the janitors may have staged a strike, or they may have begun a car pool. Several controls for history are possible, perhaps the best being to add a no-treatment control group. But, though advisable, this is not always necessary. For instance, Lawler and Hackman's unobtrusive measure of absenteeism was calibrated into weekly intervals, and the historical events that can explain an apparent treatment effect are fewer with weekly intervals than with monthly or yearly ones. Also, if records are kept of all plausible effect-causing events that could influence respondents during a quasi-experiment, it should be possible to ascertain whether any of them were operative between the last pretest and the first posttest. If they were not, history is less plausible as a threat.

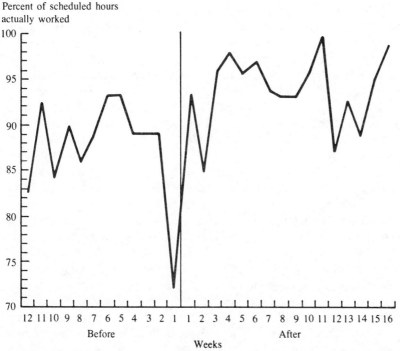

Figure 5.2. Mean attendance of the participative groups for the 12 weeks before the incentive plan and the 16 weeks after the plan. Attendance is expressed in terms of the percentage of hours scheduled to be worked that were actually worked. (From Lawler and Hackman, 1969.)

Another threat is instrumentation. A change in administrative procedures will sometimes lead to a change in the way records are kept. In particular, persons who want to make their performance look good can simply change bookkeeping procedures to redefine performance or satisfaction. Or, persons with a mandate to change an organization may interpret this to include making changes in the way that records are kept or in the way that criteria of success and failure are defined. This seems to have happened, for instance, when Orlando Wilson took charge of the Chicago police. By redefining how crimes should be classified, he appeared to have caused an increase in crime. But the increase was spurious, reflecting record-keeping changes and not changes in criminal behavior. In time-series work it is exceedingly dangerous not to pay particular attention to the definition of constructs and to possible changes in record-keeping procedures. Uncritical acceptance of a series of numbers that purport to measure a possible effect can lead to spurious inferences, for the numbers suppose a constancy of definition which they may not always reflect. As a further instance, note the experience of Kerpelman et al. (1978). As part of their study of the effects of a lawn mower safety campaign, they used time-series data about accidents that are reported to hospitals. Some hospitals routinely monitor accidents and their reported causes. Kerpelman et al. wanted to discover if the monthly accident rate attributable to lawn mowers decreased after the safety campaign was launched. At one site, the data looked to simple visual inspection as though the campaign had backfired, for accidents seemed higher after the campaign than for the two years before it. Since this result was surprising, the hospital records were checked, and it was discovered that record keeping changed at the time of the campaign. It seems that the persons responsible for compiling the data became much more conscious of "lawn mower accidents" as an important category for assigning causes after they learned that a lawn mower safety campaign was under way in their district and that the data they provided would be used as part of the evaluation of the campaign. When they went back to the basic data for all three years and recoded them with the same care across all years, Kerpelman et al. found that the magnitude of the apparent negative effect was less after the reanalysis than before it and that it was probably not statistically significant. (The small number of time intervals makes the statistical analysis problematic.) In this case, the shift in the record-keeping system at the time of the intervention probably affected error as much as bias, but the change was enough to make a visually strong negative effect into what was at the very most a weak negative one.

Another threat is simple selection. This occurs when the composition of the experimental group changes abruptly at the time of the intervention. Usually, this will be because the treatment causes attrition from the measurement framework. When this happens, it will not be possible without further analyses to disentangle whether the treatment caused an interruption in the series or whether the interruption was due to different persons being in the pretreatment series when compared to the posttreatment series. The simplest solution to the selection problem, where available, is to restrict at least one of the data analyses to the subset of units which were measured at each time period. But repeated measurement on the same units is not always possible (e.g., where the third-grade achievement scores over 20 years from a single school are involved). In such cases it is more difficult to deal

with selection. Nonetheless, background characteristics of units can sometimes be analyzed in order to ascertain whether there is a sharp discontinuity in the profile of the units when the treatment was introduced. If there is, selection is a problem. If there is not, then selection is not likely to be a serious threat unless the background characteristics are poorly measured or are not appropriate for describing shifts in the units that could have affected the dependent variable of the series.

A final threat to internal validity is worth reiterating, even though we previously mentioned it in discussing the Farmer study. Time series are subject to many influences of a cyclical nature, including seasonal variation in performance, attitudes, or communication patterns; and these influences can be inadvertently interpreted as treatment effects. In the Lawler and Hackman quasi-experiment, it is not clear at what point in the year the study of janitors was conducted or how performance is normally related to temporal cycles. Just suppose, however, that the study began in December when the weather is cold, illness more prevalent, and absenteeism higher. Twelve weeks later, when the treatment was implemented, it would be March or April when the weather is better, health improved, and absenteeism lower. If the treatment was indeed introduced in December (and we have no evidence that it was), then the decrease in absenteeism which the authors obtained might be due to a recurrent seasonal change rather than to the novel decision-making scheme of theoretical and practical interest. Since controlling for cyclical change obviously requires estimating what the cyclical pattern is, a long time series is required to test this particular threat.

The prevalence of cyclical patterns of behavior indicates the importance of displaying interrupted time-series data so that cyclical variation has been removed and the series is expressed as deviations from an expected cyclical pattern. Consider seasonality, the most frequent cyclical pattern, which reflects the systematic way behavior fluctuates during the seasons. For instance, retail sales peak every year in December and decline in January; the use of outdoor recreational facilities peaks in the third quarter of the year (summer) and declines in the first and last quarters (late fall, winter, and early spring). Several methods for removing seasonal variation have been advocated. The modeling tradition of Box and Jenkins (1976) will be presented in the next chapter since, in our opinion, it is probably the best single method. However, other methods are used, including dummy variables (see Johnston, 1972, pp. 186–92) and the ratio-to-moving average method (see Hickman and Hilton, 1971, chapter 19).

As far as statistical conclusion validity is concerned, Lawler and Hackman analyzed their data comparing the collapsed pretest hours worked with the collapsed posttest hours. But in doing this, they did not use the full data from the pretest, posttest, and the statistical test they employed is only appropriate for comparing two independent groups and not the same group at two times. They would have done better to use the methods outlined in the next chapter, though their series is rather short for them. In any event, we cannot be sure from the analysis the authors conducted that there is any statistically significant decrease in absenteeism as a result of the treatment.

As far as construct validity is concerned, reactive arrangements are only likely to hinder interpretation of the data for a single time series if (1) the same respondents are repeatedly measured and (2) they know when the treatment was imple-

mented. In most archival studies it is unlikely that both these conditions will be met, so that reactivity-related threats to construct validity are not revelant. But such threats are more likely in clinical or other operant studies, especially if the time interval between observations is short and respondents can remember their past responses. Each time-series experiment has to be carefully examined on its own merits to determine the viability of the interpretation that the observed results are due to evaluation apprehension or some similar threat to construct validity.

Typically, there will be only one operationalization of the treatment and effect in time-series work. This raises other problems of construct validity, particularly if the treatment is not closely tailored to a well-specified construct and is not independently measured. As always, it is easier to have more than one measure of an effect construct than a treatment construct. But, nonetheless, the difficulty of obtaining multiple measures of an effect should not be underestimated. This is because most archives are set up to store information about indicators. Concerns about expense or old-fashioned definitional operationalist thinking often led the persons who set up archives to measure academic achievement, or burglary, or unemployment in one particular way. Contrast this with the situation where the researcher collects his own dependent variable data and can add more questions or observations to the measurement framework. In cases where one does have multiple measures of an effect, each of which is reasonably reliably measured, the time series for each measure can be examined separately or, if the measures are highly correlated, a composite index can be formed.

Concerning external validity, it is sometimes possible in archival studies to use available data on the background characteristics of units in order to stratify them into, say, males and females, persons aged 18–35, 36–50, 51–65, 65+, or the like. Then, the series for each subgroup can be separately examined to assess whether an effect holds across the various subgroups. Of course, there is no need to restrict the stratification to person variables. Setting variables can also be used like person variables in order to specify the range of an effect. This disaggregation has to be accomplished with caution, for statistical power is reduced by creating subgroups. Moreover, in archival research one has a restricted flexibility for creating the kinds of subgroups one wants. One is restricted to the variables in the system and to the particular cutting points in the record. Thus, if the last age category is 65+ and one is interested in studying the so-called "old-old" (75+), one cannot do so.

INTERRUPTED TIME SERIES WITH A NONEQUIVALENT NO-TREATMENT CONTROL GROUP TIME SERIES

Consider the addition to the simple time-series design of a time series from a nonequivalent no-treatment control group. The resulting design is diagrammed below:

O_1	O_2	O_3	O_4	O_5 X O_6	O_7	O_8	O_9	O_{10}
O_1	O_2	O_3	O_4	O_5 O_6	O_7	O_8	O_9	O_{10}

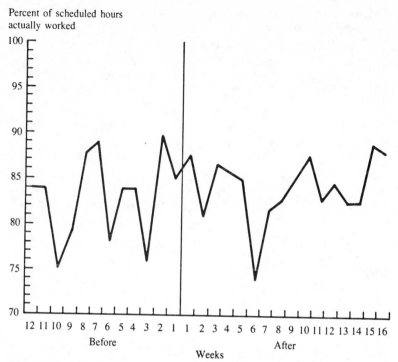

Figure 5.3. Mean attendance of the imposed groups for the 12 weeks before the incentive plan and the 16 weeks after the plan. Attendance is expressed in terms of the percentage of hours scheduled to be worked that were actually worked. (From Lawler and Hackman, 1969.)

Lawler and Hackman (1969) actually incorporated an untreated control group into their experiment since one set of work groups was given the same bonus as the experimentals but did not participate in the decision about setting rates. The relevant data from the control group are in Figure 5.3, which should be compared with the time series from the treatment group in Figure 5.2 above. Visual inspection suggests that absenteeism may have declined by more in the group with participative decision making than in the group without it.

Since the experimental and control groups worked over the same time period, it is unlikely that a treatment-correlated historical event caused the apparent decrease in absenteeism in the treatment group. If it had done so, we would have expected a decrease in the control group as well. The ability to test for the threat of history is the major strength of the control group time-series design. Local history (selection × history) can be problematic, though, if the groups differ from each other considerably; one group may well experience a set of unique events that the other does not. Note that the problem is not one of unique history in general; the internal validity threat can only come from a unique historical event *at*

the time of the intervention. Such an event is unlikely with groups as comparable as Lawler and Hackman's, but more likely with less comparable groups.

The untreated control series normally also allows tests of the other threats to internal validity that operate on the single time series. There is no obvious reason in the Lawler and Hackman case, for example, why the measurement instrument should have differed between the treatment and control groups. Nor is there an obvious reason why each group should be experiencing a different cyclical pattern of absenteeism. However, as groups get increasingly noncomparable, each of these threats becomes more plausible. This is why it is always worthwhile to check the pretreatment series for indications of differential cyclical patterns and to check the data sources to probe whether any shifts in definition or recording behavior can be remembered. Given a no-treatment control series, the possibility of differential regression can be simply explored by seeing if there is an immediate pretreatment shift in one series but not the other. If there is not, regression is not a problem.

Since threats to internal validity are more problematic the less comparable the groups, it might be thought that matching the two series at the point of the intervention will produce comparability and reduce threats. This is not the case, however, for such matching can cause spurious effects. Consider a study of the effects of television on, say, library circulation where we have two nonequivalent sets of communities, one of which gets television in 1953 and the other does not. The particular communities in each set can be selected by matching per capita library circulation in 1953 (i.e., by choosing communities from each set that are "close" matches). When this is done, the data might appear as in the hypothetical Figure 5.4, which should be contrasted with the unmatched series in Figure 5.5. It can be seen that the matching is successful and that the television and nontelevision groups have similar library circulation figures at the point of the intervention. But, given errorful measures of circulation, it can also be seen that the two groups differ in the same direction before and after 1953. The lower library circulation in the set of television communities after 1953 is probably not due to television. Rather, it is probably due to statistical regression, since the nonequivalent groups are drifting apart to their true (population) values. In other words, the match in 1953 is achieved by capitalizing on error—to achieve matches, communities tend to be chosen for the experimental group because error inflates their scores, while communities tend to be chosen for the control group because error deflates their scores. Matching can have the same regression consequences in time-series work as with simpler nonequivalent control group designs.

The threats to external validity that apply to the simple time series also apply to the control group time series. Consider the interaction of populations and treatments. The data of Lawler and Hackman (1969) suggest relatively flat pretest slopes with considerable "noise" (the immediate pretreatment pretest value in the experimental group being a salient example). Let us assume, therefore, that the pretest trends are flat for the sake of exposition. If so, work attendance during the pretest was higher in the treatment groups (average of 12 weeks = 88%) than among controls (average over 12 weeks = 83%). This difference would have been even more marked if the one deviant pretest value had been removed from the

experimental time series. Hence, the effect in the treatment group may reflect the restriction that participative decision making is more effective with conscientious persons who attend work regularly than with others. The probability of an interaction of treatment and population would have been reduced if the intact groups of janitors had been matched on pretest averages and then randomly assigned to the different conditions. While the number of groups in Lawler and Hackman's study was so low that matching plus randomization would not have ensured pretest equivalence, it would have at least reduced pretest differences.

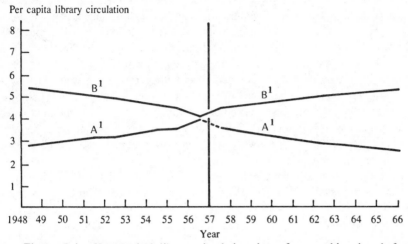

Figure 5.4. Hypothetical library circulation data after matching just before a treatment is introduced.

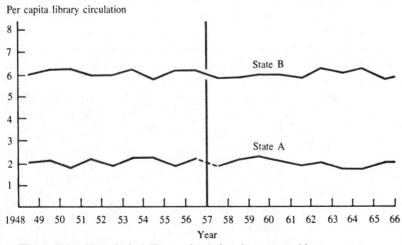

Figure 5.5. Hypothetical library circulation data prematching.

Lawler and Hackman's study also illustrates that the frequency of posttest measures should not be confused with their temporal duration. The dangers of such confounding are well illustrated by the follow-up study by Scheflen, Lawler, and Hackman (1971). The latter investigators used the same groups as Lawler and Hackman but assessed absenteeism from 53 to 64 weeks after the treatment. The major finding was that the bonus scheme developed through participative decision making had been removed from two of the three treatment groups by disgruntled managers. More importantly for the present discussion, the researchers also found that in the one group where the bonus scheme was retained, the average attendance for the 53rd to the 64th weeks after the treatment (93%) did not differ from the immediate posttreatment average and was 5% higher than during the pretest. But in the control groups where the bonus scheme was imposed by management, the average attendance between the 53rd and 64th weeks was 87%, which was a rise of 4% over the 83% average from the pretest phase. Thus, assuming that the 5% and 4% rises were not different from each other, the 53–64-week data support the conservative conclusion that participative decision making was not demonstrably more effective than was imposed decision making over the long term—a conclusion that has to be tempered by the knowledge that change may not have been as easy from the 88% pretest level in the treatment group as from the 83% level in the no-treatment controls. Without the control group it would have been much more difficult to assess the temporal persistence of treatment effects since, with a single experimental time series, persistence is confounded with both history and maturation. No-treatment control groups are generally indispensable for making inferences about the temporal persistence of any treatment effects.

INTERRUPTED TIME SERIES WITH NONEQUIVALENT DEPENDENT VARIABLES

We have previously mentioned how history is the main threat to internal validity in a single time series and how the effect of history can sometimes be examined by minimizing the time interval between measures or by including a no-treatment control group in the design. History can also be examined, and the construct validity of the effect enhanced, by collecting time-series data for some dependent variables that should be affected by a treatment and for others that should not. Of course, the restriction holds—as it did in examining the nonequivalent dependent variables design earlier—that the dependent variables must be conceptually related. The design in question is diagrammed as:

$$O_{A1} \quad O_{A2} \quad O_{A3} \quad O_{A4} \quad O_{A5} \; X \; O_{A6} \quad O_{A7} \quad O_{A8} \quad O_{A9} \quad O_{A10}$$
$$O_{B1} \quad O_{B2} \quad O_{B3} \quad O_{B4} \quad O_{B5} \; X \; O_{B6} \quad O_{B7} \quad O_{B8} \quad O_{B9} \quad O_{B10}$$

An example of the use of this design comes from a study of the effectiveness of the British breathalyser crackdown (Ross, Campbell, and Glass, 1970). Use of the breathalyser was an attempt to curb drunken driving in the hope that this would lead to a reduction in serious traffic accidents. One feature of British drinking laws is that pubs can be open only during certain hours. Thus, if we are prepared to assume that a considerable proportion of British drinking takes place

in pubs rather than at home, we might predict, if the breathalyser were effective, that the number of serious traffic accidents should decrease during the hours pubs are open, particularly during weekend nights, and should be less affected during commuting hours when pubs are closed. The importance of the distinction between serious accidents when pubs are open or closed derives from the fact that most history alternative interpretations of a decrease in serious accidents are interpretations that should affect *all* serious accidents *irrespective of the time of day.* Such alternative interpretations might include weather changes, the introduction of safer cars, a police crackdown on speeding, contemporaneous newspaper reports of high accident rates of particularly gory accidents, and so forth.

It is obvious from visual inspection of Figure 5.6 that there is a marked drop in the accident rate at weekends but there is much less of a drop during nondrinking hours in the week. Statistical analysis corroborated the decrease in 1967 in the weekend-nights time series (and also in the all-hours-and-days series). It is very

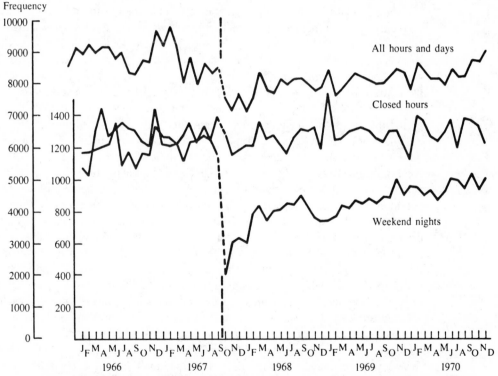

Figure 5.6. British casualties (fatalities plus serious injuries) before and after the British breathalyser crackdown of October 1967, seasonally adjusted. Adapted from "Determining the Social Effects of a Legal Reform: The British 'Breathalyser' Crackdown of 1967'' by H. L. Ross, D. T. Campbell, and G. V. Glass in *AMERICAN BEHAVIORAL SCIENTIST* March/April 1970, 13 (4): 493–509. Reprinted by permission of the Publisher, Sage Publications, Inc.

difficult to fault either the internal or statistical conclusion validity of these data.

As always, however, questions can be raised about external validity. An obvious question is: Would the same results be obtained in the United States? Another concerns whether the effects are stronger with some kinds of drivers than others. Other questions relate to possible unanticipated side effects of the breathalyser. How did it affect accident insurance rates, sales of liquor, public confidence in the role of technological innovations for solving social problems, the sale of technical gadgetry to the police, the way the courts handled drunken driving cases? Many such issues are examined in Ross (1973).

Ross's major concern in his important 1973 paper is in assessing construct validity. If we consider Figure 5.6 more carefully, it is apparent that not all of the initial decrease in serious accidents during the weekend is maintained. That is, the accident rate drops at first but then continually rises toward the level in the control time series, though the two trends still do not meet by the last measure. Thus, the effect construct needs modifying to point out that it is a *temporary* reduction in serious accidents.

The fact that "something" inflated the effects of the breathalyser at the time it was introduced or deflated its effects after it was introduced suggests that the causal agent was not the breathalyser alone. The breathalyser was introduced into Britain with much nationwide publicity, and the publicity may have made the general public especially mindful of the desirability of not driving after drinking. Or it may have made the police especially vigilant in controlling the speed of traffic, especially during and immediately after pub hours. Ross (1973) also suggested that use of the breathalyser may have reduced the overall number of hours driven, may have cut down on drinking, or may have led drunken drivers to drive more carefully. He very ingeniously ruled out some of these explanations. He took the regular surveys by the British Road Research Laboratory of miles driven, converted the number of serious accidents and fatalities to the number of accidents per mile driven, and showed that the introduction of the breathalyser was still associated with a decrease in accidents when the estimate of accidents per mile driven was used. Hence, to the extent the estimate is valid, we can rule out the explanation that the breathalyser's effect is due to a reduction in the number of miles driven. Ross also examined the sale of beer and spirits before and after the breathalyser and could find no evidence of a discontinuity in sales when the instrument was introduced. This ruled out the interpretation that the breathalyser had reduced drinking. He was also able to show for ten months after the breathalyser that more persons reported walking home after drinking than had been the case in the equivalent ten months preceding the breathalyser. Finally, he also showed that fewer of the postbreathalyser traffic fatalities had high alcohol levels in their blood than had the corpses of the prebreathalyser fatalities. These last data indirectly supported the explanation that the causal construct was a reduction in the number of heavy drinkers driving, rather than a significant reduction in either aggregate drinking or driving.

The attempts by Ross to use data to rule out alternative explanations of the causal construct should alert us to the importance of doing this, the difficulty and expense encountered, and the number of irrelevancies associated with the intro-

duction of new practices. Having claimed that the breathalyser caused a decrease in driving by heavy drinkers which led to fewer serious accidents, Ross was then faced with the problem of explaining why the effects of the breathalyser were not more permanent. His analysis suggested to him that the British courts increasingly failed to punish drinkers detected by the breathalyser so that it lost its deterrent power. Thus, Ross's final inference took the highly useful form: A breathalyser will help reduce serious traffic accidents when it is used to restrict drunken driving, but it will have this effect only if the courts enforce the law about drinking and driving.

INTERRUPTED TIME SERIES WITH REMOVED TREATMENT

Two of the units in the Scheflen, Lawler, and Hackman following study had the treatment removed from them. When restricted to these groups, the modified design can be diagrammed in the fashion below with X indicating the treatment and $\overline{X}$ its removal. (It would actually be more accurate to put Xs in each interval between O_5 and O_9 since the treatment remained in place for this period.)

$$O_1 \quad O_2 \quad O_3 \quad O_4 \quad O_5 X O_6 \quad O_7 \quad O_8 \quad O_9 \overline{X} O_{10} \quad O_{11} \quad O_{12} \quad O_{13}$$

The design is essentially two interrupted time series. The first, from O_1 to O_9, is designed to permit assessing the effects of the presence of a treatment, and the second, from O_5 to O_{13}, is supposed to test the effects of the absence of the treatment. The most powerful pattern of effects for inferential purposes would, of course, be if the intercept or slope changed in one direction between O_4 and O_5 and then changed in the opposite direction between O_9 and O_{10}. Seen from the perspective of two separate time series, the overall design must have at least the strengths of a simple time series. The question is: Which advantages of interpretation accrue because of the last part of the series where the treatment is removed?

An obvious advantage is that the threat of history is reduced because the only relevant historical threat is one that operates in different directions at different times or involves two different historical forces operating in different directions at different times. Simple selection is also less of a threat, since the only viable selection threat requires different kinds of attrition at different time points. Instrumentation is also less likely, though it will be worthwhile exploring whether a spurious effect occurred when the treatment was introduced (say, a history-related effect) while a simple ceiling or floor effect caused an inflection in an upward or downward general trend at the point when the treatment was removed. If there are no instrumentation effects related to the removal of the treatment, instrumentation is in general not likely to be a threat. Even when it is a threat it may be judged as an implausible one insofar as the same instrumentation effect cannot account for both an increase and decrease at different times.

Given this design and effects in opposite directions at X and $\overline{X}$, it will often be plausible to argue that the disappearance of the original effect is not due to removing the treatment but is due instead to resentful demoralization at having the treatment removed, or to selection-maturation. The latter would occur if the posttreatment trend were used by decision makers as a criterion for removing the

treatment, perhaps because the immediate posttreatment trend suggested an ever-quickening dissipation of the original effect. In the Scheflen, Lawler, and Hackman case, one might wonder whether the particularly high levels of absenteeism after the participative decision making was revoked by managers was due to losing the money, losing control over their lives, or due to the fact that absenteeism was beginning to accelerate anyway. Clearly, removed treatment designs are more interpretable the less salient the treatment is to respondents. But that is not the major point. What is especially worth noting is that such explanations for the effects of removing the treatment do not by themselves threaten the interpretation of effects attributable to introducing the treatment. When the removed treatment design produces results in different directions, one needs two *different* alternative interpretations to invalidate a causal inference.

Great care should be exercised before embarking upon a deliberately chosen plan to remove a treatment. Ethics aside, the major technical fear has to be that removing the treatment will prejudice the simple interrupted time series that precedes the removal because the series is shortened and sensitive statistical analysis is precluded. In our opinion, treatments should not be deliberately removed if, in so doing, it would be difficult to reliably estimate monthly, quarterly, or even annual cyclical patterns in the preremoval data.

INTERRUPTED TIME SERIES WITH MULTIPLE REPLICATIONS

In some controlled settings it is possible to introduce a treatment, remove it, reintroduce it, remove it again, and so on, according to a planned schedule. This design can be diagrammed as:

$$O_1 \quad O_2 X O_3 \quad O_4 \overline{X} O_5 \quad O_6 X O_7 \quad O_8 \overline{X} O_9 \quad O_{10} X O_{11} \quad O_{12} \overline{X} O_{13} \quad O_{14}$$

A treatment effect would be suggested if the dependent variable responded in similar fashion each time the treatment was introduced and in a similar fashion each time it was removed. However, the direction of responses must be different in the case of introductions when compared to removals.

A salient issue with this design concerns the scheduling of treatments and their removal. This is probably best done randomly, though in such a way as to preserve the alternation of X and $\overline{X}$. A random distribution rules out the threat of cyclical maturation, i.e., the series would have exhibited a regular cycle of ups and downs even in the absence of a treatment. Where such cyclicity is ruled out by theory or a long untreated part of the series, the scheduling of the treatments can be more systematic. This design is obviously a very powerful one for inferring causal effects. Moreover, it can easily be modified to compare different treatments, with X_1 being substituted for the global X and X_2 for $\overline{X}$. It would even be possible to add an interaction factor $X_1 X_2$.

The major limitations of the basic design diagrammed above are practical. First, it can be implemented only where the initial effect of the treatment is expected to dissipate rapidly. If there were any persistence of the effect in the treatment's absence, it would be difficult to obtain any dissipation of the effect when the treatment was removed. Also, the design normally requires a degree of experimental control which can rarely be achieved outside of laboratory settings or

enclosed institutional settings like schools and prisons. It is our distinct impression that the design has been most often used by researchers in mental health, particularly those with a behavior modification bent. In these cases the therapeutic problems attacked in such research allow investigators the very control over respondents that the design requires.

INTERRUPTED TIME SERIES WITH SWITCHING REPLICATIONS

Imagine two nonequivalent samples, each of which receives the treatment at different times so that when one group receives the treatment the other serves as a control, and when the control group later receives the treatment the original treatment group serves as the control. The design can be diagrammed as:

$$O_1 \quad O_2 \quad O_3 \quad O_4 \quad O_5 \quad O_6 \quad O_7 \quad O_8 X O_9 \quad O_{10} \quad O_{11}$$
$$O_1 \quad O_2 \quad O_3 X O_4 \quad O_5 \quad O_6 \quad O_7 \quad O_8 \quad O_9 \quad O_{10} \quad O_{11}$$

The power of the design derives from its control for most threats to internal validity and from its potential in extending external and construct validity. External validity is enhanced because an effect can be demonstrated with two populations in at least two settings at different moments in history. Moreover, there are likely to be different irrelevancies associated with the application of each treatment and, if measures are unobtrusive, there need be no fear of the treatment's interacting with testing.

Figure 5.7 gives previously unpublished data from a study which used the replicated time-series design (Parker, Campbell, Cook, Katzman, & Butler-Paisley, 1971). The treatment was the introduction of television into various Illinois communities, and the hypothesis was that television would cause a decrease in library circulation (Parker, 1963) because it would serve as a substitute for reading. Thus, the dependent variable was the annual per capita circulation of library books. The unique feature of this particular quasi-experiment is the sharp differentiation of the treatment groups. This occurred because the Federal Communications Commission stopped issuing new licenses for television stations in 1951. This split Illinois communities into two groups: an urban, wealthy group with growing population that had television before the freeze (the so-called early TV communities) and a rural, poor group with static population growth that received television only after the freeze was lifted in 1953 (the so-called late TV communities). It can be seen from Figure 5.7 that library circulation declined about 1948 for the early TV group and during 1953 for the late TV group. The Glass, Tiao, and Maguire (1971) statistic confirmed that each of these decreases was statistically significant. This corroborated the hypothesis, and it is noteworthy that the design involved archival measures, distinctly different populations, different historical moments for introducing the treatment (in nonreactive fashion), different irrelevancies associated with how the treatment was introduced, and repeated measures to ascertain if an initial effect can be generalized over time.

But even the replicated time-series design can have problems of internal validity. Paperback books may have been introduced earlier into the rich early TV communities than into the poor late TV communities. If so, the declines in library

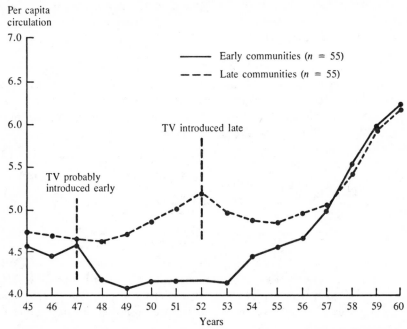

Figure 5.7. Per capita library correlation in two sets of Illinois communities as a function of the introduction of television. (From Parker et al., 1971.)

circulation in 1948 and 1953 might have been due to historical differences in the availability of paperbacks—an interaction of history and selection. This alternative interpretation could be ruled out by collecting data on the circulation of paperbacks in each set of communities. This would be a laborious but worthwhile operation for someone with a vested interest in knowing that the introduction of television *caused* a decrease in library circulation. A different strategy, following the example of Parker (1963), would be to split the library circulation into fiction and nonfiction books. Television, as a predominantly fictional medium, would be expected to have a greater effect on the circulation of fiction than of fact books. Using nonequivalent dependent variables in this way would render the paperback explanation less plausible because we would have to postulate that fiction books were introduced into the different communities at different times but that nonfiction books were not. This is not impossible—only relatively implausible.

The switching replications design is also useful because it can help detect effects that have an unpredictable delay period. Assuming an equal delay of effect in each group, we would expect a discontinuity at an earlier date in one series than in the other. We would also expect the period between the discontinuities to be equal to the known period that elapsed between implementing the treatment with different groups. However, in some cases it will not be possible to accept the assumption of equal delay intervals, particularly (1) when the nonequivalent

groups are highly dissimilar and/or (2) when the gap between implementing a treatment in one group and then another is large. Many treatments may interact in complex ways with history and group characteristics to determine how long it takes for an effect to manifest itself. Therefore, it is more realistic to look for relative differences in when an apparent treatment effect appears in each group than it is to look for an exact match between the difference in time when each group received the treatment and the difference in time when effects became manifest. The switching replications design is useful for probing delayed causal effects where there is no strong theory of the length of expected delay. However, it is most interpretable in the case where the time difference between when the groups receive the treatment exactly matches the time period between when effects appear in each group.

The replicated time-series design is clearly powerful for ruling out most validity threats. But is it practical? We think it is wherever a time-series design with a no-treatment control group is feasible. If treatments of an ameliorative nature have been successful, then it is likely that their utilization will be of benefit to the groups or organizations which served as no-treatment controls. Representatives of these groups can be approached to see if they will agree to an experiment that has once before produced desirable consequences. Consider the consequences if Lawler and Hackman (1969) had been able to persuade the persons who authorized their participative decision-making study that the resulting bonus scheme had reduced costly absenteeism and that it might do the same for the control groups where there was no participation. Then, a participative decision-making scheme might have been introduced into the control groups at a later date, and Lawler and Hackman would not have had the problem of a threat to external validity based on the interaction of populations and treatments. Nor would they have had as many other problems of external validity. Their final design would have had a replicated time series with each condition receiving the treatment *at its own level of pretest absenteeism*.

SOME FREQUENT PROBLEMS WITH INTERRUPTED TIME-SERIES DESIGNS

The foregoing discussion may give readers an oversimplified view of the practical and inferential difficulties in conducting interrupted time-series research. A number of problems frequently arise that cannot be handled as easily as our discussion implies. First, many treatments are not implemented rapidly. Instead, they slowly diffuse through a population so that the treatment is better modeled as a diffusion ogive than as a step function. Second, many effects are not instantaneous but occur with unpredictable time delays which may differ among populations and from one historical moment to the next. Third, though many data series are longer than those considered in chapters 3 and 4, they are nonetheless much shorter than the 50 or so observations usually recommended for statistical analysis. Fourth, many archivists are difficult to locate and, once contacted, are reluctant to release data. Moreover, any released data might involve time intervals that are longer than one would like; some data may be missing or look suspicious; and there may be undocumented definitional shifts.

Gradual Rather Than Abrupt Interventions

In most of the examples we have discussed thus far, interventions began at a known point in time and quickly diffused through the relevant population. Thus, the time of onset was close to the time when most people would have a chance to be affected by the treatment. But we know from many studies that innovations diffuse at different rates—some abruptly and others very gradually. If we reconsider the television and library circulation example based on Illinois counties, indirect evidence suggests that the diffusion of television was less abrupt than it might appear. In a study of the effects of the introduction of television on crime indicators which used cities (rather than states) as the unit of analysis, Hennigan, Del Rosario, Heath, Cook, Calder and Wharton (1979) showed that television was first introduced into some cities about 1948 but did not reach 75% household saturation until 1952. Similarly, the communities that began to get television after the FCC freeze was lifted in 1953 did not reach 75% saturation levels until 1957. Some of the annual household saturation figures for this period (see Figure 5.8) show diffusion ogives rather than the single abrupt line that was used in earlier examples in this chapter to represent the treatment.

Treating a diffusion curve as though it were a step function can create serious problems. First, one can create false effects by capitalizing upon chance and positioning the intervention at a discrete point during the intervention period when a

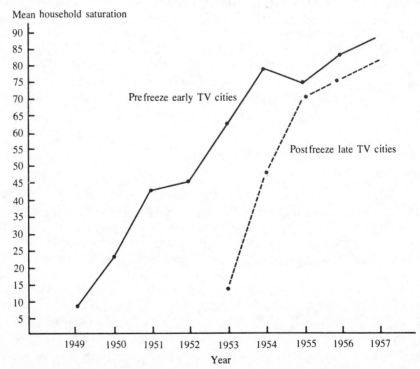

Figure 5.8. Household television saturation for 1949 to 1957 in communities that had TV before and after the FCC freeze on new stations.

larger-than-normal chance deviation occurs. Statistical regression will then result. Second, one can overlook true effects by assuming that the onset of the intervention (1953 for the late TV cities in Figure 5.8) occurred at the maximal point for potential impact (not reached until about 1957). Third, even when the researcher is careful not to confuse the onset of the treatment with its widespread availability, he or she is constrained to look for patterns of effects that mirror the pattern of the implementation of the treatment. However, to expect such patterns is often naive, since causal thresholds can operate to make the manifestation of an effect dependent on reaching at least a certain level of the treatment. The best one can do is to look for delayed effects sometime after the onset of the treatment. The difficulty here is ruling out the historical effects that could have operated between the onset of the treatment and the manifestation of what might be an effect.

In this respect, it is worth considering why the breathalyser data were so clearcut. Some laws, when changed, are not well publicized, or are poorly enforced. Hence, we would expect a gradual buildup in the public's reaction to a change in the law, and we would not expect to find the kind of visually dramatic decrease in serious traffic accidents that is displayed in Figure 5.6. Fortunately, we know from background data that the British breathalyser was widely publicized, as was the date at which the police would begin to use it. This probably speeded up the usual process of informing the public about the use of the breathalyser and also contributed to policemen using it at frequent intervals right after the publicized date for its implementation. Under these conditions the actual diffusion process better approximated a step function than many other diffusion ogives do.

When it is anticipated that an intervention will be disseminated slowly throughout a population, it is desirable to collect data for the purpose of describing the diffusion process. Such data can then be plotted together with the outcome data of major concern to see whether the buildup of the treatment corresponds with a buildup of the outcome variable. More importantly, transfer function analyses of the multiple time series (Box and Jenkins, 1976) can be carried out in which the treatment is treated as a more complex function than the preintervention zeros and the postintervention ones that correspond to a step function. The fortunate feature of a slow diffusion process is that, if we can assume instantaneous causation (i.e., for the individuals who receive a treatment the effect appears quickly), then a change in slope should be apparent at the onset of the treatment. To visualize this, consider the simplest hypothetical case in which there is an annual increase of 20% in the population who receive the treatment, leading to total saturation in five years. If there is instantaneous causation, then 20% of the pool of respondents will have changed scores immediately after the onset of the treatment. Assuming further that the effects persist from one measurement wave to the next and that annual data are at issue, then a total of 40% will have changed scores by the next year, and so on. Thus, a treatment that diffuses through a population can result in slope changes at the treatment's onset even if only a minority of the potential respondents in the treatment group have received it.

Delayed Causation

Not all change is instantaneous. Delayed causation can be involved even when a treatment is homogeneously implemented. Indeed, in some medical contexts

delayed causation is more normal than instantaneous causation, as perhaps with some carcinogens. There is little problem with delayed causation when strong background theory permits us to predict a lag. Many times, however, no such theory exists, and examination of the data suggests that no effect is apparent at the point of the intervention but an effect may have occurred at some plausible later date. Once the time-series data have been plotted, it is remarkably easy to generate plausible causal rationales for belated shifts in the series.

When delayed causation is expected but the causal lag is not known, a switching replications design can be useful. It permits the researcher to examine whether the replications show similar delay intervals between the treatment onset and the manifestation of an effect. If they do, the obvious threat of history is reduced, a threat that operates wherever a single series is examined and causation may be delayed. However, the difficulty is that the criterion of equal delay across replications presumes that the treatment does not interact with either the different kinds of units that receive the treatment or the different historical moments at which each group experiences the treatment. Should there be such interactions, we would expect group differences in the delay between treatment onset and effect manifestation. However, such differences by themselves are not "proof" of an interaction, because they may be due to different historical forces or to chance.

When the problems of delayed causation are added to the problems associated with treatments that affect a population slowly, causal inference is particularly difficult. This is because no knowledge exists of where to place the onset of the expected or desired effect, and effects might be expected at any point after treatment is implemented. The longer the time after implementation, the more plausible it becomes to interpret a possible delayed treatment effect in terms of historical factors.

"Short" Time Series

Textbooks dealing with the statistical analysis of time-series data suggest different rules of thumb for the number of time points required to perform a competent analysis. Most suggest about 50 observations, on grounds that this is usually (though not invariably) sufficient for estimating the structure of the correlated error in the series. Situations frequently arise, in research practice, in which many fewer observations than this are possible but many more are available than with a single pretest. As one might imagine from our analysis in chapter 3 of the advantages of adding only a second pretest, adding more than two pretest and posttest observations to create a short series is particularly advantageous. This holds even if statistical analysis by the Box-Jenkins techniques outlined in the next chapter is not possible.

Some of the advantages of an abbreviated interrupted time series are apparent in Figure 5.9 which shows how attendance in a job training program during 1964 affected subsequent earnings for males and females who are black or white. The data were first presented by Aschenfelter (1978), who obtained the control group data from the 0.1 percent Continuous Work History Sample of the Department of Labor. Being in the work force, the controls had higher initial incomes. (The income data were taken from Social Security records.) Figure 5.9 suggests a prompt causal impact. Imagine now that only the 1963 and 1965 data had been

Dollars (× 1000)

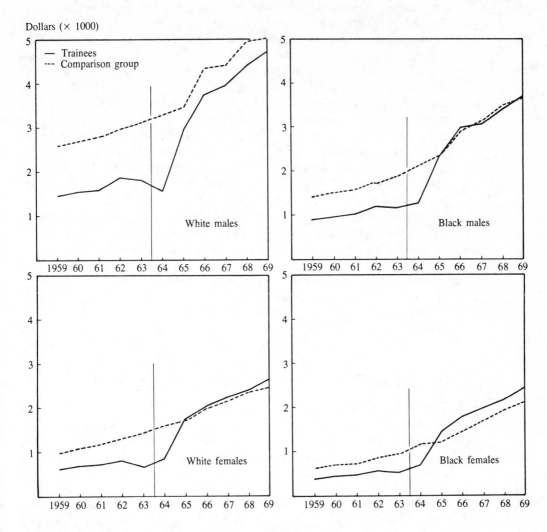

Figure 5.9. Attendance in job training program and subsequent earnings.

available, the first full years before and after the program. An increase in earnings would still be suggested, but such a causal inference would only be warranted if certain threats could be ruled out. Consider selection-maturation. Without the short pretest series, one would perhaps have to rule out the threat on plausibility grounds, perhaps emphasizing the implausibility of selection-maturation because the greatest improvement is in the group that starts further behind (see Figure 3.4 of chapter 3). The argument continues that selection-maturation would have been more problematic had the lower-scoring group fallen even further behind. With even a short additional series one can directly examine the plausibility of group differences in maturation.

Consider, next, the threat of regression. The persons eligible for job training programs in 1964 were those who were out of work in 1963. This would obviously depress estimates of 1963 earnings for trainees. Now if the selection of persons into programs was based on those considered most likely to benefit from training, this group may have increased their earnings anyway after a short period of unemployment. Having 1963 as the sole pretest point does not allow us to estimate the plausibility of regression, but even a few years of prior data does. In this case, while regression might have added to the apparent visual effect of the training program, it cannot account for all of it.

It is also interesting to note in Figure 5.9 that without the later posttest years one would not have been able to ascertain whether the effect of the training program is of any significant duration or merely a temporary result of the program. Also, without the pretest series one might wonder, from consideration of only the years 1962 through 1965, whether earnings shift in a four-year cycle and whether the apparent change in earnings from 1962 to 1965 merely reflects a four-year cycle within a general upward trend. The years from 1959 to 1962 help rule out this possibility, for they show no evidence of cyclical patterns.

A final point has to be made about these figures, particularly when they are contrasted with Aschenfelter's complex econometric analyses of the same data. They are readily credible and can be easily understood by most intelligent laymen; they need no confusing or intimidating statistical analysis to tell their story. In addition, an analysis in the abbreviated time-series form we have presented will have none of the inferential dangers of other (econometric) modes of analysis that are frequently used to estimate treatment effects when the least advantaged persons are given the treatment. (Such dangers are detailed in chapter 7.)

Limitations of Much Archival Data

Most of the data used in time-series analyses comes from archives kept by public and private institutions. In the last decade, the collection and use of economic, social, and even subjective social indicators has become a minor growth industry in academic, governmental, and business life. Data for time-series research will become increasingly available in the future.

Using archives for research purposes is not without its problems, since finding the variables one wants is more difficult than turning to what is available. Moreover, determining what is available can be troublesome; guides to archives are not easily obtained beyond what federal and state governments publish. Gaining access to data from the private business sector or from local institutions (e.g., schools and city governments) can be even more difficult. Indeed, a researcher may be assured that some particular data were available, may travel to the archive, and find that the data were not on hand.

More important, perhaps, than the difficulties of locating data is the systematic bias in their content. Since most data that are collected and stored are used for monitoring purposes, variables that have an "outcome" rather than a "process" flavor are stressed. Direct archival measures of psychological and small-group processes are rare. Consequently, current archives may not be useful to those who favor testing causal explanations involving psychological constructs.

All archived data needs close scrutiny. Operational definitions need to be critically examined, and one should not assume that the construct label applied to a particular measure is necessarily a good fit. Inquiries have to be made about shifts in definition over the time a record is kept; where possible, the nature of the shift needs documenting. Of course, the possibility of shifts in definition will become apparent as soon as the data are plotted; but in our experience it is more convenient to document such shifts when the data are first collected. In many cases, the data for some years or months will be missing and, if the problem is not too serious, will have to be estimated. In other cases, the plotted data show suspicious regularities, as values remain the same for a section of the series or the increase per time unit is constant. The suspicion is that the data have not been properly collected, and someone has interpolated values for the missing observations. Conversely, the data may vary widely and resist any rescaling to reduce the variability—a situation that at times can be attributed to sloppy data collection procedures rather than inherently unstable phenomena.

In our estimation, the major difficulty with archival data is their inflexibility. Often, the researcher would like to have monthly or quarterly data. These data provide longer series than annual; they are more sensitive for detecting immediate causal impacts of short duration; and they are more fitted for ruling out historically based alternative interpretations. But if the data are collected and stored in annual form, disaggregation into finer time units is not possible. The researcher would also like to be able to disaggregate data by a whole host of social variables, including demographic characteristics. Such disaggregation permits an examination of whether an effect is apparent with groups that received a treatment but not with groups that received none. Thus, disaggregation by respondent type can provide a no-treatment control series, with all the advantages described earlier. For instance, in studying the effects of introducing television it would be highly advantageous if the data could be broken down by whether particular households did or did not have television sets. In studying the effects of the breathalyser it would be useful to break the data down into drinkers versus nondrinkers, or even Mormons versus members of religious groups that do not proscribe drinking. Unfortunately the researcher is constrained in his or her analyses by the particular classifications developed by archivists. Often, it would aid the researcher if more dependent variables were available; he or she could then implement a nonequivalent dependent variables design which rules out many threats to internal validity. Once again, though, the researcher has to be content with what the archive contains.

We should not be pessimistic about the rigidity of archives and the sometimes dubious quality of their data. As our examples in this chapter and the next, and in Glass, Willson, and Gottman (1975); Riecken and Boruch (1974); and Campbell (1975) make clear, interrupted time-series designs that permit a high degree of confidence in causal inferences can often be implemented. Moreover, with sufficient ingenuity and perseverance, the researcher may uncover data one would not expect to find in an archive, as is made clear by the breakdown of the breathalyser data into accidents on different days and at different times. In a recent project, Cook, Calder, and Wharton (1979) obtained 25-year series covering a wide range

of variables that can be classified under the general headings of consumption, leisure, political behavior, work-force participation, local economic structure, public health, and crime. Though some of the data came from federal archives, the majority came from obscure state records that seem to be rarely consulted for research purposes. Of course, states differ in the quality of the records they maintain. To cover a substantive area adequately, the researcher may have to collect some variables in one state and others in another. However, a surprising amount of time-series data is already available, and more will be as the pressure for indicators increases. On the assumption that recent and future data are of better technical quality than was sometimes the case in the past, we can expect to see an increasing use of time-series analyses based on federal, state and local data sources.

6

The Statistical Analysis of the Simple Interrupted Time-Series Quasi-Experiment

by LESLIE J. McCAIN *and* RICHARD McCLEARY

INTRODUCTION

This chapter is concerned with the statistical analysis of a single time series with an interruption at a known time point.[1] The purpose of the analysis is to assess the magnitude and statistical significance of any shifts in the series following the interruption. In a sense, the chapter deals with assessing whether the statistical analysis corroborates the less disciplined "eyeball tests" one uses when time-series data are first plotted (and which were used in the previous chapter). The reader should not forget that, while the role of magnitude estimates and significance tests is far from trivial, they do not provide sufficient evidence of a causal relationship. The statistical procedures we shall outline help only in ruling out the threats to inference previously listed under statistical conclusion validity. Statistical analysis per se contributes little to ruling out threats to internal, external, and construct validities.

What follows is a *practical* guide to the analysis of interrupted time-series data from a single series. The how-to questions are emphasized throughout. Hopefully, our guide will give the reader enough knowledge of the basic concepts to analyze an interrupted time-series quasi-experiment or, at the very least, to read more advanced texts on the topic (e.g., Box and Jenkins, 1976; Glass, Willson and Gottman, 1975; Hibbs, 1977). Also, understanding of the analysis for a single series will make it easier to graduate to more advanced issues associated with analyzing more complex time-series designs which have no-treatment control series or switching replications.

Many readers may be disconcerted when they first approach the statistical analysis of time-series data because the analysis seems so different from the statistical work they are used to. The differences are more superficial than real, and to

---

[1]Box and Tiao (1975) and Hibbs (1977) analyze multiple interventions in a single series. See Wharton (1978, pp. 12–28, 45–88, 109–30, 222–29, appendices A and C) for a discussion and examples of the analysis of switching replications designs.

try to help the reader, we have organized the chapter to minimize the algebraic burden and to stress interpreting visual output from time-series computer programs. Our hope is that the chapter presentation will be close to the experiences that readers will actually have when they come to analyze time-series data. To make the presentation even more concrete, the chapter will close with examples of interrupted time-series analyses that were carried out according to the principles described in the main body of the text. Any difficulties that readers may have in understanding the main body should be dispelled by a careful reading of the examples and by using them as guides for reviewing the analysis sequence outlined in the text.

The main body of the text prior to the examples is in five sections. The first details why conventional statistical methods based on ordinary least squares (OLS) are inappropriate for analyzing time-series data. Among other reasons, this is because OLS methods assume independent errors while the errors at any one point in a time series are usually related to the errors at adjacent points. The second section deals with how we can recognize the particular structure of the systematic component of the errors in a given time series. This systematic component is then modeled explicitly, to leave only the uncorrelated error component which meets the requisite statistical assumptions. The third section deals with estimating seasonal patterns in the time series and removing them from the data so as to make sure that seasonal variations do not masquerade as treatment effects. The fourth section is concerned with transfer functions, in which we attempt to specify the form of an intervention effect in order to estimate its magnitude and to test its statistical significance. The fifth section integrates the four preceding ones. The final section includes interrupted time-series analyses which exemplify the use of the methods which we advocate.

THE PROBLEM WITH ORDINARY LEAST SQUARES REGRESSION

When Campbell and Stanley (1963; Campbell, 1963) first described the interrupted time-series quasi-experiment, they suggested several approaches to significance testing. None of these approaches has proved satisfactory because each relied on ordinary least squares (OLS) regression. OLS regression requires an assumption that residuals, or error terms associated with each time-series observation, be independent. When naturally occurring events or behavior are observed repeatedly over time, however, events closer to each other in time tend to be more correlated with each other than with events further removed in time. Since time is the independent variable of an OLS time-series regression, it follows that the error terms of consecutive observations are usually correlated.

The consequences of performing OLS regression when error terms are serially correlated (or as it is sometimes called, autocorrelated) are worth noting. First, the regression equations per se are unbiased. This means that in the long run, a regression equation will neither overestimate nor underestimate such parameters as the pretreatment level and slope and the posttreatment level and slope. However, we are concerned primarily with the statistical significance of these parameters. We use the *standard deviations* of parameter estimates to make the decision, and these will be biased whenever error terms are correlated.

To illustrate this consequence, consider the simple *t*-statistic that is often used to test the significance of time-series changes:

$$t = \frac{\textit{estimated change in the posttreatment series}}{\textit{standard deviation}}$$

If the bias in our estimate of standard deviation is downwards, as it most often is in social science time series, then the *t*-statistic will be inflated[2] and treatments will appear to be more effective than they actually are. We will restate this important fact with emphasis. *While OLS regression estimates of time-series parameters are not biased per se, the estimates of standard deviations (and hence, of significance tests) are biased.*

AUTOREGRESSIVE INTEGRATED MOVING AVERAGE (ARIMA) MODELS

We recommend that interrupted time-series analysts use the *au*toregressive *in*tegrated *m*oving *a*verage (ARIMA) models and the associated modeling techniques developed by Box and Jenkins (1976).[3] These techniques were designed to permit unbiased estimates of the error in a series. To understand this principle, one must first be familiar with the distinction between the deterministic and stochastic components of a time series.

The Deterministic and Stochastic Components of a Time Series

All statistical procedures require a model, i.e., an equation or set of equations purporting to describe a naturally occurring process. Time-series models have two components. The first component describes the systematic behavior of a time series and is often called the *deterministic* component.

---

[2]The conventional wisdom here is that, if the *t*-statistic is "large enough," serial autocorrelation is not a real threat to statistical conclusion validity. This is a dangerous fallacy. Hibbs (1974) approximates the bias in the estimate of variance for the ARIMA (1,0,0) model—we will explain what this is shortly—as:

$$s^2 = \sigma^2/K \text{ where } K = (1+\phi)/(1-\phi)$$

Thus if $\phi = .7$, a value not uncommon in social science time series, the *t*-statistic would be inflated by 265%! Conceivably, then, a treatment effect could be statistically insignificant even though the *t*-statistic is as large as 6.0! Of course, when ϕ is negative, as it sometimes is, the estimate of variance will be biased downwards and the effect will be underestimated.

[3]There are some interrupted time-series designs where procedures other than the Box-Jenkins transfer function approach will be more appropriate. Specifically, it is difficult to use the ARIMA modeling procedures with fewer than 50 to 100 observations. Therefore, if the number of time-series observations is small and the errors are independent, repeated measures analysis of variance may be most suitable for evaluating the significance of an intervention effect. If the number of observations is small but the errors are correlated, MANOVA (Bock, 1963; 1975, pp. 447-89; Pothoff and Roy, 1964) or repeated measures ANOVA with the Geisser and Greenhouse (1958; Greenhouse and Geisser, 1959) correction to degrees of freedom may be the relevant analytic technique. In the rare instances when at least 50 to 100 observations are available and the errors are uncorrelated, conventional methods based on ordinary least squares regression may be used. When the series contains a large number of observations whose errors are correlated, pseudo-generalized least squares regression can be used to evaluate simple constant intervention effects and two-stage pseudo-generalized least squares regression can be used to test the significance of the dynamic, i.e., nonconstant, intervention effects (Hibbs, 1974).

The deterministic component is represented by all parameters of the time series that are not dependent on the error structure. Deterministic parameters do not perfectly predict the values of the observed time series because, while the underlying process may be systematic "in the long run" or "on the average," a given observation will always deviate from its expected value.

The second component describes an underlying process of unobserved errors which make the observed time series somewhat unpredictable. Ignoring for the moment just how one might go about describing something that is "unobserved," we will call this the *stochastic* (or "noise") component of the model.

The stochastic component follows certain laws of probability and has two parts, one systematic (but nevertheless unobserved) and the other unsystematic. The systematic part is responsible for the autocorrelation in a time series, and a major goal of the statistical analysis is to discover the *structure* of the systematic part of the stochastic component. With its structure known, we can then incorporate the autocorrelation into our model, representing it in the corresponding equation. This leaves only the unsystematic part of the stochastic component unaccounted for by the time-series model. As a result, we can calculate unbiased estimates of standard deviations and can draw correct inferences from our significance tests.

Defining ARIMA (p,d,q)

ARIMA (p,d,q) models describe a time series as the realization of a stochastic or "noise" process. A particular ARIMA (p,d,q) model is characterized by three structural parameters, p, d, and q. For example, ARIMA $(0,1,1)$ is the name of the model where $d = q = 1$ and $p = 0$. The integer values of p, d, and q are specified through a simple statistical analysis, called *identification*, which we shall describe later. In the next section, we will be concerned with the meaning of p, d, and q. We begin with the concept of *stationarity*, the time-series property associated with the structural parameter d. Then we shall deal with the concepts of autoregression, associated with p, and with moving average, related to q.

Stationarity

ARIMA (p,d,q) models are appropriate only for time series that are stationary or nonstationary in the homogeneous sense. For all practical purposes, we can say that a stationary series is one that has no secular trend—i.e., there is no systematic increase or decrease in the level of the series as it drifts upwards or downwards. Most of the time series encountered in the social sciences *do* have secular trends and, hence, are *non*stationary. This would ordinarily mean that the ARIMA (p,d,q) models we recommend have little utility. Fortunately, almost every time series can be made stationary by differencing. A nonstationary time series that can be made stationary by differencing is technically said to be *nonstationary in the homogeneous sense*.

To illustrate what differencing does to a time series, consider the sequence of integers:

$$1, 2, 3, 4, 5, \ldots, N$$

If we treat this sequence as a time series, it will have a secular trend and is

nonstationary. But if we *difference* the series, that is, subtract the first observation from the second, the second from the third, the third from the fourth, and so on

$$2 - 1 = 1$$
$$3 - 2 = 1$$
$$4 - 3 = 1$$
$$5 - 4 = 1$$
$$\cdot$$
$$\cdot$$
$$\cdot$$
$$\cdot$$
$$N - N\text{-}1 = 1$$

we get a new time series

$$1, 1, 1, 1, \ldots, 1$$

which has no secular trend and, hence, is stationary. Thus, whenever we have a time series exhibiting secular trend, we will difference it before we fit an ARIMA (p,d,q) model to it.[4]

The question now is: If we detrend a time series by differencing it, do we change any of the deterministic parameters, *especially those representing intervention effects which we wish to test for significance?* The answer, fortunately, is that differencing does not affect these parameters and only affects the manner in which they are represented in the model.

To demonstrate this, consider the sequence of integers:

$$2, 4, 6, 8, 10, \ldots, 2N$$

Treating the sequence as a time series, we see that it has a secular trend. We could model this trend quite easily with the equation

$$Y_t = 2t$$

where the slope is 2. But we could also represent this same trend with the equation

$$Y_t = Y_{t-1} + 2$$

and this is true because

$$Y_2 = Y_1 + 2$$
$$= 2 + 2 = 4$$
$$Y_3 = Y_2 + 2$$
$$= 4 + 2 = 6$$
$$Y_4 = Y_3 + 2$$
$$= 6 + 2 = 8$$

---

[4]First-differencing accounts for a linear trend in the time series. Second-differencing accounts for a quadratic trend. Time series seldom have to be differenced more than once. We have never seen a time series that had to be differenced more than twice. Finally, note that our definition of stationarity is only conceptual. For a more rigorous definition, see Dhrymes (1974, p. 385), Malinvaud (1970, chapter 11.1), or Granger and Newbold (1977, chapter 1.2).

and so on. What we have here are two equations that say the same thing but in different ways. The first equation, an explicit trend equation, and the second equation, a first-order linear difference equation, are identical.

Now recall what we are doing when we difference a time series. We subtract the first observation from the second, the second from the third, the third from the fourth, and so on.

$$Y_2 - Y_1$$
$$Y_3 - Y_2$$
$$Y_4 - Y_3$$
.
.
.
.
$$Y_N - Y_{N-1}$$

and in the general case, this gives us

$$Y_t - Y_{t-1}$$

which is the differenced series. Now the arithmetic operations we performed on the sequence of integers always resulted in a constant series. We can thus set the differenced series equal to a constant

$$Y_t - Y_{t-1} = \theta_0$$

or

$$Y_t = Y_{t-1} + \theta_0$$

and know from the specific case above where $\theta_0 = 2$ that this is the same as:

$$Y_t = \theta_0 t$$

So by differencing a series, we do not remove its trend. We simply give it a different representation in the time-series model.

Whenever a time series exhibits a secular trend, we difference it. However, we must then add another parameter to the time-series model—a constant. By convention, this constant is represented by θ_0, thus

$$Y_t - Y_{t-1} = \theta_0$$

and the parameter θ_0 is interpreted as the *slope* of the series.

The structural parameter d then indicates the number of times a series has to be differenced before it is made stationary. An ARIMA $(p,0,q)$ model implies that the time series is already stationary, that it need not be differenced. An ARIMA $(p,1,q)$ model implies that the time series is nonstationary but that it can be made stationary by differencing it once. An ARIMA $(p,2,q)$ model implies that the series can be made stationary by differencing it twice, that is, by differencing the first differences. Time series that have to be differenced two or more times are rare.

Autoregressive Models

The structural parameter p indicates the autoregressive order of an ARIMA (p,d,q) model. Some time series *are characterized by a direct relationship between adjacent observations*. When this happens, the value of p exceeds zero.

For the sake of exposition, we will represent a stationary time series—or one that has been made stationary by differencing—as Y_t. An ARIMA $(1,d,0)$ model will have a single autoregressive term (i.e., $p = 1$) and can be written as:

$$Y_t = \phi_1 Y_{t-1} + a_t$$

Here, ϕ_1 is a correlation coefficient describing the magnitude of the dependency between adjacent time-series observations.[5] That is, the size of ϕ_1 indicates the extent to which the previous value in the series, Y_{t-1}, allows us to predict the current value of the series Y_t. Since only one previous observation is used to predict the current observation, there is only one autoregressive term with its corresponding autoregressive weight ϕ_1. The a_t term in the formula is a residual or error term of the prediction which we will call "white noise" or "random shock."[6] It is the unsystematic part of the stochastic component.

The essence of the autoregressive model is the direct dependency of successive time-series observations. If we know the value of the previous observation, Y_{t-1}, we can predict the value of the present observation, Y_t. If we know the value of the present observation, Y_t, we can predict the value of the future observation, Y_{t+1}. Furthermore, if ϕ_1 is relatively large, the degree of dependency from observation to observation is large. And if ϕ_1 is positive, large values of the series are followed by large values, small values by small values. If ϕ_1 is negative, large values of the series are followed by small values and vice versa.

An ARIMA $(2,0,0)$ model has two autoregressive terms. The current time-series observation, Y_t, is described as portions of the two preceding observations, $\phi_1 Y_{t-1}$ and $\phi_2 Y_{t-2}$, plus a random shock. We write this as

$$Y_t = \phi_1 Y_{t-1} + \phi_2 Y_{t-2} + a_t$$

where ϕ_1 and ϕ_2 are correlation coefficients.[7] In theory, an ARIMA $(p,d,0)$ process could have three or more autoregressive terms. However, in practice, ARIMA $(3,d,0)$ processes are rare.

---

[5]Because ϕ_1 is a correlation coefficient, it must lie in the segment:

$$-1 < \phi_1 < +1$$

This segment is called the "bounds of stationarity." When $|\phi_1| \geq +1$ the series is nonstationary. Note that differencing the time series is equivalent to positing $\phi_1 = 1$.

[6]The random shocks, a_t, have the property $a_t \sim NID(0,\sigma^2)$, that is, they are distributed normally and identically with zero mean and constant variance.

[7]For an ARIMA $(2,0,0)$ process, ϕ_1 and ϕ_2 cannot be interpreted literally as correlation coefficients, although conceptually they play the same role. The bounds of stationarity are:

$$\phi_2 + \phi_1 < 1$$
$$\phi_2 - \phi_1 < 1$$
$$|\phi_2| < 1$$

The stationarity bounds for higher-order autoregressive models can be found in Box and Jenkins (1976, chapter 3.2.1).

Moving Average Models

The structural parameter q indicates the moving average order of an ARIMA (p,d,q) model. Some time series *are characterized by the persistence of a random shock* from one observation to the next. These time series are well described by the moving average models, in the class of models where q exceeds zero.

An ARIMA $(0, d, 1)$ model, for example, predicts the current time-series observation, Y_t, from the previous random shock, a_{t-1}. This model can be written as

$$Y_t = a_t - \theta_1 a_{t-1}$$

where θ_1 is a correlation coefficient.[8]

As was the case for autoregressive processes, higher-order moving average models incorporate more than one weighted term into the prediction equation. An ARIMA $(0,0,2)$ model predicts the current time-series observation, Y_t, from the preceding random shocks, a_{t-1} and a_{t-2}. We write this as

$$Y_t = a_t - \theta_1 a_{t-1} - \theta_2 a_{t-2}$$

where θ_1 and θ_2 are correlation coefficients.[9]

Mixed Models

So far, we have considered only models where p or q is zero. But in theory, a time series can have both autoregressive and moving average terms. For example, an ARIMA $(1,0,1)$ model describes a time series where the current observation, Y_t, is predicted from both the preceding observation, Y_{t-1}, and the preceding random shock, a_{t-1}. We write this as:

$$Y_t = \phi_1 Y_{t-1} - \theta_1 a_{t-1} + a_t$$

If our experiences are typical, mixed processes are rarely found in the time series most social scientists will analyze. We have never seen a mixed process, although, in theory, they exist.

Noise Model Identification

For any given time series, the analyst has to be able to identify the systematic part of the stochastic component so that it can be described by an ARIMA (p,d,q) model. The autocorrelation function (ACF) and the partial autocorrelation function (PACF) are used for this purpose. Once a likely model has been *identified,* the model parameters (values of ϕ or θ) are *estimated* with special nonlinear computer software. The ACF and PACF for the residuals of this model are then used to *diagnose* the adequacy of the model. If diagnosis indicates that the model is inadequate, a new ARIMA (p,d,q) model must be identified, its parameters estimated, and its residuals diagnosed. This three-stage procedure of identification, estimation and diagnosis is repeated until an adequate ARIMA (p,d,q) model is gen-

---

[8]The parameter θ_1 is also restricted to the segment:

$$-1 < \theta_1 < +1$$

For a moving average process, this segment is called the "bounds of invertibility."

[9]The invertibility bounds for θ_1 and θ_2 are the same as the stationarity bounds for ϕ_1 and ϕ_2.

erated. This model will be the most parsimonious, adequate model for the time series, although not necessarily the "true" model.

Every stochastic process has a distinctive autocorrelation function (ACF) and partial autocorrelation function (PACF). The interpretation or reading of these distinctive signatures is called identification. The ACF is simply the correlation between the time series and its *lags*. "Lagging a time series forward by k units" means pushing the entire series forward. For example, the series

Lag 0 Y_1 Y_2 Y_3 Y_4 Y_5 Y_6 Y_7 Y_8 .   .   .

when lagged once is

Lag 1   . Y_1 Y_2 Y_3 Y_4 Y_5 Y_6 Y_7 Y_8 .   .

when lagged twice is

Lag 2   .   . Y_1 Y_2 Y_3 Y_4 Y_5 Y_6 Y_7 Y_8 .

when lagged three times is

Lag 3   .   .   . Y_1 Y_2 Y_3 Y_4 Y_5 Y_6 Y_7 Y_8

and so forth. Specifically, the lag k ACF, r_k, for a time series, Y_t, is computed from the formula

$$(1) \qquad r_k = \frac{\displaystyle\sum_{t=1}^{N-k} (Y_t - \bar{Y})(Y_{t+k} - \bar{Y})}{\displaystyle\sum_{t=1}^{N} (Y_t - \bar{Y})^2} \qquad \text{for } k = 1, 2, 3, \ldots$$

which we recognize as the familiar Pearson product-moment correlation coefficient. Note that this formula amounts to computing r_1 as the correlation between the time series and its own lag 1, r_2 as the correlation between the time series and its own lag 2, r_3 as the correlation between the time series and its own lag 3, and so forth.

When a time series, like the eight observations above, is lagged once, a pair of observations, Y_1 and Y_8, are lost from the computation of r_1, the lag 1 ACF. When a time series is lagged twice, two pairs of observations are lost from the computation of r_2, the lag 2 ACF. For each lag, another pair of observations are lost, so successive lags of the ACF are estimated from fewer pairs of observations. This means that we will have less confidence in our estimates of the ACF for higher lags. Fortunately, identification for most time series relies mainly on the first few lags of the ACF.

The PACF, r_{kk}, is closely related in meaning to the ACF. However, we cannot offer a simple formula definition such as (1). The PACF is estimated as a solution of the Yule-Walker equation system (see Box and Jenkins, 1976, p. 64). Widely

available computer programs solve this equation system and print out the values of the r_{kk}, so we need not be concerned with the algorithm used. Instead, we are concerned with what the ACF and PACF tell us about the nature of time series.

A stochastic process leaves a distinct signature in its ACF and PACF. More important, every ARIMA (p,d,q) model has a characteristic ACF and PACF. The trick to identification is to recognize similarities between the ACF and PACF of a real time series and the ACF and PACF that would be generated by a particular ARIMA (p,d,q) model. In the next sequence of figures, we show graphs of the ACFs and PACFs for simulated data generated from common ARIMA (p,d,q) models. Careful study of these figures (called "correlograms") and of the accompanying text will prove valuable.

The ACFs and PACFs shown in these figures are the actual computer output from the time-series software package we use (Pack, 1978; Hay et al., 1978). These visual plots are indispensable, and in most cases, the correct ARIMA (p,d,q) model can be identified from an inspection of the plots alone. But it often happens—often enough to be a problem—that a visual plot is ambiguous. In many cases, the analyst will have to know whether a particular r_k or r_{kk} value is *effectively* zero. This is an empirical question that the analyst decides by testing the value of r_k or r_{kk} for statistical significance.

All tests of statistical significance involve variance criteria. When the ACF and PACF are estimated, there is a certain amount of error or variance involved in the estimate. Most time-series computer programs calculate standard deviations for the ACF and PACF which can be used to test the statistical significance of each r_k and r_{kk} value.[10] Our computer program plots the standard deviations as confidence bands around each lag of the ACF and PACF. The parentheses in these figures, "(" and ")", are the upper and lower confidence limits. Two standard deviation units roughly delimit the 95% confidence region. Any value of r_k or r_{kk} that lies within these limits is presumed to be not statistically significant at the .05 level.

Nonstationary Processes

Time series that are nonstationary in the homogeneous sense, or time series that exhibit secular trends, must be differenced before an ARIMA (p,d,q) model can be identified. In Figure 6.1(a), we show the ACF and PACF of a nonstationary process. The ACF dies out slowly. Such persistently large ACF values and a lag 1 PACF value which almost equals $+1$ indicate nonstationarity. After the time

---

[10]Standard deviations for the r_k are estimated from the formula:

$$s = \sqrt{1/N\left\{1 + 2 \sum_{j=1}^{k} r_j^2\right\}} \quad \textit{for lag } k$$

Standard deviations for the r_{kk} are estimated from the formula:

$$s = \sqrt{1/N} \quad \textit{for all lags}$$

When using these estimates to evaluate autocorrelations computed from residuals (during the diagnosis steps), they should be considered only as rough upper bounds to the standard error limits. Otherwise, the analyst is likely to overlook evidence of lack of fit (Box and Pierce, 1970).

Autocorrelations of lags 1-30.

```
    -1.000                        0.                              1.000
    .+++++++++.+++++++++.+++++++++.+++++++++.+++++++++.+++++++++.
 1                       (    IXX)XXXXXXXXXXXXXXXXXXXXXXXXX
 2                     (     IXXXXX)XXXXXXXXXXXXXXXXXXXXXXX
 3                    (      IXXXXXX )XXXXXXXXXXXXXXXXXXXX
 4                    (      IXXXXXXX)XXXXXXXXXXXXXXXXXX
 5                   (       IXXXXXXXX)XXXXXXXXXXXXXXXX
 6                   (       IXXXXXXXXX)XXXXXXXXXXXXXX
 7                  (        IXXXXXXXXXX)XXXXXXXXXXXX
 8                  (        IXXXXXXXXXX)XXXXXXXXXXXX
 9                 (         IXXXXXXXXXXX)XXXXXXXXXX
10                 (         IXXXXXXXXXXX )XXXXXXXX
11                (          IXXXXXXXXXXXX)XXXXXXX
12                (          IXXXXXXXXXXXX)XXXXXX
13               (           IXXXXXXXXXXXXX)XXXX
14               (           IXXXXXXXXXXXXX )XXXX
15               (           IXXXXXXXXXXXXX)XXX
16               (           IXXXXXXXXXXXXX)XX
17               (           IXXXXXXXXXXXXX)X
18               (           IXXXXXXXXXXXXX*
19               (           IXXXXXXXXXXXXX)
20               (           IXXXXXXXXXXXXX)
21               (           IXXXXXXXXXXXXX  )
22              (            IXXXXXXXXXXXXX   )
23              (            IXXXXXXXXXXXX    )
24              (            IXXXXXXXXXXXX    )
25              (            IXXXXXXXXXXXX    )
26              (            IXXXXXXXXXXX     )
27              (            IXXXXXXXXXXX     )
28              (            IXXXXXXXXXXX     )
29              (            IXXXXXXXXXXX     )
30              (            IXXXXXXXXXXX      )
                -2 SD                    +2 SD
```

Partial autocorrelations of lags 1-30.

```
    -1.000                        0.                              1.000
    .+++++++++.+++++++++.+++++++++.+++++++++.+++++++++.+++++++++.
 1                              (   IXX)XXXXXXXXXXXXXXXXXXXXXXXXXX
 2                              (  IXX)
 3                              ( XI  )
 4                              (  I  )
 5                              (  IX )
 6                              (  IXX*
 7                              (XXI  )
 8                              (  I  )
 9                              (  I  )
10                              (  I  )
11                              ( XI  )
12                              (  IXX)
13                              (  IX )
14                              (  IX )
15                              ( XI  )
16                              (XXI  )
17                              (  I  )
18                              (XXI  )
19                              (  IXX)
20                              (  I  )
21                              *XXI  )
22                              (  IXX*
23                              (  IXX)
24                              (  I  )
25                              (  I  )
26                              ( XI  )
27                              (  IXX*
28                              (  IX )
29                              (  I  )
30                              (  I  )
                              -2 SD +2 SD
```

Autocorrelations of lags 1-30.

```
    -1.000                        0.                              1.000
    .+++++++++.+++++++++.+++++++++.+++++++++.+++++++++.+++++++++.
 1                              (   IX  )
 2                              (XXI  )
 3                              (XXI  )
 4                              (XXI  )
 5                              *XXXI   )
 6                              (   IXX )
 7                              (   IX  )
 8                              (   IX  )
 9                              (   IX  )
10                              (  XXI  )
11                              *XXXI  )
12                              (  XI  )
13                              (  XI  )
14                              (   IXX )
15                              (   IXX )
16                              (  XI  )
17                              (   IX  )
18                              (XXXI  )
19                              (   IX  )
20                              (   IXX )
21                              (XXXI  )
22                              (  XI  )
23                              (   IX  )
24                              (   I  )
25                              (   I  )
26                              (  XXI  )
27                              (   I  )
28                              (   IX  )
29                              (   IXX )
30                              (   IX  )
                              -2 SD   +2 SD
```

Partial autocorrelations of lags 1-30.

```
    -1.000                        0.                              1.000
    .+++++++++.+++++++++.+++++++++.+++++++++.+++++++++.+++++++++.
 1                              (   IX  )
 2                              (XXI  )
 3                              (XXI  )
 4                              (XXI  )
 5                              X(XXI  )
 6                              (   IXX)
 7                              (   I  )
 8                              (   IX  )
 9                              (   I  )
10                              (XXI  )
11                              *XXI  )
12                              ( XI  )
13                              ( XI  )
14                              (   IX  )
15                              (   I  )
16                              (XXI  )
17                              (   IX  )
18                              *XXI  )
19                              (   IXX)
20                              (   IXX)
21                              X(XXI  )
22                              (XXI  )
23                              (   I  )
24                              (   I  )
25                              (   I  )
26                              *XXI  )
27                              (   I  )
28                              (   IX  )
29                              (   IX  )
30                              (   IXX)
                              -2 SD +2 SD
```

Figure 6.1(a). The ACF and PACF of a non-stationary process.

Figure 6.1(b). The ACF and PACF of a white noise process.

series has been approximately differenced, the ACF will die out quite rapidly, usually after four or five lags.

White Noise Process

In Figure 6.1(b), we show the ACF and PACF of a white noise process. The key to identifying this process is that the ACF and PACF are effectively zero for all lags. A white noise process, or an ARIMA (0,0,0) model, consists entirely of random shocks, which, by definition, are uncorrelated with each other.

A sufficient test for white noise is that each value of r_k and r_{kk} lies within the plotted confidence limits. However, there is a problem with this test. For a white noise process, we expect the ACF to have one or two significant spikes in 30 lags by chance alone. What we must do in this case is test all 30 lags of the ACF simultaneously. The Q-statistic is used for this purpose. The Q-statistic is essentially a chi-square goodness-of-fit test for the ACF. If the estimated ACF is a good fit to the ACF expected of a white noise process, then the Q-statistic will not be significant. But if the estimated ACF is not a good fit to the ACF expected from a white noise process, then the Q-statistic is significant. This implies that the time series is not a white noise process.[11]

Most computer programs automatically calculate the Q-statistic for each ACF. Each of the ACFs shown in these figures has a Q-statistic as well as the level of statistical significance associated with the value of Q. By this criterion, the ACF shown in Figure 6.1(b) clearly indicates a white noise process.

Autoregressive Processes

For ARIMA (1,0,0) models, the ACF is expected to die out exponentially. For example, if $r_1 = .7$, then

$$r_2 = (r_1)^2 = (.7)^2 = .49$$
$$r_3 = (r_1)^3 = (.7)^3 = .343$$
$$r_4 = (r_1)^4 = (.7)^4 = .2401$$

and so forth. In Figure 6.1(c), we show the ACF and PACF for an ARIMA (1,0,0) process. The ACF clearly decays exponentially. The PACF, on the other hand, has only one significant spike in the early lags. Most subsequent lags of the PACF are effectively zero.

This is also true when r_1 is negative, although for negative autoregression the ACF shows a different pattern of decay. Successive lags are alternately negative and

---

[11]The Q-statistic is computed from the formula

$$Q = N \sum_{j=1}^{k} r_j^2$$

for an ACF of k lags. The critical value of Q is read from a table of values for the chi-square with degrees of freedom equal to the number of lags minus the number of parameters. The number of parameters is the sum $p + q + P + Q$ if the trend parameter θ_0 is not included in the model and is the sum $p + q + P + Q + 1$ if θ_0 is included in the model. (The meaning of P and Q will be provided in the section on seasonal models.) If the calculated Q-statistic exceeds the tabled critical value, then the correlogram is not white noise.

Autocorrelations of lags 1-30.

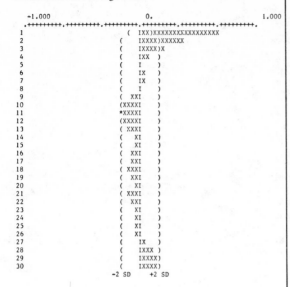

Partial autocorrelations of lags 1-30.

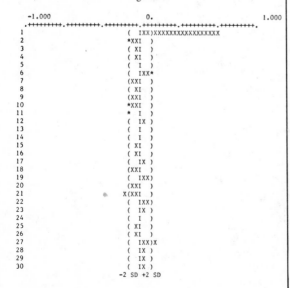

Figure 6.1(c). The ACF and PACF of an ARIMA (1,0,0) process where ϕ_1 is positive.

Autocorrelations of lags 1-30.

Partial autocorrelations of lags 1-30.

Figure 6.1(d). The ACF and PACF of an ARIMA (1,0,0) process where ϕ_1 is negative.

Autocorrelations of lags 1-30.

```
  -1.000                  0.                             1.000
  .+++++++++.+++++++++.+++++++++.+++++++++.+++++++++.+++++++++.
1                          (  IXX)XXXXXXXXXXXXX
2                          (  IXXX)
3                        *XXXI    )
4                       *XXXXI     )
5                       (XXXXI     )
6                          (   I     )
7                          (   IXX   )
8                          (   IXX   )
9                          (   I     )
10                         (XXXXI     )
11                       X(XXXXI     )
12                         ( XXXI     )
13                         (  XI     )
14                         (   IXX   )
15                         (   IXX   )
16                         (   I     )
17                         (  XI     )
18                         ( XXI     )
19                         (   I     )
20                         (   I     )
21                         ( XXI     )
22                         ( XXI     )
23                         (   I     )
24                         (   I     )
25                         (  XI     )
26                         ( XXI     )
27                         (   I     )
28                         (   IXX   )
29                         (   IXXXX)
30                         (   IXXXX)
                        -2 SD      +2 SD
```

Autocorrelations of lags 1-30.

```
  -1.000                  0.                             1.000
  .+++++++++.+++++++++.+++++++++.+++++++++.+++++++++.+++++++++.
1          XXXXXXXXXX(XXI   )
2                   (  XI   )
3                   (   I   )
4                   (   I   )
5                 *XXXI    )
6                   (  IXXX*
7                   (  XI   )
8                   (   I   )
9                   (  IX   )
10                  (  XI   )
11                  ( XXI   )
12                  (  IX   )
13                  (  XI   )
14                  (  IX   )
15                  (  IXX  )
16                  ( XXI   )
17                  (  IXXX )
18                *XXXI    )
19                  (  IX   )
20                  (  IXXX)
21                (XXXI    )
22                  (  XI   )
23                  (  IXX  )
24                  (  XI   )
25                  (  IX   )
26                  ( XXI   )
27                  (  IX   )
28                  (   I   )
29                  (  IX   )
30                  (  XI   )
                  -2 SD    +2 SD
```

Partial autocorrelations of lags 1-30.

```
  -1.000                  0.                             1.000
  .+++++++++.+++++++++.+++++++++.+++++++++.+++++++++.+++++++++.
1                          (  IXX)XXXXXXXXXXXXX
2                  XXXXXX(XXI   )
3                       *XXI   )
4                       *  I   )
5                       (XXI   )
6                          (  IXX*
7                          ( XI   )
8                          (  I   )
9                          (XXI   )
10                       X(XXI   )
11                          ( XI   )
12                          (  I   )
13                          (  I   )
14                          (  IX  )
15                          ( XI   )
16                          (XXI   )
17                          (  IX  )
18                          ( XI   )
19                          (  IXX)
20                       *XXI   )
21                       X(XXI   )
22                          (  IXX)
23                          (  I   )
24                          ( XI   )
25                          (XXI   )
26                          (XXI   )
27                          (  IXX*
28                          (  IX  )
29                          (  IXX)
30                          (  IXX)
                        -2 SD +2 SD
```

Partial autocorrelations of lags 1-30.

```
  -1.000                  0.                             1.000
  .+++++++++.+++++++++.+++++++++.+++++++++.+++++++++.+++++++++.
1          XXXXXXXXXX(XXI   )
2             XXXXX(XXI   )
3               XX(XXI   )
4                 *XXI   )
5                 (XXI   )
6                 *XXI   )
7                 (XXI   )
8                 ( XI   )
9                 (  IX  )
10                (   I   )
11                (XXI   )
12                (XXI   )
13              *XXI   )
14                ( XI   )
15                (  IX  )
16                (XXI   )
17                (  IXX)
18              *XXI   )
19                (XXI   )
20                (  IXX*
21                ( XI   )
22                (XXI   )
23                ( XI   )
24                ( XI   )
25                (  IXX)
26                (XXI   )
27                (XXI   )
28                ( XI   )
29                ( XI   )
30                ( XI   )
                -2 SD +2 SD
```

Figure 6.1(e). The ACF and PACF of an ARIMA (2,0,0) process where ϕ_1 is positive and ϕ_2 is negative.

Figure 6.1(f). The ACF and PACF of an ARIMA (0,0,1) process where θ_1 is positive.

positive, though dying out exponentially. This is so because, for $r_1 = -.7$,

$$r_2 = (-.7)^2 = .49$$
$$r_3 = (-.7)^3 = -.343$$
$$r_4 = (-.7)^4 = .2401$$

and so forth. In Figure 6.1(d), we show the ACF and PACF of a negative autoregressive process. The ACF decays exponentially, although the successive lags alternate negative and positive, and the PACF has only one significant spike at lag 1.

For autoregressive processes, the ACF will typically decay rapidly, that is, after four or five lags. The PACF, in contrast, will have a few spikes at the early lags. The number of spikes in the PACF indicates the order of autoregression, that is, the value of p. The PACFs shown in Figures 6.1(c) and 6.1(d) indicate ARIMA $(1,0,0)$ models because there is only a single spike in the early lags of these PACFs. In Figure 6.1(e), we show the ACF and PACF of an ARIMA $(2,0,0)$ process. Again, the ACF decays exponentially but the PACF has spikes at lag 1 and lag 2 while most successive lags of the PACF are effectively zero. *In general, we will use spikes in the first few lags of the PACF to identify an ARIMA (p,0,0) model. We then use the number of initial spikes to identify the value of* p.

Moving Average Processes

The role of the ACF and PACF in identifying ARIMA $(0,0,q)$ models, or moving average models, is the reverse of what it was for ARIMA $(p,0,0)$ models. In Figure 6.1(f), we show the ACF and PACF of an ARIMA $(0,0,1)$ process. Here the PACF dies out exponentially while the ACF has a single spike at lag 1.

In Figure 6.1(g), we show the ACF and PACF of an ARIMA $(0,0,2)$ process. Here again, the PACF dies out rapidly while the ACF has two spikes, one at lag 1 and one at lag 2. *In the general case, we will use spikes in the first few lags of the ACF of a time series to identify an ARIMA (0,0,q) model. We will then use the number of spikes to identify the value of* q.

In nearly all cases, a time series will be either autoregressive *or* moving average; in these cases, identification is a relatively simple task. The reader should compare the ACFs and PACFs for the autoregressive processes with the ACFs and PACFs of the moving average processes. In practical situations, given some experience, there is little difficulty distinguishing between these two classes of models.

Mixed Processes

Remember that a mixed process is one with both autoregressive *and* moving average components. In other words, a mixed process is an ARIMA $(p,0,q)$ process where both p and q are nonzero. As might be expected, the ACF and PACF of a mixed process both decay exponentially. There is thus no simple way to identify autoregressive and moving average orders, that is, the values of p and q. Figure 6.1(h) shows the ACF and PACF for an ARIMA $(1,0,1)$ process, and clearly, there is no evidence here for the identification of $p = q = 1$. In fact, the ACF and PACF for an ARIMA $(2,0,1)$ or ARIMA $(1,0,2)$ would look similar.

Fortunately, mixed processes are not common. Most social science time series, if our experiences are typical, will be *either* ARIMA $(p,d,0)$ *or* ARIMA $(0,d,q)$. However, should the analyst encounter a rare mixed process, it will be

Autocorrelations of lags 1-30.

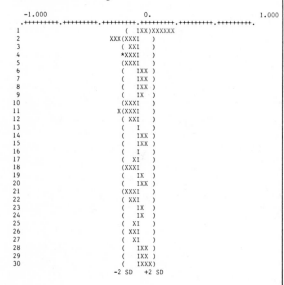

Autocorrelations of lags 1-30.

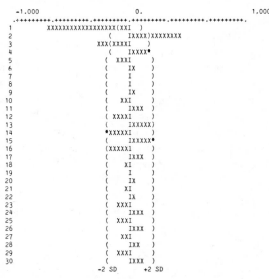

Partial autocorrelations of lags 1-30.

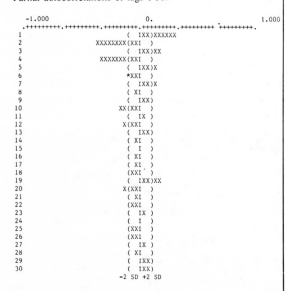

Partial autocorrelations of lags 1-30.

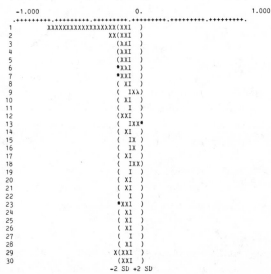

Figure 6.1(g). The ACF and PACF of an ARIMA (0,0,2) process where θ_1 is positive and θ_2 is negative.

Figure 6.1(h). The ACF and PACF of an ARIMA (1,0,1) process.

recognized immediately. Both its ACF and its PACF will exhibit decay or die out slowly. The analyst should then begin with the simplest possible mixed model, ARIMA (1,0,1). If this model proves inadequate through diagnosis—we will explain how to diagnose a model shortly—ARIMA (2,0,1) and ARIMA (1,0,2) models should be tried. The analyst continues to try more complicated models, increasing the values of p and/or q until an adequate model is found.

Using the scheme outlined in Table 6.1, we can summarize the identification procedure. First, compute the ACF and PACF from the raw time series.

If the ACF does not die out rapidly, the time series is nonstationary. This means that the series must be differenced. Difference it until the ACF dies out rapidly, indicating stationarity. The number of differences required to induce stationarity is the value of d and this will usually be one or two.

After differencing, or if the time series is already stationary and requires no differencing, look for decay in the ACF and PACF. If the ACF decays exponentially, an autoregressive model is indicated. If the PACF decays exponentially, a moving average process is indicated.

After identifying the time series as either autoregressive (decaying ACF) or moving average (decaying PACF), determine the value of p or q from the number of significant spikes in the ACF (for moving average processes) or in the PACF (for autoregressive processes). Be careful at this stage. Always start with the lowest possible values of p and q. Be conservative. If you have underestimated the value of p or q, the error will show up in diagnosis. If you have overestimated the value of p or q, however, the error may not be detected in diagnosis.

	White noise	Autoregressive	Moving average	Mixed
Autocorrelations	For all lags: zero	For all lags, starting with lag one: tails off/decays displaying a pattern like a damped exponential and/or sine wave	For first q lags: nonzero For lag k, $k>q$: zero	For lag k, $k>q-p$: damped exponential and/or sine wave
Partial autocorrelations	For all lags: zero	For first p lags: nonzero For lag k, $k>p$: zero	For all lags, starting with lag one: tails off/decays displaying a pattern like a damped exponential and/or sine wave	For lag k, $k>p-q$: damped exponential and/or sine wave

Table 6.1 Summary of the behavior of the autocorrelations and partial autocorrelations for some basic ARIMA models.

By keeping judgments conservative, the most parsimonious, adequate model is generated.

Finally, if both the ACF and PACF decay exponentially, that is, if neither shows telltale spikes, a mixed process is indicated.

Occasionally a time series cannot be identified as any ARIMA (p,d,q) model. In this case, the analyst may wish to log transform the series before identification or, more likely, after a number of unsuccessful attempts at identification.

The first case where log transformation of the series is required is the case where a time series is "explosively" nonstationary. As we noted in the previous section, first-differencing a time series accommodates a *linear* trend, that is, a trend that can be expressed as:

$$Y_t = b_1 t$$

Such a trend might consist of the sequence of integers

$$1, 2, 3, 4, 5, \ldots, N$$

with $b_1 = 1$, and differencing this sequence yields the sequence

$$1, 1, 1, 1, 1, \ldots, 1$$

which is stationary. However, consider the sequence consisting of the integer powers of 2, that is:

$$2, 4, 8, 16, 32, \ldots, 2^N$$

No matter how many times this sequence is differenced, it will be nonstationary. The reader may demonstrate this as an exercise. However, if the sequence is log transformed, it becomes

$$1(\ln 2), 2(\ln 2), 3(\ln 2), 4(\ln 2), \ldots, N(\ln 2)$$

and if this series is then differenced, we have a stationary sequence:

$$1, 1, 1, 1, \ldots, 1$$

"Explosively" nonstationary time series are not common. The analyst who encounters one will know it immediately. After differencing such a series two or three times, the ACF and PACF will still indicate that the series is nonstationary. When this happens, the analyst simply takes the natural logarithm of the series and continues with the identification procedure.

Log transformation may also be required where, in a long time series, the variance in the series appears to increase steadily. For example, the time series may be fairly regular at its start but then become erratic or irregular at some point. Such series often appear to be two different series. Unlike the case of log transformation to handle "explosive" nonstationarity, however, there is no sure and simple method of determining when a time series requires log transformation because of steadily increasing variance. Generally, such series can be fit adequately by an ARIMA (p,d,q) model, but the ACF and PACF for the residuals of the model will be "messy," indicating that the model is only *barely* adequate. We will later analyze a time series of this type to demonstrate this principle.

Estimation of ϕ and θ Values

After a tentative ARIMA (p,d,q) model has been identified, the ϕ and θ parameters of the model must be estimated. We shall not deal here with the algebra of estimation. Instead, we want to point out that most computer programs print out values for ϕ and θ and give confidence intervals which permit an assessment of whether the values differ from zero.

Sometimes, the results of the estimation stage indicate that the tentative ARIMA (p,d,q) model is inappropriate. This can happen if the ϕ and θ parameter estimates are unacceptable because they lie outside the bounds of *stationarity* and *invertibility*. In the case of ARIMA $(1,0,0)$ and ARIMA $(0,0,1)$ models, this means that the absolute values of ϕ_1 and θ_1 may not equal or exceed plus one. With ARIMA $(2,0,0)$ and ARIMA $(0,0,2)$ models, the stationarity and invertibility bounds are somewhat more complicated. For ϕ_1 and ϕ_2, these bounds are:

$$\phi_2 + \phi_1 < 1$$
$$\phi_2 - \phi_1 < 1$$
and
$$\left| \phi_2 \right| < 1$$

The invertibility bounds for θ_1 and θ_2 are the same.

When ϕ and θ estimates do not satisfy the above bounds, they are unacceptable. So, too, is the ARIMA (p,d,q) model that has been tentatively identified. In most cases, unacceptable estimates are the result of inappropriate differencing where the analyst has differenced a time series that was already stationary (over-differencing) or has failed to difference a time series that was nonstationary.

The second situation which indicates that an inadequate ARIMA (p,d,q) model has been identified is when the ϕ and θ parameters are not statistically significant. This suggests that the analyst has identified the need for a parameter but has estimated its value to be zero and so there is no need for it! Nonsignificant parameters occur most often with higher-order ARIMA (p,d,q) models. For example, identification may point to an ARIMA $(0,0,2)$ model, but if the θ_2 parameter proves in the estimation stage to be not statistically significant, then the analyst must respecify an ARIMA $(0,0,1)$ model for the series. Including nonsignificant parameters in an ARIMA (p,d,q) model amounts to overmodeling and will generally lead to an invalid test of the intervention effect. Hence, nonsignificant parameters must be dropped from the noise model.

Diagnosis

After the parameters of a tentative ARIMA (p,d,q) model have been estimated and acceptable statistically significant parameter estimates have been made, the model of the noise structure is complete. However, the purpose of noise model identification is to develop an ARIMA model that will describe the systematic component of the error and will leave only uncorrelated error unaccounted for by the model. The purpose of the diagnosis stage of the analysis is to check whether the *residuals* from the appropriate error model behave as white noise. If they do, the error modeling phase is halted; if they do not, the whole process of identification, estimation, and diagnosis is conducted again.

Most time-series computer programs will calculate the residuals from an estimated model. If these residuals are indeed white noise, then their ACF should be

uniformly zero for all lags (see Figure 6.1(b)), and the Q-statistic should not be statistically significant. But if the value of Q is statistically significant, then the residuals are not white noise and the tentative ARIMA model is inadequate. A new model must be identified.

The Q-statistic is not sensitive to where spikes appear in the ACF plot. Yet the positioning of spikes is important for identification and a tentative model may be judged inadequate even if the Q-statistic is not significant. For example, the ACF for the residuals may have a significant spike at lag 1 or lag 2, which suggests an unmodeled moving average component. Similarly, the ACF may have a significant spike at lag 12, which as we shall later see suggests unmodeled seasonality if the data are monthly observations. The analyst should thus be sensitive to spikes at lag 1 or at the seasonal lags of the ACF and should not accept any tentative model where the ACF suggests unmodeled autocorrelation.

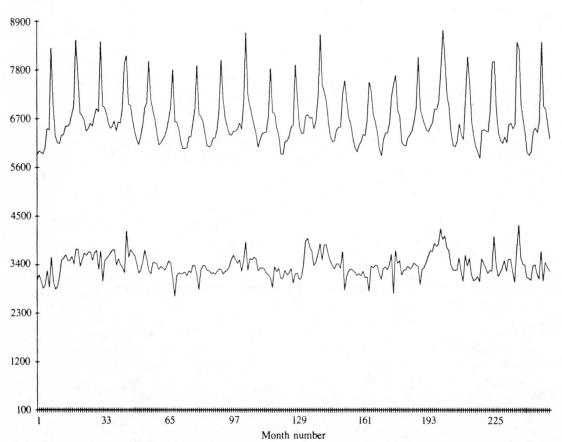

Figure 6.2. A time series before and after deseasonalization.

ARIMA SEASONAL MODELS

Multiplicative ARIMA Seasonal Models

The procedures we have discussed so far do not take into account the fact that many time series exhibit systematic periodic shifts as a pattern of behavior repeats itself. For example, monthly average temperatures rise in summer months and fall in winter months, and a plot of mean temperatures looks like a sine wave or S-curve with high and low points in July and January. The length of the period (or cycle) is 12 months. At the end of each 12-month period, the pattern of behavior repeats itself. To take another example, retail sales indicators peak in December when families shop for Christmas and decline in January. And this pattern repeats every year. To the eye, a seasonal pattern could look like the top figure in Figure 6.2, and it is obvious that if a treatment were implemented at the top part of a wave, a possible treatment effect might be inferred. Obviously, it is desirable in time-series analysis to "adjust" for seasonality and to try to infer treatment effects from a series like that at the bottom of Figure 6.2, from which the seasonal variability has been removed. In this case the level of the series was affected too, because the dummy variable regression approach to seasonal smoothing was used.

Several methods exist for dealing with seasonality, including removing the cycles by using the ratio-to-moving average algorithm (Hickman and Hilton, 1971, chapter 19) or creating dummy variables to correspond to the time units in the period cycle (eleven for a monthly seasonal pattern; three for a quarterly pattern). Another method, much "better" in some respects, is to incorporate a seasonal structure into the ARIMA (p,d,q) model. We can see how this procedure works by writing out a time series as:

$$
\begin{array}{cccccccccccc}
Y_1 & Y_2 & Y_3 & Y_4 & Y_5 & Y_6 & Y_7 & Y_8 & Y_9 & Y_{10} & Y_{11} & Y_{12} \\
Y_{13} & Y_{14} & Y_{15} & Y_{16} & Y_{17} & Y_{18} & Y_{19} & Y_{20} & Y_{21} & Y_{22} & Y_{23} & Y_{24} \\
Y_{25} & Y_{26} & Y_{27} & Y_{28} & Y_{29} & Y_{30} & Y_{31} & Y_{32} & Y_{33} & Y_{34} & Y_{35} & Y_{36}
\end{array}
$$

$$
Y_{N-11} \cdots\cdots\cdots\cdots\cdots\cdots\cdots\cdots\cdots\cdots\cdots\cdots Y_N
$$

As we have seen, autocorrelation implies a structural relationship between adjacent observations. For example, an ARIMA (1,0,0) relationship means that:

$$
Y_t = \phi_1 Y_{t-1} + a_t
$$

When a time series has a strong seasonal component (say, monthly) we will find an analogous structural dependency among observations separated by one cycle or period, that is:

$$
Y_t = \phi_{12} Y_{t-12} + a_t
$$

So we can see that there are *two types of autocorrelation*. The first type, which we

call *regular* autocorrelation, describes the structural dependency among adjacent observations. The second type, which we call *seasonal* autocorrelation, describes the structural dependency among observations separated by one period or cycle.

When we define seasonality this way, we can handle it by incorporating a seasonal structure into the stochastic component. As one suspects, there are *autoregressive, moving average,* and *mixed seasonal* structures just as there are autoregressive, moving average, and mixed *regular* structures. We denote the structural parameters of seasonal autocorrelation by an upper-case $P, D,$ and Q. These parameters are analogous to the lower-case $p, d,$ and q of regular autocorrelation. Consequently,

(1) *P specifies the number of seasonal autoregressive terms.*

(2) *D specifies the number of times a series must be seasonally differenced.*

A time series may be nonstationary from cycle to cycle as well as from observation to observation. If a time series is nonstationary in its seasonal component, that is, if its seasonal behavior increases or decreases as a trend, then the series must be seasonally differenced. For monthly data, seasonal differencing is accomplished by subtracting January 1975 from January 1976, February 1975 from February 1976, and so forth. In other words:

$$
\begin{aligned}
y_t &= Y_t - Y_{t-12} \\
y_{t+1} &= Y_{t+1} - Y_{t-11} \\
&\quad . \\
&\quad . \\
&\quad . \\
y_{t+n} &= Y_{t+n} - Y_{t+n-12}
\end{aligned}
$$

(3) *Q specifies the number of seasonal moving average terms.*

(4) *In addition to P, D, and Q, seasonal structures have a fourth parameter, S, to denote the length (or order) of the period or cycle.* The parameter S usually equals 4 for quarterly data, 12 for monthly data, 52 for weekly data, and so forth.

The conventional method for specifying a seasonal model is

$$\text{ARIMA } (p,d,q) \ (P,D,Q)_s$$

where $p, d,$ and q are the *regular* structural parameters, $P, D, Q,$ and S the *seasonal* structural parameters. When the model is specified in this way, we see that the regular and seasonal structures are coupled multiplicatively (as opposed to additively). *The regular and seasonal structures of ARIMA* (p,d,q) (P,D,Q)$_s$ *model are actually multiplied by each other.* This method of modeling seasonality has a number of advantages, but it complicates the algebra considerably.

To illustrate multiplicative seasonality, consider the ARIMA $(1,0,0)(1,0,0)_{12}$ model. This model implies that a monthly time series has one *regular* autoregressive component, that is, $p = 1$, and one *seasonal* autoregressive component, that

is, $P = 1$. If these components are modeled *additively,* this model would be written as:

$$Y_t = \phi_1 Y_{t-1} + \phi_{12} Y_{t-12} + a_t$$

But this is not the case. Instead, the components are modeled *multiplicatively,* which means that the model is written as:

$$Y_t = \phi_1 Y_{t-1} + \phi_{12} Y_{t-12} - \phi_1 \phi_{12} Y_{t-13} + a_t$$

The difference between additive and multiplicative seasonality is the cross-product term:

$$\phi_1 \phi_{12} Y_{t-13}$$

As both ϕ_1 and ϕ_{12} are fractions, numbers smaller than unity, their product, $\phi_1 \phi_{12}$, will always be smaller than either. To demonstrate that this is so, let $\phi_1 = \phi_{12} = .5$. The cross-product term, $\phi_1 \phi_{12} = (.5)(.5) = .25$, which is smaller than either ϕ_1 or ϕ_{12}. Sometimes this cross-product term is so small that it can be treated as zero. When this is the case, there is no real difference between additive and multiplicative seasonality.

Of course, the crucial difference between additive and multiplicative seasonality is the lag-13 observation. Additive seasonal models predict the current observation, Y_t, from the preceding observation, Y_{t-1}, and from the observation one period back in time, Y_{t-12}. Multiplicative seasonal models also use Y_{t-13}, the observation immediately preceding the observation one period back, to predict the current observation.

In a sense, multiplicative seasonal models use more information and, thus, are better able to model seasonality. Using common sense, we see that February's time-series observation should be related to January's observation and to *last* February's observation. However, there should also be some increase in predictability through adding *last* January's observation to the model. Just as this January's observation *controls* or *adjusts* this February's observation for autoregression, last January's observation is used to control last February's observation.

Identifying the Seasonal Model

As might be expected, seasonal ARIMA models are identified through the ACF and PACF of the time series, and the various ARIMA seasonal models have distinctive signatures analogous to those we covered earlier for the regular models. It should not be thought that all time series have seasonal components. Obviously, series using quarterly or annual data cannot have seasonal patterns of any order equal to or lower than themselves. Even with many monthly time series there is no obvious seasonal component in some of them or the observed component is so weak that it is not statistically significant. In either of these last cases, fitting a seasonal ARIMA model to the series will actually introduce seasonal variation. *A seasonal ARIMA model should not be used unless there is some evidence of substantial seasonality in the time series.*

This evidence can come from either the identification or diagnosis stage. During identification, the ACF and PACF for the series may show significant autocorrelation at the "seasonal" lags, lags 12 and 24 and so on for monthly data and

lags 4 and 8 and so on for quarterly data. Or during diagnosis it may turn out that the ACF and PACF for the residuals of a tentative model show significant autocorrelation at the seasonal lags. As a general rule, the seasonal component of the model will be of the same type as the regular component. In other words, autoregressive or moving average regular components almost always are accompanied by autoregressive or moving average seasonal components. Also, the order of the seasonal component will seldom be greater than one. With social science data, therefore, the most common season ARIMA models will be

$$\text{ARIMA } (1,0,0) \ (1,0,0)_S$$
$$\text{ARIMA } (2,0,0) \ (1,0,0)_S$$
$$\text{ARIMA } (0,0,1) \ (0,0,1)_S$$
$$\text{ARIMA } (0,1,1) \ (0,0,1)_S$$
$$\text{ARIMA } (0,1,1) \ (0,1,1)_S$$

and so forth. Our discussion of seasonal identification thus will concentrate on these simple models.

Seasonal Nonstationarity

Just as a time series may have a trend in its regular component and must be differenced, a time series may also have a trend in its seasonal component. A time series with a seasonal trend only might appear to increase in regular, annual steps:

```
                                        XXXXXXXXXXXX
                                        X
                           XXXXXXXXXXXX
                           X
              XXXXXXXXXXXX
              X
 XXXXXXXXXXXX
```

Of course, a time series may have both a regular trend *and* a seasonal trend, and in this case, the time series would have to be differenced both regularly *and* seasonally before an ARIMA model can be identified.

If a time series is nonstationary in its seasonal component, regardless of whether it is nonstationary in its regular component, the seasonal lags of the ACF will die out slowly. In Figure 6.3(a) we show the ACF and PACF of a seasonally nonstationary time series. It would have to be differenced seasonally to make it stationary. The key to the identification of seasonal nonstationarity is the existence of spikes at lags 24, 36, and 48 that are comparable in magnitude to the spike at lag 12. Since the identification of seasonal nonstationarity depends on a spike at lag 24 of the ACF, it is crucial to consider a minimum of 25 lags of the ACF when analyzing monthly time-series data. In Figure 6.3(a), we show 48 lags to demonstrate the principle underlying seasonal nonstationarity. In practice, and in later examples, we use ACFs and PACFs of only 30 lags since usually this is sufficient for establishing whether seasonal differencing is required.

Seasonal Autoregressive Processes

The most common seasonal autoregressive model is one where $p = P = 1$, the ARIMA $(1,0,0) \ (1,0,0)_S$ model. The ACF for this model decays exponentially but at the seasonal lags. In other words, for monthly data there is an exponential

Autocorrelations of lags 1-48.

```
   -1.000                    0.                                1.000
   .+++++++++.+++++++++.+++++++++.+++++++++.+++++++++.+++++++++.
 1                       (   IXX)XXXXX
 2                       (   I   )
 3                       (   IX  )
 4             XXXXX(XXXI    )
 5             XXXXX(XXXI    )
 6                 X(XXXI    )
 7             XXXXX(XXXI    )
 8             XXXX(XXXXI     )
 9                       (    IX )
10                       (    I  )
11                       (   IXXXX)XX
12                       (   IXXXX )XXXXXXXXXXXXXXXXXXXXXXX
13                      (    IXXXXXX)X
14                      (     I    )
15                      (     IX   )
16               X(XXXXXXI        )
17               X(XXXXXXI        )
18                      (  XXXXXI        )
19             XX(XXXXXXI         )
20             XX(XXXXXXI         )
21                      (     I    )
22                      (     I    )
23                      (   IXXXXXX*
24                      (   IXXXXXX )XXXXXXXXXXXXXXXXXX
25                      (   IXXXXXXX )
26            (         I         )
27            (         IX        )
28            (XXXXXXXXI          )
29            ( XXXXXXXI          )
30            (   XXXXXI          )
31            *XXXXXXXXI          )
32            *XXXXXXXXI          )
33            (         IX        )
34            (         IX        )
35            (   IXXXXXX )
36            (   IXXXXXXX )XXXXXXXXXXXXXX
37            (   IXXXXXXX    )
38            (         I         )
39            (         IX        )
40            (   XXXXXXXI        )
41            (   XXXXXXXI        )
42            (     XXXXI         )
43            (XXXXXXXXXI         )
44            (XXXXXXXXXI         )
45            (         IX        )
46            (         IX        )
47            (   IXXXXXXX )
48            (   IXXXXXXXXX )XXXXXXXXX
                -2 SD            +2 SD
```

Partial autocorrelations of lags 1-48.

```
   -1.000                    0.                                1.000
   .+++++++++.+++++++++.+++++++++.+++++++++.+++++++++.+++++++++.
 1                       (   IXX)XXXXX
 2                       *XXI  )
 3                       (   IXX)
 4             XXXXXXX(XXI    )
 5                  X(XXI    )
 6                  X(XXI    )
 7             XXXXX(XXI    )
 8             XXXXXXXX(XXI    )
 9                       *XXI  )
10             XXXXXXX(XXI    )
11                       (   I  )
12                       (   IXX)XXXXXXXXXXXXXXXXXXXXX
13                       *XXI  )
14                       (   I  )
15                       (   XI )
16                       (   IX )
17                       (   IX )
18                       (   I  )
19                       (   IXX)
20                       (   I  )
21                       (   XI )
22                       (   IXX*
23                       (   IXX*
24                      (XXI  )
25                       (   I  )
26                       (   XI )
27                       (   I  )
28                       (   I  )
29                       (   I  )
30                       (   IX )
31                       (   XI )
32                       (   XI )
33                       (   IXX)X
34                       (   I  )
35                       (   I  )
36                      (XXI  )
37                       (   IX )
38                       (   IXX)
39                       (   XI )
40                       (   I  )
41                       (   I  )
42                       (   I  )
43                       (   XI )
44                       (   IX )
45                       (   IXX)
46                      (XXI  )
47                       (   I  )
48                       (   I  )
                          -2 SD +2 SD
```

Figure 6.3(a). The ACF and PACF of a seasonally nonstationary process.

pattern involving lags 12, 24, 36, and so on which damps out quickly, and an exponential pattern beginning at each of the seasonal lags 12, 24, 36, and so on, which also dies out quickly, in addition to the exponential pattern in the initial lags. ARIMA $(p,0,0)$ $(1,0,0)_S$ models are characterized by PACF spikes at lags 1 through p and no PACF spikes after lag $p + SP$. For example, an ARIMA $(1,0,0)$ $(1,0,0)_{12}$ model will have a spike at lag 1 and will be zero after lag 13. An ARIMA $(2,0,0)$ $(1,0,0)_{12}$ model will have a spike at lags 1 and 2 and be zero after lag 14.

The ACF and PACF for some simulated ARIMA $(1,0,0)(1,0,0)_{12}$ data are shown in Figure 6.3(b). The patterns are typical for this process, although they do not exactly correspond to the theoretically expected pattern. The ACF shows an exponential pattern involving lags 1 and 12 and exponential decay beginning at both lag 1 and lag 12. By lag 24 the ACF have basically died out. As expected, there is a spike in the PACF at lag 1 and essentially the PACF have died out after lag 13. However, there is an unexplained spike at lag 27 in the PACF.

With higher-order ARIMA $(p,0,0)$ $(P,0,0)_S$ models, the pattern repeats itself in the higher-order lags. For $p = 1$, $P = 2$, and $S = 12$, we expect to see a PACF spike at lag 1 and no spikes beyond lag 25. For $p = 2$, $P = 2$, and $S = 12$, we expect PACF spikes at lags 1 and 2 and no PACF spikes beyond lag 26. If $p = 0$, that is, if there is no regular autoregressive component, the exponential decay in the ACF would occur only at the seasonal lags and not in the initial lags, as would the spikes in the PACF. Seasonal time series where $P = 2$ or greater are rare. The analyst is always better off starting with the simplest model, that is, with $P = 1$, and ruling out the simple model first.

Seasonal Moving Average Processes

In our experience, the most commonly encountered seasonal ARIMA models are the ARIMA $(0,1,1)$ $(0,0,1)_{12}$ and the ARIMA $(0,1,1)$ $(0,1,1)_{12}$ models. The time series for which these models are appropriate must be differenced regularly and/or seasonally before identification. Consequently, the remarks that follow will assume that differencing has occurred and will be addressed to the general ARIMA $(0,0,q)$ $(0,0,Q)_S$ which is the same as the ARIMA $(0,d,q)$ $(0,D,Q)_S$ after differencing.

The PACF of a seasonal moving average process is expected to decay exponentially at the seasonal lags. However, the key to identifying an ARIMA $(0,0,q)$ $(0,0,Q)_S$ model is the ACF from which the order of the moving average components (i.e., the values of q and Q) are identified. Specifically, when $Q = 1$ the ACF is expected to show spikes at lags 1 through q and lags $S - q$ through $S + q$. Thus, an ARIMA $(0,0,1)$ $(0,0,1)_{12}$ model is expected to have nonzero spikes at lags 1, 11, 12, and 13 of the ACF, and the remainder of the lags are expected to be zero.

In Figure 6.3(c) we show the ACF and PACF for a simulated ARIMA $(0,0,1)$ $(0,0,1)_{12}$ process. Essentially we see the expected patterns, although the correlations for this simulated data do not match exactly the theoretically expected behavior. In particular, while the expected spike at lag 12 in the ACF is quite evident, the expected spikes at lags 11 and 13 fail to appear.

Autocorrelations of lags 1-30.

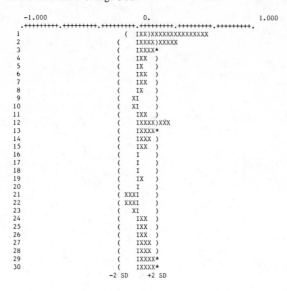

Partial autocorrelations of lags 1-30.

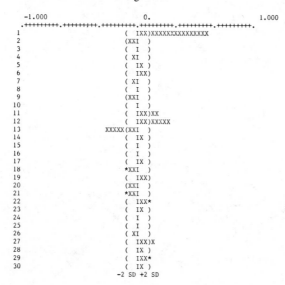

Figure 6.3(b). The ACF and PACF of an ARIMA $(1,0,0)(1,0,0)_{12}$ process.

Autocorrelations of lags 1-30.

```
       -1.000                    0.                            1.000
       .++++++++.++++++++.++++++++.++++++++.++++++++.++++++++.
    1              XXXXXXXX(XXI   )
    2                  (  XXI    )
    3                  (  XXI    )
    4                  (   I     )
    5                  (XXXI     )
    6                  (   IXXX*
    7                  (   I   *
    8                  (   I   *
    9                  (   IXXX)
   10                  (   I   )
   11                  (   IX  )
   12            XXXXXX(XXXI    )
   13                  (   IXX )
   14                  (   IXXX)X
   15                  (   IXX )
   16                  (  XXI   )
   17                  (   IXXX)
   18                  *XXXI    )
   19                 (   I    )
   20                 (   IX::X )
   21                 (  XXI   )
   22                 (   XI   )
   23                 (   IXXX )
   24                 (   I    )
   25                 (   I    )
   26                 (  XXI   )
   27                 (   XI   )
   28                 (   IX   )
   29                 (   IX   )
   30                 (   I    )
                     -2 SD     +2 SD
```

Partial autocorrelations of lags 1-30.

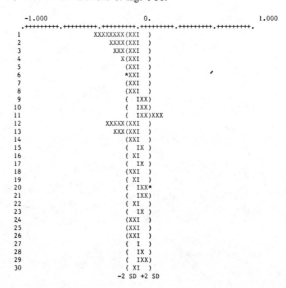

```
       -1.000                    0.                            1.000
       .++++++++.++++++++.++++++++.++++++++.++++++++.++++++++.
    1              XXXXXXXX(XXI   )
    2                XXXX(XXI   )
    3                 XXX(XXI   )
    4                   X(XXI   )
    5                    (XXI   )
    6                    *XXI   )
    7                    (XXI   )
    8                    (XXI   )
    9                    (  IXX)
   10                    (  IXX)
   11                    (  IXX)XXX
   12              XXXXX(XXI   )
   13                XXX(XXI   )
   14                   (XXI   )
   15                   (  IX  )
   16                   (  XI  )
   17                   (  IX  )
   18                   (XXI   )
   19                   (  XI  )
   20                   (  IXX*
   21                   (  IXX)
   22                   (  XI  )
   23                   (  IX  )
   24                   (XXI   )
   25                   (XXI   )
   26                   (XXI   )
   27                   (  I   )
   28                   (  IX  )
   29                   (  IXX)
   30                   (  XI  )
                      -2 SD +2 SD
```

Figure 6.3(c). · The ACF and PACF of an ARIMA $(0,0,1)$ $(0,0,1)_{12}$ process.

When Q is greater than 1, we expect to see this same pattern repeated at multiples of S. Then, an ARIMA $(0, 0, 1)$ $(0, 0, 2)$ model would have nonzero spikes at lags 23, 24, and 25 of the ACF as well as at lag 1, 11, 12, and 13. Caution is urged, however. Time series where Q is greater than 2 are rare. The analyst should always start with the simplest model, $Q = 1$, ruling that model out before larger values of Q and more complicated models are tried. We can now summarize the identification process for seasonal models.

First, make sure that a seasonal model is necessary. The evidence for this should be (1) in the ACF and PACF of the time series during the identification procedure or (2) in the ACF and PACF of the residuals for a tentative model that is being diagnosed. When in doubt, use a nonseasonal model, for if this proves inadequate during diagnosis, a seasonal component can always be added later. To use a seasonal model where there is no seasonality in the data can be dangerous because it can create spurious seasonal variation where there is none.

Next, determine whether a time series has a *non*stationary seasonal component. If this is the case, the series will have to be differenced seasonally. The evidence for seasonal nonstationarity is found in the ACF of the time series. For monthly data, lag 12 must be quite large in both the ACF and PACF and lag 24 of the ACF must also be significant. Nonstationarity, whether regular or seasonal, requires differencing. However, in our experience with social science time series, few are nonstationary in both.

The seasonal component of a time series will ordinarily be of the same type, autoregressive or moving average, as the regular component. If an autoregressive seasonal component appears likely, the PACF will spike at the seasonal lags. If a moving average seasonal component appears likely, the ACF will spike at the seasonal lags.

Always start the modeling procedure under the assumption that a lower-order seasonal component is adequate. That is, always assume that P or $Q = 1$. If this assumption is incorrect, the hypothesized model will prove inadequate during diagnosis.

THE INTERVENTION COMPONENT

Up to this point, we have not mentioned the intervention component. By fitting an ARIMA (p,d,q) model to a time series, the analyst describes the series as "noise." We can represent this conceptually as:

$$Y_t = noise$$

The noise model affords some degree of prediction and, as such, is the null case of the interrupted time-series quasi-experiment. As a next step, the analyst adds an intervention component to the model:

$$Y_t = noise + intervention$$

If the intervention component increases the model's predictability, the parameters of the intervention component will be statistically significant. This is the intervention hypothesis test, the end of the interrupted time-series quasi-experiment. Thus, the crucial issue is to establish whether the intervention adds significantly to predicting the behavior of a time series over and above the prediction that is offered through an understanding of the regular and seasonal components of the noise. Expressing the hypothesis testing component of time series in this way illustrates that the statistical analysis does not by itself test "cause." It only asks whether a statistically significant change in the series takes place at a specified point in the series. No explanations for the change are evaluated.

Box-Jenkins intervention components are called "transfer functions," a term derived from an engineering context. The three simple transfer functions we will describe here are models for (1) an abrupt, constant change in the series; (2) a gradual, constant change in the series; and (3) an abrupt, temporary change in the series.

Abrupt, Constant Change

The simplest possible intervention effect is where the time series immediately changes its level at the time of the intervention. The transfer function model for this intervention effect is

$$(2) \qquad Y_t = \omega\, I_t + noise$$

where ω is a parameter interpreted as the magnitude of the abrupt, constant change and where the noise is an ARIMA (p,d,q) model—identified, estimated and diagnosed in the manner described earlier. The independent variable I_t, meaning "intervention at time t," is a dummy variable or step function such that

$$I_t = 0 \ before\ the\ intervention,\ t < i$$
$$= 1 \ after\ the\ intervention,\ t \geq i$$

where i is the time of the intervention.

The intervention effect pattern of equation (2) is

```
                    XXXXXXXXXXXXXXXXXXXXX
                    X
                    X
XXXXXXXXXXXXXXXXXXXXX
```

pretreatment : posttreatment

when the estimated value of ω is positive and

```
XXXXXXXXXXXXXXXXXXXX
                    X
                    X
                    XXXXXXXXXXXXXXXXXXXXX
```

pretreatment : posttreatment

when the estimated value of ω is negative.

Equation (2) describes an intervention that is both abrupt and constant. The effect is a simple shift in level of the time series from pre- to posttreatment. The

magnitude of the shift is ω, so the intervention hypothesis test amounts to a test of significance for the ω parameter.

Gradual, Constant Change

Another intervention effect can be generated by adding a second independent variable to the transfer function

(3) $$Y_t = \delta Y_{t-1} + \omega I_t + noise$$

where δ is a parameter to be estimated from the data.

Equation (3) does not have as simple an explanation as equation (2). However, we will go through the arithmetic of this model slowly, showing exactly what the intervention looks like. For the sake of exposition, suppose that the noise component of (3) is uniformly zero and suppose further that the pretreatment level of the series is also zero. Then at the moment of intervention, I_t changes from zero to one and:

$$
\begin{aligned}
Y_i &= \delta Y_{i-1} + \omega I_i \\
&= \delta(0) + \omega(1) \\
&= \omega
\end{aligned}
$$

The level of the series changes from zero to ω at the moment of intervention. In the next time point:

$$
\begin{aligned}
Y_{i+1} &= \delta Y_i + \omega I_{i+1} \\
&= \delta(\omega) + \omega(1) \\
&= \delta\omega + \omega
\end{aligned}
$$

The level of the series changes again. In the next time point:

$$
\begin{aligned}
Y_{i+2} &= \delta Y_{i+1} + \omega I_{i+2} \\
&= \delta(\delta\omega + \omega) + \omega(1) \\
&= \delta^2\omega + \delta\omega + \omega
\end{aligned}
$$

We can see the progression here. In the *nth* postintervention time point, the level of the series will be:

$$Y_{i+n} = \delta^n\omega + \delta^{n-1}\omega + \ldots + \delta^2\omega + \delta\omega + \omega$$

Since the parameter d is restricted to an absolute value smaller than unity (and since numbers smaller than unity grow smaller when raised to higher powers), equation (3) generates the following pattern of intervention effect.

```
                                              X
                                      X       X
                                      X       X
                              X       X       X
                              X       X       X
                              X       X       X
                      X       X       X       X
                      X       X       X       X
                      X       X       X       X
                      X       X       X       X
                      X       X       X       X
                      X       X       X       X
          X   X   X   X   X   X   X   X
      ... i-4 i-3 i-2 i-1  i  i+1 i+2 i+3 ...
```

That is, the time series changes its level gradually beginning at time i, the point of intervention; the increments from one posttreatment time period to another become smaller and smaller until eventually the increment is nearly zero. The ultimate or asymptotic change in level is given by the formula:

$$change\ in\ level\ =\ \frac{\omega}{1-\delta}$$

The parameters ω and δ are no longer interpreted as simple measures of posttreatment change as they were in equation (2). The change in level at the moment of intervention is now ω and the rate of change from moment to moment, or from series observation to series observation, is $\delta^n\omega$. In equation (3), the parameter δ in effect determines how gradually the series will change its level. When δ is quite large, say $\delta = .9$, the series changes its level substantially over a long period of time. It reaches its asymptotic posttreatment level slowly. When δ is quite small, say $\delta = .1$, the series reaches its asymptotic level almost immediately. Of course, when $\delta = 0$, equations (2) and (3) are identical. The intervention hypothesis test for equation (3) is a test of significance for both δ and ω.

There are many interrupted time-series phenomena where patterns of intervention like this one are thought to occur. For example, Box and Tiao (1975) analyzed a time series of air pollution levels in Los Angeles before and after the passage of a pollution control act. We would not expect to see an abrupt change in this indicator. Rather, the level of air pollution would be expected to decrease gradually over time. Their findings showed an intervention effect of the type modeled by equation (3). Hibbs (1977) analyzed a time series of unemployment rates, positing a change in unemployment every time a presidential regime changed. Again, we would not expect the level of unemployment to shift abruptly with a new president, since changes in macroeconomic policy thought to cause changes in unemployment take effect gradually. Using the transfer function of equation (3), Hibbs found that unemployment dropped, but gradually, whenever a Democratic president took office. This is the strength of the transfer function approach to the interrupted time-series quasi-experiment. We can detect, measure, and test for statistical significance a wide range of intervention effects.

Abrupt, Temporary Change

The last of the three simple transfer function models describes an abrupt but *temporary* intervention effect. This pattern of effect is generated by equation (3) where I_t is defined as a pulse function. That is:

$$I_t = 0\ before\ the\ intervention,\ t < i$$
$$= 1\ at\ the\ moment\ of\ intervention,\ t = i$$
$$= 0\ thereafter,\ t > i$$

We will go through the arithmetic slowly again, showing exactly what happens to the time series. First, prior to the intervention, $I_t = 0$, so the level of the pretreatment series is uniformly zero. But then at the moment of intervention, I_t changes from zero to one and:

$$Y_i = \delta Y_{i-1} + \omega I_i$$
$$= \delta(0) + \omega(1)$$
$$= \omega$$

The level of the series changes from zero to ω. After this, however, I_t changes back to zero and:

$$Y_{i+1} = \delta Y_i + \omega I_{i+1}$$
$$= \delta(\omega) + \omega(0)$$
$$= \delta\omega$$

In the next moment

$$Y_{i+2} = \delta Y_{i+1} + \omega I_{i+2}$$
$$= \delta(\delta\omega) + \omega(0)$$
$$= \delta^2\omega$$

and so forth. The progression here is apparent. In the *nth* moment after intervention, the level of the series is

$$Y_{i+n} = \delta^n\omega$$

and recalling that δ is smaller than unity in absolute value, we see that the pattern of effect is the following.

```
                    x
                    x
                    x
                    x
                    x
                    x
                    x       x
                    x       x
                    x       x
                    x       x       x
                    x       x       x       x
          x    x    x   x   x       x       x       x
   . . . i-4  i-3  i-2 i-1  i     i+1     i+2     i+3    i+4 . . .
```

This pattern of effect can be called a decaying spike. The intervention causes a profound change in level at the moment of intervention and the magnitude of this change, the height of the spike, is ω. But thereafter, the effect erodes until, after a period of time, the series has returned to its preintervention level. The parameter δ is interpreted as the momentary rate of decay. When δ is large, say $\delta = .9$, the treatment effect persists for a long period of time, eroding slowly.

Which Transfer Function Should Be Used?

The analyst will sometimes have an a priori notion as to the nature of the hypothesized effect and will choose a transfer function accordingly. If the effect is expected to be abrupt, the analyst will use equation (2). If the effect is expected to be nonabrupt, or gradual, the analyst will use equation (3). And if the effect is expected to be temporary, the analyst will define I_t as a pulse function rather than as a step function.

The analyst may believe the shape of the intervention effect to be more complex than those handled in equations (2) or (3). In that case, one of the more

elaborate transfer functions, such as those tabled in Box and Tiao (1975), may be more suitable for use as the initial tentative model instead of the simple transfer functions described here.

But in many cases, the analyst will have no a priori notion as to the nature of the hypothesized effect. It may be abrupt or gradual, permanent or only temporary. In such a case, the analyst may be interested in *the general hypothesis that there was an effect regardless of its nature*. The transfer function approach is ideal for this task because the shape or nature of the effect depends upon the value of the parameter δ.

To test the general hypothesis, the analyst may begin with equation (3), positing a gradual but permanent effect. But if the estimated value of $\delta = 0$ or is very nearly zero, the analyst may assume that an *abrupt* but constant model of impact is more appropriate. The relationship between equations (2) and (3) in this context can be made explicit. Comparing them

(2) $$Y_t = \omega I_t$$
(3) $$Y_t = \delta Y_{t-1} + \omega I_t$$

it is clear that (2) is the special case of (3) where $\delta = 0$.

By starting with equation (3), the analyst need not make an a priori choice between gradual or abrupt patterns of impact. Similarly, if the analyst does not wish to make an a priori choice between permanent and temporary effects, the analysis should begin with equation (3) where I_t is defined as a pulse function; that is, the analysis should begin with an abrupt but temporary model of impact. If a permanent model is more appropriate, the estimated value of $\delta = 1$ or very nearly so, say, $\delta = .9$. The reader may work through the arithmetic as an exercise to show that when $\delta = 1$, the abrupt but temporary model of impact takes the following form.

XXXXXXXXXXXXXXXX
X
XXXXXXXXXX

It is clear from this that equation (2) is also a special case of the abrupt but temporary model of impact where $\delta = 1$.

In light of these relationships, the analyst need not make any a priori choices or preclude any possibilities. Instead, the analyst may start with equation (3) where I_t is defined as a pulse function; that is, with an abrupt but temporary model of impact. If the estimated value of δ is relatively small, the analysis stops. But if the estimated value of δ is relatively large, say $\delta = .9$ or larger, the analyst will take this as evidence of a permanent effect. The analysis is then replicated, using equation (3) but with I_t defined as a step function. Again, if the estimated value of δ is relatively large, the analysis stops. But if the estimated value of δ is relatively small, say $\delta = .1$ or smaller, the analyst takes this as evidence that the effect is both permanent and abrupt. The analysis is then replicated with equation (2). Using this logic, the analyst need never make an a priori choice among models of impact.

Our discussion up to this point has been necessarily technical and may have been difficult to follow. Therefore, we will summarize the modeling strategy in

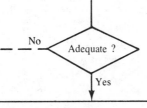

(1) IDENTIFICATION

An ACF and PACF are computed from the time-series observations. If these indicate that the series is nonstationary, the series is differenced and new ACF and PACF are computed from the differenced series. These statistics are used to select a tentative ARIMA model for the series.

(2) ESTIMATION

The ϕ and θ parameters for the tentative model are estimated.

(3) DIAGNOSIS

An ACF and PACF are computed from the residuals of the estimated tentative model, and these statistics are used to decide whether the tentative model is adequate. If there are no spikes at lag 1 and the seasonal lags of the ACF and PACF, and if the Q-statistic is not significant, the model is adequate.

No   Adequate ?

Yes

(4) INTERVENTION HYPOTHESIS TESTING

Specify a tentative transfer functional model. Estimate the joint transfer function-ARIMA model parameters—ϕ, θ, δ, and ω. If the size of the intervention effect is large, diagnose the adequacy of the joint transfer function-ARIMA model. Interpret the intervention effect parameters.

Figure 6.4. The modeling strategy.

this section, and in the next section, analyze a number of time series following the strategy we recommend. The strategy is outlined as a flow chart in Figure 6.4. This strategy should be followed very closely in conducting analyses of interrupted time series, for when shortcuts are used, even the most experienced analyst can make serious errors.

As Figure 6.4 shows, we recommend identifying the stochastic component of the model first. This three-stage process is reiterated until an acceptable model is reached. Once the stochastic component has been modeled, a transfer function should be incorporated into the model, and the parameters δ and ω should be tested for statistical significance. This is a general overview of the strategy, and we will now summarize the steps of the analysis.

SUMMARY OF THE MODELING STRATEGY

Identification

As a first step, compute the ACF and PACF from the time series. Use these statistics to determine whether the time series is stationary and, if so, which ARIMA (p,d,q) model might adequately reflect its stochastic component. If the time series is *not* stationary, its ACF and PACF will have particularly large values at lag 1 and the ACF will be slow to die out. Difference the series until the ACF dies out rapidly, indicating that the differenced series is stationary. The number of times the series must be differenced indicates the value of d. Examine the patterns of decay and spiking in the ACF and PACF to determine the likely values of p and q. (We have summarized the behavior of these statistics in Table 6.1.) Identify a likely ARIMA (p,d,q) model or ARIMA (p,d,q) $(P,D,Q)_S$ model if seasonality is indicated. Remember that *this is only a tentative model*. If it proves inadequate or otherwise inappropriate, we will return to this step to identify another tentative model.

Estimation

Estimate the values of the ϕ and θ parameters for the tentative model. Special nonlinear software is needed for this step. The software we recommend and use for our example analyses (Hay et al., 1978; Pack, 1978) has been designed especially for analyses using the strategy we recommend. The software computes the ϕ and θ parameters for a specified ARIMA model, 95% confidence intervals for the parameters, and the model residuals. If one or more of these parameters proves to be not statistically significant, the model is inadequate. The analyst must then return to the *identification* step. If the ϕ and θ parameters *are* statistically significant, the residuals from the tentative model are used in the next step.

Diagnosis

Compute the ACF and PACF for the residuals of the tentative model. If the model is adequate, these statistics will meet two basic criteria.

> The ACF and PACF will have no significant spikes at early lags or at the seasonal lags. If this criterion is not met, the model is inadequate and a new model must be identified.

The ACF and PACF will be characteristic of a white noise process. The residuals should ideally have a zero mean and the Q-statistic for the ACF should not be statistically significant. If this criterion is not met, the model is inadequate and a new model must be identified.

Note that both criteria must be satisfied. A model that meets one criterion but not the other is just as inadequate as a model that meets neither criterion.

Sometimes the ACF and PACF for the residuals of a tentative model may provide information that can be used to identify a more adequate model. This is particularly true when diagnosis indicates that a seasonal ARIMA model is required. The pattern of decay and spiking in the diagnostic ACF and PACF often point directly to a likely seasonal model.

Diagnosis yields a simple yes/no answer to the question: Is the tentative ARIMA model adequate for this time series? If the answer is yes, that is, both diagnostic criteria are satisfied, the analysis moves on to the fourth step. But if the answer is no, that is, either or both criteria are not met, the analysis returns to the first step, *identification*. A new tentative model is identified, its parameters estimated, and its residuals diagnosed. This procedure continues iteratively until an adequate ARIMA model for the time series is generated.

Intervention Hypothesis Test

The transfer function is specified. If the analyst has a strong prior notion as to the nature of the hypothesized effect, the most parsimonious function describing that shape is chosen. Otherwise, the analyst uses the general function in equation (3) as the initial tentative transfer function model.

The specified transfer function is added to the previously identified ARIMA noise model to form the tentative joint transfer function-ARIMA model. The ϕ, θ, ω, and δ parameters for the joint model are estimated.

If the size of the intervention effect appears to be large, given the natural instability of the series, the adequacy of the joint transfer function-ARIMA model fit should be diagnosed.[12] Again, the criteria for determining model adequacy are behavior of the autocorrelations, the partial autocorrelations, and the Q-statistic for the residuals. If the model is adequate, the residuals should act like white noise. If the model is not adequate, the autocorrelations will not act like white noise. Unfortunately, however, the shape of the correlogram for the residuals does not indicate how to alter the transfer function to more adequately fit the data

Finally, the tests of significance for the intervention parameters are interpreted to decide whether to reject or fail to reject the null hypothesis of no intervention effect.

---

[12]The authors disagree about the necessity of diagnostic checking at this stage in the model-building process. One considers this step necessary only when the intervention effect is large. The examples are analyzed from this perspective. The other author prefers the conservative approach advocated by Hibbs (1977) and Box and Jenkins (1976) where one always diagnoses and confirms the fit of the joint transfer function-ARIMA model before proceeding with intervention hypothesis testing.

THREE EXAMPLES

Up to this point, our discussion has been necessarily general and perhaps overly technical. In this section, we analyze three interrupted time-series quasi-experiments as examples to illustrate the general and specific principles of model building. Each example illustrates a typical problem where the interrupted time-series quasi-experiment can be used, and each series has facets demonstrating special cases and special problems for the analyst.

The first analysis concerns the effects of introducing charges for telephone calls to Directory Assistance. This example is interesting because the interruption in the time series is so marked. We have a good opportunity to illustrate the procedure of selecting an appropriate model of intervention. The second analysis concerns the effects of a flood on a local economy and will illustrate how to deal with seasonal nonstationarity by differencing the time series seasonally. Finally, we shall examine the effect of a new gun control law on the incidence of armed robbery. In this analysis, we are forced to log transform the time series before identification. The analysis also points to the importance of the iterative strategy of identification/estimation/diagnosis that we recommend.

The Effects of Charging for Calls to Directory Assistance[13]

Figure 6.5(a) shows the average daily number of Directory Assistance ("Information") calls logged each month in Cincinnati from 1962 to 1976. In March 1974, the 147th month of the series, Cincinnati Bell initiated a 20-cent charge for each Directory Assistance call. Prior research had shown that the majority of all Directory Assistance calls were requests for telephone numbers available from published sources. Cincinnati Bell hoped that by charging a nominal fee for Directory Assistance service, its use would be minimized. In the 147th month of the series, the level of Directory Assistance calls dropped abruptly, suggesting the strategy was successful. McSweeny (1978) used a static intervention effect time-series analysis to determine the statistical significance of this apparent drop. Here we will use transfer functions to analyze this data.

Identification

When an intervention is as marked as this one, the intervention distorts the estimates of the ACF and PACF. Consequently, we use only the preintervention or pretreatment observations for ARIMA noise model identification. The ACFs and PACFs presented here in steps one through three are based on only the first 146 observations of this series.

The ACF and PACF of the series, shown in Figure 6.5(b), clearly indicate nonstationarity, so the series must be differenced. The ACF and PACF of the first-differenced series, shown in Figure 6.5(c) suggest that this series may be nonstationary in its seasonal component as well. Notice the single spikes at lags

---

[13]This time series is taken from McSweeny (1978). Because of format limitations within Program SCRTIME, it was necessary to divide all the observations by 100. The results here are reported in the original data units, however. The autocorrelation, partial autocorrelation, and δ estimates are the same regardless of the transformation. The θ_0 and ω estimates generated by SCRTIME were multiplied by 100 to make these estimates comparable to the actual data units.

Average daily calls

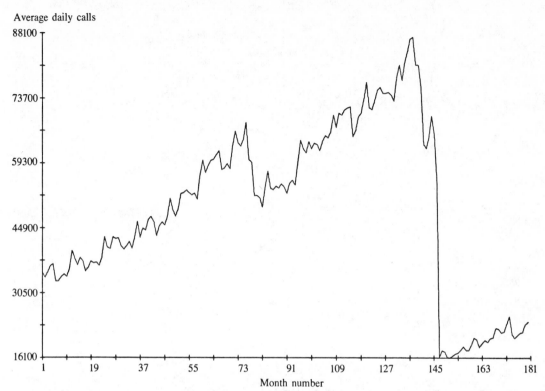

Figure 6.5(a). Average daily number of calls to Cincinnati directory assistance.

12 and 24 of the ACF which are nearly equal in size. This means that the series may have to be differenced seasonally. The ACF and PACF of the series after regular *and* seasonal differencing are shown in Figure 6.5(d). The ACF and PACF indicate that an ARIMA $(0,1,0)$ $(0,1,1)_{12}$ model may be appropriate for these data. The key to this identification is the single spike at lag 12 of the ACF and the rough pattern of decay beginning at lag 12 of the PACF. This model is somewhat unusual in that it posits autocorrelation only in the seasonal component, not in the regular component. However, it is only a tentative model. If it is inappropriate, we will identify another model.

Estimation[14]

Parameter estimates for an ARIMA $(0,1,0)$ $(0,1,1)_{12}$ model are:

$$\theta_0 \ = -58.06 \ \textit{with t-statistic} \ = -1.08$$
$$\theta_{12} \ = \ \ \ .85 \ \textit{with t-statistic} \ = \ \ 15.30$$

---

[14]Neither Hay et al. (1978) nor Pack (1978) provides *t*-values for the parameter estimates. Instead, the programs provide 95% confidence intervals. These *t*-values were computed by the authors.

Autocorrelations of lags 1-30.

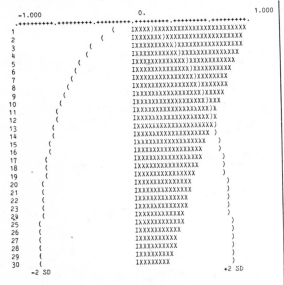

Autocorrelations of lags 1-30.

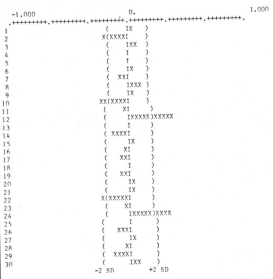

Partial autocorrelations of lags 1-30.

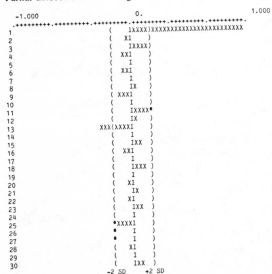

Figure 6.5(b). The ACF and PACF of the preintervention series.

Partial autocorrelations of lags 1-30.

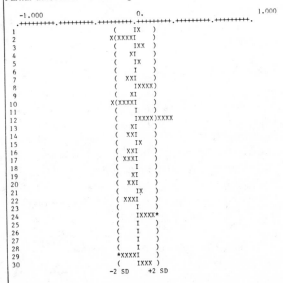

Figure 6.5(c). The ACF and PACF of the first differences of the preintervention series.

The trend parameter, θ_0, is not statistically significant, so it is dropped from our model. The seasonal moving average parameter, θ_{12}, is statistically significant. Moreover, its value is within the bounds of invertibility for moving average parameters.

Diagnosis

Our tentative model for this time series is ARIMA $(0,1,0)$ $(0,1,1)_{12}$ without a trend parameter, θ_0. Dropping the trend parameter in this case does not mean that the series has no trend. It means rather that the trend is so slight that it cannot be measured. It is not statistically different than zero. To diagnose this model, we compute the ACF and PACF for the model residuals as shown in Figure 6.5(e). There is a spike at lag 6 of the ACF but nothing else. In this sense, the tentative model meets our first diagnostic criterion. The larger criterion, however, is that these residuals must be white noise, and we use the Q-statistic to test this hypothesis. For these residuals, $Q = 14.649$ with 29 degrees of freedom, a value of Q corresponding to a .988 level of significance. As the Q-statistic is not significant, we accept the null hypothesis that the residuals from our tentative model are white noise. By inference, we accept the ARIMA $(0,1,0)$ $(0,1,1)_{12}$ model for this time series.

Before proceeding to the intervention hypothesis test, we note that our ARIMA noise model identification, estimation, and diagnosis steps were based on the first 146 observations only. Our motives for not using the postintervention segment of the series concern the magnitude of the intervention. The intervention effect is so large that it will overwhelm our identification statistics and, thus, cause us to identify an incorrect model.

To demonstrate these consequences, consider the ACF and PACF shown in Figure 6.5(f). These statistics are for the first differences of the whole 180-observation series. Here, $Q = 26.744$ with 30 degrees of freedom, a value of Q corresponding with a .637 probability level. Both the visual pattern and the Q-statistic for the differenced series indicate that, after differencing, the series is white noise. Had we used all 180 observations of this series for building the noise model, we would have identified an ARIMA $(0,1,0)$ model. The intervention, the change in level at the 147th month, is so large that it obscures the seasonal autocorrelation of the series. In most cases, the analyst may disregard this problem. However, some caution is urged and the analyst must at least be conscious that this problem can arise whenever the intervention effect is large.

Intervention Hypothesis Test

In many time-series problems, we will be unsure as to the nature or form of the hypothesized effect. In this problem, however, we are certain that the effect is abrupt and constant. A visual inspection of the time-series plot convinces us that equation (2) is the most appropriate model of impact. Using an ARIMA $(0,1,0)$ $(0,1,1)_{12}$ model for the noise component, we estimate the intervention effect parameter as:

$$\omega = -39{,}931 \; with \; t\text{-}statistic = -17.41$$

Autocorrelations of lags 1-30.

```
      -1.000                0.                    1.000
   .++++++++.+++++++++.+++++++++.+++++++++.+++++++++.+++++++++.
 1                    (    XI    )
 2                    (    IX    )
 3                    (    IXX   )
 4                    (    I     )
 5                    (    IXXX  )
 6                    (    IXX   )
 7                    (    IX    )
 8                    (    IXXX  )
 9                    (    XI    )
10                    (    XI    )
11                    (    IXX   )
12             XXXX(XXXXI        )
13                    (    IX    )
14                    (    XI    )
15                    (    XI    )
16                    (    XXI   )
17                    (    IXXX  )
18                    ( XXXXI    )
19                    (    XXI   )
20                    (    XI    )
21                    (    IXXX  )
22                    ( XXXI     )
23                    (    XI    )
24                    (    I     )
25                    (    IX    )
26                    (    XI    )
27                    (    IX    )
28                    (    I     )
29                    (    XXI   )
30                    (    IXXXX )
                    -2 SD      +2 SD
```

Autocorrelations of lags 1-30.

```
   -1.000                0.                        1.000
 .++++++++.+++++++++.+++++++++.+++++++++.+++++++++.+++++++++.
 1                   (    XI    )
 2                   (    I     )
 3                   (    IXXX  )
 4                   (    XI    )
 5                   (    IXXXX*)
 6                   (    IX    )
 7                   (    XI    )
 8                   (    IXXX  )
 9                   (    IX    )
10                   (   XXI    )
11                   (    XI    )
12                   (    I     )
13                   (   XXI    )
14                   (    I     )
15                   (   XXI    )
16                   (  XXXI    )
17                   (    IXX   )
18                   (   XXI    )
19                   (    XI    )
20                   (    I     )
21                   (    IXXX  )
22                   (   XXI    )
23                   (   XXI    )
24                   (    XI    )
25                   (    XI    )
26                   (    IXX   )
27                   (    XI    )
28                   (   XXI    )
29                   (    XI    )
30                   (    IXX   )
                   -2 SD      +2 SD
```

Partial autocorrelations of lags 1-30.

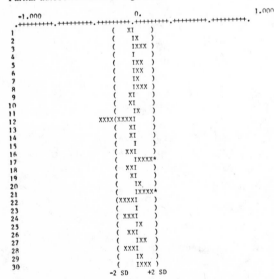

Partial autocorrelations of lags 1-30.

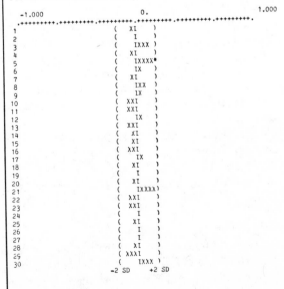

Figure 6.5(d). The ACF and PACF of the regular and seasonal differences of the preintervention series.

Figure 6.5(e). The ACF and PACF of the ARIMA $(0,1,0)$ $(0,1,1)_{12}$ residuals for the preintervention series.

Autocorrelations of lags 1-30.

```
      -1.000                0.                    1.000
      .+++++++++.+++++++++.+++++++++.+++++++++.+++++++++.
  1                       (    IXXX*              )
  2                       (    XI    )
  3                       (    XI    )
  4                       (    I     )
  5                       (    I     )
  6                       (    IXXXX* )
  7                       (    IX    )
  8                       (    IX    )
  9                       (    IXXX )
 10                       (  XXXI    )
 11                       (    XI    )
 12                       (    IXXXX)
 13                       (  XXXI    )
 14                       (    XI    )
 15                       (    I     )
 16                       (  XXXI    )
 17                       (    I     )
 18                       (    I     )
 19                       (  XXI     )
 20                       (    I     )
 21                       (    I     )
 22                       (XXXXI     )
 23                       (    XI    )
 24                       (    IXXXX)
 25                       (    I     )
 26                       (    I     )
 27                       (    I     )
 28                       (    XI    )
 29                       (    XI    )
 30                       (    XI    )
                            -2 SD   +2 SD
```

Autocorrelations of lags 1-30.

```
      -1.000                0.                    1.000
      .+++++++++.+++++++++.+++++++++.+++++++++.+++++++++.
  1                       (    XI    )
  2                       (    XI    )
  3                       (    IXX   )
  4                       (    XI    )
  5                       (    IXXX )
  6                       (    IX    )
  7                       (   XXI    )
  8                       (    IXX   )
  9                       (    IXX   )
 10                       (   XXI    )
 11                       ( XXXI    )
 12                       (    IX    )
 13                       (   XXI    )
 14                       (    I     )
 15                       (    IX    )
 16                       (  XXXI    )
 17                       (    XI    )
 18                       (    XI    )
 19                       (    XI    )
 20                       (    XI    )
 21                       (    IXXX )
 22                       ( XXXI    )
 23                       (XXXXI    )
 24                       (    IX    )
 25                       (  XXI     )
 26                       (    IXXX )
 27                       (    I     )
 28                       (   XXI    )
 29                       (   XXI    )
 30                       (    IXXX )
                            -2 SD   +2 SD
```

Partial autocorrelations of lags 1-30.

```
      -1.000                0.                    1.000
      .+++++++++.+++++++++.+++++++++.+++++++++.+++++++++.
  1                       (    IXXX* )
  2                       ( XXI    )
  3                       (    I     )
  4                       (    I     )
  5                       (    I     )
  6                       (    IXXX)X
  7                       (    XI    )
  8                       (    IXX )
  9                       (    IXXX)
 10                       *XXXI    )
 11                       (    I     )
 12                       (    IXXX)
 13                       *XXXI    )
 14                       (    I     )
 15                       (    XI    )
 16                       (  XXI     )
 17                       (    IX    )
 18                       (  XXI     )
 19                       (    I     )
 20                       (    I     )
 21                       (    I     )
 22                       (  XXI     )
 23                       (    I     )
 24                       (    IXXX* )
 25                       (   XI     )
 26                       (    I     )
 27                       (    IX    )
 28                       (    I     )
 29                       (  XXI     )
 30                       (  XXI     )
                            -2 SD   +2 SD
```

Partial autocorrelations of lags 1-30.

```
      -1.000                0.                    1.000
      .+++++++++.+++++++++.+++++++++.+++++++++.+++++++++.
  1                       (    XI    )
  2                       (    XI    )
  3                       (    IXX   )
  4                       (    XI    )
  5                       (    IXXX )
  6                       (    IX    )
  7                       (    XI    )
  8                       (    IXX   )
  9                       (    IXX   )
 10                       (   XXI    )
 11                       (XXXXI    )
 12                       (    IX    )
 13                       (  XXXI    )
 14                       (    I     )
 15                       (    IX    )
 16                       (   XXI    )
 17                       (    XI    )
 18                       (    XI    )
 19                       (    I     )
 20                       (   XXI    )
 21                       (    IXXX )
 22                       (  XXXI    )
 23                       (XXXXI    )
 24                       (    I     )
 25                       (    XI    )
 26                       (    IXX   )
 27                       (    I     )
 28                       (    I     )
 29                       (  XXXI    )
 30                       (    IXXX )
                            -2 SD   +2 SD
```

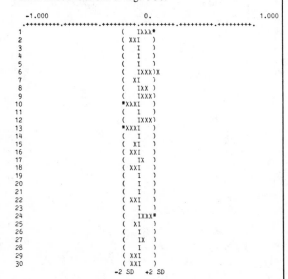
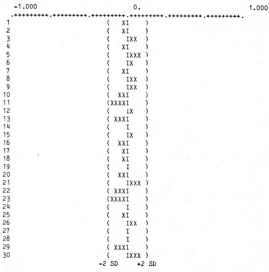
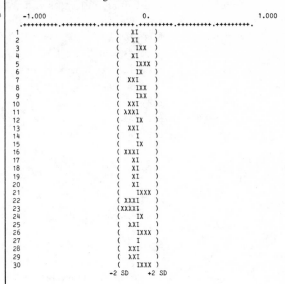

Figure 6.5(f). The ACF and PACF of the first differences for the whole series.

Figure 6.5(g). The ACF and PACF of the residuals for the full transfer function—ARIMA $(0,1,0)$ $(0,1,1)_{12}$ model.

Because of the size of the intervention effect, we will diagnose the adequacy of the joint transfer function–ARIMA model before proceeding with the intervention hypothesis testing. The autocorrelations and the partial autocorrelations for the residuals are plotted in Figure 6.5(g). For the first 30 lags, the autocorrelations and partial autocorrelations remain within the two standard error bands. For these residuals, $Q = 21.448$. With 29 degrees of freedom, the probability of obtaining this Q value is between .8 and .9. Both visual inspection and the value of the Q-statistic indicate that a white noise model could describe the residuals; there is no evidence of lack of model fit.

The intervention effect, ω, is statistically significant. We interpret these findings to mean that in the 147th month of the time series, in the month that Cincinnati Bell began charging 20 cents for Directory Assistance calls, the level of the time series dropped by over 38,000 calls per day. The new policy clearly had its intended effect.

Specifying the Transfer Function

In this example, we could see immediately that the hypothesized effect was abrupt and constant, so we knew which transfer function to use. In many cases, however, the analyst may have no idea which transfer function to use. As we know the correct or true effect in this problem, we can use it to demonstrate the general logic of transfer function specification.

Suppose that we have no real idea what form the true intervention effect in this problem will take. We are then interested in testing the general hypothesis that a measurable impact occurred regardless of its form. As a first step in this situation, we hypothesize an abrupt but temporary effect. To model this intervention, we use equation (3) but with the independent variable defined as a pulse function, that is:

$$I_t = 0 \; \textit{for the first 146 months}$$
$$= 1 \; \textit{for the 147th month}$$
$$= 0 \; \textit{for the remaining 33 months}$$

Then using the ARIMA $(0,1,0) \, (0,1,1)_{12}$ model we identified for this series, we estimate the transfer function parameters as:

$$\delta = .997 \; \textit{with t-statistic} = 94.00$$
$$\omega = -39,913 \; \textit{with t-statistic} = -17.28$$

Both parameters are statistically significant.

For this model, the parameter δ is interpreted as the rate of the impact's persistence. The effect is only temporary. It wears off or erodes, and the rate of erosion is indicated by the estimated value of δ. When δ is small, say, $\delta = .1$, the effect erodes quickly, usually after two or three months. But when δ is large, as it is in this case, the effect erodes slowly. With $\delta = .997$ the effect will not erode to any substantial degree for many years. For all practical purposes, the effect is permanent.

As our analysis has ruled out a temporary effect, we conclude that the effect is permanent. The next step is to posit a permanent but gradual effect. We use equation (3) again but define the independent variable as a step function, that is:

$I_t = 0$ *for the first 146 months*
$= 1$ *for the last 34 months*

Then using the ARIMA $(0,1,0)$ $(0,1,1)_{12}$ model we identified for this series, we estimate the transfer function parameters as:

$$\delta = -.003 \text{ } \textit{with t-statistic} = -.05$$
$$\omega = -39{,}931 \text{ } \textit{with t-statistic} = -17.30$$

Our estimate of δ is not significantly different than zero.

For this model, the parameter δ is interpreted as the rate at which the series approaches its new postintervention level. When δ is large, say, $\delta = .9$, the effect is quite gradual. And when δ is small, as it is in this case, the effect is quite abrupt. Of course, when $\delta = 0$, equations (2) and (3) are identical; in this case, we can say that δ is not statistically different than zero which implies that $\delta = 0$. For all practical purposes, the effect is abrupt.

Reviewing the logic of our analysis, we see that in the first step, we ruled out the possibility of a temporary effect. In the second step, we ruled out the possibil-

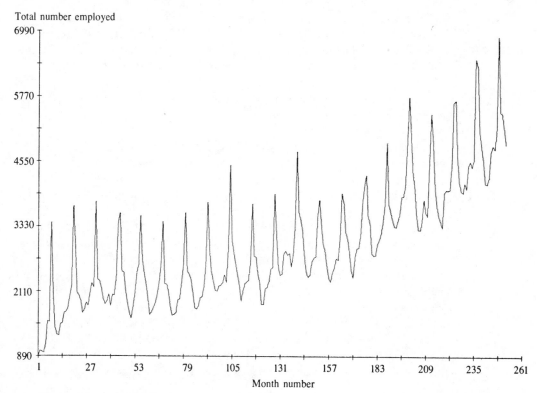

Figure 6.6(a). Sutter County workforce.

ity of a gradual effect. The only logical alternative is that the effect is both abrupt and constant, an impact associated with equation (2). In this case, of course, it was obvious from a visual inspection of the time-series plot. However, when the analyst is unsure, the method and logic illustrated here should be followed.

The Effects of a Flood on a Local Economy[15]

Figure 6.6(a) shows a time-series graph of the "work force" for Sutter County, California. The data are the total number of people working each month as reported to the U.S. Department of Commerce by employers. The series is 252 months long, starting in January 1946 and running through December 1966. At the end of December 1955, a flood forced the evacuation of Sutter County. Friesema et al. (1979) have used the interrupted time-series quasi-experiment to examine the long-range economic consequences of this flood. The questions involved in the analysis center on the length or duration of the flood's impact. As the onset of the flood was relatively abrupt, the time-series quasi-experiment is an ideal method for answering these questions.

Identification

The ACF and PACF of the time series, as shown in Figure 6.6(b), clearly indicate that this series is nonstationary and seasonal. The ACF dies slowly and we see telltale peaks at the seasonal lags. The ACF and PACF of the *differenced* series, shown in Figure 6.6(c), suggest that seasonal differencing is also required. The key to this identification is the size of the ACF at the seasonal lags. Lags 12 and 24 of the ACF are approximately .7 and .65 respectively. Lags 36, 48, and 60 of the ACF, which we do not show here, are approximately .58, .57, and .54. In other words, ACF dies out slowly at the seasonal lags, indicating that the series is nonstationary in its seasonal component.

One motive in selecting this series for analysis is that the ACF gives us perfect evidence for seasonal nonstationarity. Whenever a time series is nonstationary in its seasonal component, the ACF will die out slowly from seasonal lag to seasonal lag; that is, for monthly data, from lag 12 to lag 24, from lag 24 to lag 36, and so forth.

When seasonal nonstationarity is indicated by the ACF, the series must be seasonally differenced. A time series should not be differenced unless seasonal nonstationarity is indicated. If this point is unclear, compare this ACF to the ACFs from the lag-transformed data in the next example. In that case, the ACFs do not indicate seasonal nonstationarity. In this case, on the other hand, the ACF clearly indicates seasonal nonstationarity, so we difference the series seasonally.

The ACF and PACF for the differenced series (both regular *and* seasonal) are shown in Figure 6.6(d). These statistics suggest that an ARIMA $(0,1,1) (0,1,1)_{12}$ model might be appropriate. The basis for this identification are the lone spikes at lag 1 and lag 12 of the ACF. We also see rough patterns of decay starting at lag 1

---

[15]This time series is taken from Friesema et al. (1978).

Autocorrelations of lags 1-30.

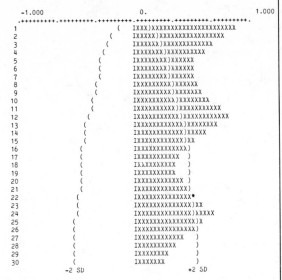

Autocorrelations of lags 1-30.

Partial autocorrelations of lags 1-30.

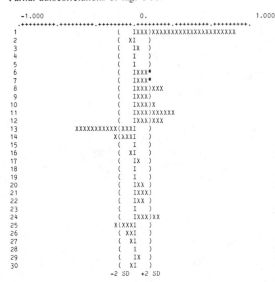

Partial autocorrelations of lags 1-30.

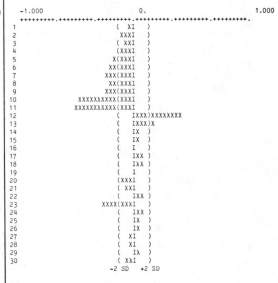

Figure 6.6(b). The ACF and PACF of the raw time series.

Figure 6.6(c). The ACF and PACF of the (regularly) first-differenced time series.

Autocorrelations of lags 1-30.

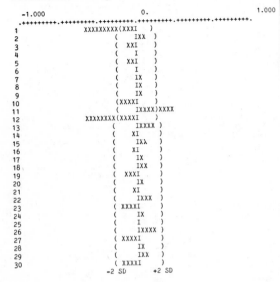

```
  -1.000                 0.                    1.000
.+++++++++.+++++++++.+++++++++.+++++++++.+++++++++.+++++++++.
1            XXXXXXXXX(XXXI    )
2                     (   IXX  )
3                     (   XXI  )
4                     (    I   )
5                     (   XXI  )
6                     (    I   )
7                     (   IX   )
8                     (   IX   )
9                     (   IX   )
10                    (XXXXI   )
11                    (   IXXXX)XXXX
12           XXXXXXXXX(XXXXI   )
13                    (   IXXXX )
14                    (   XI   )
15                    (   IXλ  )
16                    (   XI   )
17                    (   IX   )
18                    (   IXX  )
19                    (  XXXI  )
20                    (   IX   )
21                    (   XI   )
22                    (   IXXX )
23                    ( XXXXI  )
24                    (   IX   )
25                    (    I   )
26                    (   IXXXX )
27                    ( XXXXI  )
28                    (   IX   )
29                    (   IXX  )
30                    ( XXXXI  )
                      -2 SD  +2 SD
```

Autocorrelations of lags 1-30.

```
  -1.000                 0.                    1.000
.+++++++++.+++++++++.+++++++++.+++++++++.+++++++++.+++++++++.
1                     (   IX   )
2                     (    I   )
3                     (XXXI    )
4                     (   XXI  )
5                     (   XI   )
6                     (   IXX  )
7                     (   IXX  )
8                     (   IXXX)
9                     (   XI   )
10                    *XXXI    )
11                    (   IX   )
12                    (    I   )
13                    (   XI   )
14                    (   XI   )
15                    (   XXI  )
16                    (   XXI  )
17                    (   IX   )
18                    (   IX   )
19                    (   XI   )
20                    (    I   )
21                    (   XI   )
22                    (   XI   )
23                    (XXXI    )
24                    (   IX   )
25                    (   IXXX*
26                    (   IXXX)
27                    (   XXI  )
28                    (   XI   )
29                    (   IX   )
30                    (   XI   )
                      -2 SD  +2 SD
```

Partial autocorrelations of lags 1-30.

```
  -1.000                 0.                    1.000
.+++++++++.+++++++++.+++++++++.+++++++++.+++++++++.+++++++++.
1            XXXXXXXXX(XXXI    )
2                     *XXXI    )
3                     *XXXI    )
4                     (XXXI    )
5                     *XXXI    )
6                     (XXXI    )
7                     .   I    )
8                     (   IXX  )
9                     (   IXXX)
10                    (   XXI  )
11                    (   IXXX)XXXXX
12           XXX(XXXI    )
13           XX(XXXI    )
14                    *XXXI    )
15                    (XXXI    )
16                    *XXXI    )
17                    *XXXI    )
18                    *   I    )
19                    (XXXI    )
20                    (   I    )
21                    (   IXX  )
22                    (   IX   )
23                    (   IXX  )
24           X(XXXI    )
25                    *XXXI    )
26                    (   IX   )
27                    (XXXI    )
28                    *XXXI    )
29                    (   XI   )
30                    (   XXI  )
                      -2 SD  +2 SD
```

Partial autocorrelations of lags 1-30.

```
  -1.000                 0.                    1.000
.+++++++++.+++++++++.+++++++++.+++++++++.+++++++++.+++++++++.
1                     (   IX   )
2                     (   XI   )
3                     (XXXI    )
4                     (   XI   )
5                     (   XI   )
6                     (   IXX  )
7                     (   IXX  )
8                     (   IXX  )
9                     (   XI   )
10                    (XXXI    )
11                    (   IXX  )
12                    (    I   )
13                    (   XXI  )
14                    (   XI   )
15                    (   XXI  )
16                    (   XXI  )
17                    (   IX   )
18                    (   IX   )
19                    (   XXI  )
20                    (    I   )
21                    (   IX   )
22                    (   XI   )
23                    (XXXI    )
24                    (   IX   )
25                    (   IXXX)
26                    (   IXX  )
27                    (   XXI  )
28                    (    I   )
29                    (   IXX  )
30                    (   XI   )
                      -2 SD  +2 SD
```

Figure 6.6(d). The ACF and PACF of the (regularly and seasonally) first-differenced time series.

Figure 6.6(e). The ACF and PACF of the ARIMA $(0,1,1)(0,1,1)_{12}$ model residuals.

and 12 of the PACF. If the series required a higher-order moving average model, that is, $q = 2$ or $Q = 2$, we would expect to see more spikes in the ACF and patterns of decay at lag 24 of the PACF. Indeed, there seems to be some autocorrelation at lag 24 of the PACF but this is too weak to concern us at this point. If the ARIMA $(0,1,1)$ $(0,1,1)_{12}$ model is inadequate, we will see the evidence in diagnosis.

Estimation

The parameters of the tentative model are estimated as:

$$
\begin{aligned}
\theta_0 &= &-.5 &\quad \textit{with t-statistic} &= &\quad -.22 \\
\theta_1 &= &.60 &\quad \textit{with t-statistic} &= &\quad 11.38 \\
\theta_{12} &= &.68 &\quad \textit{with t-statistic} &= &\quad 13.33
\end{aligned}
$$

As the estimated value of θ_0 is not statistically significant, we drop this parameter from the tentative model. The estimated values of θ_1 and θ_{12} are both statistically significant and within the bounds of invertability, so we accept these estimates.

Diagnosis

The ACF and PACF for the residuals of the tentative model are shown in Figure 6.6(e). Aside from marginally significant spikes in the ACF at lags 10 and 25, there is nothing here to make us suspect that these residuals are not white noise. The Q-statistic for the ACF reinforces this judgment. $Q = 28.304$, and with 28 degrees of freedom, this value of Q corresponds with a .448 level of significance. The residuals meet both criteria, so we accept them as white noise and accept this model for the time series.

Intervention Hypothesis Test

In this case, we have an a priori notion as to the expected impact. It is expected to be abrupt but temporary in duration. According to Friesema et al. (1979), the economy of Sutter County is largely agricultural. The flood struck after the normal harvest season and caused little disruption. By the time of the next harvest season, most damage to local farmlands had been repaired. The transfer function model we require then is that of equation (3)

$$ Y_t = \delta Y_{t-1} + \omega I_t $$

where I_t is defined as a pulse function:

$$
\begin{aligned}
I_t &= 1 \textit{ in the } 121\text{st month} \\
&= 0 \textit{ in all other months}
\end{aligned}
$$

This impact is a decaying spike, an abrupt but temporary effect.

Using an ARIMA $(0,1,1)$ $(0,1,1)_{12}$ model for the stochastic component, we estimate the transfer function parameters as:

$$
\begin{aligned}
\delta &= &.84 &\quad \textit{with t-statistic} &= &\quad 2.64 \\
\omega &= &-276.44 &\quad \textit{with t-statistic} &= &\quad -1.36
\end{aligned}
$$

Using the formula for this transfer function, we see that the impact of the flood was short and negligible.

$$
\begin{aligned}
\text{First month's impact} &= \omega = -276.44 \\
\text{Second month} &= \delta\omega = -232.21 \\
\text{Third month} &= \delta^2\omega = -195.06 \\
\text{Fourth month} &= \delta^3\omega = -163.85 \\
&\cdot \\
&\cdot \\
&\cdot \\
\text{Twelfth month} &= \delta^{11}\omega = -40.61
\end{aligned}
$$

As the mean level of this series is nearly 3,000 employees, the initial impact of the flood amounted to a decrease of less than 10% in the work force. A year after the flood, the economy had returned to normal. Overall, as the estimated value of $\omega = -276.44$ is not statistically significant, we may say that the flood had no significant impact on this dependent measure.

The Effects of a Gun Control Law on the Incidence of Armed Robbery[16]

In 1975, the Massachusetts legislature passed a strict gun control law which, it was hoped, would reduce gun-related crime in Massachusetts. Deutsch and Alt (1977) used an interrupted time-series quasi-experiment to assess the impact of this new law on armed robbery and other crime rates in Boston. Their analysis:

> . . . indicated a statistically significant decrease in . . . armed robbery . . . in this time period. . . . Further, the specific time points in which these decreases were noted strongly suggest their probable direct association with the introduction and enactment of this law (p. 566).

However, a reanalysis of their data (Hay and McCleary, 1979) has shown that this conclusion is questionable and that Deutsch and Alt would have arrived at a different conclusion had they used the strategy we recommend.

The modeling strategy we recommend, outlined as a flow chart in Figure 6.4, leads the analyst in the direction of a parsimonious but adequate model. Let us be clear as to the role of ARIMA models in the quasi-experiment: The ARIMA model is a stochastic benchmark against which the intervention is contrasted. Each time series is described in terms of systematic and unsystematic error. The ARIMA model "explains" the systematic part of this error, and the remaining "unexplained" variance is used as the denominator of the t-statistic. The transfer function describes the changes in the pattern of the systematic error subsequent to the introduction of the intervention and is used as the numerator of the t-test:

$$
t = \frac{\textit{transfer function}}{\textit{``unexplained'' variance}}
$$

To be statistically significant, the intervention component must be relatively large compared to the "unexplained" variance.

---

[16]This time series is taken from Deutsch and Alt (1977).

It should be clear in this context that a *t*-statistic can be made arbitrarily large simply by increasing the amount of series variance "explained" by the ARIMA model. The selection of an ARIMA model for a time series thus plays a crucial, direct role in the outcome of our intervention hypothesis test. If the ARIMA model is the most parsimonious, adequate model for the time series, then the intervention hypothesis test will be fair and reasonable. But if the ARIMA model is inadequate or inappropriate, that is, if the model does not satisfy our diagnostic criteria, then the intervention hypothesis test will be biased.

There are obviously many ways to select an ARIMA model for a time series. For example, the analyst can simply "guess" at the correct model or, more likely, can "assume" that a particular model is the correct one. The identification/estimation/diagnosis method which we recommend has the virtue of leading the analyst to the most parsimonious but adequate ARIMA model. If the analyst relies solely on luck or experience, an adequate ARIMA model may be selected but there is no guarantee that this will be the most parsimonious model. As a result, the analyst may arrive at an unjustified picture of the intervention's significance.

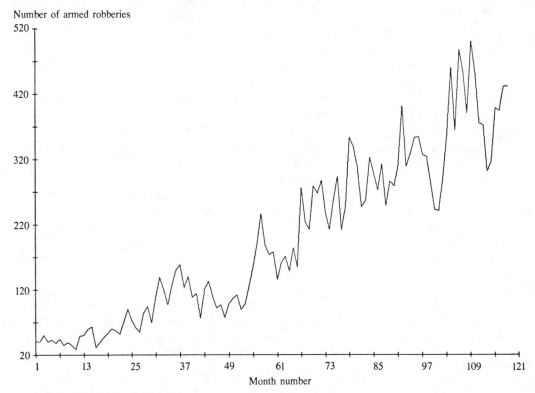

Figure 6.7(a). Boston armed robberies.

The time series graphed in Figure 6.7(a) represents the total number of armed robberies reported in Boston each month from January 1966 to October 1975. The Massachusetts Gun Control Law was enacted in April 1975, after several months of publicity. To be consistent with the Deutsch and Alt analysis, we use February 1975, the 110th month of the series, as the intervention point for the "anticipatory effect." Looking at this graph, we note that the series appears to be *non*stationary and seasonal. The number of armed robberies increases each month. Of course, we will reserve judgment on these issues until after we have seen the ACF and PACF for this series.

Identification

The ACF and PACF for this series are shown in Figure 6.7(b). There is no doubt that this series is nonstationary and must be differenced. The ACF and PACF for the differenced time series, shown in Figure 6.7(c), do not immediately suggest any simple ARIMA model for this series. Frankly, these statistics baffle us. We see no patterns of decay and/or spiking to serve as the basis of an identification. However, Deutsch and Alt have identified an ARIMA $(0,1,1)$ $(0,1,1)_{12}$ model for this series. Note that this model implies that the series is nonstationary in its seasonal component as well as in its regular component. But if this were the case, we would expect to see large spikes in the ACF at lag 12 and at lag 24. We see no such spikes and thus conclude that we will not have to difference the series seasonally.

Nevertheless, we agree with Deutsch and Alt that the ACF and PACF of the differenced series indicate a moving average component. We see one spike at lag 1 of the ACF and a pattern of rough decay in the first few lags of the PACF. We also see a pattern of rough decay at the seasonal lags of the PACF, so we tentatively identify an ARIMA $(0,1,1)(0,0,1)_{12}$ model for this time series.

In essence, we disagree with Deutsch and Alt only on the question of seasonal nonstationarity. We agree that the time series is nonstationary in its regular component and that it must be differenced. We also agree that the series is probably seasonal and that a moving average model is appropriate. The ARIMA $(0,1,1)$ $(0,0,1)_{12}$ model we have proposed is the simplest model which will incorporate these features. Of course, we admit that the ACFs and PACFs are too ambiguous at this point to give us confidence in our identification. However, we are not overly concerned about stumbling around in the dark at this stage of the analysis. If our model is inadequate, we will reject it in diagnosis.

Estimation

To demonstrate the points we have made about the modeling strategy, we will estimate the parameters of both models. For the ARIMA $(0,1,1)$ $(0,1,1)_{12}$ model proposed by Deutsch and Alt, we have:

$$\theta_0 = .31 \;\; \textit{with t-statistic} = .47$$
$$\theta_1 = .52 \;\; \textit{with t-statistic} = 6.08$$
$$\theta_{12} = .73 \;\; \textit{with t-statistic} = 8.29$$

As the *t*-statistic for θ_0 is not greater than 1.96, we drop this parameter from the model.

Autocorrelations of lags 1-30.

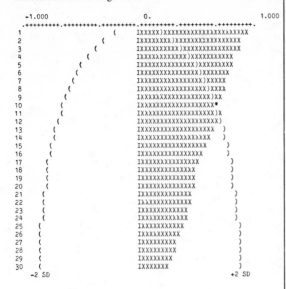

Autocorrelations of lags 1-30.

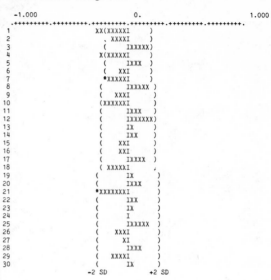

Partial autocorrelations of lags 1-30.

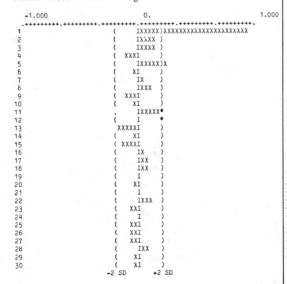

Partial autocorrelations of lags 1-30.

Figure 6.7(b). The ACF and PACF of the raw time series.

Figure 6.7(c). The ACF and PACF of the first-differenced time series.

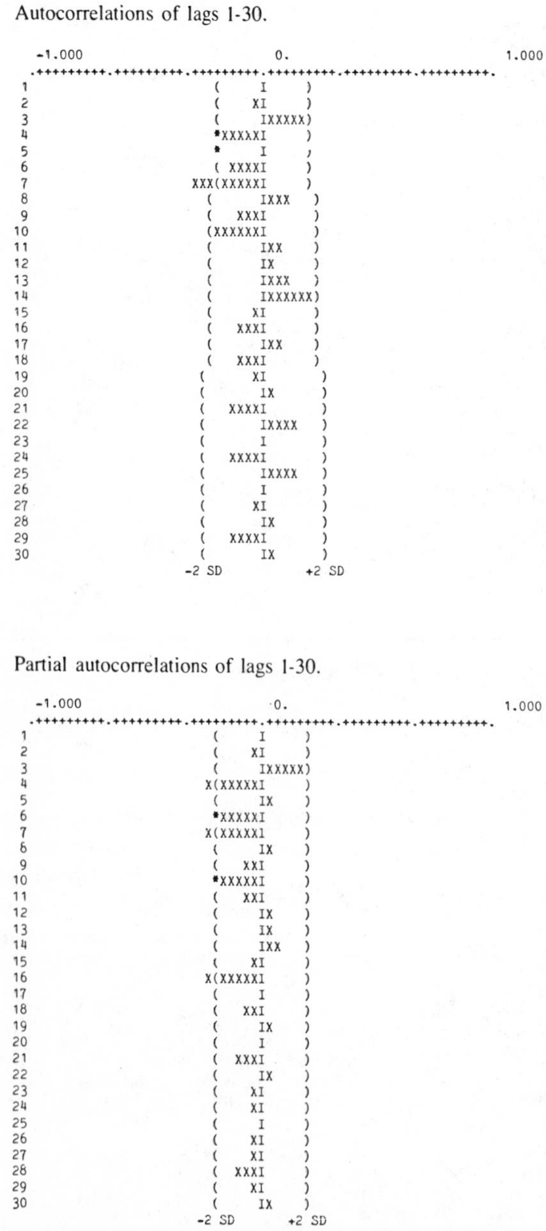

Left column

Autocorrelations of lags 1-30.

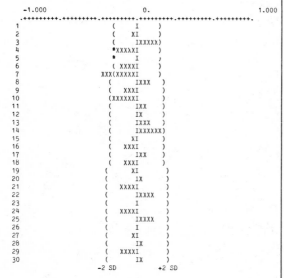

```
    -1.000              0.                1.000
    .+++++++++.+++++++++.+++++++++.+++++++++.+++++++++.
 1                    (     I     )
 2                    (    XI     )
 3                    (    IXXXXX)
 4                   *XXXXXI     )
 5                   *      I     )
 6                    ( XXXXI     )
 7                 XXX(XXXXXI     )
 8                    (     IXXX  )
 9                    (   XXXI    )
10                    (XXXXXXI    )
11                    (    IXX    )
12                    (    IX     )
13                    (    IXXX   )
14                    (    IXXXXXX)
15                    (   XI      )
16                    (  XXXI     )
17                    (    IXX    )
18                    (  XXXI     )
19                    (   XI      )
20                    (    IX     )
21                    (  XXXXI    )
22                    (    IXXXX  )
23                    (    I      )
24                    (  XXXXI    )
25                    (    IXXXX  )
26                    (    I      )
27                    (   XI      )
28                    (    IX     )
29                    (  XXXXI    )
30                    (    IX     )
                   -2 SD       +2 SD
```

Partial autocorrelations of lags 1-30.

```
    -1.000              0.                1.000
    .+++++++++.+++++++++.+++++++++.+++++++++.+++++++++.
 1                    (     I     )
 2                    (    XI     )
 3                    (    IXXXXX)
 4                  X(XXXXXI     )
 5                    (    IX     )
 6                   *XXXXXI     )
 7                  X(XXXXXI     )
 8                    (    IX     )
 9                    (   XXI     )
10                   *XXXXXI     )
11                    (   XXI     )
12                    (    IX     )
13                    (    IX     )
14                    (    IXXX   )
15                    (   XI      )
16                  X(XXXXXI     )
17                    (    I      )
18                    (   XXI     )
19                    (    IX     )
20                    (    I      )
21                    (   XXXI    )
22                    (    IX     )
23                    (   XI      )
24                    (   XI      )
25                    (    I      )
26                    (   XI      )
27                    (   XI      )
28                    (  XXXI     )
29                    (   XI      )
30                    (    IX     )
                   -2 SD       +2 SD
```

Figure 6.7(d). The ACF and PACF of the ARIMA $(0,1,1)(0,1,1)_{12}$ model residuals.

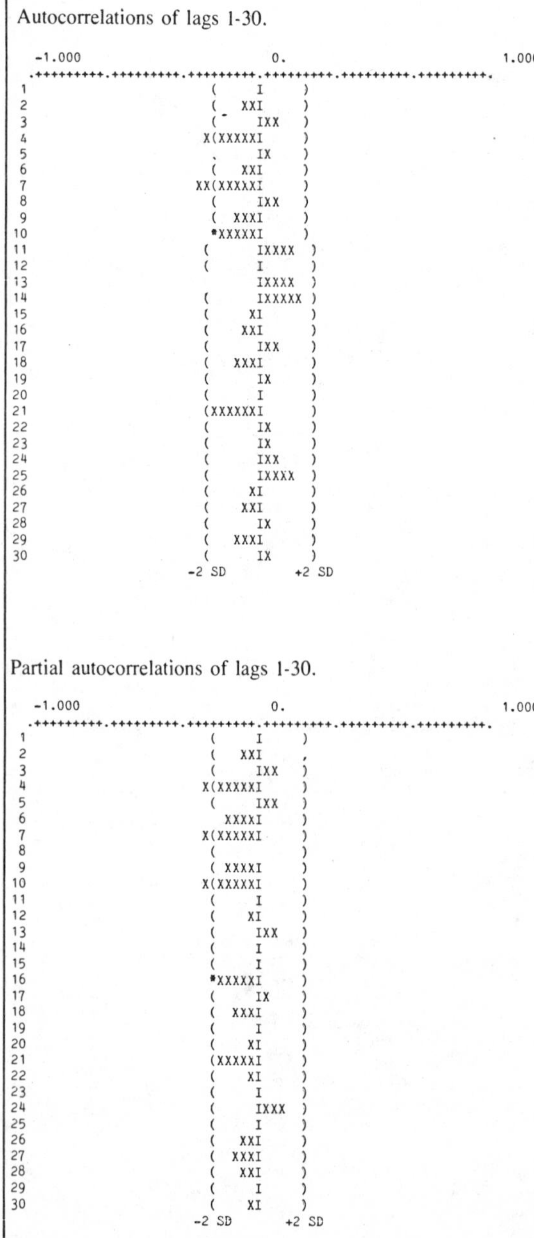

Right column

Autocorrelations of lags 1-30.

```
    -1.000              0.                1.000
    .+++++++++.+++++++++.+++++++++.+++++++++.+++++++++.
 1                    (     I     )
 2                    (   XXI     )
 3                    (     IXX   )
 4                  X(XXXXXI     )
 5                    (     IX    )
 6                    (   XXI     )
 7                  XX(XXXXXI     )
 8                    (    IXX    )
 9                    (   XXXI    )
10                   *XXXXXI     )
11                    (    IXXXX  )
12                    (    I      )
13                    (    IXXXX  )
14                    (    IXXXXX )
15                    (   XI      )
16                    (   XXI     )
17                    (    IXX    )
18                    (  XXXI     )
19                    (    IX     )
20                    (    I      )
21                    (XXXXXXI    )
22                    (    IX     )
23                    (    IX     )
24                    (    IXX    )
25                    (    IXXXX  )
26                    (   XI      )
27                    (   XXI     )
28                    (    IX     )
29                    (  XXXI     )
30                    (    IX     )
                   -2 SD       +2 SD
```

Partial autocorrelations of lags 1-30.

```
    -1.000              0.                1.000
    .+++++++++.+++++++++.+++++++++.+++++++++.+++++++++.
 1                    (     I     )
 2                    (   XXI     )
 3                    (     IXX   )
 4                  X(XXXXXI     )
 5                    (     IXX   )
 6                    (   XXXXI    )
 7                  X(XXXXXI     )
 8                    (     I     )
 9                    ( XXXXI     )
10                  X(XXXXXI     )
11                    (    I      )
12                    (   XI      )
13                    (    IXX    )
14                    (    I      )
15                    (    I      )
16                   *XXXXXI     )
17                    (    IX     )
18                    (  XXXI     )
19                    (    I      )
20                    (   XI      )
21                    (XXXXXI     )
22                    (   XI      )
23                    (    I      )
24                    (    IXXX   )
25                    (    I      )
26                    (   XXI     )
27                    (  XXXI     )
28                    (   XXI     )
29                    (    I      )
30                    (   XI      )
                   -2 SD       +2 SD
```

Figure 6.7(e). The ACF and the PACF of the ARIMA $(0,1,1)(0,0,1)_{12}$ model residuals.

For the ARIMA $(0,1,1)$ $(0,0,1)_{12}$ model we propose, the parameters are estimated as:

$$\theta_0 = 2.96 \; \textit{with t-statistic} = 1.18$$
$$\theta_1 = -.45 \; \textit{with t-statistic} = -5.60$$
$$\theta_{12} = -.40 \; \textit{with t-statistic} = -4.11$$

Again, the t-statistic for θ_0 is not greater than 1.96, so we drop this parameter from our model.

In the estimation stage of our analysis, we are interested only in two rough criteria. First, we want the parameters of our model to be statistically significant. If any parameter is not significantly different than zero, we drop that parameter from the tentative model as we have done. Second, we want the ϕ- and θ-parameters to lie within the bounds of stationarity and invertibility. What this means for first-order ARIMA models is that the absolute value of the estimated value of ϕ_1 and/or θ_1 should be smaller than unity. We see that the θ-parameters in both models meet this criterion.

Diagnosis

To diagnose a tentative model, we compute the ACF and PACF for the model residuals. These statistics are shown in Figure 6.7(d) for the ARIMA $(0,1,1)$ $(0,1,1)_{12}$ model proposed by Deutsch and Alt and, in Figure 6.7(e), for the ARIMA $(0,1,1)$ $(0,0,1)_{12}$ model we have proposed. If either of these models is adequate, we expect the model residuals to behave as white noise. If the model residuals are white noise, that is, if the model is adequate, we expect the ACF and PACF for the residuals to satisfy two criteria. First, the Q-statistic for the ACF must be small. Second, the ACF and PACF of the residuals must have no spikes either at early lags or at the seasonal lags.

With respect to the first criterion, we see that neither model is at all adequate. The Q-statistics for both models are large enough to reject the null hypothesis that the model residuals are white noise. For the ARIMA $(0,1,1)$ $(0,1,1)_{12}$ model, $Q = 41.724$. With 22 degrees of freedom, this value of Q is significant at the .007 level. For the ARIMA $(0,1,1)$ $(0,0,1)_{12}$ model, $Q = 39.913$. With 22 degrees of freedom, this value of Q is significant at the .011 level.

Both models fail to satisfy this diagnostic criterion, so we must return to the identification stage. Returning to the ACFs and PACFs shown in Figure 6.7(b), we remain convinced that this series is nonstationary, that it must be differenced. However, the ACF and PACF of the differenced series give us no real clues as to the nature of the process. One alternative would be to posit a more complicated model, for example, an ARIMA $(0,1,2)$ $(0,0,1)_{12}$ or an ARIMA $(0,1,2)$ $(0,0,2)_{12}$. Increasing the values of either q or Q will often do the trick. But we see no evidence of a higher-order moving average in these ACFs and PACFs. Moreover, the model is already too complicated and cumbersome for our tastes, and increasing the value of q or Q would simply complicate the model further.

The other alternative is to explore a transformation of the series. This series is indeed nonstationary but it may be nonstationary in a way that differencing will not cure. In a long time series, the series variance may increase or decrease systematically as time passes. If we examine the graphed series, shown in Figure

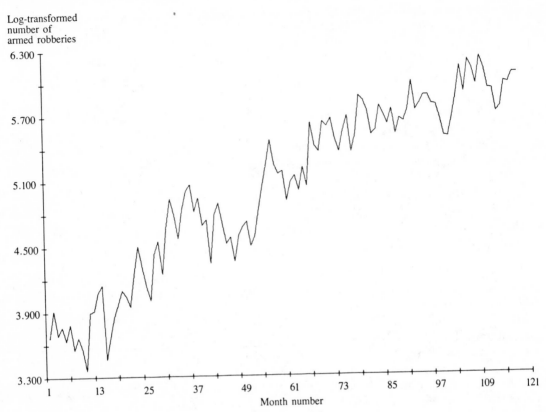

Figure 6.7(f). Log-transformed Boston armed robberies.

6.7(a), we see that this appears to be the case. The series seems to grow noisier. The second half of the series, for example, seems to be more erratic or to have a greater variance than the first half of the series. When this is a possibility, the series should be log transformed. After log transformation, a simple ARIMA model can often be identified.

In Figure 6.7(f), we show the graphed log transformation of the series. The transformation is accomplished simply by taking the natural logarithm of each series observation. It appears that log transformation has made the series variance more uniform across time. The second half of the series does not appear to be much noisier or more erratic than the first half. We can now try to identify a model for this series.

Identification

The ACF and PACF of the log-transformed time series, as shown in Figure 6.7(g), indicate nonstationarity. Even after log transformation, the series must be differenced. The ACF and PACF of the differenced series, shown in Figure

Autocorrelations of lags 1-30.

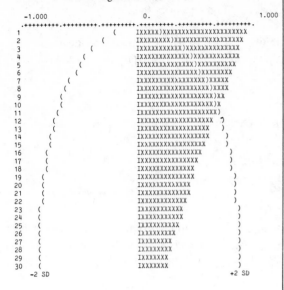

Partial autocorrelations of lags 1-30.

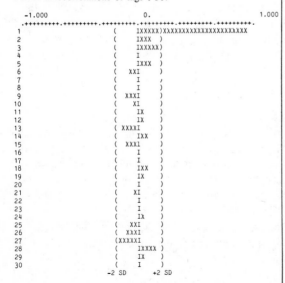

Figure 6.7(g). The ACF and PACF of the log-transformed time series.

Autocorrelations of lags 1-30.

Partial autocorrelations of lags 1-30.

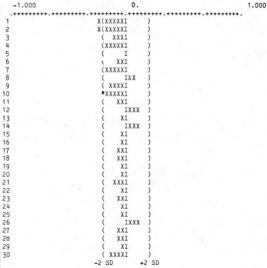

Figure 6.7(h). The ACF and PACF of the first-differenced log-transformed time series.

6.7(h), suggest a moving average process. Overall, the ACFs and PACFs of the log-transformed series are not as messy as those for the raw series. There is still some ambiguity, of course, but we see a spike at lag 1 of the ACF and a pattern of decay in the PACF. We also see a pattern of decay at the seasonal lags of the PACF, although this is not as obvious. On the basis of these statistics, we identify an ARIMA $(0,1,1)$ $(0,0,1)_{12}$ model for the *log-transformed* time series. We agree that there might be other possibilities, but this seems to be a reasonable starting point. If the tentative model is either improbable or inappropriate, we will again return to identification.

Estimation

An ARIMA $(0,1,1)$ $(0,0,1)_{12}$ model for the log-transformed time series gives us parameter estimates:

$$\theta_0 = .0195 \quad \textit{with t-statistic} = 1.57$$
$$\theta_1 = -.43 \quad \textit{with t-statistic} = -4.99$$
$$\theta_{12} = +.19 \quad \textit{with t-statistic} = +1.97$$

As the *t*-statistic for θ_0 is less than 1.96, we drop this parameter from the model. Both θ_1 and θ_{12} are acceptable estimates and statistically significant.

Diagnosis

The ACF and PACF for the model residuals, as shown in Figure 6.7(i), have no spikes at early lags or at the seasonal lags. Moreover, the Q-statistic leads us to accept the hypothesis that these residuals are white noise: $Q = 15.921$ with 22 degrees of freedom. This value of the Q-statistic is not significant at the .05 level. In fact, we would expect to see a Q-statistic this large 90% of the time by chance alone. It is clear that the ARIMA $(0,1,1)$ $(0,0,1)_{12}$ model for the log-transformed time series is adequate.

Intervention Hypothesis Testing

We would ordinarily begin this stage of the analysis with equation (3) as we have recommended. However, as there are only eight postintervention observations in this time series, we need to slightly alter the general strategy. The change is necessary because if we estimate several transfer function parameters on the basis of only eight data points, we are likely to have multicollinearity problems during estimation.[17] We can eliminate the risk of multicollinearity problems by reducing the number of parameters to be estimated. Therefore, we assume the constant change model is appropriate and specify the simpler equation (2) as the initial tentative transfer function model.

Our main point in this analysis has to do with the modeling strategy. Deutsch and Alt selected an ARIMA $(0,1,1)$ $(0,1,1)_{12}$ model for the time series; as we have demonstrated, this model is inappropriate. Using their model, we estimate the

---

[17]See Johnston (1972) or Kmenta (1971) for a discussion of multicollinearity and its associated estimation problems.

Autocorrelations of lags 1-30.

Partial autocorrelations of lags 1-30.

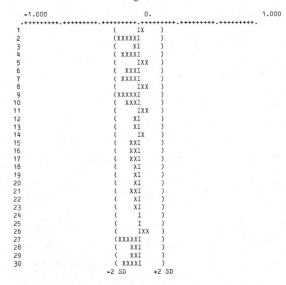

Figure 6.7(i). The ACF and PACF of the ARIMA $(0,1,1)$ $(0,0,1)_{12}$ model residuals for the log-transformed time series.

change in the level of armed robberies after enactment of the gun control law as:

$$\omega = -84.58 \ \textit{with t-statistic} = -2.86$$

This means that, beginning with the month the new law was enacted, armed robberies dropped by nearly 85 per month in Boston. Moreover, as the t-statistic for ω is less than -1.96, this change is statistically significant.

However, log transforming the series first, then using an ARIMA $(0,1,1)$ $(0,0,1)_{12}$ model, we estimated the change in level as:

$$\omega = -.20701 \ \textit{with t-statistic} = -1.33$$

Now our estimate of ω is stated in the natural logarithm metric, so we must use $e \ \omega$ as our effect. As $e^{.20701} = 1.23$, we may conclude that the ratio of the preintervention to the postintervention series is 1.23. This represents an 18.7% reduction from the preintervention to the postintervention level. Of course, as the t-statistic for ω is not less than -1.96, we conclude that this change is not statistically significant. *Overall, we cannot conclude that the Massachusetts Gun Control Law had an impact on the level of armed robbery in Boston.*

The reader may wish to go over this example again. The most significant point to be learned is the importance of the iterative identification/estimation/diagnosis modeling strategy. Deutsch and Alt apparently did not follow this strategy and, as a result, arrived at an ARIMA model which did not adequately reflect the stochastic behavior of the Boston armed robbery time series. Because their ARIMA model was inappropriate, they arrived at an incorrect estimate of the impact of the Massachusetts Gun Control Law.

More generally, this example illustrates log transformation. The reader should study the ACFs and PACFs of this example to see why log transformation was required. We suspected this was the case because we were unable to fit a lower-order ARIMA model to the time series. The ARIMA $(0,1,1)$ $(0,0,1)_{12}$ and ARIMA $(0,1,1)$ $(0,1,1)_{12}$ models failed to meet our diagnostic criteria. We then inspected the ACFs and PACFs of the differenced series and concluded that they were messy and ambiguous, indicating that this was not a "typical" time series. Finally, we inspected the plotted series and saw that the series variance appeared to increase with the level of the series. That is, the series appeared to grow erratic with time. After log transforming the series, the ACFs and PACFs were neater, and we had no trouble identifying an ARIMA $(0,1,1)$ $(0,0,1)_{12}$ model for the series. More important, this model easily satisfied our diagnostic criteria.

CONCLUSION

Our intent has been to tread the thin line between theoretical rigor and practical, unintimidating instruction. We suspect that many students are intimidated by time-series problems because they believe that learning the practical skills requires a high degree of mathematical sophistication. This is no more true of time-series analysis than it is of other statistical methods. For example, many social scientists use the analysis of variance even though they do not understand the underlying mathematics. While time-series modeling does indeed have a complicated mathe-

matical basis, its practical application mainly requires time, patience, and access to relevant computer programs.

On the other hand, mastering the theoretical basis will have long-range practical benefits. We direct the interested reader to Glass, Willson, and Gottman (1975) and to Hibbs (1977) as logical next steps. But at the same time, we urge the newcomer to go out and gain practical experience. This will build confidence which in turn will motivate the newcomer to dig deeper into the theoretical aspects. There are literally thousands of interesting time series available in any good library.

7

Inferring Cause from Passive Observation

The section of this chapter entitled "The Causal Analysis of Concomitancies in Time Series" was written for this book by Melvin M. Mark.

The previous chapters have dealt for the most part with inferring cause from manipulated changes which were arbitrarily and abruptly introduced at a specified time into a measurement and comparison setting. This enables researchers to make inferences regarding the effect of the intervention. In contrast, the methods of the present chapter try to infer causal processes based on observations of concomitancies and sequences as they occur in natural settings, without the advantage of deliberate manipulation and controls to rule out extraneous causal influences.

The methods discussed in this chapter are usually categorized under headings such as "correlational methods" or "nonexperimental methods." We have no quarrel with the latter title, but the former no longer seems appropriate. This is because correlations in the ordinary sense are what one looks for in experiments as well as in descriptive studies of the nonexperimental sort. In both cases, one is interested in discovering whether certain variables covary with others, irrespective of whether any of the variables is manipulated. Correlations in the technical statistical sense could be used to analyze data from experiments as well as from nonintrusive observational studies. The t test of the difference between means, the F test from analysis of variance or covariance, and the common multiple regression approaches are all part of the same general linear statistical model. The crucial difference between the methods discussed in this chapter and those used in experimentation is not in the choice of statistics to analyze the data. Indeed, even if only graphic or tabular means of analysis and presentation are used, these are just as applicable to the experiment as to descriptive or observational studies.

Traditionally, the term "correlational study" refers to a purely descriptive or observational study where the data are statistically analyzed. Since the terms "description" and "observation" could also apply to the data from experiments, we propose for the sake of clarity to add to them the adjective "passive," as in the title of this chapter. While we are not likely to change well-established usage,

we propose for our own use the contrasting phrases "experimental studies" and "passive-observational studies." To shorten the latter to "observational studies" alone would invite confusion with the similar distinction between "experimental" and "observational" studies in the statistics literature, under which all nonrandomized experiments—including quasi-experiments—may be classified as observational.

Passive-observational approaches may be employed for the purpose of causal inference. We have briefly alluded to this possibility in chapter 1, even while holding up deliberate, intrusive experimentation as the epitome of the meaning of causation. In chapters 5 and 6 on time series we applied experimental modes of analysis even when the "treatment" was a natural disaster rather than a planned intervention. But in this and other similar cases, we also specified that the event being evaluated had to be abrupt and precisely dated, and not a reaction to prior change in the level of the indicator. Given these restrictions, such a passive observational setting might justifiably be called a "natural experiment" since it approaches a deliberate experiment in form—a form which facilitates causal inference. In regard to the nonequivalent control group design, we could tolerate the use of the methods of chapters 3 and 4 for "treatments," such as attending a particular training program, even where the program was a permanent institution and where the researcher did not manipulate anything. However, in those chapters we added the caveat that it was crucial to render rival hypotheses implausible, such as selection-maturation interactions, and that there should be structural aspects of the setting which reduce the equivocality of causal inference normally accompanying correlational data. The settings in this sense should be quasi-experimental, substituting natural controls for those that would be introduced in deliberate experimentation. In the present chapter the goal of achieving causal inference from passive observational data is extended to include observations from settings which lack even such quasi-experimental structural controls.

In aspiring to causal inference from passive-observational data, it is essential to distinguish sharply between this goal and other uses of the same type of correlational evidence, such as forecasting. For purely forecasting purposes, it does not matter whether a predictor works because it is a symptom or a cause. For example, your goal may be simply to predict who will finish high school. In that case, entering the Head Start experience into a predictive equation as a negative predictor which reduces the likelihood of graduation may be efficient even if the Head Start experience improved the chances of high school graduation. This is because receiving Head Start training is also evidence of massive environmental disadvantages which work against completing high school and which may be only slightly offset by the training received in Head Start. In the same vein, while psychotherapy probably reduces a depressed person's likelihood of suicide, for forecasting purposes it is probably the case that the more psychotherapy one has received, the greater is the likelihood of suicide.

This chapter is *not* concerned with presenting forecasting techniques. They enter into discussion here only insofar as well-established modes of analysis developed for forecasting are still mistakenly used for causal inference. This confusion is all the more saddening because, in the first book on the subject, Blalock (1961) clearly distinguished between "prediction" and "causal inference." Moreover,

within the literature on regression techniques, one can find an explicit distinction between "predictive regression" (i.e., forecasting) and "structural regression" (i.e., causal inference or something close to it). Rogosa (1978) is able to trace such a usage back to Wald (1940) and Tukey (1954). Wold (1956) has long made a similar distinction. But in most applied statistical analyses in the social sciences this distinction is ignored. Multiple regression beta weights—for a program treatment (coded as a dummy variable, 1 for treated, 0 for untreated) or for some other antecedent variable—that are quite appropriate for forecasting purposes are mistakenly reported in causal language. For forecasting purposes, it makes no difference what the true causal path is from one variable to another, and there is no need to distinguish between symptoms and causes. Nor does it create a problem if the presumed causal variable is a complex composite of which only a part produces the correlation with the outcome variable. However, for structural regression, both error and independent factors in the covariates (the "independent variables") can produce profoundly misleading results, neglect of which can lead to *reversing* the sign of the beta weight, for example making the Head Start experience seem harmful. For predictive regression, leaving out a relevant covariate may produce a forecast less precise than it might otherwise have been but does not lead to any misstatement of the forecasting relevance of the covariates employed. For structural regression, such an omission or specification error may again lead to erroneous estimates of both the magnitudes and signs of the causal paths among the variables at hand. Thus the distinction between *causal inference* from observational data and *forecasting* from the same data is a very significant one with many concrete methodological implications. It is on the causal inference agenda that we focus in this chapter. Many readers are already fluent in the algebra and computer programs for forecasting. We ask you in particular to attend to this difference.

Behind the prevalent confusion of the two purposes may be the well-established terminological usage of calling the covariates in multiple regression "independent variables" even though many of them cannot be "independently varied" even with an all-out massing of the powers of government. How John Stuart Mill's precious and appropriate usage for deliberate manipulation (see chapter 1) could come to be so misapplied is a question for some historian of science to answer. Doubtless it occurred in that period from Mill to Russell when Hume's denial of any distinction between causation and correlation dominated the theory of science. Perhaps Karl Pearson himself was to blame, being at the same time a positivist philosopher of science, an evolutionary biologist who fought the introduction of Mendel's theory with its unobserved causal genes, and a major contributor to the development of multiple regression statistics.

In this chapter we present three or four common modes of quasi-experimental analysis that will be encountered in the research literature. For the statistically sophisticated reader, these approaches are all redundant alternative presentations of a common mathematical structure presented more elegantly in chapter 4. Yet we believe it is important to discuss the crucial issues in each of these forms of presentation, since it is in these forms that causal claims from field research will most commonly be encountered. The four sections that follow can be read in any order. Their relative difficulty will vary depending upon the statistical background of the reader. The section on "treatment as a dummy variable in a regression

analysis'' is particularly condensed and requires prior familiarity with regression and adjustments to third variables. The path analysis section attempts to provide some introductory understanding to those not previously familiar with the approach, but omits any introduction on how to do such analyses. The section on the cross-lagged panel correlation gives considerable detail on the past history of the method, since we have also taken the occasion to update our view of its historical development. The final section, on drawing causal inferences from the relationship of two time series, is only a brief sketch of what is a voluminous and growing literature.

TREATMENT AS A "DUMMY VARIABLE" IN A REGRESSION ANALYSIS

In the actual practice of applied social science, including program evaluation, the most common mode of causal inference, the most common quasi-experimental design, is to represent the treatment as a "dummy variable" (treated = 1, untreated = 0) in a regression analysis. Since the treated group differs in composition from the untreated, other variables are entered into the analysis in the expectation that they will model the selection process whereby different kinds of persons came to be in different groups, or will provide an acceptable causal model of the dependent variable. A treatment effect is inferred if there is a statistically significant regression coefficient (beta weight) relating the dummy variable to the dependent variable, after adjusting for the effect of the covariates introduced to try and correct for selection. Unfortunately, those who use this widespread practice make the error of employing forecasting techniques for causal inference.

Our main analysis of the mistaken assumptions underlying this approach is presented in Reichardt's chapter 4. Here we discuss a commonsense illustration stated in the terms of regression analysis. For the older generation of readers, we will use the language of partial correlation, asking the (misleading) question, e.g., What is the correlation between the treatment (T) and achievement (A) when we have "partialed out" the effects of social class (S), family income (F), education (E), etc. (i.e., what is $r_{AT \cdot SFE}$)? For those with more modern training in multivariate statistics, we will speak in terms of adjusted regression coefficients, or betas, $\beta_{AT \cdot SFE}$. We are addressing this illustration, remember, not to the best methodology articles and texts in applied social science, but to a common practice which is all the more entrenched because of handy computer programs that generate "impressive" output.

Table 7.1 presents a hypothetical set of correlations based upon a model situation in which most users of multivariate regression techniques would expect these techniques to work. In this hypothetical simulation, let us imagine that the population is from middle management. The pretest (Pr), which we will not use for most of this simulation, and posttest (Po) are similar measures of executive aptitude. These scores have 80% of their variances determined by the same underlying "social advantage" factor. The experimental treatment (T) could be a year in a graduate school of management, intentionally awarded to the most promising, and on the whole, to those highest on a latent social advantage factor. In our hypothet-

ical example, this factor accounts for half of the variance in assignment to treatment and is the sole source of the .505 correlation between treatment and pretest. Since T is a dichotomous variable, this correlation is lower than it would otherwise be. In terms of shared components of variance, it corresponds to the .632's found between the pretest and the covariate in Table 7.1. Similarly, the .399's in that table are reduced by T's dichotomous character from the .500's that would be obtained if both variables were continuous. The correlation between the treatment and pretest shows that those who received the treatment were already ahead of the others in executive aptitude. For our hypothetical case, the treatment has had no real effect on executive ability. Thus the correlation of the treatment with the pretest is identical to its correlation with the posttest and is again due to the shared social advantage factor as reflected in selection of candidates for the program, rather than the beneficial effects of the program.

	(Pr)	Po	T	C_1	C_2	C_3
Po	(.800)					
T	(.505)	.505				
C_1	(.632)	.632	.399			
C_2	(.632)	.632	.399	.500		
C_3	(.632)	.632	.399	.500	.500	

Table 7.1. Hypothetical intercorrelations among variables for regression adjustment demonstration.

Shown also in Table 7.1 are three excellent covariates tapping the same latent social advantage factor which determines 50% of the variance of each. To make these illustrations more concrete, imagine that C_1 is father's income, C_2 mother's educational level, and C_3 the socioeconomic level of the candidate's home neighborhood. Let us now use these covariates to adjust the relationship between the treatment and the posttest measure of executive ability in the hope of removing the effects of the social advantage factor that determined who received the treatment—a treatment that we simulated to be ineffective. Table 7.2 shows such adjustments for a version of our hypothetical illustration in which no pretest is available. The first row gives the starting values, with no covariates employed. The adjusted mean differences are stated in terms of standard score units for the pooled population of those who received the treatment and those who did not. These differences directly correspond to the partial correlations and beta weights also presented in the table.

Using one covariate substantially reduces the apparent effect of the program. Each covariate added helps reduce the apparent effect still more. With three of these unusually powerful covariates, the adjusted mean difference is down to .33, the partial correlation $r_{PoT \cdot C_1 C_2 C_3} = .230$, the regression coefficient $\beta_{PoT \cdot C_1 C_2 C_3} = .167$. But these values are still of a magnitude that would be mistakenly reported as impressive results for the training program. If the study were based on 500 cases, half receiving the training, these differences would be significant beyond the $p < .0001$ level. Even if we had ten such marvelous covariates measuring social advantage, with 500 cases the adjusted mean difference would still be significant at the posttest ($p < .02$) level. Thus even in this apparently optimal situation for the use of regression adjustments, they fail. The underadjusted residuals left could be mistakenly reported as treatment effects. The only way such covariates can provide an adequate adjustment is for one or more of them to be a perfectly reliable and valid measure of the latent common factor. Such covariates simply do not exist, and most covariates available have much weaker relevance than do those of this hypothetical illustration.

Number of covariates	Adjusted regression coefficient $\beta_{PoT \cdot C_1 - C_n}$	Partial correlation $r_{PoT \cdot C_1 - C_n}$	Adjusted mean difference on posttest
0	(.505)	(.505)	(1.01)
1	.301	.356	.60
2	.214	.278	.42
3	.167	.230	.33
10	.065	.105	.13

Table 7.2. Regression adjustments on the matrix of Table 7.1 (see text).

What if we do have the pretest and adjust on it? The adjusted mean difference would be .271, $\beta_{PoT \cdot Pr} = .136$, $r_{PoT \cdot Pr} = .195$, all of which spuriously suggest a treatment effect. What if we use both the pretest and the three other covariates? The adjusted mean difference becomes .175, $\beta_{PoT \cdot Pr C_1 C_2 C_3} = .111$, $r_{PoT \cdot P_r C_1 C_2 C_3} = .136$. All of these, though small, still have a magnitude frequently reported as treatment effects. It is especially worth noting that our illustration has assumed but one underlying latent factor. If the factorial pattern is more complex, both multivariate regression adjustments and partial correlation are equally inappropriate. Only by a chance combination of circumstances can they give the correct adjustment.

Two striking reanalyses of previous multivariate regression estimates of program effects have recently been published that questioned the initial analyses which found compensatory educational efforts *harmful*. Magidson (1977) reanalyzed data designed to evaluate Head Start. While his alternative analysis has come under attack (Bentler and Woodward, 1978; Magidson, 1978), it should be noted that the quarrel is about whether a plausible alternative analysis shows statistically significant beneficial effects. In both Magidson (1977) and Bentler and

Woodward (1978) the sign for the treatment effect is positive and is opposite to that obtained from the earlier multivariate regression analyses which led to conclusions about harmful effects. Director (1979) called attention to the misleading conclusions of regression analyses of Job Corps training, which again have found such training a liability. Having in one study three waves of measurement with no training between the first two, Director was able to apply the standard regression approach to a "dry run" estimate of the effect of the training program before it was ever implemented. The approach resulted in significantly harmful effects from the nonexistent training. Director's alternative analyses removed the appearance of harmful effects in all cases, but failed to find significantly positive effects from such programs. The point to be emphasized here is that the use of standard regression approaches often results in unwarranted conclusions of harmful treatment effects when "compensatory" treatments are evaluated where the persons receiving the treatment do less well than controls at the pretest. Similarly, they often lead to unwarranted conclusions of beneficial impact when programs are evaluated where the initially more fortunate group has greater exposure to the treatment, as was the case in the hypothetical example above.

CAUSAL MODELING BY PATH ANALYSIS

In the last decade techniques for causal inference from nonexperimental data have emerged as dominant within sociology, economics, and political science under such names as causal models, path analysis, and structural equation models. The dominance of these methods can be easily verified by consulting contemporary theory-related empirical studies in sociology as well as methodological journals such as *Sociological Methods and Research* and *Social Science Research*. Indications are that this dominance will increase rather than decrease during the next few years. This is not the place to begin an education in path analysis, nor are we appropriate teachers. Blalock (1961, 1971), Duncan (1975) and Heise (1975) provide good starting points, while the Goldberger and Duncan (1973) text is more advanced. Nonetheless, it seems useful to present some of the basic ideas at their simplest level and to use this important language of explanation and analysis to restate some of the concerns that have been raised throughout this book.

In practice, most of the detailed methodology of path analysis deals with estimating path coefficients and paths from correlation coefficients computed on observational data. Didactically, however, it is simpler to start as though the path coefficients were known and generate the correlation coefficients that would result from them. This is particularly true when illustrating methodological problems. No matter what the complexity of an assumed path model, one can always generate the relevant correlation coefficients. This is true even in cases in which it would be impossible to do the reverse and deduce path coefficients from the manifest correlational data.

Let us start with a very simple three-variable model, Figure 7.1, where A causes B and B in turn causes C, there being no direct causal connection from A to C: i.e., $A \rightarrow B \rightarrow C$. The two path coefficients generate the three correlations as follows: First, the path coefficient itself gives the correlation between two directly connected variables (except as this value is modified by a correlation mediated

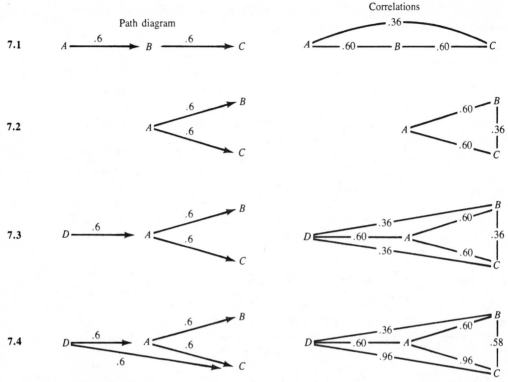

Figures 7.1, 7.2, 7.3, and 7.4. Illustrative causal path diagrams and the corresponding correlation coefficients.

indirectly by common causes which the two variables share, as in subsequent examples). Thus $r_{AB} = .60$ and $r_{BC} = .60$. Second, mediated causal relations generate correlation components equal to the product of the path coefficients of the links that connect them. Thus $r_{AC} = .6 \times .6 = .36$. Note that this same pattern of correlations would be generated by these alternative paths: $A \leftarrow B \leftarrow C$ and $A \leftarrow B \rightarrow C$. Like the $A \rightarrow B \rightarrow C$ model under test, these other models imply no path from A to C. Thus if one found that $r_{AC} = .36$, this would imply no causal path from A to C, but it would not allow one to differentiate among the three causal models unless there was background information or trusted theory which allowed one to rule out some of the models on a priori grounds. (Regression coefficients can be used to test simple models like this. Assuming the model is correct, $\beta_{AC \cdot B} = 0$.)

Figure 7.2 shows another three-variable case, to which we will add more variables to illustrate further computational rules. In Figure 7.3 B and C now share a remote common cause D as well as the direct common cause A. But this does not add to the correlation between B and C since the routes from D to B and from D to C *both* have to go through A. Therefore A already transmits all of the correlation-

generating causal efficacy of D, and D's addition does not change r_{BC}. However, if we add a direct causal path from D to C as in Figure 7.4, r_{BC} is changed. The new path creates a supplementary channel for D's influence on r_{BC}. To the .36 correlation points contributed by the fact that both B and C share A as a cause, mediated through the loop BAC, are added the .22 correlation points generated by D as a common cause, mediated through the new loop $BADC$ (.6 $\times$ .6 $\times$ .6 = .216) summing to the new value, r_{BC} = .58. This new path also changes two of the correlations corresponding to direct paths. The correlation r_{AC} becomes .96, composed of the direct path .60 plus the influence of their shared cause D, via loop ADC, .6 $\times$ .6 = .36. The value for r_{DC} also becomes .96 via DAC as well as DC.

We have moved in the easy deductive way from known path coefficients to resultant correlation coefficients. We will not attempt here to teach how to move in the inductive direction from the correlation coefficients (plus the assumed paths) to estimates of the path coefficients. For all of the cases of Figures 7.1 through 7.4 it can readily be done. Since in each case there are more correlation coefficients than hypothesized paths, the models are "over-identified." This means that there are enough degrees of freedom not only to estimate the paths but also to test the goodness of fit of the model. Where the number of coefficients and the number of paths are equal, the model is just-identified, and one can estimate coefficients but not test the fit. Where, as in later examples, there are more paths than correlation coefficients, the path coefficient cannot be estimated. Even in such cases, however, drawing up path diagrams using the best available background information, the most trusted theories, and making plausible guesses as to path coefficients can be of fundamental help in the theory-relevant interpretation of correlational data.

In discussing the examples of Figures 7.1 through 7.4, we have not specified how measurement errors (unreliability) and reliable irrelevant components of variables (invalidity) enter into consideration. However, one way of conceptualizing the totality of such unique or unshared components is already implicit in these path models. Figure 7.5 provides a more explicit version of Figure 7.1 to clarify this conceptualization. In path analysis, the variables have all been "standardized," with the variance of each variable being transformed to 1.0. The causal paths impinging upon a variable usually leave much of that variance unexplained. The unexplained residual can be attributed to unique components, spelled out in

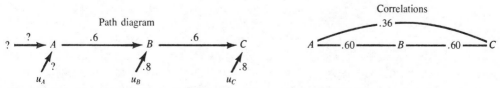

Figure 7.5. A version of Figure 7.1 with the unique components (*u*) of measured variables made explicit. (Lower case letters represent unobserved variables.)

Figure 7.5 using u for unique components, with the letter in lower case to indicate that it is an unobserved variable. (For B and C, values for the path from u have been set at .8 so that the sum of the squares of impinging paths will equal 1.00 ($.8^2 + .6^2$) and no remote sources of correlation complicate the picture. For A, which is unexplained in this model, the path $u_A \rightarrow A$ is indeterminate, and could be set from .00 to 1.00 without affecting the rest of the model.) As noted for variable D in Figure 7.3, a cause which enters a network through only one variable can be omitted without affecting the paths or correlations among the other variables. Especially where such causes are unobserved variables, it simplifies the presentation to leave them out (as in Figure 7.1). They do not affect the computational aspects of the method either for deducing correlations from path coefficients or for *inferring* path coefficients from observed correlation coefficients. However, putting them in (as we have in Figure 7.5) does make more explicit the nature of the conceptual model. It also helps explain why in the most advanced presentations of causal modeling this is *not* the recommended approach for representing error and unique variance in variables, even though it is the one approach implicit in most of the older and many of the current research applications of path analysis.

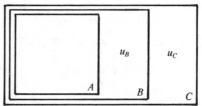

Figure 7.6. Shared variance overlap diagram corresponding to Figures 7.1 and 7.5.

In the model of Figure 7.5 (and Figure 7.1), the unique components of B, u_B, are not irrelevant to C, but become a causally efficacious part of B impinging on C fully as much as those components deriving from A. The overlapping-area diagram, Figure 7.6, using an older approach to understanding correlation, may help make this clearer for some readers. All of the variance of A is contained in (i.e., causally effective in) B, and all of the variance of B is contained in C. The correlation between A and B is less than perfect only because of u_B, the unique components of B. Similarly, it is u_C, not u_B, which keeps r_{BC} down to .60 instead of being 1.00. But this is a very implausible model. In most situations, we know that our variables are measured imperfectly, with both irrelevant systematic sources of variance as well as haphazard error of which "methods factors" (Campbell and Fiske, 1959) are only one type. Except in those rare instances in which a measurement is itself directly used in a social decision process (which we discuss in regard to the regression-discontinuity design in chapter 3), it is not reasonable to regard these incidental components of the measure's variance as being causally efficacious. Furthermore, we know that in practice correlations are apt to be atten-

uated by the unique components of the "cause" fully as much as by the unique components of the "effect." The model of Figures 7.1, 7.5, and 7.6 make the mistake, discussed in previous chapters, of assigning all the error to the "dependent" variable, treating an "independent" variable as though it were a perfect measure.

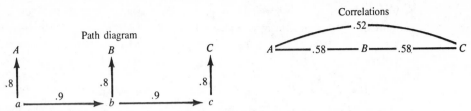

Figure 7.7. Path model with the preferred representation of unique variance in measured variables. (Capital letters represent measured variables, lower case are unobserved.)

Figure 7.7 shows a much more appropriate way of modeling the unique variance in measured variables. Here the causally efficacious relations are among the unmeasured or latent variables *a, b,* and *c,* rather than the observed *A, B,* and *C.* (Since much of the unique variance that attenuated relations in Figures 7.1 and 7.5 is now moved up out of the causal path, the path coefficients relating *a, b,* and *c* have been set at larger values. To avoid confusion, paths from unique components have been omitted.)

While this model is no doubt more realistic, it is much less "convenient." There are five paths to estimate from only three observed correlation coefficients; thus the model is seriously underidentified. Only by making further assumptions could one begin to estimate causal paths. For example, one might assume that the reliability-validity of each of the variables was the same, so that $a \rightarrow A = b \rightarrow B = c \rightarrow C$. This reduces to three the number of path coefficients to be estimated, and the model becomes just-identified. While this is an unreasonable assumption, almost certain to be wrong unless *A, B,* and *C* are three forms of the same intelligence test, it is clearly a more reasonable approximation than to assume the model of Figures 7.1, 7.5, and 7.6 where *A* is measured without uniqueness, and *B*'s uniqueness from *A* is causally efficacious in *C.*

If the true but unknown model of causal relationships takes the form of Figure 7.7, but we misinterpret it and test the model in Figure 7.1, we are led to the seriously mistaken conclusion that there must be a direct causal path between *A* and *C,* inasmuch as $\beta_{AC \cdot B} = .27$ rather than zero.

Practical approaches are being developed regarding the problem of unique variance in measured variables. These involve causal models for unobserved variables, and in our judgment this development is essential if path analysis and structural equation modeling is to minimize misleading conclusions. The work of Jöreskog, Sörbom, and Goldberger (Jöreskog, 1970, 1973, 1974, 1977; Jöreskog and Sörbom, 1976, 1978; Jöreskog and Goldberger, 1975; Goldberger, 1972, 1973; Long, 1976) seems particularly important. Such models in practice will

often involve assumptions that one knows are oversimplifications. Nonetheless, such assumptions will almost always be more appropriate than those made in the simpler form of path analysis and in ordinary regression analysis, namely, that the causal variables and other covariates have been measured without unique irrelevant variance. Note that in the vigorous exchange already cited between Magidson (1977, 1978) and Bentler and Woodward (1978) on Head Start reanalyses, both are employing the Jöreskog–Sörbum techniques.

We can continue this introductory presentation of path analysis by using it to model one of the imperfect compensatory examples referred to in the first section of this chapter. In school systems covering a range of educational advantages in the homes of its pupils, the observed correlation between Head Start attendance (*HS*) and first-grade achievement (*Ach*) will be negative. If we use $HS \rightarrow Ach$ as a complete causal model, we would conclude that the path coefficient is negative and that Head Start has a harmful effect on school achievement. But such a simple model is guilty of a specification error, since it has omitted at least one important causal variable that influences achievement. We can call this the educational advantage *(EA)* associated with home and neighborhood environments. Specification error is an important problem for causal modeling but we will not elaborate on it here. It is enough to say that valid causal modeling is dependent on functionally complete specification and that whenever path coefficients are taken seriously as a research product complete specification has to be assumed. Omitting a relevant cause not only can produce an erroneous estimate of the size of the path coefficients among the variables attended to, it can also lead to the sign of the path coefficient being wrong, mistaking negative causation for positive and harmful effects for beneficial ones. In the very simple Head Start case above, this type of omission occurred.

Figure 7.8. A model for educational advantage (EA), Head Start (HS), and school achievement (Ach), lacking proper representation of the unique components of the measured variables.

Figure 7.8 illustrates a somewhat more complete model. Head Start has been offered to those from the least advantaged homes, hence the negative path coefficient between *EA* and *HS*. Moreover, we know from past research that children from the most advantaged homes do better in first-grade achievement, hence the positive path coefficient between *EA* and *Ach*. Assume now that the Head Start experience improves first-grade achievement, resulting in the positive coefficient from *HS* to *Ach*. The resultant correlation between Head Start and achievement is

made up of this direct causal component .30, and the indirect component due to the common cause, educational advantage, shared by *HS* and *Ach*. This indirect component (.7 × −.7) is −.49, the net correlation between *HS* and *Ach* is therefore −.19. However, if such a model were correct, one could successfully control for the effect of educational advantage by a regression adjustment, $\beta_{AchHS \cdot EA} =$ .30, showing positive benefits from Head Start in accordance with the model.

But the model of Figure 7.8 has not represented the unique components in the measured variables adequately. If we try to do this, an example such as Figure 7.9 results. (In assigning the path coefficient between *ea* and *EA*, we have been guided by our impression of the validity of such measures. For *hs* → *HS* we have used .9 rather than 1.0, in awareness of errors in school records and cases of near zero attendance.)

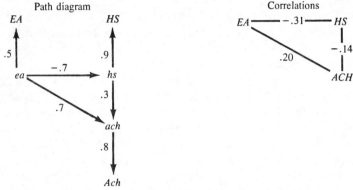

Figure 7.9 A preferred model for representing unique components in measured educational advantage, Head Start, and school achievement.

In this case, where unique variance in measured variables is more appropriately modeled, the regression adjustment does *not* correct the direction of effect. Indeed, $\beta_{Ach \cdot EA} = -.08$, a value that still suggests small but harmful effects in the same direction as the simple correlation between *HS* and *Ach*. Similar models could of course be supplied for other illustrations, such as the probably higher suicide rate for those who have received more psychotherapy, or the lower calculus grades for those with more tutoring, and other instances of valid compensatory efforts that do not offset initial disadvantages.

As a contribution to competent causal theory building in complex real-world settings, path analysis can perform two quite different functions: theoretical clarification and estimation of specific causal impacts. As a tool for theoretical clarification, it has our strong approval. Starting from one's theoretical, empirical, and commonsense knowledge of a problem, one maps all of the latent variables one believes to be present and the probable causal links among them, indicating which paths are positive and which negative. One adds in the measured variables already available and those that might be obtained. While the path-analytic language uses

linear relationships, at this stage one can even note links that are believed to be nonmonotonically curvilinear (where, for example, A's maximum effect in increasing B is at an intermediate value of A). By adding in estimated path coefficients, one can derive predictions about the size and direction of the correlation coefficients that one would expect between available measured variables. Such derivations often produce surprises such as *negative* correlations connecting two variables linked by a *positive* causal path, thus showing how deceptive common habits of drawing causal inferences from correlational evidence can be. (In Figures 7.8 and 7.9, the relation between Head Start and achievement provides a simple example of such an outcome.) Used in this way, drawing up causal pathway maps as complete and complex as the real-world setting itself can be an enormously valuable preparation for field work, whether of a quantitative or qualitative nature. And with regard to the specific issues of this book, path analysis used this way increases awareness of the equivocality of causal inference from passive observational data and, by contrast, of the great advantages in reducing equivocality of experimental control, randomization, comparable comparison groups, and pretests similar to posttests. It is a flexible language in which the precautionary messages about third-variable causation and the other dangers of inferring causation from correlation can be clearly expressed.

This use of path modeling for making explicit what one knows about a real-world causal nexus is rare, but it is no doubt sometimes used in unpublished stages of research. However, it is antithetical in spirit to the commoner goal of producing estimates of specific causal path coefficients. Such estimates require greatly reduced complexity, wholesale elimination of plausible causal connections, and usually the elimination of the distinction between measured variables and the causally effective variance they contain. The estimates of specific causal paths may occasionally be plausible and valid, but the pressure to come up with a model permitting their estimation results in omissions which render most of these conclusions suspect. In terms of the concerns of this book, the omissions of error and unique variance in the causal variables are particularly serious.

These cautionary notes are of course not ours alone. They are to be found in Blalock's (1961) book and its successors. It is fitting to close this section with two quotations from Duncan's (1975) recent text:

> We distinguish sharply between (1) statistical description, involving summary measures of the joint distributions of observed variables, which may serve the useful purpose of data reduction, and (2) statistical methods applied to the problem of estimating coefficients in a *structural model* (as distinct from a "statistical model") and testing hypotheses about that model. One can do a passably good job of the former without knowing much about the subject matter (witness the large number of specialists in "multivariate data analysis" who have no particular interest in any field). But one cannot even get started on the latter task without a firm grasp of the relevant scientific theory, because the starting point is, precisely, the model and not the statistical methods (pp. 5–6).
>
> It is the gravest kind of fallacy to suppose that, from a number of competing models involving different causal orderings, one can select the true model by finding the one that comes closest to satisfying a particular test of overidentifying restrictions. (Examples of such a gross misunderstanding of the Simon-

Blalock technique can be found, among other places, in the political science literature of the mid-1960s.) In fact, a test of the causal ordering of variables is beyond the capacity of any statistical method; or, in the words of Sir Ronald Fisher (1946), "if . . . we choose a group of social phenomena with no antecedent knowledge of the causation or absence of causation among them, then the calculation of correlation coefficients, total or partial, will not advance us a step toward evaluating the importance of the causes at work" (p. 50).

CROSS-LAGGED PANEL CORRELATIONS

The cross-lagged panel correlation technique is much less widely used than path analysis or structural equation modeling. It is restricted to a much narrower set of passive observational settings, where two or more variables have been measured on a number of persons (or other units) on two or more occasions. The method was initially proposed independently of the path analysis tradition, and its preferred measure of cause has been the comparison of correlation coefficients between measured variables rather than latent path coefficients. However, when its assumptions are made explicit, they can be presented in path analysis form. We give this technique disproportionate attention here, including commentary on its historical development, because the predecessors of this book (Campbell and Stanley, 1963, 1966; Cook and Campbell, 1976) have been a major channel for disseminating information about cross-lagged panel correlations. While these earlier presentations have treated the technique with skeptical advocacy, this presentation carries still more skepticism and even less advocacy.

Beginning some 30 years ago, Lazarsfeld (e.g., 1947, 1948, 1972; Lipset, Lazarsfeld, Barton and Linz, 1954. See Lazarsfeld, 1978, for a history) argued that repeated measurement of the same two variables potentially should provide information about the direction of any causal asymmetries between them. His "16-fold table" (two dichotomous variables at two successive times generating 16 cells) probably finds its best modern descendant in Goodman (1973, 1978). In an effort to convert the 16-fold table for use with continuous variables and to relate it to the use of lagged correlations in economics, Campbell (1963; Campbell and Stanley, 1963) devised the cross-lagged panel correlation method. Working independently, and with more impressive illustrations, Pelz and Andrews (1964) developed essentially the same model. Kenny has contributed many further developments (1973, 1975b, in press).

Figure 7.10 presents the set of terms and images we will use in this presentation. The letters A and B represent two variables, each measured at two times—1 and 2—on the same persons (i.e., a "longitudinal" study or, in social survey terms, a "panel study"). The initial question at issue was whether A is a stronger cause of B than B is of A? A careful note should be made of the question, and it should be differentiated from the concern in previous chapters which can best be summarized as: Is A a cause of B? The synchronous correlations, $r_{A_1B_1}$ and $r_{A_2B_2}$, and the test-retest correlations, $r_{A_1A_2}$ and $r_{B_1B_2}$, provide the interpretative framework for the two cross-lagged correlations, $r_{A_1B_2}$ and $r_{B_1A_2}$. If A is a stronger cause of B than B is of A, and if there are real storage processes (such as bank accounts and memories) spreading out the causation in time, then it might be

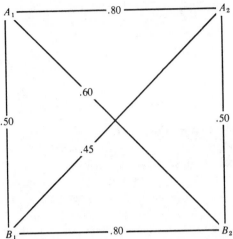

Figure 7.10. Hypothetical cross-lagged and background correlations between two variables (A and B) measured at two successive time periods (1 and 2) on the same sample.

expected that $r_{A_1 B_2}$ would be larger than $r_{B_1 A_2}$. Such a case is illustrated in Figure 7.10 where a clear-cut $A \to B$ causation of a positive nature seems to be indicated (i.e., increases in A_1 cause increases in B_2). Because $r_{A_1 B_2}$ is also larger than $r_{A_1 B_1}$ or $r_{A_2 B_2}$, and because the latter two are equal, this illustration avoids many of the sources of equivocality that will be discussed below.

Built into the presumptions of the method is a bias in favor of regarding A and B as symptoms of a common or third variable rather than as specific causes. Whereas in cross-sectional path analysis the synchronous correlations of A and B—which equal .50 in Figure 7.10—would suggest cause, in cross-lagged panel analysis they are treated as sharing variance due to a third factor. That is, they are considered symptomatic of an $A \leftarrow z \to B$ model rather than an $A \to B$ or $B \to A$ model.

Initially, Campbell (1963) was only willing to infer causation where the synchronous correlation was increasing, that is, $r_{A_1 B_1} < r_{A_2 B_2}$; but subsequently it has seemed that interpretability is maximum when a condition of "stationarity" exists, that is, when the componential or causal model remains the same at each time period. One symptom of stationarity is that the synchronous correlations be stable, although with only two waves of measurement, the assumption of stationarity is poorly tested. Another consideration in the model is "temporal erosion" (Kenny, 1973). It is ubiquitously observed that relationships are lower over longer lapses of time. For example, an intelligence test might correlate .90 over a one-year lapse but only .50 over a five-year gap, with intermediate periods having intermediate values. Cross-trait correlations show a comparable diminution over time. Figure 7.11 shows an extension of the hypothetical case of Figure 7.10

illustrating both stationarity and a homogeneous temporal erosion process. It also illustrates an $A \rightarrow B$ causal effect that persists over longer lags but in diminished degree. Thus over one interval, the lagged correlations are .60 and .45, while over two intervals they are .54 and .40.

The rate and pattern of temporal erosion are matters to be determined empirically. In the simple case of Figure 7.11, A and B are equally reliable and have the same rate of temporal erosion. In this hypothetical case, each has an "instantaneous" reliability of .89 (not shown in Figure 7.11) and a temporal erosion rate of .90 per unit of time. Thus $r_{A_1A_2} = .89 \times .90 = .80$, $r_{A_1A_3} = .80 \times .90 = .72$, $r_{A_1A_4} = .72 \times .90 = .65$, and so on. This conforms to the autoregressive model known as a first-order Markov process, which is probably a reasonable model for many time-series data in economics and the other social sciences. The rates of temporal erosion are expected to vary for the differing components of systematic variance making up each variable. The erosion rate for the components generating the A-B correlation are of special importance since they provide the basis for estimating what the lagged cross-correlations would be in the absence of any

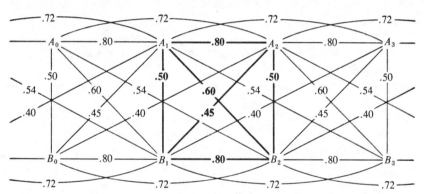

Figure 7.11. The hypothetical cross-lagged panel correlations from Figure 7.10 extended as a stationary process in repeated measures. (To avoid confusion, lags beyond two time periods have not been included in the diagram.)

$A \rightarrow B$ or $B \rightarrow A$ causation. In the simple case of Figures 7.10 and 7.11 where the overall erosion rates of A and B are the same, it may seem reasonable to assume that the erosion rate of their shared component is the same as the two overall rates. On this basis, the values $r_{B_1A_2} = .45$, $r_{B_1A_3} = .41$, $r_{B_1A_4} = .36$, and so on, represent no causation, just temporally attenuated cosymptomicity.

Making such estimates in practice turns out to be a difficult problem. However, if the assumption of stationarity is appropriate, the expected values for $r_{A_1B_2}$ and $r_{B_1A_2}$ are the same if there is no specific $A \rightarrow B$ or $B \rightarrow A$ causation. This is because the effect of the unknown attenuation would be equal on $r_{A_1B_2}$ and $r_{B_1A_2}$. In the absence of any cross-causation, these correlations should be equal. Thus, it would be appropriate to compare these two values directly, without estimation of erosion rates. Whereas in Figures 7.10 and 7.11 one of the cross-lagged values is higher than the synchronous values, causal inference is suggested no matter what

estimate of temporal erosion is used. And when the synchronous values are zero (as in a randomized experiment and occasionally in cross-lagged panel correlations), no further erosion is possible, clarifying cross-causational inference.

But stationarity is not always the case, and the assumption is not met when variables change in reliability, as happens in longitudinal studies with children where reliability increases over time. When such changes are uniform across all variables, they may not bias the comparison of cross-lagged values. If, however, one variable is changing at a different rate from the others, mistaken inferences can result. Other things being equal, a variable that is increasing in reliability will be mistakenly judged to be an effect rather than a cause. (For example, if A_2 is more reliable than A_1, all correlations involving A_2 will tend to be higher than those involving A_1, including $r_{B_1A_2} > r_{A_1B_2}$.) If appropriate reliability estimates are available (it is not clear that internal consistency reliability estimates are appropriate), correction for attenuation may restore stationarity. Kenny (1973) has developed a "correction for communality" for use where many variables are involved. Using factor-analytic logic, though not performing a factor analysis, estimates of reliability ratios are based on the inter-trait correlations. An application and exposition of Kenny's approach is found in Crano, Kenny, and Campbell (1972). Figure 7.12 illustrates the best of their many cross-lagged panel correlations, showing that vocabulary is a stronger cause of spelling than vice versa. (Since in this case the correction for communality did not change the picture, the original correlations are presented.)

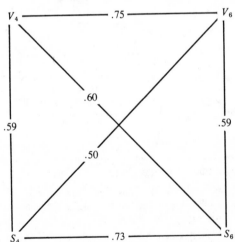

Figure 7.12. Cross-lagged correlation pattern between vocabulary and spelling scores from the Iowa tests of basic skills, Milwaukee Public Schools, grades 4 and 6, $n = 5,495$. The t for the comparison $r_{V_4S_6} > r_{S_4V_6} = 9.32$. (After Crano, Kenny, and Campbell, 1972.)

INFERRING CAUSE FROM PASSIVE OBSERVATION

The presentation so far and the original presentations of Pelz and Andrews (1964) and Campbell (1963) have implied that only two causal hypotheses are in competition: $A \rightarrow B$ and $B \rightarrow A$. But a causal relation between two variables can be either negative or positive. Increases in A can result in increases in B, or in decreases in B. Expanding our symbolism, there are at least four hypotheses: $A \overset{+}{\rightarrow} B$, $A \overset{-}{\rightarrow} B$, $B \overset{+}{\rightarrow} A$, and $B \overset{-}{\rightarrow} A$. Some examples will help clarify this. Rozelle and Campbell (1969) set out to probe the method by confirming that in an achievement-oriented suburban high school, high attendance caused high grades, testing this against the unlikely alternative (for this population) that high grades caused high attendance. They surprised themselves by also concluding that high grades in one semester caused lower attendance in the following, which made sense in terms of high grades giving a student freedom to join his parents on a winter vacation or to cut one class to study for another. (All correlations were very low. The synchronous correlations were essentially zero, making noticeable the sign difference between $r_{A_1 G_2} = .08$ and $r_{G_1 A_2} = -.06$. With an n of 1,000, this difference is highly significant.) Thus their significant difference between $r_{A_1 G_2} > r_{G_1 A_2}$ was best interpreted as a pooled effect of two causal processes. Inspecting Pelz and Andrews's (1964) wide range of illustrations provides other examples. In the analysis of data from the Survey Research Center panel on economic trends, intentions-to-purchase at one time no doubt "caused" purchases a later year. For television sets, $r_{I_1 P_2} = .75$, $r_{P_1 I_2} = -.57$. But certainly some of this 132-point difference in correlation is due to a negative component: purchases one year reduce subsequent intentions. (In their results on intentions-to-purchase pooled over a wide range of household durables, $r_{I_1 P_2} = .33 > r_{P_1 I_2} = .09$, the negative component $P \overset{-}{\rightarrow} I$ is less noticeable because both signs are positive, but it is no doubt still there.)

Rozelle and Campbell (1969) attempted to solve the problem of confounding negative and positive causation by computing a "no-cause comparison base" against which each of the cross-lagged values could be separately compared. Thus in the case of Figure 7.11 using the lagged autocorrelations (test-retest correlations) and the synchronous cross-correlations, one would estimate what each of the cross-lagged correlations would be in the absence of an $A \rightarrow B$, $B \rightarrow A$ causation. The obtained cross-lagged correlations would each be separately compared with this value, rather than directly with each other. One could confirm two separate causal hypotheses at one time, and each of these could be one of two types, positive or negative. In Figure 7.11 (and 7.10), had both $r_{A_1 B_2}$ and $r_{B_1 A_2}$ been .60, with the no-cause comparison base .45, the two conclusions would have been $A \overset{+}{\rightarrow} B$ and $B \overset{+}{\rightarrow} A$. Had each been .30, the two conclusions would have been $A \overset{-}{\rightarrow} B$ and $B \overset{-}{\rightarrow} A$. Had $r_{A_1 B_2}$ been .60 and $r_{B_1 A_2}$ .30, the conclusions would have been $A \overset{+}{\rightarrow} B$ and $B \overset{-}{\rightarrow} A$, and so on. (Some outcomes will be incompatible with the requirement of stationarity.) The use of a "no-cause comparison base" would be appropriate if there were reasonable grounds for estimating it. Rickard (1972) and Kenny (1973) have, however, persuasively rejected Rozelle and Campbell's estimation procedure, which involved treating temporal erosion as though it were a characteristic of a variable as a whole. When A and B differed in erosion rate, Rozelle and Campbell recommended using the geometric mean of the two as the rate at which the synchronous correlations would erode to become the lagged

cross-correlations under no-cause conditions. Rickard and Kenny correctly point out that the relevant temporal erosion is that of the shared latent factors producing the synchronous correlation and that there is no logical reason why that should be an average. (In Rozelle and Campbell's data, since the synchronous correlations were essentially zero, the niceties of estimating erosion rates and no-cause comparison bases did not affect their substantive conclusions.)

As a result, Kenny advocated a less ambitious version of cross-lagged panel analysis, in which the two cross-lagged correlations are compared directly with each other. In many instances some of the four causal hypotheses will be so implausible that (à la path analysis) they can be ruled out on a priori grounds. In Crano et al. (1972) it seemed a real question whether the preponderant causal direction was from intelligence to achievement or from achievement to intelligence—Piaget's theories being invoked for the latter. But it was inconceivable that either had a negative effect on the other; thus in Figure 7.12 $V \stackrel{-}{\to} S$ and $S \stackrel{-}{\to} V$ could be disregarded. Where this is not so, the cross-lag differences reflect on the preponderance of two composite effects. Had Rozelle and Campbell (1969) found a substantial synchronous correlation between grades and achievement (as would have been expected from a general conscientiousness factor), then the finding that $r_{A_1 G_2} > r_{G_1 A_2}$ would have had to be interpreted as merely showing that the composite effect of $A \stackrel{+}{\to} G$ and $G \stackrel{-}{\to} A$ was greater than the composite $G \stackrel{+}{\to} A$ and $A \stackrel{-}{\to} G$. Of these four only the last is inconceivable (and this perhaps inconceivable only to us educators). In such a case, a rather frustrating degree of equivocality would remain even if a striking cross-lag differential were found.

Conceding these sources of equivocality, it was nonetheless assumed that the relative magnitude of the cross-correlations was a dependable indicator of the relative strengths of $A_1 \stackrel{+}{\to} B_2$ and $B_1 \stackrel{+}{\to} A_2$ where (1) only $A \stackrel{+}{\to} B$ and $B \stackrel{+}{\to} A$ are plausible, (2) the synchronous correlations are constant thus showing stationarity, and (3) it is plausible to assume no synchronous cross-causation (to assume $A_1 \to B_1 = 0$, $B_1 \to A_1 = 0$, $A_2 \to B_2 = 0$, $B_2 \to A_2 = 0$). This was assumed to hold true even where A and B differed in their "stability," test-retest or autocorrelation (that is, even where $r_{A_1 A_2} \neq r_{B_1 B_2}$). However, Rogosa (1978) and Reichardt (personal communication), using path analysis models, have pointed to the existence of plausible path models meeting these three specifications where comparing the absolute magnitudes of the cross-lagged correlation coefficients $r_{A_1 B_2}$ and $r_{B_1 A_2}$ is misleading as to the causal paths between $A_1 \to B_2$ and $B_1 \to A_2$. Reichardt provides the illustration in Figure 7.13 which shows causal paths extended over several time periods in a context of stationarity. Note that variable A has higher "stability" ($A \to A$ causal path) than variable B and that there are no synchronous causal paths nor direct paths spanning more than one time period. Note, finally, that A and B have equal cross-variable causal paths to each other, so that there is no differential causal predominance.

Figure 7.14 translates the path coefficients of Figure 7.13 into correlational terms. Note, now, that the three past requirements for use of the cross-lagged panel correlation are met and that from the comparison of the cross-lagged correlation values, our past interpretation rules would give causal predominance to $B_1 \to A_2$ over $A_1 \to B_2$. However, in the path model from which the correlations were generated there was no causal predominance at all. The source of the dif-

INFERRING CAUSE FROM PASSIVE OBSERVATION

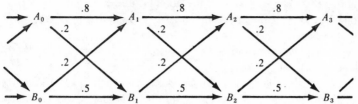

Figure 7.13. Path diagram for Reichardt's counter example for the cross-lagged panel correlation.

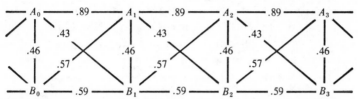

Figure 7.14. Correlation coefficients corresponding to the path diagram of Reichardt's example in Figure 7.13.

ference in results between the path analytic and correlational analysis can be found in certain of the indirect paths connecting A_1 and B_2, and B_1 and A_2, which go through the $A_1 \rightarrow A_2$ and $B_1 \rightarrow B_2$ routes. We can spell out some of these routes for the final cross-lagged correlation pair presented in the second figure. As Figure 7.13 shows, $r_{A_2B_3}$ and $r_{B_2A_3}$ get .20 units of correlation from the two direct paths. In addition, both correlations are augmented by both A_1 and B_1 as common causes. Let us arrange these in mirror symmetry to show more clearly how the inequality comes about:

$$r_{A_2B_3}, \text{ cause } A_1, \text{ route } A_2A_1B_2B_3 = .8 \times .2 \times .5 = .08$$
$$r_{B_2A_3}, \text{ cause } B_1, \text{ route } B_2B_1A_2A_3 = .5 \times .2 \times .8 = .08$$
$$r_{A_2B_3}, \text{ cause } B_1, \text{ route } A_2B_1B_2B_3 = .2 \times .5 \times .5 = .05$$
$$r_{B_2A_3}, \text{ cause } A_1, \text{ route } B_2A_1A_2A_3 = .2 \times .8 \times .8 = .128$$

Going back one more generation, both are augmented by A_0 and B_0 as common causes:

$$r_{A_2B_3}, \text{ cause } A_0, \text{ route } A_2A_1A_0B_1B_2B_3 = .8 \times .8 \times .2 \times .5 \times .5 = .032$$
$$r_{B_2A_3}, \text{ cause } B_0, \text{ route } B_2B_1B_0A_1A_2A_3 = .5 \times .5 \times .2 \times .8 \times .8 = .032$$
$$r_{A_2B_3}, \text{ cause } B_0, \text{ route } A_2A_1B_0B_1B_2B_3 = .8 \times .2 \times .5 \times .5 \times .5 = .02$$
$$R_{B_2A_3}, \text{ cause } A_0, \text{ route } B_2B_1A_0A_1A_2A_3 = .5 \times .2 \times .8 \times .8 \times .8 = .0512$$

Summing these five components for each:

$$r_{A_2B_3} = .20 + .08 + .050 + .032 + .0200 = .382$$
$$r_{B_2A_3} = .20 + .08 + .128 + .032 + .0512 = .4912$$

With each generation farther back, the augmenting contributions are smaller, and taper off at the asymptotic values of .43 and .57.

(Note that there is a substantial correlation of .46 between A_3 and B_3, and so on even though there is no direct causal path. To show how this is composed would be even more tedious. Factors A_3 and B_3 are linked by one route each to both A_2 and B_2, by two routes each to both A_1 and B_1, by four routes each to both A_0 and B_0, and so forth.)

For many models where there are *no* causal paths between A and B, the cross-lag comparisons will be undisturbed by differentials in test-retest or autocorrelation levels. But where cross-causation paths are added, the source of the autocorrelation differential operates so as to produce differential indirect components of cross-correlation. This outcome of our implicit model has been overlooked in previous presentations. Let us illustrate this again with an extremely simple autoregressive third-variable model, Figure 7.15, where all of the correlation between A and B (between A_1 and A_2 and so on) is due solely to the unobserved third variable z. In Figure 7.15, the higher autocorrelation for A than B (.58 versus .23) is a result of A being a purer representative of z than is B. However, this has no differential effect on the cross-lag values. Both $r_{A_2B_3}$ and $r_{B_2A_3}$ are due to the

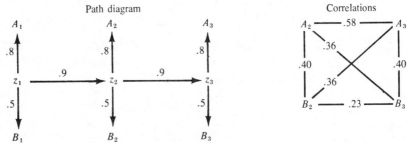

Figure 7.15. An autoregressive latent common factor model with no cross-variable causation.

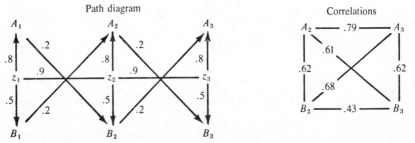

Figure 7.16. Equal cross-variable causal paths added to the autoregressive latent common factor model of Figure 7.15.

indirect path through $z_2 \rightarrow z_3$, and both use a path $z \rightarrow A_1 = .8$ and a path $z \rightarrow B_1 = .5$, although in different order.

In Figure 7.16, two small equal A-B causal paths are added to the model of Figure 7.15. While the correlations presented are the asymptotic ones from an indefinitely long set of prior stages in the stationary series, we can note the source of the differential in the indirect causal chains involving just one prior wave. Note first that both $r_{A_2B_3}$ and $r_{B_2A_3}$ get .2 of correlation from two direct diagonal paths. Note next that both share z_2 as a common cause and get equal contributions from it:

For $r_{A_2B_3}$, route $A_2z_2z_3B_3 = .8 \times .9 \times .5 = .36$
For $r_{A_2B_3}$, route $B_2z_2z_3A_3 = .5 \times .9 \times .8 = .36$

However, note that when one looks at the contribution from z_1, a differential appears:

For $r_{A_2B_3}$, route $A_2B_1z_1z_2z_3B_3 = .2 \times .5 \times .9 \times .9 \times .5 = .04$
For $r_{B_2A_3}$, route $B_2A_1z_1z_2z_3A_3 = .2 \times .8 \times .9 \times .9 \times .8 = .10$

For z_0 no differential appears, but for z_{-1} there is again a differential in this same direction, and so on back to infinity.

In unpublished and published studies, several dozen sets of data involving some hundred pairs of variables have been explored for cross-lagged correlation differentials. It is our overall experience that statistically significant differences and differences of interesting magnitude are very rare. The method has in this sense been conservative in contributing causal laws. Probably third-variable causation with no causal asymmetries between the measured variables, or a causal influence in only one direction has been the general case, and for this the method may be reasonably dependable. But for such cases as well as others, we now see no advantage in reporting the results in the descriptive language of correlation coefficients if a plausible path model can be applied and the conclusions stated in path coefficient terms. Remaining at the correlation coefficient level no longer seems a less presumptive route to causal inference.

Our general impression from experience with many data sets is that stationarity seems a reasonable assumption in a majority of cases where the estimates are computed on large numbers of cases. Being able to make such an assumption is of course as much of an advantage to a path analysis approach as to any other, for it enables one to fix parallel sets of path coefficients as equal, thus greatly reducing the number of parameters to be estimated. When the number of waves of measurement can be extended to three and more, a greater capacity to estimate complex and realistic path models is achieved.

With this increased awareness of the equivocality of the method, of the many plausible alternative latent causal models available and of the need to uncover and explicitly model all of the assumptions implicit in previous interpretative rules, let us look at some recent examples of the use of cross-lagged correlation patterns in causal inference. Under the former interpretational guidelines, all of the examples would qualify as exemplary for inferring cause. Given the recently identified ambiguities in the method we cannot be so sure. We therefore invite our readers to study the examples and determine if they can generate plausible competing models of cause.

Jessor and Jessor (1977) offer the example shown in Figure 7.17, depicting a study of the relationship between attitudes and marijuana usage. Using our previous interpretative rules, a redundant confirmation of a causal direction from attitudes to behavior is shown. Stationarity assumptions are probably not seriously violated. The autocorrelation (test-retest) values are approximately the same for each variable. Longer lags confirm the pattern shown for shorter lags. (Yet do we not also know that trying out marijuana increases the tolerance for that particular deviance, if not the tolerance for deviance in general?) Jessor and Jessor (1977, p. 243) use their cross-lagged panel analysis as only one of ten modes of data analysis and are commendably cautious about drawing causal conclusions:

> Taken together, the ten strategies have generated a high degree of convergence, and the logical structure they comprise is coherent. Consonance of results from the separate strategies—for example, the commonality between the variables that are associated cross-sectionally with problem behavior and those that predict its onset over time—makes for strong conviction about the

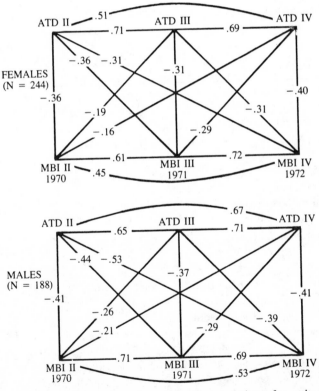

Figure 7.17. Cross-lagged panel correlations for attitudinal tolerance of deviance (ATD) and marijuana behavior involvement (MDI) for Years II, III, and IV, High School Study. (Jessor and Jessor, 1977, p. 242)

explanatory relevance of the variables. But it needs to be emphasized that none of the strategies, separately or together, does more than document an association, even where temporal order is known, and therefore *causal influence* has not been demonstrated.

Lave and Seskin (1977) present the example shown in Figure 7.18, relating air pollution and mortality rate for 81 metropolitian areas. Under the previous interpretative rules, this pattern would seem to confirm a causal influence from air pollution to mortality, showing up in spite of the long, nine-year lag. Again, this

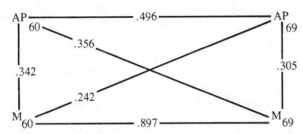

Figure 7.18. Cross-lagged cross-sectional analysis of air pollution (AP) and mortality (M) in 81 SMSAs. (From Lave and Seskin, 1977, p. 136)

is a minor part of their argument, supporting extensive traditional economic analyses of time series and cross-sectional data. (While the fact that the autocorrelation for *M* (.897) is much higher than that for *AP* (.496) could explain the differential in lags through a model such as Figures 7.13 and 7.16, we can probably rule out in advance any causal path from mortality to air pollution as long as bodies have been properly embalmed and buried, and cremation is rare.)

Humphreys and his associates (Atkin, Bray, Davison, Herzberger, Humphreys, and Selzer, 1977) have developed what can be called the cross-lagged multiple-correlation approach. Their approach can be explained by outlining an analysis they conducted using data from the Educational Testing Service's massive Growth Study, a longitudinal study measuring 16 cognitive variables at grades 5, 7, 9, and 11. The authors computed a multiple correlation between each individual variable at each testing and the composite of the 15 other variables on each of the waves. They used the composite of the latter as though it were a single variable, computing these lagged multiple correlations across all four waves of measurement, separately for males and females and for blacks and whites. In the two-variable, two-wave form, 24 CLPCs were generated for each single variable versus the composite of others. The largest and most consistent pattern of cross-lag differences emerging from this analysis suggested the causal priority of listening over other tests (listening was constructed like a reading test except that a sample of prose was presented aurally rather than in writing). Figure 7.19 shows the results for listening for the longest time lag, spanning grades 5 to 11.

It should be noted, first, that a high degree of stationarity holds and, second, that the differences in cross-lagged correlations are consistent across groups of

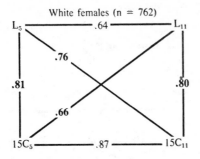

White females (n ≐ 762)

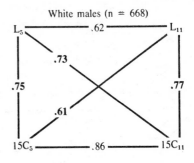

White males (n ≐ 668)

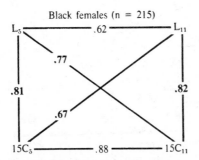

Black females (n = 215)

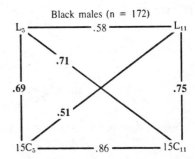

Black males (n = 172)

Figure 7.19. Cross-lagged multiple correlations between Listening (L) and 15 other cognitive measures (15C) at grades 5 and 11 (Atkin, Bray, Davison, Herzberger, Humphreys, and Selzer, 1977). Boldface values are multiple correlations.

children. The results are consistent across the shorter time periods for each of the four subsamples.

This causal pattern was discovered by a blind search process using up lots of degrees of freedom rather than by a priori theory. Nonetheless, the strength and consistency of findings are much too great to be explained away by chance, and the authors have provided a theoretical rationale for expecting a gain in aural skills to cause a gain in other cognitive skills. It should be noted that earlier explorations of the same data using simple cross-lagged panel correlations with individual variables showed similar trends; however, they were too inconsistent to support the strong conclusions encouraged by this multiple-correlational analysis. It is not likely that a model along the lines of Figure 7.13 or 7.16 can explain the results in terms of the weakness in stability of the listening variable (test-retest correlation or autocorrelation). At the single-variable level, listening is well above the average of the 16 variables, being among the top five. While its stability is clearly less than that of the composite (as shown in Figure 7.19), any explanation along that line would also have to explain why the other single variables do not appear causally to dominate their composites, especially the weakest variables. (Atkin et

al., 1977, present a detailed comparison analysis for one of the weakest tests, Recreation.)[1]

THE CAUSAL ANALYSIS OF CONCOMITANCIES IN TIME SERIES

This section is concerned with statistical methods for making causal inferences about two variables measured as time series, where the interest is in testing whether changes in one variable cause later changes in the other rather than in testing whether a discrete intervention has any causal impact. For example, the section deals with problems such as "Do changes in the national unemployment rate cause changes in the rate of suicides?" The discussion assumes a familiarity with chapter 6 of this volume and the preceding part of this chapter.

The goals of this section are modest. The first is to provide an overview of alternative approaches to the statistical analysis of concomitancies in time series, describing each approach and illustrating some of its major problems. The second goal is to outline several of the major strengths and limitations inherent in the causal analysis of all noninterrupted time series. The reader should be forewarned that we only provide an introduction to the topic here and that other sources are more comprehensive. Moreover, while we can point to serious flaws in certain approaches and can suggest that some approaches are superior to others, we cannot as yet identify a single approach as *the* method of analysis. Given current interest in time series and the current investment in more and more economic and social indicators, as well as subjective social indicators, we can confidently predict that work on the causal analysis of time-series data will expand considerably in the coming years and that methodological advances will be plentiful. Despite the low level of current knowledge, the analysis of concomitancies in time series has great potential; even today tentative conclusions about cause are sometimes possible.

Eight approaches to the causal analysis of concomitancies in time series will be briefly described, beginning with the simplest and moving to the more complex. Except as noted, the approaches discussed first share the difficulties that will be outlined in later discussions of different approaches. Thus, if we deal with few problems in analyzing the first method, this does not mean that only these shortcomings are associated with the method. On the contrary, the first method shares nearly all of the flaws outlined later for other modes of analysis.

Ordinary Least Squares (OLS) Regression
When Trend or Seasonality Is Present

The simplest approach to the statistical analysis of concomitancies in time series is the correlation of two untransformed series. The correlation between two series, X and Y, is estimated as

$$r_{xy} = \frac{(X_t - \overline{X})(Y_t - \overline{Y})}{\sqrt{(X_t - \overline{X})^2 (Y_t - \overline{Y})^2}} \quad ,$$

---

[1]Humphreys and Parsons (1979) have provided a simple model for these data implemented by successive orthogonal diagonal factor extraction. It is to be hoped that a more direct fitting of the correlation matrix by an autoregressive model can be applied to the problem (Jöreskog, 1969, 1970; Werts, Linn, and Jöreskog, 1977).

which can be recognized as the common correlation coefficient. The correlation between two series is sometimes referred to as the cross-correlation, to distinguish it from the autocorrelation function, which indicates the degree of temporal dependence in a *single* series.

An equivalent method of relating two series is to conduct a bivariate (i.e., two variable) regression analysis. Series Y is regressed on series X, where X is the presumed cause of Y. That is, the value X_t (i.e., X at time t) is used to predict Y_t and the regression parameters are computed as in any OLS regression. The simple cross-correlation and the bivariate OLS regression give identical results concerning the strength of the covariation between two series. In the following discussion, these related procedures are discussed interchangeably.

A simple OLS regression of two time series is frequently rendered uninterpretable by the presence of secular trend or seasonality in the data. (See chapter 6 for the definition of secular trend and seasonality.) As an example, consider the rela-

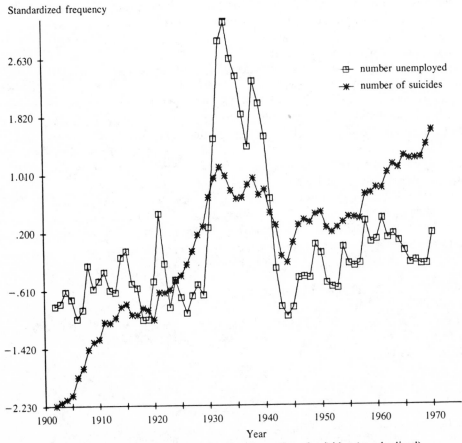

Figure 7.20. Number of unemployed and number of suicides (standardized).

tionship between unemployment and suicides in the United States, illustrated in Figure 7.20. The simple correlation between these two series is .53. This large and statistically significant correlation might be taken to support the hypothesis that increased unemployment leads to increased suicides. Though much of this correlation appears to be attributable to the increase in both series during the Great Depression of the 1930s, some of the correlation may be attributable to a general upward trend in the number of unemployed and the number of suicides. This is due to a general increase in the U.S. population over time, and many causally unrelated, untransformed aggregate social variables will be positively correlated because of this historic increase. (A convincing demonstration is to show that the negative correlation between the number of people unemployed and the number of people employed is far from unity. This occurs because, as the population increases over time, so does the *number* of people in each of these categories, which attenuates the negative relationship.)

It is obvious that the trends in Figure 7.20 should be removed from the variables prior to causal analysis. However, it is worth noting that population growth is not the only potential cause of trend. For instance, many indicators of economic expenditures would show trend even after population growth was controlled for, largely because of inflation. Thus, the variable would have to be expressed as "per capita expenditures in constant dollars." In other cases, the rationale for detrending may be less clear. If unemployment and suicides were expressed as rates per 1,000 population and still exhibited the trend in Figure 7.20, would it be necessary to detrend? More generally, is detrending always necessary whenever trend occurs? The answer to this question is almost always yes, whatever the cause or probable cause of the trend is presumed to be.

Let us consider why trends should be removed prior to causal analysis. First, for virtually any case of trend, plausible historical explanations of the trend exist other than that it is the result of the causal relationship between X and Y. So long as such explanations can be imagined, the obtained relationship between trended series may be spurious. Second, removal of trend is necessary to meet the assumption of stationarity (see chapter 6) which underlies the most sophisticated methods of time-series analysis. Finally, the removal of trend is necessary to meet rigorous standards for the assessment of covariation.

One such standard is conceptually related to the criterion described in chapter 6 for the assessment of an intervention effect. In that chapter, McCain and McCleary point out that the statistical test of an intervention effect determines whether the intervention component adds significantly in predicting the behavior of a time series over and above the predictability offered by the ARIMA model of the series. A similar criterion can be proposed for the assessment of covariation between two series: tests of covariation should be based on whether series X adds significantly in predicting the behavior of series Y over and above the predictability arising from Y's own orderly behavior, i.e., from its deterministic and stochastic components. This criterion, which has been formalized by Granger (1969), can be supported using the logic of plausible rival hypotheses: As a general rule, it is equally or more plausible—and certainly more parsimonious—that present values of Y are due to regularity in the behavior of Y over time than that they are due to the effects of some other variable X.

In pointing out the common inferential flaws which usually render simple OLS regression inappropriate for the analysis of concomitancies in time series, we have focused on the problem of secular trend. Seasonality, which is almost always present in daily, monthly or quarterly data, poses a similar problem. Seasonality should be removed prior to causal analysis for the same reasons that secular trend should be removed.

We will not describe the inferential problems associated with trend and seasonality further, though they can also arise in the context of GLS regression (described below). However, it should be remembered that trend and seasonality are not the only flaws in the simple OLS regression approach, which shares most of the problems described later in this section.

OLS Regression When Trend and Seasonality Are Absent or Removed

Early social science time-series analysts (e.g., Hooker, 1901; Yule, 1906) recognized the inferential ambiguity introduced by the presence of trend and seasonality. Their preferred approach was to correlate series from which these components have been removed. Ogburn and Thomas (1922) provide a relevant historical example. They examined the relationship between a composite economic index and an estimate of the suicide rate for 100 U.S. cities for the period 1900–1920. They fit trend lines independently to both series and computed correlations between deviations from these estimated trends. The synchronous correlation they obtained was $-.74$. Figure 7.21 presents an updated example. Unemployment and suicides are presented as rates, which removes most of the secular trend in Figure 7.20. The synchronous cross-correlation is .59. (Note that Ogburn and Thomas's composite index consisted of so-called procyclical indicators such as employment while Figure 7.21 includes the countercyclical indicator, *un*employment. This difference in economic indicators accounts for the opposite signs of the two correlations just presented.)

A critical issue for this approach concerns the method by which trend and seasonality are removed. Early analysts usually computed deviations from OLS regression lines. That is, they regressed a series on time, or some function of time, and used the residuals from this regression in correlations—or OLS regressions—with other series. Alternative techniques for removing trend include differencing, the use of rates or similar transformations (e.g., the use of constant dollars), and the use of logarithmic or other power transformations.

At least three major problems exist in computing an OLS regression between two series after trend and seasonality are removed. First, the techniques used to remove trend and seasonality may underadjust. When OLS regression lines are fit to remove trend, a best—not a perfect—fit is achieved. Rates, which are sometimes used to remove trend, are based on imperfect measures of population. (Additionally, the error in most population measures contain systematic error. Population is estimated better during census years, and estimates are worst midway between censuses.) In short, no adjustment will perfectly represent the underlying cause of the trend or the seasonality. When certain adjustment procedures are used, this may result in underadjustment. As a result, some part of the trend or

the seasonality may remain in the series and spuriously affect the correlation. To guard against this, one should always test the adequacy of the adjustment procedures, as when one tests for seasonality in deseasonalized data. It is especially advisable to cross-check using methods other than those originally employed to test for seasonality and trend. For example, Nerlove (1964) used spectral analysis (described below) to test the adequacy of Bureau of Labor Statistics seasonal adjustment techniques, which were based on other analytic procedures. Such a cross-checking strategy does not test equally well for the possibility that some adjustment procedures, because they are "best fit" techniques, may overadjust and remove from a series variability which is not truly attributable to trend or seasonality. Overadjustment of this sort is sometimes referred to as "throwing out the baby with the bath water."

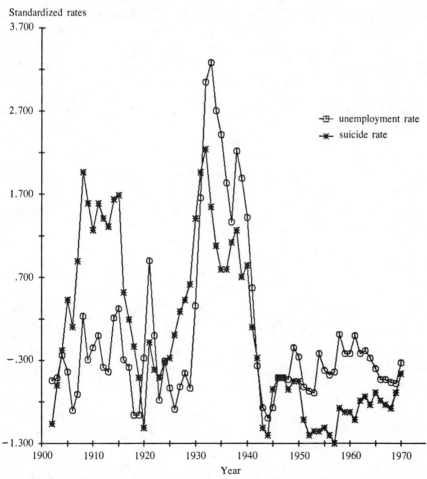

Figure 7.21. Unemployment rate and suicide rate (standardized).

A second problem with OLS approaches is that they are usually used to test only for a synchronous relationship. That is, X_t is used to predict Y_t. The relationship of X and Y over various leads and lags is not examined, even though a correlation between X at one time and Y at a later time is a stronger indication of causality than a simple synchronous correlation. Without information about the temporal ordering of X and Y, causal inference is not generally warranted. This flaw is ironic, because the study of time-series data is particularly suited to the probing of temporal precedence. However, as we shall see, the use of data from which only trend and seasonality have been removed is not appropriate for this task.

A third problem with OLS approaches is associated with autocorrelated errors. In chapter 6, McCain and McCleary discussed the problem of autocorrelated errors in the context of *interrupted* time series. Autocorrelated error can also be a problem in the analysis of noninterrupted time series. When X_t is used to predict Y_t in a regression equation, Y_t is not completely predicted. The difference between the real value and the predicted value is the error term, ϵ_t. These errors can be autocorrelated: that is, ϵ_t can be correlated with ϵ_{t+1}, ϵ_{t+2}, and so on. As McCain and McCleary point out, OLS estimates of regression coefficients are not biased in the presence of autocorrelated error. However, they are not efficient or asymptotically efficient (see Kmenta, 1971, section 8.2), and estimates of their standard error are biased. In the usual case of positive autocorrelation, the standard error is spuriously underestimated, resulting in an inflated t-statistic for regression coefficients and in an inflated r and R^2 (Hibbs, 1974). Autocorrelated error thus often leads to spurious cross-correlations.

These three shortcomings are sufficiently serious to render the OLS approach, after trend and seasonality have been removed, inadequate for the causal analysis of most time series. Further, if the approach is extended in obvious ways to overcome some of the three shortcomings, other serious problems can arise.

Generalized Least Squares (GLS) Regression

Ordinary least squares regression assumes that errors are not autocorrelated. This assumption (and the OLS regression assumption of homoskedasticity) is not required for the Generalized Least Squares (GLS) regression model, which is called "generalized" because it includes other models, including OLS, as special cases. Technically, GLS requires prior knowledge of the autocorrelated error structure, which is of course not available in practice. Instead, most so-called GLS techniques (e.g., Durbin, 1960; Cochrane and Orcutt, 1949) *estimate* the autocorrelated error structure, and so are called pseudo-GLS by Hibbs (1974). Essentially, these methods estimate the degree of autocorrelation structure from the OLS residuals and use this estimate to transform the data so that the errors are independent. For a more detailed description of these techniques, the reader can consult any standard econometrics text, such as Kmenta (1971, section 8.2) or Johnston (1972). GLS regression approaches are usually, but not always, conducted using detrended and deseasonalized data, thereby avoiding the difficulties inherent in working with data that has trends and seasonal variation.

Though GLS regression avoids some problems, it is subject to other serious criticisms. First, these methods often make assumptions about the nature of the

error structure. In practice, it is frequently assumed that the autocorrelation in the errors is described by a first-order autoregressive model. This assumption will not always be valid, and the transformations made may not adequately control for the autocorrelated error if it is of a different type. Second, in the GLS approach the direction of cause is assumed a priori. As a result, no evidence is generated as to the temporal ordering of variables. Third, while an adjustment is made for auto-correlated error, autocorrelation can remain in each of X and Y. Recall that auto-correlated error refers to the autocorrelation in ϵ_t, which are the residuals from an OLS regression. Autocorrelated error is not simply equivalent to the autocorrelation in X and Y. In fact, it is possible for the OLS regression of two highly autocorrelated series to result in white noise residuals.

The GLS regression approaches adjust for autocorrelated error so that significance tests of the regression parameters are not biased, but X and Y can still each be autocorrelated. We have previously suggested that one might consider X a possible cause of Y only if X adds significantly in predicting Y over and above the predictability arising from Y's own orderly behavior. Because the autocorrelation of Y is part of Y's orderly behavior, it should not be available for prediction by X. Further, as we shall see shortly, autocorrelation in X and Y can obscure whether changes in Y follow changes in X, or vice versa.

Distributed Lag Models

In a distributed lag model, the independent variable is included in the equation predicting Y not only synchronously but also in lagged form. That is, Y_t is predicted using X_t, X_{t-1}, X_{t-2}, . . . X_{t-d}. This finite series of X values is often constrained to conform to some form, such as a first- or second-order polynomial. Distributed lag regression models are often but not always estimated with a GLS procedure to remove autocorrelated error.

It might seem that distributed lag models would provide useful information about the temporal ordering of variables. However, in practice useful information is almost never obtained because the regression is conducted with one variable specified, a priori, as the causal agent. Y is regressed on X but X is not regressed on Y, so we learn very little about the relative ordering of X and Y. Other problems associated with GLS or OLS approaches also hold, e.g., autocorrelated error can spuriously inflate significance estimates and is usually assumed to follow a first-order autoregressive model, and so on. In addition, even if a distributed lag regression were conducted regressing Y on X and X on Y, the functional form to which a distributed lag regression is usually constrained (e.g., polynomial lag, geometric lag, Pascal lag) would obscure the precise relationship of X and Y at each lag and would spuriously favor the most reliable indicator as the overall cause of the other.

The Simple Cross-Correlation Function

A criticism common to the preceding methods is that the temporal precedence of variables is not established. The cross-correlation function is a relatively simple attempt to remedy this. In 1901, Hooker suggested that causal analysis of time series be based on an inspection of the cross-correlation coefficients for X leading Y and for Y leading X over several lags. That is, the correlation of X_t with Y_{t+1},

Y_{t+2}, Y_{t+3}, and so on and the correlation of Y_t with X_{t+1}, X_{t+2}, X_{t+3}, and so on are examined in addition to the synchronous correlation. (The correlation of X_t with Y_{t+1} is the correlation of X in one time period, say a year, with the next year's Y.) Hooker reasoned that if X causes Y, correlations should be larger when X leads Y than when it lags behind Y. This asymmetry occurs because, when X causes Y, changes in X should be manifest in later values of Y. The reverse should not be true if cause is unidirectional. Hooker's approach has been neglected as a method of causal analysis until recent attention by Campbell (1976; Lee, 1977), who supported the method with a logic similar to that previously underlying the cross-lagged panel correlation.

Number of years the unemployment rate leads the suicide rate	Cross-correlation	Number of years the suicide rate leads the unemployment rate	Cross-correlation
0	.590	0	.590
1	.461	1	.591
2	.315	2	.554
3	.210	3	.508
4	.146	4	.416
5	.074	5	.341
6	.033	6	.306
7	−.012	7	.246
8	−.095	8	.142
9	−.152	9	.050
10	−.182	10	−.058

Table 7.3. Cross-correlations between unemployment rate and suicide rate.

The cross-correlations between the unemployment rate and the suicide rate are given in Table 7.3. The left side of the table gives the cross-correlations when the unemployment rate leads the suicide rate. The right side of the table gives the cross-correlations for the suicide rate leading unemployment. (The synchronous cross-correlation is given on both sides.) As an example, the cross-correlation when suicides lead two years is .554. The data in Table 7.3 could alternatively be presented in graphic form, similar to the autocorrelogram, and we would call this graphical representation the cross-correlogram. By convention, the cross-correlation at lag K is represented as $r_{xy}(K)$, where K is the number of observations by which X leads Y. Note that a negative K would indicate that Y is leading X.

A critical feature of the cross-correlation function is that, in contrast to the autocorrelation function, it need not be symmetrical. A series correlated with itself is symmetrical, which is why the autocorrelograms in chapter 6, which dealt with the analysis of a single series, presented autocorrelations only for positive lags. (Consider: When two identical series are cross-correlated, which is essentially what occurs when the autocorrelation function is estimated, it does not matter if X leads Y or Y leads X; the two are the same.) However, when two different series are cross-correlated, the value of the cross-correlation is likely to differ depending on which series is leading. For instance, the cross-correlation is .46 when the

unemployment rate leads the suicide rate by one year, while the correlation increases to .59 when the suicide rate leads one year. It is the asymmetry in the cross-correlation function which suggests that cross-correlations are uniquely useful, for causal inference is more appropriate when changes in one variable precede changes in the other. Such a temporal order, one might expect, would lead to an asymmetrical cross-correlation function which peaks toward one side of the synchronous—the side where the causal series leads the outcome series.

The dependence of causal inference on the *asymmetry* of the cross-correlation function suggests that certain of the problems described above may not be important for cross-correlogram analysis. One might expect that the effects of trend and autocorrelated error—and perhaps of any shared third-variable cause—would be constant across the autocorrelation function. While these forces would lead to spurious correlation, there might appear to be little reason to suppose that they would affect the correlation more at one lag than at another. Therefore, one might assume that the relative difference between correlations for X leading Y and correlations for Y leading X would not be affected. That is, no asymmetry in the cross-correlation function would be expected as a result of these forces. Thus, no incorrect causal inference should occur. (Note, however, that asymmetry would be expected if different seasonal patterns are present in the two series.)

The similarity to the cross-lagged panel correlation should be apparent here, with the same predisposition to see synchronous correlations as the result of third variables rather than cause and the same predisposition to test for causal significance with asymmetrical differences rather than single values. Moreover, the possibility of correlation due to trend or other shared third variables means that the expected value of the cross-correlation is unknown, just as the expected value of the cross-lagged correlations is unknown. Consequently, in neither case does a no-cause baseline exist against which to compare the obtained correlations, be they cross-lagged panel correlations or cross-correlations of time series.

The similarity between cross-lagged panel correlations and cross-correlations suggests that autocorrelation will pose a major problem for the cross-correlogram as it does for the cross-lagged correlation. Indeed, the very same problem holds as that described in the previous section for the cross-lagged panel correlation, as is made immediately clear by extending back the number of observations in Figures 7.13 and 7.14. Autocorrelation can obscure the underlying causal relationship between two series to the point of suggesting the wrong direction of causality!

In Table 7.3, for example, the asymmetry in the cross-correlation function would strongly suggest that changes in the suicide rate precede changes in the unemployment rate. This is because the highest level of cross-correlation occurs when suicides lead by one year, and the coefficients for a one-year lag are strikingly larger when suicide leads unemployment than vice versa. In fact, all the coefficients are higher when suicide leads—e.g., when the suicide rate leads by three years, the cross-correlation remains above .50, while when the unemployment rate leads by three years, the cross-correlation declines to .21.

The positive relationship between the unemployment rate and the suicide rate is consistent with the OLS regression results and with our intuition, but the asymmetry in the cross-correlations runs contrary to expectations. These expectations are based on the claims of past researchers that unemployment (or whatever

aspects of the economy it stands for) causally affects the suicide rate, and on the commonsense observation that the number of suicides is so small relative to the total work force that suicides could not plausibly affect the unemployment rate. Additionally, were the direction of cause to be from suicides to unemployment, we would expect the relationship to be negative: A large number of suicides should lead to *lower* unemployment, because the number of people in the labor force would be reduced. The anomolous pattern of cross-correlations between unemployment rates and suicide may be attributable to the pattern of autocorrelation in each time series. It is important, therefore, to consider an approach which attempts to control for artifacts related to the nature of the autocorrelation within each series.

Prewhitening by the Presumed Cause

Perhaps an obvious means to alleviate problems due to autocorrelation would be to adjust each series for its pattern of autocorrelation prior to cross-correlation. This would involve *prewhitening* the series. Though the term prewhitening sometimes has slightly different meanings in the literature, we use it here to refer to the process of identifying the ARIMA model of a series and then transforming the series into a white noise process. Prewhitened series could be cross-correlated, with causal inference based on asymmetry in the cross-correlation function.

Two major approaches have been proposed which use the cross-correlation of prewhitened series, one by Box and Jenkins (1976), the other by Haugh and Box (1977). Other closely related approaches, such as that of Sims (1972), are described by Pierce and Haugh (1977). Box and Jenkins (1976) were interested in using the cross-correlations between two series to identify a dynamic regression or transfer function model of the relationship. Because their work was focused on engineering contexts, Box and Jenkins were able to identify a priori one series as the cause of the other. To increase mathematical efficiency, they suggested that the causal series should be prewhitened and that the other series should be transformed according to the ARIMA model identified for the causal series. Note that by this method the outcome series will not be transformed to white noise unless it is adequately fit by the ARIMA model of the presumed causal series.

Vigderhaus (1977) followed the Box-Jenkins approach and constructed a transfer function model of the relationship between the unemployment rate and the suicide rate of white males. He first prewhitened the presumed causal series, unemployment, and applied the same transformation to white male suicides. Vigderhaus's cross-correlations are reported in Table 7.4. Vigderhaus chose to make his causal inference depend on the synchronous correlation; thus he concluded that unemployment influences the rate of suicides. However, it can be seen that, when cognizance is taken of temporal precedence, the asymmetry in cross-correlations suggests that suicides cause unemployment!

The pattern of asymmetry in Vigderhaus's cross-correlations can perhaps be attributed to two shortcomings in the Box-Jenkins approach. First, it requires that one series be specified as the cause and the other series as the effect. This simply cannot be done in much social science research using time-series data where part of the aim is to probe which changes in which series cause changes in the other series. Second, the application of the same transformation to both series means

Number of years the unemployment rate leads the suicide rate	Cross-correlation	Number of years the suicide rate leads the unemployment rate	Cross-correlation
0	.613	0	.613
1	.013	1	.399
2	.072	2	.184
3	.190	3	.186
4	.094	4	.211
5	.155	5	−.126
6	.135	6	.075
7	.174	7	.079
8	.071	8	.216
9	.069	9	.002
10	.129	10	.011

Table 7.4. Cross-correlations between unemployment rate and white male suicide rate using Box-Jenkins prewhitening strategy. (From Vigderhaus, 1977)

that the presumed outcome series in all likelihood will still be autocorrelated, and that the autocorrelation which remains can obscure the underlying parameters. (Vigderhaus's results may also be partly due to his misspecification of the ARIMA model for unemployment. The parameters of the ARIMA [2,0,0] model he fit to the data exceeded the bounds of stationarity.)

That the presumed outcome series remains autocorrelated will not be problematic if causation is in fact unidirectional from the presumed cause. When the underlying causal system involves feedback, misleading conclusions can occur of the sort described in the previous section on cross-lagged panel correlations. One could perform two analyses, first treating one variable as the causal variable and then treating the other variable as the causal variable, but the following strategy will often be preferable.

The Independent Prewhitening of Both Series

An alternative to the Box-Jenkins prewhitening strategy has been suggested by Haugh and Box (1977). Working in the context of transfer function model building, they proposed that each series be prewhitened independently. That is, the ARIMA model which best describes a single series is used to transform that particular series to white noise, and there is no requirement that the same model be used for both series. The two prewhitened series are then cross-correlated.

The Haugh-Box approach is preferable to that of Box-Jenkins for several reasons. First, it is not necessary to specify, a priori, which is the causal series. Second, it is easier to detect feedback effects, in which X_t affects later values of Y, and Y_t also affects later values of X. Third, the ambiguity about temporal ordering that autocorrelation creates is often reduced, though it will not be completely removed. (After all, the autocorrelation parameters are imperfectly estimated with "best fit" procedures. As a result, the causal parameters may be underestimated under some conditions.) Nonetheless, prewhitening each series before computing cross-correlations satisfies the criterion that covariation should be inferred only when X adds to the predictability of Y over and above the predictability arising

from the orderly behavior of Y. The final advantage of the Haugh-Box approach is that a simple significance test exists. Haugh (1972, 1976) has shown that, under the null hypothesis of no relationship, the cross-correlations between prewhitened series are normally and independently distributed with zero mean and standard deviation $1/\sqrt{N}$. The significance of a cross-correlation between prewhitened series can be judged against this standard error.

The combined advantages of the cross-correlation of prewhitened series make it one of the stronger statistical approaches for causal inferences. Unfortunately, it is not a perfect method, and several of its drawbacks are serious. Among the most serious are those which would appear to be inherent in all currently available methods of analyzing noninterrupted time series. We shall discuss these shortly. However, a unique drawback is that the method relies on ARIMA modeling. As McCain and McCleary point out, in ARIMA modeling several decision points are involved where the analyst's judgments reek of "art." This problem, while real, should not be exaggerated. Our own experience is that, with adequate training, an acceptable degree of reliability across analysts can be obtained. Even higher agreement should occur when the iterative model-building procedure described in chapter 6 is followed. Further, decision rules can be formalized to provide an automatic evaluation of alternative models, as Ozaki (1977) has recently done. Finally, it is our experience that the different judgments that ARIMA modelers are most likely to make (in terms of model specification) may result in similar white noise series, because the alternative models will usually be mathematically similar. Nonetheless, the criticism is a serious one and is given weight when ARIMA model misspecifications are uncovered in published work.

A second problem with the Haugh-Box approach is that the causal relationship between variables will sometimes be underestimated. When prewhitened series are cross-correlated, true values of X and Y are not related to each other. Instead, *estimated disturbances* or *innovations* in X (i.e., the assumed random shock) are correlated with the estimated disturbances or innovations in Y. Claims have been made that the cross-correlation of these innovations preserve the causal relationships underlying X and Y (e.g., Pierce, 1977). However, further analytic study and simulations appear necessary to determine the conditions under which this is true. The disturbances are not directly known and must be estimated from the data. This estimation is of course imperfect and it appears that for some underlying models (as when Y is autocorrelated only because it is generated by autocorrelated X), the Haugh-Box approach will underestimate true causal parameters. Also of interest is the possibility that imperfectly estimated innovations, under some conditions, will be sufficiently autocorrelated to create spurious cross-correlations. Again, further study is necessary.

A third shortcoming of the approach is the absence of a statistic which can provide an adequate test of the overall relationship of X and Y, rather than the relationship of X and Y at a single lag. Pierce (1977) has suggested a statistic which is conceptually and computationally similar to the Q-statistic of ARIMA modeling. However, he admits that the problem deserves further study.

Table 7.5 presents the cross-correlation between the prewhitened unemployment rate and the prewhitened suicide rate, based on the same data presented earlier. Though the synchronous correlation is .50, suicides do not appear to lead

Number of years the unemployment rate leads the suicide rate	Cross-correlation	Number of years the suicide rate leads the unemployment rate	Cross-correlation
0	.500	0	.500
1	−.070	1	−.019
2	−.255	2	.001
3	−.234	3	.276
4	.052	4	−.100
5	−.205	5	−.151
6	−.009	6	.272
7	.175	7	.202
8	−.202	8	−.051
9	−.150	9	.207
10	.054	10	.066

Table 7.5. Cross-correlations between prewhitened unemployment rate and prewhitened suicide rate.

unemployment when autocorrelation is adequately controlled for. Thus, the anomalous finding of earlier analyses is not obtained. However, since unemployment does not appear to cause suicides, the presumption may be that prewhitening decreases the sensitivity for detecting any lagged effect.

Several cross-correlations in Table 7.5 other than the synchronous are significant. One of the reasons for this appears to be the isolated spikes of autocorrelation in the prewhitened series. Even in a white noise series, significant autocorrelation is expected to occur at isolated lags by chance alone, and this can contribute to significant cross-correlations. Isolated cross-correlations due to residual autocorrelation are of course less likely the better a series is fit by its ARIMA model. One might be able to decide whether the cross-correlation of two series at a given lead or lag is spurious: (1) by testing whether the errors, ϵ_t, from the regression at that lag are autocorrelated; (2) by examining the scatterplot of the cross-correlation residuals for outliers; and (3) by examining the autocorrelation functions of the prewhitened series to see how much autocorrelation remains. However, a more systematic solution would be preferable. Spectral analysis, the final method to be considered, may offer that solution.

Spectral Analysis Methods

A relatively abstruse class of approaches to time-series analysis is classified under the category "spectral analysis." The autocorrelation and cross-correlation functions examine the process underlying a time series in the *time domain*. That is, the process is described by the temporal relationships of observations X_t with X_{t+1}, X_{t+2}, and so on (in the univariate case). Spectral analysis, on the other hand, focuses on the *frequency domain* representation of a series. That is, a time-series process is described in terms of sine and cosine waves of different frequencies.

It is beyond the scope of this presentation to describe spectral methods in detail. Rather, some of the more important concepts will be described, often in terms of their relationship to more familiar concepts discussed in this book. For a broader introduction to spectral analysis, the reader is referred to Mayer and

Arney (1974). More mathematically sophisticated presentations are given by Granger and Hatanaka (1964), Jenkins and Watts (1968), and Granger (1969).

Spectral methods are based on the application of Fourier analysis to the behavior of time series. Fourier analysis is a technique for decomposing a series into its frequency components. That is, a time series is decomposed by Fourier transformation into a set of frequency bands. Interestingly, the most important aspects of spectral analysis arise, not from the direct Fourier analysis of time series, but from the Fourier analysis of the autocovariance and cross-covariance functions. (These are the numerators of the autocorrelation and cross-correlation functions, respectively.)

Let us introduce some basic concepts from spectral analysis. The *power spectrum* $\Gamma xx(f)$ of a series X is the Fourier transform of the autocovariance function. Briefly, the power spectrum measures the relative importance of different frequency bands in terms of their contribution to the overall variance of the series. The *cross-spectrum* $\Gamma xy(f)$ is the Fourier transform of the cross-covariance function of the two series X and Y. It measures the relative importance of different frequency bands and their contribution to the overall covariation of the two series.

When the power spectrum is estimated from the autocovariance function of an empirical series, the result is likely to have a large variance and to be erratic in appearance. For this reason, smoothing procedures are often used in spectral analysis. The primary smoothing techniques are functions called *spectral windows*. Spectral windows essentially provide for a weighted averaging over some given number of frequencies. In other words, spectral windows determine the width of the frequency bands examined and the relative weighting assigned to each frequency within the band.

One primary method of expressing the relationship between two series in spectral terms is analogous to the cross-correlation function obtained when two series are prewhitened according to the ARIMA model of the presumed causal series. First, the power spectrum and the cross-spectrum are estimated, with spectral windows probably being applied for smoothing. The value $V(f)$ is computed:

$$V(f) = \frac{\Gamma xy(f)}{\Gamma xx(f)}$$

This is the proportion of the smoothed estimated cross-spectrum to the smoothed estimated power spectrum of X. The series X is here presumed to be the cause of Y, although, as with Box-Jenkins–type cross-correlations, it is possible to perform two analyses, treating each series as the cause in turn.

The value $V(f)$ gives the strength of the relationship from X to Y at each frequency f. A more interesting function can be derived by taking the inverse Fourier transform of $V(f)$. This gives us the impulse response function, which is the equivalent of (unstandardized) regression weights for the regression of Y on X (i.e., for the synchronous lag and for lags with X leading).

This method is conceptually similar to the Box-Jenkins cross-correlation approach. Dividing the cross-spectrum by the power spectrum of X is like applying the prewhitening model of X to both series prior to cross-correlating. The impulse response weights generated with the method should be proportional to the

Box-Jenkins cross-correlations (1976, Appendix A 11.1). Impulse response weights can also be computed using Box-Jenkins methods. These would be equal to the weights derived with spectral methods were it not for the effects of (1) smoothing the power spectrum and cross-spectrum; (2) the slightly greater mathematical efficiency of spectral methods; and (3) possible ARIMA model misspecification in the Box-Jenkins approach. These three provide the major advantages of spectral methods over the methods described in the previous subsection.

Through these three effects, spectral methods overcome two of the more serious criticisms specific to cross-correlations with prewhitened series. Because of the computational approach taken in spectral analysis, it is not necessary to identify an ARIMA model of the series and to transform the data on the basis of that model. Thus, the "art" of ARIMA modeling is not a required step. In addition, the smoothing techniques of spectral analysis can be used to reduce the occurrence of spurious cross-correlations due to deviant spikes in the autocorrelation function of the prewhitened series. Nonetheless, we must be aware of the possibility that excessive smoothing may obscure the actual lead-lag structure.

As the spectral method under discussion is the Fourier equivalent to Box-Jenkins cross-correlation approach, we expect it to share whatever shortcomings of that method are not resolved by the computational niceties of spectral analysis. In particular, Box-Jenkins and related approaches have difficulty when feedback occurs, because the autocorrelation remaining in the presumed outcome series can obscure the real causal parameter. Feedback systems similarly can create inferential ambiguity when common spectral methods are applied. Conducting separate analyses, treating each series as the cause in turn, will often indicate that a two-variable system involves feedback, but at present no completely satisfactory solution is available. Our impression is that ongoing study will lead to more satisfactory means of identifying and estimating causal systems when feedback is possible, involving both spectral and nonspectral techniques.

Our description of spectral methods has been brief and will only give the reader a flavor of the richness and the complexity of spectral analysis. It is also meant to convey the notion that developments in the area of spectral analysis are likely to lead to analytical methods superior to those currently available.

Some Generic Problems

Eight approaches to the statistical analysis of concomitancies in time series have been discussed. Most of them are associated with shortcomings, such as trend, seasonality, autocorrelated error, and autocorrelation, which make causal analysis inappropriate. The cross-correlation of prewhitened series was seen to overcome most problems under at least some conditions and further meets the criterion that X should be considered a possible cause of Y only if it adds to the predictability of Y over and above the predictability arising from Y's own orderly behavior. Additionally, spectral analysis was presented as an approach which may eventually fulfill even more of the requirements for a rigorous method of analysis. However, each of these methods has shortcomings particular to it. The optimal analytic strategy at present may be to conduct several types of analysis, relying on the strengths of one approach to compensate for the weaknesses of the others.

No strategy, though, can allow completely confident causal inferences. As a passive observational technique, ambiguity about causal relationships is usually unavoidable in noninterrupted time-series analysis. The major source of ambiguity is the inability to completely rule out third-variable causation. An asymmetrical cross-correlation function, with significant cross-correlations $r_{xy}(2)$, $r_{xy}(1)$, and $r_{xy}(0)$ might reflect a causal relationship between X and Y, as diagrammed in Figure 7.22. Alternatively, it could reflect the causal relationship of some third variable, z, with both X and Y, as illustrated in Figure 7.23. For instance, a significant cross-correlation between unemployment and suicides synchronously and with unemployment leading one, two, and three years could be interpreted as evidence that unemployment causes suicide. However, the possibility still has to be ruled out that some third variable, such as confidence in the political system, does not account for the obtained relationship. We might expect such confidence to affect unemployment and suicides both synchronously and for the following years (though not necessarily with the same pattern for both unemployment and suicides).

The plausibility of third-variable alternative explanations can sometimes be examined directly, if a measure of the third variable is available in time-series form. In other cases, the plausibility of a third-variable cause can be examined

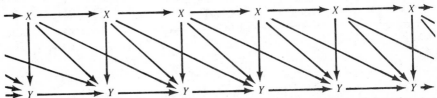

Figure 7.22. Illustrative causal model in which significant cross-correlations between prewhitened X and prewhitened Y are generated by the causal relationship $X \rightarrow Y$.

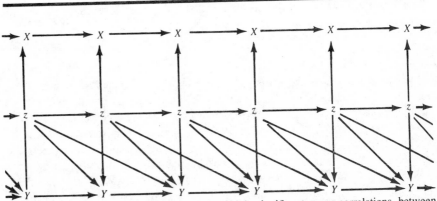

Figure 7.23. Illustrative causal model in which significant cross-correlations between prewhitened X and prewhitened Y are generated by a third variable z.

indirectly by means of analysis of subgroup data[2] and nonequivalent measures, some of which should be affected by third variables and others which should not be. Yet no precaution can completely rule out the logical possibility of third-variable causation.

Another apparent limitation of the careful analysis of time series is related to the criterion we have suggested for the assessment of covariation in time series. The criterion is that to be judged a possible cause of Y, X must add to the predictability of Y over and above the predictability arising from the orderly behavior of Y itself over time. Covariation cannot therefore be inferred when a series is perfectly deterministic (Granger, 1969). For instance, consider a variable D which increases 7% every year. Thus, D is perfectly predictable from its own past behavior; greater predictability cannot be achieved by using another predictor. This restriction means that we will not infer causation when two series share only orderly, long-term patterns. While this may seem unfortunate, it is necessary for responsible causal inferences. The argument can be made that in holding to this criterion, we are "throwing out the baby with the bath water," that is, removing from consideration those aspects of variables which are of greatest interest and which are likely to be causally related to other variables. It is true that time-series components of potential causal interest, such as secular trend, are excluded from causal analysis by our stringent criterion. However, these are components for which so many plausible alternative explanations exist that causal inferences can rarely be justified.

Another restriction inherent in "hard-headed" time-series analysis is a bias against inferring causal relationships on the basis of synchronous covariation alone. This reluctance has two sources. First, synchronous cross-correlations do not indicate the direction of cause. Second, a single isolated cross-correlation is more likely to be spurious than a pattern of contiguous cross-correlations. In some cases, we might attempt to make a causal inference on the basis of a synchronous cross-correlation, especially where we have longer spacings between observations than the causal lag is presumed to be. Thus, if the suicide and unemployment data are annual, but unemployment is assumed to affect suicide within four months, one-year lags will give at best an attenuated assessment of any causal impact. Synchronous correlations will be better. Moreover, plausibility can sometimes be invoked to interpret synchronous correlations causally (e.g., suicide can hardly increase unemployment). But the assumption in such a case is that no third variable is operating to cause the synchronous unemployment-suicide relationship. This last point should not be forgotten, even when examining cross-correlations, for the investigator is trying to infer cause from correlations that reflect a myriad

---

[2]A special type of design feature frequently used in time-series investigation, and which could be considered a type of nonequivalent dependent measure, is the analysis of subgroups. In subgroup analysis, the relationship of a variable X to a variable Y is more precisely specified by examining the series Y broken down into different classes of measurement units (usually individuals). For instance, the relationship of unemployment to suicides could be examined for different groups, such as white males aged 17 to 22, nonwhite females aged 65 and over, and so on. Subgroup analyses can be useful for differentiating among alternative theoretical explanations of a relationship between X and Y, because different explanations often make different predictions for the pattern of response across subgroups.

of systematic processes rather than from manipulanda over whose distribution he or she has some control.

Another limitation of time-series analysis is based on the type of information which is available in time-series form. For construct validity purposes, it is often impossible to differentiate among alternative causal mechanisms which might explain the relationship between X and Y. Available time series usually reflect aggregates of discrete social actions like unemployment or suicide. We surmise that such variables are not causally related in direct fashion. Rather, their causal relationship is mediated by other, often inter- or intrapersonal, variables. Unfortunately, such process variables are rarely archived and so are usually not available in time-series form unless the investigator collects the relevant data. It is rare that we can determine the micro-level social and psychological processes mediating causal relationships between more macro-level archived measures.

Finally, it is worth noting that the magnitude of the relationship between two time series depends on the extent to which the observations in any one series are factorially equivalent. It is reasonable to assume in most series that this assumption is not met, particularly with series which cover long time spans. For instance, how likely is it that the forces which cause shifts in unemployment are the same over 80 years? We would guess that a high degree of factorial similarity is unlikely and that each observation contains many, sometimes unique, sources of irrelevancy and error. The effect of such irrelevancy and unique error will be to attenuate the obtained relationships between series X and series Y.

This recital of the difficulties inherent in the causal analysis of noninterrupted time series may seem to indicate that we are predominantly pessimistic about the general method. On the contrary, we consider that the need for such a method is great in light of the nation's expanding store of archived social and economic measures. Because of this, we expect rapid conceptual progress in methods for the causal analysis of concomitancies in time series. The currently available methods of analysis are admittedly somewhat rudimentary. This fact demands a particularly thoughtful use of the stronger methods and a frank recognition in written reports of the limitations of any chosen method or methods. We would be saddened, however, if the limitations of the methods discouraged their use, just as we are saddened when we read of instances where the fallible methods we have described are used and their limitations are not explicitly acknowledged in a language that is easily understood by all.

Issues Not Addressed

Many important issues are beyond the scope of this presentation. Our focus has been on the identification of causal relationships between series, and not on the specification or estimation of models of the form and magnitude of relationships—causal or not—between series (cf. Box and Jenkins, 1976). The pooling of time-series and cross-correlational data, a subject of growing interest in the econometrics literature (see Hannan and Young, 1977; Nerlove, 1971) has unfortunately been ignored. Nor have we considered the study of growth—that is, the study of concomitancy in the secular trends of two or more series—because such study is generally not amenable to causal analysis. Only general approaches to time-series analysis have been discussed, and specific variants on each approach

have not been given adequate attention (cf. Pierce and Haugh, 1977). The error-in-measurement problem has not been addressed directly, although it is discussed elsewhere in this book. These and many other issues would be addressed in a more complete discussion of the analysis of concomitancies in time series.

CONCLUDING COMMENTS ON MOVING FROM PASSIVE OBSERVATION TO DELIBERATE MANIPULATION

While we have explicitly carried over into this chapter our concerns with unique variance, regression artifacts and third-variable causation, we have not systematically gone through our full armamentarium of threats to validity. Had we done so, many more plausible rival hypotheses would have become apparent and would raise serious questions about the techniques discussed here that have been used to generate causal inference from passive observational data. Instead, we have presented these techniques, however briefly, primarily in their own terms, raising the threats to validity that have appeared in their respective literatures.

In chapter 1 we presented the task of diagnosing causal relations in terms of effects that could be achieved were one able to manipulate the cause. While the advocates of path analysis, causal modeling, and cross-lagged panel correlation are not always clear on this point, we judge that for the most part their use of causal terminology indicates a similar orientation. Be that as it may, the causal conclusions that are being drawn by many social scientists using passive observational methods could often be used to justify policy changes and, in that sense, may lead to deliberate efforts to manipulate change.

We offer several recommendations regarding such developments. First, we hope that social scientists and government administrators collaborate in trying to make policy changes so that the causal assertions buttressing these changes can be cross-validated—for these changes may often be of great significance but founded on precarious, passive methods. The political settings in which such changes are implemented will contain many ambiguities as far as causal inference is concerned, but deliberate manipulation is involved nonetheless and the methods described in the other chapters of this book will be appropriate for assessing the effectiveness of the deliberate change.

Our second recommendation is more easily put into practice. It is that in studies employing passive observational approaches, the social scientist should extend the discussion of results to examine how diagnosed causes could be manipulated and what the likelihood is that the effects claimed from such analyses of passive data will also be obtained when the diagnosed causes are translated into concrete policy actions. Consequently, there should be discussions of any differences between the causal variable as it has impinged in the natural setting and what it would be like when deliberately manipulated. Such discussions would increase the probability of the social scientists' conclusions being validly applied. They would also complicate and purify the causal analyses, thereby improving the quality of the scientific knowledge achieved whether used for policy or not.

8

The Conduct
of Randomized
Experiments

INTRODUCTION

The Functions of Random Assignment

As previously noted, randomization serves two principal functions in the social sciences. The first is to draw samples that are representative of a known population within limits of sampling error; the second is to draw samples that are comparable to each other within known limits of sampling error. This latter function, which helps facilitate causal inferences, is the focus of this chapter.

Random assignment achieves comparability by equating the average unit within each treatment group, irrespective of whether the units are individual persons, neighborhood blocks, or classrooms. In the simplest design with a single experimental and control group, assigning units to conditions on a chance basis means that units with a given idiosyncracy which are assigned to one group will, on the average, be counterbalanced by units with comparable (but not necessarily identical) idiosyncracies in the other group. Thus, if individuals are the unit of assignment and some individuals are extremely tall, taller individuals will be represented about equally in each of the groups if assignment is, say, by coin toss. Randomization does not, of course, remove the idiosyncracy from any one unit; Abraham Lincoln remains Abraham Lincoln, as it were. But prior to the treatment and after random assignment, the average score of all the persons in a particular group should not differ from the average score in the other group. Hence, the pretest means of the different treatment groups should not differ; or, said differently, the biserial correlation of the pretest and the treatment (scored as 1 or 0—a dummy variable) should not be different from zero.

The equivalence achieved by random assignment is probabilistic. Thus it is not inevitable that a correctly implemented randomization procedure will result in groups that do not differ. Obviously, with a small initial sample of persons who differ widely on a dependent variable of interest, random assignment may result in dissimilar groups. (If you have difficulty imagining this, think of only five per-

sons, whose individual weights are 120, 130, 140, 150, and 160 pounds. A simple randomization procedure might result in the two lightest persons being in one group [average weight 125 pounds] and the three heaviest in the other [average weight 150 pounds].) Even with large samples and dependent variables of low variability, the pretest means will not be identical; and statistically significant differences will sometimes be obtained by chance alone. Nonetheless, a properly implemented random assignment procedure will usually result in initially comparable experimental groups and will avoid most of the threats to internal validity discussed in chapters 3 through 7.

Random assignment is not a panacea that inevitably rules out all threats to internal validity. We saw in chapter 2 how random assignment creates focused inequities between the ways various individuals are treated. This may exacerbate pressures on either the experimentals or controls to act atypically. Such pressures (e.g., compensatory rivalry) can obscure true differences or create effects in the control group (i.e., resentful demoralization) that may be misinterpreted as effects in the treatment group. Though random assignment does serve to make *most* things equal between the different experimental groups—so that selection, selection-maturation, regression, and the like are equal in each group—it does not necessarily make *all* things equal. The case for random assignment has to be made on the grounds that it is better than the available alternatives for inferring cause and not on the grounds that it is perfect for inferring cause.

Random assignment serves two more minor functions in addition to creating initial probabilistic equivalence. First, as we saw in chapter 4, it creates the conditions for which the best known statistical models were created. Tests of differences between randomly formed groups are less biased and more powerful than tests with nonequivalent groups. We therefore have greater faith both in magnitude estimates of effects and in inferences about rejecting the null hypothesis. Second, many experiments involve the distribution of scarce and desired resources such as income supplements, educational opportunities, or new drugs. Ethical decisions have to be made about who should receive the desired resources. Often a good case can be made for distribution by chance—with no one person among the eligibles having a better chance than anyone else. This is in distinction to allocative procedures such as "to each according to need or merit," or "first come, first served," or "it is who you know that counts and not what you know or what you need or deserve." Random assignment sometimes serves, then, as a means of solving the ethical issues that arise when we must distribute valuable but scarce resources.

What Random Assignment Does Not Do

A successfully implemented random assignment procedure does not guarantee that the initial comparability between groups will be maintained over the course of an experiment. There are many reasons why the attrition from an experiment may be systematically related to treatments, the major one being that treatments are often chosen precisely because they differ in desirability. Since decisions about cause depend on the *posttest* comparability of treatment groups on all dimensions other than receiving the treatment, it is obvious that a procedure like random assignment which results in comparability at the *pretest* does not inevitably

achieve the most *relevant* comparability of groups. Consequently, we can anticipate that an important component of all randomized experiments is the collection and analysis of data to test whether attrition from an experiment has been systematically related to treatments.

If one is prepared to assume that the attrition has been random, one can continue with the analysis of the data as coming from a randomized experiment. If one assumes that the attrition is systematic, then one has to try and describe the ways in which it is systematic, and try to control for these factors in the statistical analysis. Most of the quasi-experimental analyses required after systematic attrition has taken place call for the measurement of control variables that describe how the groups differ and of variables that may have affected posttest scores. Therefore, it is always useful to design randomized experiments in light of (1) expectations derived from past research, theory, and common sense about the direction of attrition, and (2) the reliable measures needed for a fallback quasi-experimental analysis in case the randomized experiment breaks down because units drop out of the study in ways that are correlated with the assignment to treatments.

Though random assignment is germane to the research goal of assessing whether the treatment may have *caused* any observed effects, it is conceptually irrelevant to all other research goals. Consequently, if a randomized experiment is conducted with a sample of units that does not correspond to the population of theoretical or policy interest, this weakens the usefulness of the research but is not an argument against randomized experimentation. Thus, Rossi and Lyall's (1976) critique of the New Jersey Negative Income Tax Experiment in terms of the respondents being working poor when most guaranteed incomes in a national scheme would go to the jobless poor is irrelevant to issues concerned with random assignment. Similarly, the critique by Cook et al. (1975) of Ball and Bogatz (1970) for manipulating the level of social encouragement to view "Sesame Street" instead of manipulating viewing "Sesame Street" without such encouragement is irrelevant to random assignment. Larson (1976) criticized the Kansas City Patrol Experiment (1974) because he discovered that the amount of police patrolling in the high patrolling condition was less than is currently the case in New York. He also found that the contrast between high and low patrolling areas in Kansas City was much less than planned since squad cars crossed atypically often over the low patrol areas with flashing lights and screaming sirens. However, these criticisms of the experiment had nothing to do with random assignment. One can have experiments where the questions, samples, treatments, comparisons, and measures are chosen poorly or well. But these aspects of the experiment have no implications for assessing the desirability of random assignment, which is only relevant to improving causal inferences.

Perhaps the best way to understand what random assignment does not do is to think of it as *part* of the experimental design, which is itself only *part* of the overall research design. Experimental design involves the scheduling of observations, the choice of treatments and comparisons, the selection of measured control variables, and the manner of assigning units to treatments. Random assignment deals with only the last of these issues—the manner of assignment. Research design is broader than experimental design and is concerned with asking relevant

research questions, including the determination of which outcome variables should be measured and who should be the respondents. To assign at random does not guarantee a useful experimental or research design, for random assignment relates only to causal inferences and causal inference is only one goal of experimentation, although the most unique goal that clearly differentiates its origins from those of other social science methods.

Another way to think of what random assignment does not do is to compare it to other means of testing causal propositions. As we saw at many points in this book, with most quasi-experiments and nonexperiments assumptions have to be accepted before confident causal inferences can be drawn, although considerable differences exist between types of quasi-experiments and nonexperiments in the number and plausibility of the assumptions on which causal inference depends. Random assignment does not make causal inference infallible. It is still dependent on accepting assumptions—e.g., that random assignment resulted in initial comparability, that resentful demoralization or systematic attrition did not occur, and so forth. Moreover, as with quasi-experiments and nonexperiments, the careful researcher has to think through these assumptions and assess their plausibility. He or she then attempts to rule them out by design or to measure them and either show that a particular possible threat did not in fact operate or that it operated but failed to affect the dependent variable in a manner which makes a treatment effect unlikely. *The difference between random and systematic assignment to conditions lies in the number and plausibility of the assumptions that have to be accepted for causal inference.* A moment's reflection should illustrate that the assumptions are fewer in number for randomized experiments than for other forms of design (e.g., no need exists to think of, say, regression as a threat) and are less plausible in nature for randomized experiments than for other forms of design (e.g., selection is less likely and can be checked by examining pretest means). Moreover, the possibility exists that, even where assumptions cannot be met after random assignment (e.g., if there has been systematic attrition), the magnitude of the resulting threat—and hence its plausibility as an alternative interpretation—may be less than it would have been had systematic assignment initially taken place.

When Random Assignment Is Not Feasible or Desirable

Usually a considerable time elapses between planning a randomized experiment and obtaining the results. Major research questions have to be developed and validated, pilot work (or formative research) has to be conducted, the pretest measurements have to be made, the rest of the data collected, cleaned and ordered, the analysis conducted, and the first drafts of reports carefully scrutinized. Thus, it should not be surprising that typically several years pass between the conception of an experiment and the availability of results. When decisions have to be made rapidly, randomized experiments may not be suitable, and some form of quasi-experiment or nonexperiment may have to be undertaken that uses naturally occurring variability for defining the independent variable. To take just one example, in a study of the effects of job placement versus income supplements for ex-convicts, the alternative to a randomized experiment would be to seek out persons who had themselves found jobs soon after release from prison or had been helped by social

services which provide income supplements. The recidivism rates for each group could then be examined. A moment's reflection should reveal that such a procedure is considerably weaker for inferring cause than a randomized experiment, but it may be more timely. This is the crux of the issue, for the advantages of accumulating data rapidly have to be weighed against the disadvantages of misinterpreting treatment effects, either in terms of a treatment being effective or more effective than some alternative. What would be the cost of inferring that one release program is better than another if neither is actually effective or if the program that is deemed more effective is actually less so?

Randomized experiments cannot be designed to answer questions about certain kinds of possible causal variables. For instance, it is not possible to assign persons at random to different chronological ages, or physical body states, or race (though contrived randomized experiments can be conducted with people strapped in wheelchairs or treated chemically to change their skin pigmentation). It is also not possible for ethical reasons to assign persons at random to most kinds of events that cause suffering. For instance, physical disasters cannot be staged, except under clearly labeled conditions that indicate a simulation is under way. Quasi-experimental analyses are, therefore, required for anyone wanting to study disasters. Randomized experiments cannot be carried out retrospectively, except under the most unusual circumstances (Notz, Staw and Cook, 1971). If one wanted to examine the effects of the death of President Kennedy or of the Depression in the 1930s, designs other than a randomized experiment would be required. Indeed, the study of many social and economic structural factors precludes randomization. Can we imagine feasible randomized experiments where the independent variable is "unemployment rate" or "proximity to a metropolitan area"?

It is rarely desirable to conduct an experiment before preliminary conceptual or empirical work has been done to ensure that the manipulations are exactly the ones of interest. "Planned variations" studies aside, the vast majority of experiments have only one or two treatments in addition to a no-treatment control group. To conduct a randomized experiment with hastily chosen treatments is a waste of resources; one has results about a treatment of little interest or a treatment that had little promise of resulting in effects. Consider evaluating the health services offered by the Peace Corps, with a view to discovering which particular health services are successful and worth expanding into other countries. It would not be advisable to sit in an armchair and think of three ways of, say, controlling surface water to attack mosquitoes. Nor would it be particularly advisable merely to consult experts about what should be done. Rather, if the need for decisions is not pressing, it might be better to conduct a correlational study to test, in approximate fashion, which kinds of existing health services seem to be related to higher health outcome levels. Only after this step would one conduct a randomized experiment in which the next volunteers are randomly assigned to one of the particular health services that seemed for the correlational analysis to be most promising. Since so much in experimental research depends on the choice of the independent variable, preexperimental exploratory research helps to avoid the problem of premature experimentation which arises when treatments are implemented, whose operational stability is untested and whose theoretical or practical significance is underexamined.

Hollister (1979) has argued that randomized experiments are likely to be more expensive than nonexperimental or quasi-experimental alternatives. We can see no reason why randomized experiments should be more expensive than other forms of experimentation since the major expense is usually the cost of the treatment itself—a fixed expense for any given treatment. However, all forms of experiments are likely to be more expensive than those nonexperiments which capitalize upon naturally occurring versions of what appears to be a particular treatment. For instance, it is obviously less costly to study the effects of sudden income supplements using the winners of state lotteries than it is to use experimental resources for providing the supplements. Also it is less costly to study children who view "Sesame Street" for different amounts of time in their own homes than it is to provide cables at random to the homes of persons who live in areas where the show can only be received via cable.

The argument about financial cost highlights another kind of cost—that of being wrong in one's conclusions about the direction of causality. One can readily see how, with sufficient ingenuity, one can conduct a less expensive (and usually, more timely) study using nonexperimental or simple quasi-experimental methods. However, as chapters 3 through 7 emphasized, one runs the risk with such methods of drawing false causal inferences. The exact degree of risk depends on the strength of the implemented design and measurement framework for ruling out specific threats to internal validity. Tukey (1977) and Gilbert, McPeek, and Mosteller (1977) have discussed this issue with respect to experimentation with medical innovations. They have concluded that the social costs of being wrong about whether, say, a drug is effective outweigh the ethical and financial costs associated with experimenting and deliberately withholding possibly effective treatments from some persons in order to create control groups. In the area of criminal justice research, Zimring (1976) has advocated strong experiments over other means for assessing the effectiveness of treatments, explicitly preferring—in his own words—"the slow but careful tortoise over the speedy but less reliable hare." Campbell and Boruch (1975) have made the same advocacy in the area of compensatory education. Every researcher should carefully weigh the costs of being wrong in a causal inference, for decisions to implement randomized experiments over their sometimes more timely alternatives depend on these anticipated costs more than on any other single factor.

This Chapter

In the sections that follow, we will not spend much time outlining research designs that can be used with randomly formed groups. Appropriate models are contained in classical texts on experimental design (e.g., Walker and Lev, 1953; Winer, 1961; Edwards, 1963; Hays, 1963; Kirk, 1968; McNemar, 1975). Instead, we shall concern ourselves with (1) outlining obstacles in implementing and maintaining randomly formed groups in field settings; (2) listing strategies to overcome these obstacles; and (3) developing a list of situations that are most conducive to randomization. Therefore, our stress is on *problems of implementing randomized experiments* in field settings rather than on the *interpretation of the results obtained from randomized experiments*.

Most of the discussion that follows focuses on the simplest possible design in which a treatment and a no-treatment control group are compared. This restriction is for heuristic convenience only. It should not be interpreted as a lack of enthusiasm for factorial designs (where levels of more than one factor are "crossed") or parametric designs (where many levels of a particular factor are experimentally varied). Indeed, we are firm believers in such designs because they provide more information than the simple experimental-control comparison, and because each unit is usually provided with some kind of treatment. However, the simpler designs seem to be more prevalent in field settings. Moreover, many of the problems that beset factorial or parametric designs also beset experimental-control designs, and the latter designs permit a simpler exposition of the basic points we want to make.

MAJOR OBSTACLES TO CONDUCTING RANDOMIZED EXPERIMENTS IN FIELD SETTINGS

It is difficult to gain and maintain access to research populations in field settings, irrespective of whether randomized experiments or quasi-experiments are contemplated. The problem of access can probably best be conceptualized in terms of social power. Access is more likely if one has power over the persons determining access. This can be a power based on the ability to reward or punish, on being personally respected or being sponsored by respected research institutions, on belonging to the same membership groups as persons determining access, on promising research that might benefit an organization, or on being the kind of person who can successfully badger, cajole, or charm others into compliance with one's wishes. This is not to say that negotiations about access should only be conducted with the persons responsible for authorizing immediate entry into an organization. Obtaining access and maintaining good field relationships may well depend on a study being explicitly or implicitly endorsed by the lower-level persons from whom data are collected or by representatives of such persons. Endorsement of this kind would probably help prevent some of the problems that arise when respondents think they are being studied without their consent.

We will not concern ourselves with the problem of access as it affects all field experimentation. Rather, we shall concentrate on the special problems of access and implementation that face investigators *who plan to use random assignment*.

Withholding the Treatment from No-Treatment Control Groups

Nature of the Problem

In many instances, the investigator's request for randomization will be accompanied by a request that the treatment be deliberately withheld from some respondents or be given to them in smaller amounts. These requests may seem ethically questionable if potentially beneficial treatments are withheld from persons who might need or deserve them. A prime example of this is in medical research where, because an experimental drug's effectiveness is not known, sick patients are not given the drug which might help them. However, this is only one instance of the more general problem that arises when valuable resources are allocated by

chance instead of by the more widely accepted criteria of need, merit, cronyism, or the like.

The decision about access has a public relations aspect as well as an ethical one. Both Bishop and Hill (1971) and Hand and Slocum (1972) have attributed unexpected decrements in performance and attitude in no-treatment control groups to the group's resentment when comparing their own lack of a treatment to the treatment received by others. We suspect that the persons who authorize access to field populations often anticipate such resentment. If they do, the works cited above suggest that their anticipation may at times be justified, though we do not yet know the conditions under which such apprehension is warranted.

Solutions

Withholding the treatment is less problematic in designs where multiple treatments are implemented and contrasted to assess their relative effectiveness. Atkinson (1968) provides an ingenious example of this in a study of computer-assisted instruction (CAI). It would have been difficult, within schools, to have had some children receive CAI and others not receive it. So, all the students in a class were randomly assigned to receive computerized instruction in either mathematics or English, and each group took tests of their knowledge of both subjects. Consequently, the groups "switched" experimental and control topics, with mathematics being the experimental and English the control topic for some students, while the reverse was true for other children.

This design is available where one has multiple problems for ameliorative action, a common treatment that can take a variety of forms (e.g., computer-assisted instruction), and where the particular form of one treatment (computer-assisted instruction in English) would not be expected to affect tests measuring the effects of some other form of the treatment (e.g., computer-assisted instruction in mathematics). This design is not without problems. For instance, a teacher might know that some children are receiving special mathematics instruction via computer and may concentrate on teaching them English, because he or she knows that they are getting no special instruction in this topic. If so, performance in English would improve among students in the mathematics group, and an evaluation of computerized instruction in English would run the risk of leading to false negative conclusions about the treatment's effectiveness. Probably the best way of assessing the plausibility of this threat would be to supplement the study with quasi-experimental data from cohorts from the same class in previous years. If performance in English differed between these cohorts and children in the experiment who received computerized instruction in mathematics, this would serve as presumptive evidence that the controls for English were inadequate "no-cause baseline controls" and that the children might have received special unplanned instruction in English.

Withholding a treatment is also less of a problem when several treatments of approximately equal desirability are aimed at solving the same problem. This is optimal, for the investigator can assign a different treatment to each respondent. He or she can then compare the various treatments to find the ones that most affect the dependent variable measures reflecting some correction of the problem. This is

sometimes called the strategy of "planned variations," and Rivlin and Timpane (1975) have a book on this topic.

One difficulty when multiple treatments are targeted on a common problem is the absence of a no-cause baseline, making it difficult to test hypotheses about "absolute" cause as opposed to hypotheses about differential impact. Adding a no-treatment control group would get around this problem. But it would also mean that the treatment has to be withheld from some persons, thereby creating the very ethical and public relations problem that "planned variations" is partly meant to solve. Thus, for no-cause baseline purposes it is often worthwhile exploring the possibility of giving some groups irrelevant treatments that are aimed at different sorts of problems than the target one.

A more serious concern with planned variations experiments is that the different treatments are often not targeted at exactly the same kind of problem. Imagine a comparative study of different ways of increasing academic achievement. One educational innovation may focus on improving achievement directly. But another treatment may focus on academic self-concept in the anticipation that cognitive performance will increase once the student feels better about his or her ability. Even within the cognitive domain, one new curriculum may focus on algebra, though it covers the other aspects of elementary mathematics, while another may have different priorities, though it also covers the other major aspects of elementary mathematics. To be sensitive to the particular aspirations and presumed strengths of any innovation requires tailoring the measures to the unique aspects of the innovation. Yet planned variation logically requires that the measures are equally appropriate to each innovation, and it implies that the innovations have been tailored to the particular objectives embodied by the measures. Clearly, sensitively planned variation studies have to tap into *both* the common *and* the particular lower-order goals of programs which at first glance appear to be targeted at the same problem. This will usually require that additional resources be used for measurement purposes.

The problem of withholding a treatment is also partially solved in designs like that of Bishop and Hill (1971). Here, a change is given to the control group which is not expected to affect the performance being examined and which is conceptually different from the other treatments in the experiment unlike Atkinson's switching of the conceptually related English and mathematics instruction by computer. A control group receiving an irrelevant treatment is often called a "placebo control group." Such a group is useful because it differentiates the effects of any change from the effects of a specific change that was introduced for experimental reasons. For example, Bishop and Hill had experimental respondents experience a job enlargement treatment while the controls had their jobs changed but not enlarged by the addition of new tasks. This meant that the construct "job enlargement" could be distinguished from the construct "change in the job," the latter being an inevitable but irrelevant correlate of job enlargement. More important for our present purpose, the job change among the controls meant that all respondents received a treatment.

The problem of withholding treatments is reduced, of course, when resources are scarce and it is simply not possible to provide everyone with the treatment. In

this case, the investigator knows that there will have to be no-treatment controls. But he or she has no guarantee that these controls will be equivalent to the treatment group, since in many settings there will be pressure to distribute the treatment to those who are thought to merit or need it most rather than to a randomly selected group. Knowing this, the investigator has to use all of his or her persuasive powers to inform the persons controlling access that we *hope* a treatment will have ameliorative consequences but *we do not know* if it will; that, if we did know, there would be no need to conduct an experiment; and that, since we do not know, to conduct any study other than a randomized experiment would decrease the likelihood of learning whether the treatment had solved the practical or theoretical problem to which it was addressed. The investigator should further add that he or she would like to provide the treatment, or a refinement of it, to the no-treatment controls at a later date if the treatment proves to be successful. This information should help the persons who control access because it ensures that everyone will finally receive a treatment if it turns out to be useful. However, it would also benefit investigators who would have a chance to replicate previous findings or even, if the appropriate permission were obtained, to add to already existing knowledge by modifying the replication.

The problems associated with withholding treatments are serious and often difficult to resolve. In the last analysis, the investigator has two principal resources: his or her own ingenuity in trying to think through socially and ethically acceptable ways in which no-treatment controls can receive some sort of treatment, either during or after an experiment; and his or her own persuasive powers so that gatekeepers might be convinced to permit random assignment. However, persuasion is more likely to be successful with persons who are genuinely concerned about the ethical and practical problems associated with withholding treatments than with persons who use these problems to justify their reluctance to randomize or to conduct any kind of research.

Faulty Randomization Procedures

Problem

The most common method of drawing random samples is probably to use a book of edited random numbers like the one published by Rand (1955). These random numbers can be incorrectly used. So, too, can mechanical procedures, such as dice, shuffled cards, spinners, roulette wheels, and the like. For example, Fienberg (1971) and Notz, Staw, and Cook (1971) have commented upon the bias in the 1969 military draft lottery. Slips of paper bearing different birth dates were drawn out of an urn, and the order in which dates were drawn fixed the order in which men would be called up for service in the armed forces. Bias arose because the urn was not sufficiently shaken, with the result that the numbers put into it last (those of December, November, October) lay on the top and were drawn out first. (There have also been cases where slips of paper have adhered to the sides of a vessel.) It is also possible to obtain nonequivalent samples when using computerized random number generator programs. For instance, one large city school system assigns eligible students at random to either a regular city school or a new and innovative Magnet School which spends four times more per pupil than the

average city school. A study of how the Magnet School affected achievement and attitudes (Zigulich, 1977) showed that random assignment was correctly carried out one year but that, after attempts had been made to make the computerized random number generator more efficient, the assignments it made were biased!

Solutions

In most contexts ethical and practical concerns will dictate informing respondents about the random assignment procedure. Clearly, a frank and simple explanation of the rationale for randomization will have to be presented. Unfortunately, evidence is accumulating which suggests that, at least under some conditions, respondents do not believe that a truly random procedure was conducted, particularly when they lose in the selection (Wortman and Rabinowitz, in press). (Perhaps it was to improve the credibility of random assignment that the second American draft lottery involved selection from the urn by a young man of draft-eligible age, i.e., by someone who appeared to have a vested interest in a fair selection and with whom the potential draftees could identify.) Every effort should be made to have the drawing of lots for treatment assignments either public or at least open to public scrutiny by interested parties or their representatives. While this heightens awareness of being in a research experiment, it can also make random assignment more understandable and credible.

	1–4	5–8	9–12	13–16	17–20	21–24	25–28	29–32	33–36	37–40
1	77 66	88 40	86 61	96 70	78 75	29 77	21 94	12 37	66 11	53 42
2	74 81	53 71	16 61	59 13	33 02	25 95	92 37	03 18	46 26	37 86
3	05 88	20 12	10 45	80 22	38 70	94 11	22 02	08 37	74 87	49 04
4	05 79	76 95	69 00	48 70	60 14	53 11	06 57	06 26	60 31	06 74
5	79 98	70 98	97 94	55 99	44 04	75 89	69 50	64 03	96 68	17 89
6	55 09	79 15	11 56	65 88	08 16	96 95	33 17	60 45	81 31	50 46
7	79 19	16 49	99 08	80 01	56 35	41 42	72 58	20 39	33 53	85 26
8	28 70	12 06	71 02	34 50	30 16	83 58	39 98	84 01	27 85	17 35
9	54 44	53 59	34 44	49 93	61 75	19 87	34 93	85 16	18 79	65 94
10	93 69	31 43	93 93	77 39	72 40	66 32	90 86	65 88	41 19	36 86
11	24 94	65 41	64 64	95 13	46 97	43 12	86 02	79 50	67 90	14 19
12	04 07	67 01	59 03	27 37	83 20	17 82	11 80	46 08	32 68	60 26
13	67 24	63 38	76 53	29 14	02 47	70 31	20 88	24 31	14 65	23 35
14	69 06	90 51	48 94	89 77	41 66	54 60	66 95	46 73	76 59	20 05
15	66 56	20 91	61 48	91 73	98 80	96 94	45 09	93 21	90 40	03 01
16	36 48	02 01	88 94	20 08	07 64	08 84	26 41	25 54	43 65	82 24
17	62 93	85 57	12 06	07 88	22 37	03 84	80 69	93 29	22 34	67 88
18	94 01	05 57	71 98	47 26	58 99	72 11	69 93	22 46	72 52	75 62
19	52 94	18 97	82 49	76 84	86 83	05 27	53 27	16 40	94 34	81 86
20	27 43	78 39	71 17	16 72	43 37	60 73	83 41	31 32	61 05	37 89
21	46 00	19 71	63 06	75 27	01 57	59 61	86 70	33 35	54 77	81 38
22	29 58	01 44	39 62	83 16	97 46	31 27	27 43	67 66	35 08	86 34
23	19 31	80 79	63 47	80 56	00 71	06 17	49 70	26 75	55 43	46 84
24	02 52	31 23	74 12	16 62	21 19	76 63	33 43	17 16	96 00	42 50
25	06 00	13 63	57 37	51 83	45 58	21 01	02 89	88 07	74 32	21 87

Table 8.1. Page from a table of random numbers.

The technical process of random assignment implies two basic steps. First, the investigator needs a list of the units in some population of relevance; the list may be of persons, families, classrooms, schools, precincts, and the like. Second, the investigator will need a procedure for the random selection of units from the list.

It is simple to create a list of unique numbers for oneself, but sometimes such lists are available, e.g., a voter registration list, a school attendance roster, a list of administrative units, and so forth. Each sampling unit on the list should then be assigned a unique number. The requirements for such numbers are not restrictive, and gaps in the number system create no problem. For instance, individual employee identification numbers would be acceptable even if there are gaps and certain of the digits represent, say, specific departments. The important part is that no unit should have the same number as any other unit.

The second step is to use a table of random numbers (Rand, 1955) to guide the selection of the sample from within the list. For example, if the maximum number in the list was 2,557, we would select from a table of random numbers a column four digits wide and start reading down, selecting as our sample those numbers appearing in the table which correspond to units in the population. Table 8.1 shows a sample from a page of random numbers. Let us start at the upper left corner and read down. Since 2577 is the highest number on our list, 77 66 should be skipped since it is larger than any in our sample, as is 74 81. However, 05 88 is in our range and would be selected if it were on our list but passed over if the list had gaps which included 05 88. Look now to the 12th number, 04 07, which could also enter our sample, as could 19 31, 02 52, and so forth. If we needed 100 units in the experimental group and 100 in the control group, we would proceed as above until 200 were selected and perhaps several pages of random numbers had been used. Then, the first 100 units might be designated as the experimental group, and the second 100 as controls.

Such a procedure represents simple random sampling *without replacement* (Kish, 1965). It is "simple" because no prior stratification has taken place, and it is "without replacement" because any unit selected will be treated as a blank if its number comes up a second time in the random number listing.[1] The purpose of the procedure is to create two samples that are probabilistically equivalent to each other. They will also be representative of the total list which might, or might not, itself be a universe of particular significance.

We have previously mentioned the desirability of drawing stratified random samples. When stratification is possible, the listing and randomization process would be carried out separately for each stratum or block of the population, as with, say, sex or race. Where matching is to be done, an abbreviated version of the same procedure can still be used. For example, suppose in a given experiment four treatment types are to be compared: *A, B, C,* and *D.* One might judgmentally select sets of four units which are as alike as possible within sets. One or many variables can be used in such matching. One could then number the units arbi-

---

[1] In our illustration, we started at the very beginning of a random number table. Statisticians would prefer such niceties as a random starting point instead of such a systematic one. At the very least, one should not reuse the same page.

trarily within each set as 1, 2, 3, and 4, looking to some column in a random number table to see which of these four numbers comes up first. The one that does is assigned to A, the second to B, and so on. Thus, if we were using the extreme right column of the sample table above, number two comes in the first row, getting assigned to A, number four comes in the third row and is therefore assigned to B. We then draw many blanks and repeats, but by row 15 we come to a number one, and it goes into treatment C. By elimination, number three goes to treatment D. This procedure can then be repeated, with a new column of random numbers for each set. Where there are just two treatments, experimental and control, the decision rule would be even simpler—whichever number comes up first goes into the experimental group, the other into the control.

Stratifying or blocking in advance is better than randomization editing after initial assignment. Nonetheless, the latter process can improve comparability if it is accomplished before any treatments are delivered. Thus if background or pretest data are available along with the lists of units assigned to each treatment, one can check whether the preexperiment profile of one group is like the other's. If the assignment seems biased, the whole random number assignment can be gone through again, starting on a new page of the table of random numbers, until one gets apparent pretest equivalence of the groups. For example, in an experiment with, say, 200 juvenile offenders who are to receive a counseling program, it might eventuate that, despite randomization, all 15 mental retardates ended up in the 100-person counseled group. Mental retardates differ from other persons in many respects, and if they are all represented in a single group, they will bias many comparisons. If such a bias were noted before the treatment assignments were implemented, one could then rerandomize instead of persisting with the initial random assignment. Of course, initial blocking, whereby half of the retardates would be in the experimental group and half in the controls, would be even better than simple random sampling.

Not all random assignment is done directly from tables of random numbers. The draft lotteries, for instance, were accomplished by placing numbers corresponding to birth dates in an urn and then shaking the urn. The first lottery was biased, and the persons conducting the draft lottery might have been well advised to check on their procedure by examining the relationship of number to birth dates after, say, 50 numbers had been drawn. Evidence of bias could then have led to a reshaking and redrawing. When computers are used for random assignment, the supposition is made that the numbers are stored in random fashion. This supposition can be wrong, as the Magnet School evaluation by Zigulich suggested. Our advice is that all random number programs should be checked prior to being used in an experiment for implementing the random assignment procedure. Such checking can easily be accomplished with simulated units.

Conner (1977) has suggested some organizational factors that may contribute to implementing randomization. His analysis of 12 projects where randomization was planned tentatively identified that randomization was *less* likely under the following conditions: If the implementation plan was carried out by outside researchers rather than by researchers working for the project being evaluated; if the random assignment was controlled by operating personnel from the agency being studied rather than by researchers; if loopholes were identified for exempt-

ing some individuals from random assignment so that they could be assigned systematically; and if the implementation was carried out by several persons rather than a single individual. The hypotheses at issue here are that in-house research personnel have more credibility than outsiders, that researchers understand the rationale for random assignment better than others, that allowing loopholes legitimizes an implementor's own implicit theory of how particular experimental resources should be allocated, and that having many implementors increases the likelihood of some persons deliberately or inadvertently departing from the planned assignment schedule.

As far as organizational arrangements are concerned, once permission to randomize has been obtained the most important feature is that researchers should carry out the procedure on a day-to-day basis. This avoids the difficulties that can arise when untrained personnel do not fully understand how to randomize, or think that little harm will be done if they assign some units to treatment conditions because of a special need or merit. Sometimes, however, the implementation of random assignment has to be in the hands of nonresearch personnel. When this is the case, the researchers should develop and carry out a monitoring scheme to detect deviations from random assignment. This will involve regularly screening the lists of persons randomized, which ensures that at least the percentage of persons in each condition follows the experimental plan. Other archival data can be routinely scrutinized for comparability, including any demographic or other data that are collected at the pretest. In keeping with one of Conner's points, we also think it desirable to have one trained researcher implement the random assignment plan.

Sampling Variability and the Number and Choice of Units for Randomization

Problem

Considerations of both statistical power and the effectiveness of randomization for ensuring the comparability of experimental groups incline most statisticians to prefer to have as many units as possible in the randomization process. Consequently, if 1,000 students were to be in an experiment, a statistician might prefer the assignment of 1,000 distinct units as opposed to, say, 50 classes with an average of 20 students in each, or 10 schools with an average of 100 students each. Assigning only 10 schools to two conditions would mean 5 schools per condition—not a state of affairs that would generate confidence in the comparability of the two groups, particularly since significant variability among schools can usually be anticipated.

Though large numbers are desirable for statistical reasons, there are also practical and scientific considerations for randomly assigning larger units than the individual, perhaps whole workrooms or buildings. The experiments of Lawler and Hackman (1969) and Broadbent and Little (1960) exemplify this, for it would not have been practical to isolate each worker and give him or her a unique treatment. If this had happened, resentful demoralization or imitation of the treatment might have been rampant. Hence, intact groups were assigned to treatments in these experiments. Consider, next, the first evaluation of "Plaza Sesamo" by Diaz-

Guerrero and Holzmann (1974). The study required that some individual children in Mexican day-care centers be randomly assigned to watch "Plaza Sesamo" in small groups. They were in a special room with two adult monitors who focused attention on the show. At the same time, other children watched cartoons in larger groups in the regular room with no special monitors. (The controls also had to stay at the day-care center for two hours longer than the experimentals so that the controls would not be at home during hours when "Plaza Sesamo" was available.) Since treating classmates in these different ways may well have led to a focused inequity, think how much more desirable the experimental situation would have been if the experimenters' resources had permitted them to assign intact classes to treatments, rather than individuals within classes.

The research question also determines at which level of aggregation units should be randomized. Obviously, if effects on individuals are under study, the individual should be the unit. But if school or neighborhood phenomena are involved, the unit of randomization must reflect the aggregate-level question and cannot be at a level of aggregation less than itself. Thus, if one is investigating whether the frequency of police car patrols deters crime in a neighborhood, one has to assign different amounts of patrolling to several neighborhoods and not, say, blocks within neighborhoods. The latter might make it difficult to detect effects, and it might lead to the situation where crime is apparently reduced in the experimental blocks but is really displaced from the experimental blocks into adjacent blocks. The use of neighborhoods as units would reduce (but not eliminate) such a displacement effect and would permit studying *neighborhood* crime.

Solutions

The problems associated with having a small sample of units can be reduced by matching the units before randomization. Indeed, given the high variability associated with field research, such prerandomization matching is always advisable. In most cases, the best matching variable will be pretest scores on the principal dependent variable measure. Consider, once again, the Lawler and Hackman (1969) time-series study. There were nine work groups, five in one experimental condition and four in the other. The conditions differed at the pretest, as we saw earlier, despite what may have been random assignment. Inferential problems resulted from this difference. What would have happened if the authors had been able to rank their janitorial groups by pretest absence rate from work (the dependent variable of major interest), and if they had then been able to assign the groups to conditions from within blocks of two janitorial groups each? The answer is simple. The pretest differences would have been less than what they were without any stratification prior to randomization, and the resulting inferential problems would have been less.

A second and obvious solution to the problem of sample size which results from highly aggregated units is to increase the number of units. After all, it does not inevitably follow from multi-person units that there have to be so few of them that pretest comparability is endangered, even though collecting more data means higher cost. Alternatively, a small sample experiment can be conducted at first; if its results seem promising, it can be replicated in a different setting with more

units. Worchel and Mitchell (1972) did this in their test of the effectiveness of a culture assimilator.

A persistent error of data analysis runs through many of the field experiments we have studied in which units larger than individuals were assigned to conditions. The data were analyzed with the degrees of freedom in the error term based on the number of respondents and not the (smaller) number of assigned units. This error is sometimes made deliberately on the grounds that the low number of degrees of freedom in the error term precludes a sensitive statistical analysis. (Just think for the moment of the t value required for statistical significance at the .05 level with 5, 10, 25, and 50 degrees of freedom.) To avoid this problem, it will be possible at times to reconceptualize the design and transform it either into a time series (by adding additional pretest and posttest observations) or into an experiment where the treatment is faded in and out at different times. Occasionally, it will also be possible to collect repeated measures between the pretest and the final posttest. Such measures permit a test of the treatment's main effect on scores that are particularly reliable, not only because they are formed by summing across all the individuals within units, but also because each unit's score is based on the sum of all the repeated posttest observations. The advantages of repeated measurement are most obvious, however, when the treatment effect is expected to increase with time, as is often the case. Under those conditions it makes sense to examine the interaction of the treatment and the time of testing to see if the difference between experimental and control means is progressively increasing before asymptote is reached. Fortunately, the degrees of freedom for testing this interaction will be higher than for testing the treatment's main effect. Thus, in a design with seven times of testing and nine units (five in one treatment group and four in the other) there would be six degrees of freedom for the interaction of the treatment and time of testing, and 42 for the error term to test this last crucial interaction. Such a test would, of course, be positively biased, because of the correlated error problem due to repeated measurement. However, Greenhouse and Geisser (1959) have demonstrated that the effect of treatments and times of testing will be bracketed by a test with 6 and 42 degrees of freedom and a test with 1 and 7 degrees of freedom. Thus, even though the true effect cannot be estimated, its limits can be.

Treatment-Related Refusals to Participate in the Planned Experiment

Problem

Sometimes experimental units will be randomly assigned to treatments and some individuals will refuse to receive the treatment that was scheduled for them. For instance, Ball and Bogatz (1970) randomly assigned preschool classes to two groups—those who were encouraged and those who were not encouraged to view "Sesame Street." However, some teachers assigned to the not-encouraged group insisted on receiving television sets and having their children view the show while others originally assigned to the encouraged group insisted on their children not being encouraged to view. Hence, some teachers self-selected themselves into treatments and vitiated that part of the design which dealt with studying the effects of "Sesame Street" in the school setting. Alternatively, there may be personal or political pressures on investigators to ensure that certain individuals or groups

receive the treatment or be excluded from it, and it may not always be possible to withstand such pressure.

Solutions

The solutions to this problem can perhaps best be understood by considering the stages at which randomization, and refusals to be in the experiment, could occur. The following discussion of these issues is taken from Riecken and Boruch (1974) and is based on three stages at which randomization could occur. Not all of them occur explicitly or separately for each project, but they are nonetheless involved. The stages are:

1. Once a list of eligible units is achieved, randomization to treatment conditions could follow.

2. Once potential respondents have agreed to cooperate in the measurement activities (pretests, posttests, and the like) which are to be shared by the experimental and control groups alike, random assignment could then follow. Note that this would be assignment from among persons who have agreed to cooperate with measurement but have not had the treatments described to them.

3. Once potential respondents have agreed to accept assignment to either the experimental or control treatments, random assignment could then follow. Note that this would be assignment from among persons who have had all of the treatments described to them and would be willing to accept any of them, including those that are less desirable.

Random assignment can occur any place in this sequence. The important point to bear in mind is that the bias due to treatment-correlated refusals will decrease the later in this three-stage sequence random assignment comes. Riecken et al. (1974) made the three steps explicit in a discussion of the New Jersey Negative Income Tax Experiment, and we cite their text below:

> An early decision had been made that the experiment could not be distributed randomly on a nationwide basis, but had to be concentrated in a single area where it could be serviced by a single delivery and research staff. Representative sampling of sites was thus precluded; instead, a judgmental sample of several sites was chosen, designed to exemplify a wide range of eligible recipients. Within the several New Jersey and nearby Pennsylvania cities thus chosen, the universe for sampling was all the poverty areas designated by the 1960 Census plus all other areas judged to have become poverty areas since then. Within these areas, modern public opinion polling procedures of randomized cluster sampling were employed. Residential blocks were chosen at random. For these blocks, all residences were listed. From these listings individual households were selected at random, in numbers estimated to be sufficient to find enough eligibles. Members of these households were then approached for a screening interview to ascertain the eligibility of the family for the program. At this stage, 20% refused to be interviewed and 21% could not be found at home after four tries. Of those who completed the screening interview, 18% were judged eligible and were then approached for a detailed

preenrollment interview; 7% of the interviews attempted resulted in refusals at this stage, and 14% were lost through changes of address and so on. As a result of this process, a list of eligible families was achieved.

From this list, random assignment was used to create eight experimental groups ranging in size from 48 to 138 families, totaling 725 families, and one control group of 632 families. Those assigned to the experimental groups were then approached with a request to cooperate with the income supplement system, the required record keeping, and the quarterly interviews. At this stage, 8.6% declined, with more declining in the less remunerative treatments. Those assigned to the control group were later approached for cooperation on the occasion of the first quarter interview, at which time 7.9% declined.

This brief scenario then leads to a suggestion about when randomization should be scheduled. The authors suggest:

> Since both experimental and control groups share the same measurement framework of quarterly interviews, one could first ask the entire sample to agree to this interviewing procedure, and then randomly assign those agreeing to experimental and control groups. Subsequently, the experimental groups would be invited to participate in an income support plan. If all accepted, the comparability would be maximum. The reports of the New Jersey researchers indicate, however, that a small number refused on grounds of unwillingness to accept charity. This could produce a bias, although similar persons might remain in the control group. Had things been scheduled in this way, it would have been desirable to keep those that rejected the experimental treatment in the repeated measurement study which they had agreed to. In later analyses, if one wanted to be absolutely sure that such differential dropout did not explain the obtained results, one would analyze these households *as though they had received the treatment,* that is, according to the random assignment, even though they rejected the treatment. A strong effect would survive such dilution. The analysis is conservative, leaning over backwards to avoid a pseudo-effect (pp. 58-59).

A second alternative mentioned later in the book (p. 175) would be to postpone the randomization one step further until all of the experimental and control treatments have been explained to each person, and he or she is asked to participate to *any* treatment group to which he or she might be randomly assigned. Only the persons who agreed to be in any of the conditions would be in the experiment, thereby making differential refusals all the less likely.

This extreme postponement of randomization has several disadvantages that restrict its utility under some conditions. One problem is that generalization can only be to volunteers. However, given the high dropout rate in many experiments, this problem is less acute than it appears at first, for external validity is restricted in any study where participants drop out. A second problem is that since participants are aware of all the treatment conditions, members of groups receiving less desirable treatments may envy recipients of the more generous treatments. This may lead to problems of compensatory rivalry or resentful demoralization that would make it difficult to draw confident inferences about cause. Yet such confident inferences provide the very rationale for the random assignment that produces the envy! In addition, we should not forget that the extreme postponement of randomization will not prevent all differential dropout, though it may be relatively more effective than the alternatives in reducing it.

The extreme postponement of randomization cannot, therefore, be recommended as a palliative that guarantees comparability. Instead, a practical compromise has to be made in each concrete situation between the advantages of initial group comparability and the anticipated disadvantages of treatment-correlated envy. Where it is decided that the consequences of envy or of reactivity in general are too great to tolerate, individuals should not be told of the other treatments unless ethical concerns demand this. However, no respondent should remain ignorant about the particular individual treatment he or she is to receive and about any adverse consequences that might follow from it.

Giving full details about the comparison of treatments seems most feasible where alternative attempts to solve a well-defined problem are being compared, rather than when a particular attempt is being compared with no attempt at all. Consider this in the context of research on the effectiveness of psychotherapy. The researcher could honestly stress how little we reliably know about the benefits of the therapies being contrasted. He or she could then guarantee to everyone in the experiment that, if they wish, they will receive the most effective experimental treatment after the experiment is ended. These same arguments can be made, of course, when a single therapy is contrasted with no therapy. But our suspicion is that it will be harder to convince respondents that we do not know whether a particular therapy is likely to be beneficial at all (else why do the experiment?) than it would be to convince them that we do not know which of several therapies is more beneficial than any other.

When randomly assigning organized social units such as schools, we would normally recommend assignment from among volunteers who agree to receive any treatment. This is because one is usually dealing with so few units that the loss of any of them after randomization has serious consequences for the design. Moreover, since experimental treatments often involve receiving desired funds while control group status is only an administrative burden, it might seem unfair to some persons if the experimental boon is given to units that will refuse to be controls if the randomization goes against them. Under these conditions, the assignment might take place at the latest step. Every effort should be made to anticipate and deal with both the reluctance of administrators to have their schools be in the experiment and the envy of teachers and students who receive less desirable treatments.

There are clearly a host of practical concerns that differ with each research effort and affect when randomization should take place. There can be no hard-and-fast rules about this important issue. But every researcher should be sensitive to the available options so that his or her final decision about when to randomize increases the probability of treatment groups staying equivalent.

Treatment-Related Attrition from the Experiment

Problem

Experimental treatments differ in their attractiveness to respondents, so that the number and nature of persons remaining in an experiment may differ between conditions if the experiment lasts any period of time. For instance,

respondents in the New Jersey Negative Income Tax Experiment were given guaranteed incomes of different amounts, and it is not surprising that persons who received the lower guarantees were more likely to drop out of the experiment (Kershaw and Fair, 1976; Watts and Rees, 1977a, 1977b). Indeed, the basic question guiding the research *demanded* treatments of differential attractiveness, thereby inevitably inviting the danger of treatment-correlated refusal and attrition.

In another study, Rosen and Turner (1971) compared two training programs for the hard-core unemployed and found that one of them led to less turnover than the other. This is entirely attributable to the difference between the treatments and is an important finding in its own right. But it also means that the two groups would not be comparable for testing other possible treatment effects. The same point is also made in the evaluation of computer-assisted instruction packages aimed at students in community colleges, for one of the hopes is that the computer will reduce the very high rate of attrition found in these colleges. If it did so in randomized experiments, the differential attrition in experimental and control groups would be of practical significance. However, it might also make it difficult to ascertain the achievement consequences of the computer-assisted instruction package since the various experimental groups would not be equivalent after differential attrition. The point is this: While differential attrition is itself interpretable as a treatment effect, any other posttest differences between the groups that remain will be hard to interpret because the groups will no longer be comparable by the end of the experiment.

Another point is worth noting about the difficulty of maintaining comparable groups over time. No matter how late in the sequence randomization is deferred, still further attrition is bound to occur when the treatments differ in desirability. This is especially true for individuals, but is probably also true when larger units, such as schools, have been randomized, for the differential loss of students within classes can still produce pseudo-effects. For example, the experimental treatment might be so attractive that it motivates families to remain in the experimental school districts, thus reducing classroom turnover in the experimental schools but not in the controls. Differential vigilance on the part of the research team in following up experimentals versus controls can have a similar effect: more experimentals may remain in the study than no-treatment controls.

The discussion of attrition here and the earlier discussion of nonresponse and refusals to cooperate make it clear that many randomized experiments in practice move toward quasi-experiments in which pretreatment differences are to some extent confounded with treatments. Nonetheless, it should not be forgotten that these same biases usually exist to a greater degree in more natural, less well-controlled exposures to treatments where systematic selection and recruitment biases determine allocation to treatments rather than randomization and subsequent differential attrition. It is likely, therefore, that initial randomization can often reduce the overall magnitude of posttest bias when compared to more casual quasi-experimental approaches.

Solutions

Analyzing for bias in attrition. Lost cases will almost certainly differ on the average from those remaining in the sample. Insofar as the dropouts are of the

same type in the various treatment groups, they bias sample representativeness rather than the comparison of treatments. Hence, they are a threat to external rather than internal validity. But how can one know that the attrition is similar across groups?

The first analysis is to test whether the rate or percentage of attrition is equal in all groups. If it is, the experimenter can usually be confident that no comparative bias exists and that the forces leading to attrition are of the same nature and of the same degree in all groups. While this may be true in most cases, examining the specifics of the setting and experiment may indicate otherwise. For example, in the pretreatment losses in the New Jersey Negative Income Tax Experiment as discussed above, the control group losses may occasionally have been mainly the result of low economic motivation to cooperate, while the experimental losses may in some part have resulted from the unwillingness to accept charity. If so, equivalent attrition rates (7.9 versus 8.6) may be the product of different selection factors which could potentially produce group differences on subsequent measures. Thus it is important to look for evidence of differential attrition other than by computing the percentage of those who drop out.

A second analysis, therefore, should be made of the reasons respondents have given for dropping out of the experiment. The purpose is to test whether the reasons are different for experimental and control groups.

A third analysis should be made using the prerandomization background data on the units remaining in the study. The purpose of this is to test whether the units remaining in each treatment group were comparable on these measures before the study began.

Finally, "pretest" measures should be studied, these being the pretreatment measures that will subsequently be used as indicators of a treatment effect. Such measures have a special role to play: they can often be presumed to have approximately the same factorial structure as the posttest measures. Therefore, they provide the best available single estimates of bias. This, in combination with the difficulty of maintaining randomly formed groups over time in complex field settings, is one reason why we recommend the use of pretests, even though they are not strictly necessary if randomization is successfully initiated and maintained.

Jurs and Glass (1971) have detailed analyses of the pretest data that are worth conducting to see how mortality affects internal and external validity. Their method can perhaps be most simply illustrated by imagining a 2×2 matrix with one factor being treatment condition (say, experimental versus control) and the other being attrition or mortality (still in the experiment at the posttest versus providing only pretest data). The dependent variable is the pretest mean of each of these four groups. If sample sizes are sufficiently large in each cell, a main effect of those who drop out versus those who remain can indicate a threat to external validity. A statistical interaction of the mortality and treatment factors suggests differential mortality and a threat to internal validity, for the kind of unit dropping out of the experimental group is different from the kind of unit dropping out of the controls.

If sample sizes do not readily permit a sensitive analysis of this type, then it is possible to compare just the pretest data of experimentals and controls

who remain in the study and provide posttest data. If such an analysis produces significant effects, this strongly suggests that attrition has produced pseudo-effects. Moreover, *under assumptions of stationarity*, broadly conceived, the pretest difference of experimental and control units who remain gives the best available estimate of the magnitude of the pseudo-effect that would be expected at the posttest. It will not be a perfect estimate, of course, and it will usually be impossible to correct for all of the differential attrition that may have occurred. The best one can usually do is to assess the direction of attrition empirically and then conduct a variety of different analyses of the principal outcome data, each of which is based on different plausible assumptions about the nature of the bias resulting from treatment-correlated attrition.

It is important to note that within the same study different measures, or different sets of measures, may have different attrition patterns. Because of this each set of measures should be treated as though it provided the only data available. This is in contrast to using one set of outcome measures to estimate the attrition pattern for another set or to using any procedure that results in a single composite body of data with a single attrition pattern. For instance, in the New Jersey Negative Income Tax Experiment, Internal Revenue Service records might have been used to provide measures of labor force participation which would probably have had a different attrition pattern from, say, the questionnaire measures of labor force participation that the researchers actually used. There would, of course, have been overall attrition from the IRS measurement framework because many persons do not earn enough income so that taxes are withheld or FICA deductions made and because government records are not yet organized for ready access by social security number or name. However, the pattern of attrition might have been different from that found using periodic interviews where attrition was most strongly related to the financial value of the experimental treatment. The important points about the IRS measures for the present discussion are (1) that the attrition pattern should *not* be caused by a lack of motivation to continue cooperating with the study, as was the case with the quarterly interviews; and (2) that any underrepresentation would probably affect experimentals and controls alike, which was not the case with the quarterly interviews.

An analysis using IRS files would not be perfect, of course. First, it would be naive to assume that all earnings would be detected by using IRS files. Such an erroneous assumption would be particularly serious in its consequences if the persons guaranteed larger incomes did less moonlighting work during the experimental period, for this source of income would not show up in any year's withholding tax. Second, the government records would not be as good or complete as the survey data collected by the project personnel in the field, and they would not be tailored as closely to the researchers' goals. And third, the data analysis of IRS files, while less likely to be biased by selection, would be conservative, for it would include all the experimentals who dropped out of the study but continued to file income data with IRS for nonexperimental reasons. Large effects would survive conservative analyses, but many researchers are reluctant to be conservative. So it is best to conduct both a conservative analysis and an analysis that is restricted to the experimentals who provided data at all measurement times.

Attrition from treatment but not from measurement. Some experiments are conducted to take advantage of an established record-keeping or measurement framework which has been developed and is maintained independently of the experiment per se. For some investigators (e.g., Stapleton and Teitelbaum, 1972; Empey and Lubeck, 1971; and Empey and Erickson, 1972), court records provided a frame, while for others records about withholding tax provide the frame. The advantage of such archives is that, while a respondent may drop out of the experiment or even refuse to participate from the very beginning, he or she is still included in the measurement system, and so posttest data can be collected from him or her.

The growing emphasis upon voluntarism and informed consent in social experimentation will lead to an ever-increasing number of experiments that use randomized *invitations* to treatments rather than randomized *assignment* to treatments. This means that an experiment which is planned to have two groups will have at least three: those who are invited and accept the treatment; those who are invited but refuse the treatment and are hence untreated; and those who are the intended controls. A widespread error in analysis is to compare the treated either with the controls, or with the invited-untreated, or with a pool of invited-untreateds and controls. Each of these strategies can obviously capitalize upon selection and result in pseudo-effects.

When a measurement framework exists, the selection problem can be dealt with in conservative fashion by preserving the original assignment to treatments and including the units who were randomly invited but refused as though they had in fact been treated. This will inevitably lower the chances of inferring a treatment effect because some units are considered to have received the treatment but did not. Many experimenters and sponsors of research do not want to underestimate effects by conducting an analysis that preserves the original invitation to treatments, though some persons have shown exemplary insight and commitment in doing just this (e.g., Rosenberg, 1964; Empey and Lubeck, 1971). However, when effects can be inferred from the analysis despite the conservative bias, conclusions about treatment effects are relatively easy to make.

The utility of the conservative analysis becomes apparent when comparing its consequences to those which result from the most frequent alternative quasi-experimental analysis. In this, all the units that receive the treatment are compared to all those that do not. This usually leads to "creaming" whereby the most able persons, who are more likely to take up invitations to novel experiences, receive the treatment. Since they are the ones who will look best after the treatment (even without the treatment), such "creaming" will result in pseudo-effects in nearly all quasi-experimental analyses. (Since "creaming" is a way of making programs look better than they are, it is sometimes deliberately used to create a spurious impression of efficacy—see Empey and Erickson, 1972, pp. 73–95.)

Using hypotheses about the nature of differential attrition. As we have said, there is no purely statistical way of correcting for differential attrition once it has occurred, since the violation of randomness also involves a violation of assumptions underlying the relevant tests of statistical significance. In some cases, how-

ever, we may correctly judge that these violations are of trivial importance. If so, our judgments about the consequences of attrition have to be made on the basis of scientific hypotheses about the real attrition processes involved, not on purely statistical grounds.

It will improve present data analytic practices if we make hypotheses about attrition processes explicit in the context of our own particular data about a project, and if we then conduct a variety of analyses under different assumptions about the nature of attrition, finishing up with a range of estimates of effect. In some situations, all of the estimates will be in essential agreement and final inference will be easy. But in others, the estimates will bracket a range of contradictory outcomes and will thus serve as a warning that attrition artifacts may be masquerading as treatment effects.

Though attrition processes are highly particularistic and bound to specific data sets, some general patterns of attrition can be presumed to be fairly widespread. These include the following:

> The children dropping out of control groups in education experiments in urban settings are likely to be the more able whose parents are disappointed with the regular schools and move out of the city or send their children to private schools.

> The children in educational experiments who persist in voluntary exposure to an educational innovation will be the more able, and the less able will drop out in greater numbers.

> The individuals who drop out of Job Corps programs, which guarantee an income during training, are likely to be the more able, because they are more likely than others to find work that pays well.

> The individuals who drop out of parole programs will be those who have the lowest chance of "rehabilitation."

> The persons most willing to cooperate with long-term follow-up will be those experimentals who received the most desirable treatments and feel most grateful to the experimenters.

> The individuals who drop out of, say, an experimental group designed to evaluate the effectiveness of day care for the elderly will be the oldest and most infirm and those who are less gregarious.

> The persons whose addresses are most up to date for follow-up purposes will be the experimentals, for they have usually had most initial contact with the experimenters.

These are only a small sampling of the many systematic processes that contribute to differential attrition, and more could be added from what is known in particular substantive areas. However, it should not be forgotten that even with the examples above special instances will arise where the bias is in the opposite direction from the one we indicated. In addition, while background knowledge permits us to anticipate the usual direction of biases associated with differential attrition, it

does not permit us to estimate specific values for the amount of bias found with specific populations on specific measures in a particular study. Nonetheless, to be able to anticipate the most likely direction of bias is useful, for the direction can be taken into account in drawing final tentative causal inferences.

Because comparability is more important than completeness for drawing causal inferences, it is more important to have similar attrition patterns in both the experimental and control groups than it is to eliminate some of the experimental attrition at the cost of causing differential attrition and bias. Thus, every practical effort should be made to anticipate processes like the above and to prevent them from subverting the randomization. For instance, it would be useful if the persons who collected the follow-up data were not the experimenters, for this would reduce the problem that arises when the same person delivers treatments and collects data. In addition the experimentals may feel greater loyalty or obligation to this person than the controls do. In a similar vein, the follow-up efforts should be restricted to the same addresses and background information for both experimentals and controls, even if up-dated information is available about the new addresses of the experimentals. Our general recommendation does not, of course, necessarily preclude special efforts to follow up the missing alumni of the treatment program. But this would be for conducting weaker quasi-experimental analyses of effects using the data from all the alumni who differed among themselves in the extent of their exposure to the treatment. Such analyses would not be readily interpretable by themselves, but they are more interpretable together with the results from the randomized experiment.

Finally, a concentrated effort should be made before each experiment begins to explicate all of the reasons why control group members might differentially drop out of an experiment. Where possible, means can be taken to block off some of the paths that lead to attrition. For instance, Hudson (1969) wanted to test the effectiveness of an autotelic teaching machine on economically disadvantaged children, but he was faced with the problem that the experimental children and their parents had to travel many miles to use the machine. It seemed, therefore, that more of the experimental children would drop out of the experiment than the controls. So, Hudson arranged for the experimental children to be transported by bus to the teaching machine—a simple but effective move that reduced treatment-correlated attrition, though it may also have affected construct validity.

Another more general hypothesis about attrition is always worth considering. This is that treatment-correlated attrition is restricted to certain subgroups of respondents or sites. If examination of the pretest data and attrition rates does suggest that there are instances where pretest comparability can reasonably be assumed, then these particular instances deserve special attention in the data analysis. For instance, Cook et al. (1975) were able to demonstrate that the planned random assignment of children to encouraged and nonencouraged groups resulted in comparable pretest groups at some, but not all, of the sites involved in the evaluation of "Sesame Street." These sites therefore become particularly prominent in the data analysis. But while the search for randomly comparable subgroups is worthwhile, it must be done cautiously. Subgroup analyses mean that sample sizes will be reduced and problems of statistical conclusion validity arise. None-

theless, if used carefully, the strategy of disaggregation will sometimes lead to salvaging some true experimental comparisons from what would otherwise be exclusively quasi-experimental comparisons.

Heterogeneity in the Extent of Treatment Implementation

Problem

Mullen, Chazin, and Feldstein (1972) tested whether a demonstration program of counseling for those who had just gone on welfare was more effective than the traditional program available to them. The authors found that, over 14 months, the number of face-to-face interviews with the counselor in the demonstration group varied from 1 to 129 with a median of 15 and that the number of telephone and letter contacts varied from 0 to 81 with a median of 9.5. It is obvious in such a case that there was considerable variability in the extent to which the treatment was received, and it would be unrealistic to expect counseling effects from individuals who had hardly received any counseling. Similarly, in situations where managers, foremen, or teachers are expected to implement treatments we might expect them to differ in the extent to which they comply across all the clients with whom they come into contact. There are many reasons for this very prevalent problem of heterogeneity in the way an apparently similar treatment is implemented—dependence on old habits, the absence of local approval for the new treatment, concerns about the identity of the sponsors of the research, the personal effort the treatment requires, and so forth. What makes this point all the more important is that analyses of effects by the number of sessions attended immediately becomes quasi-experimental, and plausible selection or selection-maturation hypotheses can usually be invoked to explain posttest differences.

Solutions

The problem of treatment heterogeneity is decreased, but not eliminated, when treatments are standardized. This would occur, for example, if the treatments were delivered by machines, as in some industrial or education experiments (e.g., Alderman, 1978). Even so, there may be some variability in the frequency of exposure to the treatment because of absences or differences in the motivation to use the machine, as Alderman discovered in his evaluation of the computer-assisted instruction system TICCIT. Moreover, machines are not appropriate for delivery in most treatments of interest.

Treatments are more likely to be standardized if they are delivered by trained research personnel as opposed to persons who regularly work in the environment where the experiment is taking place. This is largely because the research personnel will not fall back on their preexperimental habits of behavior as the organization's employees well might. However extensive the training for the organization's employees, it will usually not be perfect, even if it includes behavioral simulation of treatment implementation. Standardization is also more likely if there is intensive monitoring of the treatment to check on how it is being implemented. Indeed, one of the primary tasks of the monitoring staffs should be to develop and carry through a system for the *early* detec-

tion of "excessive" variability in the degree to which a planned treatment is actually implemented or adopted by respondents. Corrective action can then be taken which is based upon the monitors' analysis of the reasons for the variability. In addition the investigator or his or her staff should be available to answer questions from the persons responsible for implementing the treatment so that their motivation can be kept high. In some cases even a newsletter may help in which useful information about treatment implementation is presented and where individuals can exchange experiences regarding difficulties they have met in implementing their treatment or procedures they have adopted for alleviating these problems.

It is in the spirit of some of our earlier remarks to note that a more homogeneous treatment should often be implemented even at the cost of some restriction to external validity. Part of the problem of variability in the treatment actually experienced is due to the fact that potential recipients do not want the treatment. In some social welfare experiments in particular, recipients may only attend arranged sessions once or twice in order to enroll or make themselves eligible for benefits or meet some minimal eligibility requirement. One partial solution to this problem is to postpone randomization until all the treatments have been described to all the potential clients. Then, random assignment can take place from among the persons who state an interest in extended exposure to the treatment. It is not necessary, of course, that the data analysis be restricted to experimentals and controls from such a select subpopulation. Final inferences about treatment effects should also depend on the results of quasi-experimental analysis of the data from the subset of persons who choose to receive the treatment in different amounts. In other words, a comprehensive data analysis should involve multiple probes of the treatment effects. Some probes should be with a subpopulation of persons successfully randomized—analyses high in internal but perhaps low in external validity. Other probes should be with the subpopulation of persons who, for one reason or another, self-selected themselves into receiving the treatment in very different "dosages."

The Treatment in the No-Treatment Control Group

Problem

It is naive to consider groups without an experimenter-planned treatment as experiencing nothing between a pretest and posttest. Numerous events can happen to the controls over and above spontaneous maturation. For instance, Rosen and Turner (1971) had planned to use a company-controlled orientation program for the hard-core jobless as a control for a quasi-therapeutic package developed by a university team and designed to help the hard core adjust to work by finding group-based solutions to common problems. The authors discovered that the company-sponsored program was not a passive, information-centered approach as was thought. Instead, it had become a program with individual counseling and concrete behavioral support for the employee in his on-the-job difficulties with others. Thus, the control group became a treatment group. This may have been a response by the company to the knowledge that the other treatment existed (compensatory rivalry). In a similar vein, Ball and Bogatz (1970) randomly assigned children to

groups who were encouraged or not encouraged to view "Sesame Street" in the hope that encouraged children would view more than nonencouraged children. But the success of "Sesame Street" was so great that the nonencouraged children viewed the show quite heavily, thereby becoming more than the planned no-treatment control group (diffusion of treatment). Feshbach and Singer (1971) attempted to assess the effects of watching high-violence television programs on the aggressiveness of children by randomly assigning institutionalized children to watch programs with either a high or a reduced amount of violence. They found that the high-violence groups were reported as less aggressive. But this difference may have been due to the low-violence controls being frustrated because they were not allowed to watch their regular amount of televised violence. Thus, they were probably not an appropriate no-violence control group and they may have received a violence-causing frustration treatment.

Solutions

When there are grounds for suspecting that the control group fails to serve its no-cause baseline function, it is nonetheless important at first to analyze the data as though they came from a randomized experiment. For example, Ball and Bogatz (1970) believed that they were forced to use quasi-experimental methods in evaluating "Sesame Street" because some of the control group children viewed the show. Cook et al. (1975) took the same data, preserved the original distinction between the randomly formed encouraged and nonencouraged groups and demonstrated that, though some of the nonencouraged children did view "Sesame Street," the average amount of viewing was less than in the encouraged group. This meant that the planned experimental distinction could be maintained and that the data could be analyzed as coming from a randomized experiment.

Rosen and Turner (1971) suspected that unexpected events had affected their supposed no-treatment controls. Nonetheless, they treated their data as though they had come from a randomized experiment, and they showed that the intended controls outperformed the intended experimentals by the posttest! The authors were then faced with the difficulty of deciding how they should label the treatment in the control group because this seemed to be more important than what had happened in the experimental group. Indeed, the authors found it difficult to decide whether any effects at all had occurred in the original treatment group.

It is important to be able to detect unexpected reactions in control groups at an early date. Some may be anticipated at the earliest design stages before data are collected, and the research can be designed so as to minimize their effect. Others will become apparent during pilot tests, which are crucial if problems of unexpectedly large variability in treatment implementation and unexpected causal forces in control groups are to be detected. Without pilot work, the likelihood of premature experimentation is increased considerably.

Even if considerable discussion and pilot testing have taken place, this still does not eliminate the need for closely monitoring the controls to detect the unexpected and to react to it before it is too late. Indeed, this reason alone is sufficient for recommending that as much attention be devoted to monitoring controls as

experimentals. (This is a recommendation that also follows from the experimental desideratum of treating experimentals and controls in absolutely identical ways except for the presence of the treatment.)

If the controls do behave unexpectedly, despite preventative efforts, it is worthwhile trying to establish whether this is because of inadvertent treatment diffusion or because the controls are generally in rivalry with their counterparts (as in the Rosen and Turner example). The former process means that the experimentals and controls have had similar experiences, but the latter process can mean that they have had qualitatively different experiences. This is a point worth bearing in mind in any quasi-experimental data analysis which pools the planned experimental and control groups and then stratifies the units according to the length of their reported exposure to the treatment. Such analyses will be problematic in many ways under most circumstances. But they are likely to be all the more problematic if they are not sensitive to the possibility of unanticipated group differences in the qualitative nature of the treatment experienced in the planned treatment and control groups.

Unobtrusive Treatment Implementation

Problem

Most of the previously cited experiments were obtrusive because respondents knew that a treatment was being implemented even if they did not always know which outcome measures were being collected. It is technically desirable that treatments be unobtrusive, for this rules out many reactivity-based threats to both internal and construct validity. However, from ethical and perhaps legal perspectives, much technically feasible unobtrusive experimentation is not desirable since it violates the ethical requirement of "informed consent." It may also violate United States laws, though the issues are not yet clear on this last point (Silverman, 1975).

There are some innocuous but valuable field experiments where little time or effort is demanded of potential respondents and where respondents run no danger that could reasonably be foreseen (e.g., when experimenters drop letters addressed to mainstream political parties or extremist parties and then check the percentage of lost letters returned). Campbell (1969a) has commented favorably on such experiments which typically last only a few minutes for any one respondent and where the treatment falls within the range of the respondent's "normal" experience. Hence, a major problem with unobtrusive field experiments is that they are likely to be restricted in scope—that is, they are likely to be based on fleeting encounters between persons in organizations or on the street or to be based on mail or telephone experiments. They are not likely to deal with significant changes in respondents' lives or with unusual experiences, the reactions to which might be damaging. Though there are some published field experiments that do involve unusual acts (e.g., falling down in a subway car with blood coming from one's mouth), many people may find it hard to justify them and easier to justify more innocuous treatments.

Silverman (1975) has commented on the legal problems that unobtrusive field experiments might run into. He presented two lawyers with the details of ten

published experiments and asked them if they found any possible legal violations. A defense lawyer found few problems, but the other, an expert in prosecuting medical liability cases, consistently found possible legal infringements, particularly with respect to trespass, harassment, disorderly conduct, and criminal negligence. Though the determination of courts on such issues is not yet known, the general question is a grave one worth more study.

These are not the only legal issues. Consider one experiment from an excellent series by Feldman (1968). He had compatriots or foreigners in Boston, Athens, and Paris give too much money to taxi drivers; he was interested in determining how the city and the passenger's nationality affected the taxi drivers' honesty. Most of the drivers took more money than they were entitled to, and if individual drivers had been identified, they could have had problems with employers or with the law. If so, they might have been able to argue that they had been "trapped" by the experimenter and they could have used the "entrapment" issue to fight an indictment. Of course, Feldman did not report the identity of individual drivers, and it would have been desirable if he had not collected such data. However, if cab numbers had been recorded, he could have been subpoenaed for them, and since social scientists do not yet enjoy the "testimonial privilege" of doctors and lawyers, he would have had to produce his records or go to jail. There are, therefore, three legal issues: experimenters' violations of the law during an experiment, their protecting records from subpoena after an experiment, and their discovery of illegal acts by respondents during an experiment.

(Perhaps the most famous example of the last two problems comes from an obtrusive study, the New Jersey Negative Income Tax Experiment, where a Mercer County Grand Jury, suspecting that some respondents were fraudulently receiving both experimental payments and welfare, subpoenaed the experimenters' records in order to identify respondents. This placed the experimenters in a difficult dilemma: in order to protect possible lawbreakers who had been promised that their responses would be kept confidential, the experimenters would have had to break the law. However, the dilemma never reached the point of concrete decision making, for a legal settlement was made by the experimenters out of court. Though we have only just begun to scratch the surface of the relationship between the social sciences and the law, it is clear that unobtrusive treatments and measures lead to special legal problems, the ramifications of which we are not yet well aware of. But notwithstanding this, any experimenter would do well not to keep records that identify individuals or institutions in easily understandable form or for any longer time period than he or she has to.)

Restricting the range of unobtrusive field experiments to the innocuous and the unquestionably ethical and legal often leads to a problem of reduced treatment salience. This would occur, for example, if we varied the nature of signs in a factory, or sent out letters with different kinds of appeals for some prosocial end like blood donating, or varied the physical layout of offices, or arranged for different kinds of seat-belt appeals to be televised to different communities. In most experiments of this type one runs the risk that some respondents will not even see the treatment and that others will pay scant attention to it even if they do see it. After all, one characteristic of the "mundane" treatments that are unquestionably

permissible is that they are mundane—they do not stand out. Consequently, there will be a problem of statistical conclusion validity.

One example that we think typifies the problem comes from Bryan and Test's (1967) experiment on modeling and helping that was conducted on a Los Angeles freeway. The dependent variable was whether motorists stopped to help a female whose tire was flat, and the independent variable was whether the motorist could or could not have seen someone helping a second stranded motorist about one-quarter of a mile before they came upon the stranded test car. We wonder how many persons in the modeling condition were concentrating on the road ahead of them and failed to notice the first stranded car, especially motorists in the outside lanes or at busier times of the day. Or, if they noticed it, how many paid enough attention that the first car was still salient one-quarter of a mile later? In mail experiments, how many target persons do not even receive the letter if other members of the family get the mail first, open it, and consign it to the "junk and wastebasket" category. Or, if the target person receives it, how likely is it that he will read it closely rather than briefly getting the gist of it?

Solutions

One answer to the problem of the low treatment salience is to conduct large sample research, and the feasibility of this depends on the financial cost of additional observations. (Bryan and Test, 1967, actually followed this strategy and found that of about 2,000 motorists in the model condition 58 stopped, whereas 35 of 2,000 stopped in the nonmodeling condition $-.01 < p < .05$.) Another answer is to enhance the salience of the treatment. For instance, Bryan and Test could have conducted their experiment on a one- or two-lane road and positioned their first stranded car at a bend where it is harder not to see it. And in the mail experiments one does better to have individually addressed and personally signed letters sent by first-class mail that tie into the interests of the addressee. In some cases even special delivery letters or telegrams might be called for. The problem of low treatment salience is widespread in ethical unobtrusive experiments, but it can frequently be reduced as a problem even though it cannot always be eliminated.

SITUATIONS CONDUCIVE TO RANDOMIZED EXPERIMENTS

We have previously commented upon the possibility of control group members comparing themselves to experimentals and reacting differently because they know that they are being treated differently from experimentals. A similar problem also arises when persons receiving different treatments observe these differences and can communicate freely with each other about them. This is most likely to happen where the units are in close proximity and can communicate with each other or when individuals have common institutional affiliations, however distant they may be. For instance, in an experiment on the effects of job change and job enlargement, Bishop and Hill (1971) had manipulations administered to persons within work groups—all the work groups came from the same employment center for the handicapped. It is conceivable, therefore, that the respondents discussed why some persons' jobs were not changed, others were changed but not

enlarged, while others were both changed and enlarged. The effects of such treatment contamination are difficult to assess. However, it is at least possible that respondents in the job enlargement condition were led by the comparison with the job change condition to define their new work as a job change rather than as a job enlargement. This would then explain the data pattern that Bishop and Hill interpreted as indicating that job change and job enlargement do not have noteworthy differences for employees' performance.

We shall deal in detail with strategies for avoiding the contamination problem in the section that follows, paying particular attention to equivalent time samples designs and spatially separated units. The section is devoted to an explication of the situations that are most conducive to conducting randomized experiments in field settings. Once again, it must be stressed that they do not guarantee that a randomized experiment can be carried out. They only increase the probability of it.

When Lotteries Are Expected

Randomized experiments are lotteries in which each unit has an equal chance of being in a particular treatment condition. Occasionally, but all too rarely, lotteries are used as a socially accepted means of distributing scarce resources. When they occur, a randomized experiment is created, and the investigator must use his or her ingenuity to decide how to exploit the opportunity.

For example, Siegel and Siegel (1957) noted that a lottery was used to assign female students at Stanford to a dormitory for their last three college years. They also noted that some dormitories were associated with higher levels of authoritarianism than others and that the more authoritarian dorms were in greater demand by students. Siegel and Siegel therefore used the Stanford housing lottery to examine how joining a living group led to the adoption of the "personality style" of that group. To do this, they obtained measures of authoritarianism both before the women entered their dormitories and after they had been there for a year. As expected, the level of reported authoritarianism varied with the level of authoritarianism in the dormitory to which random assignment had been made.

Staw (1974) used the 1970 draft lottery to examine the effects of a randomly allocated reward (freedom from the draft) on organizational performance and on attitudes towards the organization. He did this by selecting ROTC program where some students had already legally committed themselves to military service before learning their draft number while other students had not. Staw reasoned that persons without any legal commitment would leave ROTC in greater numbers (and would be less inclined to join in the first place) if their draft number exempted them from military service. These effects were indeed obtained among students without a legal commitment. But Staw also reasoned that, if the theory of cognitive dissonance were correct, students who were legally bound to go into military service whatever their draft number would have a stronger need to justify their being in ROTC if their lottery number exempted them from service than if it did not. He also reasoned that being in ROTC could be justified if students generated enthusiasm for the program and performed well in it. Hence, he related draft numbers to ROTC grades and to satisfaction with ROTC among the students who were legally bound to enter the service. He found positive relationships which

indicated that men whose draft numbers would have exempted them from military service if they were not already committed to it liked ROTC more and performed better in it. Moreover, attrition from ROTC was not related to draft number among the legally committed, thereby increasing our confidence in the comparability of the students with different draft numbers who provided the data for analysis.

Sechrest (1970) has been attempting to use public lotteries as experiments on the long-term effects of income supplements, using small prize winners as randomly equivalent controls for large prize winners whose incomes are greatly supplemented. Obviously, such a goal has some overlap with what the negative income tax experiments have tried to accomplish. Hafeez Zaidi and Lee Sechrest (personal communication) are attempting to use Pakistan's land lotteries in a similar way.

A particularly important example of the use of lotteries for policy purposes is afforded by Zigulich (1977). Much of the literature on integrating black and white children in schools suggests that the achievement of black children is hardly enhanced by integration and that cross-race prejudice and stereotyping may be initially increased. A major metropolitan community has a Magnet School designed as a showcase of what urban education can be at its best. The school has a new building; a per pupil expenditure four times the average; fixed ratios of children from white, black, and Hispanic backgrounds; volunteer teachers; an innovative open-class format; and children whose parents are willing to see them bussed from various parts of the city in order to gain a quality education. It can be argued, therefore, that these are optimal conditions for school integration, and that if it does not achieve its goals in such an atypical setting, it will be hard to achieve them anywhere. Given the desirability of the Magnet School to urban parents and the publicity surrounding it, it is not surprising that the demand for places in the school outstripped the supply.

To deal with this situation, the school board authorities assigned children to the school at random from within racial strata. It must be stressed that the randomization was not done for research purposes. Its purpose was to meet ethical standards and to be politically acceptable. Whatever the motive, by testing children who were selected for the Magnet School and children whose parents volunteered them for the school but who *did not* get selected, one has an excellent context for evaluating the consequences of school integration at its best. To be sure, there are inferential pitfalls—the possibility of differential attrition, inadequate initial randomization, and a heavy reliance on archival measures. But these are all surmountable with enough foresight, ingenuity, and luck. Indeed, some of them are important "effects" in their own right. Differential attrition, for example, can mean that parents whose children do not get into a Magnet School leave the school district.

Here, then, are examples of the creative use of natural randomization to test hypotheses of distinct relevance to the social sciences. However, since formal social lotteries do not occur frequently, they cannot be relied upon as a means of creating probabilistically equivalent groups. This does not mean that we should ignore them when they do occur, since they can have both a theoretical and policy dividend.

When Demand Outstrips Supply

One signpost indicating the potential for randomization arises when demand for some resources outstrips supply. When this happens, there will be arguments to the effect that certain groups need the resources more than others and should have priority. Alternatively, it may be argued that some persons cannot under any circumstances benefit from the resources and should not get them, or that yet others particularly merit the treatment and should get it. Sometimes such appeals are specious, merely aimed at promoting particular interests. But if they are not, or if the only means of regulating conflicting interests is to call for a lottery, then randomization can be invoked as a credible rationale for the fair distribution of resources—a rationale that might carry weight both with those wanting the experimental resource and those dispensing it. Certainly, excessive demand is more likely to lead to randomization than oversupply. In the latter case, the person dispensing resources generally will be reluctant to create a no-treatment control group because he or she knows that sufficient resources exist and some persons want, merit, or need them. Moreover, in many programs financial reimbursement to those providing services is tied to how many places are filled rather than to how many are available.

Excessive demand often pertains in organizational settings. Consequently, randomized experiments could be conducted on such issues as who is allowed to participate in training programs outside the firm, which classes get additional teachers' aides, which economically disadvantaged parents get job training or fill vacancies, which applicants for early retirement can be allowed to retire, which factory work areas should have videophones, or the like.

Some practical problems associated with excessive demand issues are worth exploring. An operating agency cannot usually afford to have vacancies, and they typically have to confront the implications of rejected applicants' right to reapply for a vacancy in the organization. This means the creation of waiting lists, whether it be for day-care space, Job Corps training, or for special retirement home opportunities. Even in situations where there is acceptance of randomized admissions on the grounds of equity, it would be difficult to forbid an applicant from entering the lottery a second time, since such a prohibition violates the very sense of fairness that justified the initial randomization. Yet reapplication can produce systematic selection biases. (Before discussing such biases it is also worth noting that persons on a waiting list or in a reapplicant status are far from ideal no-treatment controls, for they may very well suspend the self-help and search alternatives that they would have undertaken had the program not existed at all. Such persons would not therefore provide an appropriate baseline against which to measure program effectiveness.)

If reapplication is permitted but left up to individual initiative, then successful reapplicants will be a biased subsample of the original control group who were not assigned to the treatment in the initial randomization. In this situation one could follow the conservative lead of Sherwood, Greer, Morris, and Sherwood (1972) and treat successful reapplicants as though they were untreated controls, thereby avoiding selection bias at the expense of underestimating the experimental-control difference. (Such a conservative analysis need not be the *only* data analysis, of course. Other analyses with biases in the opposite direction could be conducted so

as to bracket the true effect (Cook et al., 1975).) Another alternative would be to fill new openings in the program by randomly selecting persons from the entire original control group. However, this will avoid *all* the bias only if every invited person accepted the offer at the later date. Some might not, for they may be satisfied with the arrangements they made (retirement plans, day care, employment or training status, and the like) once they knew they were not to enter the program the first time around. To want an opportunity at one time does not necessarily mean that one will want it later.

Perhaps the best way to avoid the above problems would be to use the initial randomization to create two nonexperimental but equivalent groups. One would be an explicit waiting-list group, told that they are given priority for program space, new openings, or the next session of the training program. The other would be told that randomization has failed to place them in either the treatment group or the waiting group, their applications have been cancelled and it will be useless to reapply, and they should seek other solutions to their problems. This latter group would be the control group, and the data from persons in the waiting-list group need not be analyzed at all. Of course, persons from this last group can be used to fill any vacancies that occur in the program.

The details on how to handle the waiting-list group would have to be negotiated in the light of local conditions. Complicating issues include whether the waiting-list persons are to be given priority over new applicants who were not in the first lottery, as new applicants must usually be allowed for. Or should the waiting-list group be pooled with the new applicants for new lottery drawings? Or for age-specific programs such as day care, Job Corps, and retirement homes, should waiting-list status be limited to younger applicants and only for a specific time period so that applicants can be rotated off the list? Or should popular concepts of equity, such as "first come, first served," be invoked in some conditions to give the waiting-list group total precedence over new applicants? These issues have to be faced in the light of local circumstances.

When an Innovation Cannot Be Delivered in All Units at Once

When an innovation has been decided upon, it often happens that it is physically or financially impossible to introduce the innovation simultaneously to all units. This makes it possible deliberately to plan an *experimentally staged introduction,* with chance determining in what order the innovation is received. This then means that the units changed first and last are probabilistically equivalent and can provide an experimental and control comparison. Situations like this frequently arise in education as curricula are slowly changed or as new teaching devices filter down through the schools in a system. They also arise in other organizational settings, as when computers are introduced or new training schemes are implemented.

For many ongoing treatment programs, it is not even possible to introduce innovations into parts of the organization at different discrete, planned times. Instead, openings and applicants occur on a daily basis, and since beds or spaces cannot be left vacant for long, waiting times for those accepted must be kept short. Under such conditions, admission decisions often must be made for each applicant as he or she appears or for small groups of applicants each week. Due to

the vagaries of supply and demand, treatment-control proportions cannot be held fixed indefinitely at, say, 50–50 or 70% experimentals and 30% controls. If they were, the waiting lists would become too long or unused vacant spaces would pile up. Empey and Lubeck (1971, pp. 316–19) have provided a frank discussion of such problems, and the difficulties these problems can produce in implementing an experimental design.

If admissions decisions can be postponed for a weekly decision day, one might still fit the selection ratio to the vacancies each week. But pooling the applicants for several weeks into one composite would create problems. These problems are best understood if one recognizes that each week is basically a separate experiment, the pooling of data being superimposed to provide statistical stability and a summary estimate. For example, suppose that a series of weeks provided these assignments: 5E–5C, 7E–0C, 1E–1C, 6E–2C, 2E–6C, and so forth. Week-to-week or seasonal changes in the character of the applicants must be assumed. Thus, the data from the second week (7E–0C) cannot be used at all, for it provides no control group to compare with the experimental group. The subsequent characteristics of the 7Es are an undecipherable amalgam of the unique selection characteristics of that week and the treatment effect. Similarly, one should not lump the last two sets of E–C groups as they are, for the penultimate set might be assigned the week before payday, while the last group is assigned the week after, for example. They might therefore draw quite different applicants. Such differences can masquerade under simple lumping as a treatment difference while they are really the result of varied selection from batch to batch. A concrete illustration of this may help. Suppose that there is no treatment effect, and in week four applicants in both the experimental and control groups get an average score of 10, while in week five both average 20. If we simply lump these two groups, the experimentals average 12.5, $(6\times10 + 2\times20)/8$, while the controls average 17.5, $(2\times10 + 6\times20)/8$.

One simple solution to the problem is to discard cases randomly so that each weekly batch contributes experimentals and controls in the same proportion. Thus, if one were sampling to achieve a 50–50 proportion between experimentals and controls, the following allocation of cases would result: 5E–5C, 0E–0C, 1E–1C, 2E–2C, 2E–2C. Probably more efficient composites can be achieved. Certainly, computing the mean E and the mean C *for each weekly batch* and then using these averages *as a single observation* is acceptable. But weighting each weekly average proportionately to its number of cases will reproduce the simple selection bias if the number of experimental and control cases are separately considered.

Where a decision must be made on an applicant basis as opposed to a weekly basis, then a fixed rate of randomized admission must be used for a period of time. This rate should be chosen on the basis of expectations and prior experience with vacancy and applicant rates, but it would usually be unrealistic to expect an exact fitting of individuals to vacancies so that all the slots will be filled most of the time. Instead, a randomization process should be used which, on the average, would produce the target rate while hopefully keeping most of the slots filled much of the time. The target rate can be achieved by a reverse use of the table of random numbers. That is, applicants, as they come in, are assigned the next two-digit number in the column of the table being used. If the selection ratio were .35

experimental, .65 control, then all the applicants who get randomly chosen numbers of 35 and below would go into the experimental group, and all larger into the control. If the results of this process produced lengthy waiting lists or too many vacant slots, then the rate could be changed on the basis of the experience gained. If the rate were changed, the experimentals and controls selected under any one rate would be treated as a single batch, and the batches corresponding with different rates would be combined as above.

When Experimental Units Can Be Temporarily Isolated:
The Equivalent Time Samples Design

The art of designing nonreactive randomized experiments is to capitalize upon the natural variation in a potential cause so as to schedule when a group of respondents receives a treatment, or to schedule which of several treatments they receive. We shall now discuss several contexts in which natural variation in time can be capitalized upon.

One of the easiest situations for conducting randomized experiments is when there are multiple rotations—that is, when one group of persons undergoes an experience and goes away, another group comes and goes, a third group comes and goes, and so on. Each of these groups is isolated from the others in time and perhaps in space (if they come from different areas), and each group can be given a different treatment. For example, Mase (1971) was fortunate enough to be able to randomly assign one of two kinds of sensitivity training to 24 groups of persons who came for separate two-week stays at a center for pastoral counseling. Thus, 12 groups received each treatment in a blocked design where each of the treatments was twice represented in each block, and there were six such blocks.

Kerr (1945) used time in a different way that involved only one group of respondents. They received one treatment at one set of times and a second treatment at an equivalent set of times. The experiment took place in a factory, and its purpose was to test whether the presence or absence of background music affected productivity. Consequently, the work days were listed and then randomly selected to have music or not. Campbell and Stanley (1963) called the Kerr experiment an "Equivalent Time Samples Design" in order to highlight that the time periods when the treatment was present were made equivalent via randomization to the time periods when it was absent. The design is altogether useful under two conditions: first, the effect is not expected to be of long duration—otherwise, there could be no decrease in the magnitude of the treatment's impact once the treatment is withdrawn. Second, the effect has to be modifiable by continued exposure to the treatment—otherwise, there would be no increase in the effect after the treatment was received for the first time.

The equivalent time samples design is useful because it can be employed when the investigator has access to only a single institution. Consider the problem that Doob, Carlsmith, Freedman, Landauer, and Tom (1969) tackled. They hypothesized that discounting an article would increase initial sales but decrease long-term sales of various products. Their hypothesis was based on the assumption that customers bought the product because of the discount and not because they liked it. So, very creatively, the authors went to 12 discount houses, matched them for sales volume, and then randomly assigned them to discount or not discount

various items. As hypothesized, discounting led to lower long-term sales. Imagine, for the moment, that Doob et al. had only had access to one store. They might then have arranged that, for a given period, one random set of items would be discounted and another random set not discounted. After sufficient time had elapsed so that both the initial increase and the long-term drop were evident, they could then have replicated the study by having the previously nondiscounted items discounted and the previously discounted items sold at the regular price.

In much the same way, persons with a social reform intention could establish whether or not agencies were doing their duty. For instance, some organizations send white and nonwhite couples to real estate agents to see if they are given the same lists of houses for sale or rent. If there is a target real estate operator in mind, it would be possible to send in white and nonwhite couples on the same or adjacent days. This procedure could then be repeated at a later date with different samples of couples until a series of equivalent time samples was obtained. Or, if someone wanted to test whether police discriminated against certain classes of persons, he or she might drive a car on some days with, say, a Black Panther bumper sticker and on other equivalent days with a Support Your Local Police sticker (Heussenstamm, 1971). The dependent variable in this experiment would be the number of stoppings by police, and it would be imperative that the sticker be affixed without the driver knowing which sticker is on the car (Gordon and Myers, 1970). If he or she knew, this might bias the method of driving so that the number of times the car is stopped could be a response to the manner of driving rather than to the nature of the bumper sticker.

High internal validity results when treatments are randomly assigned to time samples, providing, of course, that there is an adequate number of time samples. Moreover, if random assignment takes place in an ordered sequence so that the different treatments or the presence and absence of the treatment are randomized within blocks of, say, four time samples, the data can be analyzed as coming from as many different replications of the experiment as there are blocks. Such an analysis would increase external validity. However, external validity is low in those instances where the design is used because of its feasibility with a single sample of persons in a single setting. (Of course, the design is not restricted to such contexts; it is merely most useful in them.) Finally, the design is vulnerable to threats of construct validity if respondents were to notice that the presence and absence of a particular treatment was related to time. For this reason, it is probably best to use the design when treatments are nonobtrusive or when the scheduling of treatments is random within larger time blocks so that no simple pattern of presence/absence can be ascertained by respondents.

When Experimental Units Are Spatially Separated or Interunit Communication Is Low

The actual experiment by Doob et al. (1969) on the effects of discounting on subsequent sales was made possible because discount houses are geographically separated from each other and the personnel may have minimal contact with one another. This makes it relatively easy to match discount houses and then randomly assign them to the various conditions. Lawler and Hackman (1969) were helped in their study of participative decision making among groups of janitors because the

different groups never met. Rather, each group received a new job assignment when it was already on a job. The members then reported to the new job without having to check back to some common headquarters where the members of different groups might have met and discussed the different treatments.

Robertson, Kelley, O'Neill, Wixom, Eiswirth, and Haddon (1972) were able to conduct a randomized experiment on the effects of a televised seat-belt campaign because homes in mountainous Pennsylvania towns receive television by cable and because advertising researchers had used two cables (A and B) to divide one town into two essentially random samples. This made it possible to assign the televised seat-belt-wearing commercials to half of the people. Observers were then posted at stop signs, and they noted seat-belt wearing and license plate numbers. Through state records, the licenses were identified with house numbers and thus with Cable A or Cable B. (It is not reported whether neighbors were ever aware that they were getting different commercials.)

In their randomized experiment on "Sesame Street," Bogatz and Ball (1971) provided either television cables or a UHF adapter to a randomly selected group of neighborhood blocks in areas where "Sesame Street" could not otherwise be picked up. Their reason for using blocks was that treatment contamination would be less likely than if assignment were by, say, homes within individual streets.

It is worthwhile pointing out a second strength of some of the above experiments besides the spatial isolation of experimental units. We expect there to be variability in which items in a store are discounted or in which public service ads are on TV; part of the experimenter's skill lies in tempering the naturalness of these features to deliver interpretable treatment schedules in unobtrusive fashion. Contrast this with introducing participative decision making or providing homes with special TV cables or UHF adapters. Such treatments are likely to be obtrusive because we do not normally expect changes in our lives to include participative decision making or obtaining a TV cable. Because of this, respondents will often demand explanations for such one-time changes, and in many cases the explanations will have to be research related. A change in TV ads or in the items discounted, on the other hand, is less obtrusive because we expect these things to vary in our everyday lives.

There are, of course, instances where the treatment is deliberately designed to stand out from what respondents expect. In these instances construct validity is not threatened as it is where unexpectedness is not part of the intended treatment. For example, Ivancevich and Donnelly (1971) conducted a randomized experiment to determine if telephoning persons who had just accepted jobs would decrease the percentage of persons who accepted a job but later failed to appear for it. Hence, the researchers had cooperating firms call a random half of the new hirings to answer any questions the latter might have had about the job and firm. The no-treatment control group was not telephoned, and more of the controls failed to show up for the job than the experimentals. What is worth noting here is, first, that the job acceptees were socially isolated from each other, and second, that the experimental manipulation was deliberately designed to make respondents feel that they were being treated in an out-of-the-ordinary way.

Spatially isolated treatment units are potentially available when organizations have multiple branches. This occurs with supermarkets, industries whose special-

ized units produce a common product, units in the armed forces, university alumni, schools within school districts, wards within hospitals, residential units of religious orders, branches of health clubs in large cities, dealerships that sell automobiles, appliances, and the like. What counts is that there be spatially isolated units and little communication among units. Of course, spatial isolation does not guarantee low levels of communication, and care should be taken to check that this is indeed the case.

When Change Is Mandated and Solutions Are Acknowledged to Be Unknown

A mandate for change can be issued when a situation is generally acknowledged to be less desirable than it should be. Often, it is not clear which changes should be made despite passionate advocacy of certain alternatives by interested parties. From the perspective of someone in charge of an organization it might not be at all clear which changes are worth making, and he or she might want to try out several alternatives. We suspect that formal experimentation is especially likely when change is required, no single solution is known or preferred, and several alternative kinds of change are possible.

The 1960s witnessed a powerful mandate for change in some aspects of the educational system in the United States, though much of the change took the form of haphazard nonexperimental program changes or quasi-experiments that could not be evaluated. However, some of the changes took the form of systematically planned variations. For example, Head Start was a response to the problem that, even before lower-class children enter school, middle-class children outperform them on standardized achievement tests. Hence, some of the Head Start programs were primarily aimed at teaching lower-class children basic cognitive skills, and some of these programs were evaluated by means of randomized experiments (Bereiter and Engelmann, 1966; Weikart, 1972). Performance Contracting experiments were also conducted in order to see if outside contractors could enter schools with prepackaged learning programs that would lead to a year's cognitive growth in a year's schooling. Unfortunately, though it was intended to set up the performance contracting experiments as randomized experiments, they were in fact implemented as quasi-experiments. The report on these quasi-experiments (Ray, 1972) does not allow one to infer without reasonable doubt which programs met their learning goals and which programs were more successful than others (see Gramlich and Koshel, 1975). Nonetheless, the strategy of planned variations was evolved and proposed as a response to a problem whose solution was not clear.

Though planned variation studies promise important results, they can have one severe drawback. While each variation might be partly aimed at solving the same problem, it will be rare that the persons responsible for each variation would define their goals *exclusively* in terms of the target problem. In addition, it is not always clear that the directors of the various projects would agree on the measures to be used as a means of determining what they are commonly trying to change. Planned variation does not make sense if apples and pears are being contrasted or if different kinds of apples are involved and no one can agree on an "apply taste test"!

When a Tie Can Be Broken

We previously advocated the regression-discontinuity design when "awards" are distributed to the meritorious or needy. Some scale of merit or need is obviously required to implement the design. It is realistic, we think, to assume that the scale will be unreliable and to postulate that there will be some persons above the cutting point whose true score lies below it, that there will be some persons below the point whose true score lies above it, and that, in addition, there will be cases of tied scores at the cutting point where the true scores are different—some above and some below the point. In other words, there is a region of uncertainty in which one does not know if certain individuals or groups fall above or below the cutting point. This is a prime situation for implementing a randomized design.

In 1967, the University of Illinois decided to admit students on a random basis. Their policy would have inadvertently permitted an assessment of the effects of attending that university if it had been possible to follow the controls to whichever college or university they attended for undergraduate work or to whichever job they took instead of attending a college or university. A public outcry ensued when the random allocation procedure became known to the public. The reaction was probably due to feelings that some meritorious students would be denied entry and that an inequitable criterion based on chance had been substituted for an equitable criterion based on merit (Menges, 1976). How different would the public reaction have been, we wonder, if University of Illinois authorities had (1) ranked students according to the university's established criteria of merit, (2) admitted as many of the highest scorers as were required to fill, say, 75% of the places at the university, (3) honestly pointed out the fallibility of the merit measures, (4) designated an equal number of merit scores on each side of the obtained cutting point as ambiguous, and (5) randomly chosen the remaining 25% of the students to attend the university from the sample around the obtained (and hence unreliable) cutting point. We suspect that, with careful public statements about this procedure, University of Illinois officials would have been able to randomize and test the university's effect on students in a particular merit range. They might also have been able to educate some members of the public about reliability!

A limitation to tie-breaking experiments is that generalization is restricted to persons scoring around the unreliable cutting point. While this is a very important class of persons when program expansion or contraction is being considered, we suspect that officials of many organizations believe that they are better at teaching the best students (or new members) than those who just manage to meet the established criteria. If so, officials may feel that their institution is not being sensitively evaluated. Fortunately, it will sometimes be possible to link a tie-breaking experiment with some form of interpretable quasi-experiment. If so, final inferences should be based on correspondences in outcome across the samples studied in different ways using different kinds of experimental methods.

When Some Persons Express No Preference Among Alternatives

Many organizations that would like to monitor how various parts of their system "work" have an opportunity to do this even if considerations of ethics or public relations require that assignment to the various parts of the system be by

choice rather than by lottery. This is because some persons will not want to express a preference to work in building A or B or to receive curriculum X or Y. The assignment of those who have no clear preferences can then be done by chance.

For example, Valins and Baum (1973) wanted to study some effects of "crowding." Freshmen enter one of two kinds of living quarters at Stony Brook. These quarters do not differ in terms of the immediate living space per person, but do differ in terms of the number of persons whom one is likely to meet in every-day interactions because of the building layout (more than 30 versus 6). The authors restricted their study to a population of 30% of the freshmen who had indicated to university authorities before coming that they had no preference for the kind of housing they lived in and whom the authorities had assigned to living units on a haphazard (but not formally random) basis. It would presumably have been easy to have had the assignment done absolutely randomly, which would then permit strong inferences about the different ways the living units affected students.

Whenever surveys are conducted to elicit preferences, it is advisable to include a "no preference" option so that later experimental evaluations can be made of the effects of the various resources about which no preference was stated. But any conclusions about cause from such an experiment could not be generalized beyond the kinds of persons who have no preference on the issue. Thus, if it were especially important to know how "keen" or "decisive" persons use resources, one cannot restrict a study to persons with no preferences, for the "keen" and "decisive" will have preferences. If the "keen" and "decisive" are of special interest, an inferentially powerful randomized experiment of limited generalizability should be conducted together with the best possible quasi-experiment that utilizes a wider range of respondents. Then, the results of the studies can be impressionistically compared, for the weakness of the one is the strength of the other. Where the results coincide, a global overall inference will be easy. Where they do not, a final uncertainty will be engendered about the quasi-experiment, but not about the limited causal relationship corroborated in the randomized experiment.

When You Can Create Your Own Organization

Many experiments on equity theory have involved investigators creating their own organization (e.g., Adams, 1965; Pritchard, Dunnette, and Jorgenson, 1972). Respondents in Adams's experiments came to work for him by answering his newspaper advertisement and had no idea they were involved in research. Having his own organization enabled Adams to control many of the respondents' experiences—the particular treatment they received, the fact that they worked in an isolated room where error-inflating distractions were held to a minimum, and the fact that they unobtrusively provided measures of the quantity and quality of work. Adams had this much control because the organization was tailored to meet his research needs. This was not the normal case where research has to be modified to suit realistic organizational constraints.

There are some other contexts where organizations can be created to facilitate random assignment. For example, it is difficult to evaluate the relative effectiveness of different drug abuse programs. There are many reasons for the difficulty—

different programs often have varying goals and attrition rates; they may provide different opportunities for creating appropriate control groups; and there may be much hostility to being evaluated, especially in terms of the researcher's criteria of success rather than one's own (see Cook, 1974a). Moreover, different kinds of persons are attracted to various programs for reasons of program philosophy, friendship, and convenience. Some of these problems could be reduced by setting up city-wide clearinghouses so that all new referrals have to go through the city- or state-controlled clearinghouse. If there were special reasons for assigning certain persons to specific programs, this could and should be done. But the remaining persons would be assigned to programs on a random basis and would form the population of experimental respondents. With sufficient tact, perseverance, and luck, such persons could be used to assess the relative efficacy of different programs.

The establishment of a clearinghouse could be used in some contexts for assigning elderly persons to nursing homes, children to day-care centers, or soldiers to units. It must be repeated that this assignment need not be coerced. Selection could come from a pool of persons who do not mind where they are assigned. Restricting the population to volunteers (but volunteers to be in *any* program) would decrease external validity. But it would not restrict personal freedom, and it would enhance internal validity over quasi-experimental alternatives for honestly assessing the relative efficacy of various solutions to a problem.

When You Have Control over Experimental Units

Being able to establish one's own organization is an extreme in control, and it confers many of the advantages of the laboratory. (The laboratory is, after all, a special case of establishing one's own organization in order to schedule events and treatments to suit research goals.) But most field researchers do not have the same control opportunities as their laboratory counterparts or the founders of organizations. They are more likely to be guests than hosts, and they may derive many of their possibilities for control from being associated with their powerful hosts.

Strong links to the host or to the host's benefactors increase the chance of randomization. We might, therefore, expect randomization whenever major funders of organizations insist that a randomized experiment has to be conducted. This tendency makes institutions like the Office of Education (OE), the Department of Defense, and the large foundations major catalysts of randomized experiments. However, the organizational separation of the implementing branch from the evaluator branch in OE, though justified in leading to unbiased evaluation (Williams and Evans, 1969), makes experimental implementation all the more difficult to achieve. So, too, do traditions of local autonomy. These dictate, for example, that states or school districts can spend funds as they want within certain constraints. Since it is not normal to require randomization, we suspect that some state or local officials would object if it were added to any list of constraints. It would seem to them like yet another encroachment on their sphere of authority and discretion.

Control is "the name of the game" in most organizations where subordinates expect to receive and carry out orders. The demands of experimentation fit neatly into this pattern, for control over treatments, measures, time schedules, aspects of

the physical environment, and the like are part of the stock-in-trade of experimenting. This aspect of experimentation has recently come under attack (for a review see Kelman, 1972). This is because, first, it involves the manipulation of people for ends that may benefit the researcher and his sponsors more than the respondent. Second, manipulation may take place without the respondent's consent and in a way that will make him or her feel like a pawn in the investigator's elaborate game. "Informed consent" is one way of alerting respondents to the risks they may be running, and this type of consent is now required for projects receiving federal funds. Informed consent means that experiments may be more reactive in the future and that random assignment may have to be from populations of research volunteers. But as things stand now, many experiments still take place in field settings where investigators have considerable control over respondents (more exactly, they have it conferred on them by their sponsors), and where respondents have little obvious counter-power. Hence, field experiments will probably continue to take place with children in schools; with the handicapped, aged, and infirm in institutions; with soldiers of low rank in the army; with factory workers who have weak unions or none at all; and with economically disadvantaged children and adults.

The relationship between experimentation, control, and the absence of effective counter-power is a sobering one that should indicate the long-term danger of abusing the control opportunities that are afforded to investigators who come as guests into host organizations. Even if we leave aside the important ethical problems and look only at pragmatic issues, it may be self-defeating to conduct one's randomized experiment today in a way that directly or indirectly demeans respondents. For in the future, we shall need volunteers—and the motivation to volunteer tomorrow may well be related to how we treat respondents in experiments today. To have absolute control in an organization one has founded; to have a large measure of control in organizations managed by friends or acquaintances or in organizations on whom one has been gently or not-so-gently forced by outside agencies that dispense funds; to have some, albeit circumscribed, measure of control as a guest in organizations to which one was invited—all of these relationships imply, to different degrees, that one will be able to conduct a randomized experiment. They also imply that one should be aware of how this control is used.

CONCLUSION

The case for random assignment cannot be made on the grounds that it is a general facilitator of high-quality research. By itself, randomization does not speak to such crucial research issues as asking relevant theoretical or practical questions, or having a close fit between operations and targets of generalization. Random assignment is relevant to only one of the many issues in research design: the quality of inferences about whether a causal relationship can reasonably be postulated from one variable to another. Nor can the case for random assignment be made on the grounds that it guarantees valid causal inference, for as we have seen, chance, systematic attrition, resentful demoralization, and the like are in many contexts plausible alternative interpretations not ruled out by random assignment. Rather, the case for random assignment has to be based on the claim that it is a better means of ruling out threats

to internal validity and statistical conclusion validity than most quasi-experimental and nonexperimental alternatives—i.e., fewer and less plausible assumptions about alternatives usually need to be made after a randomized experiment than after a quasi-experiment or a nonexperiment.

An interest in causal statements can be assumed in anyone who designs an experiment of whatever form, since the *raison d'etre* of experiments is causal inference. After all, if one wanted to collect data primarily for descriptive or hypothesis-generating purposes, one would use surveys or participant observation and not experiments. But inferring cause is not the sole purpose of experiments since most causal propositions with theoretical or policy implications refer to specific constructs and populations. Since some means of strengthening causal inference restrict construct—and particularly external—validity, one crucial question is: What determines the extent to which one should assign higher priority to internal validity over other kinds of validity? The answer is quite simple: The interests of internal validity are paramount when the cost of being wrong about a causal inference is high—e.g., when, because of experimental results, an ineffective policy could be implemented widescale or an effective one reduced in scope.

A second issue is: How does one minimize the damage caused by compromising one type of validity with another? Our answer throughout this chapter has stressed basing causal inferences on analyses of data from more than one set of comparison samples—e.g., from randomly created groups representing perhaps a restricted population and from a systematically assigned sample of persons not included in the randomized experiment who represent a somewhat different, though overlapping, population. Cook and Gruder (1978) deal with this matter in greater detail.

The desirability of randomized experiments in field settings is less in question than their feasibility. This chapter has included many examples of successfully implemented randomized experiments, and this by itself refutes extreme statements about the low feasibility of randomized experiments. So, too, does the list of initially mounted randomized experiments of Boruch, McSweeny, and Soderstrom (1978) which covers experiments in education, social services, law, medicine, mass media, mental health, labor force participation, and the like. Moreover, we have learned considerably from the "teething" troubles of the first generation of systematic field experimentation (post-1960). The present identification of both obstacles to randomization and of situations conducive to randomization would not have been possible without the efforts of the early pathfinders. The second generation should find random assignment easier to implement in the field and better understood by the persons who help determine access. Though there are clearly some situations where random assignment is neither feasible nor desirable (see the introduction to this chapter), the number of completed experiments suggests the feasibility of some experimentation with randomly formed groups.

It would be naive, however, to deny that many experiments which are initially implemented in random fashion subsequently break down and that the data have to be analyzed in quasi-experimental fashion. While such breakdowns will occur less often with effective field monitoring, monitoring will not inevitably prevent the breakdown of randomization when treatments differ in intrinsic desirability. However, we strongly suspect that a debased randomized experiment will still be supe-

rior to its feasible quasi-experimental and nonexperimental alternatives for inferring cause, since the assignment to conditions prevailing at the final posttest will still be partly based on randomization. With quasi-experiments the final assignment will be much more closely tied to biased self-selection factors or to the biased allocation preferences of administrators. If we are correct in this suspicion, the final magnitude of bias is likely to be less in debased randomized experiments than in their alternatives.

Nonetheless, each person who designs a randomized experiment would be well advised to think through all of the ways in which debasement can occur, to design ways of circumventing these where possible, and to incorporate into the design fallback quasi-experimental models to attempt to deal with anticipated patterns of debasement. The researcher should also implement field-monitoring procedures to detect anticipated and *unanticipated* sources of debasement early enough to modify the design. Moreover, he or she should try to measure sources of debasement and to analyze the final data using several methods to take into account plausible (and hopefully measured) ways in which the planned randomized experiment broke down. Designing a randomized experiment should never preclude the simultaneous design of fallback quasi-experiments which will use the same data base as the randomized experiment. Measures should be collected that will improve our inevitably partial understanding of any selection process which results because the random assignment has broken down.

References

Ackermann, R. *The philosophy of science*. New York: Pegasus, 1970.

Adams, J. S. Inequity in social exchange. In T. Berkowitz (Ed.), *Advances in experimental social psychology* (Vol. 2). New York: Academic Press, 1965.

Alderman, D. L. *Evaluation of the TICCIT computer-assisted instructional system in the community college*. Princeton, N.J.: Educational Testing Service, 1978.

Aschenfelter, O. The effect of manpower training on earnings: Preliminary results. *Proceedings of the 27th Annual Meeting of the Industrial Relations Research Association*, 1974.

Aschenfelter, O. *Estimating the effect of training programs on earnings with longitudinal data*. Paper presented at the Conference on Evaluating Manpower Training Programs, May 6–7. Industrial Relations Section, Princeton University, 1976.

Aschenfelter, O. Estimating the effect of training programs on earnings. *The Review of Economics and Statistics*, 1978, *LX*, 47–57.

Atkin, R., Bray, R., Davison, M., Herzberger, S., Humphreys, L. G., & Selzer, U. Cross-lagged panel analysis of sixteen cognitive measures at four grade levels. *Child Development*, 1977, *48*, 944–52.

Atkinson, R. C. Computerized instruction and the learning process. *American Psychologist*, 1968, *23*, 225–39.

Atiqullah, M. The robustness of the covariance analysis of a one-way classification. *Biometrika*, 1964, *51*, 365–72.

Ball, S., & Bogatz, G. A. *The first year of Sesame Street: An evaluation*. Princeton, N.J.: Educational Testing Service, 1970.

Barnow, B. S. *The effects of Head Start and socioeconomic status on cognitive development of disadvantaged students* (Doctoral dissertation, University of Wisconsin, 1973). *Dissertation Abstracts International*, 1974, *34*, 6196A. (University Microfilms No. 74-470, 268)

Bechtoldt, H. P. Construct validity: A critique. *American Psychologist*, 1959, *14*, 619–29.

Bem, D. J. Self-perception theory. In L. Berkowitz (Ed.), *Advances in experimental social psychology* (Vol. 6). New York: Academic Press, 1972.

Bentler, P. M., & Woodward, J. A. A Head Start reevaluation: Positive effects are not yet demonstrable. *Evaluation Quarterly*, 1978, *2*, 493–510.

Bereiter, C., & Englemann, S. *Teaching disadvantaged children in the preschool*. Englewood Cliffs, N.J.: Prentice-Hall, 1966.

Bergmann, G. *Philosophy of science*. Madison, Wis.: University of Wisconsin Press, 1958.

Berkson, J. Are there two regressions? *Journal of the American Statistical Association*, 1950, *45*, 164–80.

Bhaskar, R. *A realist theory of science*. Leeds, England: Leeds Books, 1975.

Bhaskar, R. On the possibility of social scientific knowledge and the limits of naturalism. *Journal for the Theory of Social Behavior*, 1978, *8*, 1, 1–28.

Bishop, R. C., & Hill, J. W. Effects of job enlargement and job change on contiguous but non-manipulated jobs as a function of worker's status. *Journal of Applied Psychology*, 1971, *55*, 175–81.

Blalock, H. M., Jr. *Causal inferences in nonexperimental research* (1st ed.). Chapel Hill, N.C.: The University of North Carolina Press, 1961.

Blalock, H. M., Jr. *Causal inference in nonexperimental research*. Durham, N.C.: The University of North Carolina Press, 1964.

Blalock, H. M., Jr. (Ed.). *Causal models in the social sciences*. Chicago: Aldine, 1971.

Bock, R. D. Multivariate analysis of variance of repeated measures. In C. W. Harris (Ed.), *Problems in measuring change*. Madison, Wis.: University of Wisconsin Press, 1963.

Bock, R. D. *Multivariate statistical methods in behavioral research*. New York: McGraw-Hill, 1975.

Bogatz, G. A., & Ball, S. *The second year of "Sesame Street": A continuing evaluation*. Princeton, N.J.: Educational Testing Service, 1971.

Boring, E. G. The nature and history of experimental control. *American Journal of Psychology*, 1954, *67*, 573–89.

Boruch, R. F., & Gomez, H. Sensitivity, bias and theory in impact evaluation. *Professional Psychology*, 1977, *8*, 411–34.

Boruch, R. F., McSweeny, A. J., & Soderstrom, E. J. Randomized field experiments for program planning, development, and evaluation. *Evaluation Quarterly*, 1978, *2*, 655–95.

Box, G. E. P., & Jenkins, G. M. *Time-series analysis: Forecasting and control*. San Francisco: Holden-Day, 1976.

Box, G. E. P., & Pierce, D. A. Distribution of residual autocorrelations in autoregressive-integrated moving average time series models. *Journal of the American Statistical Association*, 1970, *65*, 1509–26.

Box, G. E. P., & Tiao, G. C. A change in level of nonstationary time series. *Biometrika*, 1965, *52*, 181–92.

Box, G. E. P., & Tiao, G. C. Intervention analysis with applications to economic and environmental problems. *Journal of the American Statistical Association*, 1975, *70*, 70–92.

Bracht, G. H., & Glass, G. V. The external validity of experiments. *American Educational Research Journal*, 1968, *5*, 437–74.

Brand, M. *The nature of causation*. Urbana, Ill.: University of Illinois Press, 1976.

Brannon, R., Cyphers, G., Hesse, S., Hesselbart, S., Keane, R., Schuman, H., Viccaro, T., & Wright, D. Attitude and action: A field experiment joined to a general population survey. *American Sociological Review*, 1973, *38*, 625–34.

Bridgman, P. W. *The logic of modern physics*. New York: Macmillan, 1960. (Originally published, 1927.)

Broadbent, D. E., & Little, E. A. J. Effects of noise reduction in a work situation. *Occupational Psychology*, 1960, *34*, 133–40.

Bryan, J. H., & Test, M. A. Models and helping: Naturalistic studies in aiding behavior. *Journal of Personality and Social Psychology*, 1967, *6*, 400–407.

Bryk, A. S., & Weisberg, H. I. Value-added analysis: A dynamic approach to the estimation of treatment effects. *Journal of Educational Statistics*, 1976, *1*, 127–55.

Bryk, A. S., & Weisberg, H. I. Use of the nonequivalent control group design when subjects are growing. *Psychological Bulletin*, 1977, *85*, 950–62.

Bunge, M. *Causality*. Cambridge, Mass.: Harvard University Press, 1959.

Cain, G. G. Regression and selection models to improve nonexperimental comparisons. In C. A. Bennett & A. A. Lumsdaine (Eds.), *Evaluation and experiment: Some critical issues in assessing social programs*. New York: Academic Press, 1975.

Campbell, D. T. Factors relevant to the validity of experiments in social settings. *Psychological Bulletin*, 1957, *54*, 297–312.

Campbell, D. T. Recommendations for APA test standards regarding construct, trait, or discriminant validity. *American Psychologist*, 1960, *15*, 546–53.

Campbell, D. T. From description to experimentation: Interpreting trends as quasi-experiments. In C. W.

Harris (Ed.), *Problems in measuring change*. Madison, Wis.: University of Wisconsin Press, 1963.

Campbell, D. T. Pattern matching as an essential in distal knowing. In K. R. Hammond (Ed.), *The psychology of Egon Brunswik*. New York: Holt, Rinehart, 1966.

Campbell, D. T. Prospective: Artifact and control. In R. Rosenthal & R. L. Rosnow (Eds.), *Artifact in behavioral research*. New York: Academic Press, 1969. (a)

Campbell, D. T. Reforms as experiments. *American Psychologist*, 1969, *24*, 409–29. (b)

Campbell, D. T. Herskovits, cultural relativism, and meta-science. In M. J. Herskovits, *Cultural relativism*. New York: Random House, 1972.

Campbell, D. T. Evolutionary epistemology. In P. A. Schilpp (Ed.), *The philosophy of Karl Popper* (Vol. 14, 1 & 2). *The library of living philosophers* (Vol. 14, 1). La Salle, Ill.: Open Court Publishing, 1974.

Campbell, D. T. "Degrees of freedom" and the case study. *Comparative Political Studies*, September 1975, pp. 178–93.

Campbell, D. T. *Theory of social experimentation measurement, and program evaluation*. Research proposal to the National Science Foundation, 1976.

Campbell, D. T., & Boruch, R. F. Making the case for randomized assignment to treatments by considering the alternatives: Six ways in which quasi-experimental evaluations tend to underestimate effects. In C. A. Bennett & A. A. Lumsdaine (Eds.), *Evaluation and experience: Some critical issues in assessing social programs*. New York: Academic Press, 1975.

Campbell, D. T., & Erlebacher, A. E. How regression artifacts in quasi-experimental evaluations can mistakenly make compensatory education look harmful. In J. Hellmuth (Ed.), *Compensatory education: A national debate* (Vol. 3). *Disadvantaged Child*. New York: Brunner/Mazel, 1970.

Campbell, D. T., & Fiske, D. W. Convergent and discriminant validation by the multitrait-multimethod matrix. *Psychological Bulletin*, 1959, *56*, 81–105.

Campbell, D. T., & Stanley, J. C. Experimental and quasi-experimental designs for research on teaching. In N. L. Gage (Ed.), *Handbook of research on teaching*. Chicago: Rand McNally, 1963. (Also published as *Experimental and quasi-experimental designs for research*. Chicago: Rand McNally, 1966.)

Campbell, D. T., & Tyler, B. B. The construct validity of work-group morale measures. *Journal of Applied Psychology*, 1957, *41*, 2, 91–92.

Campbell, N. R. *Physics: The elements*. Cambridge, England: Cambridge University Press, 1920. (Reprinted as *Foundations of science*. New York: Dover, 1957.)

Cicirelli, V. G., et al. *The impact of Head Start: An evaluation of the effects of Head Start on children's cognitive and affective development*. Athens, Ohio: Ohio University and Westinghouse Learning Corporation, 1969.

Cochran, W. G. Matching in analytical studies. *American Journal of Public Health*, 1953, *43*, 684–91.

Cochran, W. G. Analysis of covariance: Its nature and uses. *Biometrics*, 1957, *13*, 261–80.

Cochran, W. G. The planning of observational studies of human populations (with discussion). *Journal of the Royal Statistical Society*, Series A, 1965, *128*, 234–66.

Cochran, W. G. The effectiveness of adjustment by subclassifications in removing bias in observational studies. *Biometrics*, 1968, *24*, 295–313. (a)

Cochran, W. G. Errors of measurement in statistics. *Technometrics*, 1968, *10*, 637–66. (b)

Cochran, W. G. The use of covariance in observational studies. *The Journal of the Royal Statistical Society*, Series C, 1969, *18*, 270–75.

Cochran, W. G. Some effects of errors of measurement on linear regression. *Proceedings of the 6th Berkeley Symposium on Mathematical Statistics and Probability I*, 1970, 527–39.

Cochran, W. G. Observational studies. In T. A. Bancroft (Ed.), *Statistical papers in honor of George W. Snedecor*. Ames, Iowa: Iowa State University Press, 1972.

Cochran, W. G., & Rubin, D. B. Controlling bias in observational studies: A review. *Sankhyā*, Series A, 1973, *35*, 417–46.

Cochrane, D., & Orcutt, G. W. Application of least squares regression to relationships containing autocorrelated error terms. *Journal of the American Statistical Association*, 1949, *44*, 32–61.

Cohen, J. *Statistical power analysis for the behavioral sciences*. New York: Academic Press, 1970.

Coleman, J. S., Campbell, E. Q., Hobson, C. J., McPortland, J., Mood, A. M., Weinfeld, F. D., & York, R. L. *Equality of educational opportunity*. Washington, D.C.: U.S. Government Printing Office, 1966.

Collingwood, R. G. *An essay on metaphysics*. Oxford, England: Clarendon Press, 1940.

Conner, R. F. Selecting a control group: An analysis of the randomization process in twelve social reform programs. *Evaluation Quarterly*, 1977, *1*, 195–244.

Cook, D. *The impact of the Hawthorne effect in experimental designs in educational research* (U.S. Office of Education, No. 0726, June, 1967). Washington, D.C.: U.S. Government Printing Office, 1967.

Cook, T. D. The potential and limitations of secondary research. In M. W. Apple, M. J. Subkoviak, & H. S. Lufler, Jr. (Eds.), *Educational evaluation: Analysis and responsibility*. Berkeley, Calif.: McCutchan, 1974. (a)

Cook, T. D. The medical and tailored models of evaluation research. In J. G. Ebert & M. Kamrass (Eds.), *Social experiments and social program evaluation*. Cambridge, Mass.: Ballinger, 1974. (b)

Cook, T. D., Appleton, H., Conner, R., Schaffer, A., Tamkin, G., & Weber, S. J. *"Sesame Street" revisited: A case study in evaluation research*. New York: Russell Sage Foundation, 1975.

Cook, T. D., Calder, B. J., & Wharton, J. D. *How the introduction of television affected a variety of social indicators*. Report in 4 volumes to the National Science Foundation, February 1979.

Cook, T. D., & Campbell, D. T. The design and conduct of quasi-experiments and true experiments in field settings. In M. Dunnette (Ed.), *Handbook of industrial and organizational psychology*. Skokie, Ill.: Rand McNally, 1976.

Cook, T. D., & Cook, F. L. Comprehensive evaluation and its dependence on both humanistic and empiricist perspectives. In R. S. French (Ed.), *Humanists and policy studies: Relevance revisited*. Washington, D.C.:

George Washington University, Division of Experimental Programs, 1977.

Cook, T. D., Crosby, F., & Hennigan, K. M. The construct validity of relative deprivation. In J. M. Suls & R. L. Miller (Eds.), *Social comparison processes: Theoretical and empirical perspectives*. Washington, D.C.: Hemisphere Publishing, 1977.

Cook, T. D., Del Rosario, M. L., Hennigan, K. M., Mark, M. M., & Trochim, W. M. K. *Evaluation studies review annual* (Vol. 3). Beverly Hills, Calif.: Sage Publications, 1978.

Cook, T. D., & Flay, B. R. The persistence of experimentally induced attitude change. In L. Berkowitz (Ed.), *Advances in experimental social psychology* (Vol. 11). New York: Academic Press, 1978.

Cook, T. D., & Gruder, C. L. Metaevaluation research. *Evaluation Quarterly*, 1978, *2*, 5–51.

Cook, T. D., Gruder, C. L., Hennigan, K. M., & Flay, B. R. The history of the sleeper effect: Some logical pitfalls in accepting the null hypothesis. *Psychological Bulletin*, 1979, *86*, 662–79.

Cook, T. D., & Reichardt, C. S. (Eds.). *Qualitative and quantitative methods in evaluation research*. Beverly Hills, Calif.: Sage Publications, in press.

Costner, H. L., & Schoenberg, R. Diagnosing indicator ills in multiple indicator models. In A. S. Goldberger & O. D. Duncan (Eds.), *Structural equation models in the social sciences*. New York: Seminar Press, 1973.

Cox, D. R. The use of a concomitant variable in selecting an experimental design. *Biometrika*, 1957, *44*, 150–58.

Crano, W. D., Kenny, D. A., & Campbell, D. T. Does intelligence cause achievement? A cross-lagged panel analysis. *Journal of Educational Psychology*, 1972, *63*, 258–75.

Cronbach, L. J. *Designing educational evaluations*. Book in preparation.

Cronbach, L. J., & Furby, L. How we should measure "change"—or should we? *Psychological Bulletin*, 1970, *74*, 68–80.

Cronbach, L. J., Glesser, G. C., Nanda, H., & Rajaratnam, N. *The dependability of behavioral measurements: Theory of generalizability for scores and profiles*. New York: Wiley, 1972.

Cronbach, L. J., & Meehl, P. E. Construct validity in psychological tests. *Psychological Bulletin*, 1955, *52*, 281–302.

Cronbach, L. J., Rogosa, D. R., Floden, R. E., & Price, G. G. *Analysis of covariance in nonrandomized experiments: Parameters affecting bias*. (Occasional paper.) Berkeley, Calif.: Stanford University, Stanford Evaluation Consortium, 1977.

Cronbach, L. J., & Snow, R. E. *Aptitudes and instructional methods*. New York: Irvington Publishers, 1976.

DeGracie, J. S., & Fuller, W. A. Estimation of the slope and analysis of covariance when the concomitant variable is measured with error. *Journal of the American Statistical Association*, 1972, *67*, 930–37.

Deutsch, S. J., & Alt, F. B. The effect of Massachusetts' gun control law on gun-related crimes in the city of Boston. *Evaluation Quarterly*, 1977, *1*, 543–68.

Dhrymes, P. J. *Econometrics*. New York: Springer-Verlag, 1974.

Diamond, S. S. *Hawthorne effects: Another look*. Unpublished manuscript, University of Illinois at Chicago, 1974.

Diaz-Guerrero, R., & Holtzman, W. H. Learning by televised "Plaza Sesamo" in Mexico. *Journal of Educational Psychology*, 1974, *66*, 632–43.

Diaz-Guerrero, R., Reyes-Lagumes, I., & Witzke, D. B. *Educational television for preschool in Mexico: A systematic and experimental summative of "Plaza Sesamo."* Final report submitted to Ford Foundation, 1976.

Director, S. M. Underadjustment bias in the quasi-experimental evaluation of manpower training (Doctoral dissertation, Northwestern University, Graduate School of Management, 1974). *Dissertation Abstracts International*, 1975, *35*, 6303A. (University Microfilms No. 75-7903, 193)

Director, S. M. Underadjustment bias in the evaluation of manpower training. *Evaluation Quarterly*, 1979, *3*, 190-218

Doob, A. N., Corlsmith, J. M., Freedman, J. L., Landauer, T. K., & Tom, S., Jr. Effect of initial selling price on subsequent sales. *Journal of Personality and Social Psychology*, 1969, *11*, 345–50.

Draper, N. R., & Smith, H. F. *Applied regression analysis*. New York: Wiley, 1966.

Duhem, P. *The aim and structure of physical theory*. New York: Atheneum, 1962. (Originally published, 1908.)

Duncan, O. D. *Introduction to structural equation models*. New York: Academic Press, 1975.

Durbin, J. Estimation of parameters in time series regression models. *Journal of the Royal Statistical Society*, Series B, 1960, *22*, 139–53.

Edwards, A. L. *Experimental design in psychological research*. New York: Holt, Rinehart, 1963.

Elashoff, J. D. Analysis of covariance: A delicate instrument. *American Educational Research Journal*, 1969, *6*, 383–401.

Elashoff, J. D., & Snow, R. E. *Pygmalion reconsidered*. Worthington, Ohio: Charles A. Jones Publishing Co., 1971.

Empey, L. T., & Erickson, M. L. *The Provo experiment: Life and death of an innovation*. Lexington, Mass.: Heath, 1972.

Empey, L. T., & Lubeck, S. G. *The Silverlake experiment*. Chicago: Aldine, 1971.

Farmer, E. *A comparison of different shift systems in the glass trade* (Report No. 24, Medical Research Council, Industrial Fatigue Research Board). London: Her Majesty's Stationery Office, 1924.

Feldman, R. Reponse to compatriot and foreigner who seek assistance. *Journal of Personality and Social Psychology*, 1968, *10*, 202–14.

Feldt, L. S. A comparison of the precision of three experimental designs employing a concomitant variable. *Psychometrika*, 1958, *23*, 335–53.

Feshbach, S., & Singer, R. D. *Television and aggression*. San Francisco: Jossey-Bass, 1971.

Feyerabend, P. *Against method: Outline of an anarchist theory of knowledge*. London, England: New Left Books, 1975.

Fienberg, S. E. Randomization and social affairs: The 1970 draft lottery. *Science*, 1971, *171*, 255–61.

Fischoff, B. Hindsight ≠ foresight: The effect of outcome knowledge on judgment under uncertainty. *Journal of Experimental Psychology: Human Perception and Performance*, 1975, *1*, 288–99.

Friesema, H. P., Caporaso, J., Goldstein, G., Lineberry, R., & McCleary, R. *Aftermath: communities after natural disasters*. Beverly Hills, Calif.: Sage Publications, 1979.

Gadenne, V. *Die Gültigkeit psychologischer unterscichungen*. Stuttgart, Germany: Kohlhammer, 1976.

Gasking, D. Causation and recipes. *Mind*, 1955, *64*, 479–87.

Geisser, S., & Greenhouse, F. W. An extension of Box's results on the use of F-distribution in multivariate analysis. *Annals of Mathematical Statistics*, 1958, *29*, 885–91.

Gilbert, J. P., McPeek, B., & Mosteller, F. Statistics and ethics in surgery and anaesthetics. *Science*, 1977, *198*, 684–89.

Glass, G., Peckham, P. D., & Sanders, J. R. Consequences of failure to meet assumptions underlying the analysis of variance and covariance. *Review of Educational Research*, 1972, *42*, 237–88.

Glass, G., Tiao, G. C., & Maguire, T. O. Analysis of data on the 1900 revision of German divorce laws as a time-series quasi-experiment. *Law and Society Review*, 1971, *4*, 539–62.

Glass, G., Willson, V. L., & Gottman, J. M. *Design and analysis of time-series experiments*. Boulder, Colo.: Colorado Associated University Press, 1975.

Glenn, N. *Cohort analysis*. Beverly Hills, Calif.: Sage Publications, 1977.

Goldberger, A. S. Maximum-likelihood estimation of regression containing unobservable independent variables. *International Economic Review*, 1972, *13*, 1–15. (a)

Goldberger, A. S. *Selection bias in evaluating treatment effects: Some formal illustrations* (Discussion Paper 123-72). Madison, Wis.: University of Wisconsin, Institute for Research on Poverty, April 1972. (b)

Goldberger, A. S. *Selection bias in evaluating treatment effects: The case of interaction* (Discussion Paper 129-72). Madison, Wis.: University of Wisconsin, Institute for Research on Poverty, June 1972. (c)

Goldberger, A. S. Structural equation models: An overview. In A. S. Goldberger & O. D. Duncan (Eds.), *Structural equation models in the social sciences*. New York: Seminar Press, 1973.

Goldberger, A. S., & Duncan, O. D. *Structural equation models in the social sciences*. New York: Seminar Press, 1973.

Goodman, L. A. Causal analysis of data from panel studies and other kinds of surveys. *American Journal of Sociology*, 1973, *78*, 1135–91.

Goodman, L. A. *Analyzing qualitative/categorical data: Log-linear models and latent-structure analysis* (J. Magidson, Ed.). Cambridge, Mass.: Abt Books, 1978.

Gordon, H. C., & Myers, J. L. *Methodological recommendations for extensions of the Heussenstamm bumper sticker study*. Duplicated report, Northwestern University, Center for Urban Affairs, September 1970.

Gramlich, E. M., & Koshel, P. D. *Educational performance contracting: An evaluation of an experiment*. Washington, D.C.: The Brookings Institution, 1975.

Granger, C. W. Investigating causal relations by econometric models and cross-spectral methods. *Econometrica*, 1969, *37*, 424–38.

Granger, C. W., & Hatanaka, M. *Spectral analysis of economic time series*. Princeton, N.J.: Princeton University Press, 1964.

Granger, C. W., & Newbold, P. *Forecasting economic time series*. New York: Academic Press, 1977.

Greaney, V., Kellaghan, T., Takata, G., & Campbell, D. T. Regression-discontinuities in the Irish "Leaving Certificate." In preparation.

Greenhouse, S. W., & Geisser, S. On methods in the analysis of profile data. *Psychometrika*, 1959, *24*, 95–112.

Guttentag, M. Models and methods in evaluation research. *Journal for the Theory of Social Behavior*, 1971, *1*, 75–95.

Guttentag, M. Evaluation of social intervention programs. *Annals of the New York Academy of Sciences*, 1973, *218*, 3–13.

Hand, H. H., & Slocum, J. W., Jr. A longitudinal study of the effects of a human relations training program on managerial effectiveness. *Journal of Applied Psychology*, 1972, *56*, 412–17.

Hannan, M. T., & Young, A. A. Estimation in panel models: Results on pooling cross-sections and time series. In D. R. Heise (Ed.), *Sociological methodology 1977*. San Francisco: Jossey-Bass, 1977.

Hanson, N. R. *Patterns of discovery: An inquiry into the conceptual foundations of science*. Cambridge, England: Cambridge University Press, 1958.

Harré, R., & Madden, E. H. *Causal powers: A theory of natural necessity*. Oxford, England: Blackwell, 1975.

Haugh, L. D. *The identification of time series interrelationships with special reference to dynamic regression* (Doctoral dissertation, Department of Statistics, University of Wisconsin, 1972). *Dissertation Abstracts International*, 1972, *33*, 2399B. (University Microfilms No. 72-23,054,198)

Haugh, L. D. Checking the independence of two covariance stationary time series: A univariate residual cross-correlation approach. *Journal of the American Statistical Association*, 1976, *71*, 378–85.

Haugh, L. D., & Box, G. E. P. Identification of dynamic regression (distributed lag) models connecting two time series. *Journal of the American Statistical Association*, 1977, *72*, 121–30.

Hay, R. A., Berk, R., & Reagan, M. *SCRUNCH: An interactive system for correlation, regression, and time series analysis*. Evanston, Ill.: Northwestern University, Department of Sociology and Vogelback Computing Center, 1978.

Hay, R. A., & McCleary, R. On the specification of Box-Tiao time series models for impact assessment: A comment on the recent work of Deutsch and Alt. *Evaluation Quarterly*, 1979, *3*, 277–314.

Hays, W. L. *Statistics for psychologists*. New York: Holt, Rinehart, 1963.

Heider, F. Social perception and phenomenal causality. *Psychological Review*, 1944, *51*, 358–74.

Heise, D. R. *Causal analysis*. New York: Wiley, 1975.

Hennigan, K. M., Del Rosario, M. L., Heath, L., Cook, T. D., Calder, B. J., & Wharton, J. D. *How the introduction of television affected the level of violent and instrumental crime in the United States*. Report to National Science Foundation, February 1979.

Herskovits, M. J. *Cultural relativism*. New York: Random House, 1972.

Heussenstamm, F. Bumper stickers and the cops. *Transaction*, 1971, *8*, 32–33.

Hibbs, D. A., Jr. Problems of statistical estimation and causal inference in time-series regression models. In H. L. Costner (Ed.), *Sociological methodology 1973–1974*. San Francisco: Jossey-Bass, 1974.

Hibbs, D. A., Jr. On analyzing the effects of policy interventions: Box-Jenkins vs. structural equation models. In D. R. Heise (Ed.), *Sociological methodology 1977*. San Francisco: Jossey-Bass, 1977.

Hickman, J. P., & Hilton, J. G. *Probability and statistics*. Scranton, Pa.: Intext, 1971.

Hollister, R. Comments on Cook and McAnany. In Klein, R. E., Read, M. S., Riecken, H. W., Brown, J. A., Jr., Pradilla, A., & Daza, C. H. (Eds.), *Evaluating the impact of nutrition and health programs*. New York: Plenum, 1979.

Hooker, R. H. Correlation of the marriage rate with trade. *Journal of the Royal Statistical Society*, 1901, *64*, 485–92.

Hudson, W. W. *Project breakthrough: A responsive environment field experiment with preschool children from public assistance families*. Chicago: Cook County Department of Public Aid, 1969.

Hultsch, D. F., & Hickey, T. External validity in the study of human development: Theoretical and methodologized issues. *Human Development*, 1978, *21*, 76–91.

Humphreys, L. G., & Parsons, C. K. A simplex process model for describing differences between cross-lagged correlations. *Psychological Bulletin*, 1979, *86*, 325–34.

Ivancevich, J. M., & Donnelly, J. H. Job offer acceptance behavior and reinforcement. *Journal of Applied Psychology*, 1971, *55*, 119–22.

Jenkins, G. M., & Watts, D. G. *Spectral analysis and its applications*. San Francisco: Holden-Day, 1968.

Jessor, R., & Jessor, S. L. *Problem behavior and psychosocial development: A longitudinal study of youth*. New York: Academic Press, 1977.

Johnston, J. *Econometric methods* (2nd ed.). New York: McGraw-Hill, 1972.

Jöreskog, K. G. *Factoring the multitest-multioccasion correlation matrix* (Research Bulletin 69-62). Princeton, N.J.: Educational Testing Service, 1969.

Jöreskog, K. G. Estimation and testing of simplex models. *The British Journal of Mathematical and Statistical Psychology*, 1970, *23*, 121–45. (a)

Jöreskog, K. G. A general method for analysis of covariance structures. *Biometrika*, 1970, *57*, 239–51. (b)

Jöreskog, K. G. A general method for estimating a linear structural equation system. In A. S. Goldberger & O. D. Duncan (Eds.), *Structural equation models in the social sciences.* New York: McGraw-Hill, 1973.

Jöreskog, K. G. Analyzing psychological data by structural analysis of covariance matrices. In R. C. Atkinson, D. H. Krantz, & P. D. Suppes (Eds.), *Contemporary developments in mathematical psychology* (Vol. 2). San Francisco: W. H. Freeman, 1974.

Jöreskog, K. G. Structural equation models in the social sciences: Specification, estimation and testing. In P. R. Krishnaiah (Ed.), *Application of statistics.* Amsterdam: North Holland, 1977.

Jöreskog, K. G., & Goldberger, A. S. Estimation of a model with multiple indicators and multiple causes of a single latent variable. *Journal of the American Statistical Association*, 1975, *10*, 631–39.

Jöreskog, K. G., & Sörbom, D. Some models and estimation methods for analysis of longitudinal data. In D. J. Aigner & A. S. Goldberger (Eds.), *Latent variables in socioeconomic models.* Amsterdam: North Holland, 1976. (a)

Jöreskog, K. G., & Sörbom, D. *LISREL–Estimation of linear structural equation systems by maximum likelihood methods.* Chicago: International Educational Services, 1976. (b)

Jöreskog, K. G., & Sörbom, D. *LISREL IV: Analysis of linear structural relationships by the method of maximum likelihood: User's guide.* Chicago: International Educational Services, 1978.

Jurs, S. G., & Glass, G. V. The effect of experimental mortality on the internal and external validity of the randomized comparative experiment. *Journal of Experimental Education*, 1971, *40*, 62–66.

Keat, R., & Urry, J. *Social theory as science.* London: Routledge & Kegan Paul, 1975.

Keesling, J. W., & Wiley, D. E. *Measurement error and the analysis of quasi-experimental data, Version IV.* Unpublished manuscript, University of Southern California, 1976.

Kelman, H. C. The rights of the subject in social research: An analysis in terms of relative power and legitimacy. *American Psychologist*, 1972, *27*, 989–1016.

Kenny, D. A. Cross-lagged and synchronous common factors in panel data. In A. S. Goldenberger and O. D. Duncan (Eds.), *Structural equation models in the social sciences.* New York: Seminar Press, 1973.

Kenny, D. A. Cross-lagged panel correlations: A test for spuriousness. *Psychological Bulletin*, 1975, *82*, 887–903. (a)

Kenny, D. A. Panel data analysis of the first year of "Sesame Street" Unpublished research report, Harvard University, Department of Psychology, 1975. (b)

Kenny, D.A. A quasi-experimental approach to assessing treatment effects in the nonequivalent control group design. *Psychological Bulletin*, 1975, *82*, 345–62. (c)

Kerlinger, F. N., & Pedhazur, E. J., *Multiple regression in behavioral research.* New York: Holt, Rinehart, 1973.

Kerpelman, L. C., Fox, G., Nunes, D., Muse, D., & Stoner, D. *Evaluation of the effectiveness of outdoor power equipment information and education programs.* Final report of Abt Associates to U.S. Consumer Product Safety Commission, 1978.

Kerr, W. A. Experiments on the effect of music on factory production. *Applied Psychology Monographs*, 1945, *5*.

Kershaw, D., & Fair, J. Operations, surveys, and administration. *The New Jersey Income Maintenance Experiment* (Vol. 3). New York: Academic Press, 1976.

Khatri, C. G. A note on a MANOVA model applied to problems in growth curves. *Annals of the Institute of Statistical Mathematics*, 1966, *18*, 75–86.

Kirk, R. E. *Experimental design procedures for the behavioral sciences.* Belmont, Calif.: Brooks/Cole, 1968.

Kish, L. *Survey sampling.* New York: Wiley, 1965.

Kmenta, J. *Elements of econometrics.* New York: Macmillan, 1971.

Kruglanski, A. W., & Kroy, M. Outcome validity in experimental research: A re-conceptualization. *Journal of Representative Research in Social Psychology*, 1975, *7*, 168–78.

Kuhn, T. S. *The structure of scientific revolutions.* Chicago: University of Chicago Press, 1962.

Kuhn, T. S. Theory-change as structure-change: Comments on the Sneed formalism. *Erkenntnis*, 1976, *10*, 179–99.

Lana, R. C. Pretest sensitization. In R. Rosenthal & R. L. Rosnow (Eds.), *Artifact in behavioral research.* New York: Academic Press, 1969.

Larson, R. C. What happened to patrol operations in Kansas City? *Evaluation*, 1976, *3*, 117–23.

Lave, L. B., & Seskin, E. P. *Air pollution and human health.* Baltimore: Resources for the Future, Johns Hopkins University Press, 1977.

Lawler, E. E., III, & Hackman, J. R. Impact of employee participation in the development of pay incentive plans: A field experiment. *Journal of Applied Psychology*, 1969, *53*, 467–71.

Lazarsfeld, P. F. *The mutual effects of statistical variables.* Duplicated report, Columbia University, Bureau of Applied Social Research, 1947.

Lazarsfeld, P. F. The use of panels in social research. *Proceedings of the American Philosophical Society*, 1948, *92*, 405–10.

Lazarsfeld, P. F. Mutual effects of statistical variables. In P. F. Lazarsfeld, A. K. Pasanella, & M. Rosenberg (Eds.), *Continuities in the language of social research.* New York: Free Press, 1972.

Lazarsfeld, P. F. Some episodes in the history of panel analysis. In D. B. Kandel (Ed.), *Longitudinal research on drug abuse.* New York: Hemisphere Press, 1978.

Lee, S. H. *Cross-correlogram and the causal structure between two time series.* Unpublished manuscript, Northwestern University, 1977.

Lewin, K. *Field theory in social sciences.* New York: Harper, 1951.

Lieberman, S. The effects of changes in roles on the attitudes of role occupants. *Human Relations*, 1956, *9*, 385–402.

Lindley, D. V. Regression lines and the linear functional relationship. *Journal of the Royal Statistical Society,*

Series B, 1947, *9*, 218–24.

Lindquist, E. F. *Design and analysis of experiments in psychology and education.* Boston: Houghton Mifflin, 1953.

Linn, R. L., & Werts, C. E. Analysis implications of the choice of a structural model in the nonequivalent control group design. *Psychological Bulletin,* 1977, *84*, 229–34.

Lipset, S. M., Lazarsfeld, P. F., Barton, A. H., & Linz, J. The psychology of voting: An analysis of political behavior. In G. Lindzey (Ed.), *Handbook of social psychology* (Vol. 2). Reading, Mass.: Addison-Wesley, 1954.

Lohr, B. W. *An historical view of the research on the factors related to the utilization of health services.* Duplicated research report, Bureau for Health Services Research and Evaluation, Social and Economic Analysis Division, Rockville, Md., January 1972.

Long, J. S. Estimation and hypotheses testing in linear models containing measurement error: A review of Jöreskog's model for the analysis of covariance structures. *Sociological Methods and Research,* 1976, *5*, 157–206.

Lord, F. M. The measurement of growth. *Educational and Psychological Measurement,* 1956, *16*, 421–37. (See also Errata, *ibid.,* 1957, *17*, 452.)

Lord, F. M. Further problems in the measurement of growth. *Educational and Psychological Measurement,* 1958, *18*, 437–54.

Lord, F. M. Large-sample covariance analysis when the control variable is fallible. *Journal of the American Statistical Association,* 1960, *55*, 307–21.

Lord, F. M. Elementary models for measuring change. In C. W. Harris (Ed.), *Problems in measuring change.* Madison, Wis.: University of Wisconsin Press, 1963.

Lord, F. M. A paradox in the interpretation of group comparisons. *Psychological Bulletin,* 1967, *68*, 304–5.

MacCorquodale, K., & Meehl, P. E. On a distinction between hypothetical constructs and intervening variables. *Psychological Review,* 1948, *55*, 95–107.

Madansky, A. The fitting of straight lines when both variables are subject to error. *Journal of the American Statistical Association,* 1959, *54*, 173–205.

Magidson, J. Towards a causal model approach for adjusting for pre-existing differences in the nonequivalent control group situation: A general alternative to ANCOVA. *Evaluation Quarterly,* 1977, *1*, 399–420.

Magidson, J. Reply to Bentler and Woodward: The .05 significance level is not all-powerful. *Evaluation Quarterly,* 1978, *2*, 511–20.

Malinvaud, E. *Statistical methods of econometrics.* Amsterdam: North Holland, 1970.

Mandelbaum, M. *Philosophy, science, and sense perception.* Baltimore: Johns Hopkins University Press, 1964.

Mase, B. F. *Changes in self-actualization as a result of two types of residential group experience.* Unpublished doctoral dissertation, Northwestern University, 1971.

Maxwell, G. Russell on perception: A study in philosophical method. D. Pears (Ed.) *Russell: A collection of critical essays.* New York: Doubleday Anchor Books, 1972.

Mayer, T. F., & Arney, W. R. Spectral analysis and the

study of social change. In H. L. Costner (Ed.), *Sociological methodology 1973-1974.* San Francisco: Jossey-Bass, 1974.

McCall, W. A. *How to experiment in education.* New York: Macmillan, 1923.

McNemar, Q. A critical examination of the University of Iowa studies of environmental influences upon the I.Q. *Psychological Bulletin,* 1940, *37*, 63–92.

McNemar, Q. *Psychological statistics* (5th ed.). New York: Wiley, 1975.

McSweeny, A. J. The effects of response cost on the behavior of a million persons: Charging for directory assistance in Cincinnati. *Journal of Applied Behavior Analysis,* 1978, *11*, 47–51.

Menges, R. J. College admissions by lottery: A case of resistance to random selection. *Evaluation,* 1976, *3*, 40–42.

Michotte, A. *The perception of causality* (1st English ed.). New York: Basic Books, 1963.

Minton, J. H. The impact of Sesame Street on reading readiness of kindergarten children. (Doctoral dissertation, Fordham University, 1972.) *Dissertation Abstracts International,* 1973, *33*, 3396A. (University Microfilms No. 73-1516, 168)

Minton, J. H. The impact of Sesame Street on reading readiness of kindergarten children. *Sociology of Education,* 1975, *48*, 141–51.

Mitroff, I. I., & Bonoma, T. V. Psychological assumptions, experimentation, and old world problems: A critique and an alternative approach to evaluation. *Evaluation Quarterly,* 1978, *2*, 235–60.

Mitroff, I. I., & Kilman, R. H. *Methodological approaches to social science.* San Francisco: Jossey-Bass, 1978.

Morrison, D. F. *Multivariate statistical methods* (2nd ed.). New York: McGraw-Hill, 1976.

Morse, N. C., & Reimer, E. The experimental change of a major organizational variable. *Journal of Abnormal and Social Psychology,* 1956, *52*, 120–29.

Mullen, E. J., Chazin, R. M., & Feldstein, D. M. Services for the newly dependent: An assessment. *The Social Service Review,* 1972, *46*, 309–22.

Myers, J. L. *Fundamentals of experimental design* (2nd ed.). Boston: Allyn and Bacon, 1972.

Nerlove, M. Spectral analyses of seasonal adjustment procedures. *Econometrica,* 1964, *32*, 241–85.

Nisbett, R. E., & Kanouse, D. E. Obesity, food deprivation, and supermarket shopping behavior. *Journal of Personality and Social Psychology,* 1969, *12*, 289–94.

Northrop, F. S. C. *The logic of the sciences and the humanities.* New York: Meridian Books, 1959.

Northrop, F. S. C., & Livingston, H. H. (Eds.). *Cross-cultural understanding: Epistemology in anthropology.* New York: Harper & Row, 1964.

Notz, W. W., Staw, B. M., & Cook, T. D. Attitude toward troop withdrawal from Indochina as a function of draft number: Dissonance or self-interest? *Journal of Personality and Social Psychology,* 1971, *20*, 118–26.

Ogburn, W. F., & Thomas, D. S. The influence of the business cycle on certain social conditions. *Journal of the American Statistical Association,* 1922, *18*, 324–40.

Ozaki, T. On the order of determination of ARIMA

models. *Journal of the Royal Statistical Society,* Series B, 1977, *26*, 290–301.

Pack, D. J. *A computer program for the analysis of time-series models using the Box-Jenkins philosophy.* Hatboro, Pa.: Automatic Forecasting Systems, 1978.

Parker, E. B. The effects of television on public library circulation. *Public Opinion Quarterly,* 1963, *27*, 578–89.

Parker, E. B., Campbell, D. T., Cook, T. D., Katzman, N., & Butler-Paisley, M. *Time-series analysis of effects of television on library circulation in Illinois.* Unpublished paper, Northwestern University, 1971.

Pearson, K. *The grammar of science.* New York: Meridian Books, 1937. (Originally published, 1892.)

Pelz, D. C., & Andrews, F. M. Detecting causal priorities in panel study data. *American Sociological Review,* 1964, *29*, 836–48.

Pierce, D. A. *R² measures for time series.* Special studies paper. Washington, D.C.: Federal Reserve Board, 1977.

Pierce, D. A. & Haugy, L. D. Causality in temporal systems: Characterizations in a survey. *Journal of Econometrics,* 1977, *5*, 265–93.

Popper, K. R. *The logic of scientific discovery.* New York: Basic Books, 1959. (Originally *Die Logik der Forschung,* 1935.)

Popper, K. R. *Objective knowledge: An evolutionary approach.* Oxford, England: Clarendon Press, 1972.

Porter, A. C. *The effects of using fallible variables in the analysis of covariance.* (Doctoral dissertation, University of Wisconsin, 1967.) *Dissertation Abstracts International,* 1968, *28*, 3517B. (University Microfilms No. 67-12, 147, 144)

Porter, A. C. *Analysis strategies for some common evaluation paradigms.* Paper presented at American Educational Research Association convention, 1973.

Porter, A. C., & Chibucos, T. R. Selecting analysis strategies. In G. D. Borich (Ed.), *Evaluating educational programs and products.* Englewood Cliffs, N.J.: Educational Technology Publication, 1974.

Pothoff, R. F., & Roy, S. N. A generalized multivariate analysis of variance models useful especially for growth curve problems. *Biometrika,* 1964, *51*, 313–26.

Pritchard, R. D., Dunnette, M. D., & Jorgenson, D. O. Effects of perceptions of equity and inequity on worker performance and satisfaction. *Journal of Applied Psychology,* 1972, *56*, 75–94.

Quine, W. V. *From a logical point of view.* Cambridge, Mass.: Harvard University Press, 1953.

Rand. *A million random digits.* Santa Monica, Calif.: Rand Corporation, 1955.

Ray, H. W. *Final report on the Office of Economic Opportunity experiment in educational performance contracting.* Columbus, Ohio: Battelle Columbus Laboratories, 1972.

Reichardt, C. S. *The design and analysis of the nonequivalent group quasi-experiment.* Unpublished doctoral dissertation, Northwestern University, 1979.

Rickard, S. The assumptions of causal analyses for incomplete sets of two multilevel variables. *Multivariate Behavioral Research,* 1972, *7*, 317–59.

Riecken, H. W., Boruch, R. F., Campbell, D. T., Coplan, W., Glennan, T. K., Pratt, J., Rees, A., & Williams, W. *Social experimentation: A method for planning and evaluating social innovations.* New York: Academic Press, 1974.

Rindskopf, D. M. Using structural equation models to analyze nonexperimental data. In R. F. Boruch & P. M. Wortman (Eds.), *Secondary analysis.* San Francisco: Jossey-Bass, 1978.

Rivlin, A. M. *Systematic thinking for social action.* Washington, D.C.: Brookings Institution, 1971.

Rivlin, A. M., & Timpane, P. M. (Eds.). *Planned variation in education.* Washington, D.C.: The Brookings Institution, 1975.

Robertson, L. S., Kelley, A. B., O'Neill, B., Wixom, C. W., Eiswirth, R. S., & Haddon, W. *A controlled study of the effect of television messages on safety belt use.* Washington, D.C.: Insurance Institute for Highway Safety, 1972.

Roethlisberger, F. S., & Dickson, W. J. *Management and the worker.* Cambridge, Mass.: Harvard University Press, 1939.

Rogosa, D. Causal models in longitudinal research: Rationale, formulation and interpretation. In J. R. Nesselroade & P. B. Baltes (Eds.), *Longitudinal research in human development: Design and analysis.* New York: Academic Press, 1978.

Rosen, H., & Turner, J. Effectiveness of two orientation approaches in hard-core unemployed turnover and absenteeism. *Journal of Applied Psychology,* 1971, *55*, 296–301.

Rosenberg, M. *The pretrial conference and effective justice.* New York: Columbia University Press, 1964.

Rosenberg, M. J. The conditions and consequences of evaluation apprehension. In R. Rosenthal & R. L. Rosnow (Eds.), *Artifact in behavioral research.* New York: Academic Press, 1969.

Rosenthal, R. *On the social psychology of the self-fulfilling prophecy: Further evidence for Pygmalion effects and their mediating mechanisms.* Unpublished manuscript, Harvard University, 1972.

Ross, H. L. Law, science and accidents: The British Road Safety Act of 1967. *Journal of Legal Studies,* 1973, *2*, 1–75.

Ross, H. L., Campbell, D. T., & Glass, G. V. Determining the social effects of a legal reform: The British "breathalyser" crackdown of 1967. *American Behavioral Scientist,* 1970, *13*, 493–509.

Rossi, P. H., & Lyall, K. *Reforming public welfare: A critique of the negative income tax experiment.* New York: Russell Sage Foundation, 1976.

Rozelle, R. M., & Campbell, D. T. More plausible rival hypotheses in the cross-lagged panel correlation technique. *Psychological Bulletin,* 1969, *71*, 74–80.

Rubin, D. B. Matching to remove bias in observational studies. *Biometrics,* 1973, *29*, 159–83. (a)

Rubin, D. B. The use of matched sampling and regression adjustment to remove bias in observational studies. *Biometrics,* 1973, *29*, 185–203. (b)

Rubin, D. B. Multivariate matching methods that are equal percent bias reducing, I: Some examples. *Biometrics,*

1976, *32*, 109–20. (a)

Rubin, D. B. Multivariate matching methods that are equal percent bias reducing, II: Maximum on bias reduction for fixed sample sizes. *Biometrics*, 1976, *32*, 121–32. (b)

Rubin, D. B. Assignment to treatment group on the basis of a covariate. *Journal of Educational Statistics*, 1977, *2*, 1–26.

Russell, B. On the notion of cause. *Proceedings of the Aristotelian Society* (New Series), 1913, *13*, 1–26.

Ryan, T. A. Multiple comparisons in psychological research. *Psychological Bulletin*, 1959, *56*, 26–47.

Sacks, J., & Ylvisaker, D. *Linear estimation for approximately linear models* (Discussion Paper 9). Evanston, Ill.: Northwestern University, Center for Statistics and Probability, 1976.

Saretsky, G. The OEO P.C. experiment and the John Henry effect. *Phi Delta Kappan*, 1972, *53*, 579–81.

Scheffé, H. *The analysis of variance*, New York: Wiley, 1959.

Scheflen, K. C., Lawler, E. E., III, & Hackman, J. R. Long-term impact of employee participation in the development of pay incentive plans: A field experiment revisited. *Journal of Applied Psychology*, 1971, *55*, 182–86.

Schuman, H., & Duncan, O. D. Questions about attitude survey questions. In H. L. Costner (Ed.), *Sociological methodology 1973–1974*. San Francisco: Jossey-Bass, 1974.

Scriven, M. The logic of cause. *Theory and Decision*, 1971, *2*, 49–66.

Scriven, M. Causation as explanation. *Noûs*, 1975, *9*, 3–16.

Scriven, M. Maximizing the power of causal investigation: The modus operandi method. In G. V. Glass (Ed.), *Evaluation studies review annual* (Vol. 1). Beverly Hills, Calif: Sage Publications, 1976.

Seaver, W. B. Effects of naturally induced teacher expectancies. *Journal of Personality and Social Psychology*, 1973, *28*, 333–42.

Seaver, W. B., & Quarton, R. J. Regression-discontinuity analysis of Dean's List effects. *Journal of Educational Psychology*, 1976, *68*, 459–65.

Sechrest, L. *Dissipating and snowballing effects in social amelioration: Lotteries as true experiments*. Duplicated memorandum, Northwestern University, 1970.

Sherwood, S., Greer, D. S., Morris, J. N., & Sherwood, C. C. *The Highland Heights Experiment*. (Final report, contract H 1275, to the Department of Housing and Urban Development.) Boston: Department of Social Gerontological Research, Hebrew Rehabilitation Center for the Aged, May 1972.

Siegel, A. E., & Siegel, S. Reference groups, membership groups, and attitude change. *Journal of Abnormal and Social Psychology*, 1957, *55*, 360–64.

Silverman, I. Nonreactive methods and the law. *American Psychologist*, 1975, *30*, 764–69.

Sims, C. A. Money, income, and causality. *American Economic Review*, 1972, *62*, 540–52.

Smith, H. F. Interpretation of adjusted treatment means and regressions in analysis of covariance. *Biometrics*, 1957, *13*, 282–308.

Snow, R. E. Representative and quasi-representative designs for research on teaching. *Review of Educational Research*, 1974, *44*, 265–91.

Sörbom, D. Detection of correlated errors in longitudinal data. *British Journal of Mathematical and Statistical Psychology*, 1975, *28*, 138–51.

Sörbom, D. An alternative to the methodology for analysis of covariance. *Psychometrika*, in press.

Spiegelman, C. H. *Two techniques for estimating treatment effect in the presence of hidden variables: Adaptive regression and a solution of Reiersol's problem*. (Doctoral dissertation, Northwestern University, 1976.) *Dissertation Abstracts International*, 1977, *37*, S703B. (University Microfilms No. 77-9958, 47)

Stapleton, W. V., & Teitelbaum, L. E. *In defense of youth*. New York: Russell Sage Foundation, 1972.

Staw, B. M. Attitudinal and behavioral consequences of changing a major organizational reward: A natural field experiment. *Journal of Personality and Social Psychology*, 1974, *29*, 742–51.

Stegmüller, W. *The structure and dynamics of theories*. New York: Springer-Verlag, 1976.

Stouffer, S. A. Some observations on study design. *American Journal of Sociology*, 1950, *55*, 355–61.

Strenio, J. F., Bryk, A. S., & Weisberg, H. I. An individual growth model perspective for evaluating educational programs. *Proceedings of the Social Statistics Section*, American Statistical Association, 1977.

"Student" (1931) The Lanarkshire milk experiment. *Biometrika*, 1931, *23*, 398–406.

Suppes, P. *A probabilistic theory of causality*. Amsterdam: North Holland, 1970.

Theil, H. *Principles of econometrics*. New York: Wiley, 1971.

Thorndike, R. L. Regression fallacies in the matched groups experiment. *Psychometrika*, 1942, *7*, 85–102.

Toulmin, S. E. *Foresight and understanding: An inquiry into the aims of science*. Bloomington: Indiana University Press, 1961.

Toulmin, S. E. *Human understanding: The collective use and evolution of concepts* (Vol. I). Princeton, N.J.: Princeton University Press, 1972.

Tubbs, J. D., Lewis, T. V., & Duran, B. S. A note on the analysis of the MANOVA model and its application to growth curves. *Communications in Statistics*, 1975, *4*, 643–53.

Tukey, J. Causation, regression, and path analysis. In O. Kempthorne (Ed.), *Statistics and mathematics in biology*. Ames, Iowa: Iowa State College Press, 1954.

Tukey, J. Some thoughts on clinical trials, especially problems of multiplicity. *Science*, 1977, *198*, 679–84.

Tversky, A., & Kahneman, D. Judgment under uncertainty: Heuristics and biases. *Science*, 1974, *185*, 1124–31.

Valins, S., & Baum, A. Residential group size, social interaction, and crowding, *Environment and Behavior*, 1973, *5*, 421–39.

Vigderhaus, G. Forecasting sociological phenomena: Application of Box-Jenkins methodology to suicide rates. In K. F. Schuessler (Ed.), *Sociological methodology 1978*. San Francisco: Jossey-Bass, 1977.

Wald, A. The fitting of straight lines if both variables are subject to error. *Annals of Mathematical Statistics,* 1940, *11,* 284–300.

Walker, H., & Lev, J. *Statistical influence.* New York: Holt, Rinehart, 1953.

Wallace, W. *Causality and scientific explanation* (2 vols.). Ann Arbor, Mich.: The University of Michigan Press, 1972, 1974.

Watts, H. W., & Rees, A. Labor supply responses, *The New Jersey Income Maintenance Experiment* (Vol. 2). New York: Academic Press, 1977. (a)

Watts, H. W., & Rees, A. Expenditures, health, and social behavior; and the quality of the evidence. *The New Jersey Income Maintenance Experiment* (Vol. 3). New York: Academic Press, 1977. (b)

Webb, E. J., Campbell, D. T., Schwartz, R. D., & Sechrest, L. *Unobtrusive measures.* Skokie, Ill.: Rand McNally, 1966.

Weber, S. J., & Cook, D. T. Subject effects in laboratory research: An examination of subject roles, demand characteristics, and valid inference. *Psychological Bulletin,* 1972, *77,* 273–95.

Weber, S. J., Cook, T. D., & Campbell, D. T. *The effects of school integration on the academic self-concept of public school children.* Paper presented at the meeting of the Midwestern Psychological Association, Detroit, 1971.

Weikart, D. P. Relationship of curriculum, teaching, and learning in preschool education. In J. C. Stanley (Ed.), *Preschool programs for the disadvantaged.* Baltimore: Johns Hopkins University Press, 1972.

Weiss, R. S., & Rein, M. The evaluation of broad-aim programs: Experimental design, its difficulties, and an alternative. *Administrative Science Quarterly,* 1970, *15,* 97–109.

Werts, C. E., & Linn, R. L. A general linear model for studying growth. *Psychological Bulletin,* 1970, *73,* 17–22.

Werts, C. E., Linn, R. L. & Jöreskog, K. G. A simplex model for analyzing academic growth. *Educational and Psychological Measurement,* 1977, *37,* 745–56.

Wharton, J. D. *An investigation of some effects of the introduction of television on consumer purchase behavior.* Unpublished doctoral dissertation, Northwestern University, 1978.

Whitbeck, C. Causation in medicine: The disease entity model. *Philosophy of Science,* 1977, *44,* 619–37.

Wilder, C. S. *Physician visits, volume, and interval since last visit, U.S., 1969.* Rockville, Md.: National Center for Health Statistics, July 1972. (Series 10, No. 75; DHEW Pub. No. (HSM) 72-1064.)

Williams, W., & Evans, J. W. The politics of evaluation: The case of Head Start. *The Annals,* 1969, *385,* 118–32.

Winch, R. F., & Campbell, D. T. Proof? No! Evidence? Yes! The significance of tests of significance. *American Sociologist,* 1969, *4,* 140–43.

Winer, B. J. *Statistical principles in experimental design.* New York: McGraw-Hill, 1961.

Wold, A. Causal inference from observational data: A review of ends and means. *Journal of the Royal Statistical Society,* Series A, 1956, *119,* 28–61.

Worchel, S., & Mitchell, R. R. An evaluation of the effectiveness of the culture assimilator—Thailand and Greece. *Journal of Applied Psychology,* 1972, *56,* 472–79.

Wortman, C. B., & Rabinowitz, V. Randomization: The fairest of them all. In L. Sechrest (Ed.), *Evaluation studies review annual* (Vol. 4). Beverly Hills, Calif.: Sage Publications, in press.

Wright, G. H. von. *Explanation and understanding.* Ithaca, N. Y.: Cornell University Press, 1971.

Yule, G. V. On changes in the marriage and birth rates in England and Wales during the past half century. *Journal of the Royal Statistical Society,* 1906, *49,* 88–132.

Zajonc, R. B., & Markus, H. Birth order and intellectual development. *Psychological Review,* 1975, *82,* 74–88.

Zigulich, J. *A comparison of elementary school environments: Magnet Schools versus traditional schools.* Unpublished doctoral dissertation, Northwestern University, School of Education, 1977.

Zimring, F. E. Field experiments in general deterrence: Preferring the tortoise to the hare. *Evaluation,* 1976, *3,* 132–35.

NAME Index

Ackermann, R., 23
Adams, J. S., 382
Alderman, D. L., 366
Alt, F. B., 282, 284, 287, 292
Andrews, F. M., 309, 313
Arney, W. R., 333
Aschenfelter, O., 46, 228, 230
Atiqullah, M., 153n
Atkin, R., 319–20
Atkinson, R. C., 348
Austin, G., 28

Ball, S., 129–30, 195, 343, 356, 367–68, 379
Barnow, B. S., 91
Barton, A. H., 309
Baum, A., 382
Bechtold, H. P., 14
Bem, D. J., 70
Bentler, P. M., 91, 193, 300, 306
Bereiter, C., 380
Bergmann, G., 13
Berkson, J., 163n
Bhaskar, R., 15, 92
Bishop, R. C., 348–49, 371
Blalock, H. M., Jr., 296, 301, 308
Bock, R. D., 148, 203, 235n
Bogatz, G. A., 129–30, 195, 343, 356, 367–68, 379
Bonoma, T. V., 92
Boring, E. G., 3, 14, 19
Boruch, R. F., 43, 45, 90, 181, 185, 191, 346, 357, 385
Box, G. E. P., 195, 207, 213, 227, 233, 235, 239n, 242, 264, 269n, 330–31, 338
Bracht, G. H., 71, 111
Brand, M., 10

Brannon, R., 79
Bray, R., 319–20
Bridgman, P. W., 13
Broadbent, D. E., 103, 119–20, 354
Brunswick, E., 87
Bryan, J. H., 371
Bryk, A. S., 160, 196
Bunge, M., 10
Butler-Paisley, M., 223

Cain, G. G., 168
Calder, B. J., 226, 231
Campbell, D. T., 1, 6, 14, 18, 23, 28, 30, 36–39, 45, 61, 70–71, 74, 80, 82, 85–88, 90, 92–93, 96, 108, 115, 132, 143, 181, 185, 207, 218–19, 229, 234, 304, 309–10, 312–14, 328, 346, 369, 377
Campbell, N. R., 10–12
Carlsmith, J. M., 377
Chazin, R. M., 366
Chibucos, T. R., 183n, 191
Cicirelli, V. G., 91
Cochran, W. G., 155n, 157n, 163n, 169–70, 176n, 179–81, 190, 197, 201
Cochrane, D., 326
Cohen, J., 42
Coleman, J. S., 91
Collingwood, R. G., 25–28, 32, 34
Comte, A., 13, 18
Conner, R. F., 353
Cook, A. F. L., 92
Cook, D., 66
Cook, T. D., 14, 45, 61, 64, 74, 81–82, 92, 108, 112, 196,

200–201, 223, 226, 231, 309, 345, 350, 365, 368, 375, 383, 385
Costner, H. L., 188, 193
Cox, D. R., 177, 183n
Crano, W. D., 312, 314
Cronbach, L. J., 14, 38, 42, 61, 70, 85, 89, 92, 160, 166, 168, 184n, 191, 193–94, 200
Crosby, F., 61

Davison, M., 319–20
DeGracie, J. S., 190n
Del Rosario, M. L., 81, 226
Deutsch, S. J., 282, 284, 287, 292
Dhrymes, P. J., 237n
Diamond, S. S., 66
Diaz-Guerrero, R., 354
Dickson, W. J., 123
Director, S. M., 191, 301
Donnelly, J. H., 379
Doob, A. N., 377–78
Draper, N. R., 204n
Duhem, P., 14, 21, 23–24
Duncan, O. D., 9, 79, 301, 308
Dunnette, M. D., 382
Duran, B. S., 195
Durbin, J., 326

Edwards, A. L., 346
Einstein, A., 23
Eiswirth, R. S., 379
Elashoff,. D., 44, 153n, 183n
Empey, L. T., 363, 376
Englemann, S., 380
Erickson, M. L., 363
Erlebacher, A. E., 115, 181
Evans, J. W., 383

Fair, J., 360
Farmer, E., 209, 213
Feldman, R., 69, 88, 370
Feldstein, D. M., 366
Feldt, L. S., 177, 183n
Feshbach, S., 368
Feyerabend, P., 23–24
Fienberg, S. E., 350
Fischoff, B., 93
Fiske, D. W., 14, 61, 304
Flay, B. R., 45, 64
Floden, R. E., 193
Freedman, J. L., 377
Friesema, H. P., 278
Fuller, W. A., 190n
Furby, L., 166, 184n, 191

Gadenne, V., 85
Gasking, D., 15–16, 25, 27
Geisser, S., 235n, 356
Gilbert, J. P., 345
Glass, G., 71, 111, 151, 153n,
  207, 218–19, 223, 229, 233,
  293, 361
Glenn, N., 127
Glesser, G. C., 61
Goldberger, A. S., 168, 205, 301,
  305
Gomez, H., 43
Goodman, L. A., 309
Gordon, H. C., 378
Gottman, J. M., 207, 229, 233,
  293
Gramlich, E. M., 380
Granger, C. W., 235n, 323, 334,
  337
Greaney, V., 143
Greenhouse, S. W., 235n, 356
Greer, D. S., 374
Gruder, C. L., 45, 92, 385
Guttentag, M., 92

Hackman, J. R., 103, 210–11,
  213, 215–18, 221–22, 225,
  354–55, 378
Haddon, W., 379
Hand, H. H., 348
Hannan, M. T., 338
Hanson, N. R., 18, 23–24
Harré, R., 25
Hatanaka, M., 334
Haugh, L. D., 330–32, 339
Hay, R. A., 242, 268, 271n, 282
Hays, W. L., 346
Heath, L., 226
Heider, F., 28
Heise, D. R., 9, 301
Hennigan, K. M., 45, 61, 81, 226
Herskovitz, M. J., 92
Herzberger, S., 319–20
Heussenstamm, F., 378

Hibbs, D. A., 195, 207, 233,
  235n, 264, 269n, 293, 326
Hickey, T., 85, 89, 92
Hickman, J. P., 213, 253
Hill, J. W., 348–49, 371
Hilton, J. G., 213, 253
Hollister, R., 346
Holtzmann, W. H., 355
Hooker, R. H., 324, 327
Hudson, W. W., 365
Hultsch, D., 85, 89, 92
Hume, D., 10, 13, 18, 20, 23,
  297
Humphreys, L. G., 319–20, 321n

Ivancevich, J. M., 379

Jenkins, G. M., 195, 207, 213,
  227, 233, 235, 239n, 241, 269n,
  330, 334, 338
Jessor, R., 318
Jessor, S. L., 318
Johnston, J., 157n, 213, 290n, 326
Jöreskog, K. G., 192, 193n, 195,
  305, 321n
Jorgenson, D. C., 382
Jurs, S. G., 361

Kahneman, D., 93
Kanouse, D. E., 134–36
Kant, I., 23, 30
Katzman, N., 223
Keat, R., 92
Keesling, J. W., 193
Kellaghan, T., 143
Kelley, A. B., 379
Kelman, H. C., 384
Kenny, D. A., 168, 184–85, 201,
  309–10, 312–14
Kerlinger, F. N., 203
Kerpelman, L. C., 116, 212
Kerr, W. A., 377
Kershaw, D., 360
Khatri, C. G., 195
Kilman, R. H., 92
Kirk, R. E., 346
Kish, L., 71, 352
Kmenta, J., 290n, 326
Koshel, P. D., 380
Kroy, M., 85
Kruglanski, A. W., 85
Kuhn, T. S., 23–24, 94

Lana, R. C., 42, 68
Landauer, T. K., 377
Larson, R. C., 343
Lave, L. B., 319
Lawler, E. E., III, 103, 210–11,
  213, 215–18, 221–22, 225,
  354–55, 378
Lazarsfeld, P. F., 309

Lee, S. H. 328
Lev, J., 346
Lewin, K., 17
Lewis, T. V., 195
Lieberman, S., 103, 122
Lindley, D. V., 169
Lindquist, E. F., 42, 151
Linn, R. L., 183n, 193, 321n
Linz, J., 309
Lipset, S. M., 309
Little, E. A. J., 103, 119–20, 354
Livingston, H. H., 92
Lohr, B. W., 143–44, 146
Long, J. S., 192, 305
Lord, F. M., 148, 160, 165, 184n,
  190, 197
Lubeck, S. G., 363, 376
Lyall, K., 343

MacCorquodale, K., 13
Mach, E., 13
Madansky, A., 190
Madden, E. H., 25
Magidson, J., 91, 193, 300, 306
Maguire, T. O., 223
Malinvaud, E., 235n
Mandelbaum, M., 92
Mark, M. M., 81
Mase, B. F., 377
Maxwell, G., 17, 92
Mayer, T. F., 333
McCain, L., 323, 326, 332
McCleary, R., 282, 323, 326, 332
McNemar, Q., 49, 100, 346
McPeek, B., 346
McSweeny, A. J., 270, 385
Meehl, P. E., 13–14, 38, 61, 70
Menges, R. J., 381
Michotte, A., 28
Mill, J. S., 1, 4, 18–19, 31–32,
  297
Minton, J. H., 127, 129–30, 201
Mitchell, R. R., 356
Mitroff, I. I., 92
Morris, J. N., 374
Morrison, D. F., 195
Morse, N. C., 124–25
Mosteller, F., 346
Mullen, E. J., 366
Myers, J. L., 177, 378

Nanda, H., 61
Nerlove, M., 325, 338
Newbold, P., 235n
Newton, I., 21–23
Nisbett, R. E., 134–36
Northrop, F. S. C., 92
Notz, W. W., 345, 350

Ogburn, W. F., 324
O'Neill, B., 379

Orcutt, G. W., 326
Ozaki, T., 332

Pack, D. J., 242, 268, 271n
Parker, E. B., 69, 223–24
Parsons, C. K., 321n
Pascal, B., 3–4
Pearson, K., 10, 297
Peckham, P. D., 151, 153n
Pedhazur, E. J., 203
Pelz, D. C., 309, 313
Pierce, D. A., 242n, 330, 332, 339
Polanyi, M., 24
Popper, K. R., 1, 18, 20, 22–24, 31, 92
Porter, A. C., 183n, 190–92
Pothoff, R. F., 195, 235n
Price, G. G., 193
Pritchard, R. D., 382

Quarton, R. J., 139, 142
Quine, W. V., 20–21, 23

Rabinowitz, V., 351
Rajaratnam, N., 61
Rand Corporation, 350, 352
Ray, H. W., 380
Rees, A., 360
Reichardt, C. S., 92, 194, 314
Reimer, E., 124–25
Rein, M., 92
Rickard, S., 313–14
Riecken, H. W., 146, 207, 229, 357
Rindskopf, D. M., 193
Rivlin, A. M., 9, 349
Robertson, L. S., 379
Roethlisberger, F. S., 123
Rogosa, D. R., 193, 297, 314
Rosen, H., 360, 367–69
Rosenberg, M., 363
Rosenberg, M. J., 67
Rosenthal, R., 67, 85
Ross, H. L., 218–21
Rossi, P. H., 343
Roy, S. N., 195, 235n
Rozelle, R. M., 36, 313–14
Rubin, D. B., 170, 179–82, 189, 197
Russell, B., 10–12, 16, 297
Ryan, T. A., 42–43

Sacks, J., 204
Sanders, J. R., 151, 153n
Saretsky, G., 55, 59, 131–32
Scheffé, H., 43, 151, 176n
Scheflen, K. C., 218, 221–22
Schoenberg, R., 188, 193
Schuman, H., 79
Scriven, M., 27, 97
Seaver, W. B., 135–36, 139–40, 142
Sechrest, L., 373
Selzer, U., 319–20
Seskin, E. P., 319
Sherwood, S., 374
Sherwood, C. C., 374
Siegel, A. E., 372
Siegel, S., 372
Silverman, I., 369
Sims, C. A., 330
Singer, R. D., 368
Slocum, J. W., Jr., 348
Smith, H. F., 169n, 204n
Snow, R. E., 42, 89, 183n
Soderstrom, E. J., 385
Sörbom, D., 188, 190n, 193n, 305
Spiegelman, C. H., 204
Stanley, J. C., 1, 14, 18, 37, 39, 70–71, 85–88, 92, 133, 234, 309, 377
Stapleton, W. V., 363
Staw, B. M., 345, 350, 372
Stegmüller, W., 24
Stouffer, S. A., 6
Strenio, J. F., 196
"Student", 47
Suppes, P., 11, 15, 17, 25
Sween, J., 140

Takata, G., 143
Teitelbaum, L. E., 363
Terman, L., 14
Test, M. A., 371
Theil, H., 157n
Thomas, D. S., 324
Thorndike, R. L., 181, 192
Tiao, G. C., 207, 223, 233n, 264
Timpane, P. M., 349
Tom, S., Jr., 377
Toulmin, S. E., 22–23, 94
Trochim, W. M. K., 81
Tubbs, J. D., 195
Tukey, J., 43, 297, 346

Turner, J., 360, 367–69
Tversky, A., 93
Tyler, B. B., 61

Urry, J., 92

Valins, S., 382
Vigderhaus, G., 330–31

Wald, A., 297
Walker, H., 346
Wallace, W., 10
Watts, D. G., 334
Watts, H. W., 360
Webb, E. J., 14
Weber, S. J., 66, 109
Weikart, D. P., 380
Weisberg, H. I., 160, 196
Weiss, R. S., 92
Werts, C. E., 183n, 193, 321n
Wharton, J. D., 226, 229, 233n
Whitbeck, C., 25
Wilder, C. S., 143, 146
Wiley, D. E., 193
Williams, W., 383
Willson, V. L., 207, 229, 233, 293
Winch, R. F., 80
Winer, B. J., 346
Wittgenstein, L. J., 28
Wixom, C. W., 379
Wold, A., 297
Woodward, J. A., 91, 193, 300–301, 306
Worchell, S., 356
Wortman, C. B., 351
Wright, G. H. von, 25

Ylvisaker, D., 204
Young, A. A., 338
Yule, G. V., 324

Zaidi, H., 373
Zajonc, R. B., 128
Zigulich, J., 351, 353, 373
Zimring, F. E., 346

SUBJECT Index

ACF. *See* Autocorrelation function
Activity theory of causation, 25–28, 31
Analysis of causation, eight statements, 32–36
Analysis of covariance, 149
Analysis of covariance, multiple covariates, 170–75
  bias, 171–75
  comparison, ANOVA/ANCOVA, 171–75
  model, 170–71
Analysis of covariance, single covariate, 153–70
  bias, 159–70
  comparison, ANOVA/ANCOVA, 153, 156–64, 167–68
  model, 153–59
Analysis of variance, 149, 150–52
  bias, 152
  error in, 151
  model, 150–52
Analysis of variance with blocking, 175–82
  bias, 178–82
  comparison, ANOVA/ANCOVA, 178
  model, single pretest, 175–78
  multiple pretests, 182
Analysis of variance with gain scores, 182–85
  bias, 184
  comparison, ANOVA/ANCOVA, 182–83
  model, 182–84
  standardized, 184–85
ANCOVA. *See* Analysis of covariance
ANOVA. *See* Analysis of variance

ARIMA *(p,d,q)*, definition, 236–40
  autoregressive models, 239
  mixed models, 240
  moving average models, 240
  stationarity, 236–38
ARIMA *(p,d,q)*, modeling strategy, 267–69
  deterministic and stochastic components, 235–36
  diagnosis, 251–52, 268–69
  estimation, 251, 268
  intervention hypothesis test, 269
  noise model identification, 240–50, 268
  three examples, 271–92
ARIMA seasonal models, 253–61
  identifying seasonal models, 255–61
  multiplicative models, 253–55
Autocorrelation function, 241–52, 255–61, 268–75, 278–92
Autocorrelation, two types of, 253–55
Autoregressive integrated moving average, 235–93. *See also* ARIMA

Basement or "floor" effects, 42
Blocking or matching, 175–82
Bracketing procedure, 200–201
British breathalyser experiment, 218–21, 227
British Industrial Fatigue Research Board, 209

CAI. *See* Computer-assisted instruction
Causal analysis, concomitancies in time series, 321–39

distributed lag model, 327
generic problems of, 335–38
GLS regression, 326–27
independent prewhitening, 331
OLS regression, trend and seasonality removed, 324–26
prewhitening by presumed cause, 330–31
simple cross-correlation function, 327–30
simple OLS regression, 321–24
spectral analysis methods, 333–35
Causal modeling, path analysis, 301–9
  with direct causal path, 303
  estimates of specific paths, 307–8
  imperfect compensatory examples, 306–7
  models "over identified," 303
  remote and direct common cause, 302
  unique components, 303–4
  with more variables, 302–3
Causation, 10–36
  activity theory of, 25–28
  essentialist theories of, 14–18
  evolutionary critical-realist perspective on, 28–30
  implications of analysis, 30–36
  Mill, John Stuart, on, 18–20
  Popper and falsificationism, 20–25
  positivist tradition of, 10–14
Ceiling effect, 52
Cincinnati Directory Assistance, ARIMA model, 270–78
Cohort, 127

Cohort designs, 126–34
    no treatment partitioning, 131–33
    treatment partitioning, 127–31
Coleman Report, 91
Compensatory equalization of
    treatments, 54
Compensatory rivalry, 54–55
Computer-assisted instruction, 348;
    system (TICCIT), 366
Confounding, 38n, 39, 59–60, 85;
    levels of constructs, 67
Constant conjunction, 10
Construct and external validity, 82
Construct underrepresentation, 64
Construct validity, putative
    cause/effect, 38, 59–70, 81–82
    introduction, 59–64
    preexperimental/postexperimental,
        68–70
    threats to, 64–68
Control, 7–9; ruling out threats,
    8–9
Controlled settings, 7
Convergence, 61
Correlational study, 295
Covariation, inferring cause, 37
Creaming, 363
Critical-realist mode, 29;
    philosophy, 92
Cross-lagged panel correlations,
    309–21
    confounding negative/positive
        causation, 313
    correction for communality, 312
    Lazarsfeld's 16-fold table, 309
    with other methods, 318–21
    no-cause comparison base,
        313–14
    temporal erosion, 310–12
Cross-spectrum, 334
Crossover pattern, 165
Curvilinear regression, 140–42

Data analysis, 196–202
    conclusions and results, 201–2
    planning and design, 198–99
    random assignment, 196–98
Definitional operationalism, 14, 71,
    92
Delayed causation, 15–17
Deliberate manipulations, 3, 339
Deliberate sampling, 75–77
Dependent variables, 4
Designs with and without
    controlled selection, 147
Deterministic components, 235–36
Developmental sequences, construct
    validity, 62
Differential mortality, 57–58
Differential statistical regression,
    105

Direction of causal influence,
    ambiguity of, 53–54
Distributed lag models, 327
Divergence, 61
Dummy variable, 298
Dynamic equilibrium, 165

Educational Testing Service, 112;
    growth study, 319
Effect, 9, 149
Effects, types of, 208–9
Empiricist monism, 13–14
Errors, Types I and II, 42
Essentialist theories of causation,
    14–18
ETS. See Educational Testing
    Service
Evaluation apprehension, 67
Evolutionary critical-realist
    perspective, 28–30, 31
Experiment, 2–3
Experimental design, 4–9
Experimenter expectancies, 67, 81
"Explosively" nonstationary time
    series, 250
External validity, 37–39, 70–80,
    81–82
    discussion of, 37–39
    introduction, 70–73
    models increasing, 74–80
    threats to, 73–74

F test, 176, 191, 295
Factorial experiments, 7
Fallback quasi-experiment, 134
Falsificationism, 20–25
Fan-spread pattern, 184–85
First-order Markov process, 311
Fishing and error rate problem,
    42–43
Forecasting or predictive
    regression, 296–97
Fourier analysis, 334
Frequency domain, 333

Gain scores, analysis of variance
    with, 182–85
Generalized least squares, 326–27
Generalizability, across constructs,
    68
GLS. See Generalized least squares
Graduate Record Examination, 138
Grand mean, 151

Haugh-Box approach, 331–32;
    shortcomings, 331
Hawthorne effect, 39, 60, 66, 125
Hawthorne studies, 123–24, 209
Head Start, 91, 296, 380
    path analysis of, 306–7, 308
    regression analysis of, 300–301

Hypothesis guessing, 66–67, 81

Identifiable subpopulations, 165
Identification, statistical analysis,
    236, 268
Identifying seasonal ARIMA
    models, 255–61
    autoregressive processes, 256
    moving average processes, 258
    nonstationarity, 256
Imitation or diffusion of treatments,
    54
Impressionistic modal instance,
    77–78
Inadequate preoperational
    explication, 64–65
Independent prewhitening, 331–33;
    Haugh-Box approach, 331–32
Independent variables, 4, 297
Inferring cause, Mill's conditions,
    18, 31
Inferring cause from passive
    observation, 295–339
    causal analysis, time series,
        321–39
    causal modeling, path analysis,
        301–9
    cross-lagged panel correlations,
        309–21
    introduction, 295–98
    treatment as "dummy variable,"
        298–301
Informed consent, 369, 384
Instability, 80
Instrumentation, 52
Interaction of different treatments,
    67–68
Interaction of history and time, 74
Interaction of selection and
    treatment, 73
Interaction of testing and treatment,
    68
Interactions with selection, 53
Internal validity, 37–38, 50–59,
    80–81
    defined, 37–38
    estimating in randomized and
        quasi-experiments, 55–56
    plausibility of threats, 58–59
    threats to, 51–55
    threats not ruled out, 56–58
Intervention component, ARIMA
    models, 260–68
Intervention hypothesis test,
    ARIMA models, 269
Interrupted time series. See
    individual entries under
    Quasi-experiments, interrupted
    time-series designs
Interrupted time-series analysis,
    207

Interrupted time-series designs, 6
Intervention component, ARIMA
  (p,d,q), 261–68
  abrupt, constant change, 262–63
  abrupt, temporary change,
    264–65
  gradual, constant change, 263–64
  transfer function, 265–68
Invalidity, 37

John Henry effect, 55
Job Corps, 364; regression
  analysis, 301

Kansas City Patrol Experiment,
  343

Language of experimentation, 1–9
  control, 7–9
  experiment, 2–3
  independent variable, 4
  interrupted time-series design, 6
  outcomes, dependent variables, 4
  quasi-experiments, 6
  random assignment, 5
  randomized experiments, 5–6
  treatments, 4
  trial, 3–4
Lazarsfeld's 16-fold table, 309
Linear regression, 140–42
Logical positivism, 92
Low statistical power, 42

Magnet School, 76, 353, 373
Magnitude estimates, 41
MANOVA. *See* Multivariate
  analysis of variance
Massachusetts Gun Control Law,
  ARIMA model, 282–92
Maturation, 52
Medicaid, 142, 144–46
Medicare, 145
Methodology of path analysis, 301
Metropolitan Readiness Test, 127,
  129
Micromediation, 32–36
Mill, John Stuart, on causation, 4,
  18–20, 31
  on Method of Agreement, 18
  on Method of Concomitant
    Variation, 4, 18–19
  on Method of Difference, 4, 18–19
Mixed models, ARIMA, 240,
  247–50
Modus operandi approach, 97
Molar causal laws, 33–36
Mono-method bias, 66, 71, 81
Mono-operation bias, 65
Mortality, 53
Moving average models, ARIMA,
  240

Moving average processes,
  ARIMA, 247
Multiple definitional
  operationalism, 71
Multiple formal definitionalism,
  61–62, 63
Multiple operationalism, 61–62, 63
Multiplicative ARIMA seasonal
  models, 253–55
Multivariate analysis of variance,
  195–96

National Science Foundation, 138
New Jersey Negative Income Tax
  Experiment, 343, 357–58,
  361–62, 370
Noise model identification,
  ARIMA, 240–50
  autoregressive processes, 244–47
  mixed processes, 247–50
  moving average processes, 247
  nonstationary processes, 242–44
  white noise processes, 244
Nomological net, 70
Nomological validity, 38
Nonequivalent, 148
Nonequivalent control group
  designs. *See entry under*
  Quasi-experiments
Nonequivalent group designs, 6
Nonexperimental or correlational
  methods, 295
Nonlinear regression lines, 169–70
Nonparallel regression lines, 170
Nonstationary processes, ARIMA
  (p,d,q), 242–44
Notational system,
  quasi-experimental designs, 95
Null hypothesis, 44–50

Observational studies, 296
OLS. *See* Ordinary least squares
One-group designs
  posttest only, 96–98
  pretest-posttest, 99–103
Operationally unique
  pretest-posttest measures, 169
Ordinary least squares, 234–35,
  321–26

PACF. *See* Partial autocorrelation
  function
Partial autocorrelation function,
  241–52, 255–61, 268–75,
  278–92
Passive observational approaches,
  295–339
Peace Corps, 345
Pearson product-moment correlation
  coefficient, 241

Performance Contracting
  Experiment, 131
Philosophy of social sciences,
  objections to, 91–94
Placebo control group, 349
Plaza Sésamo, 354–55
Positivist tradition of causation,
  10–14
Postexperimental specification,
  68–70
Postpositivists, 23–25
Posttest-only design
  nonequivalent groups, 98–99
  higher-order interactions, 134–36
Posttreatment time series, effects,
  208–9
  continuous, 208
  delayed, 209
  discontinuous, 208
  drift, trend or slope change, 208
  instantaneous, 209
  level or intercept change, 208
Popper and falsificationism, 20–25,
  31
Power spectrum, 334
Predictive regression, 296–97
Preexperimental tailoring, 68–70
Prewhitening, 330
  Box-Jenkins, 330–31
  by presumed cause, 330–31
Priority among validity types,
  82–85
  for applied research, 83
  for theory testing, 83

Quasi-experiments, 6
Quasi-experiments, interrupted
  time-series designs, 207–32
  effects, 208–9
  frequent problems, 225–32
  introduction, 207–8
  simple interrupted time series,
    209–14
  with multiple replications,
    222–23
  with nonequivalent, dependent
    variables, 218–25
  with nonequivalent, no-treatment
    time series, 214–18
  with removed treatment, 221–22
  with switching replications,
    223–25
Quasi-experiments, nonequivalent
  control group designs, 95–146
  cohort designs, 126–33
  nonequivalent, dependent
    variables, 118–20
  notational system, 93
  posttest-only, higher order
    interaction, 134–36
  regression-discontinuity, 137–46

removed treatment, 120–23
repeated treatment, 123–24
reversed treatment with
    pretest/posttest, 124–26
three designs, 95–103
untreated with pretest, 117–18
untreated with pretest/posttest,
    103–12
untreated with proxy pretest,
    112–15
untreated with separate
    pretest/posttest, 115–17
Quasi-experiments, three designs
    where interpretation is often
    difficult, 95–103
one-group posttest-only design,
    96–98
one-group pretest-posttest design,
    99–103
posttest-only design,
    nonequivalent groups, 98–99
Quine-Duhem thesis, 20–21, 23

Random assignment, 5, 85–86,
    341–46
limitations, 342–46
principal functions, 341–42
use not feasible or desirable,
    344–46
Random irrelevancies, experimental
    setting, 44
Random heterogeneity of
    respondents, 44
Random sampling, 75
Randomized experiments, 5–6,
    341–86
Randomized experiments, conduct
    of, 341–86
conclusion, 384–86
introduction, 341–47
major obstacles to, 347–71
situations conducive to, 371–84
Randomized experiments, major
    obstacles to, 347–71
faulty procedures, 350–54
heterogeneity, treatment
    implementation, 366–67
sampling variability, number and
    choice of units, 354–56
treatment, control group, 367–69
treatment-related attrition, 359
treatment-related refusals,
    356–59
unobtrusive treatment
    implementation, 369–71
withholding treatment, 247–50
Randomized experiments, situations
    conducive to, 371–84
breaking a tie, 381
control over experimental units,
    383
creating an organization, 382–83

demand outstrips supply, 374–75
equivalent time-samples design,
    375–77
experimental units separated,
    378–80
lotteries, 372
mandated change, 380
no preference expressed, 381–82
staged introduction of
    innovation, 375–77
Rationales, statistical analysis. *See
    entry under* Statistical
    analysis
Reductionism, 15
Referent validity, 89
Regression analysis "dummy
    variable," 298–301
Regression-discontinuity designs,
    137–46, 147, 202–5
analysis of, 202–5
quantified multiple control
    groups, 143
similar-appearing pretest
    measures, 139–43
Regular autocorrelation, 254
Relay Assembly Row Experiment,
    123
Reliability of measures, 43
Reliability of treatment
    implementation, 43–44
Removed-treatment design, 120–23
Repeated-treatment design, 123–24
Resentful demoralization, 55
Reversed-treatment, nonequivalent
    design, 124–26
ROTC program, 372–73

Scientism, 91–92
Seasonal autocorrelation, 254
Seasonal autoregressive processes,
    256–58
Seasonal nonstationarity, 256
Seasonal moving average
    processes, 258–61
Selection, 53
Selection-maturation, 104, 106–8,
    110, 112
Sesame Street, 61, 63–64, 127–31,
    200–201, 343, 354–55, 356,
    365, 368, 379
Shaped variance overlap diagram,
    305
Signed cause, 97–98
Simon-Blalock technique, 308–9
Simple cross-correlation function,
    327–30
Simple interrupted time series,
    209–14
Simple OLS regression, 321–24;
    trend and seasonality removed,
    324–26
Spectral analysis methods, 333–35

application of Fourier analysis,
    334
ARIMA model, 335
cross-spectrum, 334
power spectrum, 334
spectral windows, 334
Stanford Achievement Test, 135
Stanford Binet Test (1916), 14
Stationarity in ARIMA (p,d,q),
    236–38
Statistical analysis, nonequivalent
    group designs, 147–205
introduction, 147
rationales, 185–96
without controlled selection,
    148–202
Statistical analysis, rationales,
    185–96
causal model of posttest, 187–88
Cronbach et al. formulation,
    193–94
model of assignment process,
    188
models of change or growth,
    194–96
Statistical analysis,
    regression-discontinuity design,
    202–5
Statistical analysis, simple
    interrupted time series, 233–92
ARIMA modeling strategy,
    267–69
ARIMA models, 235–52
ARIMA seasonal models,
    253–55
intervention component, 261–69
introduction, 233–34
OLS regression, 234–35
three examples, 270–92
(*See also individual entries*)
Statistical analysis, without
    controlled selection, 148–202
ANCOVA with blocking,
    . 175–82
ANCOVA with gain scores,
    182–85
ANCOVA with multiple
    covariates, 170–75
ANCOVA with single covariate,
    153–70
general guidelines, data analysis,
    196–202
(*See also individual entries*)
Statistical conclusion validity, 37,
    39–50, 80–81
introduction, 39–41
major threats to, 41–44
null hypothesis in, 44–50
Statistical power, 39–40
Statistical regression, 52–53
Stochastic component, 236
Strategy of planned variations, 349

Surplus construct irrelevancies, 64
Sutter County flood, ARIMA
  model, 278–82

t statistic, 235
t test, 295
Testing, 16, 52
Theory-ladenness, 23–24
Threats to validity. *See individual*
  entries under Construct
  validity, External validity,
  Internal validity, Statistical
  conclusion validity
Time domain, 333
Time series, 207
Time-series analysis, generic
  problems in, 335–39

Time series, causal analysis of,
  321–39
Trait instability and irrelevance,
  165–66
Trait validity, 38
Transfer functions, 262, 265–68
Treatment as "dummy variable,"
  regression analysis, 298–301
Treatment effect, 151
Treatments, 4; limitations of,
  54–55
Trial, 3–4

Untreated control group design,
  103–18
  pretest, more than one time
    interval, 117–18
  proxy pretest measures, 112–15

separate pretest/posttest samples,
  115–17

Validity, 37
Validity, relationships among
  types, 80–91
  construct and external, 81–82
  internal and statistical
    conclusion, 80–81
  objections to distinctions, 85–91
  priority among types, 82–85

White noise or random shock,
  239–40
White noise processes, ARIMA
  (0,0,0), 244

Yule-Walker equation, 241